D1666635

GERMAN LAW ACCESSIBLE

Happ/Habbe

Deployment of External Personnel in Germany

Deployment of External Personnel in Germany

by

Daniel Happ

Dr. Sophia Habbe

Martin Gliewe

Janine Fischer

Karolin Fitzer

2021

C.H.BECK

www.beck.de

ISBN 978 3 406 74560 7

© 2021 Verlag C.H.Beck oHG
Wilhelmstraße 9, 80801 München
Druck: Westermann Druck Zwickau GmbH
Crimmitschauer Straße 43, 08058 Zwickau
Satz: Fotosatz Buck
Zweikirchener Str. 7, 84036 Kumhausen
Umschlaggestaltung: Druckerei C.H.Beck, Nördlingen

chbeck.de/nachhaltig

Gedruckt auf säurefreiem, alterungsbeständigem Papier
(hergestellt aus chlorfrei gebleichtem Zellstoff)

Vorwort

In einem zunehmend flexiblen und schnelllebigen Arbeitsmarkt vollbringen Unternehmer regelmäßig den Spagat zwischen ihrem wirtschaftlichen Bedürfnis nach einer optimierten Personalstruktur und den geltenden rechtlichen Anforderungen. Der allgegenwärtige Wunsch nach einem gezielten Erwerb von Fachwissen und Fertigkeiten muss mit den komplexen rechtlichen Rahmenbedingungen des Fremdpersonaleinsatzes in Einklang gebracht werden. Das vorliegende Buch soll aufzeigen, dass diese rechtlichen Anforderungen weit über das Arbeitsrecht, das Strafrecht, das Sozialversicherungsrecht und das Steuerrecht hinausgehen.

Von der Vertragsgestaltung über die tatsächliche Umsetzung bis hin zur Beendigung von Vertragsverhältnissen mit Fremdpersonal stehen die Führungskräfte und Personalverantwortlichen vor vielfältigen Herausforderungen. Jeder dieser Schritte birgt weitreichende und oft unterschätzte Risiken. Erhebliche Haftungsfolgen, zivilrechtliche Sanktionen und die sich häufig ändernde Rechtsprechung werden zu Fallstricken beim Einsatz von Fremdpersonal. Zu diesen eher rechtlichen Risiken gesellen sich wirtschaftliche Risiken, insbesondere in Form von Zahlungsverpflichtungen bezüglich Lohnsteuer und Sozialversicherungsbeiträgen sowie Bußgelder und Geldstrafen.

Angesichts der zahlreichen zuvor genannten Risiken ist es für die Verantwortlichen entscheidend, mit den verschiedenen Formen des Fremdpersonaleinsatzes vertraut zu sein, aber auch die jeweiligen rechtlichen Rahmenbedingungen und Anforderungen zu erkennen. Dies hilft den Unternehmen die rechtlichen und betriebswirtschaftlichen Herausforderungen zu bewältigen, um vom Einsatz externen Personals zu profitieren.

Ziel dieses Buches ist es, dem Leser eine Darstellung und Analyse der rechtlichen Aspekte des Fremdpersonaleinsatzes in Deutschland zu geben. Die Intention ist es, der Leserschaft einen praktischen Leitfaden für das Tagesgeschäft zu bieten, geschrieben in britischem Englisch.

Ein herzliches Dankeschön an Christina Werner, Hannah Wilhelm, Philipp Zinndorf und Nadine Vogt.

Frankfurt am Main, Dezember 2020

Daniel Happ
Dr. Sophia Habbe

Preface

In an increasingly flexible and fast-moving labour market, entrepreneurs regularly perform a balancing act between their commercial need for an optimised personnel structure and the corresponding legal requirements. The omnipresent request for a targeted acquisition of specialist knowledge and skills must be reconciled with the complex legal framework of the deployment of external personnel. As to be seen in the course of this book, these legal requirements widely range from employment law, criminal law, social security law, and tax law.

The management personnel and human resources directors face various challenges, from drafting contracts to its actual implementation and termination of contractual relationships with external personnel. Each of these stages entails far-reaching and often underestimated risks. Considerable liability consequences, commercial law sanctions, and the frequent changes in case law become pitfalls in the deployment of external personnel. These rather legal risks are accompanied by commercial risks. In particular, in the form of payment obligations regarding wage tax and social security contributions and administrative and criminal fines.

In light of the numerous risks previously mentioned, it is crucial for the responsible bodies to be able to identify the different forms of deployment of external personnel but also to recognise their relevant legal framework and requirements. This helps business undertakings navigate the legal and commercial challenges that have to be taken to benefit from the deployment of external personnel.

This book aims to provide the reader with a description and analysis of the legal aspects of external personnel's deployment in Germany. The intention is to offer the readership a practical guidance for the day to day business, written in British English.

Warm and everlasting gratitude to Christina Werner, Hannah Wilhelm and Philipp Zinndorf.

Frankfurt on the Main, December 2020

Daniel Happ
Dr. Sophia Habbe

Autoren

Daniel Happ ist Partner im Frankfurter Büro von Noerr und Mitglied der Praxisgruppe Employment & Pensions. Er berät deutsche und internationale Unternehmen in allen arbeitsrechtlichen Angelegenheiten. Insbesondere berät er Unternehmen bei der Beschäftigung von Fremdpersonal, vertritt sie in arbeitsrechtlichen Streitigkeiten und berät und verteidigt sie in sozialversicherungsrechtlichen Auseinandersetzungen mit der Deutschen Rentenversicherung.

Julia Sophia Habbe ist Partnerin im Frankfurter Büro von Noerr und co-leitet die Praxisgruppe Compliance & Interne Ermittlungen. Sie verfügt über umfangreiche Erfahrung bei behördlichen und internen Untersuchungen und berät im Nachgang hierzu im Bereich des Prozess- und Krisenmanagements. Sie vertritt börsennotierte und inhabergeführte Unternehmen und deren Organe bei Compliance-Vorfällen, insbesondere im Bereich der Organverantwortung und in Haftungsfragen.

Martin Gliewe ist Rechtsanwalt und Fachanwalt für Arbeitsrecht. Er berät nationale und internationale Unternehmen in allen Fragen des individuellen und kollektiven Arbeitsrechts. Neben der alltäglichen Beratung liegt ein Schwerpunkt seiner Tätigkeit in der Beratung zu sämtlichen Formen des Fremdpersonaleinsatzes, insbesondere der Arbeitnehmerüberlassung und dem Einsatz von „Freelancern" oder Interim Managern.

Karolin Fitzer berät nationale und internationale Mandanten in allen Arten von Compliance-Angelegenheiten, z. B. bei der Überprüfung vorhandener Compliance-Strukturen sowie der Entwicklung und Einführung von Compliance-Programmen/Richtlinien. Daneben berät sie Unternehmen zu allen wirtschaftsstrafrechtlichen Fragestellungen mit einem besonderern Beratungsschwerpunkt im Bereich des Arbeits- und Steuerstrafrechts.

Janine Fischer beriet als Mitglied der Praxisgruppe Employment & Pensions im Frankfurter Büro von Noerr nationale und internationale Unternehmen in Fragen des individuellen und kollektiven Arbeitsrechts. Ein Fokus ihrer Tätigkeit lag dabei auf der Durchführung von internen Untersuchungen im Bereich des Fremdpersonaleinsatzes und der Beratung zu Fragen der Arbeitnehmerüberlassung und Scheinselbständigkeit. Aktuell ist sie als Strafrichterin am Amtsgericht Hanau tätig.

Authors

Daniel Happ is a partner at Noerr's Frankfurt office and member of the Employment & Pensions practice group. He has been advising national and international clients on all aspects of labour law. In particular, he advises companies on the employment of external personnel, represents them in labour law disputes and advises and defends them in social security law disputes with the German Pension Insurance Fund.

Julia Sophia Habbe is a partner at Noerr's Frankfurt office and co-heads the Compliance & Internal Investigations practice group. She has extensive experience in compliance regulatory and internal investigations and advises on process and crisis management after such investigations. She represents listed and family-owned companies and their management bodies in compliance cases, in particular in the area of their accountability and liability.

Martin Gliewe is a lawyer and certified specialist in employment law. He advises national and international companies on all matters of individual and collective labour law. Besides providing day-to-day advice, his work also focuses on all forms of deploying external personnel, especially temporary agency work and the use of freelancers or interim managers.

Karolin Fitzer advises national and international clients in all kinds of compliance matters, e. g. on the review of existing compliance structures and the development and introduction of compliance programs/guidelinese. In addition she advises companies on all questions of commercial criminal law with emphasis on labor criminal law and criminal tax law.

Janine Fischer advised national and international companies on questions of individual and collective labor law as member of the Employment & Pensions practice group at Noerr's Frankfurt office. One focus of her work was on conducting internal investigations in the area of deployment of external personnel and advising on questions of temporary agency employment and false self-employment. At present she is a criminal judge at the Hanau district court.

Overview

Table of Contents

Table of Figures

List of Abbreviations

AEntG	Posted Workers Law
AG	stock corporation
AGG	General Equal Treatment Act
AktG	Stock Corporation Act
AO	Tax Code
ArbGG	Labour Court Act
ArbSchG	Health and Safety at Work Act
ArbZG	Working Time Act
Art.	Article
AÜG	Act on Temporary Employment
BAG	Federal Labour Court
BetrVG	Works Constitution Act
BGB	German Civil Code
BUrlG	Federal Vacation Act
cf.	conferatur
DrittelbG	One-Third Participation Act
EFZG	Act on Payment of Wages and Salaries on Holidays and in Case of Illness (Continuation of Remuneration Act)
e.g.	exempli gratia
EStG	Income Tax Act
etc.	et cetera
et seq.	et sequentes
GG	Basic Law
GmbH	limited liability company
HAG	Home Employment Act
half-sent.	half-sentence
HGB	German Commercial Code
i.e.	id est
KSchG	Dismissal Protection Act
lit.	littera
marginal no.	marginal number
MitbestG	Codetermination Act

NachwG . . . . Law on Documenting Essential Applicable Conditions for Employ-
                       ment Relationship
no./nos. . . . . number/numbers

para. . . . . paragraph

SCEBG . . . . Law on the Participation of Employees in a European Cooperative
                        (SCE participation Act)
SEBG . . . . Law on the Participation of Employees in a European Company (SE
                        participation Act)
sec. . . . . section
sent. . . . . sentence
SGB . . . . Social Security Code

TFEU . . . . Treaty on the Functioning of the Euro-pean Union
TVG . . . . Collective Bargaining Agreements Act
TzBfG . . . . Part-Time and Fixed-Term Employment Act
var. . . . . variant
VAT . . . . value added tax

ZPO . . . . Code of Civil Procedure

PART 1
OVERVIEW

A. Forms of Deployment of External Personnel

Due to the rising demands of global competition on the flexibility of companies and **1** the increasing division of labour in the economy, companies are increasingly tending not only having tasks performed by their own employees but also outsource work or partially realising work results by using external personnel. This affects all stages of the value chain, i. e. the pursuit of the actual purpose of the company as well as secondary or auxiliary activities such as IT, canteen, cleaning and plant security/safety. In addition, the use of external personnel is often determined by the fact that the company is unable to cover its specific need for specialist knowledge and/or skills in sufficient quantities, on economic terms, in the appropriate time or not with its own employees.

Within the framework of his constitutionally protected rights, an entrepreneur is **2** fundamentally free to decide how and by whom he has the work carried out in his undertaking. In this context, he has to take the provisions of simple law into account to protect the constitutional rights of other people, to which the German legal system gives validity with a comprehensive and multi-layered sanctions regime and a high density of controls. The basic model is the use of the undertaking's own labour or the use of own employees with whom the entrepreneur concludes an employment contract within the meaning of sec. 611a of the German Civil Code ("**BGB**"). In practice, the entrepreneur often appears in the form of a legal entity under private law, for instance, in the form of a limited liability company (GmbH) or a stock corporation (AG). According to German law, this legal entity is to be qualified as an employer, if the legally appointed representative concludes an employment contract with the potential employee on behalf of the legal entity.

For the entrepreneur, it is also conceivable and legally permissible to employ external **3** personnel in his own company to promote and pursue his corporate purpose. Under this form of employment, the work is not accomplished by the company's own staff or by its own employees, but by external third parties. This is commonly understood as the use of external personnel.

The use of external personnel is possible in various forms. The classic forms of external **4** personnel deployment are the service contract, the contract to produce a work, and the temporary agency employment, which are dealt with in the following. Besides these, there are further deployment models that have gained significance in recent years. These will be explained after the classic forms of external personnel deployment.

I. Temporary Agency Employment

One way of reducing an undertaking's existing need for personnel or closing capacity **5** gaps is temporary agency employment, often also referred to as *temporary employment*.

The deployment of external personnel by means of temporary agency employment is **6** characterised by the fact that (temporary) employees are made available to a third party (hirer) as a worker for a limited period of time by their employer (temporary work agency). The hirer pays a fee to the temporary work agency for the period of the assignment. Consequently, the hirer can dispose of the temporary agency workers' manpower within the framework of the contractual agreement with the temporary work agency. The hirer can therefore use the temporary agency workers integrated into his own establishment as if they were his own employees. Particularly, he is entitled to exercise the right to issue instructions in relation to the job. However, even while working for the hirer, the temporary agency workers are exclusively in an employment relationship with the temporary work agency. The temporary work agency thus continues to have the disciplinary right of direction. If the relationships of the parties mentioned are visualised, a triangular relationship is created.

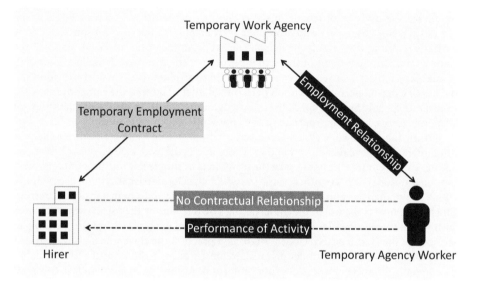

Figure 1: Illustration of temporary agency employment

7   The peculiarities of the temporary agency employment mean that temporary agency workers are often indistinguishable from the hirer's own employees when carrying out their work in the hirer's establishment. However, this special form of employment may have negative consequences for temporary agency workers in certain situations as they remain exclusively employed by the temporary work agency even while carrying out this activity.

8   The legislator has also recognised this general circumstance and considered it worthy of protection to such an extent that the Act on Temporary Agency Employment (*Gesetz zur Regelung der Arbeitnehmerüberlassung* – "**AÜG**") allows the practice of temporary agency employment only if numerous conditions are met.

9   For the first time, a legal definition of temporary agency employment was introduced with the new reform from April 1st, 2017 in sec. 1 sent.2 AÜG. In accordance with this, employees are leased if they are integrated into the work organisation of the hirer and are subject to his instructions. Although the legal definition does not fully correspond to the definition that has been developed in case law for years, it does take up the essential conditions. Hence, the legal definition has not changed the previous legal situation.

A violation of the requirements of the AÜG can lead to drastic consequences for all   **10**
parties involved (see marginal no. **320/ 572** et. seq.). Therefore, it is essential to be aware of
the requirements to be complied with when it comes to the legally compliant structuring
and implementation of temporary agency employment. Furthermore, the legal requirements are equally important when it comes to choosing a certain method of employing
external personnel to cover the need for external personnel.

1. Legal Basis

Like many other areas of law, temporary agency employment needs to increasingly be   **11**
seen in a European context. It is therefore not surprising that temporary agency employment is object to legislative acts of both the national and the European legislator.

For instance, Article 31 of the Charter of Fundamental Rights of the European Union,   **12**
as well as Title IV, Part Three of the Treaty on the Functioning of the European Union
("TFEU"), addressing the free movement of persons, services, and capital, have implications on temporary agency employment at the level of European law. Additionally,
the European legislator enacted Directive 2008/104/EC on Temporary Agency Work on
November 19th, 2008 („**Leiharbeits-Richtlinie**"), which is a specific legal act establishing
a harmonised framework at Community level for the protection of temporary agency
workers.

The German legislator has mainly summarised its requirements for temporary agency   **13**
employment in the AÜG. The requirements of the AÜG regarding the obligation to obtain
a permit date back to 1972. The provisions of the current AÜG serve both to implement
the Temporary Employment Directive and to establish exclusively national requirements.
The Act aims to provide social protection for temporary agency workers as well as to
pursue labour market policy objectives.

Therefore, the AÜG is the pivotal law in Germany concerning the provision of tem-   **14**
porary agency workers. To a large extent, it lays down public-law regulations including
civil and labour-law consequences. Nevertheless, the AÜG is not conclusive; it (merely)
contains provisions and legal consequences specifically applicable to the temporary
agency employment. Further legal consequences may also result from different laws or
legal principles.

Thus, the parties to the three-person relationship mentioned above are entitled, subject   **15**
to a violation of other legal provisions, to organise their legal relations under the AÜG in
accordance with the principle of private autonomy.

2. Legal Relations

Temporary agency employment is characterised by the specific structure of the tripar-   **16**
tite employment relationship, with the result that the three parties involved (temporary
work agency, hirer, and temporary agency worker) each relate to one another in diferrent
ways.

These relationships are characterised by very specific and besides different rights and
obligations, characterising the contractual constellation as temporary agency employment
overall.

a) Temporary Work Agency – Temporary Agency Worker

The provision of sec. 1 para. 1 sent. 3 AÜG stipulates that the temporary agency em-   **17**
ployment is only permissible if an employment relationship exists between the temporary
work agency and the temporary agency worker. The so called (temporary) employment

contract thus characterises the legal relationship between the temporary work agency and the temporary agency worker. Consequently, it results in numerous primary and secondary obligations for the parties.

18   aa) (Temporary) Employment Contract. First of all, it can be stated that German labour law does not recognise the concept of a (temporary) employment contract or a separate type of contract with this designation. A (temporary) employment contract is an employment contract according to sec. 611a BGB (see marginal no. 253 et. seq.), which rights and obligations are adapted to the unique features of temporary agency employment.

19   (1) *Formal Requirements.* In section 1, paragraph 1, sentence 3 of the AÜG is the existence of an employment relationship as an essential requirement for temporary agency employment laid down. Still, it does not initially define the criteria for such a relationship any further. The legislator instead refers to the form of employment relationship generally used in German labour law within the meaning of sec. 611a BGB.

20   Accordingly, the same conditions apply to the conclusion of a (temporary) employment relationship as to the conclusion of any other employment relationship. Therefore, an examination of the actual implementation of the contractual relationship in its entirety is also decisive for the status qualification of the contractual relationship between the temporary work agency and the temporary agency worker (sec. 611a para. 1 sent. 5 and 6 BGB). In case the (contractual) relationship between the parties is therefore lived out as an employment relationship within the meaning of sec. 611a BGB, then it must necessarily be qualified as such. It applies regardless of whether the parties share this assessment, whether they wanted it, or whether they have designated the contract accordingly.

21   Besides, it follows from the application of the provisions applicable within the framework of sec. 611a BGB that it is also possible to conclude a (temporary) employment contract without any formalities. The parties can, therefore, conclude the contract purely verbally, for example. However, such a procedure is strictly discouraged not only for reasons of legal certainty. In the employment relationship context, the Law on Documenting Essential Applicable Conditions for Employment Relationship (*Nachweisgesetz* "**NachwG**") applies to the contractual relationship of these persons. According to sec. 2, para. 1,sent. 1 NachwG, the employer (temporary work agency) must, no later than one month after the agreed commencement of the employment relationship, lay down the necessary contractual conditions in writing, sign the minutes and hand them over to the employee. Thus, if a (temporary) employment contract has been effectively concluded orally between the parties, it would have to be drawn up in writing in any case after one month at the latest. Sec. 11 para. 1 sent. 1 AÜG expressly clarifies that the obligations to provide information under the NachwG also apply to temporary employment relationships.

22   Furthermore, the temporary work agency also has extended obligations to provide evidence to a "normal" employer, resulting from the specific nature of the employment within the scope of temporary agency employment. According to sec. 11 para. 1 sent. 2 AÜG, the temporary work agency must include the following information in the written contract additionally to the requirements of the NachwG (i) the name and address of the temporary work agency, (ii) the licensing authority, (iii) the place and date of issue of the temporary agency employment permit according to sec. 1 para. 1 sent. 1 AÜG, and (iv) the type and amount of benefits for periods during which the temporary agency worker is not on loan.

In individual cases, the peculiarities of the notified contract design may result in further requirements for the contract's conclusion and, in particular, its form. Suppose the temporary work agencies and temporary agency workers intend to conclude a fixed-term employment contract. In that case, according to sec. 14 para. 4 Part-Time and Fixed-Term Employment Contracts Act (*Teilzeit- und Befristungsgesetz* "**TzBfG**"), the fixed-term agreement must be in writing within the meaning of sec. 126 BGB in order to be effective. In case the fixed term is legally ineffective due to a violation of the formal requirement, the employment contract is deemed to have been concluded for an indefinite period (sec. 16 para. 1 TzBfG).

(2) Limits of the Private Autonomous Freedom of Design. Temporary work agencies **23** and temporary agency workers enjoy the protection of private autonomy in the shaping of their relationship. They are, therefore, in principle entitled to freely shape the contractual relationship between them and the rights and obligations arising from it. However, the freedom of the parties granted by the principle of private autonomy is not unlimited.

In addition to the general limits of the law applicable to all employment contracts, **24** particularly the general protective regulations under labour law, including the Dismissal Protection Act (*Kündigungsschutzgesetz* "**KSchG**"), specific limits also result from the AÜG. Thus, according to sec. 11 para. 4 sent. 1 AÜG, the provision of sec. 622 para. 5 sent. 1 no. 1 BGB is inapplicable in an employment relationship between a temporary work agency and a temporary agency worker. Sec. 622 para. 5 sent. 1 no. 1 BGB usually gives the parties to the employment contract the possibility of agreeing shorter notice periods than those laid down by law if the employee is hired for temporary help. The peculiarities of temporary agency employment and, mainly the inherent purpose of the employees' assignment to cover an occasionally short-term need required the protection of temporary agency workers at this point.

Also, due to a particular need for protection, sec. 11 para. 4 sent. 2 AÜG, provides that **25** the temporary agency worker's right to remuneration cannot be revoked or limited by a contractual agreement in the event of a so-called default of acceptance by the temporary work agency. Pursuant to sec. 615 sent. 1 BGB, the employee may – in deviation from sec. 275 para. 1, sec. 326 para. 1 BGB – demand the remuneration agreed in his employment contract even if he has not performed any work because the employer has not accepted it. This provision principally assigns the employer operational risk. However, such a claim is abdicable under the general rules. With temporary agency employment, it is not the case for good reasons. This is because it is a matter of the so-called non-employment periods between assignments to hirers, which, according to the German model of temporary agency employment, are assigned to the hirer as an economic risk.

Furthermore, the (temporary) employment contract cannot contain any provision **26** prohibiting the temporary agency worker from concluding an employment contract with the hirer if the employment relationship between the temporary work agency and the hirer no longer exists (cf. sec. 9 para. 1 no. 4 AÜG). In this respect, the private autonomy of the contracting parties is limited– also to protect the temporary agency worker from himself.

bb) Obligations of the Temporary Agency Worker. The temporary agency worker's **27** obligation under the (temporary) employment contract does not differ in their basic form from the obligations of other employees. The temporary agency worker is obliged to perform work bound by instructions and determined by others in personal dependence in the service of another person.

In contrast to other employees, however, the temporary agency worker is principally **28** obliged to perform services of the kind mentioned above also for third parties according to their instructions. By providing these services to third parties, the temporary agency worker fulfills his contractual obligations to the employer. Thus, the temporary agency worker owes his employer (temporary work agency) an activity to third parties, persons outside the employment contract. The selection of the third person is the responsibility of the temporary work agency. Within the scope of his authority, he assigns the temporary agency worker to a hirer. The temporary agency worker is then obliged to appear at the place of employment assigned to him by the hirer and to perform his work in his establishment. In doing so, he is integrated into the hirer's work organisation and must follow the hirer's instructions regarding place, time, content and performance.

29 Since a (temporary) employment contract is an employment contract it is subject to private autonomy within the meaning of sec. 611a BGB and not a type of contract of a separate kind (see marginal no. **18**). Therefore, the primary service obligations do not have to be limited to the work as a temporary agency worker. Instead, the employee can also undertake himself in the contract to perform normal work for the temporary work agency and give the employer the opportunity to hire the employee out.

30 Besides, the temporary agency worker is also subject to a variety of general ancillary service obligations, such as the general obligation to consider the interests of the employer (see marginal no. **261**).

31 **cc) Obligations of the Temporary Work Agency.** The temporary work agency's primary service obligation under the (temporary) employment contract is to pay the remuneration owed (sec. 611a para. 2 BGB). Additionally, the parties may also agree on further contractual obligations depending on the requirements, provided they do not move outside the legal framework with that.

32 Like the temporary agency worker, the temporary work agency also has a whole range of ancillary service obligations (see marginal no. **263**). Besides, the temporary work agency must also observe special ancillary service obligations arising from the AÜG due to the specifics of the temporary agency employment.

33 According to sec. 11 para. 2 sent. 1, the temporary work agency is obliged to provide the temporary agency worker with an information leaflet from the licensing authority (Employment Agency) on the Act on Temporary Employment's essential content when the contract is concluded. Suppose the employment relationship is concluded with a non-German temporary agency worker. In that case, the latter can demand that the information leaflet is issued in his native languange (sec. 11 para. 2 sent. 2 AÜG). The information sheet is available on the homepage of the Federal Employment Agency (see "*helpful weblinks*" on page 413). In case the information sheet is not available in a language the temporary agency worker speaks. Then the temporary work agency must have the information sheet translated at its own expense (sec. 11 para. 2 sent. 3 AÜG).

34 Besides, the temporary work agency is obliged to inform the temporary agency worker without delay if the temporary work agency's temporary agency employment permit ceases to apply (sec. 11 para. 3, sent. 1 AÜG). The information can be provided informally and thus, in principle, verbally. In practice, however, written information is recommended to avoid difficulties in providing evidence.

35 **dd) Works Constitution Law.** Sec. 14 para. 1 AÜG stipulates that temporary agency workers continue to be members of the establishments of the temporary work agency within the meaning of the Works Constitution Act (*Betriebsverfassungsgesetz* "**BetrVG**") even during the period of their employment with a hirer. Accordingly, temporary agency workers are also entitled to vote and are eligible for election during the assignment in the hirer's establishment under the prerequisites of sec. 7, 8 BetrVG. The provisions mentioned before regulate the allocation of temporary agency workers under works constitution law and, thus, it answers a question that arises due to the division of employer powers between the temporary work agency and the hirer.

36 With regard to participation and codetermination rights, it means the following: If there is a works council in the temporary agency work's establishment, the codetermina-

tion rights of the works council need to be preserved insofar as their prerequisites are met. Furthermore, they need to be maintained insofar the measure at issue concerns temporary agency workers, not currently employed in the temporary work agency's establishment. For example, the employer must preserve the works council's right of codetermination pursuant to sec. 99 para. 1 BetrVG, if he or she wishes to regroup the employee (within the temporary work agency's establishment). Also, with a dismissal, that the temporary work agency intends to express towards the temporary agency workers, a right of codetermination of the works council is to be selected (sec. 102 para. 1 sent. 1 BetrVG). Furthermore, the operating agreements valid in the temporary work agency apply, as far as in the area of application, no deviating regulation was met.

ee) Social Security Law. In the German legal system, social insurance is a statutory   **37** insurance system whose task it is to secure the standard of living of every insured person in life situations threatening their existence. In the statutory social security, there is a fundamental obligation to insure. Consequently, those affected by compulsory insurance have to deduct social security contributions from their remuneration to benefit from social security benefits in the event of a claim.

The social security system provides for social security obligations for both the employ-   **38** ee and the employer. An employer in the sense of labour law and social security law is any natural or legal person or partnership with legal capacity that employs other natural persons (i. e., the employee) in an employment relationship subject to instructions, others directed, and in personal dependence. Employment is any non-autonomous work, particularly the activity within the scope of an employment relationship, sec. 7 para. 1 sent. 1 Social Security Code, Fourth Book (*Sozialgesetzbuch, Viertes Buch* "**SGB IV**"). As soon as activity falls under the employee concept of sec. 7 SGB IV, the obligation to be insured in social security comes into effect immeadeatly by law.

The social security obligations of the temporary work agency and the temporary   **39** agency worker do not differ from the obligations to which other employers and their employees are subject.

Under social security law, the temporary work agency is initially exempted from   **40** the registration requirements under sec. 28a SGB IV vis-à-vis the office responsible for collecting the social security contribution (so-called collecting agency). The collecting agency is not the same for every temporary agency worker. Indeed, the collecting agency is the statutory health insurance fund with which the individual temporary agency worker is insured or – if no longer insured by the statutory health insurance fund – was last insured. In addition to other notification obligations, the temporary work agency must notify the collecting agency of the commencement of employment of a temporary agency worker subject to compulsory insurance. In particular, this notification must include the employee's insurance number, name, and date of birth (for further requirements, see sec. 28a para. 3 SGB IV). Moreover, the temporary work agency must report changes of employment, such as termination, change of the collecting agency, and the start of a partial retirement. The temporary agency worker has an obligation to cooperate under sec. 28o SGB IV. The employee must submit the required documents for the notification to the temporary work agency and must also inform the temporary work agency of any further employment with third party employers.

Furthermore, social security law provides for a monthly payment obligation of the   **41** temporary work agency and the temporary agency worker. They both pay the social security contribution in equal parts, i. e., half each. Also, the temporary work agency has to pay the contributions to the statutory accident insurance, sec. 150 continuing Social Security Code, Seventh Book (*Sozialgesetzbuch, Siebtes Buch* "**SGB VII**"). The employee's and employer's social insurance contributions form together with the accident insurance contribution the so-called total social insurance contribution. The total social insurance contribution is paid solely by the temporary work agency, sec. 28e SGB IV. The temporary work agency must calculate the social insurance contribution monthly and notify the collecting agency of this calculation on the fifth last bank working day of the current month. Furthermore, the temporary work agency shall deduct the employee's social security contributions from the wages to be paid to the leased employee. It shall transfer them together with his own employer's contributions to the statutory health insurance fund of the respective temporary agency worker. The social insurance contribution must be paid no later than the third last bank working day of the current month, sec. 23 para. 1 sent. 2 SGB IV.

42   **ff) Tax Law.** Just as in the area of social security law, the tax obligations of the temporary work agency and the temporary agency worker do not differ from those of other employers and employees.

43   Therefore, the temporary agency worker is under sec. 1, 2, 38 para. 2 of the Income Tax Act (*Einkommenssteuergesetz*"**EStG**") subject to wage tax liability, a specific form of income tax collection. Even if the employee is the debtor of the wage tax, the temporary work agency must withhold the wage tax monthly from the wages paid to the employee and pay it to the local tax office, sec. 41a para. 1 EStG. At the same time, the temporary work agency must make a wage tax registration. The wage tax registration and payment must generally occur on the tenth day after the end of each month. In the case of smaller wage sums (payments of less than EUR 1,080 in the previous calendar year), payment can also be made quarterly on request. The amount of income tax determines by the employee's salary and tax class. Employees are assigned to one of six wage tax classes:
1. Wage tax class I:
   unwed and divorced employees as well as widowed employees, provided they do not fall into wage tax classes II or III
2. Wage tax class II:
   unwed, divorced and widowed employees who are entitled to a relief amount for lone-parents
3. Wage tax class III:
   married employees, civil partner, and widowed employees, but only for the calendar year following the year of death of the spouse/civil partner
4. Wage tax class IV:
   married employees and civil partners, if both spouses/civil partners get a wage
5. Wage tax class V:
   one of the spouses/civil partners (in the place of wage tax class IV), if the other spouse/civil partner is classified in wage tax class III
6. Wage tax class VI:
   employees who are simultaneously paid by several employers.

44   Even if the temporary agency worker is according to sec. 38 EStG, the original debtor for a wage tax, the temporary work agency, is also liable for wage tax under sec. 42d para. 1 EStG. Temporary agency workers and temporary work agencies are in this respect jointly and severally liable debtors under sec. 42d para. 3 EStG.

45   However, no value-added tax is incurred in the employment relationship.

b) Temporary Work Agency – Hirer

46   The legal relationship between the temporary work agency and the hirer is decisively characterised by the rights and obligations which the parties agree upon in their contractual relationship in the temporary agency employment contract.

aa) Temporary Agency Employment Contract. In the case of external personnel 47
deployment by way of temporary agency employment, a so-called temporary agency
employment contract is concluded between the temporary work agency and the hirer.
A temporary agency employment contract is a subset of the so-called service provision
agreement. According to this contract, the temporary work agency owes the hirer the
provision of dependent services, while the hirer owes the agreed transfer remuneration.
Formal as well as substantive requirements are placed on the validity of such a contract.

(1) Formal Requirements. Divergent to a regular service provision agreement, sec. 12 48
para. 1 sent. 1, AÜG formally subjects the temporary agency employment contract to a
written form requirement. The temporary agency employment contract must, therefore,
be concluded in writing.

In this respect, the German legislator stipulates that the written form is only satisfied 49
if the contract has been signed by both parties on the same deed either by hand through
a personal signature or a notarially certified hand mark (sec. 126 para. 1, 2 sent. 1 BGB).
Only if both parties to the contract receive a copy of the contract – which in practice
should probably be the rule – it is sufficient for each party to sign by personal signature
the copy intended for the other party (sec. 126 para. 2 sent. 2 BGB). The case that often
occurs in practice, namely the digitisation of the contract with simultaneous destruction
of the original, is therefore not sufficient for evidentiary purposes. Such a procedure is
not advisable in practice.

This written form requirement applies to all essential contractual agreements of the 50
parties in the temporary agency employment contract. This also includes the information required by the AÜG concerning such a contract (see marginal no. 58). Thus, on
the one hand, the declaration of the temporary work agency is covered by the written
form requirement that he owns the required permission. On the other hand, the hirer's
information concerning the required qualifications of the temporary agency worker and
the essential working conditions in his establishment must also be recorded in writing. A
violation of the written form requirement leads to the invalidity of the concluded contract
(sec. 125 sent. 1 BGB).

Besides, sec. 1 para. 1 sent. 5 AÜG requires that the contract between the temporary 51
work agency and the hirer must expressly designate the temporary agency workers' provision as temporary agency employment. This requirement, which appears marginal at first
glance, must be given sufficient attention (see marginal no. 386 et seq.) when structuring
the temporary agency employment against the background of the far-reaching legal
consequences of a breach (see marginal no. 482 et seq.). In particular, this also applies to
individual agreements for the respective temporary agency employment case, basing on
a framework contract. Such individual agreements must also comply with the written
form requirement. The same applies to extensions or extensions of the original temporary
agency employment contract.

(2) Limits of the Private Autonomous Freedom of Design. Here as well, as it already 52
the case for the employment agreement, there may be limits to the parties' fundamental
freedom to conclude the contract. Such limits can be found in general form, for example,
in sec. 117, 134, and 138 BGB. Furthermore, there are also special statutory requirements
regarding the content of a temporary agency employment contract, in particular for the
protection of temporary agency workers.

The AÜG sets out various substantive requirements for this purpose. The temporary 53
agency employment contract must contain a declaration by the temporary work agency,
stating that the temporary work agency has the required permission for the temporary
agency employment according to sec. 1 para. 1 sent. 1 AÜG. Furthermore, the hirer is

the addressee of various content requirements. Sec. 12 para. 1 sent. 4 AÜG stipulates a decisive demand. According to this, the parties must state in the contract what specific characteristics the activity intended for the temporary agency worker has and what professional qualifications he requires for it. The claim relates to the individual temporary agency worker and must be in writing.

54   Also, the agreement must contain information on the fundamental working conditions, including wage, applicable in the hirer's establishment to a comparable employee of the hirer. In this context, it may be sufficient if the temporary agency employment contract refers to the full extent to collective bargaining agreements or works agreement, and includes a copy of these. However, further information is indispensable if other essential working conditions do not result from the documents referred to (see marginal no. **138**).

55   Moreover, the AÜG prohibits agreements that prohibit the hirer from hiring the temporary agency worker at a point in time at which the latter's employment relationship with the temporary work agency no longer exists (Sec. 9 para. 1 no. 3 half-sent. 1 AÜG). This does not cover the agreements between the temporary work agency and the hirer on appropriate remuneration for the after the previous hiring out or through the previous hiring out occurring placement mediation that took place after previous lending or by means of previous lending.

56   **bb) Obligations of the Temporary Work Agency.** The temporary work agency's primary service obligation is, in accordance with the requirements, to provide the hirer with suitable and willing temporary agency workers for the desired period. This is a so-called indeterminate obligation. Within the scope of such a debt, the obligor is solely obliged to perform from a specific class of services. However, the obligee cannot demand any performance in particular. Therefore, the temporary work agency's contractual obligation towards the hirer ends when he has duly selected the employee and made him available to the hirer for work performance.

57   Thus, the temporary work agency's service obligation must be clearly distinguished from the obligation of the temporary agency worker to work. The temporary work agency does not owe the hirer the performance of his temporary agency worker's work. Instead, the performance of an activity is the temporary agency worker's main service obligation resulting from the employment contract between the temporary agency worker and the temporary work agency (see marginal no. **27** et seq.). The temporary work agency only owes the provision of an employee. Therefore, the temporary ageny worker is not an assistant of the temporary work agency for the work itself. Consequently, the temporary work agency is not liable for the temporary agency worker's poor performance, but only for the duly selection.

58   In addition to the usual or individual cases agreed upon ancillary service obligations, the temporary work agency is also subject to ancillary service obligations that arise specifically from the AÜG. According to sec. 12 para. 2 sent. 1 AÜG, the temporary work agency is obliged to inform the hirer without delay of the expiry of his temporary agency employment permit. Further obligations to inform also exist in cases of non-renewal, withdrawal or revocation of the permit sec. 12 para. 2 sent. 2 AÜG). If a temporary agency employment permit is not extended, the permit continues to be valid for the execution of the contracts concluded under its validity. However, this continued permit is no longer than twelve months valid (sec. 2 para. 4 sent. 4 AÜG). The temporary wor agency must also inform the hirer of the periods in question in this context (sec. 12 para. 2 sent. 2 AÜG).

59   **cc) Obligations of the Hirer.** The hirer's primary service obligation is to pay the assignment remuneration agreed in the temporary agency employment contract.

Besides, the hirer is also subject to the usual contractual ancillary service obligations. Against the background of temporary agency employment, the obligation to cooperate on the hirer's part for the correct execution of temporary agency employment can be counted among the (ancillary) obligations program of the hirer.

dd) Social Security Law. By the temporay agency worker's activity in the hirer's establishment within the framework of temporary agency employment, the hirer does not become an employer. The employer status, which is the original connecting point of the social-legal obligations program, remains with the temporary work agency for its entire duration of the activity. In principle, the contractual connection between the temporary work agency and the hirer does not result in the hirer's direct obligations under social security law. 60

However, to protect temporary agency workers and the contributor's community, the legislator has made special rules for the case of temporary agency employment. 61

It is true that, in principle, according to sec. 28e para. 1 SGB IV, the temporary work agency, as the employer, is liable for the total social security contributions. However, sec. 28e para. 2 sent. 1 SGB IV provides a certain degree of protection: In addition to the temporary work agency, the hirer is liable for the temporary work agency's original obligation to pay the total social insurance contribution like a directly liable surety. This applies to the extent that the temporary agency employment contract between the temporary work agency and the hirer has been effectively concluded and that the hirer has actually been provided with employees for work performance against remuneration. The ordering of the hirer's liability as a directly liable surety means that the hirer is obliged to pay and can be directly claimed against by the collecting agency without the defence of unexhausted remedies being available to him as a means of defence (sec. 771 sent. 1, 773 para. 1 no. 1 BGB). Therefore, the collecting agency can claim the total social security contribution directly from the hirer and does not have to take action against the temporary work agency beforehand without success by way of execution. However, the hirer is not entirely unprotected in this context. According to sec. 28e para. 2 sent. 2 SGB IV, the hirer can refuse the payment as long as the collecting agency has not reminded the temporary work agency and a set reminder period has not expired. Such a reminder obligation does not apply if insolvency proceedings are opened against the temporary work agency. 62

The amount of the hirer's payment obligation is not alone limited to the in arrears' social insurance contributions. According to sec. 28e para. 4 SGB IV, any interests on arrears that are payable due to the breach of duty and interests on deferred contributions, are also included in the liability of the hirer. However, the hirer's liability is limited to the extent that it applies only to the temporary agency workers provided explicitly to him and only for the loan period. 63

To effectively ensure the protection of the temporary agency workers and the contribution community, the hirer's liability is regardless of negligence or fault. Neither the temporary work agency nor the hirer can exclude the hirer's liability, not even under private law. Such an agreement would be null and void, sec. 32 Social Security Code, First Book (*Sozialgesetzbuch, Erstes Buch* "**SGB I**"). The hirer is obliged to pay even if he has paid the remuneration agreed in the temporary agency employment contract full to the lender. 64

Insofar as the hirer has fulfilled the collecting agency's claim, the claim of the collecting agency is transferred to the hirer, according with sec. 774 para. 1 sent. 1 BGB. Consequently, the hirer has a right of recourse against the temporary work agency in the amount of his payment to the collecting agency. 65

ee) Tax Law. Even from a tax law perspective, being an employer is the connecting point of the obligations program. Since the hirer does not become an employer of the 66 temporary agency worker in the temporary agency employment context, he is not affected by the obligations under wage tax law at first.

67   Like social security law, the legislator has also made a special rule here, which places the hirer explicitly under the (tax law) obligation.

68   According to the rules of sec. 42d para. 6 sent. 1 and 5 EStG, the hirer is next to the actual employer (temporary work agency) a jointly and severally liable debtor for the correct payment of wage tax. This to the extent that temporary agency workers have been assigned to him within the meaning of sec. 1 AÜG. The liability is limited to the outstanding wage tax solely for the periods in which the respective temporary agency workers were actually provided to the hirer, sec. 42d para. 6 sent. 4 EStG. In contrast to liability in the social law area, however, liability is more differentiated from a tax law perspective. According to sec. 42d para. 6 sent. 6 EStG, the hirer may only be claimed for payment if enforcement against the employer's domestic movable assets has failed or does not promise success. Therefore, the local tax office must generally contact the temporary work agency at first Besides, the hirer's tax liablitiy is – in contrast to social security law – not a liability of negligence or fault. The hirer is not liable according to sec. 42d para. 6 sent. 3 EStG if he erred about the existence of temporary agency employment without fault. The hirer is in error without fault if he has exercised reasonable care when legally classifying the contract. In particular, those cases are excluded from liability in which temporary agency employment actually exists, but the parties have wrongly made a different legal classification of the contractual relationship. The hirer must prove the error. The exclusion of liability explicitly does not include the error regarding the existence of an employee leasing permit according to sec. 1 para. 1 AÜG.

c) Hirer – Temporary Agency Worker

69   The legal relationship between the hirer and the temporary agency worker is the only relationship in the three-person relationship created in the temporary agency employment contract, which is characterised by the absence of a contractual link. Although there is no contractual obligation, the parties have mutual rights and obligations. These stem both from contractual relationships with third parties and directly from the law.

70   **aa) Allowance Relationship.** Looking at the constellation of the parties' relationships in the three-person relationships, as they are necessarily established in the temporary agency employment context, the relationship between the hirer and the temporary agency worker is presented as a so-called allowance relationship. Besides, there is a so-called cover relationship, consisting of the labour relationship between the temporary work agency and the temporary agency worker. Also, a so-called underlying debt relationship exists in the form of the temporary agency employment contract between the temporary work agency and the hirer.

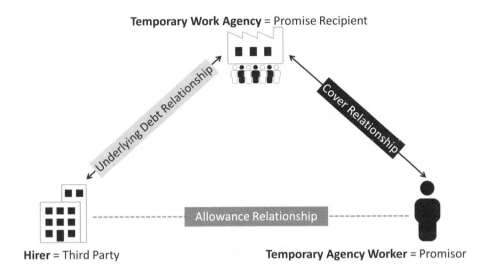

Temporary Work Agency = Promise Recipient

Hirer = Third Party

Temporary Agency Worker = Promisor

Figure 2: Legal Relations between the parties (temporary agency work)

No contractual relationship between the hirer and the temporary work agency results 71
from temporary agency employment; in particular, there is no employment contract between the parties within the meaning of sec. 611a BGB. However, from an overall view of
all existing obligations of the parties the relationship between the hirer and the temporary
agency worker can most certainly be described as a legal relationship similar to a contract.

The relationship between the hirer and the temporary agency worker is indirectly 72
regulated by the (temporary) employment contract contents and the temporary agency
employment contract. Thus, the hirer does not merely accept the work performance of
the temporary agency worker. Instead, he has his right to demand it from the temporary
agency worker and adapt it to his ideas and objectives by exercising his right of direction. Furthermore, ancillary service obligations, protection, and care obligations, and
the principles of the employee liability privilege apply. Moreover, the labour courts are
competent for disputes between temporary agency workers and the hirer. Temporary
agency workers may also "transfer" to a new owner within the transfer of establishment
according to sec. 613a BGB.

bb) Obligations under the AÜG. The legal relationship between the hirer and the 73
temporary agency worker, which is similar to a contract, is also the connecting point for
several rights of the temporary agency worker and obligations of the hirer.

In sec. 13 AÜG, the law grants the leased employee a claim for information from the 74
borrower. The legal norm opens up the possibility for the temporary agency worker to
demand information from the hirer on the essential working conditions applicable in the
hirer's establishment to a comparable employee of the hirer. Moreover, the hirer must,
according to sec. 13b sent. 1 AÜG, grant the temporary agency worker access to the joint
facilities or joint services existing in the hirer's undertaking. Unless justified by objective reasons, the access needs to be granted on the same terms and conditions as those
imposed on comparable employees of the establishment in which the temporary agency
worker is employed. Community facilities or services within the legal norm's meaning are
in particular childcare facilities, community catering, and means of transport (sec. 13b
sent. 2 AÜG). In this respect, the hirer has an obligation of equal treatment.

75   Further, the hirer has an oligation to inform pursuant to sec. 13a sent. 1 AÜG. According to this, the hirer must inform the temporary agency worker about vacant workplaces in his establishment. The information does not have to occur in person. Instead, the hirer may provide the information at a suitable place in his establishment accessible to the temporary agency worker (sec. 13 sent. 2 AÜG). Therefore, the announcement of vacant workplaces can happen, for example, by posting a notice on the notice-board, on the job portal, or the intranet.

76   If the temporary agency worker becomes active in the hirer's establishment, the hirer has health and safety obligations to the temporary agency worker (sec. 11 para. 6 sent. 1 AÜG). The activity is subject to public law prescriptions of health and safety law applicable to the hirer's establishment. The employer's obligations resulting from this are incumbent on the hirer, without affecting the employer's position and the resulting obligations of the temporary work agency. In this context, the hirer must inform the temporary agency worker about risks to health and safety he may be exposed to during his performance, particularly before the start of employment, as well as when changes in his field of work occur. Furthermore, the hirer has to inform the temporary agency worker about measures and facilities to avert the dangers mentioned above. Additionally, the hirer must inform the temporary agency worker about the need for special qualifications or professional skills or special medical supervision and increased workplace-specific risks.

77   **cc) Works Constitution Law.** The use of temporary agency workers in the hirer's establishment is also important from the Constitution Act's point of view. On the one hand, this concerns, the decision itself to have temporary agency workers work in the hirer's establishment. On the other hand, the effects that the employment of temporary agency workers can have on the works constitution of the establishment in which they are employed.

78   In this context, sec. 14 para. 2 sent. 1 AÜG stipulates that temporary agency workers whose activity is longer than three months are entitled to vote actively in elections to the works council of the hirer's establishment (active voting right). Only insofar as the general requirements are met (Sec. 7 BetrVG). However, the temporary agency workers in the hirer's establishment are still not allowed to stand for election as works council members. Therefore, temporary agency workers are the only group of employees who are entitled to vote but not eligible for election.

79   Furthermore, the employment of a temporary agency worker is an individual personnel measure subject to codetermination in the sense of sec. 99 BetrVG. In this regard, sec. 14 para. 3 sent. 1 AÜG expressly stipulates that the works council of the hirer's undertaking must be involved before a temporary agency worker is hired to perform work according to sec. 99 BetrVG. The consequences of not proper participation of the works council depend on the general legal consequences of sec. 99 para. 1 BetrVG. Furthermore, it must be noted that the hirer is also subject to specific obligations to inform. Thus, the hirer must submit to the works council within the participation scope the written explanation of the temporary work agency about the possession of a temporary agency employment permit (sec. 14 para. 3 sent. 2 AÜG). If, besides, the temporary work agency informs the hirer that his temporary agency employment permit is no longer valid (see marginal no. **58**), the hirer is obliged to inform the works council immediately of this circumstance (sec. 14 para. 3 sent. 3 AÜG).

80   In addition to temporary agency workers' employment as a matter of decision-making subject to codetermination, their use also has other sometimes serious consequences under works constitution law for the hirer's undertaking.

81   According to sec. 14 para. 2 sent. 4 and 5 AÜG, the temporary agency workers employed in a hirer's undertaking, must then be considered if legal consequences under code-

termination right require a certain number or proportion of employees. For example, this becomes relevant, in the context of the German Codetermination Act (*Mitbestimmungs-gesetz* "**MitbestG**"). The undertaking's temporary agency workers are counted within the determination of the threshold above which a co-determinated supervisory board must be formed (Sec. 1 para. 1 MitbestG in conjunction with Sec. 14 para. 2 sent. 5 AÜG). Therefore, the use of temporary agency workers can be decisive in determining whether or not a supervisory board with codetermination needs to be formed. For the provisions of the Codetermination Act, Coan & Stell Co-Determination Act, the Supplementary Codetermination Act, the One-Third Participation Act, the Act on the Codetermination of Employees in Cross-Border Mergers, the SE and SCE Participation Act or the electoral regulations issued based on the respective laws, the number of active temporary agency workers only needs to be taken into account if their period of employment exceeds six months (sec. 14 para. 2 sent. 6 AÜG).

The requirement of a six-month period of employment is to be understood in relation **82** to the workplace. This means that an undertakinge that uses temporary agency workers to fill positions for six months is obliged to include the temporary agency workers in calculating the threshold value.

Furthermore, there are many special regulations under works constitution law regard- **83** ing the information and consultation of temporary agency workers or the right of appeal.

dd) Social Security Law. By the activity of temporary agency workers in the hirer's **84** establishment, the hirer does not become the temporary agency workers' employer. In principle, the contractual relationship between the temporary work agency and the hirer does not result in the hirer's direct obligation under social security law. However, the social security law contains a special liability element on protecting temporary agency workers and the community of contributors (see marginal no. **61** et seq.).

ee) Tax Law. For the effects of the allowance relationship on the hirer's obligations **85** under wage tax law, reference can be made to social security law statements. In practice, the hirer is only obliged to do so in exceptional cases (see marginal no. **66** et seq.).

3. Scope of Application of the AÜG

Suppose the type of external personnel deployment chosen by the parties is temporary **86** agency employment within the meaning of the AÜG. In that case, the legal relations between the parties are subject to far-reaching provisions of the AÜG. The regulations refer to both public-law requirements for the obligation to obtain a permit and practical requirements for implementing temporary agency employment. Not only cases of overt temporary agency employment come within the scope of applying the strict regulations of the AÜG, but also cases of concealed temporary agency employment (see marginal no. **572/652** et seq.). The subsequent obligations must be complied with in both cases.

a) Permission Requirement for Temporary Agency Employment

The AÜG not only postulates the legal principle of the obligation to obtain permission **87** for temporary agency employment, but it also provides for exceptions.

aa) Principle: No Temporary Agency Employment without Permission. Generally, **88** employers who, as temporary work agencies, want to provide their temporary agency workers to hirers to perform work require a permit to do so, according to sec. 1 para. 1 sent. 1 AÜG.

The regulatory technique used by the German legislator here is a so-called preventive **89** prohibition in combination with subject to permission. This means that the temporary agency eployment is generally prohibited unless the hirer possesses a corresponding permit. Therefore, possession of a valid temporary agency employment permit is a mandatory prerequisite for legal temporary agency employment in Germany. Through this type of "access restriction to the market", the legislator secures a central control position for itself, which is intended to counteract the abuse of temporary agency employment.

90   However, the effects of this reservation of permission on the temporary work agencies' business are not as serious as it may seem at first glance. On the one hand, the temporary work agency is entitled to hire out all of its employees within its permit scope, which means that it is not necessary to apply for a new licence for each assignment. On the other hand, the criteria under which a permit must be issued by the responsible authority (Employment Agency) are transparent. Furthermore, the authorities do not have a completely free discretion within the framework of their decision, but only a so-called bound discretion. If the legal requirements for the granting of a temporary agency employment permit are met, the authority must issue it (see marginal no. **100** et seq.). A further advantage for undertakings is that so-called mixed operation can also apply for a temporary agency employment permit. It means for undertakings that even if only a small part of temporary agency employment is carried out, the permit can be granted. There is no need for genuine temporary employment agencies that have specialised in temporary agency employment.

91   However, the consequences of the permit requirement are serious in cases where this legal requirement is violated. If the temporary work agency outhires an employee without the necessary permit, this has far-reaching consequences for all parties involved (see marginal no. **320/572** et seq.).

92   **bb) Exemptions for Small Businesses and for the Construction Business.** The obligation to obtain permission does not apply absolutely, as the AÜG contains both positive and negative deviations from the principle. Sec. 1a AÜG privileges the so-called colleague assistance, whereas sec. 1b AÜG provides for restrictions for the construction industry.

93   According to sec. 1a para. 1 AÜG, an employer with less than 50 employees who hand over an employee to another employer to avoid short-time work or dismissals, does not require permission. A further requirement is that the lent employee is not hired and employed for temporary agency employment. If these prerequisites are met, temporary agency employment for up to twelve months is permissible even without a temporary agency employment permit if the hirer has notified the Federal Employment Agency in writing in advance to temporary agency employment. The individual details which the notification must contain are regulated in sec. 1a para. 2 AÜG. According to this legal norm, temporary agency employment should only be permitted in exceptional cases and only to bridge economic difficulties. This results from the core requirement, requiring that the employee not be hired and employed for temporary agency employment. Suppose the employee is hired or employed for temporary agency employment's purpose. In that case, temporary agency employment reflects the intended field of application of the employee and is not the employer's reaction to an unforeseen exceptional situation. With the hiring out in such a constellation, the employer obviously pursues monetary goals; the assignment does not primarily serve to secure the employee's job. However, if the requirements are met, this form of temporary agency employment is not subject to approval.

94   According to sec. 1b sent. 1 AÜG, temporary agency employment is not permitted if the temporary agency worker is to be provided to establishments in the construction business and would be entrusted there with work that is usually carried out by (construction) workers. The prohibition presupposes that the hirer's undertaking is an establishment in the construction business, which means that construction work is carried out there. This includes establishments in the main construction business and establishments in the scaffolding and roofing trades, as well as in gardening and landscaping. The prohibition also covers mixed operations if construction work is predominantly performed in the establishment or in the operating department. Since the prohibition is linked to an activity usually performed by workers in the hirer's establishment, temporary agency employment to corresponding establishments is also covered by the prohibition. If, for example, a possible temporary agency worker in the construction establishment was entrusted with commercial activities, the prohibition of sec. 1b sent. 1 AÜG does not apply.

The counter-exception of sec. 1b sent. 2 lit. a AÜG permits temporary agency employ- **95**
ment from establishments in any business to establishments in the construction business if a collective bargaining agreement, which has generally been declared binding, permits the temporary agency employment. The collective bargaining agreement must expressly permit temporary agency employment. In contrast, sec. 1b sent. 2 lit. b AÜG also allows the temporary agency employment between establishments in the construction business if the lending establishment has demonstrably been covered by the same framework and social security fund collective bargaining agreements or by their generally binding nature for at least three years.

A further exception to the partial prohibition of the temporary agency employment **96**
in establishments in the construction business can be found in sec. 1b sent. 3 AÜG for establishments in the construction business having their registered office in another Member State of the European Economic Area. In case the foreign establishments are not covered y German framework, and social security fund collective bargaining agreements (sec. 1b sent. 2 lit. b AÜG) or generally binding declared collective bargaining agreements (sec. 1b sent. 2 lit. b AÜG), temporary agency employment can still be permitted. It can be permitted if the foreign establishments can prove that they have predominantly been engaged for at least three years in activities covered within the scope of the same framework, and social security fund collective bargaining agreement the hirer's establishment falls under as well.

According to the AÜG, the exceptions mentioned above are exceptions under trade **97**
law or a restriction of the obligation to obtain permit per se. However, a distinction must be made between these exceptions and the privileged possibilities for temporary agency employment (see marginal no. **179** et seq.).

For other restrictions affecting the application of the AÜG as a whole, see margin- **98**
al no. **171** et seq.

cc) Exception in the Meat Processing Industry. During the corona pandemic there **99**
were repeated outbreaks of infection in meat processing factories in 2020. In the extremely intensive media coverage of these events, the massive use of temporary agency workers and contractors was repeatedly mentioned as a possible cause for these outbreaks. This brought the working conditions in the industry, which had already been criticised as precarious, into broad public focus. The German government reacted to this by passing a special law prohibiting the use of temporary agency workers and the performance of work by contractors. Under sec. 6a para. 2 of the Act on Safeguarding Workers' Rights in the Meat Industry (*Gesetz zur Sicherung von Arbeitnehmerrechten in der Fleischwirtschaft* – "**GSA-Fleisch**"), the operator of a meat-processing business may only have slaughtering and cutting work carried out by employees who are employed by him. There is thus a ban on the supply of temporary agency workers in the meat processing industry with effect from 1 January 2021. The same applies mutatis mutandis to the use of service contracts and contracts to produce a work.

dd) Incurrence: Application for a Permit. A temporary agency employment permit, **100**
as required by sec. 1 para. 1 sent. 1 AÜG, is issued by the responsible authority after the conclusion of an appropriate administrative procedure.

101   For the desired permit to be granted, the applicant must submit a written application (sec. 2 para. 1 AÜG) in German. This application must be submitted to an appropriate authority. According to sec. 17 para. 1 sent. 1 AÜG, the Federal Employment Agency is fundamentally responsible for implementing the AÜG and, thus, for granting a temporary agency employment permit. Since the statute does not contain any prescriptions on further factual and/or local responsibilities, the application for a permit can be submitted to any Employment Agency. Due to the internal distribution of tasks, a responsibility arises for the Employment Agencies in Düsseldorf, Kiel and Nuremberg, depending on the federal state or country of the applicant. To avoid unnecessarily delays in the application procedure, the respective competence of the Agencies should be considered (see „*helpful adresses*" on page **415**).

102   In the context of the application process, various details and numerous documents are required. All information on the required information and the papers to be submitted can be found on the application form provided online by the Federal Employment Agency (see „*helpful weblinks*" on page **413**). In addition to personal information on the temporary work agency, the following additional documents must be submitted with the application:
→ Copy of the current excerpt from the commercial register
→ Copy of the articles of incorporation
→ Copy of the business registration
→ Evidence of application for a certificate of good conduct for presentation to an authority
→ Information from the central register of trade – GZR 3 – for the applicant or – in the case of persons other than natural persons – for the representatives according to the law/statute/articles of incorporation, and branch managers
→ Information from the central register of trade – GZR 4 – for legal entity or body of persons
→ Certificate of a employer's liability insurance association (accident insurer)
→ Certificates from health insurance funds
→ Statements of all business accounts, and credit confirmations where appropriate
→ Model temporary employment contract, respectively, an employment contract with a supplementary agreement for temporary agency workers according to sec. 11 AÜG
→ Model of a temporary agency employment contract according to sec. 12 AÜG

103   After receiving all necessary documents and information by the responsible authority, the latter will verify whether the conditions for granting the permit are fulfilled and whether there are serious grounds for refusing to approve the permit. In particular, this examination shall assess whether the applicant is considered eligible and whether the establishment's setting up and the establishment's organisation meets the requirements. If the Employment Agency concludes that there are no grounds for refusing to grant a temporary agency employment permit, it issues the permit by means of an administrative act. The permit shall contain the declaration of the issue and the period for which the permit is valid. In principle, the permit, according to sec. 2 para. 4 sent. 1 AÜG is initially limited to one year. Pricipally, the authority can also grant the permit under conditions and subject to conditions (sec. 2 para. 2 AÜG). If no application for renewal is submitted, the permit expires without further action on the part of the authority or the temporary work agency.

104   According to sec. 2 para. 4 sent. 2 AÜG, an application for the permit's extension must be submitted at least three months before the end of the year in which the permit expires. In the case of three consecutive years of granting a temporary agency employment permit, the temporary work agency may apply for an unlimited permit for the first time.

b) Disclosure Statement

With the reform of the AÜG on 1 April 2017, the legislator has included the so-called **105** disclosure statement, consisting of obligations to label and concretise, in the AÜG. In addition to these obligations, it has added information requirements on the temporary work agency's part towards the temporary agency worker. The legislative intention behind the introduction of a disclosure statement was to avoid abusive formations of the use of external personnel in the form of the concealed temporary agency employment through an open commitment of the parties to the contract's form.

aa) Obligation to label. Part of the disclosure statement is contained in sec. 1 para. 1 **106** sent. 5 AÜG with the so-called obligation to label. According to this, temporary work agencies and hirers must expressly designate the hiring out of temporary agency workers in their contracts as temporary agency employment.

The designation as a temporary agency employment contract does not necessarily **107** have to be in the contract's title, even if this is advisable. However, the contract's subject must be expressly designated as temporary agency employment, at least in the contract's text. It is, therefore, not sufficient if this only results indirectly from the agreed contractual obligations. Declarations by the parties outside the contractual document are also insufficient to comply with the obligation to label since the designation must be made in the contract between the temporary work agency and the hirer; also, the temporary agency employment contract is subject to the written form requirement under sec. 12 para. 1 sent. 1 AÜG (see marginal no. **48**). Instead, an express reference must be made in the actual temporary agency employment contract.

According to the explicit wording, the obligation's addressee is both the temporary **108** work agency and the hirer. Furthermore, the wording clearly states that this obligation must be fulfilled before temporary agency workers are hired out by the temporary work agency or start to perform for the hirer. It follows that the disclosure of temporary agency employment must be made before the actual start of work. However, a later contract supplement or contract amendment is not sufficient to cure a breach that has already occurred. It should be noted that this also applies to cases in which a service agreement or contract for work and labour only develops into a temporary agency employment contract in the course of the contract's execution. Therefore, the parties are forced to determine the type of contract in a binding manner before the contract. Due to the often difficult question of the correct legal assessment and conversion of the contractual relationship, this regularly puts the parties to the contract in a difficult position. In particular, as the time of such a change of the legal relationship can often not be determined exactly, the client and contractor bear the risk of a legal misjudgement (see marginal no. **386/614** et seq.).

The obligation to label is mandatory. It can neither be waived nor restricted by an **109** agreement.

bb) Obligation to concretise. The other part of the disclosure statement is found in **110** sec. 1 para. 1 sent. 6 AÜG with the so-called obligation to concretise. According to this, the person of the temporary agency worker must be concretised regarding the temporary agency employment contract before the temporary agency employment starts. This obligation applies to every employed temporary agency worker. For example, suppose the temporary work agency wants to exchange a temporary agency worker who has already been hired out for another temporary agency worker. In that case, concretisation must occur before the temporary agency worker is used in the hirer's establishment. It must happen in such a way that the identity of the temporary agency worker can be established beyond doubt. It will be sufficient to state the first name, surname and birth date in many cases. However, in individual cases, it may be necessary to add further details such as personal/official ID number, address, etc.

111   According to the law, the obligation to concretise is per se not subject to any formal requirement. According to the principle of freedom of form, concretisation is possible without observing a form (e. g., verbally). However, it is not advisable to concretise verbally not only to provide evidence in potential disputes but also to meet the obligations to produce supporting documents imposed on the temporary work agency by the AÜG (sec. 7 para. 2 AÜG). This also applies concerning the stricter formal requirements of labeling (sec. 1 para. 5, 12 AÜG). The concretisation should at least follow in text form (sec. 126b BGB – e. g. e-mail).

112   Concretisation does not have to occur in the temporary agency employment contract, per se. On the one hand, this already results from the wording of the obligation, which states that the concretisation must be carried out "…with reference to this contract…". Furthermore, this also results from the intention of the legislator. According to the explanatory memorandum, the obligation to concretise is aimed at the framework contracts of temporary agency employment, which are often encountered in practice.[1] In these agreements, the temporary work agency undertakes to provide the hirer with a contingent of employees for a particular period. In this case, the specific temporary agency worker is not necessarily certain when the framework contract is concluded. In order not to leave a gap in the disclosure statement at this point, the law requires that the personnel concretisation of the temporary agency worker takes place before the actual hiring out.

113   The obligation to concretise is also mandatory and can neither be waived nor restricted by an agreement.

114   **cc) Information Requirement.** With the reform of the AÜG, the temporary work agency's information requirement according to sec. 11 para. 2 sent. 4 AÜG has been added to the disclosure statements.

115   Before each hiring out to a hirer, the temporary work agency must inform the temporary agency worker that he is acting as a temporary agency worker. It is not sufficient to refer to the temporary employment activity only when the employment contract is concluded, but not before the corresponding assignment to the hirer. This means that in the case of multiple assignments, the information requirement must be repeated. In practice, the information is regularly provided with the deployment assignment to the hirer's establishment.

116   Such an information requirement is only triggered if there is actually a temporary agency employment contract.

117   The information requirement is not subject to any formal requirement. This means that the temporary agency worker can also be informed formless. However, it is not only advisable for evidentiary purposes to comply with the information requirement, at least by observing the written form (sec. 126 BGB). It is sufficient to inform the temporary agency worker in an e-mail to comply with the written form.

c) Maximum Assignment Length

118   Principally, the German legislator recognises the undertakings' need for external personnel in temporary agency employment. However, to avoid competition with the hirer's so-called permanent staff, the new reform of the AÜG only permits the temporary agency employment for a limited period.

---

[1] German Bundestag Drucksache 18/9232, p. 19 et seq.

aa) Principle. The AÜG postulates the principle of a maximum assignment length in   **119**
sec. 1 para. 1b sent. 1 AÜG. The legislator has opted for a rigid deadline with the possibility of deviation. According to the legal standard, the temporary work agency must not
assign the same temporary agency worker to the same hirer for more than 18 consecutive months. The hirer must not, mirror-invertedly, employ the same temporary agency
worker for more than 18 straight months. Therefore, the maximum assignment length is
addressed to both the hirer and the temporary work agency.

According to the wording, the maximum assignment length clearly refers to the   **120**
individual temporary agency worker. It is therefore open to the hirer to exchange the
temporary agency worker for another temporary agency worker at the end of the respective maximum assignment length. In practice, this means that permanently changing
temporary agency workers can also be used at the respective establisment. The legislator
has thus consciously decided in favour of an employee reference.

Concerning the respective hirer, it depends on the hirer's undertaking and not on the   **121**
respective establishment. The legislator has thus prevented temporary agency workers
from changing from one establishment to another.

Overall, the calculation of the maximum assignment length is not defined in detail   **122**
by law. With regard to the beginning and the end of the maximum assignment length
the general rules of sec. 187 para. 2 and sec. 188 para. 2 BGB must, therefore, be applied.
Accordingly, the period begins with the first day of the actual employment at the hirer,
whereby this day already counts. Whether in individual cases, the temporary agency
worker is hired out for individual days or full-time or part-time is irrelevant for the
maximum assignment length according to the law's wording. As soon as the maximum
assignment length is exceeded by one day, this constitutes a violation of the AÜG.

When determining the maximum permissible assignment length, periods of previous   **123**
assignments by the same or another temporary work agency to the same hirer shall be
fully considered. This is only the case if no more than three months elapse between the
assignments (sec. 1 para. 1b sent. 2 AÜG). This means that a renewed hiring out of the
specific temporary agency worker to the same hirer after the maximum assignment length
has been reached is only possible after the expiry of a three-month waiting period. After
this period has expired, the maximum assignment length of 18 months can again be fully
utilised. On the other hand, reaching the maximum assignment length does not affect
the temporary agency worker's intended employment to another hirer. According to the
legislator's intentions, these regulations shall prevent possible circumvention strategies
concerning the maximum assignment length.

bb) Exceptions. However, even the principle of a maximum assignment length postu-   **124**
lated by sec. 1 para. 1b sent. 1 AÜG is not without its exceptions. The AÜG itself provides
scope for extended assignment periods under certain conditions. These possibilities for
exceptions regulated by the AÜG itself are conclusive. Therefore, the parties cannot provide for more extended temporary agency employment periods, such as in the (temporary)
employment contract or the temporary emplyment contract.

(1) Derogation by Collective Bargaining Agreement. Sec. 1 para. 1b sent. 3 AÜG gives   **125**
the parties to a collective bargaining agreement in the respective sector of employment,
the possibility of agreeing, through a collective bargaining agreement on the maximum
assignment length deviating from the statutory requirement.

The decisive factor for uning the law's exception is that the hirer's industry's collective   **126**
bargaining agreement provides for a maximum assignment length, actually deviating
from the legal requirement. On the one hand, this means that the collective bargaining
agreement that is willing to deviate must also contain a maximum assignment length.

Here, too, the completely unlimited hiring out is inadmissible. On the other hand, the collective bargaining agreement must be that of the hirer's industry, and the collective bargaining agreement must bind the hirer. Therefore, it is not sufficient if the exception to the maximum assignment length is regulated in a collective bargaining agreement of the temporary agency employment sector.

127   In practice, it can be observed that the legislator makes frequent use of this leeway. Regulations regarding deviating the maximum assignment length can be found, for example, in the metal and electrical industry, the electrical trade or the steel industry. However, a deviation is possible in association with corporate collective bargaining agreements and an in-house collective bargaining agreement.

128   *(2) Derogation by Works or Operating Agreement.* In addition to the possibility of deviation through a collective bargaining agreement, the provisions of sec. 1 para. 1b sent. 4, 5, 6 AÜG also open up the possibility of deviating from the maximum assignment length in works or operating agreements. However, these possibilities are more restrictive to the extent that they generally presuppose the existence of a collective bargaining agreement containing regulations on the maximum assignment length.

129   For example, sec. 1 para. 1b sent. 4 AÜG provides that hirer's undertakings not bound by collective bargaining agreements may adopt deviating provisions of collective bargaining agreements by concluding works or operating agreement. This only applies insofar as they are subject to the scope of the collective bargaining agreement. To be able to utilise this exception, the hirer must be covered by a deviating collective bargaining agreement's territorial, technical, and temporal scope, but not be collectively bound (otherwise, the exception from sec. 1 para. 1b sent. 3 AÜG would already apply, see marginal no. 125 et seq.). Furthermore, he must transfer the collective bargaining agreement regulations fully to his establishment through works or operating agreement. Collective bargaining agreement regulations regularly represent an indivisible unit and can only be adopted in their entirety and without any changes to their content.

130   Besides, deviations from the maximum assignment length are also possible in cases where the collective bargaining agreement itself does not specify a different maximum assignment length but allows the parties to works or operating agreement to make differing arrangements. These are cases where the collective bargaining agreement contains a so-called opening clause for regulation by a works or operating agreement. However, a mere silence of the collective bargaining agreement on this issue is not sufficient in this respect.

131   Sec. 1 para. 1b sent. 5 AÜG provides for such an exception. According to this, the differing maximum assignment length can be validly specified in works or operating agreement if a collective bargaining agreement of the employment sector entitles this. The prerequisite for using this exception is an opening clause in a collective bargaining agreement to which the hirer is bound. A further perequisite is that based on this, the different maximum assignment length is stipulated in works or operating agreement.

132   Furthermore, such a possibility is also offered to establishments of a hirer not bound by collective bargaining agreements. According to sec. 1 para. 1b sent. 6 AÜG, the maximum assignment length can also deviate in such establishments if an opening clause is contained in a collective bargaining agreement relevant to the areal, technical, and time. The hirer not bound by this collective bargaining agreement completes the opening clause in his establishment through provisions in works or operating agreement. In contrast to a hirer bound by a collective bargaining agreement, however, the hirer not bound by the collective bargaining agreement must only provide a deviation from the maximum assignment length up to a maximum of 24 months. However, this maximum limit of 24 months does not apply if the opening clause stipulates a maximum assignment length.

Since all of the options above require the conclusion of works or operating agreement, **133** they are closed to companies with no corresponding codetermination body. In such establishments, the only exception of the maximum assignment length is that referred to in marginal no. **125** et seq. above.

d) Equal Pay and Equal Treatment

Sec. 8 para. 1 sent. 1 AÜG contains the so-called principle of equal treatment, known in **134** German as the equal pay/equal treatment principle. According to this principle, the temporary agency worker must not be disadvantaged concerning their working conditions, and the remuneration received compared to the hirer's establishment employees. Exceptions and restrictions are only permitted by or based on a collective bargaining agreement.

aa) Principle. As a general rule, sec. 8 para. 1 sent. 1 AÜG states that the temporary **135** work agency is obliged to provide the temporary agency worker, for the duration of temporary agency employment to the hirer, with the necessary working conditions applicable in the hirer's establishment to a comparable worker of the hirer. This also and in particular applies to remuneration.

It is a specific prohibition of discrimination within the framework of the AÜG for the **136** duration of temporary agency employment. Therefore, the principle of equal treatment only benefits the temporary agency worker for such periods during which he is actually hired out to a hirer. During the not hired out time, the working conditions, including remuneration, are governed exclusively by the working conditions in which the temporary work agency and the temporary agency worker have agreed in the (temporary) employment contract (see marginal no. 31 et seq.).

The principle of equal treatment shall apply from the first day of the temporary agency **137** employment unless there is a permissible deviation. From a practical point of view, it is imperative to clarify the criteria according to which the principle of equal treatment requirements is determined.

(1) Essential Working Conditions. Although the AÜG postulates equality, there is no **138** indication as of which elements of the working conditions are regarded as essential within the meaning of the equal treatment principle. Under recourse to art. 3 para. 1 lit. f of the Directive on Temporary Agency Work, it can be stated that this includes all working conditions laid down by law, regulation, administrative provision, collective bargaining agreement or other binding provisions of a general nature applicable to the hirer. These relate to working hours, overtime, breaks, rest periods, night work, holidays and days off.

Besides, the legislator – freely following the solution of "equal pay for equal work" – **139** expressly clarifies in sec. 8 para. 1 sent. 1 AÜG that remuneration also counts among the essential working conditions. However, in this respect, the Act does not indicate which should cover potential remuneration components. The legal norm wording merely shows in sec. 8 para. 1 sent. 3 AÜG that the legislator wants to see remuneration in kind understood as part of remuneration. Due to the lack of a sufficient statutory provision, the remuneration covers all that the temporary agency worker would have received if employed by the hirer to perform the same work.

Consequently, this includes all cash benefits and benefits in kind, not only current benefits but also all bonuses and allowances and entitlements to continued remuneration and all other remuneration components that a comparable employee of the hirer receives the return for his work. The non-cash benefits to incoporate are all benefits that are not in cash but have an economic value. For example, these include providing a mobile phone, a company car or a railcard for private use, job tickets, discounted childcare or canteen use, staff discounts, stock options, and subsidies for accommodation and dwelling. Due to practical circumstances, such benefits in kind can be valued in euros within margin call with the principle of equality (sec. 8 para. 1 sent. 3 AÜG). In this respect, the temporary agency worker may not be discriminated against in terms of value, but they are not entitled to receive the non-cash benefits per se.

140   *(2) Comparable Employees.* The reference object of the principle of equality is a comparable employee working for the hirer. In practice, however, the exact determination of a comparable employee sometimes causes difficulties.

141   First of all, the starting point is the temporary agency worker's actual activity at the hirer and not a (deviating) definition of the activity in the temporary agency employment contract or the (temporary) employment contract. In this respect, the hirer and temporary work agency cannot make use of the equality principle's legal provisions. If this connecting factor is determined, a hypothetical consideration is required to determine a comparable employee. The essential working conditions of a comparable employee are then those which would apply to the temporary agency worker if the hirer had directly employed him at the same workplace for the duration of temporary agency employment.

142   According to this, determining a comparable worker is generally possible without any problems if regular employees also carry out the temporary agency worker's work in the hirer's establishment. Suppose the essential working conditions, including the permanent employees' remuneration, as often in practice, are linked to other factors (e.g., special qualifications or duration of employment in the establishment), and these do not depend solely on the type of work performed. In that case, these factors must be taken into account. Therefore, a temporary agency worker does not need to be treated in the same way as workers whose (more favourable) working conditions result from the presence of specific characteristics that the temporary agency worker does not meet.

143   This often results in a situation where no employee can be identified who can be considered comparable within the principle of equal treatment. This applies particularly to cases where the temporary agency worker is the only member of the establishment who carries out such work. In such cases, a comparable worker for determination is an employee engaged in similar work. In this context, activity is to be classified as similar if it is not identical but is carried out at the same hierarchical level and makes comparable demands in terms of the qualifications, skills, sense of responsibility, and physical strain on the workers. Suppose there is no permanent employee comparable to the temporary agency worker in the hirer's establishment even according to these requirements. In that case, the usual working conditions of comparable employees according to a collective bargaining agreement applicable to the establishment or the respective branch of industry or a remuneration scheme applicable there must be taken into account.

144   In practice, however, the parties involved may also face the opposite problem. Especially in inconsistent, respectively fragmented remuneration structures, several comparable employees may be found in the hirer's establishment. In such cases, it is not permitted to classify exclusively as a reference object the permanent employee with the supposedly most unfavorable working conditions. Instead, the reference object must always be the permanent employee who was last hired. It must be assumed that the temporary agency worker would also have been hired under these conditions unless peculiar circumstances justify a deviation.

145   *(3) Comparability.* In addition to the difficulties of determining the comparable employee, the comparability of the main working conditions also causes problems in practice. Especially due to the differentiation by functional groups and the conversion of non-monetary remuneration into euros, a comparison is not always easy.

Comparing the respective working conditions occurs within the framework of a func- **146** tional group comparison for the respective duration of temporary agency employment. For example, the existing regulations on leave must be compared in their entirety. A comparison of individual regulations across the functional groups – a kind of "cherry-picking" – is not permitted. A supposedly more favourable holiday regulation of the temporary work agency, for example, does not compensate for the lack of a company pension scheme which the hirer grants to his employees.

Within the framework of this regularly very labor-intensive determination of a com- **147** parable employee's essential working conditons, the law contains a significant simplification of the principle of equal treatment in sec. 8 para. 1 sent. 2 AUG. However, this only applies concerning the requirement to grant comparable remuneration. According to this provision, the law presumes that the temporary agency worker is on an equal footing about remuneration if they receive the collective bargaining agreement remuneration of a comparable employee in the hirer's establishment. If there is no comparable employee, the presumption also applies if the employee gets a collectively agreed remuneration applicable to comparable employees in the hirer's employment industry.

The legislator works with fiction at this point. If the prerequisites for this are met, the **148** temporary gency worker is considered to be treated equally, regardless of whether they are actually treated equally to employees in the hirer's establishment. However, it should be noted that this fiction is not absolute but merely refutable. Suppose the temporary agency worker can demonstrate that the remuneration of a comparable permanent employee in the hirer's establishment is higher than the remuneration owed under the relevant collective bargaining agreement or the remuneration owed in the employment industry. In that case, the temporary agency worker will continue to be entitled to equal treatment.

bb) Exceptions. The principle of equal treatment in sec. 8 para. 1 sent. 1 AÜG is also **149** not without its exceptions. Deviations are permitted by collective bargaining agreements.

(1) Derogation by Collective bargaining agreement. According to sec. 8 para. 2 sent. 1 **150** AÜG, the principle of equal treatment does not apply if a collective bargaining agreement is applicable in the temporary work agency's and temporary agency worker's relationship. The mentioned collective bargaining agreement regulates the latter's working conditions and thereby lays down rules which deviate from the provisions of the principle of equal treatment. The collective bargaining agreement does not have to define the deviating regulations in detail; it can also permit deviating regulations by the parties to the employment contract and/or the establishment through an opening clause.

At this point, the legislator accepts the need for a uniform arrangement of the working **151** conditions because of an activity's special circumstances within the temporary agency employment's framework. Collective working conditions for temporary agency workers employed by different hirers must continue unchanged as in a regular employment relationship. This takes into account that, for example, the holiday entitlement of a temporary agency worker should not depend on the hirer with whom he has been employed in the last three months.

In order to make use of the exception, the effective collective bargaining agreement **152** must actually cover the temporary employment relationship. Therefore, the temporary employment relationship must fall within the collective bargaining agreement's territorial, temporal, professional, and personal scope. Suppose such a collective bargaining agreement is not originally applicable to the temporary employment relationship because the collective bargaining agreement does not bound the temporary work agency or the temporary agency worker. In that case sec. 8 para. 2 sent. 3 AÜG nevertheless allows them to deviate from the provisions of the principle of equal treatment. This possibility exists if the temporary employment relationship falls within the (territorial, temporal and professional) scope of applying a different collective bargaining agreement. Moreover, when the parties to the (temporary) employment contract agree to use the collective bargaining agreement.

153   So-called mixed operations, i. e., establishments that pursue other establishment purposes besides temporary agency employment, also have the possibility of deviation. The prerequisite here is that the collective bargaining agreement of the temporary agency employment's industry, which deviates from the principle of equal treatment, is applied at least for the period during which the temporary agency worker is hired out.

154   Irrespective of the fulfilment of the conditions mentioned above, such a collective bargaining agreement cannot deviate from the principle of equal treatment if the respective temporary agency worker was in an employment relationship with the hirer in the last six months before the hiring out. This also applies if the temporary agency worker was not an employee of the hirer during the period mentioned before but was in an employment relationship with an employer who forms a group of companies with the hirer within the meaning of sec. 18 of the German Stock Corporation Act (*Aktiengesetz* „**AktG**") (sec. 8 para. 3 AÜG). This provision, also referred to as the «revolving door clause», is intended to prevent the misuse of temporary agency employment, which sometimes occurred in practice until its introduction. In this context, employees were dismissed. Within a short period, they (sometimes immediately after dismissal) were reinstated as temporary agency workers in their former undertaking or in another undertaking of the same group, but under worse working conditions.

155   Furthermore, a deviation under the collective bargaining agreement is also invalid if its application results in the minimum remuneration fixed in a statutory instrument according to sec. 3a para. 2 AÜG being undercut (sec. 8 para. 2 sent. 1 AÜG).

156   *(2) Special Features of the Deviation from the Equal Pay Principle.* Suppose a deviating collective bargaining agreement is also intended to regulate remuneration for the temporary agency worker that does not comply with the provisions of the principle of equality. In that case, this is only permissible from 1 April 2017 onwards if further prerequisites are observed. Therefore, the following prerequisites are always not to be honored if the collective bargaining agreement is to deviate from other essential working conditions but not from the remuneration.

157   According to the provision of sec. 8 para. 4 sent. 1 AÜG, a collective bargaining agreement may deviate from the principle of equality concerning remuneration only in the first nine months of an assignment to the respective hirer. The decisive period's determination is based on the specifications that are also to be used to determine the maximum assignment length (see marginal no. **122**). Therefore, in each case, it must be examined based on a person- or hirer-related consideration regarding the undertaking of how long the specific temporary agency worker was loaned to the same hirer's undertaking.

158   A more prolonged deviation is only permissible, according to sec. 8 para. 4 sent. 2 no. 1 AÜG if at least a remuneration is achieved, which itself is defined in the collective bargaining agreement as equivalent to a comparable employee's remuneration in the industry of employment. This must occur according to the deviating collective bargaining agreement's provision 15 months of an assignment, the latest. The collective bargaining agreement must therefore stipulate a remuneration which it regards as equivalent by definition. The collective bargaining agreement must also provide that the initially deviating remuneration level after a familiarisation period of no more than six weeks will gradually approach the remuneration which the collective bargaining agreement defines as equivalent and must be achieved after 15 months at the latest.

If these conditions are met and the temporary work agency, after a gradual adjustment period of no more than 15 months, grants the temporary agency workers the remuneration defined as equivalent in the collective bargaining agreement, a permanent deviation from the statutory principle of equality may be made. The actual remuneration of a comparable employee in the hirer's undertaking is then no longer of significance. Thus, the parties to the collective bargaining agreement are allowed to replace the statutory Equal-Pay principle by granting a "Equal-Pay under a collective bargaining agreement". **159**

Here, too, it applies that despite the fulfillment of the conditions mentioned before in such a collective bargaining agreement, no deviation from the principle of equality may be made if the respective temporary agency worker was in an employment relationship with the hirer in the last six months before the assignment. This also applies if the temporary agency worker was in an employment relationship with an employer forming a group of companies with the hirer within the meaning of sec. 18 AktG (sec. 8 para. 3 AÜG) during the period mentioned before. **160**

Furthermore, a deviation under the collective bargaining agreement is also ineffective if this would result in the minimum remuneration fixed in a statutory ordinance according to sec. 3a para. 2 AÜG falling below (sec. 8 para. 2 sent. 1 AÜG). **161**

(3) Handling of Possible Deviations in Practice. In practice, there is an enormous need to make use of the possibility mentioned above of collective deviation. The statutory equal pay is almost impossible to implement in practice and causes hardly solvable calculation problems. Therefore, the application of equal pay under a collective bargaining agreement is the only possibility of deploying temporary agency workers for more than nine months at the same hirer from the practical point of view starting with 1 April 2017. **162**

In practice, this need is met by so-called sectoral collective bargaining agreements/ industry surcharge agreements. As can be seen from their title, these collective bargaining agreements provide for surcharges for the use of temporary agency workers in specific industries. Therefore, the temporary employment agency is obliged to pay remuneration, increased by the corresponding supplement, if it hires out one of its temporary agency workers in an industry for which the collective bargaining agreement provides for a supplement. By regulating the corresponding industry surcharges, the parties to the collective bargaining agreement make use of their authority to determine a level of remuneration that is considered equivalent to the level of remuneration of employees in the industry of employment (sec. 8 para. 4 sent. 2 no. 1 AÜG). The sectoral collective bargaining agreements, therefore, determine the "collectively agreed equal pay". **163**

Due to the above-mentioned circumstances, such sectoral collective bargaining agreements are very widespread and are the rule rather than the exception. In practice, there are practically no more collective bargaining agreements available that allow the hiring out to all (hirer) industries without industry surcharges. The collective bargaining agreements of the two major employers' associations, the Association of German Temporary Employment Agencies (*Interessenverband Deutscher Zeitarbeitsunternehmen „iGZ"*) and the Federal Employers' Association of Personnel Service Providers (*Bundesarbeitgeberverband der Personaldienstleister „BAP"*) with the German Federation of Trade Unions (*Tarifgemeinschaft Deutscher Gewerkschaftsbund „DGB"*), contain industry surcharge regulations for all major industries that apply "automatically" when these collective bargaining agreements are used and when in companies in these industries is hired out. This also applies when collective bargaining agreements do not bind the parties to the temporary agency employment relationship, but the collective bargaining agreements are nevertheless applicable by reference under employment law. **164**

e) Other Documentation/Registration Requirements

165 In addition to the general requirements of the NachwG, the AÜG itself also imposes documentation and resgistration requirements. In contrast to the NachwG, these affect both the temporary work agency and the hirer.

166 Special registration requirements of a hirer based within the Federal Republic of Germany to the customs administration's responsible authority may result from sec. 17b para. 1 and 2 AÜG. The prerequisite for this is that the temporary work agency is domiciled abroad. A further prerequisite ist that a binding lower-wage limit for the temporary agency worker's activity has been set by the Federal Ministry of Labour and Social Affairs' statutory order under sec. 3a AÜG. Suppose these conditions of the registration requirement are met. In that case, the hirer must submit a written declaration in German language containing the information listed in sec. 17b para. 1 sent. 1 no. 1 to 7 AÜG to the customs authorities before the beginning of each assignment. The notification must be made individually for each temporary agency worker and be on hand no later than one working day before the start of work. If information once submitted to the customs administration changes, the hirer is obliged under sec. 17b para. 1 sent. 2 AÜG to notify the changes immediately, i. e., without undue delay. Besides, under sec. 17b para. 2 AÜG, the hirer must add an affirmation from the temporary work agency to the temporary agency worker's registration to the customs administration. In this document, the temporary work agency must assure that he meets his obligations under sec. 8 para. 5 AÜG and provides his temporary agency workers with at least the remuneration prescribed in the relevant statutory order according to sec. 3a AÜG. This notification is generally made online via the "Minimum Wage Notification Portal" (see "*helpful weblinks*" on page 413). However, the notification can also be sent by post or fax.

167 Insofar as a statutory ordinance on a lower wage limit for temporary agency employment, according to sec. 3a AÜG, applies to an employment relationship, the hirer is also subject to certain retention requirements, additionally to the registration requirements described above.

168 The hirer is obliged to record the beginning, end, and duration of the temporary agency worker's daily working hours, sec. 17c para. 1 AÜG. The working hours' recording is intended to enable the Federal Employment Agency or the customs authority to determine whether the hirer pays its temporary agency workers the minimum hourly remuneration laid down by the statutory order.

169 The responsible authority must deduce from the records the number of working hours the temporary agency worker has actually worked. Working hours means the time for which the temporary agency worker gets remuneration. Thus, the temporary work agency must document the start and end of work as well as the time that is subject to remuneration under the employment contract or collective bargaining agreement or under a works agreement. This can also include, for example, travel time or on-call time. For a proper calculation to occur, breaks that are not classified as working hours must also be recorded.

170 In terms of time, the recording must be made up to seven days after the day of work performance. An extension of this period is not possible. If the recording has been made, the hirer must keep it for at least two years, sec. 17c para. 1 AÜG.

Besides, according to sec. 17c para. 2 AÜG, each temporary work agency is also obliged to keep the documents required for checking compliance with a statutory instrument according to sec. 3a AÜG in German for the entire duration of the temporary agency worker's actual employment, but no longer than two years in total. At the audit authority request, the documents must also be kept available at the place of employment. The latter sec. 17c para. 2 sent. 2 AÜG may thus result in the foreign temporary work agency's obligation to retain employee-related documents in the respective establishment of the hirer in Germany.

4. Exceptions from the Scope of the AÜG

Employers who, as temporary work agencies, wish to hire out employees (temporary 171 agency workers) to third parties (hirers) for work in the course of their business activities require permission under sec. 1 para. 1 sent. 1 AÜG (see marginal no. **88**). In addition to the obligation to obtain a permission, the AÜG regulates further extensive rights and obligations of the parties involved. There are also cases in which hiring out is either not regarded as temporary agency employment in the sense of the AÜG or the AÜG is not applied for other reasons. If such a case exists, it follows that an employee may be hired out to another undertaking without a permission, and the other legal consequences of the AÜG do not have to be observed.

a) Other Forms of Deployment of External Personnel

The legal consequences of the AÜG apply only to temporary agency employment with- 172 in the meaning of sec. 1 para. 1 sent. 1 AÜG. Firstly, from this follows that other forms of external personnel deployment that do not meet the requirements of the definition of temporary agency employment in the AÜG are not subject to the provisions of the AÜG.

For this reason, forms of deployment of external personnel that deviate fundamentally 173 from the definition of temporary agency employment are excluded from the scope of application. This applies particularly to genuine service contracts or contracts to produce a work and temporary agency employment in a joint establishment.

aa) Service Contract and Contracs to Produce a Work.
If the contractual relation- 174 ship of the parties involved consists of a service contract (sec. 611 BGB) or a contract to produce work (sec. 631 BGB) and if this type of contract does not only exist on paper but is actually lived, this excludes the scope of application of the AÜG. The rights and obligations to which the contracting parties are subject in the case of a service contract or contract to produce a work differ so fundamentally from the rights and obligations of the parties within the framework of temporary agency employment that temporary agency employment is excluded in such cases.

Within the framework of a service contract, the service provider undertakes to provide 175 the promised services, and in the case of a contract to produce a work, the production of the promised work (see for a detailed description of mutual obligations marginal no. **236** et seq. for the service contract and marginal no. **267** et seq. for the contract to produce a work). On the other hand, in temporary agency employment, as required by sec. 1 para. 1 AÜG, the employer (temporary work agency) hires out his employees to a third party (hirer), who are then integrated into the work organisation of the hirer and are subject to his instructions (see marginal no. **16** et seq.).

bb) Joint Establishment.
The deployment of workers to a joint establishment (see 176 marginal no. **297** et seq.) and temporary agency employment are also mutually exclusive for technical legal reasons. Temporary agency employment is deemed to exist if the temporary agency worker concerned is integrated into a foreign business organisation and is subject to the hirer's instructions under labour law. The temporary agency worker's temporary work agency promotes exclusively the hirer's business purposes through the hiring out. In the case of a joint establishment, on the other hand, there is a collective operating organisation, so that the very concept of integration into a "foreign" organisation cannot be assumed. The employee's right to issue instructions is also not exercised

by a third party (hirer). In a joint establishment, the right to issue instructions is rather incumbent on the uniform management apparatus, in which the employee's contractual employer is also involved. Ultimately, the employee's activity in the joint establishment also serves at least the operational purposes of the employer and not exclusively those of a third party (hirer).

177   cc) **Deployment to a Consortium.** Sec. 1 para. 1a sent. 1 AÜG provides that the deployment of employees to a consortium formed for the purpose of the manufacture of a work is no temporary agency employment if the employer is a member of the consortium formed. Additionally, all consortium members must be subject to collective agreemens in the same branch of industry. Furthermore, all members must be obliged to provide contractual services independently based on the consortium agreement. Through the last two conditions mentioned above, the legislator prevents, for example, pure temporary agencies and mixed operations, limiting themselves to making temporary agency workers available to the consortium from benefiting from the regulation. Even if solely one of the conditions mentioned before is missing, there is no exception. This has the consequence that temporary agency employment with all the consequences connected with it is present.

178   An exception for this is found in sec. 1 para. 1a sent. 2 AÜG for employers with a registered office in another European Union member state. Such undertakings also benefit from the exception mentioned above if they are not subject to German collective bargaining agreements in the same branch of industry as the other consortium members; but meet the other requirements of sec. 1 para. 1a sent. 1 AÜG.

b) Privileged Temporary Agency Employment

179   Apart from the exceptions mentioned, the AÜG itself also excludes external personnel deployment forms from its main scope of application, although these forms meet the requirements of the definition of temporary agency employment in sec. 1 para. 1 sent. 1 AÜG.

aa) Temporary Agency Employment to Avoid Short-time Work and Redundancies.
180 According to sec. 1 para. 3 sent. 1 of the AÜG, the AÜG generally does not apply to temporary agency employment between employers in the same industry branch with the purpose of avoiding short-time working or redundancies if a collective bargaining agreement applicable to the hirer and temporary work agency provides for precisely this possibility.

181   The collective bargaining agreement must expressly provide the possibility of temporary agency employment to avoid short-time work or redundancies.

182   Regarding content, it concerns the occasional assignment of employees if employees who cannot be employed in the hirer's establishment due to a cyclical or seasonal decline in orders are hired out for a transitional period in order to reinstate them if their undertaking employment situation improves. Consequently, the assignment must actually be made to avoid short-time work or redundancies. However, a purely subjective intention to avoid redundancies or short-time work on the employer's part is insufficient. In objective terms, an extensive short-time work or dismissal situation must actually exist. Moreover, temporary agency employment is also objectively suitable to prevent short-time work or redundancies in the concrete situation.

183   **bb) Deployment of Employees in the Group (Group Privilege).** The scope of application of the AÜG also does not cover constellations of temporary agency employment where employees concerned are hired out between companies that belong to a group within the meaning of sec. 18 AktG (sec. 1 para. 3 no. 2 AÜG). However, this is subject to the condition that the employees hired out are neither hired out for temporary agency employment nor employed for this purpose.

This exception is intended to create flexibility between group-affiliated companies, for example, to react to fluctuating personnel requirements. The purpose of the exception is to avoid bureaucratic formalities in cases where the law's protective purpose is guaranteed even without permission. From the legislator's point of view, only the Group's internal labor market is affected, and the social protection of temporary agency workers is therefore not endangered.

Particular attention must be paid to the stipulation that employees must not be hired **184** and employed for temporary agency employment's purpose. The sole purpose of the exception is to allow employee's temporary deployment at other group companies without bureaucratic hurdles (i. e., without a temporary agency employment permit). On the other hand, the restriction is not intended to exempt permanent deployment of employees from one group company to another, respectively, purely temporary employment companies within a group from the application of the AÜG. Intra-group temporary agency employmnet by personnel management companies, the purpose of which is the employment and assignment of personnel to other group companies, is therefore not covered by the exception. It should also be noted that the exception's requirements are not fulfilled if the employee concerned is employed for temporary agency employment's purpose. In this way, the legislator wants to ensure that it is not only the performance content determined at the time of the conclusion of the employment contract that matters, but also that the employee is not subsequently employed for temporary agency employment. This means that the group privilege ceases to apply, if the employer hirers out the employee exclusively to other group companies without reinstating them in the meantime with the contractual employer (temporary work agency). It is irrelevant whether it was already planned at the time of the contract's conclusion or whether this circumstance arose later after the employment.

Finally, it should be noted that, even if the prerequisites of the matter of fact mentioned **185** above are met, its application should be applied with caution. In the legal literature it is predominantly assumed that group privilege is not compatible with applicable European law. If the company's personnel deployment is significantly based on group privilege, this risk should be kept in mind.

cc) **Solely Occasional Temporary Agency Employment.** A further exception to the **186** scope of application of the AÜG is in sec. 1 para. 3 sent. 2a AÜG. According to this provision, temporary agency employment is not subject to the regulatory regime of the AÜG if temporary agency employment is only occasional and the employee is not hired and employed for the temporary agency employmnet's purpose.

Temporary agency employment is only occasionally provided if it does not take place regularly. This requirement applies to both the temporary work agency and the hirer, i. e., the temporary work agency may only supply his employees to a particular hirer or different hirers for work in exceptional cases and not specifically or repeatedly. If, on the other hand, temporary agency employment occurs on schedule recurrent, there is no longer an occasional temporary agency employment. Furthermore, even in this exception, the employee may not be hired or purpose of the temporary agency employment's purpose. Like the group privilege, this exception has no equivalent in the Directive on Temporary Agency Work 2008/104/EC. The regulation is, therefore, also at this point in conflict with European law. Concerning the latter requirement and the conformity of the regulation with European law, reference can be made to the comments on group privilege (see marginal no. **183** et seq.).

dd) **Provision of Personnel in the Public Sector.** The personnel's provision is the **187** permanently invested employment of an employee with a third party under the existing employment relationship's continuance. The term is particularly relevant to restructuring in the public sector. Suppose a public employer relocates the activities previously performed by it to an institution under private law. In that case, the employee affected by this measure must, under continued employment relationship at the employer's request, perform the work owed under the employment contract to a third party (sec. 4 para. 3 sent. 1 Collective Bargaining Agreement for Public Sector – *Tarifvertrag für den öffentlichen Dienst* "**TvöD**"). However, the legislator has expressly excluded this form of external personnel deployment, which is principally covered by the definition of temporary agency employment within the meaning of the AÜG, from the scope of application of the AÜG (sec. 1 para. 3 no. 2b AÜG). This exception consider that the personnel provision is functional to be regarded as a peculiar form of devolution and is carried out in interest on grandfathering by employees affected by the devolution. The risks typically associated with employment as a temporary agency worker do not exist in these cases, and protection under the AÜG is therefore not necessary.

188   **ee) Legal Persons under Public Law.** An exception from the scope of application of the AÜG also exists for legal persons under public law. According to sec. 1 para. 3 no. 2c AÜG, the provisions of the AÜG do not apply to temporary agency employment between public law employers. However, this only applies to the extent that the employers in a question apply collective bargaining agreements of the public service or regulations of the public-law religious communities.

189   The scheme covers assignments within the public sector and thus assignments in perfoming public service tasks. Both on the temporary work agency and the hirer side, there are legal persons under public law who are constitutionally bound to an extraordinary degree by law and statute and have a special constitutional status. The legislator does not see employees exposed to any dangers which must be counteracted by the AÜG's validity, even during an assignment within this framework.

190   **ff) Use of Temporary Agency Workers in a Joint Establishment Abroad.** Finally, sec. 1 para. 3 no. 3 AÜG, provides that the AÜG does not apply if temporary agency employment is carried out abroad. A further condition is that the temporary agency worker is hired to a German-foreign joint establishment that originated based on intergovernmental agreements to which the temporary work agency has a stake.

191   In such joint establishments, it regularly happens that the participating companies' employees are deployed to the foreign joint establishment, as this is necessary for organisational and economic reasons. To avoid having to go the way of a "local" foreign employment contract under the German employment contract suspension, the posting of German employees abroad while maintaining the German employment contract shall not be made more difficult by the additional restrictions and obligations under the AÜG.

5. Particular Case: Temporary Agency Employment within International Scope

192   The external personnel deployment through temporary agency employment is not limited to purely inner German situations. There is often a cross-border constellation. For example, the temporary work agency may have its registered office or a branch abroad, or the hirer may be a foreign undertaking or the temporary agency worker's place of employment may be abroad. The constellations mentioned above can occur not only individually but also cumulatively.

193   In these cases, the question to which extent German legal norms, notably the AÜG, apply is a particular challenge. This question cannot be answered uniformly. Temporary

agency employment under the AÜG affects various areas of law such as trade law, debt law, labour law, social security law, and tax law. Conflict of laws must be differentiated according to the respective norms. This is because the applicability of trade law – it exemplarily includes the obligation to obtain permission under sec. 1 para. 1 sent. 1 AÜG – follows different rules than the norms concerning the temporary employment relationship or the contractual relationship between the hirer and the temporary work agency. The applicable tax and social security law is subject to other conflict-of-law rules.

In the following, the main types of foreign deployment and the respective hurdles will be briefly described. **194**

a) Temporary Agency Employment Abroad („*Outbound*")

The question of the applicability of German law in connection with temporary agency employment abroad arises particularly in cases where a temporary work agency with its registered office in Germany hires out temporary agency workers abroad for work performance to a hirer in the course of its economic activities. These cases are also referred to as *outbound* cases. **195**

aa) Applicability of the AÜG on the Obligation to Obtain Permission.
The AÜG is part of public law and is subject to the obligation to obtain permission. In cross-border deployment, the question arises as to how far this obligation to obtain permission applies. Since the AÜG is about public law and the so-called territorial principle applies, this also applies to the AÜG. The territorial principle means that public law provisions are applicable if the facts of the case, i.e., temporary agency employment, have a so-called domestic connection. Generally, such a domestic connection exists in all cases in which **196**

(i) the assignment occurs in Germany, including hiring out from abroad into Germany;

(ii) temporary agency workers from Germany are hired out abroad and

(iii) the asssignment from a temporary work agency based abroad to a hirer based abroad provided that the temporary agency workers become active in Germany.

On the other hand, it is not sufficient for the determination of a domestic reference if a foreign temporary work agency hires out employees to a German hirer; but the employees hired out work exclusively abroad. **197**

Consequently, there is sufficient domestic reference in *outbound* cases, which means that the provisions of the AÜG also apply to such instances of temporary agency employment. For example, a temporary work agency with its registered office in Germany must also have a valid temporary agency employment permit according to sec. 1 para. 1 sent. 1 AÜG when hiring out employees abroad. On the other hand, the foreign temporary work agency also requires a permit to hire out temporary agency workers to Germany. **198**

However, the applicability of the AÜG concerning the obligation to obtain permission does not necessarily mean that foreign national law does not also have to be applied. Since the other states' national public law often also aligns the scope of application of its legal norms with the territorial principle, a cross-border assignment in these cases must do justice to both regulatory regimes. If a foreign hirer's national law then also provides legal requirements for temporary agency employment, the German temporary work agency must also comply with these requirements if it hires out employees to the respective country of the hirer. This double requirement leads to considerable difficulties in practice, particularly in cases where the two states' requirements are different and sometimes contradictory. In particular, the double obligation to obtain permission often presents practical difficulties for the temporary work agencies. **199**

bb) Legal Relationships between the Parties.
Irrespective of the question of the obligation to obtain permission, the applicable law's question must be seen in the parties' **200**

respective legal relations to each other. The parties' legal relations to each other are not about public law, as in the case of the obligation to obtain permission, but general private law. Due to the border crossing, the question of which law applies to the parties' legal relations besides the mandatory applicable provisions of the AÜG complies with private international law.

201   Since the revision of international private law in 2009, the applicable law's question is uniformly assessed according to European law. In this respect, the provisions of Regulation (EC) No. 594/2008 of the European Parliament and of the Council of 17 June 2008 on the law applicable to contractual obligations ("**Rome I Regulation**") are authoritative.

202   Accordingly, the contract between the parties is, in principle, subject to the law chosen by the parties. Art. 3 para. 1 sent. 1 Rome I Regulation lays down the principle of free choice of law. The parties are, therefore, entitled to choose the law applicable to their contractual relationship freely. This choice need not be explicit; it may also be implied (Art. 3 para. 1 sent. 2 Rome I Regulation).

203   Subsequently, a distinction must be made between the (temporary) employment contract and the temporary agency employment contract.

(i) For the (temporary) employment contract, the applicable law must be determined based on objective criteria in cases where the parties have not chosen law. According to Art. 8 para. 2 of the Rome I Regulation, the applicable law is determined either by the habitual place of work or, in ambiguous cases, by the place of the employing establishment. The result may, divergent from this, be corrected within narrow limits if, given the prevailing total circumstances (exemplarily, place of residence, employee, language), there is a closer connection with another contracting state. In the case of cross-border temporary agency employment, the objective link according to art. 8 para. 2 sent. 1 Rome I Regulation leads in principle to the application of the home law of the temporary work agency and temporary agency worker. This is because the "temporary" employment in another state is harmless according to art. 8 para. 2 sent. 2 Rome I Regulation.

(ii) If there is no choice of law by the parties for the (temporary) employment contract, the contract is governed by the law of the country in which the party who has to perform the service characteristic of the contract has his habitual residence under Art. 4 para. 2 Rome I Regulation. This is usually the place where the temporary work agency has its registered office.

204   However, the applicable law determined in this way shall be restricted within the framework of Art. 9 of the Rome I Regulation for both the (temporary) employment contract and the temporary agency employment contract. Irrespective of which law is applicable on the basis of a subjective connection (i. e., based on a choice by the parties) or the basis of an objective connection (i. e., according to Art. 4 and 8 of the Rome I Regulation), it applies that the provisions of German labour law that are mandatory in the public interest must be applied in all cases, regardless of the choice of law (Art. 9 para. 1 of the Rome I Regulation). These include, in particular, the provisions of the AÜG, such as the provisions of sec. 12 AÜG concerning the legal relationship between the temporary work agency and the hirer or the provisions of the principle of equality in sec. 8 para. 1 sent. 1 AÜG concerning the temporary employment relationship.

205   Finally, it can be pointed out that although there is no employment relationship and thus no contract between the hirer and the temporary agency worker. Nevertheless, the legal relationship can be described as a legal relationship similar to a contract due to some peculiarities (see marginal no. 70 et seq.). For this legal relationship, the applicable law's determination is therefore based on Art. 3, 8 and 9 of the Rome I Regulation.

cc) Social Security Law. German social security law is part of public law. Therefore, **206** the principle of territoriality, applies, which is also expressed in sec. 3 SGB IV: The provisions on compulsory insurance in Germany apply to all persons

(i), who are employed or self-employed within the scope of this Code or

(ii), insofar as they do not require employment or self-employment, to all persons who have their residence or habitual abode within the scope of this Code.

In domestic employees' deployment abroad, the strict application of the principle of **207** territoriality would mean that the law applicable would no longer be German law but the country's law where the employee actually carries out his employment. By sec. 4 para. 1 SGB IV, the German legislature deviates from the principle of territoriality so far as it orders that an employee deployed from Germany continues to be subject to German social security law. This only applies if the deployment is limited in time due to the nature of the employment or contractually in advance. In principle, this provision also applies to the posting of a temporary agency worker abroad by a German temporary work agency.

Suppose an employee is deployed from Germany to another European country. Then **208** the question of the obligation to pay social security contributions is determined solely based on Regulation (EC) 883/2004 on the coordination of social security systems (**Regulation (EC) 883/2004**) due to the principle of primacy in application of European law. Regulation 883/2004 (EC) is directly applicable to nationals of a Member State, stateless persons and refugees residing in a Member State for who one or more Member States' legislation applies or had been applied. The Regulation of Art. 3 para. 1 of Regulation (EC) 883/2004 applies to all statutory provisions within its factual scope of application, which concern benefits in sickness, age, unemployment, etc.

In principle, the Regulation states in Art. 11 of Regulation 883/2004 (EC) that only **209** the legislation of one Member State applies in the event of cross-border operations. The Regulation thus prevents such persons from being subject to a double social security obligation. Accordingly, a person who pursues an employed or self-employed activity in a Member State is subject to the legislation of that Member State.

By way of derogation, Art. 12 para. 1 of Regulation 883/2004 (EC) contains a special **210** rule that, in practice, becomes relevant to cases of cross-border temporary agency employmnet and constitutes an exception to the principle. According to Art. 12 para. 1 of Regulation 883/2004 (EC), a person shall continue to be subject to the first Member State's legislation. This only if the person pursues an activity in a Member State o behalf of an employer typically carrying out work there and is posted by that employer to another Member State to perform work there on its behalf. This only provided that the expected duration of that work does not exceed 24 months and that the person does not replace another posted person.

In the cases of Art. 12 para. 1 of Regulation 883/2004 (EC), this means in concrete **211** terms that a temporary agency worker continues to be subject to German social security law. But only if he is employed by an employer (temporary work agency) who usually works inland and the temporary agency worker is sent to foreign European countries to carry out work there on behalf of the temporary work agency. In such a case, an A1 certificate (certificate of deployment) can be applied for by the temporary work agency as an employer for the temporary agency worker's specific deployment. In the event of an application for this certificate of deployment, the individual modalities are governed by the implementing regulation (**Regulation (EC) 987/2009**) in addition to Regulation 883/2004 (EC). The competent institution is the respective health insurance fund of the temporary agency worker. According to Art. 19 para. 2 of Regulation (EC) 987/2009, the competent institution of the Member State shall, at the request of the person concerned or of the employer (temporary work agency), certify that this legislation continues to apply and, where appropriate, for how long and under what conditions.

212   Since 1 January 2019, the certificate of deployment has been transmitted electronically by data transfer from a system-tested program or through a machine-generated completion aid. Once a decision has been made on the application and an A1 certificate has been issued, this certificate is binding for all other Member States under Art. 5 para. 1 of Regulation (EC) 987/2009 as long as the certificate has not been revoked or declared invalid. In practice, this means for the temporary agency worker that he remains liable for social security in Germany despite his cross-border assignment.

213   If the temporary agency worker remains subject to German social security law, the hirer is must comply with national social security regulations (see marginal no. 37 et seq.).

214   As far as a cross-border assignment to a third country is concerned and there is a bilateral agreement between the Federal Republic of Germany and a third country, which social security law is applicable, these agreement's provisions are decisive, as shown by sec. 6 SGB IV.

215   **dd) Tax Law.** The tax law obligations connected with the cross-border temporary agency employment are regulated in detail in the applicable double taxation agreements. Therefore, the type of taxation and the tax obligations are to be taken from the individual double taxation agreements and legally assessed in the specific case.

216   **ee) Right of Residence.** The requirements under residence law that must be met by the temporary agency employment abroad cannot be described in general terms, as they depend on the respective national requirements. Therefore, it must always be examined on a case-by-case basis to determine which requirements the national law of the state in which the temporary agency worker is to perform his work imposes on such work.

217   However, it can be stated that for work within the European Union and the European Economic Area, no special residence law requirements have to be observed based on the freedom of movement for workers as set out in Art. 45 TFEU, provided the temporary agency worker is a citizen of the European Union.

b) Temporary Agency Employment into the Country („*Inbound*")

218   Also of interest in the present context are cases where a temporary work agency with its registered office abroad hires out temporary agency workers to a hirer in Germany in its economic activities. These cases are also referred to as *inbound cases*.

Equal to the above mentioned classical inbound cases are those constellations in which

(i) both the temporary work agency and the hirer have their registered office abroad, but the temporary agency workers are employed in Germany, and

(ii) the cases in which a German temporary work agency hires out foreign temporary agency workers to Germany.

219   In the inbound cases, the unique features of cross-border deployment must also be taken into account.

220   **aa) Applicabilty of the AÜG.** The applicability of the AÜG must also be determined in inbound cases based on the principle of territoriality (see marginal no. **196**).

221   Sufficient domestic reference exists in cases where the temporary agency workers of a foreign temporary work agency work for a hirer with its registered office in Germany, and in cases where the hirer has its registered office abroad, but temporary agency workers work in Germany. This applies more than ever to cases in which a temporary work agency based in Germany employs foreign temporary agency workers in Germany. The AÜG, therefore, also applies to all these cases.

Therefore, it should also be noted that the assignment compliant to the rules according **222**
to the foreign state's law does not suspend the parties from the obligation to comply with
the AÜG's requirements.

This includes in particular, the obligation to obtain permission according to sec. 1 **223**
para. 1 sent 1 AÜG. A legally compliant temporary agency employment in the constellation of *inbound* cases is only possible if the foreign temporary work agency has a valid
temporary agency employment permit. In this context, the restriction of the mandatory
ground for refusal in sec. 3 para. 2 AÜG must be observed. According to this, the permit
or its extension must be refused mandatorily. Therefore, legal temporary agency employment in the Federal Republic of Germany is not possible in the following acse: the
activity's exercise, according to sec. 1 AÜG, is intended for establishments, plant sections,
or companion plants that are not located in a European Economic Community's member
state or another state that is a party to the Agreement on the European Economic Area.
In this context, the only relevant factor is the place where the hiring out is to be operated.
This means that temporary work agencies who have their registered office in the Federal
Republic of Germany or in a member state of the European Economic Community as
well as in another state which is a party to the Agreement on the European Economic
Area are generally not permitted to perform temporary agency employment which does
not originate from this area.

In connection with *inbound* cases, reference should also be made at this point to the **224**
registration requirements, which must occasionally be complied with (see marginal no. **165** et seq.).

bb) Legal Relationships of the Parties. In principle, private international law in the **225**
form of the Rome I Regulation rules also applies to the determination of the law governing
the parties' legal relations in *inbound* cases (see marginal no. **200** et seq.).

cc) Social Security Law. If temporary agency workers are sent to Germany by a foreign **226**
temporary work agency, they would also be subject to the German social security system
under the territoriality principle's maxim. An exception to this principle is, first of all,
sec. 5 para. 1 SGB IV, which excludes the application of German social security law, insofar as employees are only deployed to the area of application of the Social Security Code
for a limited period. Something else can also apply on the basis of bilateral agreements,
sec. 6 SGB IV.

Suppose an employee is deployed to Germany from another European country. In that **227**
case, the applicable law's question must be assessed solely based on Regulation 883/2004
(EC), as in the cases of "*outbound.*" Regularly, German social security law will not be
applicable in practice if the requirements of Art. 12 of Regulation 883/2004 (EC) are met
and an application for the corresponding A1 certificate has been submitted.

Suppose an A1 certificate has been issued by another European Member State. In **228**
that case, it shall also have binding effect in the Federal Republic of Germany, Art. 5
para. 1 of Regulation (EC) 987/2009. An A1 certificate issued by the competent institution
of a Member State shall be binding, where appropriate retroactively, on the Member State's
social security institutions in which the activity is pursued and on its courts. Even if the
certificate was issued only after the latter Member State established that the employee
concerned is compulsorily insured under its legislation.[2] Consequently, at least the State's
competent courts in which the temporary agency worker is working are not empowered
to verify the validity of the certificate.[3] Besides, suppose an A1 certificate from an EU
member state is available. In that case, the German Pension Insurance Fund cannot levy

---

[2] European Court of Justice, 6 September 2018 – C-527/16.
[3] European Court of Justice, 6 September 2018 – C-527/16.

contributions for foreign employees working in Germany within the social-law audit framework by sec. 28p para. 1 sent. 5 SGB IV. For this reason, a criminal liability, according to sec. 266a StGB, must also be ruled out.[4]

229   This binding effect applies even if the certificate is incorrect in content and has not been withdrawn or declared invalid by the Member State of origin. The only exceptions are cases of fraud or abuse of rights.[5]

230   For the foreign temporary work agency, the non-applicability of German social security law means that he is not subject to an employer's social law obligations as listed in marginal no. 37 et seq. above. He is subject to his member state's social security system and must observe its legal provisions regarding any contribution obligations or registration requirements.

231   **dd) Tax Law.** The tax obligations connected with the cross-border temporary agency employment are regulated in detail in the applicable double taxation agreements. Therefore, the type of taxation and the tax obligations are to be taken from the individual double taxation agreements and legally assessed in the specific case.

232   **ee) Right of Residence.** In case foreign temporary agency workers are employed in Germany, the respective employees' nationality is of decisive importance for the requirements to which such employment is subject under residence law.

233   Nationals of a member state of the European Union or of the European Economic Area may work in Germany without restriction because of workers' free movement as set out in Art. 45 TFEU. Therefore, a temporary agency worker with European nationality does not require a separate work permit in Germany.

234   However, the legal situation shall be assessed differently for citizens from foreign EU countries. Temporary agency workers from third countries can only be employed at a hirer in Germany under certain conditions. They must have a sufficient work permit. The foreign temporary agency worker can request a work permit from the Aliens Department with the Federal Employment Agency's assistance. But only if he presents a residence title by sec. 4 para. 3 of the Residence Act (*Aufenthaltsgesetz* "**AufenthaltsG**"), a residence title for specific purposes, toleration, or a permission under sec. 284 para. 1 of the Social Security Code, Third Book (Sozialgesetzbuch, Drittes Buch "**SGB III**"), which also entitles him to take up employment.

235   The Federal Employment Agency must formally issue the work permit in each case so that temporary agency employment with foreign temporary agency workers can be effectively carried out. If a corresponding permit is not available, it is irrelevant whether the work permit should have been issued under substantive law. Insofar, the material legal situation is not decisive for assessing temporary agency workers' effective use from third countries.

II. Service Contract

236   The entrepreneur may commission an external service provider for services' performance and conclude a service contract with him.

---

[4] Federal Supreme Court, 24 October 2006 – 1 StR 44/06.
[5] European Court of Justice, 6 September 2018 – C-527/16.

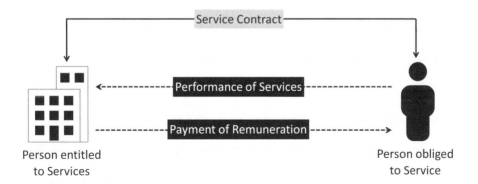

Figure 3: Illustration of a service contract

A service contract is a contract under the law of obligations aimed at exchanging   237
service and remuneration. It is therefore subject not only to the provisions of the General
Part of the Civil Code relating to legal transactions and contracts, and the provisions of
the General Part of the Law of Obligations applicable to contractual obligations but also
to the provisions on reciprocal (synallagmatic) contracts (sec. 320 et seq. BGB).

The subject of the service contract according to sec. 611 para. 2 BGB can be services   238
of any kind, such as contracts for lawyers, doctors, tax consultants, and architects (please
be aware of the existing prohibition in the meat industry, see marginal no. **99**). Contracts
with consultants or IT service providers are also regularly designed as service contracts.

While the legislator considered the inclusion of higher-level services (e.g., legal ser-   239
vices) in the type of service contract as requiring regulation, it did not recognise the
regulatory problems associated with the employees' dependent work. Soon after the BGB
came into force, the type of service contract practically broke down into two sub-cases:
the self-employed person's service contract and the employment contract of the employee
providing services dependet. This distinction was only later incorporated into the text of
the Civil Code. In some cases, provisions of the law on a service contract, such for example sec. 612a, sec. 613a, sec. 615 sent. 3, sec. 619a, sec. 620 para. 3, sec. 622, and sec. 623
BGB, according to their wording, apply direct exclusively to employment relationships.
In contrast, sec. 620 para. 3 BGB, and sec. 630 para. 4 BGB, clarify the existence of employment law outside the BGB. This development terminated by inserting sec. 611a into
the BGB with effect from 1 April 2017. The employment contract has thus been given an
independent statutory regulation.

1. Legal Basis and Legal Relations

The service contract is regulated by law in sec. 611 et seq. BGB. The parties to the   240
service contract are the person entitled to services (obligee to the service) and the person
obliged to services (obligee to the claim for remuneration).

The person entitled to services commissions the person obliged to services to perform   241
a specific service and owes the agreed remuneration for this activity, sec. 611 para. 1 BGB.

The person obliged to services is obliged to perform the promised services, sec. 611   242
para. 1 BGB. He shall make his work available to the person entitled to services in return

for the agreed remuneration. Suppose the parties have not concluded a remuneration agreement. In that case, remuneration shall be deemed to have been tacitly agreed based on sec. 612 para. 1 BGB, if the circumstances indicate that the service can only be expected in return for remuneration. The amount of remuneration is based on the usual remuneration according to sec. 612 para. 2 BGB.

243   The service contract is characterised by the personal freedom of the person obliged to services. The person obliged to services is self-employed. He is free to decide in what way or at what time he fulfils the promised services. The person obliged to services solely ows the supply of the performance ("services") and not any particular performance result. Furthermore, he is not subject to personal instructions, so that the person entitled to services cannot instruct him to perform the service at a particular time and place. According to sec. 84 para. 1 sent. 2 of the German Commercial Code (*Handelsgesetzbuch* – "**HGB**"), the commercial agent's self-employment depends on whether he is essentially able to arrange his activities freely and determine his working hours. Anyone who cannot do so is a staff member and thus an employee (sec. 84 para. 2 HGB). This origin delimitation criterion for a commercial agent's activity, now adopted in sec. 611a para. 1 sent. 3 BGB, will also help in many cases of different job performance. If the employee is subject to a comprehensive right of instruction concerning time, duration, and place of performance of the promised work, he is an employee. As a rule, dependent work is firmly bound by instructions. If the contract grants the employer the relevant disposal of the employee's manpower, this indicates the existence of an employment relationship. An employee is dependent on instructions in terms of time if he is expected to be in permanent readiness to help or if the employee is called upon to a not inconsiderable extent, even without a corresponding agreement, i. e., the working hours are ultimately "assigned" to him or her. The constant readiness for help can result from the parties' express agreements or the practical implementation of the contractual relationships. In this respect, an employee's schedule in duty rosters without prior agreement is a strong indication of employee status.

244   However, the self-employed person working based on a service contract or a contract to produce a work may have to follow instructions in the same way as the mandatary (see sec. 665, 675 BGB). The person entitled to services can therefore give professional instructions that concern the service itself. This can be, for example, the instruction to perform the services in a particular order.

245   Thus, a service contract is present if the entrepreneur providing the services explicates the services owed either in person or through his assistants under his responsibility, and according to his plan (organisation of the service, temporal scheduling, number of assistants, suitability of the assistants, etc.). The decisive factor is that the assistants are essentially free of instructions from the employer's representative of the person entitled to services concerning the service perfomance to be rendered and can determine their own working hours by themselves.

2. Social Security Law

246   As already explained in the context of temporary agency employment, the statutory social security obligations solely apply at dependent employment (see marginal no. 37 et seq.). However, the person obliged to services acts independently and is therefore not dependently employed. Therefore, there is no compulsory insurance for him or her in health, nursing, unemployment, pension, and accident insurance. The person obliged to serviceis, however, is free to insure himself voluntarily in the statutory social security, in case he or she would like to take their coverage in an insured event sec. 2 para. 1 var. 2 SGB IV.

Since the person obliged to services is not employed as a dependent employee, the 247
person entitled to services does not have any obligations under social security law, significantly, not the obligation to pay social security contributions for the person obliged
to services under sec. 28e para. 1 sent. 1 SGB IV.

3. Tax Law

According to sec. 1, 2 para. 1 EStG, the person obliged to services is liable to income 248
tax liability. He must pay tax on his income. Under sec. 25 para. 1 EStG, income tax is
generally assessed at the end of the calendar year (assessment period) based on the taxpayer's income derived during this assessment period. As a taxpayer, the person obliged
to services must submit a personally signed income tax return for the assessment period,
sec. 25 para. 3 sent. 1 EStG. Besides, the person obliged to services must make advance
payments on the expected income tax due. Payment dates are each on
- March 10th,
- June 10th,
- September 10th and
- December 10th

of each year, sec. 37 para. 1 EStG. The amount of income tax is determined, among
other things, by the amount of income.

Additonally, the person obliged to services, as far as he fulfills deliveries and other 249
services against payment as an entrepreneur within the scope of its undertaking, is subject
to the obligation to pay value-added tax according to sec. 1 para. 1 of the Value Added Tax Act (*Umsatzsteuergesetz* "**UStG**"). Entrepreneur is a person, who carries out a
trade or professional activity independently, sec. 2 para. 1 UStG. As a rule, the tax is to
be calculated according to agreed remuneration, sec. 16 para. 1 sent. 1 UStG. Insofar as
there is an obligation to pay value-added tax (VAT), the person obliged to services must
issue an invoice per the requirements of the UStG and show the VAT (19 %, respectively,
7 %) separately, sec. 14 para. 4 no. 8 UStG. An invoice must, among other things, contain
the following information:
- → Name and address of the invoicing party (here: the person obliged to services) and
  invoice recipient (here: the person entitled to services)
- → Tax number or sales tax identification number
- → Date of invoice
- → Consecutive invoice number
- → Quantity and type of delivery of the or the other service (with description of the
  service to be specified)
- → Time of delivery or the other service
- → Value-added tax amount
- → Gross total

Besides, the person obliged to services is obliged to submit a preliminary VAT return. 250
If a VAT payable amount of less than EUR 7,500 was incurred by the person obliged to
services in the previous year, the preliminary VAT return must be submitted by the end of
the tenth day of a quarter. If the previous year's VAT payable amount of the person obliged
to services was more than EUR 7,500, the preliminary VAT return must be submitted by
the end of each month's tenth day of. Preliminary VAT returns can also be submitted
online. It should be noted that every undertaking must conduct the preliminary VAT
return, therefore, even the person entitled to services.

However, consumers or small business owners do not have to charge VAT or report it 251
separately. Small businesses are establishments whose turnover (plus the tax payable on

it) did not exceed EUR 22,000 in the previous calendar year and is not expected to exceed EUR 50,000 in the current calendar year, sec. 19 UStG.

252   The person entitled to services may, in turn, deduct the value-added tax shown separately in the invoice by the person obliged to services as so-called input tax at the tax office, sec. 15 UStG (so-called *input tax deduction*). Input tax deduction must only occur under the following conditions:

-     The input tax has to result from the incoming invoices (invoice received by the person entitled to services himself) of the person entitled to services.
-     The invoices have to contain the minimum information required by sec. 14 para. 4 UStG.
-     The person obliged to services and the person entitled to services have to be entrepreneurs themselves. The invoice of a small business owner does not entitle for the input tax deduction.

4. Distinction from the Employment Contract

253   A subset of the service contract is the employment contract according to sec. 611a BGB. The distinction between service contracts with self-employed persons (service contracts in the narrower sense, "free" service contracts) on the one hand and employment contracts, on the other hand, is of considerable practical importance because the legal norms of labour law also apply to the latter. The courts for labour matters are responsible for legal disputes arising from employment contracts rather than the civil courts (see sec. 2 para. 1 no. 3 ArbGG). Above all, however, the demarcation between a service contract under sec. 611 BGB and an employment contract is of fundamental importance in practice. That is because considerable legal differences arise concerning the mutual obligations to perform and social and tax law obligations. Therefore, the typical characteristics of an employment contract according to sec. 611a BGB will be explained in the following in differentiation to a free service contract.

a) Legal Basis and Legal Relations

254   The employment contract is concluded by two concurrent declarations of intent.

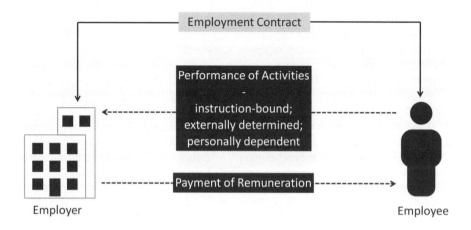

Figure 4: Illustration of an employment relationship

The two concurrent declarations of intent have to aim at establishing an employment **255** relationship and be made with the will to bind oneself legally. The employment contract is not subject to any formal requirements so that it can be concluded orally. However, one month after the agreed commencement of the employment relationship at the latest, the employer has to set down the essential contractual conditions in writing, sign the minutes and hand them over to the employee (sec. 2 NachwG). The conclusion of a written employment contract is always recommended for documentation's reasons and in case of dispute to prevent proof difficulties.

The parties may principally determine the content of the employment contract freely. **256** However, numerous legal limits are inflicted on private autonomy in German employment contract law, restricting the freedom of content, and not permitting individual contractual agreements that deviate from the law. For example, every employee is entitled to receive a salary's payment that is at least equal to the statutory minimum wage, sec. 1 para. 1 of the German Act Regulating a General Minimum Wage (*Gesetz zur Regelung des allgemeinen Mindestlohns* "**MiLoG**"). If the employer and employee reach a deviating agreement, it is invalid, according to sec. 3 MiLoG. This type of legal regulation, which cannot be waived to the employee's disadvantage, also exists in the areas of vacation (Federal Vacation Act – *Bundesurlaubsgesetz* "**BUrlG**"), continued remuneration in the event of illness (Continuation of Remuneration Act – *Entgeltfortzahlungsgesetz* "**EFZG**"), time limits or termination (for the first see the provisions of the TzBfG; see for the latter KSchG).

The employment contract results in mutual primary service obligations on both the **257** employer's and the employee's side, which differ substantially concerning the obligations arising from a service contract relationship.

To determine whether a contract is to be classified as an employment contract, an over- **258** all consideration of all circumstances must be made, sec. 611a para. 1 sent. 5 BGB. First of all, it is determined what the parties have agreed by contract, i. e., what has become its content. However, as sec. 611a para. 1 sent. 6 BGB, shows, in a second step, the contract's actual implementation is also taken into account for the assessment so that a different designation of the contract is ultimately irrelevant.

aa) Obligations of the Employee. The employment contract obliges the employee to **259** perform bound by instructions and externally determined work in personal dependence in the service of another person, sec. 611a para. 1 sent. 1 BGB. He must integrate himself into the employer's external work organisation and follow the instructions of his employer. The employer can issue instructions regarding the content, execution, place, and time of the work performance, sec. 611a para. 1 sent. 2 BGB. Limits to the right to issue instructions may indeed arise from statutory provisions, from provisions of applicable collective bargaining agreements, a works agreement, or from the employment contract itself, as is shown by sec. 106 of the German Trade Regulation Act (*Gewerbeordnung* – "**GewO**"). However, if the employer properly exercises his right to issue instructions, the employee must comply with these instructions if he does not wish to act in breach of duty.

The most crucial distinguishing feature of the employment contract from the free ser- **260** vice contract is the employee's personal dependence on his employer. The person obliged to services provides the person entitled to services solely with his manpower in the case of a free service contract but is otherwise essentially free to exercise the "how", "when,"and "where" of his activity. On the other hand, the employee is not subject to personal freedom regarding when and how he may use his workforce.

In addition to the primary service obligation, the employee is also subject to ancillary **261** service obligations, so-called fiduciary duties. The legal connecting factor is sec. 241 para. 2 BGB, which is also applicable to the employment relationship. Thus, the employee has to consider the rights, legal assets, and interests of the employer. In particular, he must observe the rules of conduct within an establishment, handle the employer's property with care, or report his incapacity to work in case of illness.

262 **bb) Obligations of the Employer.** The employer's primary service obligation is to pay the remuneration to the employee. However, the employee is obliged for advance performance, sec. 614 BGB.

263 The ancillary service obligations of the employer also find their basis in sec. 241 para. 2 BGB. The employer is obliged to employ the employee. This obligation arises from the employee's general right of personality, protected by the Basic Law, Art. 1 para. 1 in conjunction with Art. 2 para. 1 of the Basic Law (*Grundgesetz* "**GG**"). The employer is also obliged to take measures to protect the life, health and personality of the employee within the framework of the establishment organisation, for example, to provide appropriate work clothing or gender-separated changing rooms.

264 If there is an employment relationship, the entrepreneur as employer has many legally defined obligations in social security and tax law which deviate from the employment contract and which are not available to him. Therefore, the question, whether a contractual relationship is an employment relationship in the sense of sec. 611a BGB is of central importance.

b) Social Security Law

265 Regarding the employer's and employee's obligations under social security law, please refer to the comments on temporary agency employment in the relationship between the temporary work agency and the temporary agency worker (see marginal no. 37 et seq.).

c) Tax Law

266 Regarding the employer's and employee's tax law obligations, please refer to the information on temporary agency employment in the relationship between the temporary work agency and the temporary agency worker (see marginal no. 42 et seq.).

III. Contract to produce a work

267 In addition to the overt temporary agency employment and services, are work perfomances, i. e., cooperation based on a contract to produce a work, are the third basic case of external personnel deployment.

1. Legal Basis and Legal Relations

268 The contract to produce a work is regulated in sec. 631 et seq. BGB. The conclusion of the contract follows the general regulations of the BGB. Therefore, two concurring declarations of intent must be present, which are in content directed towards the conclusion of a contract to produce a work. Sec. 631 BGB names the parties to the contract to produce a work as a contractor (obligor of the work performance) and customer (obligee of the work perfomance).

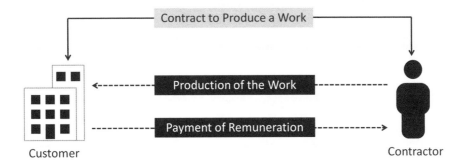

Figure 5: Illustration of a contract to produce a work

Unless a general ban prohibits the use of contracts to produce a work (see marginal no. **99** above for the prohibition in the meat industry), a contract to produce a work can generally be concluded orally. Even if there is no written form requirement concerning contracs to produce a work, the written form is recommended for documentation reasons alone.   **269**

In the law governing contracts to produce a work, there are mutual contractual primary service obligations, which differ significantly from those of the service contract.   **270**

a) Obligations of the Contractor

The contractor obliges the production of the promised work. Therefore, the contractor owes the customer to procure a particular success through his work performance. In the agreement between the parties, the promised work is specified. The contractor is self-employed. Regarding the achievement of success, the contractor is entirely free. In case of doubt, he does not have to produce the work personally but can have it produced by his employees or use another third party with whom he again concludes a contract. The contractor is free from the customer's instructions, both in terms of time and place and in his work organisation. The customer can only give the contractor factual instructions regarding the work, sec. 645 para. 1 sent. 1 BGB.   **271**

The project-related right to issue instructions under a contract to produce a work within the meaning of sec. 645 para. 1 sent. 1 BGB is factual and result-oriented, and representational limited to the work performance to be rendered. Instructions of the customer, by which the type, sequence, and single contents of different or similar work performances within the scope of the previously agreed work items are determined. These instructions do not justify the assumption of the existence of temporary agency employment as far as they are only issued in relation to the specific work. However, the instruction limit in the employment contract is exceeded if the third party only determines the subject of the work to be performed by the employee by his instruction.[6]   **272**

The regulations on the contract to produce a work do not exclude the possibility that the work to be performed is contractually agreed upon in such detail and in such a specific manner in all details concerning the execution, scope, quality, time and place of performance or creation. So that in that case, there is no leeway in decision-making left for the contractor regarding the creation of the work. The contractor is then contractually obliged to perform the work in accordance with the contract concerning all details.   **273**

---

[6] Federal Labour Court, 30 January 1991 – 7 AZR 497/89.

274   Only result-related execution instructions shall, therefore, be assigned to the right to issue instructions under the contract to produce a work. As such qualified are:
– Instructions regarding quality specifications;
– Information on the size, quantity, and type of the object to be created;
– Production methods and sequence.

275   Given the possibility for the customer to issue instructions resulting from sec. 645 para. 1 sent. 1 BGB, the contractor must still have his own technical, concrete possibility to give instructions in the sense of sec. 106 GewO for the performance of the work.

b) Obligations of the Customer

276   If the contractor has produced the work free of material defects and legal defects, the customer is obliged to accept the work and pay the agreed remuneration. Upon acceptance of the work, the contractor's claim to his wage shall become due.

c) Lessons learned

277   Based on the principles of case law above mentioned, the Federal Employment Agency has laid down the following characteristics in its business instructions (page 16 of the Technical Instructions for the Act on Temporary Employment, AÜG, valid from 1 August 2019), which speak in favour of the acceptance of a contract to produce a work:
– Agreement and preparation of a qualitatively customisable work result attributable to the contractor,
– Entrepreneurial freedom of disposition of the contractor towards the customer,
– The Contractor's right to issue instructions to his employees working in the customer's business if the work is to be created there,
– Bearing the entrepreneurial risk, in particular the warranty by the contractor and
– Success-oriented accounting of the work performance.

2. Social Security Law

278   Concerning the contractor's social security obligations, please refer to the service contract's statements (see marginal no. **246** et seq.).

3. Tax Law

279   Regarding the tax law consequences of the contract to produce a work, reference is made to the explanations above of the service contract (see marginal no. **248** et seq.).

IV. Further Practice-relevant Forms of External Personnel Deployment

280   The above mentioned forms (see marginal no. **236/267/5** et seq.) can be described as basic contractual types of external personnel deployment. Based on these basic types, a wide variety of external personnel deployment constellations have developed in practice.

1. Employment Service

281   The entrepreneur may use a placement officer to find suitable workers.

The entrepreneur and the placement officer conclude a placement contract. Here, the placement officer commits itself to look for a suitable worker according to the entrepreneur's conceptions and to place these to the entrepreneur. If the placement officer is successful, his obligation from the contract is fulfilled and he receives a placement fee.

The employment service is legally defined in sec. 35 para. 1 sent. 2 Social Security Code, Third Book ("**SGB III**"). It includes all activities aimed at bringing together persons seeking training with employers to establish a training relationship and persons seeking employment with employers to establish an employment relationship.   **282**

The placement is successful if the entrepreneur concludes a service or employment contract or a contract to produce a work with the person placed to him or her so that the external labour is available to him or her to promote the undertaking's purpose.   **283**

A contractual or other legal relationship between the placement officer and the person placed does not arise.   **284**

The prerequisites of sec. 1 para. 2 AÜG, can additionally be used to differentiate between the employment service and temporary agency employment. If the employee is hired out to third parties for work performance and the person making the employee available does not undertake the usual employer obligations or the employer risk (sec. 3 para. 1 nos. 1 to 3 AÜG). Then it is presumed according to sec. 1 para. 2 AÜG that the person making the employee available pursues employment service.   **285**

2. Home Employment

Another legally regulated form of external personnel deployment is the so-called home employment. It is a form of not self-employed work. The legal basis for home employment is the Home Employment Act (*Heimarbeitsgesetz* – **HAG**).   **286**

Homeworker is who works by way of business in a self-selected place of work (own home or self-selected business premises) alone or with his family members on behalf of tradespeople. Yet he leaves the work results' exploitation to the directly or indirectly order placing tradesman (sec. 2 para. 1 sent. 1 HAG). Work is deemed to be gainful if intended to be of a particular duration and is intended to contribute, at least in part, to earn a living. Both industrial activities and simple salaried activities can be carried out through home employment.   **287**

The homeworker is not an employee because he is neither integrated into the business organisation of an employer nor subject to personal instructions in the sense of sec. 106 GewO. The homeworker is free to choose the place, time, and scope of his work. He is only economically dependent on his principal. The homeworker is also not an independent entrepreneur because he neither bears the commercial risk of selling his goods or his work nor appears on the sales market. The utilisation of the work results is solely left to the principal. The homeworker does not use his capital or his workforce with the risk of loss.   **288**

Classification as a home employment relationship does not preclude a neccessary higher qualification of the worker for the work owed's performance.Unconsidered remains the amount of time spent working, the level of earnings, whether living is mainly earned by home employment, the need for protection of the homeworker, or the question of whether the home worker has registered a business.[7]   **289**

The legislator sees the homeworker in a similar position, worthy of protection as an employee so that the protective provisions of the Home Employment Act apply to him. In particular, sec. 29 HAG provides for a general protection against the homeworker's dismissal, the content of which is based on the provision of sec. 622 BGB. Sections 23   **290**

---

[7] Federal Labour Court, 14 June 2016 – 9 AZR 305/15.

to 27 HAG contain, for example, provisions on protection against remuneration and attachment. In addition to the HAG's protective provisions, there are special regulations in the employee protection laws in which homeworkers are treated on an equal footing with employees.

291   According to sec. 12 para. 2 SGB IV, homeworkers are regarded as personnel within the meaning of sec. 7 SGB IV. They are liable to pay contributions to health, nursing, unemployment and pension insurance. They are also entitled to statutory accident insurance. The "employer" of the homeworker is defined in social security law as the person who assigns the work directly to him. The principal is thus responsible for paying the total social security contribution, sec. 28e SGB IV. The remuneration that a homeworker receives comes from not self-employed work. For this reason, the income tax must be paid by the principal to the local tax office as wage tax, i. e., by deduction from the wage (sec. 38 para. 1 sent. 1 EStG).

292   The term "home employment" must not be equated with the term "home office". Although they are often used in the same context or as synonyms in practice, working in a home office is usually not home employment. That is because the employee does not choose his or her own place of work, but is only given the opportunity to work in the home office instead of in the employer's business by employment contract.

293   The classification of a contract as a "home employment relationship" must always be determined according to the actual business content. A different designation, such as the contract designation as "freelancing" is not relevant for the classification.

3. Interim-Management

294   Interim management describes a service model in which an executive, the so-called interim manager, works for a contractually agreed but limited period in an external undertaking. The deployment of interim managers is often project- or occasion-related and is carried out, for example, within the scope of reorganisation or restructuring measures, for handling a company purchase or sale, and generally for the handling of projects.

295   Like other external personnel deployment forms, interim management as a term is not exclusively linked to a contractual constellation behind it. Interim management can, therefore, be designed in two- or three-person relationships. Depending on the chosen model and its actual implementation, assessing the status law of the manager's work can be either as dependent employment or as self-employed.

296   Undertakings and, depending on the model chosen, the interim manager himself or an intermediate (legal) person conclude a service contract in the sense of sec. 611 BGB. The interim manager (or the intermediate person) commits himself to the agreed service; the entrepreneur commits himself as an employer to pay the agreed remuneration.

4. Joint Establishment

297   The deployment of external personnel can also be exercised in a so-called joint establishment.

298   The law does not define the concept of joint establishment. However, the legal concept's existence has been recognised by the legislator in sec. 1 para. 1 sent. 2, para. 2 BetrVG. According to the established case-law of the BAG, it can be assumed that a joint establishment exists if "*the tangible and intangible operating resources of several undertakings available at a permanent establishment are combined, ordered and used in a targeted manner for a uniform operational purpose, and a uniform management system controls the use*

of human labour."[8] Therefore, a joint establishment differs from "normal" establishments of an undertaking. The joint establishment's material and personnel resources are legally assigned not to one but to several entities.

According to the case law's specifications, three mainly features are mainl decisive for **299** the existence of a joint establishment: a *management agreement* and a *uniform management system*, and the *pursuit of a uniform and own operational purpose.*

The basis for the joint commitment of the entities in the joint establishment is the so- **300** called management agreement. This is the link under company law between the entities involved in joint establishment, with which they agree on joint management of the joint establishment. The management agreement is not subject to any formal legal requirements and can, therefore, be concluded tacitly. A management agreement does not just exist if two enterprises agree to work closely together or if there is a legal link within group law, e. g., a control agreement.

Based on the management agreement, a uniform management system controlling **301** the work processes must also be installed in the joint establishment. This management system must have the ability to legally and actually manage all the human, technical and intangible resources used to achieve the operational purpose. In the opinion of the Labour Court, it is necessary that the same institutional management must carry out the core of the employer functions in the social and also in the personnel area (e. g., keeping personnel files, drawing up employment contracts and other personal documents, recruitment, dismissals, transfers, regulation of overtime and other working time issues). However, it is not sufficient that services such as payroll accounting are carried out by one undertaking for the other. For example, even close entrepreneurial cooperation, based on a control agreement, is not principally sufficient. External control of the work process, for instance, in just-in-time production, is equally insufficient. Even such a close integration of the cooperation is not sufficient in itself to recognise a joint establishment.

Finally, the results of the work carried out in the joint establishment under uniform **302** management must serve a common purpose of the participating undertakings. This presupposes that the inter undertaking's use of personnel and resources is not limited to the mere fact that one undertaking makes the workforce of its employees available to promote the latter's business purposes. The use of the respective employees must at least also serve the undertaking's own business purposes. The decisive factor here should be the practice of cross-employer personnel deployment, which is characteristic of the ordinary course of business in a joint establishment. However, the joint establishment's undertaking does not need to participate in legal transactions in this connection to the outside. Therefore, the joint establishment's work products' economic exploitation can be carried out separately from each other in, respectively, across their respective undertakings involved.

Thus, in a joint establishment, personnel from several employers are typically em- **303** ployed. This applies in particular to joint establishments, in which two legally independent undertakings have an interest, but also to joint establishments of affiliated companies under group law. The latter is the case because German labour law does not recognise a so-called "group employment relationship". Even within a group company, employees are only in a relationship under labour law with their contractual employer. Therefore, the individual employers' interrelationship in a group under company law is irrelevant for the individual employees' assignment under labour law.

In the case of personnel deployment within the framework of a joint establishment, **304** despite the cooperation of personnel from different employers, these are not temporary agency employment cases. For technical legal reasons, the joint establishment and the

---

[8] Federal Labour Court, 11 September 2007 – 1 AZR 824/06.

temporary agency employment are mutually exclusive. Temporary agency employment is deemed to exist if the temporary agency worker in question is integrated into an external business organisation and is subject to the hirer's instructions under labour law. The temporary agency worker's temporary work agency exclusively promotes the hirer's business purposes through the hiring out. On the other hand, there is a joint business organisation in the case of a joint establishment. The very concept of integration into an "external" organisation cannot be assumed. The right to issue instructions adverse the employee is also not exercised by a third party (hirer). In a joint establishment, the authority to issue instructions is rather incumbent on the uniform management system, in which the employee's contractual employer is also involved. Ultimately, the employee's joint establishment activity also serves at least the employer's business purposes and not exclusively those of a third party (hirer).

5. Matrix Organisation

305   As with the concept of joint establishments, there is no statutory definition for the so-called matrix organisation. Furthermore, concerning the matrix organisation, it is complicated because there is a wide variety of terms in the relevant specialist literature. Furthermore, it is not possible to agree on a uniform definition. A generally valid definition of the term does not yet exist. Regardless of this, the matrix organisation can be described as an actual form of organisation in which an undertaking or several legally affiliated undertakings are jointly positioned. This form of organisation's core element of is that two or more management or reporting dimensions overlap, which refer to the same organisational unit and thus justify an equal multiple subordination of the organisational unit concerned. The consequence of this model is that, in organisational practice, there are differences between the factual structures and those that are prescribed by company/labour law.

306   For example, in a matrix structure, the employee concerned (organisational unit – OU) is no longer assigned to an establishment, there his or her department and, within that department, to a department manager and/or project manager. His classification in the matrix structure is rather oriented towards different classification criteria or dimensions. Basically, these are designed to be equivalent. For example, in the matrix, the employee is assigned to both the function-related line (for example, purchasing) and a product-related line (for example, Product A) and is subject to the instructions of his or her superior within both lines. These instructions are always activity-related instructions, whereas the disciplinary right to issue instructions remains with the contractual employer. A matrix organisation is, therefore, a multi-line organisation.

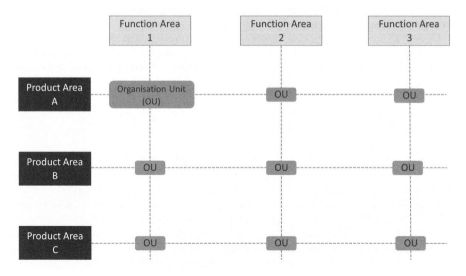

Figure 6: Illustration of a matrix organsiation

Differentiation of the cross-employer personnel deployment in matrix structures   **307**
compared to the deployment of personnel by way of temporary agency employment is a
challenge. The transfer of the right to issue activity-related instructions – fundamental for
the deployment of personnel in a matrix structure – is similar to the transfer of the right
to issue instructions in the context of temporary agency employment. In both cases, the
technical, temporal and local right to issue instructions, which the contractual employer
is entitled to under sec. 106 GewO, is transferred to another entity. A consideration of
the disciplinary right of instruction also does not lead to a delimitation. The contractual
employer does not operate its law to this effect, neither when the employee is deployed in
a matrix structure nor when the employee is hired out. This is because the disciplinary
right to issue instructions is due to the contractual employer based on his personal qualification as a party to the employment contract. This right is status-related and cannot
be transferred by the employer.

Because of the far-reaching, controversial exception provided for by the AÜG for   **308**
personnel deployment within a group structure (see marginal no. **183** et seq.), the delimitation difficulties are not as significant as they appear at first glance. Besides, the
introduction of a matrix structure in the group means that the conditions for temporary
agency employment subject to approval are not met according to the prevailing opinion.
A decisive criterion for this is missing, namely the exclusive promotion of the hirer's
business purpose. The organisation in the matrix does not lead to an employee pursuing
only one single business purpose within the third undertaking. Instead, the bundling of
tasks and responsibilities in several undertakings' interests also leads to pursuing and
promoting several interests.

6. Agile Modes of Working (e. g., Scrum)

In contrast to the constellations mentioned above, agile modes of working do not rep-   **309**
resent a typical form of external personnel deployment. Nevertheless, their description
is given in the following, because on the one hand, agile modes of working are becoming

increasingly popular. On the other hand, the deployment of external personnel in agile structures is associated with particular challenges.

310   Under the keyword "agile modes of working," different organisation and working methods can be summarised, which principally arrange establishments and undertakings more flexibly and lead faster to the desired work results. There is no uniform definition for these forms of work either. The core element of agile modes of working is the transition from classic line organisations (waterfall model) to network organisations under the dissolution of classic hierarchical structures. Flexible (project-related) put together, multi-functional teams replace the specialist departments integrated into fixed reporting lines.

311   Due to its practical importance, the representation of such an agile structure is illustrated below using Scrum's example. The originally deriving from IT development Scrum structure and the forms deduced from it are the most widespread agile modes of working in Germany. Teams working in Scrum structures are characterised by the fact that the team members organise the work process independently and without labour law instructions. Scrum is only a framework in which people can work together on complex tasks and not just as a process or methodology. This is to say: You don't work *according to the Scrum principle*", but *you become a Scrum team*. They become a Scrum team that gives itself its procedures apart from the daily meetings and, in doing so, also designs one-time superior tasks such as approval and coordination of vacation and daily working hours up to the seating arrangements.

312   The Scrum framework consists of predefined roles that qualify individual persons and rules of the concrete workflow in which the result is worked out. A Scrum team typically consists of a small, for example, a six-member interdisciplinary team and a Product Owner and a Scrum Master. There are no hierarchies in a Scrum team. The team develops the work result in several sections (sprints). Each sprint begins with the definition of the work processes to be completed (sprint planning). The actual work is preceded daily by an initial meeting (daily Scrum). In this meeting, the work for the next 24 hours is planned with the necessary brevity. This is done taking into account the progress and insights achieved since the last Daily Scrum.

313   The product owner defines the product properties to be developed at the beginning in the product backlog. The requirements for the product are entered as user stories in the product backlog. However, the product properties, and therefore the product backlog, are often adapted in the team's subsequent development process in consultation with the product owner.

314   The product owner decides whether the respective goal has been achieved in the sprint, which points still need to be worked through, and whether the product's development is complete. The Product Owner updates the product backlog and marks the backlog entries as "done". The Scrum Master is responsible as a coach to observe the rules for cooperation in the Scrum Team and supports the team in organising the way they work. He also serves the coordination between different teams. Neither the Product Owner nor the Scrum Master has the authority to issue labour law instructions. Scrum teams consist partly solely of undertaking-interal employees; somewhat, they are (also) formed by external people.

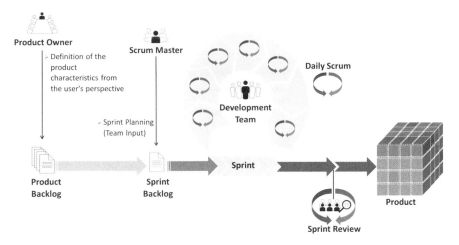

Figure 7: Illustration of Scrum

The close and largely autonomous cooperation of the team members among themselves   315
is not only the source of the such teams' flexibility and thus of the much-appreciated
advantages of agile modes of working. If the teams are made up of in-house and external
personnel, close cooperation is also the source of the problems associated with critical
external personnel deployment. In many areas, the work performed by external personnel
in agile modes of working can no longer be distinguished from the undertaking's own
employees' work. The boundaries between external personnel and employees of one's own
blur in agile modes of working like Scrum. This results in difficulties in delimitation,
leading to far-reaching consequences if a misjudgment of the people involved occurs (see
marginal no. **572/652** et. seq.). Besides, it is not generally intended that superiors can exert
influence on current work processes. Agile work structures, therefore, entail an increased
legal risk when using external personnel.

V. Summary and Tabular Overview

Due to the existing private autonomy, in Germany there are various possibilities   316
for the using the external deployment of personnel in one's undertaking. Basically, the
parties involved are free to choose the legal construction underlying their contractual
relationship. They are free to decide which of the forms above mentioned will avail for
the design of their relationship.

However, this freedom of design does not apply absolutely. The legislator considers   317
employees, in particular, to be mainly in need of protection and ties in far-reaching legal
consequences with the employee status to realise this protection. To limit abusive arrangements of the parties involved and effectuate the most outstanding possible protection of
the persons concerned, the legislator restricts the private autonomous arrangement option
to the extent that the individual case's actual circumstances are decisive for determining
the status. Suppose, the parties involved choose any of the forms mentioned above for
the deployment of external personnel, and the actual provision of services is established
differently. Then, in that case, the latter is thus decisive for the legal consequences of the
activity. This means that the parties involved should be aware of the legal consequences

of the different contract types and which form is suitable for the concrete requirement before the contract is concluded.

Types of Contracts/Forms of Employment	Contract Features/Services
Service contract, sec. 611 BGB (marginal no. **236** et seq.)	– Employee owes performance of activities, is self-employed – Entrepreneur owes payment of the remuneration
Employment contract, sec. 611a BGB (marginal no. **253** et seq.)	– Employee owes performance of work, is employed – Employer owes remuneration
Contract to produce a work, sec. 631 BGB (marginal no. **267** et seq.)	– Production of a work, prosperity is owed. The contractor is independently active – Customer owes remunertion for work

Temporary agency employment, sec. 1 AÜG (marginal no. **5** et seq.)	– Three-person relationship, consisting of temporary work agency, hirer, and temporary agency worker
	– Temporary work agency and employee: employment contract
	  • Temporary work agency owes remuneration
	  • Employee owes work performance, performs it in the hirer's establishment, is employed
	– Temporary work agency and hirer: temporary agency employment contract
	  • Temporary work agency owes the hirer the assignment of an employee to the hirer
	  • Hirer owes payment of the remuneration

Employment services (marginal no. **281** et seq.)	– Placement officer owes the placement of a foreign worker – Entrepreneur owes remuneration for the placement – Entrepreneur and a third party are subject to obligations under labour law, the type of contract is decisive
Home employment according to HAG (marginal no. **286** et seq.)	– Homeworker is gainfully employed at a self-chosen workplace; he is solely economically dependent on his principal – Utilisation of the work result is the sole responsibility of the principal
Interim-Management, sec. 611 BGB (marginal no. **294** et seq.)	– Interim manager owes service, is self-employed – Employer owes remuneration

Joint establishment, sec. 1 para. 1 sent. 2, para. 2 BetrVG (marginal no. **297** et seq.)	– Personnel are (still) employees of their respective contractual employer
	  • Owe performing activities, are dependent employees
	  • Activity is carried out within the joint establishment together with employees to the employer
	– Employer owes remuneration
	– Does not constitute temporary agency employment

Types of Contracts/Forms of Employment	Contract Features/Services

Matrix organisation (marginal no. 305 et seq.)	– Personnel are (still) employees of their respective contractual employer
	  • Owe performing activities, are dependent employees
	  • Employees are subject to the instructions of several superiors during their work
	  • Disciplinary authority remains with the contractual employer
	  • Activity can be carried out together with employees from other employers
	– Employer owes remuneration
	– Does not constitute temporary agency employment

Agile modes of working (marginal no. 309 et seq.)	– Personnel are (still) employees of their respective contractual employer
	  • Owe performing activities, are dependent employees
	  • Activity is carried out largely autonomously within agile modes of working
	  • Employer at least de facto waives exercise of the right to issue professional instructions
	  • Disciplinary right to issue instruction remains fully intact
	– Employer owes remuneration; employer/customer owes remuneration for the service/work

B. Incorrect Deployment of External Personnel – Diagnosis and Risk

318   If the law's mandatory legal provisions on temporary agency employment are violated, this can have far-reaching legal consequences for temporary work agencies, hirers, and temporary agency workers. The infringements do not solely relate to the contractual or social security level but have, particularly, criminal law implications to some extent.

319   Against the background of these far-reaching consequences, it is highly advisable to observe the legal requirements carefully. The various infringements and, in particular, their legal consequences for the parties involved are dealt with in this chapter.

I. Overt Temporary Agency Employment and its Legal Consequences

1. Definition and Meaning

320   The incorrectly implemented overt temporary agency employment is a term consisting of two parts.

321   The parties, i. e., the temporary work agency and the hirer, particularly, structure the use of external personnel openly, i. e., in a certain way recognisably, as temporary agency employment. Therefore, the parties do not choose a contractual construction that serves to conceal the use of external personnel by way of temporary agency employment.

322   Additionally, however, this overt temporary agency employment is erroneous – the defectiveness results from a violation of the relevant specific regulations of the AÜG.

323   Due to many special regulations and their level of detail, there is a particular risk for untrained legal practitioners when using external personnel through temporary agency employment. This applies in particular to legal practitioners who are not familiar with the peculiarities of German labour law. In practice, therefore, the respective requirements should be carefully checked before each assignment.

2. Case Groups and their Legal Consequences – Liability Risks

324   The respective legal consequences of a violation of individual provisions of the AÜG are described below using case groups in point.

a) Violation of the Obligation to Obtain Permission

325   If the temporary work agency is not in possession of a valid permit when assigning employees, this violates the mandatory obligation to obtain permission under sec. 1 para. 1 sent. 1 AÜG (see marginal no. 88 et seq.).

326   A violation of the obligation to obtain permission is not only present in cases where a valid temporary agency employment permit was not already available at the beginning of the temporary agency employment.

327   Instead, the circumstance of temporary agency employment without a permit may occur for the first time during the execution of temporary agency employment that has been started in conformity with the law. This is the case, for example, if a permit granted for a limited period loses its validity during the period of the assignment because the time

limit is exceeded. Furthermore, it is also possible that the competent authority revokes the temporary agency employment permit. These cases are to be considered in a more differentiated manner so that a violation of the obligation to obtain permission does not automatically occur. For example, the possibility of revocation alone is not sufficient.

The reason for a more differentiated consideration of the cases in which the permit is only canceled at a later date is explained using the example of a permit's revocation. The basis is the direct, or, in the revocation case, the corresponding application of the regulation of a permit's limited continuation for twelve months according to sec. 2 para. 4 sent. 4 AÜG (sec. 5 para. 2 sent. 2 AÜG). The revoked permit will then have an after-effect. Thus, a revoked permit is also deemed to continue to apply to the processing of already existing assignments. However, this after-effect shall not be valid for more than 12 months. Therefore, the temporary work agency is obligated to terminate or allow existing temporary agency employment contract to expire not to exceed the continuation's maximum period of validity. Those temporary agency workers who are already working in a hirer's establishment at the time of the permit's revocation may continue their work until the expiry of 12 months after the revocation. However, an exchange of these temporary agency workers is, in principle, no longer possible. Under the after-effect's validity, the temporary work agency must not conclude new temporary agency employment contracts or to extend existing contracts. **328**

In addition to revocation, the responsible authority may also revoke an illegally granted permit with effect for the future (sec. 4 para. 1 sent. 1 AÜG). However, since the provisions on temporary continuation also apply in these cases according to sec. 1 para. 1 sent. 2 AÜG, the above statements apply on the revocation accordingly. **329**

In all cases, the objective factual situation is ultimately decisive, whether the temporary work agency actually lacks the permit, and whether it is not valid under continuation. In this context, even a subsequent new grant of permission does not cure the previous assignment without a permit. Therefore, it is recommended that any legal relationship is based on new contractual foundations after the grant of a permit. **330**

There is no breach of the obligation to obtain permission if the assignemnt is possible without a permit (see marginal no. **179** et seq.). **331**

aa) Contract Law. If there is a breach of the obligation to obtain permission, the restrictions of the AÜG fundamentally interfere with the contractual constellation chosen by the parties on a privately autonomous basis in a three-person relationship and realign the existing relationships. The relevant connecting factor for violating a requirement of the AÜG is sec. 9 para. 1, sec. 10 para. 1 AÜG. In principle, sec. 9 para. 1 AÜG stipulates the contract's invalidity, whereas sec. 10 AÜG feigns a new legal relationship. This interference with the parties'contractual freedom is justified by the violating the provisions of the AÜG for the prtotection's purpose under labour law. **332**

Generally, the legal consequences that arise are not dispositive. **333**

(1) Temporary Agency Worker – Temporary Work Agency. Under sec. 9 para.1 sent. 1 half-sent. 1 AÜG, the employment contract between the temporary agency worker and the temporary work agency is invalid if the latter does not have the permit required under sec. 1 para. 1 sent. 1 AÜG. **334**

For the protection of the parties, the ineffective employment relationship continues as a so-called defective employment relationship. Mainly, this defective employment relationship constitutes the basis of claims for services already exchanged by the parties in the past. Since this legal relationship also provides a legal basis for their relationship in the past, it does not lead to a reversal of the exchange of benefits between the temporary agency worker and the temporary work agency, which is hardly possible in practice **335** anyway. The consequence of this would be that the temporary agency worker may, for example, retain the remuneration already paid by the temporary work agency in the past. When the invalidity occurs, there is also no new factual employment relationship between the temporary work agency and the hirer, which would contradict the clear intention of sec. 9 AÜG.

336   If the employment relationship between the temporary work agency and the temporary agency worker is invalid based on sec. 9 para. 1 sent. 1 AÜG, sec. 10 para. 2 sent. 1 AÜG allows the latter to claim damages from the temporary work agency. The fundamental prerequisite for this claim is, however, the existence of damage eligible for compensation. Compensable damages are those that the temporary agency worker has incurred due to trusting the validity of his employment contract with the temporary work agency. If, as a consequence of the breach of the obligation to obtain permission, an employment relationship between the hirer and the temporary agency worker is feigned (see marginal no. 337 et seq.) and this feigned employment relationship contains worse conditions than the invalid employment relationship between the temporary work agency and the temporary agency worker; this could, for example, constitute damage that could be compensated. Since the standard serves to protect legitimate expectations, it follows from this that such a claim does not exist, however, if the temporary agency worker knew the reason for the invalidity (sec. 10 para. 2 sent. 2 AÜG).

337   *(2) Temporary Agency Worker – Hirer.* As shown above, the temporary agency employment contract without the necessary permit according to sec. 9 para. 1 no. 1 half-sent. 1 AÜG leads to the invalidity of the employment contract between the temporary agency worker and the temporary work agency.

338   At the same time, sec. 10 para. 1 sent. 1 half-sent. 1 AÜG provides that in such a case, an employment relationship between the hirer and the temporary agency worker is deemed to have been concluded. At this point, therefore, an employment relationship within the meaning of sec. 611a BGB is created between the temporary agency worker and the hirer (!) through a legal fiction. The fiction's effect leads to creating the employment relationship by operation of law; a lack of knowledge or awareness is as irrelevant as a will of the parties, contrary to this legal consequence.

339   In the case of assignment without permission, the fictitious employment relationship begins with the temporary agency worker's actual assignment, i. e., with the actual commencement of work (sec. 10 para. 1 sent. 1 half-sent. 2 AÜG). If the permit does not expire until a later date, the fictitious employment relationship begins with immediate effect at that time (sec. 10 para. 1 sent. 1 half-sent. 2 AÜG). This is a crucial circumstance in practice, as company regulations often link the employee's length of service to the company. Moreover, seniority is also a sometimes significant circumstance in connection with an announced termination of this ultimately unwanted employment relationship.

340   The general restrictions apply to the termination of the fictitious employment relationship. It therefore continues to exist until it is terminated under the general provisions of labour law. A termination may be terminated by mutual agreement (termination agreement) or under the general restrictions of the KSchG. This provided that the requirements of the KSchG, the personal waiting period and the exceeding of the general threshold value are given (see sec. 1, 23 KSchG).

341   Also, the legislator makes precise specifications concerning the content of this fictitious employment relationship. Sec. 10 para. 1 sent. 2 AÜG, provides that the employment relationship is deemed limited. This applies if the temporary agency worker's activity with the hirer was only intended to be limited in time, and there is an objective justifying reason for the limitation of the employment relationship. When examining whether the deployment is limited in time, the temporary agency employment contract between the

hirer and the temporary work agency must be considered. If the specific temporary agency worker's deployment is limited according to the temporary agency employment contract's content, a time limit can be assumed. An objective reason within the meaning of sec. 14 para. 1 TzBfG, must be added. However, the written form for the objective reason is not required, as is customary in the TzBfG. Unless a limitation, and a material reason are not cumulatively present, the employment relationship shall be deemed to have been concluded for an unlimited period of time.

The working time envisaged between the temporary work agency and the hirer (!) is **342** deemed agreed (sec. 10 para. 1 sent. 3 AÜG). This has the consequence, for example, that only a part-time employment relationship exists between the hirer and the temporary agency worker if the latter is only on loan to the hirer for a part-time position. In all other respects, the content and duration of this employment relationship are determined by the provisions and other regulations applicable to the hirer's establishment. (sec. 10 para. 1 sent. 4 half-sent. 1 AÜG).

Thus, the remuneration, for example, is determined by the hirer's usual remuneration, **343** i.e., by what a regular employee of the hirer receives for comparable work in the establishment. If the hirer grants allowances in his company above the collectively agreed rate, the temporary agency worker is also entitled to these allowances via the fictitious employment relationship. In total, the temporary agency worker has at least a claim against the hirer for the remuneration agreed with the temporary work agency (sec. 10 para. 1 sent. 5 AÜG). This ensures that the temporary agency worker receives at least the remuneration he or she received.

In the absence of such comparable regulations, the regulations of comparable estab- **344** lishments apply (sec. 10 par. 1 sent. 4 half-sent. 2 AÜG).

Furthermore, this legally established employment relationship is treated in all law areas **345** as a "normal" employment relationship based on a legal transaction. Therefore, the hirer is subject to the usual employer's obligations in the field of labour law (e. g. obligations to provide evidence or obligations arising from collective bargaining agreements and works agreements).

(3) Temporary Work Agency – Hirer. Under sec. 9 para. 1 sent. 1 half-sent. 1 AÜG, **346** temporary agency employment without a valid permit also renders the temporary agency employment contract between the temporary work agency and the hirer invalid.

The ineffective assignment relationship does not establish any obligations to perform **347** between the contracting parties, the temporary work agency, and the hirer. If the permit ceases to be valid at a point at which the temporary employment is already being executed, the consequence of the invalidity also captures the permanent obligation from this point. In contrary, the temporary agency employment contract does not become invalid retroactively. From the point in time of invalidity, there are no longer any obligations to perform even in an temporary agency employment contract that is currently being executed.

If, nevertheless, services have been rendered in fulfilment of the ineffective temporary **348** agency employment contract, these are to be returned according to the principles of the law of enrichment (sec. 812 et seq. BGB). According to these principles, the person who has rendered a service without any legal reason for doing so can demand the return of the obtained advantage from the beneficiary. However, a claim for restitution can be excluded due to the special knowledge of one party about the permission's ineffectiveness.

Due to the temporary agency employment contract's invalidity, there is no legal basis **349** for the services exchanged on its basis. An "erroneous temporary agency employment relationship," similar to the erroneous employment relationship which exists between the temporary agency worker and the temporary work agency and which would prevent a rescission under the law of enrichment, does not exist at this point. Suppose the temporary work agency has rendered services to the hirer by assigning employees. This constitutes a claim under the law of enrichment, which is directed towards the replacement of the enrichment objectively incurred by the hirer. Furthermore, the temporary work agency can demand that the hirer reimburses the remuneration which the temporary work agency has paid the temporary agency worker. In return, the hirer can reclaim any assignment fee already paid from the temporary agency worker. In any legal proceedings, the claims would have to be netted out, so that such a reversal does not usually occur in practice.

350   *(4) Possibilities to Cure through a Status Quo Declaration.* The AÜG provides only very limited possibilities for the legally prescribed intervention in the parties' contractual relationships.

351   There is no possibility for the hirer and the temporary work agency to unilaterally prevent the occurrence of the legal consequences of sec. 9 para. 1 no. 1, in conjunction with sec. 10 para 1 sent. 1 AÜG. The standards lay down mandatory law for both the hirer and the temporary work agency, from which cannot be deviated by agreements. Even if a temporary work agency operating without a permit is subsequently granted the required permit, this does not lead to a retroactive cure of the committed infringements.

352   The only person who can prevent the legal consequence of sec. 10 para. 1 sent. 1 AÜG, i.e., the (temporary) employment contract's invalidity and the fiction of an employment contract between the temporary agency worker and the hirer, is the temporary agency worker himself. He is able to do so by declaring in writing to the temporary work agency or the hirer under sec. 9 para. 1 no. 1 half-sent. 2 AÜG, that he wants to abide by the employment contract with the temporary work agency (status quo declaration). This has to occur up to the expiry of one month after the time agreed between the temporary work agency and the hirer for the assignment's commencement. The temporary employment relationship then does not become invalid. An employment relationship between the hirer and the temporary agency worker is not established contrary to sec. 10 para. 1 sent. 1 half-sent. 1 AÜG.

353   The requirements for the effectiveness of a status quo declaration are very high. Before submitting the declaration in writing to the hirer or temporary work agency, the temporary agency worker must present the declaration in person at the Employment Agency premises. This is a highly personal obligation so that no substitution is possible. The staff of the Employment Agency must then mark the declaration with the date of submission and indicate that the identity of the temporary agency worker has been ascertained. The temporary agency worker must, therefore, carry an official identity document. Ultimately, even after this procedure, the status quo declaration is only effective if it is received by the hirer or temporary work agency no later than the third day after it has been submitted to the Employment Agency. The temporary agency worker must observe the written form (sec. 126 BGB), i.e., the temporary agency worker must sign the declaration in person.

354   The general one-month deadline for submitting the status quo declaration is problematic. Contrary to the law's wording, the period should not run from the point in time when the employment relationship becomes invalid or is re-established, but should additionally presuppose that the temporary agency worker is aware of the essential circumstances. Only if the temporary agency worker's declaration fulfills all of the requirements mentioned before sec. 9 para. 2 AÜG, then the legal consequence of sec. 10 para. 2 sent. 1 AÜG can be avoided. Because of these requirements, it is not difficult to see that the status quo declaration is quantitatively irrelevant in practice as a possibility to cure.

355   Regardless of this, the hirer has as little influence on this process as the temporary work agency. In particular, the temporary agency worker cannot be required to make such a declaration or even to write out one in advance, i.e., before his assignment in the hirer's establishment. In the latter case, the law expressly orders the invalidity of such a declaration in sec. 9 para. 3 sent. 1 AÜG.

Even if the employee makes an effective declaration of detention, its effect according to **356** sec. 9 para. 1 sent. 1 no. 1 half-sent. 2 AÜG extends solely to the (temporary) employment contract and the fiction of a new employment relationship with the hirer. This should, under no circumstances, be overlooked. The invalidity of the temporary agency employment contract (see marginal no. **346**) remains in force even in the context of an effective status quo declaration.

bb) Works Constitution Law. The employment relationship between the hirer and **357** the temporary agency worker fictitious in the context of sec. 10 para. 1 sent. 1 half-sent. 1 AÜG is in no way inferior to an employment relationship established in the usual way from the perspective of the works constitution.

The fictitious employment relationship is a fully-fledged connecting factor for sev- **358** eral rights/obligations under the works constitution. The employee concerned is thus principally entitled to all rights to which the hirer's regular employees are also entitled. An existing works council must be fully involved in matters concerning the respective employee within the existing framework rights.

However, under works constitution law, the connection to the temporary work agency **359** is terminated with the employment contract's invalidity.

cc) Social Security Law. Suppose an employment relationship between the hirer and **360** the temporary agency worker is feigned within the framework of the legal consequences of sec. 9, 10 AÜG. In that case, the hirer takes up the employer position, vis-à-vis the temporary agency worker. Upon assumption of the employer position, the hirer is basically subject to an employer's social security obligations (see marginal no. **37** et seq.). In particular, the hirer must pay the total social security contribution according to sec. 28e para. 1 sent. 1 SGB IV to the collecting agency.

Suppose the temporary work agency continues to pay the remuneration to the tempo- **361** rary agency worker. In that case, the temporary work agency must also pay the total social security contribution attributable to the remuneration to the collecting agency (sec. 28e para. 2 sent. 3 SGB IV). For the transfer of the social security contribution due to the paid remuneration, the temporary work agency is considered to be the employer in addition to the hirer; both are jointly and severally liable debtors (sec. 28e para. 2 sent. 4 SGB IV). Consequently, if the temporary work agency continues to pay the remuneration to the temporary agency worker and pays the total social security contributions accruing there-on to the collecting agency, the hirer is released from his obligation to pay the collecting agency. No further payment of social security contributions is required. However, t is not excluded, that the temporary work agency may have recourse to the hirer internally. In practice, in such cases, the hirer, in particular, must ensure that the temporart work agency correctly pays the total social security contributions. If the temporary work agency does not pay the total social security contribution correctly, the hirer commits a criminal offence according to sec. 266a StGB (see marginal no. **436** et seq.).

However, if the temporary agency worker effectively submits a status quo declaration **362** (see marginal no. **350** et seq.), no employment relationship between the temporary agency worker and the hirer is simulated. Therefore, the temporary work agency is still the employer, so he is obliged to pay the total social security contribution. Under social security law, the consequences of an effective temporary agency employment apply, so please refer to the above explanations (see marginal no. **60** et seq.).

dd) Tax Law. Under tax law, the fiction of an employment relationship initially has **363** no effect if the hirer continues to pay the remuneration to the employee, withholds the wage tax due on this, and pays it to the tax office. The fiction of labour law is irrelevant for the fulfillment of wage tax obligations.[9] However, the hirer is also liable in addition to the temporary work agency under sec. 42d para. 6 EStG (see marginal no. 66 et seq.).

364   **ee) Administrative Offences Law.** The assignment of temporary agency workers without a temporary agency employment permit results in legal consequences for the parties involved that are assessed in terms of fines under the AÜG and the Administrative Offences Act.

365   *(1) Administrative Offenses under the AÜG.* The assignment of temporary agency workers without a temporary agency employment permit does not preclude the implementation of administrative offences according to sec. 16 AÜG. According to sec. 16 para. 3 AÜG, the main customs offices, are responsible for prosecuting these administrative offences. Based on the existing opportunity principle in the law on administrative offences, the main customs offices can decide at their discretion whether it is necessary to prosecute the administrative offences.

366   If both the temporary work agency and the hirer are natural persons, they may be the irregularities' perpetrators. However, as such, legal persons cannot be prosecuted as perpetrators of regulatory offences or criminal offences because corporate criminal law is (still) lacking in Germany. The perpetrators, in this case, are the natural persons acting on behalf of the legal entity. According to sec. 9 of the Administrative Offences Act (*Ordnungswidrigkeitengesetz* "**OWiG**"), these are the bodies of the legal entity or members of this body (i. e., members of the executive board or management board), partners autorised to represent of a partnership with legal capacity or legal representatives of another. Furthermore, according to sec. 9 para. 2 StGB, deliberately appointed deputies can also be qualified as temporary work agencies or hirers – and thus as perpetrators. For this purpose, the representative must have been instructed by an establishment's owner or another authorised person to manage the establishment wholly or in part or perform tasks on one's own responsibility, which are incumbent on the owner. If the representative has actually performed the management function or the task assigned to him, he may be the offender. A possible person commissioned includes plant managers, chief representatives, special representatives, managing directors, authorised signatories, and heads of department (e. g., human resources department).

367   The temporary work agency (respectively, the natural person acting on behalf of the legal person) acts in breach of the regulations under sec. 16 para. 1 sent. 1 AÜG if it deliberately or negligently, contrary to sec. 1 para. 1 sent. 1 AÜG, assigns a temporary agency worker to a third party without a permit. Intention requires the knowledge and intention of the cases's facts, i. e., the temporary agency worker's assignment without a permit in the knowledge that this permit is required. Conditional intent as the weakest form of intent is sufficient for the implementation of the administrative offence. An offender acts contionally intentional when he recognises the occurrence of the actual success as possible and not entirely distant (element of knowledge) and accepts the realisation of the offence or accepts it because of the objective pursued (element of will).[10] However, suppose the temporary work agency does not know the actual circumstances of the case's facts, i. e., the requirement of temporary agency employment. In that case, he is subject to an error and does not act intentionally. In this case, however, the negligent realisation of the facts of the case is usually considered. A person acts negligent if he fails to exercise reasonable care. The negligent actor thus, unknowingly and unintentionally, carries out the facts of the case contrary to obligation.

---

[9] Federal Fiscal Court, 24 March 1999 – I R 64/98.
[10] Federal Court of Justice, 24 September 2019 – 1 StR 346/18.

A status quo declaration of a temporary agency worker under sec. 9 para. 2 AÜG (see **368** marginal no. 350 et seq.) does not legalise the breach by the temporary work agency and the hirer of the temporary agency worker's assignment without a permit. Consequently, the temporary work agency carries out the offence mentioned above despite the issue of an effective permit.

Mirror-inverted a hirer acts contrary to the regulations under sec. 16 para. 1 **369** sent. 1a AÜG if he intentionally or negligently allows a temporary agency worker provided to him by a temporary work agency without a permit to work.

The administrative offences can be punished with a fine of up to EUR 30,000 under **370** sec. 16 para. 2 AÜG. If the act is committed negligently, the maximum is halved, sec. 17 para. 2 OWiG.

In the case of intentional conduct, the limitation period is three years, sec. 31 para. 2 **371** sent. 1 OWiG in conjunction with sec. 16 para. 2 AÜG. Negligent conduct becomes statute-barred after two years, sec. 31 para. 2 no. 2, sec. 17 para. 2 OWiG.

(2) Administrative Offences under the OWiG. Suppose an administrative offence – or **372** in other cases a criminal offence – is committed within an undertaking. Then in many cases, the implementation of sec. 130 OWiG can also be considered due to obligatory supervision violations.

This concerns anyone who, as the owner of an establishment or undertaking, inten- **373** tionally or negligently fails to take required supervisory measures to prevent obligation's infringements, which affect the owner, and which violation carries a criminal penalty. This person acts contrary to regulations in a case where such contravention has been committed. The required supervisory measures include the appointment, careful selection, and monitoring of supervisory persons (sec. 130 para. 1 sent. 2 OWiG).

The natural persons named in sec. 9 OWiG can also be considered as perpetrators **374** (see marginal no. 366). Among others, members of the executive board, management members, and the Chief Compliance Officer, authorised signatories, plant managers, and heads of departments may be considered offenders.

The proprietor or the person according to sec. 9 OWiG does not have to have taken su- **375** pervisory measures required and reasonable to counter the risk of violations of establishment- or undertaking-related obligations. In the case law, the type, size, and organisation of the establishment, the various surveillance options, and the variety of regulations to be complied with are the main factors in assessing the required supervisory measure. In principle, supervision must be carried out so that the establishment-related obligations are complied with. The owner of the establishment may not only occasionally "check up on things", but must also regularly carry out supervisory measures, carefully select and instruct his employees, keep them continuously informed about legal regulations and clearly define the area of responsibility of the employees. Furthermore, the establishment owner must carry out random checks and ensure that the technical equipment are in good condition. Misconduct of individuals should also be sanctioned internally.

Besides, there must be a breach of establishment-related obligations. In the present **376** case, this is a violation of the obligation to obtain permission. Suppose the owner of the establishment has intentionally or negligently (see again marginal no. 366) not taken measures that would have prevented temporary agency employment without a permit. In that case, a fine may be imposed on the establishment owner on both the hirer's and temporary work agency's part.

In setting the fine, sec. 130 OWiG makes a distinction and differentiates according to **377** the infringement, which could have been prevented by supervision. If this infringement is punishable by a fine – i.e., a criminal offence – the fine is up to EUR 10,000,000. If the infringement is an administrative offence, as is the case with sec. 16 AÜG, the maximum fine under sec. 130 OWiG is determined by the administrative offence to be prevented. If the person subject to supervision only negligently violates his or her obligatory supervision, the respective maximum fine is reduced by half, sec. 17 para. 2 OWiG.

378 The limitation period is three years, sec. 31 para. 2 sent. 1 OWiG, and in the case of negligent offences, two years, sec. 31 para. 2 sent. 2 OWiG.

379 Under the OWiG, a fine can also be imposed on the undertaking (so-called *association fine*) if an executive body has committed an infringement. It is required that someone
→ As an authorised representative body of a legal entity or as a member of such a body,
→ As a management board of an association without legal capacity or as a member of such a body,
→ As a partner with the power of representation in a partnership with legal capacity,
→ As a chief representative or in a leading position as an authorised signatory or an authorised representative of a legal entity or an association or partnership with legal capacity

commits a criminal offence or an administrative offence and thereby violates obligations of the legal entity or association of persons or enriches the legal entity or association of persons or the act was intended to enrich the legal entity or association of persons, sec. 30 para. 1 OWiG. In the present case, the act triggering the association's fine may be the implementation of sec. 16 AÜG or sec. 130 OWiG by the group of persons just mentioned. Suppose a person from this group of persons implements sec. 16 AÜG. In that case, a fine of EUR 30,000 can also be imposed on the undertaking, sec. 16 AÜG in conjunction with sec. 30 para. 2 sent. 1 OWiG. However, suppose the person violates his or her obligatory supervision according to sec. 130 OWiG. In that case, the association fine may amount to up to EUR 300,000, sec. 130 para. 3 sent. 2 and sec. 30 para. 2 sent. 3 OWiG. In the case of negligent acts by the group of persons named, the fine is also halved for the undertaking (sec. 17 para. 2 OWiG). Case law recognises that an effective compliance management system designed to avoid legal infringements can reduce the fine.

380 In setting the fine, the prosecuting authority (such as the public prosecutor's office) may proceed as follows:
– The setting of a *cumulative association fine*: The fine may be set in combined proceedings against a person from the group of persons mentioned above and, at the same time, against the undertaking.
– Determination of an *isolated association fine*: The fine may be determined solely against the undertaking, irrespective of the prosecution of the person from the group of persons mentioned above, sec. 30 para. 4 sent. 1 OWiG.
– Determination of an *anonymous association fine*: If the specific person from the group of persons mentioned above cannot be identified, a fine may nevertheless be imposed on the undertaking. However, it must be established that an administrative offence or criminal act has been committed by a member of the group of persons mentioned above.

381 **ff) Regulatory.** Besides, the law's violations in connection with cases of erroneous temporaray agency employment may result in further indirect consequences from a regulatory perspective. The regulatory consequences are sometimes far-reaching and should never be underestimated. The following is, therefore, a non-exhaustive overview of further, often unnoticed, consequences.

382 The technical instruction of the Federal Employment Agency clearly states concerning the AÜG that violations of the provisions of the AÜG can be taken into account in the context of the reliability test (sec. 3 para. 1 no. 1 AÜG). If a permit is not available, it can be refused in the case of a subsequent application due to previous violations of the AÜG.

If a fine of more than EUR 200 is imposed for the implementation of an administrative   **383**
offence described under marginal no. **364** et seq. above, the offender shall be entered in
the central trade register under sec. 149 para. 2 no. 3 GewO. Authorities that examine the
trader's reliability when deciding whether to prohibit the trade make use of the database
and may prohibit the exercise of a trade on the grounds of unreliability.

Additionally, the entry in the central trage register can also result in a person no longer   **384**
being considered as a credit institutions' manager. According to sec. 25c of the German Banking Act (*Kreditwesengesetz* "**KWG**"), managers must be reliable. Since the
Federal Financial Supervisory Authority (*Bundesanstalt für Finanzdienstleistungsauf-
sicht* "**BaFin**") also requires an extract from the central trade register when conducting
a reliability check, it can deny a person's qualification as a manager on the grounds of
lack of reliability.

Suppose a fine of at least EUR 2,500 is imposed on the temporary work agency. In that   **385**
case, the temporary work agency shall also be entered in the Central Competition Register
according to sec. 2 para. 1 no. 2c Competition Register Act (*Wettbewerbsregistergesetz*
"**WRegG**"). As a result, the undertaking is excluded from the award of public contracts
and concessions, which can have serious economic consequences. Besides, under sec. 21
para. 1 of the Act to Combat Illegal Employment ("**SchwarzArbG**") the temporary work
agency is excluded for up to three years from participating in invitations to tender for
public supply, construction or service contracts.

b) Breach of the Disclosure Statement

If temporary work agencies and hirers do not expressly designate the hiring out of   **386**
temporary agency workers as "temporary agency employment," this constitutes a breach
of the obligation to label (see marginal no. **106** et seq.). The same applies if the temporary
work agency and the hirer do not concretise the temporary agency worker's person before
the assignment referring to the temporary agency employment contract according to
sec. 1 para. 1 sent. 6 AÜG (see marginal no. **110** et seq.). Together, the two obligations are
referred to as the disclosure statement.

The purpose of the disclosure statement introduced with the new reform was to pre-   **387**
vent the so-called "stock permit" at that time. Previously, an undertaking could escape
from illegality by holding a stock permit in the case of a concealed temporary agency
employment. This avoids labeling as a temporary work agency, as the assignment must
be disclosed. Supposed contractors or service providers are not brought into a more
favourable position by holding a permit and carrying out a so-called "covert temporary
agency employment".

aa) Contract Law. The following is a special feature if the disclosure statement is   **388**
infringed: The legal consequences of the (temporary) employment contract's invalidity
and the employment relationship's fiction with the hirer only arise in the following case.
In case the obligation to label and the obligation to concretise are infringed cumulatively,
sec. 9 para. 1 no. 1a, sec. 10 para. 1 AÜG. In this respect, sec. 9 para. 1 no. 1a AÜG expressly states that, unless the temporary agency employment is explicitly designated as such
and the person of the temporary agency worker is concretised, the (temporary) employment contract is deemed invalid. However, in a concealed temporary agency employment
(see marginal no. **236/267** et seq.) it is insufficient to simply disclose the temporary agency
worker if there is no permit to hire them out. There is already no valid "temporary agency
employment contract" to which reference could be made. In this event, the concretisation of the temporary agency employment is meaningless. In practice, an infringement
of labelling will always trigger the invalidity consequence of sec. 9 para. 1 no. 1a AÜG.

389   The disclosure statement's breach results in the overall invalidity of the (temporary) employment contract between the temporary work agency and the temporary agency worker. In this respect, reference can be made to the above explanations (see marginal no. 334 et seq.). Similarly, an employment relationship between the hirer and the temporary agency worker is concurrently simulated by law through sec. 10 para. 1 AÜG (see marginal no. 337 et seq.). Concerning the legal consequences, the point in time agreed between the temporary work agency and the hirer is not relevant. Still, the legal consequences occur from the time of the actual assignment.

390   In the absence of disclosure as temporary agency employment, temporary work agencies and hirers cannot remedy the breach by subsequently labelling the temporary agency employment or concretising the temporary agency worker in concrete terms before or even during the temporary agency worker's deployment. Nevertheless, the legal consequences under the field of civil law per sec. 9 para. 1 no. 1a, sec. 10 para. 1 AÜG apply. The invalidity and fiction of a new employment relationship with the hirer can only be prevented by the temporary agency worker's effective status quo declaration (see marginal no. 350 et seq.).

391   However, in the event of a breach of the disclosure statement, the temporary agency employment contract between the temporary work agency and the hirer remains unaffected. According to the law's wording, this does not invalidate the contract as such, sec. 9 para. 1 no. 1a AÜG. In this respect, there is a deviation from the breach of the obligation to obtain permission.

392   **bb) Works Constitution Law.** Concerning the consequences from a works constitutional law perspective, full reference can be made to the above comments on the obligation to obtain permission (see marginal no. 357 et seq.).

393   **cc) Social Security Law.** Regarding the consequences under social security law, reference can be made to the previous comments (see marginal no. 360 et seq.).

394   **dd) Tax Law.** Also, reference concerning the tax consequences can be made to the above statements (see marginal no. 363).

395   **ee) Administrative Offences Law.** The temporary agency worker's assignment without prior disclosure results in legal consequences under the AÜG and the OWiG subject to fines for the parties involved.

396   *(1) Administrative Offences under the AÜG.* Contrary to the consequences under civil law, sec. 16 AÜG stipulates a separation of the matters of fact subject to a fine into the obligation to concretise and the obligation to label.

397   The violation of the obligation to label under sec. 1 para. 1 sent. 1 sent. 5 AÜG may be punished as an administrative offence under sec. 16 para. 1 sent. 1c AÜG. The matter of fact can be realised by both the temporary work agency and the hirer.

398   Sec. 16 para. 1 sent. 1c AÜG is applicable, if temporary agency employment is not, not correctly or not in time labeled as such. This is the case if neither the title nor the wording of the contract states the "temporary agency employment". Concerning the suitable offender, the subjective elements of the offence, and the amount of the fine, reference is made to the above (see marginal no. 365 et seq.).

399   The violations of the obligation to concretise under sec. 1 para. 1 sent. 6 AÜG can be punished as an administrative offence under sec. 16 para. 1 no. 1d AÜG. The matter of fact can be realised by both the temporary work agency and the hirer.

400   Sec. 16 para. 1 no. 1d AÜG applies, if the temporary agency worker is not correctly concretised, i. e., cannot be clearly determined in the individual case. In the case of frequently occurring first names and surnames, it is, therefore, necessary to state the date

of birth. Concerning the suitable offender, the subjective elements of the offence and the amount of the fine, reference is made to the above comments (see once more marginal no. 365 et seq.).

(2) Administrative Offences under the OWiG. The violation of the obligation to label **401** under sec. 1 para. 1 sent. 5 AÜG, or the obligation to concretise under sec. 1 para. 1 sent. 6 AÜG may also lead to the implementation of administrative offences under the OWiG and even to the imposition of a fine on the association (see marginal no. 372 et seq.).

ff) Regulatory. Additionally, the law's violations in connection with erroneous tem- **402** porary agency employment cases may result in further indirect consequences from a regulatory perspective. The regulatory consequences are sometimes far-reaching and should never be underestimated (see marginal no. 381 et seq. for a non-exhaustive overview).

c) Breach of the Information Requirement

Suppose the temporary agency worker is not informed of their assignment as a tem- **403** porary agency worker by the temporary work agency before the respective assignment. In that case, this constitutes a violation of sec. 11 para. 2 sent. 4 AÜG (see marginal no. 114 et seq. for the information requirements).

aa) Contract Law. In contrast to the disclosure statement's breach, the act does not **404** impose any particular civil law consequences under sec. 9 para. 1, and sec. 10 para. 1 AÜG here. In particular, the (temporary) employment contract is neither invalid, nor is a new employment relationship with the hirer feigned.

bb) Social Security Law. There are also no consequences under social security law **405** due to the lack of contractual consequences of the breach of the information requirement. Reference can therefore be made to the above social security regulations for the temporary agency employment (see marginal no. 37/60 et seq. and 84).

cc) Tax Law. Concerning tax law, reference can also be made to the previous state- **406** ments on temporary agency employment (see marginal no. 42/66 et seq. and 85).

dd) Administrative Offences Law. Suppose the temporary work agency does not **407** inform the temporary agency worker that he is acting as a temporary agency worker before the assignment to the hirer. In that case, the temporary work agency fulfils the conditions of sec. 16 para. 1 no. 8 AÜG, which may be subject to a fine of up to EUR 1,000 in individual cases.

ee) Regulatory. Besides, the violations of the law in connection with cases of erro- **408** neous temporary agency employment may result in further indirect consequences from a regulatory perspective. The regulatory consequences are sometimes far-reaching and should never be underestimated (see marginal no. 381 et seq. for a non-exhaustive overview).

d) Breach of the Maximum Assignment Length

If in parties exceed the maximum permissible assignment length in individual cases, **409** this constitutes a violation of sec. 1 para. 1b sent. 1 AÜG (see marginal no. 118 et seq.).

Because of the adverse legal consequences of exceeding the maximum assignment **410** length, a temporary work agency should inform itself about the applicable maximum assignment length before each temporary agency worker's assignment to a hirer. In particular, sufficient attention should be paid to the calculation of the assignment's length.

411   **aa) Contract Law.** If a temporary agency worker exceeds the maximum assignment length allowed for him during his deployment, the employment contract between him and the temporary work agency becomes invalid under sec. 9 para. 1 sent. 1b AÜG. According to its wording, the invalidity *"occurs when the maximum permitted assignment length is exceeded,"* i. e., on the day after expiry of the maximum assignment length. Simultaneously, an employment relationship between the hirer and the temporary agency worker is simulated when the maximum assignment length is exceeded per sec. 10 para. 1 no. 1 AÜG. Concerning the respective legal consequences, reference is made to the above explanations on the breach of the obligation to obtain permission (see marginal no. **334/337** et seq.).

412   The ineffectiveness and fiction occur when the legal maximum assignment length is exceeded, and when a maximum assignment length determined under collective bargaining agreement is exceeded. Overall, it does not depend on temporary work agency's and the hirer's knowledge, but only on the objective infringement. Errors or wrongly incorrect calculations of time limits will also not be taken into account and will be charged to the temporary work agency.

413   The invalidity and fiction of a new employment relationship with the hirer can only be prevented by the temporary agency worker's effective status quo declaration (see marginal no. **350** et seq.).

414   As in the case of a breach of the disclosure statement, the temporary agency employment contract between the temporary work agency and the hirer remains unaffected if the maximum assignment length is violated. According to the law's wording, an invalidity does not result in the present case, sec. 9 para. 1 no. 1b AÜG a.

415   **bb) Works Constitution Law.** Corncerning the consequences from a works constitutional law perspective, full reference can be made to the above comments on the obligation to obtain permission (see marginal no. **357** et seq.).

416   **cc) Social Security Law.** Concerning the consequences under social security law, reference can be made to the above comments (see marginal no. **360** et seq.).

417   **dd) Tax Law.** Reference can also be made to the above statements regarding the tax law consequences (see marginal no. **363**).

418   **ee) Administrative Offences Law.** The temporary agency worker's assignment without a temporary agency employment permit results in legal consequences for the parties involved under the AÜG and the OWiG, which are assessed in terms of fines.

419   *(1) Administrative Offences under the AÜG.* The violation of the maximum assignment length according to sec. 1 para. 1b sent. 1 AÜG may be punished as an administrative offence under sec. 16 para. 1 no. 1e AÜG. Only the temporary work agency and not the hirer can realise the administrative offence.

420   Sec. 16 para. 1 no. 1e AÜG applies in the case of a breach of the basic statutory provision on the maximum 18-month assignment length. Suppose a longer or shorter maximum assignment length must be observed based on a collective bargaining agreement or based on a contract to produce a work or service contract based upon a collective bargaining agreement. In that case, a violation of this shall not constitute an administrative offence. Concerning the qualified perpetrator, the subjective elements of the offence, and the amount of the fine, reference is made to the above (see marginal no. **365** et seq.).

421   *(2) Administrative Offences under the OWiG.* The violation of the maximum assignment length under sec. 1 para. 1b sent. 1 AÜG can also lead to administrative offences's realization under the OWiG, and to the imposition of a fine for the association (see marginal no. **372** et seq.).

ff) Regulatory. Besides, the law's violations in connection with cases of erroneous temporary agency employment may result in further indirect consequences from a regulatory perspective. The regulatory consequences are sometimes far-reaching and should never be underestimated (see for a non-exhaustive overview marginal no. **381** et seq.). **422**

e) Breach of the Principle of Equality (Equal-Pay and Equal-Treatment)

Sec. 8 para. 1 AÜG stipulates the temporary work agency's obligation to provide the temporary agency worker with the essential working conditions, including payments, during the assignment (principle of equality, see marginal no. **134** et seq.). In this context, an agreement generally violates the principle of equality if it provides for worse working conditions to which the temporary agency worker is entitled under sec. 8 para. 1 AÜG. **423**

In this context, agreements are contracts existing between the temporary agency worker and the temporary work agency and any collective bargaining agreements that determine working conditions. With the new reform in 2017, the legislator makes legal demands on the possibilities of deviation through collective bargaining agreements for the first time. Therefore, the determination of an infringement depends on any permissible deviation from the principle of equality to a large extent. In individual cases, a deviating collective bargaining agreement must also be examined, since it is possible to deviate from the principle of equality for at least the first nine months of employment (see marginal no. **149** et seq.). **424**

aa) Contract Law

(1) Temporary Agency Worker – Temporary Work Agency. Agreements that violate the principle of equality are invalid under sec. 9 para. 1 sent. 2 AÜG. In principle, this can affect both the (temporary) employment contract and the applied collective bargaining agreement. However, the unique feature is that a violation does not necessarily lead to the total nullity of, e. g., the (temporary) employment contract. Contrary, only to the nullity (partial nullity) concerning the inadmissible provision on equal treatment. The legal regulations then take the place of the ineffective agreement on the working conditions. **425**

Thus, according to sec. 8 para. 1 sent. 1 AÜG, the temporary agency worker is entitled to the same essential working conditions as the permanent employees in the hirer's establishment in the form of a special claim for supplementary remuneration against the temporary work agency. The temporary agency worker may, therefore, demand payment in the amount of the difference. **426**

Conversely, this means that the (temporary) employment contract remains in force. In particular, the temporary agency worker remains in an employment relationship with the temporary work agency. There is no change of employer by law. For this reason, the temporary agency worker is not able to issue a status quo declaration in such cases by sec. 9 para. 2 AÜG. **427**

Additionally, the agreement remains unaffected in its entirety during non-assignemnt periods. **428**

(2) Temporary Agency Worker – Hirer. Due to the (temporary) employment contract's partial nullity, the law also does not prescribe a fiction of a new employment relationship with the hirer. A breach of equal treatment does not let the hirer become the new employer of the temporary agency worker. **429**

(3) Temporary Work Agency – Hirer. Additionally, the (partial) nullity of an agreement between the temporary work agency and the temporary agency worker, under sec. 9 para. 1 no. 2 AÜG, does not lead to the temporary agency employment contracts' invalidity concluded between the temporary work agency and the hirer. **430**

bb) Social Security Law

431   *(1) Principle.* In the field of social security law, the so-called principle of origin applies. The total social security contribution is incurred for the remuneration, which would have to be paid out under the principle of equality. Remunerations to which the temporary agency worker has a legal claim are also decisive for calculating the social security contributions, sec. 22 para. 2 SGB IV.[11] In the case of temporary agency employment, the temporary agency worker has a legal claim against the temporary work agency for the payment of remuneration, which meets the principle of equality, sec. 8 para. 1 sent. 1 AÜG. Therefore, the total social security contribution is due to the remuneration paid, and the remunerationto be paid in compliance with the principle of equality. Consequently, the temporary work agency as an employer is obliged to pay the total social security contribution on the remuneration, which would have to be paid out if the principle of equality had been observed.

432   Suppose the temporary work agency does not pay the temporary agency worker a contribution following the principle of equality's elementary laws. In that case, there is reason to suspect that the temporary agency worker will not pay the social security contribution based on the principle of equality to the collecting agency.

433   The temporary work agency must pay the unpaid portion plus an interest on arrears. The interest on arrears amounts to 12 % per annum, sec. 24 para. 1 sent. 1 SGB IV. This also applies to contributions that were not paid in the past, unless the temporary work agency can credibly demonstrate that he did not know of the payment obligation through no fault of his own, sec. 24 para. 2 SGB IV.

434   Social security contributions that were not paid negligently are still to be paid four years after the end of the calendar year in which they became due, sec. 25 para. 1 sent. 1 SGB IV. However, intentionally unpaid social security contributions must still be paid for thirty years, sec. 25 para. 1 sent. 2 SGB IV.

435   Since Germany's total social security contribution amounts almost 40 %, back-payments represent a risk for undertakings that should not be underestimated, and that in some cases, endangers their existence. The sometimes considerable length of proceedings before the social courts, which can lead to a long period of legal uncertainty, must also be considered.

436   *(2) Criminal Law Consequences: Withholding of Remuneration.* Suppose the temporary work agency does not pay the total social security contributions due (i. e., the difference between the contributions which it has paid and the contributions which would have to be paid in compliance with the principle of equality) to the collecting agencies. In that case, the possibility of the realisation of criminal offences under sec. 266a StGB may arise.

437   According to sec. 266a para. 1 StGB, it is a punishable offence for an employer to withhold the *employee's share* of the total social security contribution. Withholding is already the non-payment of employee contributions at the time they are due. The social security contributions are due on the third-last bank working day of the current month, sec. 23 para. 1 sent. 2 SGB IV. In practice, the employer will generally be a legal entity. Comparable to the law on administrative offences, legal entities cannot be offenders in criminal law. According to sec. 14 StGB, the natural person acting on behalf of the legal entity, is considered to be the offender. These can exemplarily be members of the management board, members of management, heads of department, authorised signatories, and others (the information provided under sec. 9 OWiG applies to the greatest extent possible, see marginal no. **366**). The employee's shares must have been intentionally not paid. Conditional intent is sufficient again (see also the information already provided

---

[11]   Federal Social Court, 14 July 2004 – B 12 KR 7/04.

under marginal no. **367**).[12] When regarding the employer status of sec. 266a StGB and the resulting obligation to pay social security contributions. Then with the existence of conditional intent depends on whether the offender has recognised and accepted that he has become an employer due to the circumstances and is therefore obliged to pay social security contributions.[13] He must have noticed this from his amateurish evaluation. Intentional conduct can only be assumed, however, if the offender not only knew about the actual circumstances but also understood the extra-legal assessment of labour and social security law and, despite this knowledge, has approbatory accepted the occurrence of success. If the employer is subject to an error regarding his employer position and the resulting obligation to pay social security contributions, he does not act intentionally according to sec. 16 para. 1 StGB, and cannot be punished according to sec. 266a StGB.[14] Withholding the employee's shares is punishable by imprisonment for up to five years or a fine. If the additional payment for social security exceeds EUR 100,000, a prison sentence is usually due, suspended on probation. If the additional payment of more than EUR 1,000,000 is made, a prison sentence is generally imposed, which is no longer suspended on probation.

According to sec. 266a para. 2 StGB, it is also a punishable offence for an employer to withhold **employee contributions**　**438**
- By providing incorrect or incomplete information to the collecting agency, or
- By withholding (i. e., concealment) of facts relevant to social security law from the collecting agency in breach of duty.

It is, therefore, necessary that the temporary work agency makes a declaration to the　**439** collecting agency. By not stating the correct contribution, the temporary work agency conceals significant facts. In breach of duty, the temporary work agency, therefore, withholds facts from the collecting agency relevant under social security law. Concerning the intent, reference can be made to the comments on employee's shares according to sec. 266a para. 1 StGB. The withholding of employer's shares is also punishable by imprisonment for up to five years or by a fine. The remarks on imprisonment and the suspension of sentence on probation also apply.

Both in the case of sec. 266a para. 1, and sec. 266a para. 2 StGB, the non-payment　**440** constitutes a new punishable offence every month.

The court may, however, refrain from punishment according to sec. 266a　**441** para. 1 and 2 StGB if the temporary work agency as employer notifies the collecting agency in writing of the amount of the withheld contributions. This has to occur at the latest at the time of the due date or immediately thereafter and demonstrates the impossibility of timely payment. In this case, impossibility means insolvency. This insolvency exists if the payment of the contributions would seriously endanger the establishment's existence.

The period of limitation is five years, according to sec. 78 para. 3 no. 4 StGB. The　**442** statute of limitations begins with the end of the act. According to current case law, the statute of limitations should start with the passing of the due date of the social security contributions and not only with the expiration of the obligation to pay contributions.[15]

Suppose a person named in sec. 30 para. 1 OWiG commits the offences mentioned　**443** above. In that case, this may also lead to a fine for the association under sec. 30 OWiG (see marginal no. **372** et seq.). Under sec. 30 para. 2 sent. 1 OWiG, the association's fine may be up to EUR 10,000,000.

---

[12]　Federal Court of Justice, 28 May 2002 – 5 StR 16/02.
[13]　Federal Court of Justice, 24 September 2019 – 1 StR 346/18.
[14]　Federal Court of Justice, 24 September 2019 – 1 StR 346/18.
[15]　Federal Court of Justice, 13 November 2019 – 1 StR 58/19.

cc) Tax Law

444 *(1) Principle.* A violation of the principle of equality has no effect on tax law for the time being. In contrast to the *principle of origin* applicable in social security law, the *cash method* applies initially in tax law. Tax is payable on the income paid to the employee, i. e., the income that has accrued.

445 Therefore, reference can basically be made to the above explanations as long as the temporary work agency pays the remuneration, withholds the corresponding wage tax, and pays it to the local tax office (see marginal no. **363**). A violation of the principle of equality does not initially increase the wage tax.

446 However, this is to be assessed differently if the temporary work agency subsequently realises that he would have to pay out a wage that complied with the principle of equality and now – even if only as a precaution – pays the difference to the overall social security contribution to the collecting agency. As soon as he does so, the temporary agency worker receives a remuneration, which is taxable. In tax law, the employee's share is regarded as a remuneration within the meaning of sec. 19 EStG.

447 Deliberately evaded taxes can still be determined ten years after maturity, negligently evaded taxes, however, five years, sec. 169 para. 2 sent. 2 AO.

448 If the temporary work agency also pays the difference in salary to the temporary agency worker retroactively, this must be taxed retroactively as well.

449 *(2) Criminal Law Consequences: Tax Evasion.* If the temporary work agency pays the difference in remunerations to the temporary agency worker or if the temporary work agency pays the employee's shares without having deducted them from the remunerations previously, tax evasion according to sec. 370 Tax Code (*Abgabenordnung* "**AO**") is possible.

450 An offender of a tax evasion, according to sec. 370 para. 1 no. 1 AO, is someone, who delivers incorrect data regarding substantial fiscal facts towards the tax authorities. The act under sec. 370 para. 1 no. 2 AO commits, who leaves the tax authorities in ignorance contrary to obligation over substantial tax facts. Yet again, the hirer will be a legal entity as a rule, which cannot be an offender of tax evasion. Reference is therefore made to the above comments on the offender quality of the natural person acting on behalf of the legal entity (see marginal no. **437**). As an employer, the temporary work agency must issue a wage-tax return. If this does not take place when paying remuneration or when paying the employee's share, the hirer reduces taxes according to sec. 370 para. 1 no. 2 AO. The temporary work agency leaves the tax authority in ignorance about tax-relevant facts contrary to obligation. Once again, the actor must act intentionally. Concerning the tax liability from sec. 370 AO and the resulting obligation to pay the tax, the conditional intent's existence depends on whether the offender has recognised and approbatory accepted that he has become more taxable due to the circumstances and an obligation to pay the wage tax follows from this. He must have realised this from his non-expert assessment. However, intentional action can only be assumed if the offender, additionally to knowing the actual circumstances, has also understood the extra-legal evaluations of the labour and social security law and, despite this knowledge, has approbatory accepted the occurrence of success. If the actor is subject to an error regarding his tax liability, he does not act intentionally according to sec. 16 para. 1 StGB. Simple tax evasion is threatened with imprisonment for up to five years or with a fine. A higher penalty may be imposed if a reduction is made on a large scale (from a tax evasion contribution of approximately EUR 100,000). In this case, there is no imposture of fines, but only a prison sentence of six months to ten years.

451 Tax evasion becomes statute-barred after five years, provided that no taxes of a large magnitude have been evaded (sec. 78 para. 3 no. 4 StGB). Otherwise, it becomes time-barred after ten years (sec. 78 para. 3 no. 3 StGB).

If a person named in sec. 30 para. 1 OWiG commits tax evasion, this can also lead to an association fine under sec. 30 OWiG (see marginal no. **372** et seq.). Under sec. 30 para. 2 sent. 1 OWiG, the association fine may amount to up to EUR 10,000,000. **452**

In the case of tax evasion, it should be noted that the evaded tax and the evasion interest and back payments according to sec. 233a AO and sec. 235 AO have to be paid. **453**

However, the temporary work agency can attain exemption from punishment over sec. 371 AO if he corrects incorrect data or makes up for omitted data and therefore delivers a punishment-liberating self-denunciation. Exemption from punishment does not occur after sec. 371 para. 2 AO, among other things, if the act was already discovered at the time of the delivery of the self-denunciation. The delivery of the self-denunciation is extremely complex and should take place only under consultation of legal advice. If, for example, incorrect or incomplete information is again provided within the voluntary disclosure scope, there is no room for impunity. **454**

dd) Administrative Offence Law. Due to the principle of equality's violation, the legal consequences of the AÜG, the SchwarzArbG and the OWiG may result for the parties involved. **455**

(1) Administrative Offences under the AÜG. Violation of the principle of equality under sec. 8 para. 1 sent. 1 AÜG can be punished as an administrative offence under sec. 16 para. 1 no. 7a AÜG. Solely, the temporary work agency can commit the offence. **456**

Sec. 16 para. 1 sent. 7a AÜG is given, if the temporary work agency grants the temporary agency worker worse working conditions than the comparable regular employees of the hirer during the assignment in the hirer's establishment. Concerning the suitable offender, the subjective elements of the offence, and the statute of limitations, reference may be made to the above statements (see marginal no. **365** et seq.). The act is punishable by a fine of up to EUR 500,000, sec. 16 para. 2 AÜG. If the act is committed negligently, the maximum is halved, sec. 17 para. 2 OWiG. Each month in which sec. 8 para. 1 sent. 1 AÜG is violated can be punished as a separate act that is assessed as a fine. **457**

(2) Administrative Offences under the SchwarzArbG. According to sec. 8 para. 3 SchwarzArbG anyone withholding employee's or employer's shares under sec. 266a StGB is in breach of regulations **458**
→ by providing incorrect or incomplete information to the collecting agency, or
→ by withholding (i.e., concealment) of facts relevant to social security law from the collecting agency in breach of obligation.

Contrary to the criminal offence from sec. 266a StGB, the administrative offence from sec. 8 para. 3 SchwarzArbG does not require deliberate, but rather a reckless behaviour. A person acts recklessly if he disregards the care required in traffic to a particularly severe degree. Sec. 8 para. 3 SchwarzArbG, is regarded as a catch-all offence for withholding and embezzlement of remuneration according to sec. 266a StGB (see marginal no. **372** et seq.) concerning employee's and employer's shares, if an intentional act in withholding and embezzlement of remuneration cannot be established. **459**

The action can be punished with a fine of up to EUR 50,000, sec. 8 para. 6 SchwarzArbG. The action becomes statute-barred after three years, sec. 31 para. 2 no. 1 OWiG. **460**

(3) Administrative Offences under the AO. If taxes are not intentionally, but carelessly shortened, this can be avenged according to sec. 378 AO. This also statues an administrative offence. **461**

The act can be punished with a fine of up to EUR 50,000. The action becomes statute-barred after three years, sec. 31 para. 2 no. 1 OWiG. **462**

463   *(4) Administrative Offences under the OWiG.* The violation of the principle of equality under sec. 8 para. 1 sent. 1 AÜG can also lead to the implementation of administrative offences under the OWiG and the imposition of an association fine. Concerning the commission of sec. 130 OWiG, the requirements of sec. 30 OWiG, and the statute of limitations, reference is made to the above statements (see marginal no. **372** et seq.).

464   A fine of up to EUR 1,000,000 can be imposed on the person subject to supervision in the event of a criminal offence (in this case sec. 266a StGB or sec. 370 AO) (sec. 130 para. 2 sent. 1 OWiG). If only sec. 16 para. 1 no. 7a AÜG is realised, the fine is up to EUR 500,000 (sec. 130 para. 2 sent. 2 OWiG in conjunction with sec. 16 para. 1 no. 7a AÜG). If sec. 8 para. 3 SchwarzArbG or sec. 378 AO is realised, the fine may amount to EUR 50,000. If obligatory supervision breach is committed negligently, the maximum amount is halved, sec. 17 para. 2 OWiG.

465   The maximum amount of the association fine is also increased. A fine of up to EUR 10,000,000 may be imposed if a criminal offence is committed by a person named in sec. 30 para. 1 OWiG. The same applies if this person could have prevented an offence through supervisory measures according to sec. 130 OWiG. The commission of sec. 6 AÜG itself can lead to a fine of up to EUR 500,000.

466   **ee) Regulatory.** Besides, the law's violations in connection with cases of erroneous temporary agency employment may result in further indirect consequences from a regulatory perspective. The regulatory consequences are sometimes far-reaching and should never be underestimated. For a non-exhaustive overview, see marginal no. **381** et seq. above.

467   Furthermore, it should be noted that a person cannot act as a manger of a GmbH. This applies in the case that this person commits a criminal offence according to sec. 266a StGB with the imposition of a prison sentence of up to one year for a period of five years since the judgement became legally binding, sec. 6 para. 2 sent. 2 no. 3 lit. e GmbHG. This person can also not be a member of the stock corporation's executive board under sec. 76 para. 3 sent. 1 no. 3 lit. e AktG.

f) Breach of the Prohibition of Chain Hiring

468   According to sec. 1 para. 1 sent. 3 AÜG, only temporary agency workers in an employment relationship with the temporary work agency may be hired out. Therefore, a prerequisite for the assignment is the existence of a contractual employment relationship between the temporary agency worker and the temporary work agency. The consequence of this legal requirement is that it is not permissible for the (first) hirer (and at the same time the second temporary work agency) to subcontract a temporary agency worker to a third party (prohibition of chain hiring). By hiring out the temporary agency worker, the hirer does not become his contractual employer (see marginal no. **69** et seq.). If the hirer nevertheless hires out the temporary agency worker to a third party as a temporary agency worker, this constitutes an impermissible chain hiring.

469   **aa) Contract Law.** Sec. 10a AÜG generally regulates the legal consequences under civil law. Accordingly, the chain hiring alone does not render the employment relationship ineffective and, at the same time, does not create the fiction of a new employment relationship with the hirer. Instead, the secondary temporary work agency must be in breach of the obligation to obtain permission (sec. 1 para. 1 sent. 1 AÜG), the lack of disclosure as temporary agency employment (sec. 1 para. 1 sent. 5 and 6 AÜG) or the maximum assignment length (sec. 1 para. 1b AÜG).

470   Suppose one of the above-mentioned additional infringements is present. In that case, the (temporary) employment contract with the inital temporary work agency is legally

invalid, sec. 10a, sec. 9 para. 1, sec. 10 para. 1 AÜG (see on the general consequences above under marginal no. 334 et seq.). At the same time, an employment relationship is simulated with the employing employer for which the temporary agency worker actually performs his work. In this respect, the explanations on the fiction of an employment relationship with the hirer (see marginal no. 337 et seq.) apply. The invalidity and fiction of a new employment relationship with the (final) hirer can only be prevented by the temporary agency's effective status quo declaration (see marginal no. 350 et seq.).

However, if the parties do not violate any of the additional requirements mentioned **471** before, the temporary employment relationship will neither become invalid nor will a new employment relationship be simulated.

With regard to the respective temporary agency employment contract, a differentiated **472** view is also required. The initial temporary agency employment contract will regularly be effective, as the first temporary work agency will always be in own a temporary agency employment permit. However, the initial temporary agency employment contract may also be invalid in an exeptional case. In the exeptional case that a further assignment was already initiated and thus a prohibition law is violated (sec. 134 BGB in conjunction with sec. 1 para. 1 sent. 3 AÜG).

If the secondary temporary work agency does not have a temporary agency employ- **473** ment permit, the ivalidity's matter of fact under sec. 9 para. 1 no.1 AÜG arise. In this case there is a null (secondary) temporary agency employment contract (for the legal consequences see marginal no. 346 ct seq.).

bb) Works Constitution Law. Insofar as a new employment relationship becomes **474** invalid or fictitious, it can be entirely referred to the above comments on the obligation to obtain permission (see marginal no. 357 et seq.) concerning the consequences from works constitution law.

cc) Social Security Law. Concerning the social security law consequences, reference **475** can be made to the above explanations (see marginal no. 360 et seq.), insofar as the additional infringement is established.

dd) Tax Law. Reference can also be made to the above explanations regarding the **476** tax law consequences (see marginal no. 363 et seq.), insofar as there is an additional infringement.

ee) Administrative Offences Law. Temporary agency worker's assignment within the **477** framework of a chain hiring scheme results in legal consequences under the AÜG and the OWiG for the parties involved, assessed in terms of fines.

(1) Administrative Offences under the AÜG. Violation of the prohibition of chain hir- **478** ing under sec. 1 para. 1 sent. 3 AÜG may be punished as an administrative offence under sec. 16 para. 1 no.1b AÜG. The offence can be committed by both the temporary work agency and the hirer.

Sec. 16 para. 1 no. 1b AÜG applies if a temporary work agency hires out an employee **479** who is not in an employment relationship with him or allows, as a hirer, such an employee to work for him. Regarding the possible offender, the subjective elements of the offence, and the amount of the fine, reference is made to the above (see marginal no. 365 et seq.).

(2) Administrative Offences under the OWiG. Violation of the prohibition of chain hir- **480** ing can also lead to administrative offences under the OWiG, and even to the imposition of an association fine (see marginal no. 372 et seq.).

ff) Regulatory. Furthermore, the law's violations in connection with cases of erro- **481** neous temporary agency employment may result in further indirect consequences from a regulatory perspective. The regulatory consequences are sometimes far-reaching and should never be underestimated. For a non-exhaustive overview, see marginal no. 381 et seq. above.

g) Violation of the Formal Requirements of sec. 12 AÜG

482   If the temporary agency employment contract is not in writing, there is a violation of sec. 12 para. 1 AÜG (see marginal no. 48 et. seq.).

483   **aa) Contract Law.** A violation of the formal requirements of sec. 12 AÜG, in principle, leads to the invalidity of the temporary agency employment contract according to sec. 125 sent. 1 AÜG. In this case, the temporary work agency and the hirer have not effectively established mutual service obligations.

484   The ineffective temporary agency employment relationship does not establish any service obligations between the contracting parties, the temporary work agency, and the hirer.

485   Suppose services were nevertheless rendered in fulfillment of the ineffective temporary agency employment contract. In that case, these are to be returned following the principles of the law of enrichment (sec. 812 et. seq. BGB) (for the general consequences of the reversal see marginal no. 346 et seq.).

486   The violation of the written form requirement leads imperatively to the nullity of the temporary agency employment contract according to sec. 125 sent. 1 BGB. The AÜG does not provide for a possibility to remedy the error. Nor can the contract become effective retroactively by enforcement.

487   If there is no valid temporary agency employment contract, no labelling of the assignment can usually be made in the document, sec. 1 para. 1 sent. 5, AÜG. In this case, the relevant legal consequences also apply concerning the legal relationship between the temporary agency worker and the temporary work agency and the hirer and temporary agency worker (see marginal no. 388 et seq.).

488   **bb) Social Security Law.** As there regularly is no proper labelling, please refer to the comments under marginal no. 360 et seq. concerning social security law.

489   **cc) Tax Law.** As there is regularly no proper labelling, reference should also be made to the comments under marginal no. 363 regarding tax law.

490   **dd) Administrative Offences Law.** The violation of sec. 12 AÜG in itself does not lead to the implementation of regulatory offences. However, since normally in the case of nullity, the obligation to label is also not carried out properly, reference can be made to the explanations under marginal no. 364 et seq. above.

491   **ee) Regulatory.** Moreover, the law's violations in connection with erroneous temporary agency employment cases may result in further indirect consequences from a regulatory perspective. The regulatory consequences are sometimes far-reaching and should never be underestimated. For a non-exhaustive overview, see marginal no. 381 et seq. above.

h) Breach of the Registration and Retention Requirements

492   Suppose the temporary work agency and the hirer do not comply with their registration and retention requirements under the AÜG In that case, they violate sec. 17b, sec. 17c AÜG (see marginal no. 165 et seq.).

493   **aa) Contract Law.** In contrast to the violation of the obligations in sec. 1 para. 1 and 1b AÜG, the act does not link any particular civil law consequences under

sec. 9 para. 1, and sec. 10 para. 1 AÜG to a violation of the registration and retention requirements. In particular, the (temporary) employment contract is neither invalid nor is a new employment relationship with the hirer feigned.

bb) Social Security Law. In the absence of specific consequences under contractual 494 labour law, the provisions of social security law continue to apply on temporary agency employment (see marginal no. **37/60** et. seq. and **84**).

cc) Tax Law. The general principles of temporary agency employment also apply in 495 tax law (see marginal no. **42/66** et seq. and **85**).

dd) Administrative Offences Law. Violations of the registration and retention re- 496 quirements result in legal consequences under the AÜG and the OWiG for the parties involved, assessed in terms of fines.

(1) Administrative Offences under the AÜG. The violation of the registration require- 497 ments under sec. 17b para. 1 AÜG may be punished as an administrative offence under sec. 16 para.1 sent. 14, 15, or 16 AÜG. The administrative offence can be realised solely by the hirer and not by the temporary work agency. Concerning the possible offender, the subjective elements of the offence, and the amount of the fine, reference is made to the above comments (see marginal no. **365** et seq.).

The same applies to a violation of the obligation under sec. 17c AÜG. This constitutes 498 an irregularity according to sec. 16 para. 1 nos. 17 and 18 AÜG. Only the hirer can be claimed for the retention period's breach under sec. 17c para. 1 AÜG. Still, only the temporary work agency, can be claimed to breach the obligation to hold the records in readiness under sec. 17c para. 2 AÜG.

(2) Administrative Offences under OWiG. The violation of the retention period can 499 also lead to the forfeiture of administrative offences under the OWiG, and even to the imposition of an association fine (see marginal no. **372** et seq.).

ee) Regulatory. Additionally, the law's violations connected with erroneous tem- 500 porary agency employment cases may result in further indirect consequences from a regulatory perspective. The regulatory consequences are sometimes far-reaching and should never be underestimated. For a non-exhaustive overview, see marginal no. **381** et seq. above.

i) Infringement of the Prohibition of Blocking Agreements

In practice, it is not uncommon for a temporary agency employment contract to either 501 a non-solicitation of the temporary agency worker for the hirer or to include a provision on the placement fee in the event of a temporary agency worker's successful placement in the hirer's establishment. The same applies to the underlying (temporary) employment contracts.

Such regulations can pose various legal challenges to the parties and can additionally 502 lead to a violation of sec. 9 para. 1 nos. 3, 4, and 5 AÜG in individual cases.

aa) Contract Law. The violation of the so-called blocking agreements, which prohibit 503 the temporary agency worker from changing to the hirer, regularly leads to the underlying agreement's invalidity.

(1) Temporary Agency Worker – Temporary Work Agency. Agreements that prohibit 504 the temporary agency worker from entering into an employment relationship with the hirer when the employment relationship between the temporary work agency and the temporary agency worker no longer exists are invalid under sec. 9 para. 1 sent. 4 AÜG.

According to its wording, sec. 9 para. 1 sent. 4 AÜG merely prohibits the agreement of employment bans. From a social policy perspective, temporary agency workers should find their way back into a "normal" permanent employment relationship. So that, in addition to the agreement of an employment ban, all agreements that restrict the temporary agency worker's freedom of action to establish an employment relationship with the hirer are invalid beyond the wording of sec. 9 para. 1 no. 4 AÜG.

505   By way of example, the agreement on a ban on applivcations to a hirer, or the agreement of a contractual penalty for the temporary agency worker in employment with the hirer are invalid under sec. 9 para. 3 sent. 4 AÜG.

506   Those agreements, under which the temporary agency worker has to pay a placement fee to the temporary work agency, are ineffective according to sec. 9 para. 1 no. 5, AÜG. This provision covers agreements for which remuneration shall be paid for placement in an employment relationship after the assignment ended, as well as agreements for placement as a temporary agency worker.

507   *(2) Temporary Work Agency – Hirer.* Similarly, an agreement between the temporary work agency and the hirer prohibiting the hirer from employing the temporary agency worker when his employment relationship with the temporary work agency no longer exists constitutes an infringement. Such agreements are invalid under sec. 9 para. 1 no. 3 AÜG. Sec. 9 para. 1 no. 3 AÜG, and sec. 9 para. 1 no. 4 AÜG follow the same purpose. The purpose not to make it more challenging to establish an employment relationship between the temporary agency worker and the temporary work agency. Not as challenging so that, in addition to the agreement of a prohibition of employment, all agreements that prevent or significantly impede the temporary agency worker's transfer to the hirer, are also invalid.

508   Under sec. 9 para. 1 sent. 3 AÜG, the temporary work agency, and hirer are not refused to agree on remuneration for after or through the previous hiring out The legislator has opted for the possibility of a placement fee because the placement of a temporary agency worker in a permanent employment relationship of the hirer is, in principle, worthy of remuneration. Furthermore, the admission of an agreement on a placement fee results from the aspect that the hirer obtains an economic advantage by employing an employe he has already trained and integrated into the workflow of his business. At the same time, a transfer of the temporary agency worker to the hirer may lead to an economic disadvantage for the temporary work agency who must let a by him selected, and qualified employee leave.

509   The agreement of a placement fee between the temporary work agency and the hirer is effective, as long as the placement took place after or through previous hiring out, and the fee is reasonable. When examining the fee's appropriateness, the duration of the previous hiring out, and the amount of the remuneration already paid by the hirer must be taken into account initially.

510   The temporary work agency's calculated costs for the selection, recruitment, and provision of temporary agency workers, as the duration of temporary agency employment increases, are amortised by the hiring out fee, and the economic disadvantage caused by the transfer of the temporary agency worker is also compensated for. Therefore, the charge must be graduated according to the duration of the deployment in such a way that it is reduced as the hiring out period increases. The qualification of the employee and the market level of a functionally equivalent placement must also be taken into account.

511   Suppose the temporary work agency and the hirer agree on an unreasonable placement fee. In that case, the agreement is also invalid according to sec. 9 para. 1 no. 3 AÜG, because its economic effect is likely to prevent or at least substantially impede the temporary agency worker's transfer to a (permanent) job at the hirer.

Suppose a placement fee is regulated in General Terms and Conditions (*Allgemeine* **512** *Geschäftsbedingungen* "T&C"). In that case, the user of the T&C must expect that the determination of an unreasonable remuneration according to sec. 307 para. 1 sent. 1, and sec. 307 para. 2 no. 1 BGB will be invalid and will not become part of the contract due to sec. 306 para. 2 BGB. A validity-sustaining reduction in the form of reducing the unreasonable placement fee to an appropriate fee is unfeasible. Such validity-sustaining reductions preserving the validity are incompatible with the legislator's socio-political will to avoid difficulties for the temporary agency worker's transfer to the hirer. The temporary agency worker's transfer could already be made more complicated if the temporary agency worker is taken over. In the case, if it is not yet foreseeable for the hirer what costs will actually incur to him through the assignment. If the hirer is uncertain about the costs, he will probably refrain from employing the temporary agency worker.

bb) Social Security Law. In the absence of particular consequences under the employ- **513** ment contract, the provisions of social security law on temporary agency employment continue to apply (see marginal no. **37/60** et seq. and **84**).

cc) Tax Law. The general principles of temporary agency employment also apply in **514** the field of tax law (see marginal no. **42/66** et seq. and **85**).

dd) Administrative Offences Law. The violation of the prohibition of blocking agree- **515** ments does not lead to the risk of administrative offences' realisation.

j) Special Case: Infringement in Conjunction with Temporary Agency Employment with a Foreign Connection

If a foreign temporary agency worker is hired out without a permit by the temporary **516** work agency or employed by the hirer, this constitutes a violation of sec. 15, sec. 15a AÜG (see marginal no. **192** et seq.).

In such cross-border temporary agency employment, the susceptibility to errors is **517** high if the parties, especially the temporary work agency and the hirer, disregard legal provisions.

aa) Contract Law. Even temporary agency employment with a foreign connection of **518** any kind does not alter the fact that the requirements set out above under marginal no. **86** et seq. must be fulfilled by the AÜG within its application scope. If the respective obligations are violated, the legal consequences described under marginal no. **324** et seq. may also apply to temporary agency employment with a foreign connection.

bb) Social Security Law. In the absence of any particular employment contract conse- **519** quences, the social security regulations on temporary agency employment with a foreign connection continue to apply (see marginal no. **206** et seq. and **226**). If the respective obligations of the AÜG are violated, the legal consequences under social security law described under marginal no. **324** et seq. also apply to temporary agency employment with a foreign connection.

cc) Tax Law. The general principles of temporary agency employment with foreign **520** conjunction also apply in the field of tax law (see marginal no. **215** et seq. and **231**). If the respective obligations of the AÜG are violated, the legal consequences of tax law described under marginal no. **324** et seq. once again apply to temporary agency employment with a foreign connection.

dd) Criminal Law Consequences
(1) Illegal Hiring out of Foreign Temporary Agency Workers. According to sec. 15 AÜG, **521** it is a punishable offence to assign a foreigner, as a temporary work agency, who is not in

possession of a residence title to a third party without the necessary permit to hire out employees contrary to sec. 1 AÜG. The offence is punishable by imprisonment for up to three years or by fine. Concerning the requirements of offender quality and intent, reference is made to the statements mentioned before (see marginal no. **436** et seq.).

The offence is statue-barred after five years (sec. 78 para. 3 no. 4 StGB).

522   According to sec. 11 SchwarzArbG, anyone is liable to prosecution who employs more than five foreigners without an EU work permit/residence permit or commissions them by a service contract or contract to produce a work or persistently employs foreigners without an EU work permit/residence title for specific purposes, is also liable to prosecution. The act is punishable by imprisonment of up to one year or by fine. Persistence can be assumed if the offender has clearly been informed about their irregular actions, for example through a warning or warning notice. Concerning the requirements of offender quality and intent, reference is made to the above (see again marginal no. **436** et seq.). It must be taken into account that the employee lacking a work permit or residence permit can also be considered as an offender.

The offence is statute-barred after three years (sec. 78 para. 3 no. 5, StGB).

523   *(2) Illegal Borrowing of Foreign Temporary Agency Workers.* The hirer can be punished following sec. 15a AÜG if he employs a foreigner assigned to him, who does not own a required residence title, a permit, or entitlement by sec. 4 AufenthG in conjunction with para. 4 AufenthG, a residence permit, or a toleration entitling him to exercise the employment, or does not possess a permit under sec. 284 para. 1 SGB III. Additionally, if he employs this foreigner to work under working conditions of the temporary agency employment relationship, which are conspicuously disproportionate to the working conditions of German temporary agency workers who perform the same or a comparable activity. Suppose a conspicuous imbalance is identified, for example, in the payment of remunerations. In that case, such an imbalance can be assumed if the foreign temporary agency worker receives a remuneration that is 20 % lower than that of a comparable German temporary agency worker.

524   In the second variant of the offence (sec. 15a para. 2 sent. 1 no. 1 AÜG), the hirer is liable to prosecution if he simultaneously employs more than five foreign employees lacking a work permit.

The hirer who repeatedly and persistently allows people to work without the necessary permits or titles is also punishable under sec. 15 para. 2 sent. 1 no. 2 AÜG. Persistence is assumed if the hirer has been clearly informed of his disorderly conduct, for example, through a warning or a warning notice

Concerning the requirements of offender quality and intent, reference is made to the above (see again marginal no. **436** et seq.).

The acts referred to in para. 1 shall be punishable by imprisonment for up to three years or by fine. Those referred to in para. 2 by imprisonment for up to one year or by fine. The acts shall become statute-barred within five or three years respectively, sec. 78 para. 3 StGB.

525   Additionally, the hirer can be prosecuted according to sec. 10 SchwarzArbG. Accordingly, the hirer commits an offence if he employs a foreigner without a work permit or residence title and employs foreigners under working conditions that are conspicuously disproportionate to German employees' working conditions performing the same or a comparable activity.

Regarding the requirements of offender quality and intent, reference is made to the above (see once more marginal no. **436** et seq.).

The acts of sec. 10 SchwarzArbG are punishable by imprisonment from six months to five years. The actions become statute-barred within five years, sec. 78 para. 3 StGB.

ee) **Administrative Offences Law.** Concerning the temporary work agency, the ad- 526
ministrative offences from the OWiG (see marginal no. 372 et seq.) come into consideration.

A fine of up to EUR 1,000,000 may be imposed on the party subject to supervision 527
under sec. 130 OWiG, since the acts are punishable by fine, sec. 130 para. 3 sent. 1 OWiG.
The maximum amount can be halved in the case of negligent supervisory violations,
sec. 17 para. 2 OWiG. An association fine of up to EUR 10,000,000 can be imposed (sec. 30
para. 2 sent. 1, 2 OWiG).

Regarding the hirer, the realisation of sec. 16 para. 1 no. 2 AÜG is possible. Contrary 528
to the criminal offence under sec. 15a AÜG, sec. 16 AÜG may also be committed negligently. Besides, the realisation of administrative offences of sec. 30 and sec. 130 OWiG is
possible. The offence under sec. 16 para. 1 sent. 2 AÜG may be punishable by fine of up
to EUR 500,000. In the case of negligence, the maximum amount gets reduced, sec. 17
para. 2 OWiG.

ff) **Regulatory.** Additionally, the law's violations in connection with cases of erro- 529
neous temporary agency employment may result in further indirect consequences from
a regulatory perspective. The regulatory consequences are sometimes far-reaching and
should never be underestimated. For a non-exhaustive overview, see once more marginal no. 381 et seq. above.

3. Corporate Law Responsibility and Recourse

The case groups mentioned before of incorrectly executed overt temporary agency 530
employment are also relevant under corporate law. Thus, the undertaking qualifying as
an employer makes additional claims for unpaid social security contributions and wage
tax and, if necessary, fines. The company's organs can also be the obligor of recourse for
these additional claims, provided that they have causally caused the resulting damage to
the company. In detail:

a) Liability of the Organs of the Company

aa) **Subject of Liability and Scale of Obligations.** The subject of liability can be the 531
respective institutions of the company. In the case of the limited liability company, these
are the directorate in the sense of sec. 43 GmbHG and the supervisory board in the sense
of sec. 52 GmbHG as well as the management board (sec. 93 AktG) and supervisory board
(sec. 116 AktG) in the case of the AG.

Per sec. 93 para. 1 sent. 1 AktG, the management board members are to exercise the 532
due care of a prudent manager, faithfully complying, with their duties in managing the
company's affairs. This also applies to the managing directors of the limited liability
company by sec. 43 para. 1 GmbHG. According to sec. 116 sent. 1 AktG (sec. 52 para. 1
GmbHG), this due diligence also applies to the supervisory board.

This due diligence comprises various partial aspects:

On the one hand, the management bodies carry the so-called obligation of legality. 533
This includes the observance of all legal provisions relating to the undertaking under general civil law, stock corporation and limited liability company law, criminal law, and the
administrative offences law as well as public law. It also includes the obligation to control
legality. According to this, it must be checked whether the relevant legal provisions are
being complied with at all levels in the undertaking.

Additionally, the directorate must follow the due diligence in the narrower sense. The 534
management board must manage the undertaking management assigned to it with due

care. An individual case analysis is necessary to determine the due care in each case. It depends on many different factors, including the type and size of the undertaking or its economic and financial situation. The decisive factor is how a prudent and conscientious manager of a comparable undertaking would have behaved in the very same situation.

535   Furthermore, the directorate also carries the obligation to ensure itself in an appropriate manner of the lawful and expedient conduct of subordinate members of the undertaking and its management board colleagues (obligation to monitor).

536   While the management is entrusted with the company's direction, the supervisory board has a particular monitoring responsibility, standardised in sec. 111 para. 1 AktG. Also, it applies to the supervisory board of the limited liability company via sec. 52 para. 1 GmbHG. The monitoring's object is the management of the management board, particularly whether the management board is doing everything necessary to increase the company's assets and avert damage to the company by taking timely countermeasures.

537   Expressly, compliance is understood as a component of the direction task under sec. 93 and sec. 116 AktG. The management board's responsibility to act arises from ensuring that the company complies with legal requirements. This obligation to control institution members' legality can be drawn for the AG from sec. 91 para. 2 AktG. This provision stipulates the obligation to set up a monitoring system to early detect risks for the company. Although there is no corresponding regulation in the GmbHG, it is derived from the background of sec. 130 OWiG and from the interaction between the obligation to control legality and general monitoring obligation.

Compliance is divided into preventive and repressive measures:

538   First, the directorate must take preventive action to protect the undertaking from damage. To this end, it must also set up a compliance management system regularly, which serves the early detection and avoidance of risks. The "whether" of the setup of such a compliance management system is not at the disposal of the institution members. Only the design of the system is at the discretion of the company. The compliance obligation scope depends on the type, size, and organisation of the undertaking, the regulations to be observed, and possible suspicious cases in the past.

539   The institution members must review the compliance management system regularly and as needed make adjustments in case of doubt, since compliance obligations are not limited to the one-time setup of an early detection system. They also require continuous monitoring, adjustment, and further development.

540   The supervisory board must ensure that the management introduces and uses a suitable system. It monitors both the setup and the control of the compliance organisation appropriate to the undertaking's circumstances. This monitoring also includes checking that the management board members under the rules and that their compliance performed is sufficiently efficient. However, only a plausibility check is carried out because the density of obligations must be determined so that the supervisory board members can complete their tasks within a period commensurate with their duties.

541   If suspicions of possible infringements arise in the undertaking, the obligations must be intensified. Therefore, suppose an increasing number of employment relationships occur, which indicate a concealed temporary agency employment and trigger the corresponding tax, criminal, and social security law consequences. In that case, this also falls under the institution members' compliance responsibility.

542   With the Neubürger-decision[16], the so-called duty triad was also established: Enlighten, stop, and punish. It includes the obligation of the management board to a pursue irregularities within the company actively. Therefore, in actual suspicion, the man-

---

[16] Regional Court Munich I, 10 December 2013 – 5 HK O 1387/10.

agement board is obliged to actively follow the matter and to take immediate action to clarify the situation. This duty relates to past and present clarification of the facts and is not disposable.

If the management board identifies organisational deficits that led to the compliance 543
incidents (organisational fault) during its investigations, it must remedy them. Official
clarifications do not relieve the management board of its responsibility to clarify the
matter.

In all this, the principle of omnipotence applies: According to this principle, all leaders 544
are responsible for everything. An exculpation due to the current distribution of departments is not possible. In principle, the managing director can also appoint employees
or third parties. However, even in such a delegation, the managing director will always
continue to have his obligations and, accordingly, personal liability. Even in an internal
regulation of responsibilities, the managing director has his own personal obligations to
monitor.

Whether the supervisory board has to conduct its internal investigation in case of sus- 545
picion of a breach of obligation by a member of the management board or another person
in the undertaking, depends on the potential danger to the company, and the probability
of its realisation. Suppose there is suspicion of a failure on the management board's part
in connection with the clarification of compliance violations or the management board's
possible direct involvement in such violations. In that case, the supervisory board will
have to take regular action itself. In particular, past misconduct by management board
members must be discovered and pursued by the supervisory board itself.[17]

Suppose the management board does not comply with the active duty of disclosure and 546
if this results in or increases the company's damage. Then, in this case, the management
board shall be liable for damages to the company (see marginal no. **548** et seq.).

Suppose official investigation proceedings conclude with the imposition of fines 547
against the company. In that case, these also represent a loss to the company generally
recoverable from the management board members, whereby the supervisory board must
examine whether the management board has adequately fulfilled its compliance obligation. The D&O insurance does not cover any recourse if it is based on deliberate action
by the management board members (see marginal no. **566** et seq.).

bb) Internal Liability. The liability of the institutions is linked to the obligations of 548
the respective institution. According to sec. 93 para. 2 AktG, the management board
members are obliged to pay damages. Only if they violate their obligations and the company suffers a loss as a result (for the limited liability company: sec. 43 para. 2 GmbHG).
The supervisory board is liable in this respect via sec. 93 para. 2 AktG, without having to
resort to the provisions of torts.

In distributing the burden of proof, the D&O liability procedure has some important 549
particularities compared to the Code of Civil Procedure (*Zivilprozessordnung* "**ZPO**").
The principle applies that the claimant party – the company – must prove the standard's
conditions favourable from its point of view. However, this does not apply in the case
of D&O liability procedure: A blanket distribution of the burden of proof does not take
place. Instead, the legislator and case law[18] differentiate for each individual prerequisite
for damages to who is obliged to provide evidence. The reason for this simplification of
presentation and proof is that the representative body often has a considerable information advantage over the company. The company must demonstrate and prove that a
potential obligation's breach (whether an act or omission) on the representative body's

---

[17] Federal Court of Justice, 21 April 1997 – II ZR 175/95.
[18] Regional Court Munich I, 10 December 2013 – 5 HK O 1387/10.

part was the cause of a loss incurred by the company (so-called causality) and the amount of this loss. Suppose the company succeeds in fulfilling its duty of proof. In that case, the management board must prove that there was no conduct in breach of obligation or that due diligence could not be fulfilled without fault or that the damage would also have occurred in the case of alternative conduct by duty. The institution can regularly refer to the Business Judgement Rule of sec. 93 para.1 sent. 2 AktG. According to this rule, there is no breach of duty if the management board member could reasonably assume when making a business decision, that he was acting in the best interests of the company based on appropriate information.

550   A fault is initially presupposed for liability. With fault, intent or negligence is understood. In this context, the management body is responsible for objectively required skills by the task entrusted to it. The size, economic situation and other factors of the undertaking concerned must relatively also be considered. Besides, the damage must also be based on improper conduct by the management body.

551   According to sec. 93 para. 2 sent. 1 AktG, it is not sufficient for liability that an adequate compliance organization would have significantly impeded the occurrence of the damage. Instead, in the case of a compliance violation, it must be established that with a probability bordering on certainty, no damage would have occurred if an adequate compliance organisation had been in place.

552   The compensable damage shall be determined according to the general principles of sec. 249 et. seq. BGB (differential hypothesis). This involves comparing the company's assets with those which it would have had if the damaging event, i. e., the institution's breach of obligation, had not occured.

553   Possible asset-reducing positions are:
– the company's social security contributions paid to the collecting agency according to sec. 28e SGB IV or, in successful personal claiming of the member of the institution by the collecting agency according to sec. 823 para. 2 BGB in conjunction with sec. 266a StGB – the employer's shares to social security contributions and, if applicable, interest on arrears according to sec. 24 SGB IV;
– the association's fine under sec. 130 and 30 OWiG;
– the disclosure costs/costs of an Internal Investigation, and
– possibly the back-payable wage tax.

554   The claims arising from sec. 93 para. 2 AktG sec. 43 para. 2 GmbHG, become statute-barred after five years, irrespective of knowledge (sec. 93 para. 6 AktG, sec. 43 para. 4 GmbHG). According to sec. 200 sent. 1 BGB the limitation period begins with the emergence of the claim, which is only the case with the damage's occurence on the merits. The damage need not be quantifiable. It is already sufficient that it could be asserted by way of an action for declaratory judgement. The period of limitation of sec. 43 para. 4 GmbHG, can be extended to up to 30 years within the limits of sec. 202 para. 2 BGB, within the framework of by-law or an employment contract, and can also be shortened, provided it is not a breach of obligation within the meaning of para. 3.[19] However, it is not possible to extend or shorten the statute of limitations of sec. 93 para. 6 AktG.

In unlawful conduct in the external relationship, internal liability towards the company is also regularly considered, as unlawful conduct in the external relationship also constitutes a breach of obligation in the internal relationship.

555   **cc) External Liability.** If the due diligence imposed on the institutions is violated, this can also lead to external liability towards shareholders, obligees, or other third parties.

---

[19] Federal Court of Justice, 16 September 2002 – II ZR 107/01.

In general, the principle of concentration of liability applies, which results from sec. 93 556
para. 2 AktG and sec. 43 para. 2 GmbHG. According to this, a member of an institution
is solely liable to the company for corporate breaches of obligations (the company, in
turn, is liable in the external relationship with the third party). Liability in the external
relationship is, therefore, only possible based on specific claim bases.

(1) Liability towards the Collecting Agency. Suppose the institution member is accused 557
of (conditional) intent concerning the non-payment of social security contributions. In
that case, can the collecting agency demand the employee's share of the social security
contributions from the institution member personally under sec. 823 para. 2 BGB, in
conjunction with sec. 266a StGB.

Sec. 266a StGB is thus regarded as a protective law within the meaning of sec. 823 558
para. 2 BGB. It applies at the expense of the employer and the institution member, irrespective of whether sec. 266a StGB is fundamentally directed at the undertaking as an
addressee of the standard. This is because the undertaking as a legal entity cannot act
itself, but only through its institutions. Moreover, the obligation to pay social security
contributions is incumbent on the institution members that are responsible for this under
civil law according to sec. 823 para. 2 BGB.

As an institution member, you are responsible for the payment of social security con- 559
tributions, irrespective of any internal allocation of responsibilities.[20] The other institution members must take appropriate measures to ensure that the levies are actually paid
and must monitor this. For example, specific monitoring measures are required in crisis
situations or disorderly conditions in the business' course.

The liability, according to sec. 823 para. 2 BGB in connection with sec. 266a StGB 560
presupposes the occurrence of a damage, which is causally based on the withholding
of the contribution. However, this is not the case if the insolvency administrator could
probably have successfully contested the payments to the social security fund under
sec. 129 et seq. InsO.[21]

Institution members are not liable to the collecting agency for interests on arrears as 561
sec. 24 para. 1 SGB IV is not a protective law in the sense of sec. 823 para. 2 BGB.

The social security authorities must present all circumstances and prove that the con- 562
stituent elements of the offence of sec. 266a StGB have been realized. This also extends
to the intent of the institution member.

Unpaid social security contributions are to be paid later for up to four years. 563

(2) Liability to the Financial Management. According to sec. 69, 44 AO, the institution 564
member is a jointly and severally liable debtor with the undertaking for wage tax arrears
in cases of intent and gross negligence.

dd) D&O Insurance. D&O insurance policies offer pecuniary damage liability insur- 565
ance, which is often taken out by the company for its institution members to cover the
liability risks of institution members in internal and external relationships.

According to sec. 93 para. 2 sent. 3 AktG, a deductible of at least 10% of the loss is to 566
be provided for. A cap on the deductible is permissible, but it must be at least one and a
half times the management board member's fixed annual remuneration. There is no such
regulation in the law on limited liability companies (however, such a regulation can be
regulated in the employment contract).

In the event of a claim by the company or a third party, the institution member can 567
initially only demand the legal defence costs (defence coverage). Only after a lost trial

---

[20] Federal Court of Justice, 2 June 2008 – II ZR 27/07.
[21] Federal Court of Justice, 7 April 2011 – IX ZR 137/10.

he can demand exemption from the recourse claim. The insurance cover is usually not applicable in the event of intentional breaches of obligation and criminal offences.

b) Responsibility of the Shareholders

568 A partners' liability for social security contributions in arrears is generally excluded by separating the legally independent company assets from the assets of the partners (principle of seperability).

569 A public law piercing the corporate veil is only considered exceptional if the reference to the independence of the legal entity is incompatible with good faith. The partners of a limited liability company are liable up to their registration for contributions in arrears in proportion to their shares only towards the company (internal liability), but not towards the collecting agency (external liability). This founder's liability is an internal liability. But only as long as the company relationships are ordered, the registration is still being pursued, or the company is in liquidation or insolvency but is not massless. If the registration is not intended or not seriously pursued, the liability regulations of the partnerships apply.

570 In the so-called non-genuine pre-limited liability company, the partners are personally and unrestrictedly jointly and severally liable debtors, analogous to sec. 128 HGB This applies even in the external relationship with the collecting agencies, without their respective share's magnitude in the company being of any significance.

4. Lessons learned – Overview and Checklist Temporary Agency Employment

a) Checklist Temporary Agency Employment

✓ the temporary agency employment contract is available in writing
✓ the contracting parties are named
✓ the contractual document contains the temporary work agency's declaration that he holds a temporary agency employment permit
✓ the specific characteristics of the proposed activity and qualifications are listed
✓ essential working conditions of comparable employees (principle of equality) or reference to the collective bargaining agreement applicable to the employment relationship

b) Checklist (Temporary) Employment Contract between Temporary Work Agency and Temporary Agency Worker

✓ name and address of the hirer and temporary work agency
✓ start and end of the planned assignment/employment relationship
✓ limitation/duration (if applicable)
✓ indication of the licensing authority as well as place and date of issue of the permit
✓ name and address of the temporary agency worker
✓ current professional title of the temporary agency worker
✓ applicability of collective bargaining agreements/in-house collective bargaining agreement for the concrete deployment
✓ planned place of work of the temporary agency worker for the deployment
✓ description and characterisation of the activity at the hirer's premises, including required qualifications

✓ composition of the level of remuneration including allowances, supplements, premiums, and special payments
✓ planned working time for the hirer
✓ recreational holiday
✓ legal periods of notice
✓ the possible need for deployment abroad with the hirer
✓ reference to an original employment contract for non-rental periods
✓ in addition, the temporary work agency is obliged to hand over the information sheet on temporary agency workers from the Employment Agency
✓ signatures and time of conclusion of the contract.

II. Concealed Temporary Agency Employment (Sham Service Contract/Sham Contract to Produce a Work) and its Legal Consequences

1. Definition and Meaning

Illegal temporary agency employment can occur in two forms: In the case of overt illegal temporary agency employment, the employee is hired out to a third party to perform work without the temporary agency employment permit required under sec. 1 para. 1 sent. 1 AÜG (see marginal no. 325 et seq.). 571

In concealed temporary agency employment, however, the principal and agent conclude a service contract or a contract to produce a work. Still, in an overall assessment of all circumstances, including the contract's actual execution, there is actually temporary agency employment. 572

Concealed temporary agency employment can also be intentional. In this case, the principal and agent conclude a sham service contract or a sham contract to produce a work, although they know that this is, in fact, temporary agency employment. 573

However, practically relevant and a compliance-challenge for every company are, above all, those cases in which service contracts or contracts to produce a work were initially concluded effectively and properly executed. Still, the contractual relationship's character alters to temporary agency employment as the business relationship progresses. In case the contract's character changes to temporary agency employment, it is concealed and illegally operated because all legal regulations, which would have to be observed (see marginal no. 86 et seq.), are disregarded. 574

Before the contractual relationship's commencement, the principal and agent should have clarity on the contractual form classification, as uncertainties lead to considerably disadvantageous legal consequences. Therefore, it is recommended that the contracting parties inform themselves about the contract's exact nature with its respective rights and obligations before concluding a contract and ensure that the agreement is complied with during the contract's execution. 575

Whether there is temporary agency employment or not is determined as follows: 576

Firstly, the content of the legal relationship between the principal and agent is determined based on the explicit agreements in the contract. In a second step, the practical implementation of the agreement is determined and also taken into account. If the agreement's content and its actual implementation are contradictory, the agreement's actual implementation between the principal and agent is decisive, see sec. 12 para. 1 sent. 2 AÜG. The consideration of the contract's practical execution serves to determine the 577 actual business content, i. e., the rights and obligations the contracting parties assumed when concluding the contract. However, contractual practice only allows conclusions to be drawn as to the contracting parties' actual business intent if the persons entitled to conclude the contract are aware of the contractual practice that deviates from the wording of the contract and at least approve of it.[22]

578   Since the contract's actual execution is decisive for the legal classification, the implementation modalities should be monitored closely throughout the entire duration of the business relationship. This is the only way to avoid an unconscious change of the legal regime for the business relationship. For this purpose, the organisation and information transfer within the company must be designed so that the various players in the company are equally and sufficiently informed about the type of contract and the actual implementation at all times or can easily access this information.

2. Differentiation

579   It is sometimes difficult to distinguish between concealed temporary agency employment and effectively drafted service contracts or contracts to produce a work. This is because the German legislator has always refrained from using legal criteria for delimitation. In the past, there have been several reform proposals for the legal standardisation of such criteria, most recently in a discussion draft of the Federal Ministry of Labour and Social Affairs dated 16 November 2015. In the end, the legislator refrained from a legal definition of such criteria.

580   The lack of a legal standardisation does not mean that there are no demarcation criteria in practice. The delimitation between genuine service contracts or contracts to produce a work on the one hand and concealed temporary agency employment, on the other hand, has been drawn primarily by case law, which provides guidelines for classifying the types of contracts in dispute.

581   The characteristic of the employer's right to issue instructions is of fundamental importance in determining whether a temporary agency employment exists The differentiation is based on the direction in which the right to issue instructions takes effect, whereby case law distinguishes between the execution instruction relating to the contract's subject matter and the personal instruction under labour law. Suppose the agent receives instructions from the principal relating to the contract's subject matter to specify the concrete object of performance. In that case, a contract to produce a work (or a service contract) exists.[23] In this context, it is not excluded that the principal may also issue professional instructions to the agent's viscaroius agents, insofar as this is necessary to specify the performance.[24] If it can be established that within the scope of the contractual relationship between the principal and agent, only instructions relating to the subject matter were issued, a service contract or contract to produce a work can be assumed.

582   A further characteristic for the distinction between temporary agency employment and a service contract or contract to produce a work is the undertaking's structure of the contractor, respectively, the service provider. Suppose the entrepreneur organises the actions necessary to achieve economic success according to his operational requirements and remains responsible to the third party company for the performance of the services provided for in the contract, or for the production of the work owed. In that case, this does not constitute temporary agency employment.[25] The employees used to execute the

---

[22] Federal Labour Court, 27 June 2017 – 9 AZR 133/16.
[23] Federal Labour Court, 27 June 2017 – 9 AZR 133/16.
[24] Federal Labour Court, 18 January 2012 – 7 AZR 723/10.
[25] Federal Labour Court, 20 September 2016 – 9 AZR 735/15.

service contract or a contract to produce a work are solely subject to the entrepreneur's instructions under labour law and are his viscarious agents. The agent's undertaking must have a structure indicating that it fulfills the operational and organisational prerequisites to provide the contractually agreed service.[26] This applies if the undertaking's structure enables the entrepreneur to go beyond the mere provision of employees and makes decisions typical for an employment relationship.

Suppose the entrepreneur's activity is limited in personnel terms to providing the agent with individual employees without him having to make dipositions and plan their deployment to a relevant extent. In that case, the undertaking's appearance speaks against its entrepreneurial service and in favour of temporary agency employment. **583**

The entrepreneur's limited entrepreneurial responsibility regarding the service or work performance and, at the same time, little entrepreneurial initiative on the personnel part for the organisation and implementation of the contractual performance also speaks in favour of the acceptance of temporary agency employment.[27] **584**

3. Case Groups

The demarcation between service contracts and contracts to produce a work and external personnel deployment through temporary agency employment is legally straightforwrd and too complicated. This is also because, in practice, there are often case constellations that only over time meet the requircments of a concealed temporary agency employment by being handled differently from the original concept. Against this background, it is all the more important to recognise that in all cases in which operations are carried out as part of a three-person relationship with service contracts or contracts to produce a work, there is a risk of a concealed temporary agency employment. Hence, it is of particular importance to know the case groups that are most frequently encountered in practice. **585**

a) Sham Service Contracts and Sham Contracts to Produce a Work

In practice, the classic cases of concealed temporary agency employment are those in which a contract is concluded between two undertakings to provide services or work. As a result, the person obliged to services or work (agent) undertakes to provide the respective service to its contractual partner (principal). However, the agent – often a legal entity – does not offer the service owed in person but uses the workforce of the employees employed by him. The latter are, therefore, merely vicarious agents of the agent. They have no contractual relationship whatsoever with the principal. Due to the peculiarities of the service owed by the agent, however, the principal and agent's employees often come into direct contact. This circumstance bears an enormous risk potential in the present context. **586**

---

[26] Federal Labour Court, 27 June 2017 – 9 AZR 133/16.
[27] Federal Labour Court, 27 June 2017 – 9 AZR 133/16.

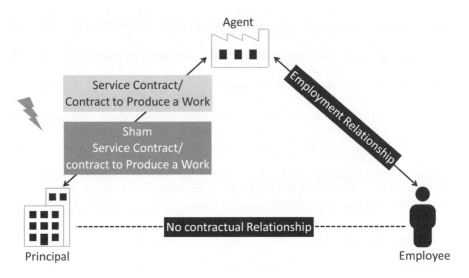

Figure 8: Illustration of sham contracts

587   If the legal assessment based on the criteria set out above (see marginal no. 579 et seq.) concludes that the actual implementation of the contractual relationship between the principal and agent is not aimed at producing the work or the perfomance of a service but at the hiring out of the agent's labour. Then in that case, concealed temporary agency employment exists.

b) Self-Hiring out of Managing directors

588   Managing directors are covered by the definition of employees under Eurpean union law.[28] For this reason, managing directors themselves can also be subject of concealed temporary agency employment. This only applies if the limited liability company managed by them concludes a service contract or contract to produce a work with a business partner, and the managing director personally performs the agreed services for the third party bound by instructions.

589   However, managing directors can only be bound by instructions if they do not simultaneously hold a majority interest in the company in whose service they are employed.[29] Therefore, the assignment of the sole shareholder and sole managing director of a temporary work agency limited liability company is not subject to the scope of application of the AÜG.

590   The majority shareholder and managing director of a limited liability company in the relationship with the limited liability company can hire themselves out to the hirer to perform the work bound by instructions to fulfill the temporary agency employment contract due to their position under company law. Even though they are not subject to its right to issue instructions under labour law. Therefore, he can independently decide whether he fulfills the temporary agency employment contract's obligation by hiring out an employee or by working for the hirer himself. Of course, this does not apply if he has already been specified by name in the temporary agency employment contract or in an-

---

[28] European Court of Justice, 9 July 2015 – C-229/14; European Court of Justice, 11 November 2010 – C-232/09.

[29] Federal Labour Court, 17 September 2014 – 10 AZB 43/14.

other agreement as the person to be provided for the work's performance, and a selection decision is thereby excluded from the outset.

On the other hand, suppose the shareholder-managing director makes the unbound, **591** autonomous decision to become active himself. In that case, this usually only affects his contractual relationship with the company without affecting the legal relationship with the hirer placed by the temporary agency employment contract. The managing director's contract of employment remains legally effective. The protective purpose of the AÜG does not prompt a new establishment of a further employment relationship with the hirer.[30]

Therefore, a managing director who does not hold a majority stake can also be a tempo- **592** rary agency worker. This may exemplarily be the case if he is entrusted by the shareholders to a company to manage its undertaking by the owners' instructions there.

Therefore, it must be ensured that the principles of legally compliant cooperation (see **593** "*checklists*" on page **101** et seq.) are strictly adhere if legal infringements and the associated drastic legal consequences are to be avoided.This shall apply to both foreigener- and shareholder-managing directors.

c) **Anglo-Saxon model (for example** *Direct Crowdworking*)

The risk of concealed temporary agency employment also exists in cases of the so- **594** called Anglo-Saxon model.

There is a direct contractual relationship between the principal and agent acting as an **595** agency or provider, in such constellations. The subject of this contractual relationship is a so-called service procurance. Within the framework of this service procurance agreement, the agent undertakes to pocure the principal with a third party's services. If this is successful, the principal subsequently concludes a contract with a self-employed service provider to provide the respective service.

This agreement will often be a service contract or contract to produce a work by its very **596** nature. Therefore, the Anglo-Saxon model is characterised by the fact that a contractual relationship affecting the notified service provision is only established between the principal and the service provider itself. The contractual relationship with the agent (agency/provider), on the other hand, has no direct connection to the service to be rendered at the principal's premises.

By way of example, such a constellation of contractual relationship exists in cases **597** of direct crowd working. In this context, the principal concludes a service procurance agreement with the crowd working platform. However, the platform does not conclude a contract for the respective service provision with the listed crowd workers. The contractual relationship between the crowd working platform and the crowd workers is limited to providing the platform for placement without final services. Subsequently, the contract for the services to be rendered is concluded directly between the principal and the crowd worker.

---

[30] Federal Labour Court, 17 January 2017 – 9 AZR 76/16.

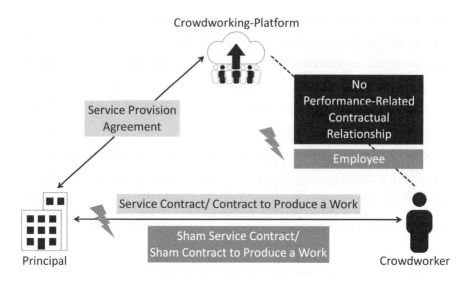

Figure 9: Illustration of direct crowdworking vs. temporary agency employment

598   The following conditions must be met so that concealed temporary agency employment exists. The relationship between the crowd working platform and the crowd worker must be so close that a legal consideration concludes that the crowd worker maintains an employment relationship with the crowd working platform (see marginal no. **253/654** et seq.). Moreover, an overall consideration should show that the crowd working platform's and the principal's contractual relationship aims at temporary agency employment (see marginal no. **579** et seq.). Finally, the contract between the principal and the crowdworker would have to be a sham service contract or sham contract to produce a work (see again marginal no. **579** et seq.).

d) Dutch model (for example *Indirect Crowdworking*)

599   In the so-called Dutch model, the agent likewise has a direct contractual relationship with the principal. In contrast to the Anglo-Saxon model's constellation, this is a service contract or contract to produce a work for the respective service to be performed. However, even the agent in the Dutch model does not intend to provide the service ultimately requested by the principal.

600   In such contractual constellations, the agent is only intermediar concerning the provision of services. In return, the agent concludes a service contract or contract to produce a work with a self-employed person to provide the service. In this downstream contract, the self-employed person undertakes to provide the service for the original principal. Nevertheless, the original agent (the direct principal's contractual partner) remains obliged to provide the service. The self-employed service provider's commissioning does not release the original agent from his obligation to perform services towards his contractual partner. He shall use only one sub-contractor for performance. There is no contractual relationship between the principal and the self-employed person actually providing the service in this form of occurence. The latter is a subcontractor of the third person.

601   By way of example, such a constellation of contractual relationships exists in cases of *indirect crowd working*. In light of this, a contract for the actual services' provision is concluded between the crowd working platform (agent) and the principal. The crowd working platform owes the provision of the service (not, as in the case of direct crowdworking (see

marginal no. **594** et seq.), merely the procurance of services). However, the Platform uses the crowd worker to fulfill its obligation and for this purpose also concludes a service contract or contract to produce a work with the crowd worker.

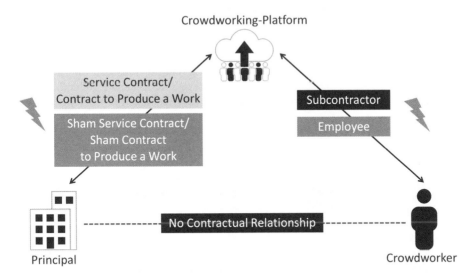

Figure 10: Illustration of indirect crowdworking vs. temporary agency employment

However, in practice, self-employed persons (freelancers, crowdworkers, etc.) often use **602** legal entities to carry out their work. If the solo self-employed person is now possible to be qualified as a false self-employed person (see marginal no. **653** et seq.), he appears as an employee in the three-person relationship. Therefore, the contractual constellation in the context of a risk assessment from the AÜG's point of view moves in dangerous proximity to cases in which the services' provision are apparently based on service contracts or contracts to produce a work (see marginal no. **586** et seq.). In practice it can be observed that the risk increases significantly with a third person's intervention and the loss of control associated with that. Consequently, the following also applies to the Dutch model's constellations: If the legal assessment of the contractual constellation described concludes that the contractual construction deviates from the actual handling, there is a risk of concealed temporary agency employment. Such a risk exists particularly if, contrary to the contractual construction, the subcontractor is not qualified as a self-employed person but rather as an employee of the agent (crowd working platform) (see marginal no. **653** et seq.). The contract concluded between the agent and principal is not qualified as a service contract or contract to produce a work. Still, the parties' contractual relationship aims to make the subcontractor's work available to the principal (see marginal no. **579** et seq.).

e) Contracting

Furthermore, the external personnel deployment through so-called *contracting* does **603** not provide any certainty against the contractual relationship's classification as concealed temporary agency employment.

Contracting is a term that cannot be clearly defined in connection with the deployment **604** of external personnel. It describes the use of self-employed service providers at the principal's premises at the behest of an intermediary personnel service provider.

605   The legal relationship between the principal and the personnel service provider often takes the form of a specific framework and/or individual project agreements. The different variations of this contractual relationship and the associated variety in quantity and quality of the personnel service provider's obligations towards the principal cause the term *contracting* to be vague. The obligations incumbent on the personnel service provider may be limited to providing a specific self-employed person. However, they may also include the personnel service provider's obligation to provide a service contract or contract to produce a work to fulfill which the personnel service provider, in turn, engages the self-employed person. If the principal and agent contract with each other, this is possible in the form mentioned above of the Anglo-Saxon and Dutch models (see marginal no. **594/599** et seq.). The parties can individually embellish the exact form of the contract.

f) Interim-Management

606   Cases of concealed temporary agency employment can also occur when using a so-called interim manager.

607   Interim management is a form of external personnel deployment, in which managers are deployed for a temporary period with a principal. The deployment of interim managers is often project- or occasion-related and is carried out, for example, within the scope of restructuring or reorganisation measures, for handling a company purchase or a sale and generally for handling projects. Like contracting, interim management as a term is not exclusively linked to an underlying contractual constellation.

608   Cases in which the interim concerning a possible concealed temporary agency employment. In practice, however, the interim manager often uses a legal entity to carry out his work. The resulting three-person relationship leads to a significant increase in the risk that the chosen contract structure is not a service contract or contract to produce a work, but a concealed temporary agency employent. Suppose the contractually chosen constellation depicts, contrary to the constellation chosen by the parties, that the interim manager is qualified as an employee of a placement officer or personal service provider. Additionally, suppose the the principal and the intermediary's relationship aims to make the interim manager's work performance available to the principal. In that case, the deployment of external personnel within the framework of interim management can, in reality, also be a concealed temporary agency employment.

609   As in the context of contracting, no general classification of which contractual relationships of the parties is fraught with risk in what way can be made for interim management due to the range of possible contractual arrangements. In this respect, however, reference can again be made to the previous explanations (see marginal no. **586/594/599** et seq.).

g) Agile Modes of Working

610   Agile modes of working are not variations of the deployment of external personnel. These modes characterise methods and/or procedures according to which employees perform their work in their respective undertakings. The core element is a flattening or eliminating hierarchy levels without replacement and an increase in flexibility (see marginal no. **309** et seq. for an example based description). Due to the expected advantages, such modes of working are becoming increasingly popular. At the same time, however, it has not been observed that the external personnel's need is decreasing noticeably. The logical consequence is that more and more external personnel will be used in teams working with agile modes of working in the future.

611   The consequence of an agile mode of working is always the service provider's very close interdisciplinary cooperation. If external personnel is used in agile teams, the principal's

employees and external personnel work together very closely in these teams and coordinate their daily work with each other. This form of cooperation is almost automatically accompanied by an increased risk of concealed temporary agency employment. This is because the external personnel can only work in the teams via service contracts or contracts to produce a work if they are not deployed in the agile teams within the framework of overt temporary agency employment. However, if the employing undertaking's employees and the external personnel are closely coordinated, many of the courts' developed indications suggest that the external personnel are integrated or bound by instructions.

In this context, the decisive question is whether the external personnel's activity is **612** externally controlled, i. e., whether their activity is organised by the principal directly or via an intermediary (auxiliary) person. This can regularly be assumed if own and external personnel work together in mixed teams based on labour division. The following prerequisite must be given so that external personnel can be legally secure deployed in agile modes of working based on contracts to produce a work or service contracts. The fundamenta; prerequisite is that individual partial tasks/sections ("tasks", "sprints") from the overall project are defined and handed over to the agent for independent completion based on an individual agreement. Regular or, if necessary, additional joint meetings in which the development status – also of the overall project – is reported and the further procedure is coordinated in terms of time and subject matter are not detrimental. These meetings only aim to concretise the object of performance and, therefore, do not justify the temporary agency employment acceptance. Admittedly, the boundaries are again fluid, and the legal evaluation of the cooperation in practice is sometimes difficult. Suppose the Scrum Owner defines the external project team's task via the Product Backlog in a concrete and temporally binding way in the Scrum model. In that case, this does not only mean the concretisation of the under service contract or contract to produce a work owed object of performance. If such specifications are made, it is rather a matter of exercising the right to issue instructions related to the activity. With such instructions, the external personnel's activity is controlled in terms of content and time, and the work processes of the external personnel are subsequently controlled externally. If the contractual employer no longer exerts any influence on its employees' the activities on-site, i. e., if it restricts itself to the personnel provision, it is considered to be temporary agency employment. As a result, the contractual arrangement for the deployment of external personnel chosen by the parties is a sham service contract or sham contract to produce a work (see marginal no. **586** et seq.).

These principles also apply to the cooperation of personnel assigned to different em- **613** ployers, but these employers are together in a group employment relationship. From the perspective of German labour law, these personnel are also (partially) "external personnel", since a group employment relationship is foreign to German labour law. Therefore, the problem is similar to differentiating between personnel deployment in a matrix organisation and temporary agency employment (see marginal no. **305** et seq.). As in this case, the consequences are mostly irrelevant due to the far-reaching effect of group privilege (see marginal no. **183** et seq.) and have so far been rather theoretical.

4. Legal Consequences – Liability Risks

Suppose the parties involved have operated with a different contractual design, and it **614** turns out that this was, in fact, a concealed temporary agency employment. In that case, this has far-reaching ipso iure consequences for all those involved.

The spectrum of these consequences ranges from a fundamental change in their relationships from a civil and labour law perspective to the associated consequences in social security law, tax law, criminal law, and administrative offence law, the personal liability of the active managers for damages and violations of the law.

a) Contract Law

615   If a case of concealed temporary agency employment is discovered, the restrictions of the AÜG fundamentally intervene in the contractual constellation chosen by the parties on an autonomous basis and realign the existing situation. With one exception, the legal consequences are not dispositive.

aa) Employee (Temporary Agency Worker) – Agent (Temporary Work Agency).

616   Sec. 1 para. 1 AÜG contains, in addition to the obligation to obtain permission in sent. 5, and 6, the so-called obligation to label and concretise. The obligation to label in sec. 1 para. 1 sent. 5 AÜG stipulates that the temporary work agency and the hirer must expressly designate the temporary agency workers ʻs assignment as temporary agency employment in the contract between them. Accordingly, the parties must disclose that they are engaged in temporary agency employment by naming the contract accordingly. This explicit designation of the contract must be made before they assign the temporary agency worker. The obligation to concretise in sec. 1 para. 1 sent. 6 AÜG provides that the temporary work agency and the hirer have to concretise the temporary agency worker prior to the assignment's commencement. This shall be done under reference to the concluded temporary agency employment contract. The concretisation must be carried out in such detail that the identity of the temporary agency worker hired out is established beyond doubt. Subsequently, possibly backdated disclosure cannot prevent the temporary agency employment contract and the fictitious employment relationship from becoming invalid. For further details of the obligations existing in this context, see marginal no. **110** et seq. above.

617   Suppose contrary to sec. 1 para. 1 sent. 5, and 6 AÜG, the temporary agency employment contract is not expressly designated as such, and the temporary agency worker has not been sufficiently specified. In that case, the temporary work agency and temporary agency worker's employment contract is invalid (sec. 9 para. 1 no. 1a AÜG). This legal consequence only occurs if there is a cumulative violation of the obligation to label and concretise. However, a mere "concretisation" – as in naming the concealed hired out employee as often in service contracts or contracts to produce a work by naming the deployed employees – does not prevent the temporary agency employment contract from being invalid according to sec. 9 para. 1 no. 1a AÜG and the fiction according to sec. 10 para. 1 AÜG. This is because the concretisation presupposes that an effective (here: temporary employment) contract exists. If the temporary agency employment contract is void due to a breach of the obligation to label, this contract cannot be concretised either. A breach of the obligation to label almost inevitably results in a violation of the obligation to concretise (see again marginal no. **110** et seq.).

618   It is precisely this effect between the use of sham contracts and an infringement of sec. 1 para. 1 sent. 5 and 6 of the AÜG that the legislator intended and the provisions to sanction such action were only recently inserted into the AÜG.[31]

619   The legal consequence of the invalidity of the existing employment contract is, in principle, mandatory. Something else only applies if the temporary agency worker expressly declares in writing that he intends to adhere to the employment contract with the lender (status quo declaration). This declaration can be made to the hirer or temporary work agency. In practice, however, this possibility, which appears to be very effective at first glance, is only of minimal use. That is because the declaration can only be declared up to

---

[31] German Bundestag Drucksache 18/9232, p. 19.

one month after the point in time agreed between the temporary work agency and hirer for the assignment's commencement (sec. 9 para. 1 no. 1a AÜG). This point in time will obviously often have elapsed due to the circumstances of reality.

Also should be noted that these legal consequences do not only occur when parties act **620** in an abusive manner from the outset. They can even happen in constellations in which a service contract or contract to produce a work has not been in a manner that is not reproachable recognised as temporary agency employment solely based on objective errors of law, and accordingly has not been designated as such.

Consequently, discovering a concealed temporary agency employment leads to the **621** invalidity of the employment relationship between the employee and the temporary work agency. In this respect, only a so-called defective employment relationship exists between them. This serves as the basis for the claim for the benefits exchanged or to be exchanged during the now ineffective employment relationship's execution.

Besides, sec. 10 para. 2 sent. 1, AÜG gives the temporary agency worker the possibility **622** to claim damages from the temporary work agency. Compensable damages are those that the temporary agency worker has suffered due to relying on the validity of his employment contract with the temporary work agency. The standard thus serves to protect confidentiality. This requires that such a claim does not exist if the temporary agency worker knew the reason for the invalidity (sec. 10 para. 2 sent. 2 AÜG).

bb) Employees (Temporary Agency Worker) – Principals (Hirer). If the obligation **623** to label and concretise is violated by operating with sham contracts (see B.II.4.a)aa), this also has far-reaching consequences for the legal relationship between the temporary agency worker and hirer.

A breach of the obligation to label and concretise in sec. 1 para. 1 sent. 5, 6 AÜG does **624** not only lead to the employment contract's nullity between the temporary agency worker and temporary work agency (sec. 9 para. 1 no. 1a AÜG). It also leads to the fiction of an employment relationship between the temporary agency worker and the hirer. According to sec. 10 para. 1 sent. 1, AÜG, an employment relationship between the hirer and temporary agency worker is deemed to have been concluded at the work commencement's point in time scheduled the hirer and temporary work agency. Only in case, the contract between the temporary work agency and temporary agency worker is invalid according to sec. 9 AÜG. If, on the other hand, the contract becomes invalid according to sec. 9 AÜG only in the course of the performance of the service, the employment relationship between the hirer and temporary agency worker is deemed to have come into existence at the time the invalidity occurs (sec. 10 para. 1 sent. 1 AÜG).

An employment relationship between the temporary agency worker and the hirer is **625** simulated based on legal order. This legally-established employment relationship is treated as an employment relationship based on legal transactions in all legal areas. Therefore, the hirer is subject to the usual employer obligations in the field of employment law (e. g., obligations to provide evidence or obligations arising from collective bargaining agreements and works agreements). The same applies to the employer's obligations in social and tax law.

The legislator also sets exact requirements concerning the content of the employment **626** relationship. Sec. 10 para. 1 sent. 2 AÜG stipulates that the employment relationship is deemed to be concluded for a limited period in the following case. In case the temporary agency worker's work for the hirer was only intended to be of limited duration and an objective reason justifying the employment relationship's limitation exists. If, for example, there is no factual reason within the meaning of sec. 14 para. 1 TzBfG, the employment relationship is deemed to have been concluded for an unlimited period. In all other respects, the working hours planned between the temporary work agency and hirer shall be deemed to have been agreed (sec. 10 para. 1 sent. 3 AÜG). Furthermore, this employment relationship's content and duration is determined by the regulations and other provisions applicable to the hirer's establishment (sec. 10 para. 1 sent. 4 AÜG). In the absence of such, those of comparable establishments apply (sec. 10 para. 1 sent. 4 AÜG). However, the temporary agency worker is at least entitled to the hirer to the remuneration agreed with the temporary work agency (sec. 10 para. 1 sent. 5 AÜG).

627   This legal consequence cannot be waived and can only be prevented by making a status quo declaration. However, the practical scope of application of this way out is limited (see marginal no. **619** et seq.).

628   **cc) Agent (Temporary Work Agency) – Principal (Hirer).** Furthermore, the concealed temporary agency employment does not remain without consequences for the existing contractual relationship between the hirer and temporary work agency.

629   The contract concluded between them is invalid. In practice, in concealed temporary agency employment, the temporary work agency will often not own a temporary agency employment permit (see marginal no. **88** et seq.). If such a case exists, the contract between temporary work agency and hirer is invalid according to sec. 9 para. 1 no. 1 AÜG. One of the legal consequences is that the legal and contractual warranty claims are void without replacement, and services already exchanged must be reversed by the so-called right of enrichment, sec. 812 et seq. BGB.

630   Should the temporary work agency have a valid permit, this will generally still lead to the contract's invalidity between the parties. However, this invalidity does not result directly from the AÜG. This is because sec. 9 para. 1 no. 1a AÜG only provides for the contract's invalidity between the temporary work agency and temporary agency worker. However, it cannot be deduced that the contract concluded between the hirer and temporary work agency is effective in every case. If the parties conclude the service contract or contract to produce a work only to cover up an actual intended temporary agency employment, this is a sham transaction. According to sec. 117 para. 2 BGB, this leads to applying the provisions applicable to the concealed legal transaction (temporary agency employment). These include, in particular, the formal requirement of sec. 12 para. 1 sent. 1 AÜG. Because the mandatory labelling did not occur in writing according to sec. 1 para. 1 sent. 5 AÜG, the contract is null and void (sec. 1 para. 1 sent. 5, sec. 12 para. 1 sent. 1 AÜG in conjunction with sec. 126, 125 sent. 1 BGB).

631   However, the situation may differ in erroneous, false designation, which is probably the most frequent case of concealed temporary agency employment. In these cases, the parties to the contract wrongly assume that there is no temporary agency employment present. Compared to the intentionally concealed temporary agency employment, there is no consensus regarding the concealed legal transaction. In this case, the requirements of sec. 117 BGB are not met. However, suppose such an error worthy of protection on the part of the parties is present. In that case, it is not easy to determine. The differentiation between a genuine service contract or contract to produce a work and cases of temporary agency employment is a highly challenging task to be performed based on the individual case, which sometimes poses challenges even to persons with in-depth background knowledge.

632   It can be established that anyone deciding in favour of a service contract or contract to produce a work because of delimitation difficulties in the individual case acts negligent. And especially in case he does so without exhausting the possibilities reasonably available to him to examine the existence of possible temporary agency employment. As a rule, it would also be reasonable to seek legal advice. Depending on the circumstances and possibilities in the individual case, further requirements must be made. It is not possible to give a general answer as to what these further measures might look like. On the other hand, however, it must be stated that a mistake worthy of protection is made by anyone

who examines the contractual constellation (and its implementation) appropriately and in line with the current state of case law.

Therefore, it is also conceivable in cases in which, despite the discovery of a concealed **633** temporary agency employment (at least for a certain period), an effective contract of service contract or contract to produce a work still exists between the temporary work agency and hirer. This is particularly important against the background of possible warranty claims of the parties.

b) Social Security Law

aa) Principle. The consequences under labour law of the concealed temporary agency **634** employment have a decisive influence on social concerning liability (see marginal no. **360** et seq.).

However, special attention is paid to the (potential) violation of the principle of equali- **635** ty. As explained under marginal no. **431** et seq., the so-called principle of origin applies in social security law. Therefore, the social security contribution is not calculated based on the remuneration paid, but on the remuneration to which the employee is entitled under sec. 8 para. 1 sent. 1 AÜG. Even if the hirer has become the temporary agency worker's employer based on the statutory fiction, the temporary work agency as contractual employer will normally continue to pay the remuneration, collect social security contributions, and deliver them to the collecting agency. This is without any problems under social security law if the temporary work agency pays a remuneration equal to or higher than the principle of equality. However, this is hugely problematic if remuneration is paid that does not comply with the principle, resulting in that a higher remuneration should have been paid. In such cases, the temporary work agency will only pay the social security contribution that is due on the remuneration paid. The temporary work agency is solely liable for this contribution (together with the hirer) according to sec. 28 para. 2 sent. 3 SGB IV. The temporary work agency is not liable for any further obligations. Consequently, the hirer alone is liable for the payment of the social security contribution, which would have been payable if the principle of equality had been observed.

Social security contributions not paid due through negligence are still to be paid four **636** years after the end of the calendar year in which they became due, sec. 25 para. 1 sent. 1 SGB IV. Intentionally unpaid social security contributions are to be paid in arrears up to the expiry of thirty years, sec. 25 para. 1 sent. 2 SGB IV.

If the hirer does not pay the social security contribution due on the difference, he **637** must pay this plus an interest on arrears. The interest on arrears is 1 % per month (sec. 24 para. 1 sent. 1 SGB IV). This also applies to contributions not paid in the past, unless the employer can credibly demonstrate that does not know the payment obligation through no fault of his own (sec. 24 para. 2 SGB IV).

Since the sum of the total social security contribution in Germany amounts to more **638** than 40 % of the respective remuneration, additional contribution demands represent a risk for undertakings that should not be underestimated, In some cases, it poses a threat to their existence. The length of proceedings before the social courts, which can be considerable in some cases, must also be taken into account, as it leads to a long period of legal uncertainty.

bb) Criminal Law Consequences: Withholding of Remuneration. Suppose the hirer **639** does not pay the total social security contributions due (i. e., the difference between the contributions paid by the temporary work agency and the contributions that would have been paid if the principle of equality had been observed) to the collecting agencies. In that case, there is a considerable risk of criminal liability under sec. 266a StGB.

640   Concerning the offence and its consequences, reference should be made to the above comments (see marginal no. **436** et seq.). The duties and the potential offences do not distinguish between the concealed or overt, incorrect temporary agency employment.

c) Tax Law

641   **aa) Principle.** Regarding tax law, the consequences of the overt temporary agency employment should also be pointed out (see marginal no. **363**).

642   Regarding a potential violation of the principle of equality, reference should be made to the previous comments on the principle of equality in the context of overt – erroneous – temporary agency employment (see marginal no. **444** et seq.). Suppose the hirer, as an employer, now pays the outstanding social security contributions in the course of its efforts to correct the situation. In that case, he must also pay tax on them and pay the wage tax to the local tax office.

643   **bb) Criminal Law Consequence: Tax Evasion.** Suppose the hirer does not fulfill his obligations under wage tax law in respect of the subsequent payment of social security contributions. In that case, reference is made to the above explanations regarding the commission of tax evasion (see marginal no. **449** et seq.). The obligations and potential criminal offences do not distinguish between the concealed or overt, incorrect temporary agency employment.

d) Other Criminal Offences

644   In the case of the foreigners' employment, the realisation of criminal offences under the SchwarzArbG cannot be excluded (see marginal no. **521/523** et seq.).

e) Administrative Offence Law

645   **aa) Administrative Offences under the AÜG.** A large number of administrative offences can also be committed under the AÜG in the area of concealed temporary agency employment. Yet again, the law does not distinguish between concealed or overt temporary agency employment, so that reference is made to the individual administrative offences under marginal no. **324** et seq. above.

646   **bb) Administrative Offences under the SchwarzArbG.** If the principle of equality is infringed, there is a risk of forfeiture of the reckless withholding of remuneration under sec. 8 para. 3 SchwarzArbG (see marginal no. **458** et seq.).

647   In foreigners' employment, administrative offences can be realised under the SchwarzArbG (see marginal no. **516** et seq.).

648   **cc) Administrative Offences under the AO.** If the principle of equality is infringed, the temporary work agency can easily evade taxes (see marginal no. **461** et seq.).

649   **dd) Administrative Offences under the OWiG.** Besides, the administrative offences from the OWiG can also be implemented, and the association fine can also be set (see marginal no. **372** et seq.).

f) Regulatory

650   Moreover, the law's violations in connection with cases of concealed temporary agency employment may result in further indirect consequences from a regulatory perspective. The regulatory consequences are sometimes far-reaching and should never be underestimated. For a non-exhaustive overview, see marginal no. **381** et seq. and **467** above.

g) Corporate Responsibility and Recours

The responsibility under company law does not differ from that of the incorrectly **651** implemented overt temporary agency employment (see margin no. 530 et. seq.).

5. Lessons learned – Overview and Checklist

a) Summary of the main legal consequences

→ Ineffectiveness of the sham contract → Remuneration and a warranty claim is not applicable

→ Invalidity of the employment contract and fiction of an employment relationship, sec. 9 para. 1 no. 1 and sec. 10 para. 1 AÜG

→ Administrative offences, sec. 16 para. 1 and 2 AÜG: fines of up to EUR 30,000 each

→ Refusal of permission due to unreliability, sec. 3 para. 1 no. 1 AÜG

→ Payment of arrears of social security contributions, sec. 28e para. 2 SGB IV

→ Criminal liability for intent, sec. 266a StGB

→ illegal employment/prohibition of hiring out.

b) Checklist: General measures to avoid concealed temporary agency employment

✓ organise the ordering process so that all stakeholders (departments, purchasing, legal, human resources, and compliance) are involved

✓ implement guidelines on external personnel

✓ training, in particular for employees who regularly commission external personnel or work with external personnel, especially on the significance of instructions regarding working hours, workplace, and work content

✓ continuous monitoring and documentation as part of a compliance management system

✓ encouraging employees to report possible violations internally (whistle-blower hotline; external ombudsperson)

✓ set sanctions regime.

c) Checklist: Concrete measures to be taken in the course of the business relationship to avoid concealed temporary agency employment

✓ avoid integration into the foreign work organisation
for example: no use of the principal's work equipment, spatial separation of the principal's staff

✓ prevent the personnel deployed from being bound by instructions
for example: intermediary of supervisors (keywords „SPOC"; „river bridge model"), the introduction of a project manager, on the principal's and agent's side, „pre-programming" of the activity

✓ treaty mechanisms for mutual control and information obligations

✓ implementation of controls
for example: establishment tours

✓ sanctions.

d) Checklist: Measures to be taken in case of self-detected non-compliance

> ✓ examination of criminal self-reports according to sec. 266a para. 6 StGB, sec. 371 AO
> ✓ if necessary, early involvement of the public prosecutor's office/social security authorities to coordinate the internal determination and the calculation method for determining
> ✓ reporting the employment relationships concerned to the collecting agency (sec. 28a SGB IV, sec. 6 DEÜV)
> ✓ payment of social security contributions during the limitation period (4 years); an attempt should be made to avoid debt-related „contribution multipliers":
> sec. 25 para. 1 sent. 2 SGB IV: 30 years limitation period in case of intent
> sec. 24 para. 1 SGB IV: interest on arrears of 1 % per month
> ✓ reporting the transactions concerned to the financial management.

III. False Self-Employment and its Legal Consequences

652   Furthermore, in cases where external personnel deployment is based on a service contract or contract to produce a work, this may conceal an actual existing employee status, referred to as so-called false self-employment. Cases of false self-employment can occur in various constellations and (at least when discovered) can have far-reaching legal consequences for all parties being involved.

1. Definition and Meaning

653   "False self-employment" describes a situation in which an agent who is supposed to provide independent services or to perform work according to the contractual relationship on which the activity is based, but actually qualifies the activity as non-self-employed work (dependent employment). Thus, the disparity between the contractual and the actual classification of the employment is characteristic. The term "false self-employment" is not a legal term, but instead describes a phenomenon of incorrect legal classification (consciously or unconsciously) of an activity.

In this context, the initial point is social security law and whether an activity is to be qualified as a non-employed activity or as a self-employed activity within the meaning of sec. 7 para. 1 Social Security Code IV (SGB IV). In this respect, an "all-or-nothing principle" applies: the distinction between employment and self-employment determines whether the employee is compulsorily included in the social security system or whether he or she is allowed to decide whether and how he or she makes provisions. Suppose the employee is compulsorily included in the social security system. In that case, the principal (who thus becomes an employer in the sense of social security law) must pay the so-called total social security contribution to the responsible collecting agency. As a rule, the total social security contribution consists of a share borne by the employee (employee share) and retained from the gross remuneration, and a share borne by the employer (employer share).

2. Delimitation

a) Identification of False Self-Employment Case

The examination of the issue of "non-self-employment" within the meaning of sec. 7 **654** para. 1 SGB IV, and thus, the distinction between self-employment and dependent employment is based on a large number of characteristics. The main characteristic is the "personal dependency" of the employee on the principal.[32] Consequently, a person is personally dependent if he or she is integrated into a foreign work organisation, performs externally determined work according to instructions, and does not work at his or her own entrepreneurial risk. On this basis, case law has developed many further, more detailed characteristics for assessment, which are presented in the following in excerpts. It should be noted, that none of the characteristics in themselves allow a reliable answer to the question of personal dependence. This answer can only be given based on an overall view, taking the traffic view into account. Even the case law does not weigh these characteristics explicitly and reliable. They rather function as components of a checklist. The overall examination leads to partial results. Like circumstantial evidence, these partial results are compiled as part of an overall assessment, situationally weighed, and lead to the decision within the framework of a weighing procedure.

The order's actual execution is always decisive for the classification and not the desig- **655** nation in an underlying contract.

Therefore, there may be cases in which the activity is initially performed independently **656** and adequately. Still, the nature of the activity changes in the course of the service's performance to provide dependent services as an employee.

A large number of detailed criteria, the weighing of which depends on the respective **657** individual case, enables the courts to take sufficient account of the overall circumstances in the separate particular case and leads to legal uncertainty on the law users' part.

Delimitation criteria (exemplary and not exhaustive; for a more detailed presentation, see "*checklists*" on page **115** et seq.):

Criteria that speak *in favour* of an **integration**: **658**
– the agent uses the principal's work material/machinery;
– the agent can only provide his services dependent on and/or together with employees of the principal;
– the principal engages employees who perform the same activities as the agent.

Criteria that speak *in favour* of the **bound by instruction**:
– the agent has no possibility of delegation to other people/must perform "in-person"; no or rare use of a possibility of delegation;
– the principal shall instruct the agent on how to carry out the delegated tasks;
– the principal may delegate an activity other than that agreed to the agent.

Criteria that speak *against* the agent's **own entrepreunerial risk**:
– the agent receives regular remuneration/the remuneration is always in the same amount/the remuneration is also paid without specific consideration (no risk of unsuccessful use of own material and personnel resources);
– the agent has not negotiated his remuneration individually (conclusion of a model contract);
– the agent is entitled to receive orders from the principal.

The determination of false self-employment has an impact on the civil, labour, or social **659** security law and on the tax law classification of the employment (see marginal no. **663** et seq.). However, the status determination is not necessarily carried out across legal ter-

---

[32] Federal Social Court, 04 June 1998 – B 12 KR 5/97 R.

ritories. The individual areas each have their own – albeit largely congruent – definitions and independent assessment responsibilities. The vast synchronisation is exemplarily clarified by the fact that sec. 7 para. 1 sent. 1 SGB IV assumes that non-self-employed work "…especially in an employment relationship…" is rendered. Additionally, the meaningful sec. 266a StGB, for instance, is accessory structured under social security law. The realisation of the criminal offence's actus reus, thus presupposes an existing obligation to contribute to social security. In case of doubt, however, a separate status assessment should be carried out in each legal area concerned.

b) Excursus: Occasions for Status Determination

660   In addition to the always non-legally binding status assessment as part of a formal compliance organisation, authorities also legally bind status statements.

661   Therefore, principals and agents can request a decision as to whether employment subject to social security contributions is present by sec. 7a para. 1 sent. 1 SGB IV. Afterward, the German Federal Pension Fund ("*Deutsche Rentenversicherung Bund*" **DRV**) made the legally binding status decision based on an overall assessment of all circumstances of the individual case. It should be noted that the decision does not have to be applied for jointly by the principal and agent. Both parties are authorised to make an application independently. Besides, a corresponding application can also be made after the completion of the service provision. This leads to the fact that with the help of the instrument of the inquiry procedure in sec. 7a SGB IV, agents often try to benefit from the protection of social security afterwards. Figures from 2016 show 22,629 inquiry procedures according to sec. 7a para. 1 sent. 1 SGB IV, which in 42.2 % of the cases ended with accepting employment subject to social security contributions.[33]

662   The German Federal Pension Fund carries out random checks on employers at least every four years by sec. 28p para. 1 sent. 1 SGB IV. The inspection subject is whether the employer fulfills its obligations under social security law, particularly concerning the correct payment of the total social security contribution, including compulsory social security notifications under sec. 28a SGB IV. Therefore, part of these recurring checks are also status checks, which regularly lead to discovering false self-employment cases.

3. Case Groups

663   Terms such as freelancer, consultant, contractor, Dutch/Anglo-Saxon model, or interim management are used to describe various forms of deployment of external personnel.

The danger of a disparity between the contractual and the actual classification of the service provision in a contractual relationship, thus the threat of false self-employment, exists with each of these forms. A fundamental distinction between two-person and three-person relationships must be made. In the latter case, there is an increased risk in the event of disruptions, since the risk of false self-employment is increased by the risk of a concealed temporary agency employment (see marginal no. 572 et seq.).

a) Two-Person Relationships

664   In a two-person relationship, the principal and agent regularly conclude a service contract or contract to produce a work.

---

[33] German Bundestag Drucksache 18/11982, sent. 3.

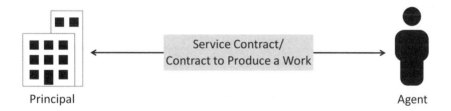

Figure 11: Illustration of a two person relationship

aa) Basic Type. The basic type of deployment of external personnel in a two-person **665** relationship is the assignment of a self-employed person (freelancer, consultant, etc.). A contractual relationship only exists between the principal and agent.

In this legal relationship, the criteria outlined above (see marginal no. **654** et seq.) must be used to determine whether the (supposedly) self-employed person's activity is actually to be assessed as self-employment or whether, contrary to the contractual arrangement, it is to be qualified as a dependent employment.

bb) Interim-Management. Interim management is a case of the deployment of **666** self-employed persons. In this case, a manager (the interim manager) is deployed for a temporary period at the principal. The deployment of interim managers is often project- or occasion-related and is carried out, for example, within the scope of reorganisation or restructuring measures, for handling a company purchase or sale and generally for handling projects.

Here, too, just as in the basic case, it must be examined based on the outlined criteria **667** (see once again marginal no. **654** et seq.) whether the (supposedly) self-employed interim manager's activity is actually to be assessed as self-employment or whether, contrary to the contractual arrangement, dependent employment is involved. Interim management's nature means that interim managers are often so closely integrated into the principal's organisation and processes that their activity can hardly be distinguished from that of an employee or institution member of the principal. The principal usually has a heightened interest in integrating the interim manager into his organisation as seamlessly as possible and integrating him into internal work processes. Due to these circumstances, there are often numerous indications in practice that the work of an interim manager may be regarded as dependent employment. Within the practice of interim management, the danger of fictitious self-employment is thus virtually immanent.

This also applies when interim managers – as it is often the case – act as the principal's **668** institution, e. g., when the interim manager is appointed managing director of a limited liability company. The managing director of a limited liability company is not an employee in the sense of labour law. However, he regularly exercises a dependent employment in the sense of sec. 7 para. 1 SGB IV, and thus gets qualified as an employee in the sense of social security law. This connection is often overlooked and leads to interim managers appointed as managing directors erroneously not registered for social security, and no social security contributions are paid for them. Therefore, they are false self-employed persons. For the legal consequences resulting from this, see marginal no. **683** et seq. below.

b) Three-Person Relationships

669   Even in a three-person relationship, the agent and principal usually conclude a service contract or contract to produce a work. The exact role of the party joining the agent and principal, and the role of the three parties among each other differs according to the chosen model and is highly variable in individual cases.

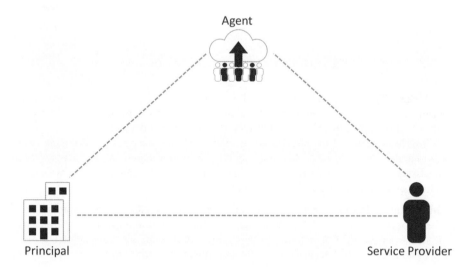

Figure 12: Illustration of a three person relationship

670   **aa) Anglo-Saxon Model (for example Direct Crowdworking).** In the so-called Anglo-Saxon model, there is a contractual relationship between the principal and the third party (agency, provider, etc.) in the form of a so-called service provision agreement. The service provision agreement's object is the procurance of services (placement) performed by a service provider. Subsequently, the principal concludes a contract (service contract or contract to produce a work) with the respective service provider regarding the specific activities to be performed. Thus, the Anglo-Saxon model is characterised by the fact that a contractual relationship concerning the precise work to be performed is only established between the principal and the service provider. The contractual relationship between the principal and the third party, on the other hand, has no direct reference to the services to be performed for the principal.

671   Such a constellation of contractual relationships occurs, for example, in cases of direct crowd working. The crowd working platform (third party) concludes a service provision agreement with the principal, but no contract regarding the respective services to be performed with the listed crowd workers. The contractual relationship between crowd working platform and crowd worker is limited to the availability of the crowd worker on the platform for placement. The contract on the precise services to be rendered is then concluded directly between the principal and the crowd worker.

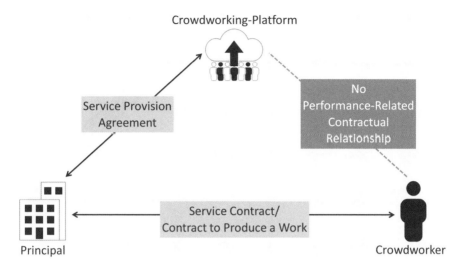

Figure 13: Legal relations between the parties (direct crowdworking)

Whether the service provider really performs his service by way of a self-employed   **672**
activity has to be examined based on the general criteria (see marginal no. 654 et seq.),
which are also applicable in the case of the Anglo-Saxon model; a risk in this context
cannot be excluded at this point. Due to the lack of a performance-related contractual
relationship between the principal and the third party, there is generally no risk of a concealed temporary agency employment (see marginal no. 572 et seq.) in the Anglo-Saxon
model's constellations.

bb) The Dutch Model (for example Indirect Crowdworking). In the so-called Dutch   **673**
model, on the other hand, the principal concludes a service contract or contract to produce a work directly with the third party (who is then, of course, the agent). The third
party then concludes a service contract or contract to produe a work with the service
provider, so that the latter performs the services owed by the principal. With this form,
there is no contractual relationship between the principal and the service provider in
contrast to the Anglo-Saxon model. The latter is a subcontractor of the agent.

Such a constellation of contractual relationships exists, for example, in cases of indirect   **674**
crowd working. A contract is concluded between the crowd working platform and the
agent for the actual provision of services. Thus, the crowd working platform basically owes
the provision of the service (and not, as in direct crowd working, merely the procurement
of services). However, the crowd working platform uses the crowd worker to fulfill its
obligation and also concludes a service contract or contract to produce a work with the
crowd worker for this purpose.

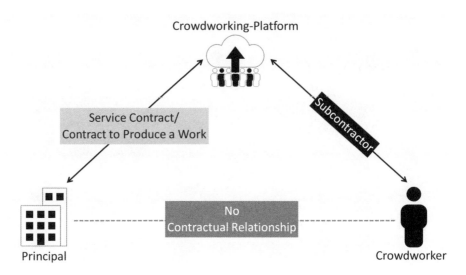

Figure 14: Legal relations between the parties (indirect crowdworking)

675   If the service is performed in the Dutch model's apperance, the status assessment of the service is also subject to the general criteria mentioned above (see once again marginal no. **654** et seq.). However, the use of the Dutch model in the contractual arrangements is associated with increased legal risks.

676   On the one hand, this is because the risk of false self-employment is twofold. Such a risk exists for the contractual relationship between agent and service provider, and between the principal and service provider. Although there is no direct contractual relationship between the principal and the service provider in the Dutch model, the service provision's overall circumstances can lead to a personal dependence of the service provider on the principal.

677   On the other hand, the Dutch model's constellations bear the risk of a concealed temporary agency employment. The structure of the parties' relations with each other is very similar to the relations within temporary agency employment (see marginal no. **17/46/69** et seq.).

678   **cc) Contracting.** Contracting does not represent a particular form that needs to be distinguished from the forms already described. Instead, it describes a collective term only the deployment of a service provider at a principal at the behest of a personnel service provider.

679   The contractual relationship between the principal and the personnel service provider often takes a specific framework and/or individual project agreements. The different variations of this contractual relationship and the associated variety in quantity and quality of the personnel service provider's service obligations towards the princpal cause the term contracting to be vague. The obligations incumbent on the personnel service provider may be limited to providing a specific self-employed person. However, they may also include the service provider's obligation to provide the service under a contract to produce a work or service contract for which's fulfilment the personnel service provider will often use the self-employed person.

680   Therefore, the term "contracting" also ultimately describes the deployment of self-employed external personnel in a three-person ratio, either in the form of the Dutch or the Anglo-Saxon model, but also in mixed forms, such as in so-called Master Vendor or

Managed Service Provider constellations. For a presentation of the risk structures, see marginal no. **670/673** et seq. above.

dd) Interim-Management. The possibilities for the contractual arrangement of in- **681** terim management are manifold. In addition to the two-person relationship mentioned before (see marginal no. **666** et seq.), interim management can also take the shape of a three-person relationship. In this case, both the Dutch and the Anglo-Saxon model are conceivable (see once again marginal no. **670/673** et seq.).

The risk of false self-employment is also inherent in the appearance of interim man- **682** agement in a three-person relationship. Besides, especially when the Dutch model is applied, the risk of a concealed temporary agency employment may also arise (see marginal no. **677**).

4. Legal Consequences – Liability Risks

If a particular case is evaluated as false self-employment, the parties involved will face **683** various legal consequences, which often occur ipso iure. The primary legal implicatons of false self-employment are described in detail below.

The following considerations refer to two-person relationships in principle (see mar- **684** ginal no. **664** et seq.). In three-person relationships, the risk of false self-employment exists for the contractual relationship between the agent and the service provider and between the principal and the service provider (see marginal no. **669**). Besides, there is a risk that such constellations will be evaluated as concealed temporary agency employment. See marginal no. **614** et seq. for details of the prerequisites and respective legal consequences.

a) Contractual Law

Suppose the parties involved wrongly assume that the service provider carries out **685** its services in a self-employed manner. In that case, this can lead to the invalidity of the underlying service contract or contract to produce a work. The contractual relationship between the parties involved can retroactively be qualified as an employment relationship (sec. 611a BGB). Subsequently, the false self-employed person is contractually bound with an employment relationship to the principal and is subject to his instructions. The classification of the false self-employed person as an employee can lead to a far-reaching change in the agreed service structure, especially when the performance of services was (planned) governed by a contract to produce a work. Furthermore, it is a consequence of the principal's entry into the legal position of the employer that the false self-employed person, who is now an employee, benefits from all employee protection provisions.

For example, the KSchG applies in the employment termination, provided that its **686** scope of application is opened up under with sec. 1 and 23 KSchG. Thus, the termination of the employment relationship requires a reason for termination. In the case of fixed-term employment (as it will often be the case within the framework of project-related service contracts or contracts to produce a work), the Part-Time and Fixed-Term Employment Act restrictions must be considered. Particularly here, the provisions of sec. 14 TzBfG must also be considered. According to these, the temporary limitation of an employment relationship is only feasible under certain conditions. If these conditions are not fulfilled, an employment relationship of indefinite duration is created. The employee is also entitled to continued remuneration on public holidays and in case of sickness (sec. 2 and 3 EFZG). Following sec. 3 para. 1 BUrlG, there is also an entitlement to at least four weeks of paid leave per year. If this entitlement can no longer be exercised in kind due to the employment relationship's termination, the employer must compensate for it. The employee can also assert pension claims resulting from an existing company pension scheme of the employer. These are only some of the employer's obligations to be fulfilled. In individual cases, there may be numerous other obligations going beyond.

b) Social Security Law

687   False self-employment of the service provider can lead to significant legal consequences for the principal if the latter contravenes its social security law-related obligation to the pay the service provider's social contributions.

688   **aa) Principle.** Unpaid or not fully paid social security contributions must be paid subsequently. The obligation to afterward pay such contributions exists retroactively for up to four years after the end of the calendar year, in which the contributions would actually have been due, sec. 25 para. 1 sent. 1 SGB IV. Suppose the employer can be proven to have acted intentionally. In that case, the contribution claims, on the other hand, only become statute-barred after a period of 30 years, sec. 25 para. 1 sent. 2 SGB IV. However, the obligation to pay social security contributions in the German social security system is to be borne equally by the employer and the employee (exception: accident insurance). Still, the employer transfers both parts to the competent collecting agency as a so-called total social security contribution, sec. 28e para. 1 sent. 1 SGB IV.

689   The employer subsequently has an entitlement to that part of the total social security contribution to be borne by the employee, sec. 28g sent. 1 SGB IV. According to sec. 28g sent. 2 SGB IV, however, this entitlement can only be asserted by deducting the employee's part of the contribution from future remuneration. Moreover, sec. 28g sent. 3 SGB IV, stipulates that such a deduction can regularly only be made for the next three salary payments. If the employment relationship has already ended, the possibility of deducting salary no longer exists. The employer then bears the burden of paying the total social security contribution on his own. Especially in the case of a false self-employed person's long-term employment, the possibilities of "recourse" are extremely limited.

690   In the German social security law, the so-called principle of origin ("Entstehungsprinzip") applies (sec. 22 para. 1 SGB IV, see marginal no. **431**). According to this principle, social security contributions are to be paid not only for those salary components which the employee actually received, but the employer must also (subsequently) pay contributions for all unpaid salary components. For example, this also applies to time-barred, forfeited remuneration or bonuses, as a claim has arisen during the employment time.

691   According to sec. 1 para. 3 SchwarzArbG, and sec. 14 para. 2 sent. 2 SGB IV, the basis for assessing the subsequent contributions is regularly the net remuneration. This means that the remuneration paid to the false self-employed person is regarded as net remuneration. On this basis, the amount of a fictitious gross remuneration is then calculated, which is used to determine the amount of social security contributions to be paid subsequently. For example, if the principal has paid the amount of EUR 2,500 for the work performed by the service provider, this can quickly result in a notional net salary of more than EUR 5,000; on this basis, the amount of the social security contributions to be paid subsequently by the principal is about approximately EUR 1,900.

692   Moreover, interests on arrears of 1 % per month may also have to be paid (sec. 24 para. 1 sent. 1 SGB IV). This applies to all contributions that have not been paid in the past, unless the employer can credibly show that he was not aware of the payment obligation without any fault of his own (sec. 24 para. 2 SGB IV).

693   Subsequent demands for contributions thus represent a risk for undertakings which should not be underestimated and, in the worst case, which could endanger their exist-

ence. One must also take the often very long duration of proceedings before the German Social Security Courts into account, which can lead to a long period of legal uncertainty.

bb) Criminal Law Consequences: Withholding of Remuneration. Furthermore, the misjudgement can also lead to serious criminal consequences for the parties involved. **694**

According to sec. 266a StGB, the employer may be liable to prosecution for withholding remuneration. Concerning the prerequisites and consequences, reference is made to the above statements (see marginal no. **436** et seq.). The only difference is that the employer did not fail to pay a part of the social security contribution due but did not pay contributions at all. **695**

c) Tax Law

aa) Principle. The incorrect legal assessment of their cooperation also results in far-reaching tax consequences for the parties involved. The treatment as a commissioned relationship between (seemingly) independent entrepreneurs results in the fact that remuneration is being paid to the principal through an invoice. In this case, the VAT is regularly stated on the invoice by the false self-employed person and paid to the respective tax office upon receipt. The principal, for his part, registers the paid VAT as input tax ("Vorsteuer") in his value-added tax return ("Umsatzsteuererklärung"). Therefore, the incorrect. Besides, the false self-employed person has declared his income incorrectly as from self-employment (sec. 18 EStG) or commercial activity (sec. 15 EStG). **696**

Deliberately evaded taxes can be assessed ten years after their due date, while negligently evaded taxes may be assessed within five years (sec. 169 para. 2 sent. 2 AO). **697**

(1) Wage Tax. If the legal classification had been correct, the income would be treated as income from non-independent employment (sec. 19 EStG). Like the mechanism in social security law, the employer would have had to pay the wage tax due to the competent tax office by deducting it from the employee (sec. 38 para. 1 EStG). In this context, the employee is indeed the original debtor of the wage tax (sec. 38 para. 2 sent. 1 EStG). However, the employer is, additionlally, fully a jointly and severally liable debtor for the tax office's claims for subsequent wage tax demands against the false self-employed person (sec. 42d para. 1 sent. 1 no. 1 and para. 3 sent. 1 EStG). However, in contrast to the consequences of subsequent payment of social security contributions, the effects of a failure to deduct wage tax are generally not as severe. This is because the false self-employed person himself regularly paid taxes to the respective tax office in the past within the scope of his self-employed or commercial business activity. The effects of the previously omitted wage tax deduction are therefore mostly limited to cases in which taxes had not (yet) been paid in a sufficient amount or the amount of the deductible items to be taken into account changes because of a different allocation of the income received by the service provider. **698**

(2) Value Added Tax (VAT). There are also consequences for both parties in connection with the processing of VAT. The false self-employed person is not an entrepreneur within the meaning of sec. 2 UStG because his work is not performed independently. Therefore, the invoices issued by him do not fulfill the legal invoice requirements according to sec. 14 para. 4 UStG. As a result, the false self-employed person is liable for the amount of value-added tax wrongly shown in his invoices, even if he mistakenly considered himself a self-employed entrepreneur (sec. 14c para. 2 UStG). The false self-employed person cannot deduct input tax at a reduced rate. As a non-entrepreneur, he was not entitled to deduct either business expenses or input tax under sec. 15 UStG. The VAT returns must therefore be corrected, and considerable additional claims may arise. **699**

On the other hand, the employer is not entitled to claim the turnover tax invoiced to him by the false self-employed person as input tax. If an input tax deduction has already **700** been made, the tax office will reverse it. This is a consequence of the lack of entrepreneurial status on the false self-employed person, even though the false self-employed person still has to pay the reported turnover tax to the respective tax office.

(3) Commercial Tax

701   Commercial tax assessments already issued are revoked by the tax office or the municipal office as a result of the amendment to the tax assessment notices. Only insofar as the false self-employed person was allegedly engaged in commercial activities before his dependent employment relationship was discovered. Commercial tax already paid will be refunded.

bb) Criminal Law Consequences: Tax Evasion

702   The misjudgments of the parties involved do not only have the tax implications mentioned above. The misjudgment in tax regulations can also lead to severe consequences under criminal tax law for those involved. A tax evasion within the scope of sec. 370 AO is possible.

703   Concerning wage tax, the false self-employed person and the employer can only conduct tax evasion. Only if deductions lead to taxable income changes. Besides that, the risk of VAT evasion through unjustified input tax deduction may arise for both of them. Concerning the prerequisites and consequences, reference is made to the previous explanations under marginal no. **449** et seq.).

704   Regarding the submission of input tax returns, the false self-employed person and the employer submit an incorrect declaration. If the submission was made without intent, it can be corrected subsequently – without committing a criminal offence – sec. 153 AO. The correction of the declaration must be made immediately, and the respective adjustments must be performed. Suppose the employer or the false self-employed person recognises the incorrectness retrospectively and both do not carry out any correction according to sec. 153 AO. In that case, they act intentionally from this point in time at the latest, so that tax evasion is possible in this regard.

705   In the event of tax evasion, not only the evaded tax is to be paid. Moreover, interests on evasion and the subsequently paid tax have also to be paid (sec. 233a AO and sec. 235 AO). Concerning the opportunities, but also the risks of a self-denunciation exempting from penalties, reference is also made to the above statements (see again margin no. **449** et seq.).

d) Administrative Offences Law

706   **aa) Administrative Offences Law under the SchwarzArbG.** If the employer does not pay the social security contributions due according to sec. 266a StGB intentionally, but only negligently, the commission of an administrative offence according to sec. 8 SchwarzArbG, can be possible. Reference is made to the previous explanations (see margin no. **458** et seq.).

707   **bb) Administrative Offences Law under the AO.** If taxes are not paid intentionally but only carelessly, this can be punished according to sec. 378 AO. Reference is made to the above explanations (see margin no. **461** et seq.).

708   **cc) Administrative Offences Law under the Administrative Offences Act.** Finally, administrative offences from the OWiG come into consideration. Except for the explanations on the AÜG, the above explanations apply likewise (see margin no. **463** et seq.).

e) Regulatory

709   Besides, the law's violations in connection with cases of false self-employment may result in further indirect consequences from a regulatory perspective. The regulatory

consequences are sometimes far-reaching and should never be underestimated (see margin no **381** et seq. and **467**).

f) Corporate Law Responsibility and Recourse

Regarding corporate law responsibilities, reference can also be made to the statements **710** above on the incorrectly or the fully concealed temporary agency employment (see in detail marginal no. **530** et seq.).

g) Secondary Liability Risks and Opportunities

aa) Direct Claims against Executive Directors by Governmental Authorities

(1) Claims in the Framework of Social Security Law. Under the German social security **711** legislation, only the employer is entitled and obliged to pay the social security contributions. If the employer is a legal entity, this remains the case even if its legal representatives, for example managers or management boards, carelessly or intentionally withhold contributions from the social security authorities. A public-legal adhesion of the responsible persons, as known in the tax law within the scope of sections 69 AO following (see below for details), does not exist within the social security legislation. In this case, a liability notice issued by a collecting agency against a managing director would therefore be illegitimate due to a lack of a legal basis.

However, this does not release the managing directors from any liability. Instead, **712** the collecting agencies may take recourse to the managers in civil court proceedings under sec. 823 para. 2 BGB in conjunction with sec. 14 para. 1 no. 1 StGB, and sec. 266a para. 1 StGB, and thereby hold themselves harmless. In contrast to public law, however, the collecting agencies are not entitled during civil court proceedings to make legally effective determinations vis-à-vis the managers through administrative acts issued by them. On the contrary, in civil court proceedings, the plaintiff authorities must prove all facts favourable to them within the scope of their asserted claim. This applies exemplarily to the intentional behaviour of the managers and to any damage caused by their actions in particular. However, damage to the respective authorities is unlikely to occur when employee's social security contributions have been paid subsequently.

Therefore, correcting one's own mistakes as well as mistakes made by possible prede- **713** cessors in the office considerably reduces liability risks. The responsibility of the managers commences with their effective appointment. There is no attribution of previous managers' conduct. Still, the manager is also liable for employee contributions to social insurance that became due before he took office if he does not pay the contributions after his appointment and thus continues to withhold them. The liability is not limited to the area of responsibility of the respective manager. Suppose a manager in a group company with divided management is exclusively concerned with technical and scientific issues. In that case, he still has obligations to monitor under his "all-around responsibility". These must prompt him to intervene if there are indications that the fulfilment of the tasks incumbent on the company's responsible manager is no longer guaranteed. Therefore, the internal rules of competence, as well as the delegation of tasks do not exclude the manager's responsibility.[34]

The liability is limited to the employee's share of the total social security contribution, **714** plus the authorities' costs incurred as a result of their legal action, and default interest and interest payable as from the commencement of proceedings, but not interest on arrears. In many cases, the liability sums in question, therefore threaten the existence of the persons concerned.

---

[34] Federal Court of Justice, 18 December 2012 – II ZR 220/10.

715   *(2) Claims in the Framework of Tax Law.* Managers are also directly liable to the tax authorities according to sec. 69 AO for claims which the authorities actually have against the employer. The managers are fully liable to the tax authorities hereafter. Only as far as claims from the employer's obligation under tax liability, resulting from intentional or grossly negligent violation of the manager's obligations, are not or not timely determined or fulfilled, or as far as tax refunds have been paid without legal reason. This liability also includes the interests on arrears as a result of the breach of obligation.

716   Thus, sec. 69 AO constitutes an obligation for managers to be liable for the employer's tax liability with their assets by public-law. The purpose of this liability is to compensate tax losses, which were caused by culpable breach of obligation of those persons. Consequently, sec. 69 AO is a claim for damages by the state.

bb) Recourse. In individual cases, the employer also has the possibility of compensating, at least in part, for financial losses caused by the employment of false self-employed persons through a recourse.

717   *(1) Differences between the Remunerations.* In the false self-employed person case, it is possible to claim compensation for the difference between the actual remuneration received and the hypothetically owed salary accordingt to sec. 812 para. 1 BGB.[35] In false self-employment cases, the false self-employed person has not rendered his services in a self-employed manner but within the framework of an employment relationship.

718   The remuneration that self-employed persons usually receive for services rendered is higher than the remuneration that employees would receive for the same activity. This is because the remuneration of persons performing self-employed activities under a contract to produce a work or service contract typically intends to cover risks that a self-employed person, unlike an employee, has to bear himself. On the one hand, this concerns risks against which the statutory social security system covers employees. On the other hand, it should be borne in mind that self-employed persons are also significantly less protected than employees regarding the loss of their entitlement to remuneration in the absence from work. For example, they are not entitled to minimum paid leave, holiday pay, or continued remuneration in the event of illness. Furthermore, many employee protection provisions, such as the Dismissal Protection Act, do not apply to self-employed persons and they do not benefit from the principles of limited employee liability and the privileges associated with it. Due to the coverage of these risks, the self-employed person's remuneration is usually higher than that of an employee.

719   In the absence of any particular indications, it cannot be assumed that the remuneration agreed between the parties (for the alleged self-employment) should also be applicable (in the actually existing employment relationship) as gross remuneration. Only in exceptional cases, which must be presented and proven by the employee, this may be otherwise.

720   The employer is, therefore, in principle, entitled to reclaim the amount in between. However, this does not apply if the employer was aware of the employee status as a false self-employed person.

721   Having said this, the practical enforcement of such claims for reimbursement can cause considerable difficulties. For example, the employer is obliged to prove how high the false self-employed person's remuneration would have been if he had carried out his work as an employee of the employer. In this regard, the courts require precise evidence. If such evidence cannot be provided, for example, because the employer employs no comparable employees, expert opinions must be obtained.

---

[35] Federal Labour Court, 26 June 2019 – 5 AZR 178/18.

(2) Wage Tax. Besides, recourse is conceivable in cases where the tax office has made   **722** a claim against the employer to the amount of the outstanding wage tax. The employer and employee are jointly and severally liable debtors for the wage tax (sec. 42d para. 3 sent. 1 EStG). Therefore, at the discretion of the tax authority from which debtor, the out- standing amount is collected. In contrast to the social security law (see marginal no. **689**), the employer may fully recourse against the employee concerning the subsequently paid wage tax. This follows from the employee's position as the original debtor of the wage tax according to sec. 38 para. 2 sent. 1 EStG and the internal relationship of the jointly and severally liable debtors according to sec. 426 para. 2 sent. 1 BGB. Under these provisions, the jointly and severally liable debtor who makes a payment to the creditor is, in principle, entitled to demand compensation for his expenses from the indemnified debtor.

IV. Checklist Dependent Employment vs. Self-Employment

1. Criteria that speak *in favour* of an integration

a)   the agent can perform his duties only by using the work material/machinery of the principal;
b)   the agent has to participate in principal's team meetings;
c)   the agent does not have its business facilities, business cards, letterheads, etc.;
d)   the agent is (obliged to be) present at the principal's business site;
e)   the agent acts externally in the name of the principal;
f)   the agent performs services for the account of the principal;
g)   the agent collects the principal's invoices from the principal's customers for payments to be made to the principal;
h)   the agent is included in the principal's duty roster (without the assignments having been agreed in advance);
i)   the agent has previously carried out the same activities as an employee of the principal;
j)   the principal has employees who carry out the same activities as the agent;
k)   the principal expects constant availability of service;
l)   the agent is called in to perform tasks to a considerable extent without any upfront agreement in this regard (tasks are effectively „assigned" to him);
m) no independent range of tasks is assigned to the service provider from which the respective requirements, and the self-responsibility of the service performed could be taken;
n)   the agent is not allowed or does actually not have the opportunity to perform his services for other principals;
o)   The agent is obliged to take over representations of the principal's employees, e. g., in cases of illness;
p)   the principal keeps a personal file of the agent.

2. Criteria that speak *in favour* of a binding by instructions

a)   the principal has the right to give instructions to the agent regarding the place and time of the performance owed (specification of place/time of work; obligation to re- cord time, if not only required for invoicing);
b)   the principal instructs the agent on how to carry out the tasks assigned;
c)   the agent has no possibility of delegation to other persons/he must perform „in-per- son"; no or rare use of the possibility of delegation despite legal existence;
d)   the agent must precisely document his activities for the principal

e) the agent is obliged to accept assignments from the principal;
f) the agent is obliged to use certain hardware and software, with which, in particular, monitoring opportunities in favour of the principal are linked;
g) low degree of flexibility for the agent, far-reaching content instructions by the principal;
h) the principal carries out regular (quality) checks on the tasks performed by the agent before the end of the contractual period;
i) the principal may assign an activity to the agent that differs from the activities stipulated in the agreement;
j) specification of the principal regarding the working material to be used by the agent (painting the car to be used with the logo of the principal).

3. Criteria that speak *against* an own business risk

a) the agent receives a recurring remuneration/the remuneration is always paid in the same amount/the remuneration is also paid without specific counter-performance (no risk of completely unsuccessful use of own material and personnel resources on the part of the agent);
b) the remuneration is mostly not performance-related;
c) the agreement between the agent and principal refers to the remuneration as a „wage" and not as a honorarium;
d) the agent has not negotiated his remuneration individually (conclusion of a model contract used by the principal);
e) the agent's remuneration is significantly lower than the usual remuneration of a self-employed person in this sector;
f) the agent is entitled to receive assignments from the principal;
g) the agent receives compensation in the event of illness and vacation;
h) the agent is subject to wage tax liability (to be clarified, if necessary, via an enquiry with the competent authority);
i) the agent does not charge any costs for the use of his own resources or the necessary travel expenses

PART 2
„LEGAL TEXTS"

I. Directive 2008/104/EC of the European Parliament and of the Concil on temporary agency work

Richtlinie 2008/104/EG des Europäischen Parlaments und des Rates vom 19. November 2008 über Leiharbeit

Stand: 19.11.2008

DAS EUROPÄISCHE PARLAMENT UND DER RAT DER EUROPÄISCHEN UNION

gestützt auf den Vertrag zur Gründung der Europäischen Gemeinschaft, insbesondere auf Artikel 137 Absatz 2,

auf Vorschlag der Kommission,

nach Stellungnahme des Europäischen Wirtschafts- und Sozialausschusses,

nach Anhörung des Ausschusses der Regionen,

gemäß dem Verfahren des Artikels 251 des Vertrags (2),

in Erwägung nachstehender Gründe:

THE EUROPEAN PARLIAMENT AND THE COUNCIL OF THE EUROPEAN UNION,

Having regard to the Treaty establishing the European Community, and in particular Article 137(2) thereof,

Having regard to the proposal from the Commission,

Having regard to the opinion of the European Economic and Social Committee,

After consulting the Committee of the Regions,

Acting in accordance with the procedure laid down in Article 251 of the Treaty,

Whereas:

(1) Diese Richtlinie steht im Einklang mit den Grundrechten und befolgt die in der Charta der Grundrechte der Europäischen Union anerkannten Prinzipien (3). Sie soll insbesondere die uneingeschränkte Einhaltung von Artikel 31 der Charta gewährleisten, wonach jede Arbeitnehmerin und jeder Arbeitnehmer das Recht auf gesunde, sichere und würdige Arbeitsbedingungen sowie auf eine Begrenzung der Höchstarbeitszeit, auf tägliche und wöchentliche Ruhezeiten sowie auf bezahlten Jahresurlaub hat.

(2) Nummer 7 der Gemeinschaftscharta der sozialen Grundrechte der Arbeitnehmer sieht unter anderem vor, dass die Verwirklichung des Binnenmarktes zu einer Verbesserung der Lebens- und Arbeitsbedingungen der Arbeitnehmer in der Europäischen Gemeinschaft führen muss; dieser Prozess erfolgt durch eine Angleichung dieser Bedingungen auf dem Wege des Fortschritts und betrifft namentlich Arbeitsformen wie das befristete Arbeitsverhältnis, Teilzeitarbeit, Leiharbeit und Saisonarbeit.

(3) Die Kommission hat die Sozialpartner auf Gemeinschaftsebene am 27. September 1995 gemäß Artikel 138 Absatz 2 des Vertrags zu einem Tätigwerden auf Gemeinschaftsebene hinsichtlich der Flexibilität der Arbeitszeit und der Arbeitsplatzsicherheit gehört.

(4) Da die Kommission nach dieser Anhörung eine Gemeinschaftsaktion für zweckmäßig hielt, hat sie die Sozialpartner am 9. April 1996 erneut gemäß Artikel 138 Absatz 3 des Vertrags zum Inhalt des in Aussicht genommenen Vorschlags gehört.

(5) In der Präambel zu der am 18. März 1999 geschlossenen Rahmenvereinbarung über befristete Arbeitsverträge bekundeten die Unterzeichneten ihre Absicht, die Notwendigkeit einer ähnlichen Vereinbarung zum Thema Leiharbeit zu prüfen und entschieden, Leiharbeitnehmer nicht in der Richtlinie über befristete Arbeitsverträge zu behandeln.

(6) Die allgemeinen branchenübergreifenden Wirtschaftsverbände, nämlich die Union der Industrie- und Arbeitgeberverbände Europas (UNICE) (4), der Europäische Zentralverband der öffentlichen Wirtschaft (CEEP) und der Europäische Gewerkschaftsbund (EGB), haben der Kommission in einem gemeinsamen Schreiben vom 29. Mai 2000 mitgeteilt, dass sie den Prozess nach Artikel 139 des Vertrags in Gang setzen wollen. Sie haben die Kommission in einem weiteren gemeinsamen Schreiben vom 28. Februar 2001 um eine Verlängerung der in Artikel 138 Absatz 4 genannten Frist um einen Monat ersucht. Die Kommission hat dieser Bitte entsprochen und die Verhandlungsfrist bis zum 15. März 2001 verlängert.

(1) This Directive respects the fundamental rights and complies with the principles recognised by the Charter of Fundamental Rights of the European Union. In particular, it is designed to ensure full compliance with Article 31 of the Charter, which provides that every worker has the right to working conditions which respect his or her health, safety and dignity, and to limitation of maximum working hours, to daily and weekly rest periods and to an annual period of paid leave.

(2) The Community Charter of the Fundamental Social Rights of Workers provides, in point 7 thereof, *inter alia*, that the completion of the internal market must lead to an improvement in the living and working conditions of workers in the European Community; this process will be achieved by harmonising progress on these conditions, mainly in respect of forms of work such as fixed-term contract work, part-time work, temporary agency work and seasonal work.

(3) On 27 September 1995, the Commission consulted management and labour at Community level in accordance with Article 138(2) of the Treaty on the course of action to be adopted at Community level with regard to flexibility of working hours and job security of workers.

(4) After that consultation, the Commission considered that Community action was advisable and on 9 April 1996, further consulted management and labour in accordance with Article 138(3) of the Treaty on the content of the envisaged proposal.

(5) In the introduction to the framework agreement on fixed-term work concluded on 18 March 1999, the signatories indicated their intention to consider the need for a similar agreement on temporary agency work and decided not to include temporary agency workers in the Directive on fixed-term work.

(6) The general cross-sector organisations, namely the Union of Industrial and Employers' Confederations of Europe (UNICE), the European Centre of Enterprises with Public Participation and of Enterprises of General Economic Interest (CEEP) and the European Trade Union Confederation (ETUC), informed the Commission in a joint letter of 29 May 2000 of their wish to initiate the process provided for in Article 139 of the Treaty. By a further joint letter of 28 February 2001, they asked the Commission to extend the deadline referred to in Article 138(4) by one month. The Commission granted this request and extended the negotiation deadline until 15 March 2001.

(7) Am 21. Mai 2001 erkannten die Sozialpartner an, dass ihre Verhandlungen über Leiharbeit zu keinem Ergebnis geführt hatten.

(8) Der Europäische Rat hat es im März 2005 für unabdingbar gehalten, der Lissabon-Strategie neue Impulse zu geben und ihre Prioritäten erneut auf Wachstum und Beschäftigung auszurichten. Der Rat hat die Integrierten Leitlinien für Wachstum und Beschäftigung (2005-2008) angenommen, die unter gebührender Berücksichtigung der Rolle der Sozialpartner unter anderem der Förderung von Flexibilität in Verbindung mit Beschäftigungssicherheit und der Verringerung der Segmentierung des Arbeitsmarktes dienen sollen.

(9) Im Einklang mit der Mitteilung der Kommission zur sozialpolitischen Agenda für den Zeitraum bis 2010, die vom Europäischen Rat im März 2005 als Beitrag zur Verwirklichung der Ziele der Lissabon-Strategie durch Stärkung des europäischen Sozialmodells begrüßt wurde, hat der Europäische Rat die Ansicht vertreten, dass auf Seiten der Arbeitnehmer und der Unternehmen neue Formen der Arbeitsorganisation und eine größere Vielfalt der Arbeitsverträge mit besserer Kombination von Flexibilität und Sicherheit zur Anpassungsfähigkeit beitragen würden. Im Dezember 2007 hat der Europäische Rat darüber hinaus die vereinbarten gemeinsamen Flexicurity-Grundsätze gebilligt, die auf ein ausgewogenes Verhältnis zwischen Flexibilität und Sicherheit auf dem Arbeitsmarkt abstellen und sowohl Arbeitnehmern als auch Arbeitgebern helfen sollen, die durch die Globalisierung gebotenen Chancen zu nutzen.

(10) In Bezug auf die Inanspruchnahme der Leiharbeit sowie die rechtliche Stellung, den Status und die Arbeitsbedingungen der Leiharbeitnehmer lassen sich innerhalb der Union große Unterschiede feststellen.

(11) Die Leiharbeit entspricht nicht nur dem Flexibilitätsbedarf der Unternehmen, sondern auch dem Bedürfnis der Arbeitnehmer, Beruf und Privatleben zu vereinbaren. Sie trägt somit zur Schaffung von Arbeitsplätzen und zur Teilnahme am und zur Eingliederung in den Arbeitsmarkt bei.

(12) Die vorliegende Richtlinie legt einen diskriminierungsfreien, transparenten und verhältnismäßigen Rahmen zum Schutz der Leiharbeitnehmer fest und wahrt gleichzeitig die Vielfalt der Arbeitsmärkte und der Arbeitsbeziehungen.

(7) On 21 May 2001, the social partners acknowledged that their negotiations on temporary agency work had not produced any agreement.

(8) In March 2005, the European Council considered it vital to relaunch the Lisbon Strategy and to refocus its priorities on growth and employment. The Council approved the Integrated Guidelines for Growth and Jobs 2005-2008, which seek, *inter alia*, to promote flexibility combined with employment security and to reduce labour market segmentation, having due regard to the role of the social partners.

(9) In accordance with the Communication from the Commission on the Social Agenda covering the period up to 2010, which was welcomed by the March 2005 European Council as a contribution towards achieving the Lisbon Strategy objectives by reinforcing the European social model, the European Council considered that new forms of work organisation and a greater diversity of contractual arrangements for workers and businesses, better combining flexibility with security, would contribute to adaptability. Furthermore, the December 2007 European Council endorsed the agreed common principles of flexicurity, which strike a balance between flexibility and security in the labour market and help both workers and employers to seize the opportunities offered by globalisation.

(10) There are considerable differences in the use of temporary agency work and in the legal situation, status and working conditions of temporary agency workers within the European Union.

(11) Temporary agency work meets not only undertakings' needs for flexibility but also the need of employees to reconcile their working and private lives. It thus contributes to job creation and to participation and integration in the labour market.

(12) This Directive establishes a protective framework for temporary agency workers which is non-discriminatory, transparent and proportionate, while respecting the diversity of labour markets and industrial relations.

(13) Die Richtlinie 91/383/EWG des Rates vom 25. Juni 1991 zur Ergänzung der Maßnahmen zur Verbesserung der Sicherheit und des Gesundheitsschutzes von Arbeitnehmern mit befristetem Arbeitsverhältnis oder Leiharbeitsverhältnis (5) enthält die für Leiharbeitnehmer geltenden Bestimmungen im Bereich von Sicherheit und Gesundheitsschutz am Arbeitsplatz.

(14) Die wesentlichen Arbeits- und Beschäftigungsbedingungen für Leiharbeitnehmer sollten mindestens denjenigen entsprechen, die für diese Arbeitnehmer gelten würden, wenn sie von dem entleihenden Unternehmen für den gleichen Arbeitsplatz eingestellt würden.

(15) Unbefristete Arbeitsverträge sind die übliche Form des Beschäftigungsverhältnisses. Im Falle von Arbeitnehmern, die einen unbefristeten Vertrag mit dem Leiharbeitsunternehmen geschlossen haben, sollte angesichts des hierdurch gegebenen besonderen Schutzes die Möglichkeit vorgesehen werden, von den im entleihenden Unternehmen geltenden Regeln abzuweichen.

(16) Um der Vielfalt der Arbeitsmärkte und der Arbeitsbeziehungen auf flexible Weise gerecht zu werden, können die Mitgliedstaaten den Sozialpartnern gestatten, Arbeits- und Beschäftigungsbedingungen festzulegen, sofern das Gesamtschutzniveau für Leiharbeitnehmer gewahrt bleibt.

(17) Außerdem sollten die Mitgliedstaaten unter bestimmten, genau festgelegten Umständen auf der Grundlage einer zwischen den Sozialpartnern auf nationaler Ebene geschlossenen Vereinbarung vom Grundsatz der Gleichbehandlung in beschränktem Maße abweichen dürfen, sofern ein angemessenes Schutzniveau gewährleistet ist.

(18) Die Verbesserung des Mindestschutzes der Leiharbeitnehmer sollte mit einer Überprüfung der Einschränkungen oder Verbote einhergehen, die möglicherweise in Bezug auf Leiharbeit gelten. Diese können nur aus Gründen des Allgemeininteresses, vor allem des Arbeitnehmerschutzes, der Erfordernisse von Gesundheitsschutz und Sicherheit am Arbeitsplatz und der Notwendigkeit, das reibungslose Funktionieren des Arbeitsmarktes zu gewährleisten und eventuellen Missbrauch zu verhüten, gerechtfertigt sein.

(19) Die vorliegende Richtlinie beeinträchtigt weder die Autonomie der Sozialpartner, noch sollte sie die Beziehungen zwischen den Sozialpartnern beeinträchtigen, einschließlich des Rechts, Tarifverträge gemäß nationalem Recht und nationalen Gepflogenheiten bei gleichzeitiger Einhaltung des geltenden Gemeinschaftsrechts auszuhandeln und zu schließen.

(13) Council Directive 91/383/EEC of 25 June 1991 supplementing the measures to encourage improvements in the safety and health at work of workers with a fixed-duration employment relationship or a temporary employment relationship establishes the safety and health provisions applicable to temporary agency workers.

(14) The basic working and employment conditions applicable to temporary agency workers should be at least those which would apply to such workers if they were recruited by the user undertaking to occupy the same job.

(15) Employment contracts of an indefinite duration are the general form of employment relationship. In the case of workers who have a permanent contract with their temporary-work agency, and in view of the special protection such a contract offers, provision should be made to permit exemptions from the rules applicable in the user undertaking.

(16) In order to cope in a flexible way with the diversity of labour markets and industrial relations, Member States may allow the social partners to define working and employment conditions, provided that the overall level of protection for temporary agency workers is respected.

(17) Furthermore, in certain limited circumstances, Member States should, on the basis of an agreement concluded by the social partners at national level, be able to derogate within limits from the principle of equal treatment, so long as an adequate level of protection is provided.

(18) The improvement in the minimum protection for temporary agency workers should be accompanied by a review of any restrictions or prohibitions which may have been imposed on temporary agency work. These may be justified only on grounds of the general interest regarding, in particular the protection of workers, the requirements of safety and health at work and the need to ensure that the labour market functions properly and that abuses are prevented.

(19) This Directive does not affect the autonomy of the social partners nor should it affect relations between the social partners, including the right to negotiate and conclude collective agreements in accordance with national law and practices while respecting prevailing Community law.

(20) Die in dieser Richtlinie enthaltenen Bestimmungen über Einschränkungen oder Verbote der Beschäftigung von Leiharbeitnehmern lassen die nationalen Rechtsvorschriften und Gepflogenheiten unberührt, die es verbieten, streikende Arbeitnehmer durch Leiharbeitnehmer zu ersetzen.

(21) Die Mitgliedstaaten sollten für Verstöße gegen die Verpflichtungen aus dieser Richtlinie Verwaltungs- oder Gerichtsverfahren zur Wahrung der Rechte der Leiharbeitnehmer sowie wirksame, abschreckende und verhältnismäßige Sanktionen vorsehen.

(22) Die vorliegende Richtlinie sollte im Einklang mit den Vorschriften des Vertrags über die Dienstleistungs- und Niederlassungsfreiheit, und unbeschadet der Richtlinie 96/71/EG des Europäischen Parlaments und des Rates vom 16. Dezember 1996 über die Entsendung von Arbeitnehmern im Rahmen der Erbringung von Dienstleistungen (6) umgesetzt werden.

(23) Da das Ziel dieser Richtlinie, nämlich die Schaffung eines auf Gemeinschaftsebene harmonisierten Rahmens zum Schutz der Leiharbeitnehmer, auf Ebene der Mitgliedstaaten nicht ausreichend verwirklicht werden kann und daher wegen des Umfangs und der Wirkungen der Maßnahme besser auf Gemeinschaftsebene zu verwirklichen ist, und zwar durch Einführung von Mindestvorschriften, die in der gesamten Europäischen Gemeinschaft Geltung besitzen, kann die Gemeinschaft im Einklang mit dem in Artikel 5 des Vertrags niedergelegten Subsidiaritätsprinzip tätig werden. Entsprechend dem in demselben Artikel genannten Grundsatz der Verhältnismäßigkeit geht diese Richtlinie nicht über das zur Erreichung dieses Ziels erforderliche Maß hinaus

HABEN FOLGENDE RICHTLINIE ERLASSEN:

(20) The provisions of this Directive on restrictions or prohibitions on temporary agency work are without prejudice to national legislation or practices that prohibit workers on strike being replaced by temporary agency workers.

(21) Member States should provide for administrative or judicial procedures to safeguard temporary agency workers' rights and should provide for effective, dissuasive and proportionate penalties for breaches of the obligations laid down in this Directive.

(22) This Directive should be implemented in compliance with the provisions of the Treaty regarding the freedom to provide services and the freedom of establishment and without prejudice to Directive 96/71/EC of the European Parliament and of the Council of 16 December 1996 concerning the posting of workers in the framework of the provision of services.

(23) Since the objective of this Directive, namely to establish a harmonised Community-level framework for protection for temporary agency workers, cannot be sufficiently achieved by the Member States and can therefore, by reason of the scale or effects of the action, be better achieved at Community level by introducing minimum requirements applicable throughout the Community, the Community may adopt measures in accordance with the principle of subsidiarity as set out in Article 5 of the Treaty. In accordance with the principle of proportionality, as set out in that Article, this Directive does not go beyond what is necessary in order to achieve that objective,

HAVE ADOPTED THIS DIRECTIVE:

Kapitel 1
Allgemeine Bestimmungen

Artikel 1
Anwendungsbereich

(1) Diese Richtlinie gilt für Arbeitnehmer, die mit einem Leiharbeitsunternehmen einen Arbeitsvertrag geschlossen haben oder ein Beschäftigungsverhältnis eingegangen sind und die entleihenden Unternehmen zur Verfügung gestellt werden, um vorübergehend unter deren Aufsicht und Leitung zu arbeiten.

Chapter 1
General provisions

Article 1
Scope

(1) This Directive applies to workers with a contract of employment or employment relationship with a temporary-work agency who are assigned to user undertakings to work temporarily under their supervision and direction.

(2) Diese Richtlinie gilt für öffentliche und private Unternehmen, bei denen es sich um Leiharbeitsunternehmen oder entleihende Unternehmen handelt, die eine wirtschaftliche Tätigkeit ausüben, unabhängig davon, ob sie Erwerbszwecke verfolgen oder nicht.

(3) Die Mitgliedstaaten können nach Anhörung der Sozialpartner vorsehen, dass diese Richtlinie nicht für Arbeitsverträge oder Beschäftigungsverhältnisse gilt, die im Rahmen eines spezifischen öffentlichen oder von öffentlichen Stellen geförderten beruflichen Ausbildungs-, Eingliederungs- und Umschulungsprogramms geschlossen wurden

(2) This Directive applies to public and private undertakings which are temporary-work agencies or user undertakings engaged in economic activities whether or not they are operating for gain.

(3) Member States may, after consulting the social partners, provide that this Directive does not apply to employment contracts or relationships concluded under a specific public or publicly supported vocational training, integration or retraining programme.

Artikel 2
Ziel

Ziel dieser Richtlinie ist es, für den Schutz der Leiharbeitnehmer zu sorgen und die Qualität der Leiharbeit zu verbessern, indem die Einhaltung des Grundsatzes der Gleichbehandlung von Leiharbeitnehmern gemäß Artikel 5 gesichert wird und die Leiharbeitsunternehmen als Arbeitgeber anerkannt werden, wobei zu berücksichtigen ist, dass ein angemessener Rahmen für den Einsatz von Leiharbeit festgelegt werden muss, um wirksam zur Schaffung von Arbeitsplätzen und zur Entwicklung flexibler Arbeitsformen beizutragen.

Article 2
Aim

The purpose of this Directive is to ensure the protection of temporary agency workers and to improve the quality of temporary agency work by ensuring that the principle of equal treatment, as set out in Article 5, is applied to temporary agency workers, and by recognising temporary-work agencies as employers, while taking into account the need to establish a suitable framework for the use of temporary agency work with a view to contributing effectively to the creation of jobs and to the development of flexible forms of working.

Artikel 3
Begriffsbestimmungen

(1) Im Sinne dieser Richtlinie bezeichnet der Ausdruck

(a) „Arbeitnehmer" eine Person, die in dem betreffenden Mitgliedstaat nach dem nationalen Arbeitsrecht als Arbeitnehmer geschützt ist;

(b) „Leiharbeitsunternehmen" eine natürliche oder juristische Person, die nach einzelstaatlichem Recht mit Leiharbeitnehmern Arbeitsverträge schließt oder Beschäftigungsverhältnisse eingeht, um sie entleihenden Unternehmen zu überlassen, damit sie dort unter deren Aufsicht und Leitung vorübergehend arbeiten;

(c) „Leiharbeitnehmer" einen Arbeitnehmer, der mit einem Leiharbeitsunternehmen einen Arbeitsvertrag geschlossen hat oder ein Beschäftigungsverhältnis eingegangen ist, um einem entleihenden Unternehmen überlassen zu werden und dort unter dessen Aufsicht und Leitung vorübergehend zu arbeiten

Article 3
Definitions

(1) For the purposes of this Directive:

(a) 'worker' means any person who, in the Member State concerned, is protected as a worker under national employment law;

(b) temporary-work agency' means any natural or legal person who, in compliance with national law, concludes contracts of employment or employment relationships with temporary agency workers in order to assign them to user undertakings to work there temporarily under their supervision and direction;

(c) 'temporary agency worker' means a worker with a contract of employment or an employment relationship with a temporary-work agency with a view to being assigned to a user undertaking to work temporarily under its supervision and direction;

(d) „entleihendes Unternehmen" eine natürliche oder juristische Person, in deren Auftrag und unter deren Aufsicht und Leitung ein Leiharbeitnehmer vorübergehend arbeitet;

(e) „Überlassung" den Zeitraum, während dessen der Leiharbeitnehmer dem entleihenden Unternehmen zur Verfügung gestellt wird, um dort unter dessen Aufsicht und Leitung vorübergehend zu arbeiten;

(f) „wesentliche Arbeits- und Beschäftigungsbedingungen" die Arbeits- und Beschäftigungsbedingungen, die durch Gesetz, Verordnung, Verwaltungsvorschrift, Tarifvertrag und/oder sonstige verbindliche Bestimmungen allgemeiner Art, die im entleihenden Unternehmen gelten, festgelegt sind und sich auf folgende Punkte beziehen:

(i) Dauer der Arbeitszeit, Überstunden, Pausen, Ruhezeiten, Nachtarbeit, Urlaub, arbeitsfreie Tage,

(ii) Arbeitsentgelt.

(2) Diese Richtlinie lässt das nationale Recht in Bezug auf die Begriffsbestimmungen von „Arbeitsentgelt", „Arbeitsvertrag", „Beschäftigungsverhältnis" oder „Arbeitnehmer" unberührt.

Die Mitgliedstaaten dürfen Arbeitnehmer, Arbeitsverträge oder Beschäftigungsverhältnisse nicht lediglich deshalb aus dem Anwendungsbereich dieser Richtlinie ausschließen, weil sie Teilzeitbeschäftigte, befristet beschäftigte Arbeitnehmer oder Personen sind bzw. betreffen, die mit einem Leiharbeitsunternehmen einen Arbeitsvertrag geschlossen haben oder ein Beschäftigungsverhältnis eingegangen sind.

(d) 'user undertaking' means any natural or legal person for whom and under the supervision and direction of whom a temporary agency worker works temporarily;

(e) 'assignment' means the period during which the temporary agency worker is placed at the user undertaking to work temporarily under its supervision and direction;

(f) basic working and employment conditions' means working and employment conditions laid down by legislation, regulations, administrative provisions, collective agreements and/or other binding general provisions in force in the user undertaking relating to:

(i) the duration of working time, overtime, breaks, rest periods, night work, holidays and public holidays;

(ii) pay.

(2) This Directive shall be without prejudice to national law as regards the definition of pay, contract of employment, employment relationship or worker.

Member States shall not exclude from the scope of this Directive workers, contracts of employment or employment relationships solely because they relate to part-time workers, fixed-term contract workers or persons with a contract of employment or employment relationship with a temporary-work agency.

Artikel 4
Überprüfung der Einschränkungen und Verbote

Article 4
Review of restrictions or prohibitions

(1) Verbote oder Einschränkungen des Einsatzes von Leiharbeit sind nur aus Gründen des Allgemeininteresses gerechtfertigt; hierzu zählen vor allem der Schutz der Leiharbeitnehmer, die Erfordernisse von Gesundheitsschutz und Sicherheit am Arbeitsplatz oder die Notwendigkeit, das reibungslose Funktionieren des Arbeitsmarktes zu gewährleisten und eventuellen Missbrauch zu verhüten.

(2) Nach Anhörung der Sozialpartner gemäß den nationalen Rechtsvorschriften, Tarifverträgen und Gepflogenheiten überprüfen die Mitgliedstaaten bis zum 5. Dezember 2011 die Einschränkungen oder Verbote des Einsatzes von Leiharbeit, um festzustellen, ob sie aus den in Absatz 1 genannten Gründen gerechtfertigt sind.

(1) Prohibitions or restrictions on the use of temporary agency work shall be justified only on grounds of general interest relating in particular to the protection of temporary agency workers, the requirements of health and safety at work or the need to ensure that the labour market functions properly and abuses are prevented.

(2) By 5 December 2011, Member States shall, after consulting the social partners in accordance with national legislation, collective agreements and practices, review any restrictions or prohibitions on the use of temporary agency work in order to verify whether they are justified on the grounds mentioned in paragraph 1.

(3) Sind solche Einschränkungen oder Verbote durch Tarifverträge festgelegt, so kann die Überprüfung gemäß Absatz 2 von denjenigen Sozialpartnern durchgeführt werden, die die einschlägige Vereinbarung ausgehandelt haben.

(4) Die Absätze 1, 2 und 3 gelten unbeschadet der nationalen Anforderungen hinsichtlich der Eintragung, Zulassung, Zertifizierung, finanziellen Garantie und Überwachung der Leiharbeitsunternehmen.

(5) Die Mitgliedstaaten informieren die Kommission über die Ergebnisse der Überprüfung gemäß den Absätzen 2 und 3 bis zum 5. Dezember 2011.

Kapitel 2
Arbeits- und Beschäftigungsbedingungen

Artikel 5
Grundsatz der Gleichbehandlung

(1) Die wesentlichen Arbeits- und Beschäftigungsbedingungen der Leiharbeitnehmer entsprechen während der Dauer ihrer Überlassung an ein entleihendes Unternehmen mindestens denjenigen, die für sie gelten würden, wenn sie von jenem genannten Unternehmen unmittelbar für den gleichen Arbeitsplatz eingestellt worden wären.

Bei der Anwendung von Unterabsatz 1 müssen die im entleihenden Unternehmen geltenden Regeln in Bezug auf

(a) den Schutz schwangerer und stillender Frauen und den Kinder- und Jugendschutz sowie
(b) die Gleichbehandlung von Männern und Frauen und sämtliche Maßnahmen zur Bekämpfung von Diskriminierungen aufgrund des Geschlechts, der Rasse oder der ethnischen Herkunft, der Religion oder Weltanschauung, einer Behinderung, des Alters oder der sexuellen Orientierung

so eingehalten werden, wie sie durch Gesetze, Verordnungen, Verwaltungsvorschriften, Tarifverträge und/oder sonstige Bestimmungen allgemeiner Art festgelegt sind.

(2) In Bezug auf das Arbeitsentgelt können die Mitgliedstaaten nach Anhörung der Sozialpartner die Möglichkeit vorsehen, dass vom Grundsatz des Absatzes 1 abgewichen wird, wenn Leiharbeitnehmer, die einen unbefristeten Vertrag mit dem Leiharbeitsunternehmen abgeschlossen haben, auch in der Zeit zwischen den Überlassungen bezahlt werden.

(3) If such restrictions or prohibitions are laid down by collective agreements, the review referred to in paragraph 2 may be carried out by the social partners who have negotiated the relevant agreement.

(4) Paragraphs 1, 2 and 3 shall be without prejudice to national requirements with regard to registration, licensing, certification, financial guarantees or monitoring of temporary-work agencies.

(5) The Member States shall inform the Commission of the results of the review referred to in paragraphs 2 and 3 by 5 December 2011.

Chapter 2
Employment and working cinditions

Article 5
The principle of equal treatment

(1) The basic working and employment conditions of temporary agency workers shall be, for the duration of their assignment at a user undertaking, at least those that would apply if they had been recruited directly by that undertaking to occupy the same job.

For the purposes of the application of the first subparagraph, the rules in force in the user undertaking on:

(a) protection of pregnant women and nursing mothers and protection of children and young people; and
(b) equal treatment for men and women and any action to combat any discrimination based on sex, race or ethnic origin, religion, beliefs, disabilities, age or sexual orientation;

must be complied with as established by legislation, regulations, administrative provisions, collective agreements and/or any other general provisions.

(2) As regards pay, Member States may, after consulting the social partners, provide that an exemption be made to the principle established in paragraph 1 where temporary agency workers who have a permanent contract of employment with a temporary-work agency continue to be paid in the time between assignments.

(3) Die Mitgliedstaaten können nach Anhörung der Sozialpartner diesen die Möglichkeit einräumen, auf der geeigneten Ebene und nach Maßgabe der von den Mitgliedstaaten festgelegten Bedingungen Tarifverträge aufrechtzuerhalten oder zu schließen, die unter Achtung des Gesamtschutzes von Leiharbeitnehmern Regelungen in Bezug auf die Arbeits- und Beschäftigungsbedingungen von Leiharbeitnehmern, welche von den in Absatz 1 aufgeführten Regelungen abweichen können, enthalten können.

(4) Sofern Leiharbeitnehmern ein angemessenes Schutzniveau gewährt wird, können Mitgliedstaaten, in denen es entweder kein gesetzliches System, durch das Tarifverträge allgemeine Gültigkeit erlangen, oder kein gesetzliches System bzw. keine Gepflogenheiten zur Ausweitung von deren Bestimmungen auf alle vergleichbaren Unternehmen in einem bestimmten Sektor oder bestimmten geografischen Gebiet gibt, — nach Anhörung der Sozialpartner auf nationaler Ebene und auf der Grundlage einer von ihnen geschlossenen Vereinbarung — Regelungen in Bezug auf die wesentlichen Arbeits- und Beschäftigungsbedingungen von Leiharbeitnehmern festlegen, die vom Grundsatz des Absatzes 1 abweichen. Zu diesen Regelungen kann auch eine Wartezeit für Gleichbehandlung zählen.

Die in diesem Absatz genannten Regelungen müssen mit den gemeinschaftlichen Bestimmungen in Einklang stehen und hinreichend präzise und leicht zugänglich sein, damit die betreffenden Sektoren und Firmen ihre Verpflichtungen bestimmen und einhalten können. Insbesondere müssen die Mitgliedstaaten in Anwendung des Artikels 3 Absatz 2 angeben, ob betriebliche Systeme der sozialen Sicherheit, einschließlich Rentensysteme, Systeme zur Lohnfortzahlung im Krankheitsfall oder Systeme der finanziellen Beteiligung, zu den in Absatz 1 genannten wesentlichen Arbeits- und Beschäftigungsbedingungen zählen. Solche Vereinbarungen lassen Vereinbarungen auf nationaler, regionaler, lokaler oder sektoraler Ebene, die für Arbeitnehmer nicht weniger günstig sind, unberührt.

(5) Die Mitgliedstaaten ergreifen die erforderlichen Maßnahmen gemäß ihren nationalen Rechtsvorschriften und/oder Gepflogenheiten, um eine missbräuchliche Anwendung dieses Artikels zu verhindern und um insbesondere aufeinander folgende Überlassungen, mit denen die Bestimmungen der Richtlinie umgangen werden sollen, zu verhindern. Sie unterrichten die Kommission über solche Maßnahmen.

(3) Member States may, after consulting the social partners, give them, at the appropriate level and subject to the conditions laid down by the Member States, the option of upholding or concluding collective agreements which, while respecting the overall protection of temporary agency workers, may establish arrangements concerning the working and employment conditions of temporary agency workers which may differ from those referred to in paragraph 1.

(4) Provided that an adequate level of protection is provided for temporary agency workers, Member States in which there is either no system in law for declaring collective agreements universally applicable or no such system in law or practice for extending their provisions to all similar undertakings in a certain sector or geographical area, may, after consulting the social partners at national level and on the basis of an agreement concluded by them, establish arrangements concerning the basic working and employment conditions which derogate from the principle established in paragraph 1. Such arrangements may include a qualifying period for equal treatment.

The arrangements referred to in this paragraph shall be in conformity with Community legislation and shall be sufficiently precise and accessible to allow the sectors and firms concerned to identify and comply with their obligations. In particular, Member States shall specify, in application of Article 3(2), whether occupational social security schemes, including pension, sick pay or financial participation schemes are included in the basic working and employment conditions referred to in paragraph 1. Such arrangements shall also be without prejudice to agreements at national, regional, local or sectoral level that are no less favourable to workers.

(5) Member States shall take appropriate measures, in accordance with national law and/or practice, with a view to preventing misuse in the application of this Article and, in particular, to preventing successive assignments designed to circumvent the provisions of this Directive. They shall inform the Commission about such measures.

Artikel 6
Zugang zu Beschäftigung, Gemeinschaftseinrichtungen und beruflicher Bildung

(1) Die Leiharbeitnehmer werden über die im entleihenden Unternehmen offenen Stellen unterrichtet, damit sie die gleichen Chancen auf einen unbefristeten Arbeitsplatz haben wie die übrigen Arbeitnehmer dieses Unternehmens. Diese Unterrichtung kann durch allgemeine Bekanntmachung an einer geeigneten Stelle in dem Unternehmen erfolgen, in dessen Auftrag und unter dessen Aufsicht die Leiharbeitnehmer arbeiten.

(2) Die Mitgliedstaaten ergreifen die erforderlichen Maßnahmen, damit Klauseln, die den Abschluss eines Arbeitsvertrags oder die Begründung eines Beschäftigungsverhältnisses zwischen dem entleihenden Unternehmen und dem Leiharbeitnehmer nach Beendigung seines Einsatzes verbieten oder darauf hinauslaufen, diese zu verhindern, nichtig sind oder für nichtig erklärt werden können.

Dieser Absatz lässt die Bestimmungen unberührt, aufgrund deren Leiharbeitsunternehmen für die dem entleihenden Unternehmen erbrachten Dienstleistungen in Bezug auf Überlassung, Einstellung und Ausbildung von Leiharbeitnehmern einen Ausgleich in angemessener Höhe erhalten.

(3) Leiharbeitsunternehmen dürfen im Gegenzug zur Überlassung an ein entleihendes Unternehmen oder in dem Fall, dass Arbeitnehmer nach beendigter Überlassung mit dem betreffenden entleihenden Unternehmen einen Arbeitsvertrag abschließen oder ein Beschäftigungsverhältnis eingehen, kein Entgelt von den Arbeitnehmern verlangen.

(4) Unbeschadet des Artikels 5 Absatz 1 haben Leiharbeitnehmer in dem entleihenden Unternehmen zu den gleichen Bedingungen wie die unmittelbar von dem Unternehmen beschäftigten Arbeitnehmer Zugang zu den Gemeinschaftseinrichtungen oder -diensten, insbesondere zur Gemeinschaftsverpflegung, zu Kinderbetreuungseinrichtungen und zu Beförderungsmitteln, es sei denn, eine unterschiedliche Behandlung ist aus objektiven Gründen gerechtfertigt.

(5) Die Mitgliedstaaten treffen die geeigneten Maßnahmen oder fördern den Dialog zwischen den Sozialpartnern nach ihren nationalen Traditionen und Gepflogenheiten mit dem Ziel,

Article 6
Access to employment, collective facilities and vocational training

(1) Temporary agency workers shall be informed of any vacant posts in the user undertaking to give them the same opportunity as other workers in that undertaking to find permanent employment. Such information may be provided by a general announcement in a suitable place in the undertaking for which, and under whose supervision, temporary agency workers are engaged.

(2) Member States shall take any action required to ensure that any clauses prohibiting or having the effect of preventing the conclusion of a contract of employment or an employment relationship between the user undertaking and the temporary agency worker after his assignment are null and void or may be declared null and void.

This paragraph is without prejudice to provisions under which temporary agencies receive a reasonable level of recompense for services rendered to user undertakings for the assignment, recruitment and training of temporary agency workers.

(3) Temporary-work agencies shall not charge workers any fees in exchange for arranging for them to be recruited by a user undertaking, or for concluding a contract of employment or an employment relationship with a user undertaking after carrying out an assignment in that undertaking.

(4) Without prejudice to Article 5(1), temporary agency workers shall be given access to the amenities or collective facilities in the user undertaking, in particular any canteen, child-care facilities and transport services, under the same conditions as workers employed directly by the undertaking, unless the difference in treatment is justified by objective reasons.

(5) Member States shall take suitable measures or shall promote dialogue between the social partners, in accordance with their national traditions and practices, in order to:

(a) den Zugang der Leiharbeitnehmer zu Fort- und Weiterbildungsangeboten und Kinderbetreuungseinrichtungen in den Leiharbeitsunternehmen — auch in der Zeit zwischen den Überlassungen — zu verbessern, um deren berufliche Entwicklung und Beschäftigungsfähigkeit zu fördern;

(b) den Zugang der Leiharbeitnehmer zu den Fort- und Weiterbildungsangeboten für die Arbeitnehmer der entleihenden Unternehmen zu verbessern.

(a) improve temporary agency workers' access to training and to child-care facilities in the temporary-work agencies, even in the periods between their assignments, in order to enhance their career development and employability;

(b) improve temporary agency workers' access to training for user undertakings' workers.

Artikel 7
Vertretung der Leiharbeitnehmer

Article 7
Representation of temporary agency workers

(1) Leiharbeitnehmer werden unter Bedingungen, die die Mitgliedstaaten festlegen, im Leiharbeitsunternehmen bei der Berechnung des Schwellenwertes für die Einrichtung der Arbeitnehmervertretungen berücksichtigt, die nach Gemeinschaftsrecht und nationalem Recht oder in den Tarifverträgen vorgesehen sind.

(2) Die Mitgliedstaaten können unter den von ihnen festgelegten Bedingungen vorsehen, dass Leiharbeitnehmer im entleihenden Unternehmen bei der Berechnung des Schwellenwertes für die Einrichtung der nach Gemeinschaftsrecht und nationalem Recht oder in den Tarifverträgen vorgesehenen Arbeitnehmervertretungen im gleichen Maße berücksichtigt werden wie Arbeitnehmer, die das entleihende Unternehmen für die gleiche Dauer unmittelbar beschäftigen würde.

(3) Die Mitgliedstaaten, die die Option nach Absatz 2 in Anspruch nehmen, sind nicht verpflichtet, Absatz 1 umzusetzen.

(1) Temporary agency workers shall count, under conditions established by the Member States, for the purposes of calculating the threshold above which bodies representing workers provided for under Community and national law and collective agreements are to be formed at the temporary-work agency.

(2) Member States may provide that, under conditions that they define, temporary agency workers count for the purposes of calculating the threshold above which bodies representing workers provided for by Community and national law and collective agreements are to be formed in the user undertaking, in the same way as if they were workers employed directly for the same period of time by the user undertaking.

(3) Those Member States which avail themselves of the option provided for in paragraph 2 shall not be obliged to implement the provisions of paragraph 1.

Artikel 8
Unterrichtung der Arbeitnehmer- vertreter

Article 8
Information of workers' representatives

Unbeschadet strengerer und/oder spezifischer einzelstaatlicher oder gemeinschaftlicher Vorschriften über Unterrichtung und Anhörung und insbesondere der Richtlinie 2002/14/EG des Europäischen Parlaments und des Rates vom 11. März 2002 zur Festlegung eines allgemeinen Rahmens für die Unterrichtung und Anhörung der Arbeitnehmer in der Europäischen Gemeinschaft hat das entleihende Unternehmen den gemäß einzelstaatlichem und gemeinschaftlichem Recht eingesetzten Arbeitnehmervertretungen im Zuge der Unterrichtung über die Beschäftigungslage in dem Unternehmen angemessene Informationen über den Einsatz von Leiharbeitnehmern in dem Unternehmen vorzulegen.

Without prejudice to national and Community provisions on information and consultation which are more stringent and/or more specific and, in particular, Directive 2002/14/EC of the European Parliament and of the Council of 11 March 2002 establishing a general framework for informing and consulting employees in the European Community, the user undertaking must provide suitable information on the use of temporary agency workers when providing information on the employment situation in that undertaking to bodies representing workers set up in accordance with national and Community legislation.

Kapitel 3
Schlussbestimmungen

Artikel 9
Mindestvorschriften

(1) Diese Richtlinie lässt das Recht der Mitgliedstaaten unberührt, für Arbeitnehmer günstigere Rechts- und Verwaltungsvorschriften anzuwenden oder zu erlassen oder den Abschluss von Tarifverträgen oder Vereinbarungen zwischen den Sozialpartnern zu fördern oder zuzulassen, die für die Arbeitnehmer günstiger sind.

(2) Die Durchführung dieser Richtlinie ist unter keinen Umständen ein hinreichender Grund zur Rechtfertigung einer Senkung des allgemeinen Schutzniveaus für Arbeitnehmer in den von dieser Richtlinie abgedeckten Bereichen. Dies gilt unbeschadet der Rechte der Mitgliedstaaten und/oder der Sozialpartner, angesichts sich wandelnder Bedingungen andere Rechts- und Verwaltungsvorschriften oder vertragliche Regelungen festzulegen als diejenigen, die zum Zeitpunkt des Erlasses dieser Richtlinie gelten, sofern die Mindestvorschriften dieser Richtlinie eingehalten werden.

Artikel 10
Sanktionen

(1) Für den Fall der Nichteinhaltung dieser Richtlinie durch Leiharbeitsunternehmen oder durch entleihende Unternehmen sehen die Mitgliedstaaten geeignete Maßnahmen vor. Sie sorgen insbesondere dafür, dass es geeignete Verwaltungs- oder Gerichtsverfahren gibt, um die Erfüllung der sich aus der Richtlinie ergebenden Verpflichtungen durchsetzen zu können.

(2) Die Mitgliedstaaten legen die Sanktionen fest, die im Falle eines Verstoßes gegen die einzelstaatlichen Vorschriften zur Umsetzung dieser Richtlinie Anwendung finden, und treffen alle erforderlichen Maßnahmen, um deren Durchführung zu gewährleisten. Die Sanktionen müssen wirksam, angemessen und abschreckend sein. Die Mitgliedstaaten teilen der Kommission diese Bestimmungen bis zum 5. Dezember 2011 mit. Die Mitgliedstaaten melden der Kommission rechtzeitig alle nachfolgenden Änderungen dieser Bestimmungen. Sie stellen insbesondere sicher, dass die Arbeitnehmer und/oder ihre Vertreter über angemessene Mittel zur Erfüllung der in dieser Richtlinie vorgesehenen Verpflichtungen verfügen.

Chapter 3
Final provisions

Article 9
Minimum requirements

(1) This Directive is without prejudice to the Member States' right to apply or introduce legislative, regulatory or administrative provisions which are more favourable to workers or to promote or permit collective agreements concluded between the social partners which are more favourable to workers.

(2) The implementation of this Directive shall under no circumstances constitute sufficient grounds for justifying a reduction in the general level of protection of workers in the fields covered by this Directive. This is without prejudice to the rights of Member States and/or management and labour to lay down, in the light of changing circumstances, different legislative, regulatory or contractual arrangements to those prevailing at the time of the adoption of this Directive, provided always that the minimum requirements laid down in this Directive are respected.

Article 10
Penalties

(1) Member States shall provide for appropriate measures in the event of non-compliance with this Directive by temporary-work agencies or user undertakings. In particular, they shall ensure that adequate administrative or judicial procedures are available to enable the obligations deriving from this Directive to be enforced.

(2) Member States shall lay down rules on penalties applicable in the event of infringements of national provisions implementing this Directive and shall take all necessary measures to ensure that they are applied. The penalties provided for must be effective, proportionate and dissuasive. Member States shall notify these provisions to the Commission by 5 December 2011. Member States shall notify to the Commission any subsequent amendments to those provisions in good time. They shall, in particular, ensure that workers and/or their representatives have adequate means of enforcing the obligations under this Directive.

Artikel 11
Umsetzung

(1) Die Mitgliedstaaten setzen die erforderlichen Rechts- und Verwaltungsvorschriften in Kraft und veröffentlichen sie, um dieser Richtlinie bis spätestens zum 5. Dezember 2011 nachzukommen, oder sie vergewissern sich, dass die Sozialpartner die erforderlichen Vorschriften im Wege von Vereinbarungen festlegen; dabei sind die Mitgliedstaaten gehalten, die erforderlichen Vorkehrungen zu treffen, damit sie jederzeit gewährleisten können, dass die Ziele dieser Richtlinie erreicht werden. Sie setzen die Kommission unverzüglich davon in Kenntnis.

(2) Wenn die Mitgliedstaaten diese Maßnahmen erlassen, nehmen sie in den Vorschriften selbst oder durch einen Hinweis bei deren amtlicher Veröffentlichung auf diese Richtlinie Bezug. Die Mitgliedstaaten regeln die Einzelheiten der Bezugnahme.

Artikel 12
Überprüfung durch die Kommission

Die Kommission überprüft im Benehmen mit den Mitgliedstaaten und den Sozialpartnern auf Gemeinschaftsebene die Anwendung dieser Richtlinie bis zum 5. Dezember 2013, um erforderlichenfalls die notwendigen Änderungen vorzuschlagen.

Artikel 13
Inkrafttreten

Diese Richtlinie tritt am Tag ihrer Veröffentlichung im *Amtsblatt der Europäischen Union* in Kraft.

Artikel 14
Adressaten

Diese Richtlinie ist an die Mitgliedstaaten gerichtet.

Article 11
Implementation

(1) Member States shall adopt and publish the laws, regulations and administrative provisions necessary to comply with this Directive by 5 December 2011, or shall ensure that the social partners introduce the necessary provisions by way of an agreement, whereby the Member States must make all the necessary arrangements to enable them to guarantee at any time that the objectives of this Directive are being attained. They shall forthwith inform the Commission thereof.

(2) When Member States adopt these measures, they shall contain a reference to this Directive or shall be accompanied by such reference on the occasion of their official publication. The methods of making such reference shall be laid down by Member States.

Article 12
Review by the Commission

By 5 December 2013, the Commission shall, in consultation with the Member States and social partners at Community level, review the application of this Directive with a view to proposing, where appropriate, the necessary amendments.

Article 13
Entry into force

This Directive shall enter into force on the day of its publication in the *Official Journal of the European Union*.

Article 14
Addresses

This Directive is addressed to the Member States.

II. Civil Code (Excerpt)

Bürgerliches Gesetzbuch – BGB (Auszug)

Stand: 21.12.2019

§ 117
Scheingeschäft

(1) Wird eine Willenserklärung, die einem anderen gegenüber abzugeben ist, mit dessen Einverständnis nur zum Schein abgegeben, so ist sie nichtig.

(2) Wird durch ein Scheingeschäft ein anderes Rechtsgeschäft verdeckt, so finden die für das verdeckte Rechtsgeschäft geltenden Vorschriften Anwendung.

§ 125
Nichtigkeit wegen Formmangels

¹Ein Rechtsgeschäft, welches der durch Gesetz vorgeschriebenen Form ermangelt, ist nichtig. ²Der Mangel der durch Rechtsgeschäft bestimmten Form hat im Zweifel gleichfalls Nichtigkeit zur Folge.

§ 126
Schriftform

(1) Ist durch Gesetz schriftliche Form vorgeschrieben, so muss die Urkunde von dem Aussteller eigenhändig durch Namensunterschrift oder mittels notariell beglaubigten Handzeichens unterzeichnet werden.

(2) ¹Bei einem Vertrag muss die Unterzeichnung der Parteien auf derselben Urkunde erfolgen. ²Werden über den Vertrag mehrere gleichlautende Urkunden aufgenommen, so genügt es, wenn jede Partei die für die andere Partei bestimmte Urkunde unterzeichnet.

(3) Die schriftliche Form kann durch die elektronische Form ersetzt werden, wenn sich nicht aus dem Gesetz ein anderes ergibt.

(4) Die schriftliche Form wird durch die notarielle Beurkundung ersetzt.

Section 117
Sham transaction

(1) If a declaration of intent that is to be made to another person is, with his consent, only made for the sake of appearance, it is void.

(2) If a sham transaction hides another legal transaction, the provisions applicable to the hidden transaction apply.

Section 125
Voidness resulting from a defect of form

¹A legal transaction that lacks the form prescribed by statute is void. ²In case of doubt, lack of the form specified by legal transaction also results in voidness.

Section 126
Written form

(1) If written form is prescribed by statue, the document must be signed by the issuer with his name in his own hand, or by his notarially certified initials.

(2) ¹In the case of a contract, the signature of the parties must be made on the same document. ²If more than one counterpart of the contract is drawn up, it suffices if each party signs the document intended for the other party.

(3) Written form may be replaced by electronic form, unless the statute leads to a different conclusion.

(4) Notarial recording replaces the written form.

§ 126a
Elektronische Form

(1) Soll die gesetzlich vorgeschriebene schriftliche Form durch die elektronische Form ersetzt werden, so muss der Aussteller der Erklärung dieser seinen Namen hinzufügen und das elektronische Dokument mit einer qualifizierten elektronischen Signatur versehen.

(2) Bei einem Vertrag müssen die Parteien jeweils ein gleichlautendes Dokument in der in Absatz 1 bezeichneten Weise elektronisch signieren.

§ 126b
Textform

[1]Ist durch Gesetz Textform vorgeschrieben, so muss eine lesbare Erklärung, in der die Person des Erklärenden genannt ist, auf einem dauerhaften Datenträger abgegeben werden. [2]Ein dauerhafter Datenträger ist jedes Medium, das es dem Empfänger ermöglicht, eine auf dem Datenträger befindliche, an ihn persönlich gerichtete Erklärung so aufzubewahren oder zu speichern, dass sie ihm während eines für ihren Zweck angemessenen Zeitraums zugänglich ist, und geeignet ist, die Erklärung unverändert wiederzugeben.

§ 127
Vereinbarte Form

(1) Die Vorschriften des § 126, des § 126a oder des § 126b gelten im Zweifel auch für die durch Rechtsgeschäft bestimmte Form.

(2) [1]Zur Wahrung der durch Rechtsgeschäft bestimmten schriftlichen Form genügt, soweit nicht ein anderer Wille anzunehmen ist, die telekommunikative Übermittlung und bei einem Vertrag der Briefwechsel. [2]Wird eine solche Form gewählt, so kann nachträglich eine dem § 126 entsprechende Beurkundung verlangt werden.

(3) [1]Zur Wahrung der durch Rechtsgeschäft bestimmten elektronischen Form genügt, soweit nicht ein anderer Wille anzunehmen ist, auch eine andere als die in § 126a bestimmte elektronische Signatur und bei einem Vertrag der Austausch von Angebots- und Annahmeerklärung, die jeweils mit einer elektronischen Signatur versehen sind. [2]Wird eine solche Form gewählt, so kann nachträglich eine dem § 126a entsprechende elektronische Signierung oder, wenn diese einer der Parteien nicht möglich ist, eine dem § 126 entsprechende Beurkundung verlangt werden.

(2) Die öffentliche Beglaubigung wird durch die notarielle Beurkundung der Erklärung ersetzt.

Section 126a
Electronic form

(1) If electronic form is to replace the written form prescribed by statute, the issuer of the declaration must add his name to it and provide the electronic document with a qualified electronic signature in accordance with the Electronic Signature Act.

(2) In the case of a contract, the parties must each provide a counterpart with an electronic signature as described in subsection (1).

Section 126b
Text form

[1]If text form is prescribed by statue, a readable declaration, in which the person is making the declaration is named, muste be made on a durable medium. [2]A durable medium is any medium that enables the recipient to retain or store a declaration included on the medium that is addressed to him personally such that is accessible to him for a peroid of time adequate to ist purpose, and that allows the unchanged reproduction of such declaration.

Section 127
Agreed form

(1) The provisions under section 126, 126a or 126b also apply, in case of doubt, to the form specified by legal transaction.

(2) [1]For compliance with the written form required by legal transaction, unless a different intention is to be assumed, it suffices if the message is transmitted by way of telecommunications and, in the case of a contract, by the exchange of letters. [2]If such a form is chosen, notarial recording in accordance with section 126 may be demanded subsequently.

(3) [1]For compliance with the electronic form required by legal transaction, unless a different intention is to be assumed, an electronic signature other than provided for section 126a also suffices an, in the case of a contract, the exchange of adeclaration of an offer and of acceptance which are each provided with an electronic signature. [2]If such a form is chosen, an electronic signature in accordance with section 126a may be demanded subsequently, or if this is not possible for one oft he parties, notarial recording in compliance with section 126.

(2) The notarial recording of the declaration replaces the official certification.

§ 130
Wirksamwerden der Willenserklärung gegenüber Abwesenden

(1) ¹Eine Willenserklärung, die einem anderen gegenüber abzugeben ist, wird, wenn sie in dessen Abwesenheit abgegeben wird, in dem Zeitpunkt wirksam, in welchem sie ihm zugeht. ²Sie wird nicht wirksam, wenn dem anderen vorher oder gleichzeitig ein Widerruf zugeht.

(2) Auf die Wirksamkeit der Willenserklärung ist es ohne Einfluss, wenn der Erklärende nach der Abgabe stirbt oder geschäftsunfähig wird.

(3) Diese Vorschriften finden auch dann Anwendung, wenn die Willenserklärung einer Behörde gegenüber abzugeben ist.

§ 133
Auslegung einer Willenserklärung

Bei der Auslegung einer Willenserklärung ist der wirkliche Wille zu erforschen und nicht an dem buchstäblichen Sinne des Ausdrucks zu haften.

§ 134
Gesetzliches Verbot

Ein Rechtsgeschäft, das gegen ein gesetzliches Verbot verstößt, ist nichtig, wenn sich nicht aus dem Gesetz ein anderes ergibt.

§ 138
Sittenwidriges Rechtsgeschäft; Wucher

(1) Ein Rechtsgeschäft, das gegen die guten Sitten verstößt, ist nichtig.

(2) Nichtig ist insbesondere ein Rechtsgeschäft, durch das jemand unter Ausbeutung der Zwangslage, der Unerfahrenheit, des Mangels an Urteilsvermögen oder der erheblichen Willensschwäche eines anderen sich oder einem Dritten für eine Leistung Vermögensvorteile versprechen oder gewähren lässt, die in einem auffälligen Missverhältnis zu der Leistung stehen.

§ 139
Teilnichtigkeit

Ist ein Teil eines Rechtsgeschäfts nichtig, so ist das ganze Rechtsgeschäft nichtig, wenn nicht anzunehmen ist, dass es auch ohne den nichtigen Teil vorgenommen sein würde.

Section 130
Effectiveness of a declaration of intent to absent parties

(1) ¹ A declaration of intent that is to be made to another becomes effective, if made in his absence, at the point of time when this declaration reaches him. ²It does not become effective if a revocation reaches the other previously or at the same time.

(2) The effectiveness of a declaration of intent is not affected if the person declaring dies or loses capacity to contract after making a declaration.

(3) These provisions apply even if the declaration of intent is to be made to a public authority.

Section 133
Interpretation of declaration of intent

When a declaration of intent is interpreted, it is necessary to ascertain the true intention rather than adhering to the literal meaning of the declaration.

Section 134
Statutory prohibition

A legal transaction that violates a statutory prohibition is void, unless the statute leads to a different conclusion.

Section 138
Legal transaction contrary to public policy; usury

(1) A legal transaction which is contrary to public policy is void.

(2) In particular, a legal transaction is void by which a person, by exploiting the predicament, inexperience, lack of sound judgement or considerable weakness of will of another, causes himself or a third party, in exchange for an act of performance, to be promised or granted pecuniary advantages which are clearly disproportionate to the performance.

Section 139
Partial invalidity

If a part of a legal transaction is void, then the entire legal transaction is void, unless it is to be assumed that it would have been undertaken even without the void part.

§ 140
Umdeutung

Entspricht ein nichtiges Rechtsgeschäft den Erfordernissen eines anderen Rechtsgeschäfts, so gilt das letztere, wenn anzunehmen ist, dass dessen Geltung bei Kenntnis der Nichtigkeit gewollt sein würde.

Section 140
Re-interpretation

If a void legal transaction fulfils the requirements of another legal transaction, then the latter is deemed to have been entered into, if it may be assumed that its validity would be intended if there were knowledge of the invalidity.

§ 186
Geltungsbereich

Für die in Gesetzen, gerichtlichen Verfügungen und Rechtsgeschäften enthaltenen Frist- und Terminsbestimmungen gelten die Auslegungsvorschriften der §§ 187 bis 193.

Section 186
Scope of applicability

The interpretation provisions of sections 187 to 193 apply to the fixing of periods of time and dates contained in statutes, court orders and legal transactions.

§ 187
Fristbeginn

(1) Ist für den Anfang einer Frist ein Ereignis oder ein in den Lauf eines Tages fallender Zeitpunkt maßgebend, so wird bei der Berechnung der Frist der Tag nicht mitgerechnet, in welchen das Ereignis oder der Zeitpunkt fällt.

(2) ¹Ist der Beginn eines Tages der für den Anfang einer Frist maßgebende Zeitpunkt, so wird dieser Tag bei der Berechnung der Frist mitgerechnet. ²Das Gleiche gilt von dem Tage der Geburt bei der Berechnung des Lebensalters.

Section 187
Beginning of a period of time

(1) If a period commences on the occurrence of an event or at a point of time falling in the course of a day, then the day on which the event or point of time occurs is not included in the calculation of the period.

(2) If the beginning of a day is the determining point of time for the commencement of a period, then this day is included in the calculation of the period. The same applies to the date of birth when the age of a person is calculated.

§ 188
Fristende

(1) Eine nach Tagen bestimmte Frist endigt mit dem Ablauf des letzten Tages der Frist.

(2) Eine Frist, die nach Wochen, nach Monaten oder nach einem mehrere Monate umfassenden Zeitraum – Jahr, halbes Jahr, Vierteljahr – bestimmt ist, endigt im Falle des § 187 Abs. 1 mit dem Ablauf desjenigen Tages der letzten Woche oder des letzten Monats, welcher durch seine Benennung oder seine Zahl dem Tage entspricht, in den das Ereignis oder der Zeitpunkt fällt, im Falle des § 187 Abs. 2 mit dem Ablauf desjenigen Tages der letzten Woche oder des letzten Monats, welcher dem Tage vorhergeht, der durch seine Benennung oder seine Zahl dem Anfangstag der Frist entspricht.

(3) Fehlt bei einer nach Monaten bestimmten Frist in dem letzten Monat der für ihren Ablauf maßgebende Tag, so endigt die Frist mit dem Ablauf des letzten Tages dieses Monats.

Section 188
End of a period of time

(1) A period of time specified by days ends on the expiry of the last day of the period.

(2) A period of time specified by weeks, by months or by a duration of time comprising more than one month – year, half-year, quarter – ends, in the case of section 187 (1), on the expiry of the day of the last week or of the last month which, in its designation or its number, corresponds to the day on which the event or the point of time occurs, or in the case of section 187 (2), on the expiry of the day of the last week or of the last month that precedes the day which corresponds in designation or number to the first day of the period of time.

(3) If, in the case of a period of time determined by months, the day on which it is due to expire does not occur in the last month, the period ends on the expiry of the last day of this month.

§ 189
Berechnung einzelner Fristen

(1) Unter einem halben Jahr wird eine Frist von sechs Monaten, unter einem Vierteljahr eine Frist von drei Monaten, unter einem halben Monat eine Frist von 15 Tagen verstanden.

Section 189
Calculation of individal periods of time

(1) A half-year is understood to mean a period of six months, a quarter is understood to mean a period of three months, and half a month is understood to mean a period of fifteen days.

(2) Ist eine Frist auf einen oder mehrere ganze Monate und einen halben Monat gestellt, so sind die 15 Tage zuletzt zu zählen.

§ 190
Fristverlängerung

Im Falle der Verlängerung einer Frist wird die neue Frist von dem Ablauf der vorigen Frist an berechnet.

§ 191
Berechnung von Zeiträumen

Ist ein Zeitraum nach Monaten oder nach Jahren in dem Sinne bestimmt, dass er nicht zusammenhängend zu verlaufen braucht, so wird der Monat zu 30, das Jahr zu 365 Tagen gerechnet.

§ 192
Anfang, Mitte, Ende des Monats

Unter Anfang des Monats wird der erste, unter Mitte des Monats der 15., unter Ende des Monats der letzte Tag des Monats verstanden.

§ 193
Sonn- und Feiertag; Sonnabend

Ist an einem bestimmten Tage oder innerhalb einer Frist eine Willenserklärung abzugeben oder eine Leistung zu bewirken und fällt der bestimmte Tag oder der letzte Tag der Frist auf einen Sonntag, einen am Erklärungs- oder Leistungsort staatlich anerkannten allgemeinen Feiertag oder einen Sonnabend, so tritt an die Stelle eines solchen Tages der nächste Werktag.

§ 194
Gegenstand der Verjährung

(1) Das Recht, von einem anderen ein Tun oder Unterlassen zu verlangen (Anspruch), unterliegt der Verjährung.

(2) Ansprüche aus einem familienrechtlichen Verhältnis unterliegen der Verjährung nicht, soweit sie auf die Herstellung des dem Verhältnis entsprechenden Zustands für die Zukunft oder auf die Einwilligung in eine genetische Untersuchung zur Klärung der leiblichen Abstammung gerichtet sind.

§ 195
Regelmäßige Verjährungsfrist

Die regelmäßige Verjährungsfrist beträgt drei Jahre.

(2) If a period of time is specified as one or more than one whole month and a half-month, then the fifteen days shall be counted last of all.

Section 190
Extension of period

If a period of time is extended, the new period is calculated from the expiry of the previous period.

Section 191
Calculation of periods of time

If a period of time is determined by months or by years with the meaning that they are not required to run consecutively, a month is counted as thirty days and a year as 365 days.

Section 192
Beginning, middle and end of a month

The beginning of the month is understood to be the first day, the middle of the month the fifteenth day, and the end of month the last day.

Section 193
Sundays and holidays; Saturday

If a declaration of intent is to be made or an act of performance to be done on a particular day or within a period, and if the particular day or the last day of the period falls on a Sunday, a general holiday officially recognised at the place of the declaration or performance, or on a Saturday, the next working day takes the place of this day.

Section 194
Subject-matter of limitation

(1) The right to demand that another person does or refrains from an act (claim) is subject to limitation.

(2) Claims based on a family-law relationship are not subject to limitation to the extent that they are directed towards creating a situation appropriate for the relationship for the future or towards consent to a genetic test to clarify biological descent.

Section 195
Standard limitation period

The standard limitation period is three years.

§ 197
Dreißigjährige Verjährungsfrist

(1) In 30 Jahren verjähren, soweit nicht ein anderes bestimmt ist,

1. Schadensersatzansprüche, die auf der vorsätzlichen Verletzung des Lebens, des Körpers, der Gesundheit, der Freiheit oder der sexuellen Selbstbestimmung beruhen,
2. Herausgabeansprüche aus Eigentum, anderen dinglichen Rechten, den §§ 2018, 2130 und 2362 BGB, sowie die Ansprüche, die der Geltendmachung der Herausgabeansprüche dienen,
3. rechtskräftig festgestellte Ansprüche,
4. Ansprüche aus vollstreckbaren Vergleichen oder vollstreckbaren Urkunden,
5. Ansprüche, die durch die im Insolvenzverfahren erfolgte Feststellung vollstreckbar geworden sind, und
6. Ansprüche auf Erstattung der Kosten der Zwangsvollstreckung.

(2) Soweit Ansprüche nach Absatz 1 Nr. 3 bis 5 künftig fällig werdende regelmäßig wiederkehrende Leistungen zum Inhalt haben, tritt an die Stelle der Verjährungsfrist von 30 Jahren die regelmäßige Verjährungsfrist.

§ 199
Beginn der regelmäßigen Verjährungsfrist und Verjährungshöchstfristen

(1) Die regelmäßige Verjährungsfrist beginnt, soweit nicht ein anderer Verjährungsbeginn bestimmt ist, mit dem Schluss des Jahres, in dem

1. der Anspruch entstanden ist und
2. der Gläubiger von den den Anspruch begründenden Umständen und der Person des Schuldners Kenntnis erlangt oder ohne grobe Fahrlässigkeit erlangen müsste.

(2) Schadensersatzansprüche, die auf der Verletzung des Lebens, des Körpers, der Gesundheit oder der Freiheit beruhen, verjähren ohne Rücksicht auf ihre Entstehung und die Kenntnis oder grob fahrlässige Unkenntnis in 30 Jahren von der Begehung der Handlung, der Pflichtverletzung oder dem sonstigen, den Schaden auslösenden Ereignis an.

(3) ¹Sonstige Schadensersatzansprüche verjähren

1. ohne Rücksicht auf die Kenntnis oder grob fahrlässige Unkenntnis in zehn Jahren von ihrer Entstehung an und

Section 197
Thirty-year limitation period

(1) Unless otherwise provided, the following are statute-barred after thirty years:

1. damage claims based on intentional injury to life, limb, health, liberty or sexual self-determination,
2. claims for return based on ownership, other real rights, sections 2018, 2130 and 2362 German Civil Code, as well as claims serving to assert the claims for return
3. claims that have been declared final and absolute,
4. claims under enforceable settlements or enforceable documents,
5. claims that have become enforceable upon being recognised in insolvency proceedings, and
6. claims to reimbursement of the costs of execution.

(2) To the extent that claims under subsection (1), nos. 3 to 5 are concerned with periodically recurring acts of performance that will fall due in the future, the standard limitation period takes the place of the period of thirty years.

Section 199
Commencement of the standard limitation period and maximum limitation periods

(1) Unless another commencement of limitation of is determined, the standard limitation period commences at the end of the year in which:

1. the claim arose and
2. the obligee obtains knowledge of the circumstances giving rise to the claim and of the identity of the obligor, or would have obtained such knowledge if he had not shown gross negligence.

(2) Claims for damages based on injury to life, body, health or liberty, notwithstanding the manner in which they arose and notwithstanding knowledge or a grossly negligent lack of knowledge, are statute-barred thirty years from the date on which the act, breach of duty or other event that caused the damage occurred.

(3) ¹Other claims for damages become statute-barred

1. notwithstanding knowledge or a grossly negligent lack of knowledge, ten years after they arise and

2. ohne Rücksicht auf ihre Entstehung und die Kenntnis oder grob fahrlässige Unkenntnis in 30 Jahren von der Begehung der Handlung, der Pflichtverletzung oder dem sonstigen, den Schaden auslösenden Ereignis an.

²Maßgeblich ist die früher endende Frist.

(3a) Ansprüche, die auf einem Erbfall beruhen oder deren Geltendmachung die Kenntnis einer Verfügung von Todes wegen voraussetzt, verjähren ohne Rücksicht auf die Kenntnis oder grob fahrlässige Unkenntnis in 30 Jahren von der Entstehung des Anspruchs an.

(4) Andere Ansprüche als die nach den Absätzen 2 bis 3a verjähren ohne Rücksicht auf die Kenntnis oder grob fahrlässige Unkenntnis in zehn Jahren von ihrer Entstehung an.

(5) Geht der Anspruch auf ein Unterlassen, so tritt an die Stelle der Entstehung die Zuwiderhandlung.

§200
Beginn anderer Verjährungsfristen

¹Die Verjährungsfrist von Ansprüchen, die nicht der regelmäßigen Verjährungsfrist unterliegen, beginnt mit der Entstehung des Anspruchs, soweit nicht ein anderer Verjährungsbeginn bestimmt ist. ²§199 Abs. 5 findet entsprechende Anwendung.

§202
Unzulässigkeit von Vereinbarungen über die Verjährung

(1) Die Verjährung kann bei Haftung wegen Vorsatzes nicht im Voraus durch Rechtsgeschäft erleichtert werden.

(2) Die Verjährung kann durch Rechtsgeschäft nicht über eine Verjährungsfrist von 30 Jahren ab dem gesetzlichen Verjährungsbeginn hinaus erschwert werden.

§241
Pflichten aus dem Schuldverhältnis

(1) ¹Kraft des Schuldverhältnisses ist der Gläubiger berechtigt, von dem Schuldner eine Leistung zu fordern. ²Die Leistung kann auch in einem Unterlassen bestehen.

(2) Das Schuldverhältnis kann nach seinem Inhalt jeden Teil zur Rücksicht auf die Rechte, Rechtsgüter und Interessen des anderen Teils verpflichten.

2. regardless of how they arose and of knowledge or a grossly negligent lack of knowledge, thirty years from the date on which the act, breach of duty or other event that caused the damage occurred.

²The period that ends first is applicable.

(3a) Claims based on the devolution of an inheritance or whose claiming is contingent on knowledge of a disposition mortis causa become statute-barred in 30 years from when the claim comes into being regardless of knowledge or of grossly negligent ignorance.

(4) Notwithstanding knowledge or a grossly negligent lack of knowledge, claims other than those under subsections (2) to (3a) become statute-barred ten years after the date upon which they arise.

(5) If the claim is for forbearance, the date of the breach of such an obligation takes the place of the date on which the claim arose.

Section 200
Commencement of other limitation periods

¹Unless another date for the commencement of limitation is specified, the limitation period of claims not subject to the standard limitation period commences when the claim arises. ²Section 199 (5) applies with the necessary modifications.

Section 202
Inadmissibility of agreements on limitation

(1) In the case of liability for intention, the limitation period may not be relaxed in advance by legal transaction.

(2) The limitation period may not be extended by legal transaction beyond a period of thirty years from the beginning of the statutory limitation period.

Section 241
Duties arising from an obligation

(1) ¹By virtue of an obligation an obligee is entitled to claim performance from the obligor. ²The performance may also consist in forbearance.

(2) An obligation may also, depending on its contents, oblige each party to take account of the rights, legal interests and other interests of the other party.

§ 242
Leistung nach Treu und Glauben

Der Schuldner ist verpflichtet, die Leistung so zu bewirken, wie Treu und Glauben mit Rücksicht auf die Verkehrssitte es erfordern.

§ 243
Gattungsschuld

(1) Wer eine nur der Gattung nach bestimmte Sache schuldet, hat eine Sache von mittlerer Art und Güte zu leisten.

(2) Hat der Schuldner das zur Leistung einer solchen Sache seinerseits Erforderliche getan, so beschränkt sich das Schuldverhältnis auf diese Sache.

§ 249
Art und Umfang des Schadensersatzes

(1) Wer zum Schadensersatz verpflichtet ist, hat den Zustand herzustellen, der bestehen würde, wenn der zum Ersatz verpflichtende Umstand nicht eingetreten wäre.

(2) [2]Ist wegen Verletzung einer Person oder wegen Beschädigung einer Sache Schadensersatz zu leisten, so kann der Gläubiger statt der Herstellung den dazu erforderlichen Geldbetrag verlangen. [2]Bei der Beschädigung einer Sache schließt der nach Satz 1 erforderliche Geldbetrag die Umsatzsteuer nur mit ein, wenn und soweit sie tatsächlich angefallen ist.

§ 254
Mitverschulden

(1) Hat bei der Entstehung des Schadens ein Verschulden des Beschädigten mitgewirkt, so hängt die Verpflichtung zum Ersatz sowie der Umfang des zu leistenden Ersatzes von den Umständen, insbesondere davon ab, inwieweit der Schaden vorwiegend von dem einen oder dem anderen Teil verursacht worden ist.

(2) [2]Dies gilt auch dann, wenn sich das Verschulden des Beschädigten darauf beschränkt, dass er unterlassen hat, den Schuldner auf die Gefahr eines ungewöhnlich hohen Schadens aufmerksam zu machen, die der Schuldner weder kannte noch kennen musste, oder dass er unterlassen hat, den Schaden abzuwenden oder zu mindern. [2]Die Vorschrift des § 278 findet entsprechende Anwendung.

§ 271
Leistungszeit

(1) Ist eine Zeit für die Leistung weder bestimmt noch aus den Umständen zu entnehmen, so kann der Gläubiger die Leistung sofort verlangen, der Schuldner sie sofort bewirken.

Section 242
Performance in good faith

An obligor has a duty to perform according to the requirements of good faith, taking customary practice into consideration.

Section 242
Obligation in kind

(1) A person who owes a thing defined only by class must supply a thing of average kind and quality.

(2) If the obligor has done what is necessary on his part to supply such a thing, the obligation is restricted to that thing.

Section 249
Nature and extent of damage

(1) A person who is liable in damages must restore the position that would exist if the circumstance obliging him to pay damages had not occurred.

(2) [2]Where damages are payable for injury to a person or damage to a thing, the obligee may demand the required monetary amount in lieu of restoration. [2]When a thing is damaged, the monetary amount required under sentence 1 only includes value-added tax if and to the extent that it is actually incurred.

Section 254
Contributory negligence

(1) Where fault on the part of the injured person contributes to the occurrence of the damage, liability in damages as well as the extent of compensation to be paid depend on the circumstances, in particular to what extent the damage is caused mainly by one or the other party.

(2) [2]This also applies if the fault of the injured person is limited to failing to draw the attention of the obligor to the danger of unusually extensive damage, where the obligor neither was nor ought to have been aware of the danger, or to failing to avert or reduce the damage. [2]The provision of section 278 applies with the necessary modifications.

Section 271
Time of performance

(1) Where no time for performance has been specified or is evident from the circumstances, the obligee may demand performance immediately, and the obligor may effect it immediately.

(2) Ist eine Zeit bestimmt, so ist im Zweifel anzunehmen, dass der Gläubiger die Leistung nicht vor dieser Zeit verlangen, der Schuldner aber sie vorher bewirken kann.

(2) Where a time has been specified, then in case of doubt it must be assumed that the obligee may not demand performance, but the obligor may effect it prior to that time.

§ 273
Zurückbehaltungsrecht

(1) Hat der Schuldner aus demselben rechtlichen Verhältnis, auf dem seine Verpflichtung beruht, einen fälligen Anspruch gegen den Gläubiger, so kann er, sofern nicht aus dem Schuldverhältnis sich ein anderes ergibt, die geschuldete Leistung verweigern, bis die ihm gebührende Leistung bewirkt wird (Zurückbehaltungsrecht).

(2) Wer zur Herausgabe eines Gegenstands verpflichtet ist, hat das gleiche Recht, wenn ihm ein fälliger Anspruch wegen Verwendungen auf den Gegenstand oder wegen eines ihm durch diesen verursachten Schadens zusteht, es sei denn, dass er den Gegenstand durch eine vorsätzlich begangene unerlaubte Handlung erlangt hat.

(3) ¹Der Gläubiger kann die Ausübung des Zurückbehaltungsrechts durch Sicherheitsleistung abwenden. ²Die Sicherheitsleistung durch Bürgen ist ausgeschlossen.

Section 273
Right of retention

(1) If the obligor has a claim that is due against the obligee under the same legal relationship as that on which the obligation is based, he may, unless the obligation leads to a different conclusion, refuse the performance owed by him, until the performance owed to him is rendered (right of retention).

(2) A person who is obliged to return an object has the same right, if he is entitled to a claim that is due on account of outlays for the object or on account of damage caused to him by the object, unless he obtained the object by means of an intentionally committed tort.

(3) ¹The obligee may avert the exercise of the right of retention by providing security. ²The providing of security by guarantors is excluded.

§ 274
Wirkungen des Zurückbehaltungsrechts

(1) Gegenüber der Klage des Gläubigers hat die Geltendmachung des Zurückbehaltungsrechts nur die Wirkung, dass der Schuldner zur Leistung gegen Empfang der ihm gebührenden Leistung (Erfüllung Zug um Zug) zu verurteilen ist.

(2) Auf Grund einer solchen Verurteilung kann der Gläubiger seinen Anspruch ohne Bewirkung der ihm obliegenden Leistung im Wege der Zwangsvollstreckung verfolgen, wenn der Schuldner im Verzug der Annahme ist.

Section 274
Effects oft the right of retention

(1) In comparison to a legal action by the obligee, assertion of the right of retention only has the effect that the obligor is to be ordered to render performance in return for receiving the performance owed to him (concurrent performance).

(2) On the basis of such an order the obligee may pursue his claim by way of execution, without effecting the performance he owes, if the obligor is in default of acceptance.

§ 275
Ausschluss der Leistungspflicht

(1) Der Anspruch auf Leistung ist ausgeschlossen, soweit diese für den Schuldner oder für jedermann unmöglich ist.

(2) ¹Der Schuldner kann die Leistung verweigern, soweit diese einen Aufwand erfordert, der unter Beachtung des Inhalts des Schuldverhältnisses und der Gebote von Treu und Glauben in einem groben Missverhältnis zu dem Leistungsinteresse des Gläubigers steht. ²Bei der Bestimmung der dem Schuldner zuzumutenden Anstrengungen ist auch zu berücksichtigen, ob der Schuldner das Leistungshindernis zu vertreten hat.

Section 275
Exclusion oft the duty of performance

(1 A claim for performance is excluded to the extent that performance is impossible for the obligor or for any other person.)

(2) ¹The obligor may refuse performance to the extent that performance requires expense and effort which, taking into account the subject matter of the obligation and the requirements of good faith, is grossly disproportionate to the interest in performance of the obligee. ²When it is determined what efforts may reasonably be required of the obligor, it must also be taken into account whether he is responsible for the obstacle to performance.

(3) Der Schuldner kann die Leistung ferner verweigern, wenn er die Leistung persönlich zu erbringen hat und sie ihm unter Abwägung des seiner Leistung entgegenstehenden Hindernisses mit dem Leistungsinteresse des Gläubigers nicht zugemutet werden kann.

(4) Die Rechte des Gläubigers bestimmen sich nach den §§ 280, 283 bis 285, 311a und 326.

§ 276
Verantwortlichkeit des Schuldners

(1) ¹Der Schuldner hat Vorsatz und Fahrlässigkeit zu vertreten, wenn eine strengere oder mildere Haftung weder bestimmt noch aus dem sonstigen Inhalt des Schuldverhältnisses, insbesondere aus der Übernahme einer Garantie oder eines Beschaffungsrisikos, zu entnehmen ist. ²Die Vorschriften der §§ 827 und 828 finden entsprechende Anwendung.

(2) Fahrlässig handelt, wer die im Verkehr erforderliche Sorgfalt außer Acht lässt.

(3) Die Haftung wegen Vorsatzes kann dem Schuldner nicht im Voraus erlassen werden.

§ 277
Sorgfalt in eigenen Angelegenheiten

Wer nur für diejenige Sorgfalt einzustehen hat, welche er in eigenen Angelegenheiten anzuwenden pflegt, ist von der Haftung wegen grober Fahrlässigkeit nicht befreit.

§ 278
Verantwortlichkeit des Schuldners für Dritte

¹Der Schuldner hat ein Verschulden seines gesetzlichen Vertreters und der Personen, deren er sich zur Erfüllung seiner Verbindlichkeit bedient, in gleichem Umfang zu vertreten wie eigenes Verschulden. ²Die Vorschrift des § 276 Abs. 3 findet keine Anwendung.

§ 280
Schadensersatz wegen Pflichtverletzung

(1) ¹Verletzt der Schuldner eine Pflicht aus dem Schuldverhältnis, so kann der Gläubiger Ersatz des hierdurch entstehenden Schadens verlangen. ²Dies gilt nicht, wenn der Schuldner die Pflichtverletzung nicht zu vertreten hat.

(2) Schadensersatz wegen Verzögerung der Leistung kann der Gläubiger nur unter der zusätzlichen Voraussetzung des § 286 verlangen.

(3) Schadensersatz statt der Leistung kann der Gläubiger nur unter den zusätzlichen Voraussetzungen des § 281, des § 282 oder des § 283 verlangen.

(3) In addition, the obligor may refuse performance if he is to render the performance in person and, when the obstacle to the performance of the obligor is weighed against the interest of the obligee in performance, performance cannot be reasonably required of the obligor.

(4) The rights of the obligee are governed by sections 280, 283 to 285, 311a and 326.

Section 276
Responsibility of the obligor

(1) The obligor is responsible for intention and negligence, if a higher or lower degree of liability is neither laid down nor to be inferred from the other subject matter of the obligation, including but not limited to the giving of a guarantee or the assumption of a procurement risk. The provisions of sections 827 and 828 apply with the necessary modifications.

(2) A person acts negligently if he fails to exercise reasonable care.

(3) The obligor may not be released in advance from liability for intention.

Section 277
Standard of care in ones own affairs

A person who owes only the care that he customarily exercises in his own affairs is not released from liability for gross negligence.

Section 278
Responsibility of the obligor for third parties

¹The obligor is responsible for fault on the part of his legal representative, and of persons whom he uses to perform his obligation, to the same extent as for fault on his own part. ²The provision of section 276 (3) does not apply.

Section 280
Damages for breach of duty

(1) ¹If the obligor breaches a duty arising from the obligation, the obligee may demand damages for the damage caused thereby. ²This does not apply if the obligor is not responsible for the breach of duty.

(2) Damages for delay in performance may be demanded by the obligee only subject to the additional requirement of section 286.

(3) Damages in lieu of performance may be demanded by the obligee only subject to the additional requirements of sections 281, 282 or 283.

§ 281
Schadensersatz statt der Leistung wegen nicht oder nicht wie geschuldet erbrachter Leistung

(1) ¹Soweit der Schuldner die fällige Leistung nicht oder nicht wie geschuldet erbringt, kann der Gläubiger unter den Voraussetzungen des § 280 Abs. 1 Schadensersatz statt der Leistung verlangen, wenn er dem Schuldner erfolglos eine angemessene Frist zur Leistung oder Nacherfüllung bestimmt hat. ²Hat der Schuldner eine Teilleistung bewirkt, so kann der Gläubiger Schadensersatz statt der ganzen Leistung nur verlangen, wenn er an der Teilleistung kein Interesse hat. ³Hat der Schuldner die Leistung nicht wie geschuldet bewirkt, so kann der Gläubiger Schadensersatz statt der ganzen Leistung nicht verlangen, wenn die Pflichtverletzung unerheblich ist.

(2) Die Fristsetzung ist entbehrlich, wenn der Schuldner die Leistung ernsthaft und endgültig verweigert oder wenn besondere Umstände vorliegen, die unter Abwägung der beiderseitigen Interessen die sofortige Geltendmachung des Schadensersatzanspruchs rechtfertigen.

(3) Kommt nach der Art der Pflichtverletzung eine Fristsetzung nicht in Betracht, so tritt an deren Stelle eine Abmahnung.

(4) Der Anspruch auf die Leistung ist ausgeschlossen, sobald der Gläubiger statt der Leistung Schadensersatz verlangt hat.

(5) Verlangt der Gläubiger Schadensersatz statt der ganzen Leistung, so ist der Schuldner zur Rückforderung des Geleisteten nach den §§ 346 bis 348 berechtigt.

§ 282
Schadensersatz statt der Leistung wegen Verletzung einer Pflicht nach § 241 Abs. 2

Verletzt der Schuldner eine Pflicht nach § 241 Abs. 2, kann der Gläubiger unter den Voraussetzungen des § 280 Abs. 1 Schadensersatz statt der Leistung verlangen, wenn ihm die Leistung durch den Schuldner nicht mehr zuzumuten ist.

§ 283
Schadensersatz statt der Leistung bei Ausschluss der Leistungspflicht

¹Braucht der Schuldner nach § 275 Abs. 1 bis 3 nicht zu leisten, kann der Gläubiger unter den Voraussetzungen des § 280 Abs. 1 Schadensersatz statt der Leistung verlangen. ²§ 281 Abs. 1 Satz 2 und 3 und Abs. 5 findet entsprechende Anwendung.

Section 281
Damages in lieu of performance for nonperformance or failure to render performance as owed

(1) ¹To the extent that the obligor does not render performance when it is due or does not render performance as owed, the obligee may, subject to the requirements of section 280 (1), demand damages in lieu of performance, if he has without result set a reasonable period for the obligor for performance or cure. ²If the obligor has performed only in part, the obligee may demand damages in lieu of complete performance only if he has no interest in the part performance. ³If the obligor has not rendered performance as owed, the obligee may not demand damages in lieu of performance if the breach of duty is immaterial.

(2) Setting a period for performance may be dispensed with if the obligor seriously and definitively refuses performance or if there are special circumstances which, after the interests of both parties are weighed, justify the immediate assertion of a claim for damages.

(3) If the nature of the breach of duty is such that setting a period of time is out of the question, a warning notice is given instead.

(4) The claim for performance is excluded as soon as the obligee has demanded damages in lieu of performance.

(5) If the obligee demands damages in lieu of complete performance, the obligor is entitled to claim the return of his performance under sections 346 to 348.

Section 282
Damages in lieu of performance for breach of a duty under section 241 (2)

If the obligor breaches a duty under section 241 (2), the obligee may, if the requirements of section 280 (1) are satisfied, demand damages in lieu of performance, if he can no longer reasonably be expected to accept performance by the obligor.

Section 283
Damages in lieu of performance where the duty of performance is excluded

¹If, under section 275 (1) to (3), the obligor is not obliged to perform, the obligee may, if the requirements of section 280 (1) are satisfied, demand damages in lieu of performance. ²Section 281 (1) sentences 2 and 3 and (5) apply with the necessary modifications.

§ 284
Ersatz vergeblicher Aufwendungen

Anstelle des Schadensersatzes statt der Leistung kann der Gläubiger Ersatz der Aufwendungen verlangen, die er im Vertrauen auf den Erhalt der Leistung gemacht hat und billigerweise machen durfte, es sei denn, deren Zweck wäre auch ohne die Pflichtverletzung des Schuldners nicht erreicht worden.

Section 284
Reimbursement of futile expenses

In place of damages in lieu of performance, the obligee may demand reimbursement of the expenses which he has made and in all fairness was entitled to make in reliance on receiving performance, unless the purpose of the expenses would not have been achieved, even if the obligor had not breached his duty.

§ 285
Herausgabe des Ersatzes

(1) Erlangt der Schuldner infolge des Umstands, auf Grund dessen er die Leistung nach § 275 Abs. 1 bis 3 nicht zu erbringen braucht, für den geschuldeten Gegenstand einen Ersatz oder einen Ersatzanspruch, so kann der Gläubiger Herausgabe des als Ersatz Empfangenen oder Abtretung des Ersatzanspruchs verlangen.

(2) Kann der Gläubiger statt der Leistung Schadensersatz verlangen, so mindert sich dieser, wenn er von dem in Absatz 1 bestimmten Recht Gebrauch macht, um den Wert des erlangten Ersatzes oder Ersatzanspruchs.

Section 285
Return of reimbursement

(1) If the obligor, as a result of the circumstance by reason of which, under section 275 (1) to (3), he has no duty of performance, obtains reimbursement or a claim to reimbursement for the object owed, the obligee may demand return of what has been received in reimbursement or an assignment of the claim to reimbursement.

(2) If the obligee may demand damages in lieu of performance, then, if he exercises the right stipulated in subsection (1) above, the damages are reduced by the value of the reimbursement or the claim to reimbursement he has obtained.

§ 286
Verzug des Schuldners

(1) ¹Leistet der Schuldner auf eine Mahnung des Gläubigers nicht, die nach dem Eintritt der Fälligkeit erfolgt, so kommt er durch die Mahnung in Verzug. ²Der Mahnung stehen die Erhebung der Klage auf die Leistung sowie die Zustellung eines Mahnbescheids im Mahnverfahren gleich.

(2) Der Mahnung bedarf es nicht, wenn

1. für die Leistung eine Zeit nach dem Kalender bestimmt ist,
2. der Leistung ein Ereignis vorauszugehen hat und eine angemessene Zeit für die Leistung in der Weise bestimmt ist, dass sie sich von dem Ereignis an nach dem Kalender berechnen lässt,
3. der Schuldner die Leistung ernsthaft und endgültig verweigert,
4. aus besonderen Gründen unter Abwägung der beiderseitigen Interessen der sofortige Eintritt des Verzugs gerechtfertigt ist.

Section 286
Default of obligor

(1) ¹If the obligor, following a warning notice from the obligee that is made after performance is due, fails to perform, he is in default as a result of the warning notice. ²Bringing an action for performance and serving a demand for payment in summary debt proceedings for recovery of debt have the same effect as a warning notice.

(2) There is no need for a warning notice if

1. a period of time according to the calendar has been specified,
2. performance must be preceded by an event and a reasonable period of time for performance has been specified in such a way that it can be calculated, starting from the event, according to the calendar,
3. the obligor seriously and definitively refuses performance,
4. for special reasons, weighing the interests of both parties, the immediate commencement of default is justified.

(3) ¹Der Schuldner einer Entgeltforderung kommt spätestens in Verzug, wenn er nicht innerhalb von 30 Tagen nach Fälligkeit und Zugang einer Rechnung oder gleichwertigen Zahlungsaufstellung leistet; dies gilt gegenüber einem Schuldner, der Verbraucher ist, nur, wenn auf diese Folgen in der Rechnung oder Zahlungsaufstellung besonders hingewiesen worden ist. ²Wenn der Zeitpunkt des Zugangs der Rechnung oder Zahlungsaufstellung unsicher ist, kommt der Schuldner, der nicht Verbraucher ist, spätestens 30 Tage nach Fälligkeit und Empfang der Gegenleistung in Verzug.

(4) Der Schuldner kommt nicht in Verzug, solange die Leistung infolge eines Umstands unterbleibt, den er nicht zu vertreten hat.

(5) Für eine von den Absätzen 1 bis 3 abweichende Vereinbarung über den Eintritt des Verzugs gilt § 271a Absatz 1 bis 5 entsprechend.

§ 287
Verantwortlichkeit während des Verzugs

¹Der Schuldner hat während des Verzugs jede Fahrlässigkeit zu vertreten. ²Er haftet wegen der Leistung auch für Zufall, es sei denn, dass der Schaden auch bei rechtzeitiger Leistung eingetreten sein würde.

§ 288
Verzugszinsen und sonstiger Verzugsschaden

(1) ¹Eine Geldschuld ist während des Verzugs zu verzinsen. ²Der Verzugszinssatz beträgt für das Jahr fünf Prozentpunkte über dem Basiszinssatz.

(2) Bei Rechtsgeschäften, an denen ein Verbraucher nicht beteiligt ist, beträgt der Zinssatz für Entgeltforderungen neun Prozentpunkte über dem Basiszinssatz.

(3) Der Gläubiger kann aus einem anderen Rechtsgrund höhere Zinsen verlangen.

(4) Die Geltendmachung eines weiteren Schadens ist nicht ausgeschlossen.

(5) ¹Der Gläubiger einer Entgeltforderung hat bei Verzug des Schuldners, wenn dieser kein Verbraucher ist, außerdem einen Anspruch auf Zahlung einer Pauschale in Höhe von 40 Euro. ²Dies gilt auch, wenn es sich bei der Entgeltforderung um eine Abschlagszahlung oder sonstige Ratenzahlung handelt. ³Die Pauschale nach Satz 1 ist auf einen geschuldeten Schadensersatz anzurechnen, soweit der Schaden in Kosten der Rechtsverfolgung begründet ist.

(3) ¹The obligor of a claim for payment is in default at the latest if he does not perform within thirty days after the due date and receipt of an invoice or equivalent statement of payment; this applies to an obligor who is a consumer only if these consequences are specifically referred to in the invoice or statement of payment. ²If the time at which the invoice or payment statement is received by the obligor is uncertain, an obligor who is not a consumer is in default at the latest thirty days after the due date and receipt of the consideration.

(4) The obligor is not in default for as long as performance is not made as the result of a circumstance for which he is not responsible.

(5) In the event of an agreement on the occurrence of default that deviates from paragraphs 1 to 3, section 271a (1) to (5) applies accordingly.

Section 287
Liability during default

¹While he is in default, the obligor is responsible for all negligence. ²He is liable for performance in the case of chance as well, unless the damage would have occurred even if performance had been made in good time.

Section 288
Default interest and other damage caused by default

(1) ¹Any money debt must bear interest during the time of default. ²The default rate of interest per year is five percentage points above the basic rate of interest.

(2) In the case of legal transactions to which a consumer is not a party the rate of interest for claims for payment is nine percentage points above the basic rate of interest.

(3) The obligee may demand higher interest on a different legal basis.

(4) The assertion of further damage is not excluded.

(5) ¹The obligee of a claim for payment shall also be entitled to the payment of a lump sum of EUR 40 in the event of default by the obligor, if the latter is not a consumer. ²This also applies if the claim for payment is a payment on account or other payment by instalments. ³The lump sum in accordance with the first sentence above shall be set off against any damages due, insofar as the damages are based on costs of legal action.

(6) ¹Eine im Voraus getroffene Vereinbarung, die den Anspruch des Gläubigers einer Entgeltforderung auf Verzugszinsen ausschließt, ist unwirksam. ²Gleiches gilt für eine Vereinbarung, die diesen Anspruch beschränkt oder den Anspruch des Gläubigers einer Entgeltforderung auf die Pauschale nach Absatz 5 oder auf Ersatz des Schadens, der in Kosten der Rechtsverfolgung begründet ist, ausschließt oder beschränkt, wenn sie im Hinblick auf die Belange des Gläubigers grob unbillig ist. ³Eine Vereinbarung über den Ausschluss der Pauschale nach Absatz 5 oder des Ersatzes des Schadens, der in Kosten der Rechtsverfolgung begründet ist, ist im Zweifel als grob unbillig anzusehen. ⁴Die Sätze 1 bis 3 sind nicht anzuwenden, wenn sich der Anspruch gegen einen Verbraucher richtet.

(6) ¹An agreement made in advance which excludes the obligee's right to claim interest on arrears is invalid. ²The same shall apply to an agreement which limits this claim or excludes or limits the creditor of a claim for remuneration to the lump sum referred to in paragraph 5 or to compensation for loss resulting from costs of legal action if it is grossly unreasonable in relation to the interests of the obligee. ³An agreement to exclude the lump sum under subsection 5 or compensation for loss resulting from legal costs shall be considered grossly unfair in case of doubt. ⁴Sentences 1 to 3 shall not apply if the claim is directed against a consumer.

§ 305
Einbeziehung Allgemeiner Geschäftsbedingungen in den Vertrag

Section 305
Incorporation of standard business terms into the contract

(1) ¹Allgemeine Geschäftsbedingungen sind alle für eine Vielzahl von Verträgen vorformulierten Vertragsbedingungen, die eine Vertragspartei (Verwender) der anderen Vertragspartei bei Abschluss eines Vertrags stellt. ²Gleichgültig ist, ob die Bestimmungen einen äußerlich gesonderten Bestandteil des Vertrags bilden oder in die Vertragsurkunde selbst aufgenommen werden, welchen Umfang sie haben, in welcher Schriftart sie verfasst sind und welche Form der Vertrag hat. ³Allgemeine Geschäftsbedingungen liegen nicht vor, soweit die Vertragsbedingungen zwischen den Vertragsparteien im Einzelnen ausgehandelt sind.

(1) ¹Standard business terms are all contract terms pre-formulated for more than two contracts which one party to the contract (the user) presents to the other party upon the entering into of the contract. ²It is irrelevant whether the provisions take the form of a physically separate part of a contract or are made part of the contractual document itself, what their volume is, what typeface or font is used for them and what form the contract takes. ³Contract terms do not become standard business terms to the extent that they have been negotiated in detail between the parties.

(2) Allgemeine Geschäftsbedingungen werden nur dann Bestandteil eines Vertrags, wenn der Verwender bei Vertragsschluss

(2) Standard business terms only become a part of a contract if the user, when entering into the contract,

1. die andere Vertragspartei ausdrücklich oder, wenn ein ausdrücklicher Hinweis wegen der Art des Vertragsschlusses nur unter unverhältnismäßigen Schwierigkeiten möglich ist, durch deutlich sichtbaren Aushang am Orte des Vertragsschlusses auf sie hinweist und
2. der anderen Vertragspartei die Möglichkeit verschafft, in zumutbarer Weise, die auch eine für den Verwender erkennbare körperliche Behinderung der anderen Vertragspartei angemessen berücksichtigt, von ihrem Inhalt Kenntnis zu nehmen,

1. refers the other party to the contract to them explicitly or, where explicit reference, due to the way in which the contract is entered into, is possible only with disproportionate difficulty, by posting a clearly visible notice at the place where the contract is entered into, and
2. gives the other party to the contract, in an acceptable manner, which also takes into reasonable account any physical handicap of the other party to the contract that is discernible to the user, the opportunity to take notice of their contents,

und wenn die andere Vertragspartei mit ihrer Geltung einverstanden ist.

and if the other party to the contract agrees to their applying.

(3) Die Vertragsparteien können für eine bestimmte Art von Rechtsgeschäften die Geltung bestimmter Allgemeiner Geschäftsbedingungen unter Beachtung der in Absatz 2 bezeichneten Erfordernisse im Voraus vereinbaren.

(3) The parties to the contract may, while complying with the requirements set out in subsection (2) above, agree in advance that specific standard business terms are to govern a specific type of legal transaction.

§ 305a
Einbeziehung in besonderen Fällen

Auch ohne Einhaltung der in § 305 Abs. 2 Nr. 1 und 2 bezeichneten Erfordernisse werden einbezogen, wenn die andere Vertragspartei mit ihrer Geltung einverstanden ist,

1. die mit Genehmigung der zuständigen Verkehrsbehörde oder auf Grund von internationalen Übereinkommen erlassenen Tarife und Ausführungsbestimmungen der Eisenbahnen und die nach Maßgabe des Personenbeförderungsgesetzes genehmigten Beförderungsbedingungen der Straßenbahnen, Obusse und Kraftfahrzeuge im Linienverkehr in den Beförderungsvertrag,
2. die im Amtsblatt der Bundesnetzagentur für Elektrizität, Gas, Telekommunikation, Post und Eisenbahnen veröffentlichten und in den Geschäftsstellen des Verwenders bereitgehaltenen Allgemeinen Geschäftsbedingungen

(a) in Beförderungsverträge, die außerhalb von Geschäftsräumen durch den Einwurf von Postsendungen in Briefkästen abgeschlossen werden,

(b) in Verträge über Telekommunikations-, Informations- und andere Dienstleistungen, die unmittelbar durch Einsatz von Fernkommunikationsmitteln und während der Erbringung einer Telekommunikationsdienstleistung in einem Mal erbracht werden, wenn die Allgemeinen Geschäftsbedingungen der anderen Vertragspartei nur unter unverhältnismäßigen Schwierigkeiten vor dem Vertragsschluss zugänglich gemacht werden können.

§ 305b
Vorrang der Individualabrede

Individuelle Vertragsabreden haben Vorrang vor Allgemeinen Geschäftsbedingungen.

§ 305c
Überraschende und mehrdeutige Klauseln

(1) Bestimmungen in Allgemeinen Geschäftsbedingungen, die nach den Umständen, insbesondere nach dem äußeren Erscheinungsbild des Vertrags, so ungewöhnlich sind, dass der Vertragspartner des Verwenders mit ihnen nicht zu rechnen braucht, werden nicht Vertragsbestandteil.

(2) Zweifel bei der Auslegung Allgemeiner Geschäftsbedingungen gehen zu Lasten des Verwenders.

Section 305a
Incorporation in special cases

Even without compliance with the requirements cited in section 305 (2) nos. 1 and 2, if the other party to the contract agrees to their applying the following are incorporated,

1. the tariffs and regulations of the railways issued with the approval of the competent transport authority or on the basis of international conventions, and the terms of transport approved under the Passenger Transport Act [Personenbeförderungsgesetz], of trams, trolley buses and motor vehicles in regular public transport services,
2. the standard business terms published in the gazette of the Federal Network Agency for Electricity, Gas, Telecommunications, Post and Railway [Bundesnetzagentur für Elektrizität, Gas, Telekommunikation, Post und Eisenbahnen] and kept available on the business premises of the user,

(a) into transport contracts entered into off business premises by the posting of items in postboxes,

(b) into contracts on telecommunications, information services and other services that are provided direct by the use of distance communication and at one time and without interruption during the supply of a telecommunications service, if it is disproportionately difficult to make the standard business terms available to the other party before the contract is entered into.

Section 305b
Priority of individually agreed terms

Individually agreed terms take priority over standard business terms.

Section 305c
Surprising and ambiguous clauses

(1) Provisions in standard business terms which in the circumstances, in particular with regard to the outward appearance of the contract, are so unusual that the other party to the contract with the user need not expect to encounter them, do not form part of the contract.

(2) Any doubts in the interpretation of standard business terms are resolved against the user.

§ 306
Rechtsfolgen bei Nichteinbeziehung und Unwirksamkeit

(1) Sind Allgemeine Geschäftsbedingungen ganz oder teilweise nicht Vertragsbestandteil geworden oder unwirksam, so bleibt der Vertrag im Übrigen wirksam.

(2) Soweit die Bestimmungen nicht Vertragsbestandteil geworden oder unwirksam sind, richtet sich der Inhalt des Vertrags nach den gesetzlichen Vorschriften.

(3) Der Vertrag ist unwirksam, wenn das Festhalten an ihm auch unter Berücksichtigung der nach Absatz 2 vorgesehenen Änderung eine unzumutbare Härte für eine Vertragspartei darstellen würde.

§ 306a
Umgehungsverbot

Die Vorschriften dieses Abschnitts finden auch Anwendung, wenn sie durch anderweitige Gestaltungen umgangen werden.

§ 307
Inhaltskontrolle

(1) ¹Bestimmungen in Allgemeinen Geschäftsbedingungen sind unwirksam, wenn sie den Vertragspartner des Verwenders entgegen den Geboten von Treu und Glauben unangemessen benachteiligen. ²Eine unangemessene Benachteiligung kann sich auch daraus ergeben, dass die Bestimmung nicht klar und verständlich ist.

(2) Eine unangemessene Benachteiligung ist im Zweifel anzunehmen, wenn eine Bestimmung

1. mit wesentlichen Grundgedanken der gesetzlichen Regelung, von der abgewichen wird, nicht zu vereinbaren ist oder
2. wesentliche Rechte oder Pflichten, die sich aus der Natur des Vertrags ergeben, so einschränkt, dass die Erreichung des Vertragszwecks gefährdet ist.

(3) ¹Die Absätze 1 und 2 sowie die §§ 308 und 309 gelten nur für Bestimmungen in Allgemeinen Geschäftsbedingungen, durch die von Rechtsvorschriften abweichende oder diese ergänzende Regelungen vereinbart werden. ²Andere Bestimmungen können nach Absatz 1 Satz 2 in Verbindung mit Absatz 1 Satz 1 unwirksam sein.

§ 362
Erfüllung

(1) Das Schuldverhältnis erlischt, wenn die geschuldete Leistung an den Gläubiger bewirkt wird.

Section 306
Legal consequences of non-incorporation and ineffectiveness

(1) If standard business terms in whole or in part have not become part of the contract or are ineffective, the remainder of the contract remains in effect.

(2) To the extent that the terms have not become part of the contract or are ineffective, the contents of the contract are determined by the statutory provisions.

(3) The contract is ineffective if upholding it, even taking into account the alteration provided in subsection (2) above, would be an unreasonable hardship for one party.

Section 306a
Prohibition of circumvention

The rules in this division apply even if they are circumvented by other constructions.

Section 307
Test of reasonableness of contents

(1) ¹Provisions in standard business terms are ineffective if, contrary to the requirement of good faith, they unreasonably disadvantage the other party to the contract with the user. ²An unreasonable disadvantage may also arise from the provision not being clear and comprehensible.

(2) An unreasonable disadvantage is, in case of doubt, to be assumed to exist if a provision

1. is not compatible with essential principles of the statutory provision from which it deviates, or
2. limits essential rights or duties inherent in the nature of the contract to such an extent that attainment of the purpose of the contract is jeopardised.

(3) ¹Subsections (1) and (2) above, and sections 308 and 309 apply only to provisions in standard business terms on the basis of which arrangements derogating from legal provisions, or arrangements supplementing those legal provisions, are agreed. ²Other provisions may be ineffective under subsection (1) sentence 2 above, in conjunction with subsection (1) sentence 1 above.

Section 362
Extinction by performance

(1) An obligation is extinguished if the performance owed is rendered to the obligee.

(2) Wird an einen Dritten zum Zwecke der Erfüllung geleistet, so findet die Vorschrift des § 185 Anwendung.

(2) If performance is rendered to a third party for the purpose of performing the contract, the provisions of section 185 apply

§ 426
Ausgleichungspflicht, Forderungsübergang

Section 426
Duty to adjust advancements, passing of claim

(1) [1]Die Gesamtschuldner sind im Verhältnis zueinander zu gleichen Anteilen verpflichtet, soweit nicht ein anderes bestimmt ist. [2]Kann von einem Gesamtschuldner der auf ihn entfallende Beitrag nicht erlangt werden, so ist der Ausfall von den übrigen zur Ausgleichung verpflichteten Schuldnern zu tragen.

(1) [1]The joint and several debtors are obliged in equal proportions in relation to one another unless otherwise determined. [2]If the contribution attributable to a joint and several debtor cannot be obtained from him, the shortfall is to be borne by the other obligors obliged to adjust advancements.

(2) [1]Soweit ein Gesamtschuldner den Gläubiger befriedigt und von den übrigen Schuldnern Ausgleichung verlangen kann, geht die Forderung des Gläubigers gegen die übrigen Schuldner auf ihn über. [2]Der Übergang kann nicht zum Nachteil des Gläubigers geltend gemacht werden.

(2) [1]To the extent that a joint and several debtor satisfies the obligee and may demand adjustment of advancements from the other obligors, the claim of the obligee against the other obligors passes to him. [2]The passing of ownership may not be asserted to the disadvantage of the creditor.

§ 611
Vertragstypische Pflichten beim Dienstvertrag

Section 611
Typical contractual duties in a service contract

(1) Durch den Dienstvertrag wird derjenige, welcher Dienste zusagt, zur Leistung der versprochenen Dienste, der andere Teil zur Gewährung der vereinbarten Vergütung verpflichtet.

(1) By means of a service contract, a person who promises service is obliged to perform the services promised, and the other party is obliged to grant the agreed remuneration.

(2) Gegenstand des Dienstvertrags können Dienste jeder Art sein.

(2) Services of any type may be the subject matter of service contracts.

§ 611a
Arbeitsvertrag

Section 611a
Employment contract

(1) [1]Durch den Arbeitsvertrag wird der Arbeitnehmer im Dienste eines anderen zur Leistung weisungsgebundener, fremdbestimmter Arbeit in persönlicher Abhängigkeit verpflichtet. [2]Das Weisungsrecht kann Inhalt, Durchführung, Zeit und Ort der Tätigkeit betreffen. [3]Weisungsgebunden ist, wer nicht im Wesentlichen frei seine Tätigkeit gestalten und seine Arbeitszeit bestimmen kann. [4]Der Grad der persönlichen Abhängigkeit hängt dabei auch von der Eigenart der jeweiligen Tätigkeit ab. [5]Für die Feststellung, ob ein Arbeitsvertrag vorliegt, ist eine Gesamtbetrachtung aller Umstände vorzunehmen. [6]Zeigt die tatsächliche Durchführung des Vertragsverhältnisses, dass es sich um ein Arbeitsverhältnis handelt, kommt es auf die Bezeichnung im Vertrag nicht an.

(1) [1]The employment contract obliges the employee to perform work in the service of another person in personal dependence and under instructions from another person. [2]The right of instruction may concern the content, performance, time and place of the work. [3]Anyone who is not essentially free to organise his activity and determine his working hours is bound by instructions. [4]The degree of personal dependency also depends on the nature of the respective activity. [5]In order to determine whether an employment contract exists, an overall consideration of all circumstances must be made. [6]If the actual implementation of the contractual relationship shows that it is an employment relationship, the designation in the contract is not relevant.

(2) Der Arbeitgeber ist zur Zahlung der vereinbarten Vergütung verpflichtet.

(2) The employer is obliged to pay the agreed remuneration.

§ 612
Vergütung

(1) Eine Vergütung gilt als stillschweigend vereinbart, wenn die Dienstleistung den Umständen nach nur gegen eine Vergütung zu erwarten ist.

(2) Ist die Höhe der Vergütung nicht bestimmt, so ist bei dem Bestehen einer Taxe die taxmäßige Vergütung, in Ermangelung einer Taxe die übliche Vergütung als vereinbart anzusehen.

§ 612a
Maßregelungsverbot

Der Arbeitgeber darf einen Arbeitnehmer bei einer Vereinbarung oder einer Maßnahme nicht benachteiligen, weil der Arbeitnehmer in zulässiger Weise seine Rechte ausübt.

§ 613
Unübertragbarkeit

[1]Der zur Dienstleistung Verpflichtete hat die Dienste im Zweifel in Person zu leisten. [2]Der Anspruch auf die Dienste ist im Zweifel nicht übertragbar.

§ 613a
Rechte und Pflichten bei Betriebsübergang

(1) [1]Geht ein Betrieb oder Betriebsteil durch Rechtsgeschäft auf einen anderen Inhaber über, so tritt dieser in die Rechte und Pflichten aus den im Zeitpunkt des Übergangs bestehenden Arbeitsverhältnissen ein. [2]Sind diese Rechte und Pflichten durch Rechtsnormen eines Tarifvertrags oder durch eine Betriebsvereinbarung geregelt, so werden sie Inhalt des Arbeitsverhältnisses zwischen dem neuen Inhaber und dem Arbeitnehmer und dürfen nicht vor Ablauf eines Jahres nach dem Zeitpunkt des Übergangs zum Nachteil des Arbeitnehmers geändert werden. [3]Satz 2 gilt nicht, wenn die Rechte und Pflichten bei dem neuen Inhaber durch Rechtsnormen eines anderen Tarifvertrags oder durch eine andere Betriebsvereinbarung geregelt werden. [4]Vor Ablauf der Frist nach Satz 2 können die Rechte und Pflichten geändert werden, wenn der Tarifvertrag oder die Betriebsvereinbarung nicht mehr gilt oder bei fehlender beiderseitiger Tarifgebundenheit im Geltungsbereich eines anderen Tarifvertrags dessen Anwendung zwischen dem neuen Inhaber und dem Arbeitnehmer vereinbart wird.

Section 612
Remuneration

(1) Remuneration is deemed to have been tacitly agreed if in the circumstances it is to be expected that the services are rendered only for remuneration.

(2) If the amount of remuneration is not specified, then if a tariff exists, the tariff remuneration is deemed to be agreed; if no tariff exists, the usual remuneration is deemed to be agreed.

Section 612a
Prohibition of victimisation

The employer may not discriminate against an employee in an agreement or a measure because that employee exercises his rights in a permissible way.

Section 613
Non-transferability

[1]The party under a duty of service must in case of doubt render the services in person. [2]The claim to services is, in case of doubt, not transferable.

Section 613a
Rights and duties in the case of transfer of business

(1) [1]If a business or part of a business passes to another owner by legal transaction, then the latter succeeds to the rights and duties under the employment relationships existing at the time of transfer. [2]If these rights and duties are governed by the legal provisions of a collective agreement or by a works agreement, then they become part of the employment relationship between the new owner and the employee and may not be changed to the disadvantage of the employee before the end of the year after the date of transfer. [3]Sentence 2 does not apply if the rights and duties with the new owner are governed by the legal provisions of another collective agreement or by another works agreement. [4]Prior to expiry of the period of time under sentence 2, the rights and duties may be changed if the collective agreement or the works agreement no longer applies or, where it is not the case that both parties are bound by a collective agreement in the scope of applicability of another collective agreement, the application of that collective agreement is agreed between the new owner and the employee.

(2) ¹Der bisherige Arbeitgeber haftet neben dem neuen Inhaber für Verpflichtungen nach Absatz 1, soweit sie vor dem Zeitpunkt des Übergangs entstanden sind und vor Ablauf von einem Jahr nach diesem Zeitpunkt fällig werden, als Gesamtschuldner. ²Werden solche Verpflichtungen nach dem Zeitpunkt des Übergangs fällig, so haftet der bisherige Arbeitgeber für sie jedoch nur in dem Umfang, der dem im Zeitpunkt des Übergangs abgelaufenen Teil ihres Bemessungszeitraums entspricht.

(3) Absatz 2 gilt nicht, wenn eine juristische Person oder eine Personenhandelsgesellschaft durch Umwandlung erlischt.

(4) ¹Die Kündigung des Arbeitsverhältnisses eines Arbeitnehmers durch den bisherigen Arbeitgeber oder durch den neuen Inhaber wegen des Übergangs eines Betriebs oder eines Betriebsteils ist unwirksam. ²Das Recht zur Kündigung des Arbeitsverhältnisses aus anderen Gründen bleibt unberührt.

(5) Der bisherige Arbeitgeber oder der neue Inhaber hat die von einem Übergang betroffenen Arbeitnehmer vor dem Übergang in Textform zu unterrichten über:

1. den Zeitpunkt oder den geplanten Zeitpunkt des Übergangs,
2. den Grund für den Übergang,
3. die rechtlichen, wirtschaftlichen und sozialen Folgen des Übergangs für die Arbeitnehmer und
4. die hinsichtlich der Arbeitnehmer in Aussicht genommenen Maßnahmen.

(6) ¹Der Arbeitnehmer kann dem Übergang des Arbeitsverhältnisses innerhalb eines Monats nach Zugang der Unterrichtung nach Absatz 5 schriftlich widersprechen. ²Der Widerspruch kann gegenüber dem bisherigen Arbeitgeber oder dem neuen Inhaber erklärt werden.

(2) ¹The previous employer is jointly and severally liable with the new owner for duties under subsection (1) to the extent that they arose prior to the date of transfer and are due before the end of one year after that date. ²If such duties are due after the date of transfer, however, the previous employer is only liable for them to the extent that corresponds to the part of their assessment period that ended on the date of transfer.

(3) Subsection (2) does not apply if a legal person or a commercial partnership ceases to exist through conversion.

(4) ¹The termination of the employment relationship of an employee by the previous employer or by the new owner due to transfer of a business or a part of a business is ineffective. ²The right to terminate the employment relationship for other reasons is unaffected.

(5) The previous employer or the new owner must notify employees affected by a transfer in text form prior to transfer:

1. of the date or planned date of transfer,
2. of the reason for the transfer,
3. of the legal, economic and social consequences of the transfer for the employees, and
4. of measures that are being considered with regard to employees.

(6) ¹The employee may object in writing to the transfer of the employment relationship within one month of receipt of notification under subsection (5). ²The objection may be addressed to the previous employer or to the new owner.

§ 614
Fälligkeit der Vergütung

¹Die Vergütung ist nach der Leistung der Dienste zu entrichten. ²Ist die Vergütung nach Zeitabschnitten bemessen, so ist sie nach dem Ablauf der einzelnen Zeitabschnitte zu entrichten.

Section 614
Due date of remuneration

¹Remuneration is to be paid after performance of the services. ²If remuneration is assessed by time periods, then it is to be paid at the end of the individual time periods.

§ 615
Vergütung bei Annahmeverzug und bei Betriebsrisiko

[1]Kommt der Dienstberechtigte mit der Annahme der Dienste in Verzug, so kann der Verpflichtete für die infolge des Verzugs nicht geleisteten Dienste die vereinbarte Vergütung verlangen, ohne zur Nachleistung verpflichtet zu sein. [2]Er muss sich jedoch den Wert desjenigen anrechnen lassen, was er infolge des Unterbleibens der Dienstleistung erspart oder durch anderweitige Verwendung seiner Dienste erwirbt oder zu erwerben böswillig unterlässt. [3]Die Sätze 1 und 2 gelten entsprechend in den Fällen, in denen der Arbeitgeber das Risiko des Arbeitsausfalls trägt.

§ 616
Vorübergehende Verhinderung

[1]Der zur Dienstleistung Verpflichtete wird des Anspruchs auf die Vergütung nicht dadurch verlustig, dass er für eine verhältnismäßig nicht erhebliche Zeit durch einen in seiner Person liegenden Grund ohne sein Verschulden an der Dienstleistung verhindert wird. [2]Er muss sich jedoch den Betrag anrechnen lassen, welcher ihm für die Zeit der Verhinderung aus einer auf Grund gesetzlicher Verpflichtung bestehenden Kranken- oder Unfallversicherung zukommt.

§ 617
Pflicht zur Krankenfürsorge

(1) [1]Ist bei einem dauernden Dienstverhältnis, welches die Erwerbstätigkeit des Verpflichteten vollständig oder hauptsächlich in Anspruch nimmt, der Verpflichtete in die häusliche Gemeinschaft aufgenommen, so hat der Dienstberechtigte ihm im Falle der Erkrankung die erforderliche Verpflegung und ärztliche Behandlung bis zur Dauer von sechs Wochen, jedoch nicht über die Beendigung des Dienstverhältnisses hinaus, zu gewähren, sofern nicht die Erkrankung von dem Verpflichteten vorsätzlich oder durch grobe Fahrlässigkeit herbeigeführt worden ist. [2]Die Verpflegung und ärztliche Behandlung kann durch Aufnahme des Verpflichteten in eine Krankenanstalt gewährt werden. [3]Die Kosten können auf die für die Zeit der Erkrankung geschuldete Vergütung angerechnet werden. [4]Wird das Dienstverhältnis wegen der Erkrankung von dem Dienstberechtigten nach § 626 gekündigt, so bleibt die dadurch herbeigeführte Beendigung des Dienstverhältnisses außer Betracht.

Section 615
Remuneration in the case of default in acceptance and business risk

[1]If the person entitled to services is in default in accepting the services, then the party owing the services may demand the agreed remuneration for the services not rendered as the result of the default without being obliged to provide cure. [2]However, he must allow to be credited against him what he saves as a result of not performing the services or acquires or wilfully fails to acquire through use of his employment elsewhere. [3]Sentences 1 and 2 apply with the necessary modifications in cases in which the employer bears the risk of loss of working hours.

Section 616
Temporary prevention from performing services

[1]The person obliged to perform services is not deprived of his claim to remuneration by the fact that he is prevented from performing services for a relatively trivial period of time for a reason in his person without fault on his part. [2]However, he must allow to be credited against him the amount he receives for the period when he is prevented under a health or accident insurance policy that exists on the basis of a statutory duty.

Section 617
Duty of medical care

(1) [1]If, in a permanent service relationship that completely or mainly takes up the economic activity of the person obliged to perform services, the person obliged is integrated into the joint household, then the person entitled to services must, in the event of illness, grant him the necessary food and medical treatment up to a duration of six weeks, but not beyond termination of his service relationship, unless the illness was caused by the person obliged by intent or gross negligence. [2]The provision of food and medical treatment may be granted by the admission of the person obliged to a hospital. [3]The costs may be credited against the remuneration owed for the period of illness. [4]If the service relationship is terminated by the person entitled to services under section 626 on the grounds of illness, then termination of the employment caused by this is not taken into account.

(2) Die Verpflichtung des Dienstberechtigten tritt nicht ein, wenn für die Verpflegung und ärztliche Behandlung durch eine Versicherung oder durch eine Einrichtung der öffentlichen Krankenpflege Vorsorge getroffen ist.

§ 618
Pflicht zu Schutzmaßnahmen

(1) Der Dienstberechtigte hat Räume, Vorrichtungen oder Gerätschaften, die er zur Verrichtung der Dienste zu beschaffen hat, so einzurichten und zu unterhalten und Dienstleistungen, die unter seiner Anordnung oder seiner Leitung vorzunehmen sind, so zu regeln, dass der Verpflichtete gegen Gefahr für Leben und Gesundheit soweit geschützt ist, als die Natur der Dienstleistung es gestattet.

(2) Ist der Verpflichtete in die häusliche Gemeinschaft aufgenommen, so hat der Dienstberechtigte in Ansehung des Wohn- und Schlafraums, der Verpflegung sowie der Arbeits- und Erholungszeit diejenigen Einrichtungen und Anordnungen zu treffen, welche mit Rücksicht auf die Gesundheit, die Sittlichkeit und die Religion des Verpflichteten erforderlich sind.

(3) Erfüllt der Dienstberechtigte die ihm in Ansehung des Lebens und der Gesundheit des Verpflichteten obliegenden Verpflichtungen nicht, so finden auf seine Verpflichtung zum Schadensersatz die für unerlaubte Handlungen geltenden Vorschriften der §§ 842 bis 846 entsprechende Anwendung.

§ 619
Unabdingbarkeit der Fürsorgepflichten

Die dem Dienstberechtigten nach den §§ 617, 618 obliegenden Verpflichtungen können nicht im Voraus durch Vertrag aufgehoben oder beschränkt werden.

§ 619a
Beweislast bei Haftung des Arbeitnehmers

Abweichend von § 280 Abs. 1 hat der Arbeitnehmer dem Arbeitgeber Ersatz für den aus der Verletzung einer Pflicht aus dem Arbeitsverhältnis entstehenden Schaden nur zu leisten, wenn er die Pflichtverletzung zu vertreten hat.

§ 620
Beendigung des Dienstverhältnisses

(1) Das Dienstverhältnis endigt mit dem Ablauf der Zeit, für die es eingegangen ist.

(2) The duty of the person entitled to services does not arise if provision has been made for the food and medical treatment by an insurance company or a public health institution.

Section 618
Duty of undertake protective measures

(1) The person entitled to services must furnish and maintain premises, devices and equipment that he must provide for performance of the services in such a way and must arrange services that must be undertaken on his order or under his supervision in such a way that the person obliged to perform services is protected against danger to life and limb to the extent that the nature of the services permits.

(2) If the person obliged has been integrated into the common household, then the person entitled to services must provide the installations and make the arrangements, with regard to the living and sleeping space, the provision of food and work and leisure time, that are required with a view to the health, morality and religion of the person obliged.

(3) If the person entitled to services fails to fulfil the duties it has with regard to the life and the health of the person obliged, then the provisions of sections 842 to 846 governing torts apply with the necessary modifications to his duty to provide damages.

Section 619
Absolute nature of welfare duties

The duties incumbent upon the person entitled to services under sections 617 and 618 may not be cancelled or restricted in advance by contract.

Section 619a
Burden of proof when the employee is liable

Notwithstanding section 280 (1), the employee must only provide the employer with compensation for damage arising from the breach of a duty under the employment relationship if he is responsible for the breach of duty.

Section 620
Termination of service relationships

(1) The service relationship ends at the end of the period of time for which it has been entered into.

(2) Ist die Dauer des Dienstverhältnisses weder bestimmt noch aus der Beschaffenheit oder dem Zwecke der Dienste zu entnehmen, so kann jeder Teil das Dienstverhältnis nach Maßgabe der §§ 621 bis 623 kündigen.

(3) Für Arbeitsverträge, die auf bestimmte Zeit abgeschlossen werden, gilt das Teilzeit- und Befristungsgesetz.

(2) If the duration of the service relationship neither is specified nor may be inferred from the nature or the purpose of the services, then either party may terminate the service relationship under the provisions of sections 621 to 623.

(3) The Part-Time Work and Fixed-Term Employment Act [Teilzeit- und Befristungsgesetz] governs employment contracts entered into for a specified period of time.

§ 621
Kündigungsfristen bei Dienstverhältnissen

Section 621
Notice periods for service relationships

Bei einem Dienstverhältnis, das kein Arbeitsverhältnis im Sinne des § 622 ist, ist die Kündigung zulässig,

In the case of a service relationship that is not an employment relationship within the meaning of section 622, termination is allowed

1. wenn die Vergütung nach Tagen bemessen ist, an jedem Tag für den Ablauf des folgenden Tages;
2. wenn die Vergütung nach Wochen bemessen ist, spätestens am ersten Werktag einer Woche für den Ablauf des folgenden Sonnabends;
3. wenn die Vergütung nach Monaten bemessen ist, spätestens am 15. eines Monats für den Schluss des Kalendermonats;
4. wenn die Vergütung nach Vierteljahren oder längeren Zeitabschnitten bemessen ist, unter Einhaltung einer Kündigungsfrist von sechs Wochen für den Schluss eines Kalendervierteljahrs;
5. wenn die Vergütung nicht nach Zeitabschnitten bemessen ist, jederzeit; bei einem die Erwerbstätigkeit des Verpflichteten vollständig oder hauptsächlich in Anspruch nehmenden Dienstverhältnis ist jedoch eine Kündigungsfrist von zwei Wochen einzuhalten.

1. if the remuneration is assessed by days, on any day to the end of the following day;
2. if the remuneration is assessed by weeks, at the latest on the first working day of a week to the end of the following Saturday;
3. if the remuneration is assessed by months, at the latest by the fifteenth of one month to the end of the calendar month;
4. if the remuneration is assessed by quarters or longer periods of time, observing a notice period of six weeks, to the end of a calendar quarter;
5. if the remuneration is not assessed by time periods, at any time; in the case of a service relationship that completely or mainly takes up the economic activity of the person obliged; however, a notice period of two weeks must be observed.

§ 622
Kündigungsfristen bei Arbeitsverhältnissen

Section 622
Notice periods in the case of employment relationships

(1) Das Arbeitsverhältnis eines Arbeiters oder eines Angestellten (Arbeitnehmers) kann mit einer Frist von vier Wochen zum Fünfzehnten oder zum Ende eines Kalendermonats gekündigt werden.

(1) The employment relationship of a wage-earner or a salary-earner (employee) may be terminated with a notice period of four weeks to the fifteenth or to the end of a calendar month.

(2) Für eine Kündigung durch den Arbeitgeber beträgt die Kündigungsfrist, wenn das Arbeitsverhältnis in dem Betrieb oder Unternehmen

(2) For notice of termination by the employer, the notice period is as follows if the employment relationship in the business or the enterprise

1. zwei Jahre bestanden hat, einen Monat zum Ende eines Kalendermonats,
2. fünf Jahre bestanden hat, zwei Monate zum Ende eines Kalendermonats,
3. acht Jahre bestanden hat, drei Monate zum Ende eines Kalendermonats,

1. has lasted for two years, one month to the end of a calendar month,
2. has lasted for five years, two months to the end of a calendar month,
3. has lasted for eight years, three months to the end of a calendar month,

4. zehn Jahre bestanden hat, vier Monate zum Ende eines Kalendermonats,
5. zwölf Jahre bestanden hat, fünf Monate zum Ende eines Kalendermonats,
6. 15 Jahre bestanden hat, sechs Monate zum Ende eines Kalendermonats,
7. 20 Jahre bestanden hat, sieben Monate zum Ende eines Kalendermonats.

(3) Während einer vereinbarten Probezeit, längstens für die Dauer von sechs Monaten, kann das Arbeitsverhältnis mit einer Frist von zwei Wochen gekündigt werden.

(4) ¹Von den Absätzen 1 bis 3 abweichende Regelungen können durch Tarifvertrag vereinbart werden. ²Im Geltungsbereich eines solchen Tarifvertrags gelten die abweichenden tarifvertraglichen Bestimmungen zwischen nicht tarifgebundenen Arbeitgebern und Arbeitnehmern, wenn ihre Anwendung zwischen ihnen vereinbart ist.

(5) ¹Einzelvertraglich kann eine kürzere als die in Absatz 1 genannte Kündigungsfrist nur vereinbart werden,

1. wenn ein Arbeitnehmer zur vorübergehenden Aushilfe eingestellt ist; dies gilt nicht, wenn das Arbeitsverhältnis über die Zeit von drei Monaten hinaus fortgesetzt wird;
2. wenn der Arbeitgeber in der Regel nicht mehr als 20 Arbeitnehmer ausschließlich der zu ihrer Berufsbildung Beschäftigten beschäftigt und die Kündigungsfrist vier Wochen nicht unterschreitet.

²Bei der Feststellung der Zahl der beschäftigten Arbeitnehmer sind teilzeitbeschäftigte Arbeitnehmer mit einer regelmäßigen wöchentlichen Arbeitszeit von nicht mehr als 20 Stunden mit 0,5 und nicht mehr als 30 Stunden mit 0,75 zu berücksichtigen. ³Die einzelvertragliche Vereinbarung längerer als der in den Absätzen 1 bis 3 genannten Kündigungsfristen bleibt hiervon unberührt.

(6) Für die Kündigung des Arbeitsverhältnisses durch den Arbeitnehmer darf keine längere Frist vereinbart werden als für die Kündigung durch den Arbeitgeber.

§ 623
Schriftform der Kündigung

Die Beendigung von Arbeitsverhältnissen durch Kündigung oder Auflösungsvertrag bedürfen zu ihrer Wirksamkeit der Schriftform; die elektronische Form ist ausgeschlossen.

4. has lasted for ten years, four months to the end of a calendar month,
5. has lasted for twelve years, five months to the end of a calendar month,
6. has lasted for fifteen years, six months to the end of a calendar month,
7. has lasted for twenty years, seven months to the end of a calendar month.

(3) During an agreed probationary period, at most for the duration of six months, the employment relationship may be terminated with a notice period of two weeks.

(4) ¹Provisions differing from subsections (1) to (3) may be agreed in collective agreements. ²Within the scope of applicability of such a collective agreement, the different collective agreement provisions between employers and employees who are not subject to collective agreements apply if the application of collective agreements has been agreed between them.

(5) ¹In an individual contract, shorter notice periods than those cited in subsection (1) may be agreed only

1. if an employee is employed to help out on a temporary basis; this does not apply if the employment relationship is extended beyond a period of three months;
2. if the employer as a rule employs not more than 20 employees with the exception of those employed for their own training and the notice period does not fall short of four weeks.

²When the number of employees employed is determined, part-time employees with regular weekly working hours of not more than 20 hours are counted as 0.5 employees and those working not more than 30 hours are counted as 0.75 employees. ³The agreement in an individual contract of longer notice periods than those stated in subsections (1) to (3) is unaffected by this.

(6) For notice of termination of employment by the employee, no longer notice period may be agreed than for notice of termination by the employer.

Section 623
Written form of termination

Termination of employment by notice of termination or separation agreement requires written form to be effective; electronic form is excluded.

§624
Kündigungsfrist bei Verträgen über mehr als fünf Jahre

¹Ist das Dienstverhältnis für die Lebenszeit einer Person oder für längere Zeit als fünf Jahre eingegangen, so kann es von dem Verpflichteten nach dem Ablauf von fünf Jahren gekündigt werden. ²Die Kündigungsfrist beträgt sechs Monate.

Section 624
Notice period in the case of contracts lasting more than five years

¹If the service relationship is entered into for the lifetime of a person or for a longer period of time than five years, then it may be terminated by the person obliged at the end of five years. ²The notice period is six months.

§625
Stillschweigende Verlängerung

Wird das Dienstverhältnis nach dem Ablauf der Dienstzeit von dem Verpflichteten mit Wissen des anderen Teiles fortgesetzt, so gilt es als auf unbestimmte Zeit verlängert, sofern nicht der andere Teil unverzüglich widerspricht.

Section 625
Tacit extension

If the service relationship is continued after the end of the service period by the person obliged with the knowledge of the other party, then it is deemed to be extended for an indefinite period of time unless the other party objects to it without undue delay.

§626
Fristlose Kündigung aus wichtigem Grund

(1) Das Dienstverhältnis kann von jedem Vertragsteil aus wichtigem Grund ohne Einhaltung einer Kündigungsfrist gekündigt werden, wenn Tatsachen vorliegen, auf Grund derer dem Kündigenden unter Berücksichtigung aller Umstände des Einzelfalles und unter Abwägung der Interessen beider Vertragsteile die Fortsetzung des Dienstverhältnisses bis zum Ablauf der Kündigungsfrist oder bis zu der vereinbarten Beendigung des Dienstverhältnisses nicht zugemutet werden kann.

(2) ¹Die Kündigung kann nur innerhalb von zwei Wochen erfolgen. ²Die Frist beginnt mit dem Zeitpunkt, in dem der Kündigungsberechtigte von den für die Kündigung maßgebenden Tatsachen Kenntnis erlangt. ³Der Kündigende muss dem anderen Teil auf Verlangen den Kündigungsgrund unverzüglich schriftlich mitteilen.

Section 626
Termination without notice for a compelling reason

(1) The service relationship may be terminated by either party to the contract for a compelling reason without complying with a notice period if facts are present on the basis of which the party giving notice cannot reasonably be expected to continue the service relationship to the end of the notice period or to the agreed end of the service relationship, taking all circumstances of the individual case into account and weighing the interests of both parties to the contract.

(2) ¹Notice of termination may only be given within two weeks. ²The notice period commences with the date on which the person entitled to give notice obtains knowledge of facts conclusive for the notice of termination. 3The party giving notice must notify the other party, on demand, of the reason for notice of termination without undue delay in writing.

§627
Fristlose Kündigung bei Vertrauensstellung

(1) Bei einem Dienstverhältnis, das kein Arbeitsverhältnis im Sinne des § 622 ist, ist die Kündigung auch ohne die in § 626 bezeichnete Voraussetzung zulässig, wenn der zur Dienstleistung Verpflichtete, ohne in einem dauernden Dienstverhältnis mit festen Bezügen zu stehen, Dienste höherer Art zu leisten hat, die auf Grund besonderen Vertrauens übertragen zu werden pflegen.

Section 627
Termination without notice in the case of a position of trust

(1) In a service relationship that is not an employment relationship within the meaning of section 622, notice of termination is allowed, even without the requirement specified in section 626, if the person obliged to perform services, without being in a permanent service relationship with fixed earnings, must perform services of a higher nature with which people are customarily entrusted on the basis of special trust.

(2) ¹Der Verpflichtete darf nur in der Art kündigen, dass sich der Dienstberechtigte die Dienste anderweit beschaffen kann, es sei denn, dass ein wichtiger Grund für die unzeitige Kündigung vorliegt. ²Kündigt er ohne solchen Grund zur Unzeit, so hat er dem Dienstberechtigten den daraus entstehenden Schaden zu ersetzen.

(2) ¹The person obliged to perform services may only give notice in such a manner that the person entitled to services can obtain the services elsewhere, unless there is a compelling reason for untimely notice of termination. ²If he should give notice in untimely fashion without such cause, then he must compensate the person entitled to services for damage arising from this.

§ 628
Teilvergütung und Schadensersatz bei fristloser Kündigung

(1) ¹Wird nach dem Beginn der Dienstleistung das Dienstverhältnis auf Grund des § 626 oder des § 627 gekündigt, so kann der Verpflichtete einen seinen bisherigen Leistungen entsprechenden Teil der Vergütung verlangen. ²Kündigt er, ohne durch vertragswidriges Verhalten des anderen Teiles dazu veranlasst zu sein, oder veranlasst er durch sein vertragswidriges Verhalten die Kündigung des anderen Teiles, so steht ihm ein Anspruch auf die Vergütung insoweit nicht zu, als seine bisherigen Leistungen infolge der Kündigung für den anderen Teil kein Interesse haben. ³Ist die Vergütung für eine spätere Zeit im Voraus entrichtet, so hat der Verpflichtete sie nach Maßgabe des § 346 oder, wenn die Kündigung wegen eines Umstands erfolgt, den er nicht zu vertreten hat, nach den Vorschriften über die Herausgabe einer ungerechtfertigten Bereicherung zurückzuerstatten.

(2) Wird die Kündigung durch vertragswidriges Verhalten des anderen Teiles veranlasst, so ist dieser zum Ersatz des durch die Aufhebung des Dienstverhältnisses entstehenden Schadens verpflichtet.

Section 628
Partial remuneration and damages in case of termination without notice

(1) ¹If after commencement of performance of the service, the service relationship is terminated on the ground of section 626 or 627, then the person obliged to perform services may demand a part of his remuneration corresponding to his services performed thus far. ²If he gives notice without being prompted to do so by action of the other party in breach of contract, or if he should prompt termination by the other party by his own action in breach of contract, then he has no claim to the remuneration to the extent that his previous services are of no interest to the other party as a result of the notice of termination. ³If remuneration is paid in advance for a later period of time, then the person obliged must reimburse it under the provisions of section 346 or, if notice of termination is given by reason of a circumstance for which he is not responsible, under the provisions on the return of unjust enrichment.

(2) If notice of termination is prompted by the conduct of the other party in breach of contract, then the other party is obliged to compensate the damage arising from the dissolution of the service relationship.

§ 629
Freizeit zur Stellungssuche

Nach der Kündigung eines dauernden Dienstverhältnisses hat der Dienstberechtigte dem Verpflichteten auf Verlangen angemessene Zeit zum Aufsuchen eines anderen Dienstverhältnisses zu gewähren.

Section 629
Time off for search for employment

After the termination of a permanent service relationship, the person entitled to services must grant the person obliged, on demand, reasonable time to seek another service relationship.

§ 630
Pflicht zur Zeugniserteilung

¹Bei der Beendigung eines dauernden Dienstverhältnisses kann der Verpflichtete von dem anderen Teil ein schriftliches Zeugnis über das Dienstverhältnis und dessen Dauer fordern. ²Das Zeugnis ist auf Verlangen auf die Leistungen und die Führung im Dienst zu erstrecken. ³Die Erteilung des Zeugnisses in elektronischer Form ist ausgeschlossen. ⁴Wenn der Verpflichtete ein Arbeitnehmer ist, findet § 109 der Gewerbeordnung Anwendung.

Section 630
Duty to provide a reference

Upon the termination of a permanent service relationship, the person obliged may demand from the other party a written reference on the service relationship and its duration. The reference must extend, on demand, to the services performed and conduct in service. The reference may not be provided in electronic form. If the person obliged is an employee, section 109 of the Trade Code [Gewerbeordnung] applies.

§631
Vertragstypische Pflichten beim Werkvertrag

(1) Durch den Werkvertrag wird der Unternehmer zur Herstellung des versprochenen Werkes, der Besteller zur Entrichtung der vereinbarten Vergütung verpflichtet.

(2) Gegenstand des Werkvertrags kann sowohl die Herstellung oder Veränderung einer Sache als auch ein anderer durch Arbeit oder Dienstleistung herbeizuführender Erfolg sein.

§632
Vergütung

(1) Eine Vergütung gilt als stillschweigend vereinbart, wenn die Herstellung des Werkes den Umständen nach nur gegen eine Vergütung zu erwarten ist.

(2) Ist die Höhe der Vergütung nicht bestimmt, so ist bei dem Bestehen einer Taxe die taxmäßige Vergütung, in Ermangelung einer Taxe die übliche Vergütung als vereinbart anzusehen.

(3) Ein Kostenanschlag ist im Zweifel nicht zu vergüten.

§632a
Abschlagszahlungen

(1) ¹Der Unternehmer kann von dem Besteller eine Abschlagszahlung in Höhe des Wertes der von ihm erbrachten und nach dem Vertrag geschuldeten Leistungen verlangen. ²Sind die erbrachten Leistungen nicht vertragsgemäß, kann der Besteller die Zahlung eines angemessenen Teils des Abschlags verweigern. ³Die Beweislast für die vertragsgemäße Leistung verbleibt bis zur Abnahme beim Unternehmer. ⁴§ 641 Abs. 3 gilt entsprechend. ⁵Die Leistungen sind durch eine Aufstellung nachzuweisen, die eine rasche und sichere Beurteilung der Leistungen ermöglichen muss. ⁶Die Sätze 1 bis 5 gelten auch für erforderliche Stoffe oder Bauteile, die angeliefert oder eigens angefertigt und bereitgestellt sind, wenn dem Besteller nach seiner Wahl Eigentum an den Stoffen oder Bauteilen übertragen oder entsprechende Sicherheit hierfür geleistet wird.

(2) Die Sicherheit nach Absatz 1 Satz 6 kann auch durch eine Garantie oder ein sonstiges Zahlungsversprechen eines im Geltungsbereich dieses Gesetzes zum Geschäftsbetrieb befugten Kreditinstituts oder Kreditversicherers geleistet werden.

§633
Sach- und Rechtsmangel

(1) Der Unternehmer hat dem Besteller das Werk frei von Sach- und Rechtsmängeln zu verschaffen.

Section 631
Typical contractual duties in a contract to produce a work

(1) By a contract to produce a work, a contractor is obliged to produce the promised work and the customer is obliged to pay the agreed remuneration.

(2) The subject matter of a contract to produce a work may be either the production or alteration of a thing or another result to be achieved by work or by a service.

Section 632
Remuneration

(1) Remuneration for work is deemed to be tacitly agreed if the production of the work, in the circumstances, is to be expected only in return for remuneration.

(2) If the amount of remuneration is not specified, then if a tariff exists, the tariff remuneration is deemed to be agreed; if no tariff exists, the usual remuneration is deemed to be agreed.

(3) In case of doubt, remuneration is not to be paid for a cost estimate.

Section 632a
Part payments

(1) ¹The contractor may demand a part payment from the customer for work carried out in accordance with the contract in the amount in which the customer has received an increased value by virtue of the work. ²The part payment may not be refused because of minor defects. ³Section 641 (3) applies with the necessary modifications. ⁴The work must be documented by a list which must facilitate a rapid, secure evaluation of the work. ⁵Sentences 1 to 5 also apply to required materials or building components that are supplied or specially prepared and made available if ownership of the materials or building components is transferred to the customer or an appropriate security is provided for this, at his option.

(2) The security pursuant to (1) sentence 6 may also be provided by a guarantee or other promise of payment from a credit institution or credit insurer authorized to conduct business within the scope of this Act.

Section 633
Material defects and legal defects

(1) The contractor must procure the work for the customer free of material defects and legal defects.

(2) ¹Das Werk ist frei von Sachmängeln, wenn es die vereinbarte Beschaffenheit hat. ²Soweit die Beschaffenheit nicht vereinbart ist, ist das Werk frei von Sachmängeln,

1. wenn es sich für die nach dem Vertrag vorausgesetzte, sonst
2. für die gewöhnliche Verwendung eignet und eine Beschaffenheit aufweist, die bei Werken der gleichen Art üblich ist und die der Besteller nach der Art des Werkes erwarten kann.

³Einem Sachmangel steht es gleich, wenn der Unternehmer ein anderes als das bestellte Werk oder das Werk in zu geringer Menge herstellt.

(3) Das Werk ist frei von Rechtsmängeln, wenn Dritte in Bezug auf das Werk keine oder nur die im Vertrag übernommenen Rechte gegen den Besteller geltend machen können.

§ 634
Rechte des Bestellers bei Mängeln

Ist das Werk mangelhaft, kann der Besteller, wenn die Voraussetzungen der folgenden Vorschriften vorliegen und soweit nicht ein anderes bestimmt ist,

1. nach § 635 Nacherfüllung verlangen,
2. nach § 637 den Mangel selbst beseitigen und Ersatz der erforderlichen Aufwendungen verlangen,
3. nach den §§ 636, 323 und 326 Abs. 5 von dem Vertrag zurücktreten oder nach § 638 die Vergütung mindern und
4. nach den §§ 636, 280, 281, 283 und 311a Schadensersatz oder nach § 284 Ersatz vergeblicher Aufwendungen verlangen.

§ 634a
Verjährung der Mängelansprüche

(1) Die in § 634 Nr. 1, 2 und 4 bezeichneten Ansprüche verjähren

1. vorbehaltlich der Nummer 2 in zwei Jahren bei einem Werk, dessen Erfolg in der Herstellung, Wartung oder Veränderung einer Sache oder in der Erbringung von Planungs- oder Überwachungsleistungen hierfür besteht,
2. in fünf Jahren bei einem Bauwerk und einem Werk, dessen Erfolg in der Erbringung von Planungs- oder Überwachungsleistungen hierfür besteht, und
3. im Übrigen in der regelmäßigen Verjährungsfrist.

(2) ¹The work is free of material defects if it is of the agreed quality. ²To the extent that the quality has not been agreed, the work is free from material defects

1. if it is suitable for the use envisaged in the contract, or else
2. if it is suitable for the customary use and is of a quality that is customary in works of the same type and that the customer may expect in view of the type of work.

³It is equivalent to a material defect if the contractor produces a work that is different from the work ordered or too small an amount of the work.

(3) The work is free of legal defects if third parties, with regard to the work, either cannot assert any rights against the customer or can assert only such rights as are taken over under the contract.

Section 634
Rights oft he costumer in the case of defects

If the work is defective, the customer, if the requirements of the following provisions are met and to the extent not otherwise specified, may

1. under section 635, demand cure,
2. under section 637, remedy the defect himself and demand reimbursement for required expenses,
3. under sections 636, 323 and 326 (5), revoke the contract or under section 638, reduce payment, and
4. under sections 636, 280, 281, 283 and 311a, demand damages, or under section 284, demand reimbursement of futile expenditure.

Section 634a
Limitation of claims for defects

(1) The claims cited in section 634 nos. 1, 2 and 4 are statute-barred

1. subject to no. 2, in two years in the case of a work whose result consists in the manufacture, maintenance or alteration of a thing or in the rendering of planning or monitoring services for this purpose,
2. in five years in the case of a building and in the case of a work whose result consists in the rendering of planning or monitoring services for this purpose, and
3. apart from this, in the regular limitation period.

(2) Die Verjährung beginnt in den Fällen des Absatzes 1 Nr. 1 und 2 mit der Abnahme.

(3) ¹Abweichend von Absatz 1 Nr. 1 und 2 und Absatz 2 verjähren die Ansprüche in der regelmäßigen Verjährungsfrist, wenn der Unternehmer den Mangel arglistig verschwiegen hat. ²Im Falle des Absatzes 1 Nr. 2 tritt die Verjährung jedoch nicht vor Ablauf der dort bestimmten Frist ein.

(4) ¹Für das in § 634 bezeichnete Rücktrittsrecht gilt § 218. ²Der Besteller kann trotz einer Unwirksamkeit des Rücktritts nach § 218 Abs. 1 die Zahlung der Vergütung insoweit verweigern, als er auf Grund des Rücktritts dazu berechtigt sein würde. ³Macht er von diesem Recht Gebrauch, kann der Unternehmer vom Vertrag zurücktreten.

(5) Auf das in § 634 bezeichnete Minderungsrecht finden § 218 und Absatz 4 Satz 2 entsprechende Anwendung.

§ 635
Nacherfüllung

(1) Verlangt der Besteller Nacherfüllung, so kann der Unternehmer nach seiner Wahl den Mangel beseitigen oder ein neues Werk herstellen.

(2) Der Unternehmer hat die zum Zwecke der Nacherfüllung erforderlichen Aufwendungen, insbesondere Transport-, Wege-, Arbeits- und Materialkosten zu tragen.

(3) Der Unternehmer kann die Nacherfüllung unbeschadet des § 275 Abs. 2 und 3 verweigern, wenn sie nur mit unverhältnismäßigen Kosten möglich ist.

(4) Stellt der Unternehmer ein neues Werk her, so kann er vom Besteller Rückgewähr des mangelhaften Werkes nach Maßgabe der §§ 346 bis 348 verlangen.

§ 636
Besondere Bestimmungen für Rücktritt und Schadensersatz

Außer in den Fällen der §§ 281 Abs. 2 und 323 Abs. 2 bedarf es der Fristsetzung auch dann nicht, wenn der Unternehmer die Nacherfüllung gemäß § 635 Abs. 3 verweigert oder wenn die Nacherfüllung fehlgeschlagen oder dem Besteller unzumutbar ist.

(2) In the cases of subsection (1) nos. 1 and 2, limitation begins on acceptance.

(3) ¹Notwithstanding subsection (1) nos. 1 and 2, and subsection (2), claims are statute-barred in the standard limitation period if the contractor fraudulently concealed the defect. ²However, in the case of subsection (1) no. 2, claims are not statute-barred before the end of the period specified there.

(4) ¹The right of revocation referred to in section 634 is governed by section 218. ²Notwithstanding the ineffectiveness of revocation under section 218 (1), the customer may refuse to pay the remuneration to the extent that he would be entitled to do so by reason of the revocation. ³If he uses this right, the contractor may revoke the contract.

(5) Section 218 and subsection (4) sentence 2 above apply with the necessary modifications to the right to reduce the price specified in section 634.

Section 635
Cure

(1) If the customer demands cure, then the contractor may, at his option, remedy the defect or produce a new work.

(2) The contractor must bear the expenditure necessary for cure, including, without limitation, transport, workmen's travel, work and materials costs.

(3) The contractor may refuse cure, without prejudice to section 275 (2) and (3), if it is only possible at disproportionate cost.

(4) If the contractor produces a new work, he may demand from the customer return of the defective work in accordance with sections 346 to 348.

Section 636
Special provisions on revocation and damages

Except in the cases of sections 281 (2) and 323 (2), there is no need for a period to be set even if the contractor refuses cure under section 635 (3) or if cure has failed or cannot be reasonably expected of the customer.

§637
Selbstvornahme

(1) Der Besteller kann wegen eines Mangels des Werkes nach erfolglosem Ablauf einer von ihm zur Nacherfüllung bestimmten angemessenen Frist den Mangel selbst beseitigen und Ersatz der erforderlichen Aufwendungen verlangen, wenn nicht der Unternehmer die Nacherfüllung zu Recht verweigert.

(2) [1]§ 323 Abs. 2 findet entsprechende Anwendung. [2]Der Bestimmung einer Frist bedarf es auch dann nicht, wenn die Nacherfüllung fehlgeschlagen oder dem Besteller unzumutbar ist.

(3) Der Besteller kann von dem Unternehmer für die zur Beseitigung des Mangels erforderlichen Aufwendungen Vorschuss verlangen.

§638
Minderung

(1) [1]Statt zurückzutreten, kann der Besteller die Vergütung durch Erklärung gegenüber dem Unternehmer mindern. [2]Der Ausschlussgrund des § 323 Abs. 5 Satz 2 findet keine Anwendung.

(2) Sind auf der Seite des Bestellers oder auf der Seite des Unternehmers mehrere beteiligt, so kann die Minderung nur von allen oder gegen alle erklärt werden.

(3) [1]Bei der Minderung ist die Vergütung in dem Verhältnis herabzusetzen, in welchem zur Zeit des Vertragsschlusses der Wert des Werkes in mangelfreiem Zustand zu dem wirklichen Wert gestanden haben würde. [2]Die Minderung ist, soweit erforderlich, durch Schätzung zu ermitteln.

(4) [1]Hat der Besteller mehr als die geminderte Vergütung gezahlt, so ist der Mehrbetrag vom Unternehmer zu erstatten. [2]§ 346 Abs. 1 und § 347 Abs. 1 finden entsprechende Anwendung.

§639
Haftungsausschluss

Auf eine Vereinbarung, durch welche die Rechte des Bestellers wegen eines Mangels ausgeschlossen oder beschränkt werden, kann sich der Unternehmer nicht berufen, soweit er den Mangel arglistig verschwiegen oder eine Garantie für die Beschaffenheit des Werkes übernommen hat.

Section 637
Self-help

(1) If there is a defect in the work, the customer may, after the expiry without result of a reasonable period specified by him for cure, remedy the defect himself and demand reimbursement of the necessary expenses, unless the contractor rightly refuses cure.

(2) [1]Section 323 (2) applies with the necessary modifications. [2] A period of time need not be specified even if cure has failed or cannot reasonably be expected of the customer.

(3) The customer may demand from the contractor advance payment of the expenses necessary to remedy the defect.

Section 638
Reduction of price

(1) [1]Instead of revocation of the contract, the customer may reduce the remuneration by declaration to the contractor. [2]The ground for exclusion under section 323 (5) sentence 2 does not apply.

(2) If the customer or the contractor consists of more than one person, reduction of price may be declared only by or to all of them.

(3) [1]In the case of reduction of price, the payment is to be reduced in the proportion which, at the time when the contract was entered into, the value of the work in a state free of defects would have had to the actual value. [2]To the extent necessary, the price reduction is to be established by appraisal.

(4) [1]If the customer has paid more than the reduced remuneration, the contractor must reimburse the surplus. [2]Section 346 (1) and section 347 (1) apply with the necessary modifications.

Section 639
Exclusion of liability

The contractor may not rely on an agreement by which the rights of the customer with regard to a defect are excluded or restricted, insofar as the contractor fraudulently concealed the defect or gave a guarantee for the quality of the work.

§ 640
Abnahme

(1) ¹Der Besteller ist verpflichtet, das vertragsmäßig hergestellte Werk abzunehmen, sofern nicht nach der Beschaffenheit des Werkes die Abnahme ausgeschlossen ist. ²Wegen unwesentlicher Mängel kann die Abnahme nicht verweigert werden.

(2) ¹Als abgenommen gilt ein Werk auch, wenn der Unternehmer dem Besteller nach Fertigstellung des Werks eine angemessene Frist zur Abnahme gesetzt hat und der Besteller die Abnahme nicht innerhalb dieser Frist unter Angabe mindestens eines Mangels verweigert hat. ²Ist der Besteller ein Verbraucher, so treten die Rechtsfolgen des Satzes 1 nur dann ein, wenn der Unternehmer den Besteller zusammen mit der Aufforderung zur Abnahme auf die Folgen einer nicht erklärten oder ohne Angabe von Mängeln verweigerten Abnahme hingewiesen hat; der Hinweis muss in Textform erfolgen.

(3) Nimmt der Besteller ein mangelhaftes Werk gemäß Absatz 1 Satz 1 ab, obschon er den Mangel kennt, so stehen ihm die in § 634 Nr. 1 bis 3 bezeichneten Rechte nur zu, wenn er sich seine Rechte wegen des Mangels bei der Abnahme vorbehält.

§ 641
Fälligkeit der Vergütung

(1) ¹Die Vergütung ist bei der Abnahme des Werkes zu entrichten. ²Ist das Werk in Teilen abzunehmen und die Vergütung für die einzelnen Teile bestimmt, so ist die Vergütung für jeden Teil bei dessen Abnahme zu entrichten.

(2) ¹Die Vergütung des Unternehmers für ein Werk, dessen Herstellung der Besteller einem Dritten versprochen hat, wird spätestens fällig,

1. soweit der Besteller von dem Dritten für das versprochene Werk wegen dessen Herstellung seine Vergütung oder Teile davon erhalten hat,
2. soweit das Werk des Bestellers von dem Dritten abgenommen worden ist oder als abgenommen gilt oder
3. wenn der Unternehmer dem Besteller erfolglos eine angemessene Frist zur Auskunft über die in den Nummern 1 und 2 bezeichneten Umstände bestimmt hat.

²Hat der Besteller dem Dritten wegen möglicher Mängel des Werks Sicherheit geleistet, gilt Satz 1 nur, wenn der Unternehmer dem Besteller entsprechende Sicherheit lei stet.

Section 640
Acceptance

(1) ¹The customer is obliged to accept the work produced in conformity with the contract, except to the extent that, in view of the quality of the work, acceptance is excluded. ²Acceptance may not be refused by reason of trivial defects.

(2) ¹A work shall also be deemed to have been accepted if the contractor has set the customer a reasonable period of time for acceptance after completion of the work and the customer has not refused acceptance within this period of time, stating at least one defect. ²If the customer is a consumer, the legal consequences of sentence 1 shall only apply if the contractor has informed the customer, together with the request for acceptance, of the consequences of an acceptance that has not been declared or has been refused without stating defects; this information must be provided in text form.

(3) If the customer accepts a defective work under subsection (1) sentence 1, even though he knows of the defect, he only has the rights designated in section 634 nos. 1 to 3 if he reserves his rights with regard to the defect when he accepts the work.

Section 641
Due date of remuneration

(1) ¹The remuneration must be paid upon acceptance of the work. ²If the work is to be accepted in parts and the remuneration for the individual parts is specified, then the remuneration is to be paid for each part when it is accepted.

(2) ¹The remuneration of the contractor for a work whose production the customer has promised to a third party is due at the latest

1. to the extent that the customer has received from the third party his remuneration or parts of his remuneration for the production of the promised work,
2. to the extent that the work of the customer has been accepted by the third party or is deemed to have been accepted, or
3. to the extent that the contractor has unsuccessfully set the customer a suitable deadline for information on the circumstances referred to in nos. 1 and 2.

²If the customer has given the third party security on account of possible defects of the work, sentence 1 applies only if the contractor gives the customer an appropriate security.

(3) Kann der Besteller die Beseitigung eines Mangels verlangen, so kann er nach der Fälligkeit die Zahlung eines angemessenen Teils der Vergütung verweigern; angemessen ist in der Regel das Doppelte der für die Beseitigung des Mangels erforderlichen Kosten.

(4) Eine in Geld festgesetzte Vergütung hat der Besteller von der Abnahme des Werkes an zu verzinsen, sofern nicht die Vergütung gestundet ist.

§642
Mitwirkung des Bestellers

(1) Ist bei der Herstellung des Werkes eine Handlung des Bestellers erforderlich, so kann der Unternehmer, wenn der Besteller durch das Unterlassen der Handlung in Verzug der Annahme kommt, eine angemessene Entschädigung verlangen.

(2) Die Höhe der Entschädigung bestimmt sich einerseits nach der Dauer des Verzugs und der Höhe der vereinbarten Vergütung, andererseits nach demjenigen, was der Unternehmer infolge des Verzugs an Aufwendungen erspart oder durch anderweitige Verwendung seiner Arbeitskraft erwerben kann.

§643
Kündigung bei unterlassener Mitwirkung

¹Der Unternehmer ist im Falle des §642 berechtigt, dem Besteller zur Nachholung der Handlung eine angemessene Frist mit der Erklärung zu bestimmen, dass er den Vertrag kündige, wenn die Handlung nicht bis zum Ablauf der Frist vorgenommen werde. ²Der Vertrag gilt als aufgehoben, wenn nicht die Nachholung bis zum Ablauf der Frist erfolgt.

§644
Gefahrtragung

(1) ¹Der Unternehmer trägt die Gefahr bis zur Abnahme des Werkes. ²Kommt der Besteller in Verzug der Annahme, so geht die Gefahr auf ihn über. ³Für den zufälligen Untergang und eine zufällige Verschlechterung des von dem Besteller gelieferten Stoffes ist der Unternehmer nicht verantwortlich.

(2) Versendet der Unternehmer das Werk auf Verlangen des Bestellers nach einem anderen Ort als dem Erfüllungsort, so findet die für den Kauf geltende Vorschrift des §447 entsprechende Anwendung.

(3) If the customer may demand remedy of a defect, he may, after becoming due, refuse to pay a reasonable portion of the remuneration; twice the costs necessary to remedy the defect are appropriate as a rule.

(4) If the remuneration is assessed in money, the customer must pay interest on it from the acceptance of the work on, except to the extent that remuneration is deferred.

Section 642
Collaboration by the customer

(1) If, in the production of the work, an act by the customer is necessary, then the contractor may demand reasonable compensation if the customer, by failing to perform the act, is in default of acceptance.

(2) The amount of compensation is assessed on the one hand on the basis of the duration of the default and the amount of the agreed remuneration, and on the other hand on the basis of what expenses the contractor saves or what the contractor can earn by employing his working capacity elsewhere.

Section 643
Termination for failure to collaborate

¹In the case of section 642, the contractor is entitled to give the customer a reasonable period of time for making up for the act to be performed by declaring that he will terminate the contract if the act is not undertaken by the end of the period of time. ²The contract is deemed to be cancelled if the act is not made up for by the end of the period of time.

Section 644
Allocation of risk

(1) The contractor bears the risk until acceptance of the work. If the customer is in default of acceptance, then the risk passes to him. The contractor is not liable for any accidental destruction or accidental deterioration of the materials supplied by the customer.

(2) If, at the demand of the customer, the contractor ships the work to a place other than the place of performance, then the provisions of section 447 governing purchase apply with the necessary modifications.

§645
Verantwortlichkeit des Bestellers

(1) [1]Ist das Werk vor der Abnahme infolge eines Mangels des von dem Besteller gelieferten Stoffes oder infolge einer von dem Besteller für die Ausführung erteilten Anweisung untergegangen, verschlechtert oder unausführbar geworden, ohne dass ein Umstand mitgewirkt hat, den der Unternehmer zu vertreten hat, so kann der Unternehmer einen der geleisteten Arbeit entsprechenden Teil der Vergütung und Ersatz der in der Vergütung nicht inbegriffenen Auslagen verlangen. [2]Das Gleiche gilt, wenn der Vertrag in Gemäßheit des § 643 aufgehoben wird.

(2) Eine weitergehende Haftung des Bestellers wegen Verschuldens bleibt unberührt.

§646
Vollendung statt Abnahme

Ist nach der Beschaffenheit des Werkes die Abnahme ausgeschlossen, so tritt in den Fällen des § 634a Abs. 2 und der §§ 641, 644 und 645 an die Stelle der Abnahme die Vollendung des Werkes.

§647
Unternehmerpfandrecht

§647a
Sicherungshypothek des Inhabers einer Schiffswerft

[1]Der Inhaber einer Schiffswerft kann für seine Forderungen aus dem Bau oder der Ausbesserung eines Schiffes die Einräumung einer Schiffshypothek an dem Schiffsbauwerk oder dem Schiff des Bestellers verlangen. [2]Ist das Werk noch nicht vollendet, so kann er die Einräumung der Schiffshypothek für einen der geleisteten Arbeit entsprechenden Teil der Vergütung und für die in der Vergütung nicht inbegriffenen Auslagen verlangen. [3]§ 647 findet keine Anwendung.

§648
Kündigungsrecht des Bestellers

[1]Der Besteller kann bis zur Vollendung des Werkes jederzeit den Vertrag kündigen. [2]Kündigt der Besteller, so ist der Unternehmer berechtigt, die vereinbarte Vergütung zu verlangen; er muss sich jedoch dasjenige anrechnen lassen, was er infolge der Aufhebung des Vertrags an Aufwendungen erspart oder durch anderweitige Verwendung seiner Arbeitskraft erwirbt oder zu erwerben böswillig unterlässt. [3]Es wird vermutet, dass danach dem Unternehmer 5 vom Hundert der auf den noch nicht erbrachten Teil der Werkleistung entfallenden vereinbarten Vergütung zustehen.

Section 645
Responsibility of the customer

(1) [1]If the work, before acceptance, is destroyed or deteriorates or becomes impracticable as the result of a defect in the materials supplied by the customer or as the result of an instruction given by the customer for the carrying out of the work, without a circumstance for which the contractor is responsible contributing to this, then the contractor may demand a part of the remuneration that corresponds to the work performed and reimbursement of those expenses not included in the remuneration. [2]The same applies if the contract is cancelled under section 643.

(2) A more extensive liability of the customer for fault is unaffected.

Section 646
Completion in lieu of acceptance

If acceptance is excluded due to the quality of the work, then, in the cases of sections 634a (2) and 641, 644 and 645, completion of the work takes the place of acceptance.

Section 647
Security right of the contractor

Section 647a
Security mortgage of the owner of a ship yard

[1]The owner of a shipyard may demand the granting of a ship mortgage on the ship under construction or the ship of the shipowner for his claims arising from the construction or repair of a ship. [2]If the work is not yet completed, he may demand the granting of a ship mortgage for a part of the remuneration corresponding to the work performed and for the expenses not included in the remuneration. [3]§ 647 shall not apply.

Section 648
Right of termination of the customer

[1]The customer may terminate the contract at any time up to completion of the work. [2]If the customer terminates the contract, then the contractor is entitled to demand the agreed remuneration; however, he must allow set-off of the expenses he saves as a result of cancelling the contract or acquires or wilfully fails to acquire from other use of his labour. [3]There is a presumption that the contractor is accordingly entitled to five percent of the remuneration accounted for by the part of the work not yet provided.

<table>
<tr><td>

§ 648a
Kündigung aus wichtigem Grund

</td><td>

Section 648a
Termination

</td></tr>
</table>

§ 648a
Kündigung aus wichtigem Grund

(1) ¹Beide Vertragsparteien können den Vertrag aus wichtigem Grund ohne Einhaltung einer Kündigungsfrist kündigen. ²Ein wichtiger Grund liegt vor, wenn dem kündigenden Teil unter Berücksichtigung aller Umstände des Einzelfalls und unter Abwägung der beiderseitigen Interessen die Fortsetzung des Vertragsverhältnisses bis zur Fertigstellung des Werks nicht zugemutet werden kann.

(2) Eine Teilkündigung ist möglich; sie muss sich auf einen abgrenzbaren Teil des geschuldeten Werks beziehen.

(3) § 314 Absatz 2 und 3 gilt entsprechend.

(4) ¹Nach der Kündigung kann jede Vertragspartei von der anderen verlangen, dass sie an einer gemeinsamen Feststellung des Leistungsstandes mitwirkt. ²Verweigert eine Vertragspartei die Mitwirkung oder bleibt sie einem vereinbarten oder einem von der anderen Vertragspartei innerhalb einer angemessenen Frist bestimmten Termin zur Leistungsstandfeststellung fern, trifft sie die Beweislast für den Leistungsstand zum Zeitpunkt der Kündigung. ³Dies gilt nicht, wenn die Vertragspartei infolge eines Umstands fernbleibt, den sie nicht zu vertreten hat und den sie der anderen Vertragspartei unverzüglich mitgeteilt hat.

(5) Kündigt eine Vertragspartei aus wichtigem Grund, ist der Unternehmer nur berechtigt, die Vergütung zu verlangen, die auf den bis zur Kündigung erbrachten Teil des Werks entfällt.

(6) Die Berechtigung, Schadensersatz zu verlangen, wird durch die Kündigung nicht ausgeschlossen.

§ 649
Kostenanschlag

(1) Ist dem Vertrag ein Kostenanschlag zugrunde gelegt worden, ohne dass der Unternehmer die Gewähr für die Richtigkeit des Anschlags übernommen hat, und ergibt sich, dass das Werk nicht ohne eine wesentliche Überschreitung des Anschlags ausführbar ist, so steht dem Unternehmer, wenn der Besteller den Vertrag aus diesem Grund kündigt, nur der im § 645 Abs. 1 bestimmte Anspruch zu.

(2) Ist eine solche Überschreitung des Anschlags zu erwarten, so hat der Unternehmer dem Besteller unverzüglich Anzeige zu machen.

Section 648a
Termination

(1) ¹Both contracting parties may terminate the contract for good cause without notice. ²An important reason exists if, taking into account all circumstances of the individual case and weighing the interests of both parties, the terminating party cannot reasonably be expected to continue the contractual relationship until the work is completed.

(2) Partial termination is possible; it must relate to a delimitable part of the work owed.

(3) Section 314 (2) and (3) shall apply accordingly.

(4) ¹After termination, either party may require the other party to cooperate in a joint determination of the state of performance. ²If one party to the contract refuses to cooperate or remains away from an agreed date or a date determined by the other party to the contract within a reasonable period for the determination of the state of performance, it shall bear the burden of proof for the state of performance at the time of termination. ³This does not apply if the contracting party is absent as a result of a circumstance for which it is not responsible and which it has immediately notified to the other contracting party.

(5) If a contractual party terminates the contract for good cause, the entrepreneur is only entitled to demand payment for the part of the work performed up to the termination.

(6) The right to claim damages is not excluded by the termination.

Section 649
Cost estimate

(1) If the contract is based on a cost estimate without the contractor guaranteeing the accuracy of the estimate and if it turns out that the work cannot be carried out without substantially exceeding the estimate, then the contractor is only entitled, if the customer terminates the contract for this reason, to the claim specified in section 645 (1).

(2) If such exceeding of the estimate is to be expected, then the contractor must notify the customer of this without undue delay.

§665
Abweichung von Weisungen

[1]Der Beauftragte ist berechtigt, von den Weisungen des Auftraggebers abzuweichen, wenn er den Umständen nach annehmen darf, dass der Auftraggeber bei Kenntnis der Sachlage die Abweichung billigen würde. [2]Der Beauftragte hat vor der Abweichung dem Auftraggeber Anzeige zu machen und dessen Entschließung abzuwarten, wenn nicht mit dem Aufschub Gefahr verbunden ist.

§666
Auskunfts- und Rechenschaftspflicht

Der Beauftragte ist verpflichtet, dem Auftraggeber die erforderlichen Nachrichten zu geben, auf Verlangen über den Stand des Geschäfts Auskunft zu erteilen und nach der Ausführung des Auftrags Rechenschaft abzulegen.

§675
Entgeltliche Geschäftsbesorgung

(1) Auf einen Dienstvertrag oder einen Werkvertrag, der eine Geschäftsbesorgung zum Gegenstand hat, finden, soweit in diesem Untertitel nichts Abweichendes bestimmt wird, die Vorschriften der §§663, 665 bis 670, 672 bis 674 und, wenn dem Verpflichteten das Recht zusteht, ohne Einhaltung einer Kündigungsfrist zu kündigen, auch die Vorschrift des §671 Abs. 2 entsprechende Anwendung.

(2) Wer einem anderen einen Rat oder eine Empfehlung erteilt, ist, unbeschadet der sich aus einem Vertragsverhältnis, einer unerlaubten Handlung oder einer sonstigen gesetzlichen Bestimmung ergebenden Verantwortlichkeit, zum Ersatz des aus der Befolgung des Rates oder der Empfehlung entstehenden Schadens nicht verpflichtet.

(3) Ein Vertrag, durch den sich der eine Teil verpflichtet, die Anmeldung oder Registrierung des anderen Teils zur Teilnahme an Gewinnspielen zu bewirken, die von einem Dritten durchgeführt werden, bedarf der Textform.

Section 665
Deviation from instructions

[1]The mandatary is entitled to deviate from the instructions of the mandator if he may assume in the circumstances that the mandator would approve of such deviation if he were aware of the factual situation. [2]The mandatary must make notification to the mandator prior to such deviation and must wait for the decision of the latter unless postponement entails danger.

Section 666
Duty of information and duty to render account

The mandatary is obliged to provide the mandator with the required reports, and on demand to provide information on the status of the transaction and after carrying out the mandate to render account for it.

Section 675
Nongratuitous management of the affairs of another

(1) The provisions of sections 663, 665 to 670 and 672 to 674 apply to a service contract or a contract to produce a work dealing with the management of the affairs of another to the extent that nothing else is provided in this subtitle and, if the person obliged is entitled to terminate without complying with a notice period, the provisions of section 671 (2) also apply with the necessary modifications.

(2) A person who gives another person advice or a recommendation, notwithstanding the responsibility that arises from a contractual relationship, a tort or another statutory provision, is not obliged to pay compensation for the damage arising from following the advice or the recommendation.

(3) A contract by means of which one party undertakes to effect the enrolment or registration of the other party to participate in games of chance operated by a third party must be in text form.

§ 771
Einrede der Vorausklage

¹Der Bürge kann die Befriedigung des Gläubigers verweigern, solange nicht der Gläubiger eine Zwangsvollstreckung gegen den Hauptschuldner ohne Erfolg versucht hat (Einrede der Vorausklage). ²Erhebt der Bürge die Einrede der Vorausklage, ist die Verjährung des Anspruchs des Gläubigers gegen den Bürgen gehemmt, bis der Gläubiger eine Zwangsvollstreckung gegen den Hauptschuldner ohne Erfolg versucht hat.

§ 773
Ausschluss der Einrede der Vorausklage

(1) Die Einrede der Vorausklage ist ausgeschlossen:

1. wenn der Bürge auf die Einrede verzichtet, insbesondere wenn er sich als Selbstschuldner verbürgt hat,
2. wenn die Rechtsverfolgung gegen den Hauptschuldner infolge einer nach der Übernahme der Bürgschaft eingetretenen Änderung des Wohnsitzes, der gewerblichen Niederlassung oder des Aufenthaltsorts des Hauptschuldners wesentlich erschwert ist,
3. wenn über das Vermögen des Hauptschuldners das Insolvenzverfahren eröffnet ist,
4. wenn anzunehmen ist, dass die Zwangsvollstreckung in das Vermögen des Hauptschuldners nicht zur Befriedigung des Gläubigers führen wird.

(2) In den Fällen der Nummern 3, 4 ist die Einrede insoweit zulässig, als sich der Gläubiger aus einer beweglichen Sache des Hauptschuldners befriedigen kann, an der er ein Pfandrecht oder ein Zurückbehaltungsrecht hat; die Vorschrift des § 772 Abs. 2 Satz 2 findet Anwendung.

§ 774
Gesetzlicher Forderungsübergang

(1) ¹Soweit der Bürge den Gläubiger befriedigt, geht die Forderung des Gläubigers gegen den Hauptschuldner auf ihn über. ²Der Übergang kann nicht zum Nachteil des Gläubigers geltend gemacht werden. ³Einwendungen des Hauptschuldners aus einem zwischen ihm und dem Bürgen bestehenden Rechtsverhältnis bleiben unberührt.

(2) Mitbürgen haften einander nur nach § 426.

Section 771
Defence of unexhausted remedies

¹The surety may refuse to satisfy the creditor as long as the creditor has not attempted without success to obtain execution of judgment against the principal debtor (defence of unexhausted remedies). ²If the surety raises the defence of unexhausted remedies, the limitation of the claim of the creditor against the surety is suspended until the creditor has attempted without success to obtain execution of judgment against the principal debtor.

Section 773
Exclusion of defence of unexhausted remedies

(1) The defence of unexhausted remedies is excluded:

1. if the surety waives the defence, including without limitation if he has assumed suretyship as principal debtor,
2. if pursuit of rights against the principal debtor is made appreciably more difficult due to a change of residence, of business establishment or of place of abode occurring after assumption of suretyship,
3. if insolvency proceedings have been opened in relation to the assets of the principal debtor,
4. if it must be assumed that enforcement of judgment against the assets of the principal debtor will not result in satisfaction of the claim of the creditor.

(2) In the cases cited in nos. 3 and 4, the defence is admissible to the extent that the creditor may satisfy his claim out of a movable thing of the principal debtor over which he has a security right or of which he has a right of retention; the provisions of section 772 (2) sentence 2 apply.

Section 774
Statutory passing of claims

(1) ¹To the extent that the surety satisfies the claims of the creditor, the claim of the creditor against the principal debtor passes to him. ²The passing of ownership may not be asserted to the disadvantage of the creditor. ³Objections by the principal debtor under a legal relationship existing between himself and the surety are unaffected.

(2) Co-sureties are only liable to each other under section 426.

§812
Herausgabeanspruch

(1) ¹Wer durch die Leistung eines anderen oder in sonstiger Weise auf dessen Kosten etwas ohne rechtlichen Grund erlangt, ist ihm zur Herausgabe verpflichtet. ²Diese Verpflichtung besteht auch dann, wenn der rechtliche Grund später wegfällt oder der mit einer Leistung nach dem Inhalt des Rechtsgeschäfts bezweckte Erfolg nicht eintritt.

(2) Als Leistung gilt auch die durch Vertrag erfolgte Anerkennung des Bestehens oder des Nichtbestehens eines Schuldverhältnisses.

Titel 27 Unerlaubte Handlungen

§823
Schadensersatzpflicht

(1) Wer vorsätzlich oder fahrlässig das Leben, den Körper, die Gesundheit, die Freiheit, das Eigentum oder ein sonstiges Recht eines anderen widerrechtlich verletzt, ist dem anderen zum Ersatz des daraus entstehenden Schadens verpflichtet.

(2) ¹Die gleiche Verpflichtung trifft denjenigen, welcher gegen ein den Schutz eines anderen bezweckendes Gesetz verstößt. ²Ist nach dem Inhalt des Gesetzes ein Verstoß gegen dieses auch ohne Verschulden möglich, so tritt die Ersatzpflicht nur im Falle des Verschuldens ein.

Section 812
Claim for restitution

(1) ¹ A person who obtains something as a result of the performance of another person or otherwise at his expense without legal grounds for doing so is under a duty to make restitution to him. ²This duty also exists if the legal grounds later lapse or if the result intended to be achieved by those efforts in accordance with the contents of the legal transaction does not occur.

(2) Performance also includes the acknowledgement of the existence or non-existence of an obligation.

Title 27 Torts

Section 823
Liability in damages

(1) A person who, intentionally or negligently, unlawfully injures the life, body, health, freedom, property or another right of another person is liable to make compensation to the other party for the damage arising from this.

(2) ¹The same duty is held by a person who commits a breach of a statute that is intended to protect another person. ²If, according to the contents of the statute, it may also be breached without fault, then liability to compensation only exists in the case of fault.

III. Act on Temporary Employment

Gesetz zur Regelung der Arbeitnehmerüberlassung – AÜG

Stand: 31.12.2019

<table>
<tr>
<td>

§ 1
Arbeitnehmerüberlassung, Erlaubnispflicht

(1) ¹Arbeitgeber, die als Verleiher Dritten (Entleihern) Arbeitnehmer (Leiharbeitnehmer) im Rahmen ihrer wirtschaftlichen Tätigkeit zur Arbeitsleistung überlassen (Arbeitnehmerüberlassung) wollen, bedürfen der Erlaubnis. ²Arbeitnehmer werden zur Arbeitsleistung überlassen, wenn sie in die Arbeitsorganisation des Entleihers eingegliedert sind und seinen Weisungen unterliegen. ³Die Überlassung und das Tätigwerdenlassen von Arbeitnehmern als Leiharbeitnehmer ist nur zulässig, soweit zwischen dem Verleiher und dem Leiharbeitnehmer ein Arbeitsverhältnis besteht. ⁴Die Überlassung von Arbeitnehmern ist vorübergehend bis zu einer Überlassungshöchstdauer nach Absatz 1b zulässig. ⁵Verleiher und Entleiher haben die Überlassung von Leiharbeitnehmern in ihrem Vertrag ausdrücklich als Arbeitnehmerüberlassung zu bezeichnen, bevor sie den Leiharbeitnehmer überlassen oder tätig werden lassen. ⁶Vor der Überlassung haben sie die Person des Leiharbeitnehmers unter Bezugnahme auf diesen Vertrag zu konkretisieren.

(1a) ¹Die Abordnung von Arbeitnehmern zu einer zur Herstellung eines Werkes gebildeten Arbeitsgemeinschaft ist keine Arbeitnehmerüberlassung, wenn der Arbeitgeber Mitglied der Arbeitsgemeinschaft ist, für alle Mitglieder der Arbeitsgemeinschaft Tarifverträge desselben Wirtschaftszweiges gelten und alle Mitglieder auf Grund des Arbeitsgemeinschaftsvertrages zur selbständigen Erbringung von Vertragsleistungen verpflichtet sind. ²Für einen Arbeitgeber mit Geschäftssitz in einem anderen Mitgliedstaat des Europäischen Wirtschaftsraumes ist die Abordnung von Arbeitnehmern zu einer zur Herstellung eines Werkes gebildeten Arbeitsgemeinschaft auch dann keine Arbeitnehmerüberlassung, wenn für ihn deutsche Tarifverträge desselben Wirtschaftszweiges wie für die anderen Mitglieder der Arbeitsgemeinschaft nicht gelten, er aber die übrigen Voraussetzungen des Satzes 1 erfüllt.

</td>
<td>

Section 1
Temporary Agency Employment, Duty to Obtain Permit

(1) Employers who, as temporary work agencies, wish to provide third parties (hirers) with employees (temporary agency employment) in the course of their business activities for the purpose of performing work (temporary agency employment) shall require permission. Employees are hired out to perform work if they are integrated into the work organisation of the hirer and are subject to his instructions. The assignment and employment of workers as temporary workers is only permitted if there is an employment relationship between the temporary work agency and the temporary worker. The assignment of workers is permitted temporarily up to a maximum assignment length in accordance with subsection 1b. The temporary work agency and the hirer must expressly designate the provision of temporary agency employment in their contract as temporary agency employment before the temporary agency worker is provided or becomes active. Before the assignment, they must concretise the person of the temporary agency worker with reference to this contract.

(1a) ¹The secondment of employees to a consortium formed for the purpose of a work's production shall not constitute temporary agency employment if the employer is a member of the consortium, if collective agreements in the same branch of industry apply to all members of the consortium and if all members are obliged to provide contractual services independently based on the consortium agreement. ²For an employer whose registered office is in another Member State of the European Economic Area, the secondment of employees to a consortium formed for the purpose of carrying out a work does not constitute temporary agency employment even if German collective agreements in the same branch of industry as those applicable to the other members of the consortium do not apply to him but he satisfies the other conditions in the first sentence.

</td>
</tr>
</table>

(1b) [1]Der Verleiher darf denselben Leiharbeitnehmer nicht länger als 18 aufeinander folgende Monate demselben Entleiher überlassen; der Entleiher darf denselben Leiharbeitnehmer nicht länger als 18 aufeinander folgende Monate tätig werden lassen. [2]Der Zeitraum vorheriger Überlassungen durch denselben oder einen anderen Verleiher an denselben Entleiher ist vollständig anzurechnen, wenn zwischen den Einsätzen jeweils nicht mehr als drei Monate liegen. [3]In einem Tarifvertrag von Tarifvertragsparteien der Einsatzbranche kann eine von Satz 1 abweichende Überlassungshöchstdauer festgelegt werden. [4]Im Geltungsbereich eines Tarifvertrages nach Satz 3 können abweichende tarifvertragliche Regelungen im Betrieb eines nicht tarifgebundenen Entleihers durch Betriebs- oder Dienstvereinbarung übernommen werden. [5]In einer auf Grund eines Tarifvertrages von Tarifvertragsparteien der Einsatzbranche getroffenen Betriebs- oder Dienstvereinbarung kann eine von Satz 1 abweichende Überlassungshöchstdauer festgelegt werden. [6]Können auf Grund eines Tarifvertrages nach Satz 5 abweichende Regelungen in einer Betriebs- oder Dienstvereinbarung getroffen werden, kann auch in Betrieben eines nicht tarifgebundenen Entleihers bis zu einer Überlassungshöchstdauer von 24 Monaten davon Gebrauch gemacht werden, soweit nicht durch diesen Tarifvertrag eine von Satz 1 abweichende Überlassungshöchstdauer für Betriebs- oder Dienstvereinbarungen festgelegt ist. [7]Unterfällt der Betrieb des nicht tarifgebundenen Entleihers bei Abschluss einer Betriebs- oder Dienstvereinbarung nach Satz 4 oder Satz 6 den Geltungsbereichen mehrerer Tarifverträge, ist auf den für die Branche des Entleihers repräsentativen Tarifvertrag abzustellen. [8]Die Kirchen und die öffentlich-rechtlichen Religionsgesellschaften können von Satz 1 abweichende Überlassungshöchstdauern in ihren Regelungen vorsehen.

(2) Werden Arbeitnehmer Dritten zur Arbeitsleistung überlassen und übernimmt der Überlassende nicht die üblichen Arbeitgeberpflichten oder das Arbeitgeberrisiko (§ 3 Abs. 1 Nr. 1 bis 3), so wird vermutet, dass der Überlassende Arbeitsvermittlung betreibt.

(3) Dieses Gesetz ist mit Ausnahme des § 1b Satz 1, des § 16 Absatz 1 Nummer 1f und Absatz 2 bis 5 sowie der §§ 17 und 18 nicht anzuwenden auf die Arbeitnehmerüberlassung

1. zwischen Arbeitgebern desselben Wirtschaftszweiges zur Vermeidung von Kurzarbeit oder Entlassungen, wenn ein für den Entleiher und Verleiher geltender Tarifvertrag dies vorsieht,

(1b) [1]The temporary work agency may not assign the same temporary agency worker to the same hirer for more than 18 consecutive months; the hirer may not assign the same temporary agency worker to work for more than 18 consecutive months. [2]The period of previous assignments by the same or another temporary work agency to the same hirer shall be fully credited if no more than three months elapse between the assignments. A collective agreement between the parties to the collective agreement in the sector of deployment may stipulate a maximum assignment length deviating from the first sentence. Within the scope of a collective agreement pursuant to sentence 3, deviating collective agreement provisions may be adopted in the business of a hirer not bound by a collective agreement by means of a works or service agreement. A maximum assignment length deviating from sentence 1 may be specified in a works or service agreement concluded on the basis of a collective agreement by parties to a collective agreement in the sector of deployment. If different provisions can be laid down in a works or service agreement on the basis of a collective agreement pursuant to sentence 5, use may also be made of such provisions in the establishments of a hirer not bound by a collective agreement up to a maximum assignment length of 24 months, unless this collective agreement stipulates a maximum assignment length for works or service agreements which differs from sentence 1. If the business of the hirer not bound by a collective agreement falls within the scope of several collective agreements when a works or service agreement is concluded pursuant to sentence 4 or sentence 6, the collective agreement representative of the hirer's branch of industry must be applied. The churches and the religious communities under public law may provide for maximum assignment length in their regulations which deviate from sentence 1.

(2) If employees are assigned to third parties to perform work and the transferor does not assume the usual employer obligations or the employer risk (Section 3 (1) Nos. 1 to 3), it shall be presumed that the transferor operates employment services.

(3) With the exception of section 1b sentence 1, section 16(1) number 1f and (2) to (5) and sections 17 and 18, this Act shall not apply to temporary agency employment

1. between employers in the same economic sector to avoid short-time working or redundancies, if a collective agreement applicable to the hirer and temporary work agency so provides

2. zwischen Konzernunternehmen im Sinne des § 18 des Aktiengesetzes, wenn der Arbeitnehmer nicht zum Zweck der Überlassung eingestellt und beschäftigt wird,

2a. zwischen Arbeitgebern, wenn die Überlassung nur gelegentlich erfolgt und der Arbeitnehmer nicht zum Zweck der Überlassung eingestellt und beschäftigt wird,

2b. zwischen Arbeitgebern, wenn Aufgaben eines Arbeitnehmers von dem bisherigen zu dem anderen Arbeitgeber verlagert werden und auf Grund eines Tarifvertrages des öffentlichen Dienstes

  (a) das Arbeitsverhältnis mit dem bisherigen Arbeitgeber weiter besteht und

  (b) die Arbeitsleistung zukünftig bei dem anderen Arbeitgeber erbracht wird,

2c. zwischen Arbeitgebern, wenn diese juristische Personen des öffentlichen Rechts sind und Tarifverträge des öffentlichen Dienstes oder Regelungen der öffentlich-rechtlichen Religionsgesellschaften anwenden, oder

3. in das Ausland, wenn der Leiharbeitnehmer in ein auf der Grundlage zwischenstaatlicher Vereinbarungen begründetes deutsch-ausländisches Gemeinschaftsunternehmen verliehen wird, an dem der Verleiher beteiligt ist.

§ 1a
Anzeige der Überlassung

(1) Keiner Erlaubnis bedarf ein Arbeitgeber mit weniger als 50 Beschäftigten, der zur Vermeidung von Kurzarbeit oder Entlassungen an einen Arbeitgeber einen Arbeitnehmer, der nicht zum Zweck der Überlassung eingestellt und beschäftigt wird, bis zur Dauer von zwölf Monaten überlässt, wenn er die Überlassung vorher schriftlich der Bundesagentur für Arbeit angezeigt hat.

(2) In der Anzeige sind anzugeben

1. Vor- und Familiennamen, Wohnort und Wohnung, Tag und Ort der Geburt des Leiharbeitnehmers,

2. Art der vom Leiharbeitnehmer zu leistenden Tätigkeit und etwaige Pflicht zur auswärtigen Leistung,

3. Beginn und Dauer der Überlassung,

4. Firma und Anschrift des Entleihers.

2. between group companies within the meaning of Article 18 of the German Stock Corporation Act (AktG), if the employee is not hired and employed for the purpose of assignment,

2a. between employers, if the assignment is only occasional and the employee is not hired and employed for the purpose of the assignment

2b. between employers, if tasks of an employee are transferred from the previous employer to the other employer and, on the basis of a collective agreement in the public sector

  (a) the employment relationship with the previous employer continues to exist; and

  (b) the work will in future be performed at the other employer,

2c. between employers, if they are legal persons under public law and apply collective agreements of the public service or regulations of the religious communities under public law, or

3. abroad, if the temporary agency worker is lent to a German-foreign joint venture established on the basis of intergovernmental agreements in which the temporary work agency has a share.

Section 1a
Notification of the Assignment

(1) An employer with fewer than 50 employees who, in order to avoid short-time work or dismissals, transfers to an employer an employee who is not hired and employed for the purpose of assignment for a period of up to twelve months, shall not require a permit if he has given prior written notification of the transfer to the Federal Employment Agency.

(2) The notification shall state

1. first and last names, place of residence and domicile, date and place of birth of the temporary agency worker

2. the nature of the work to be performed by the temporary agency worker and any obligation to provide external services

3. beginning and duration of the assignment,

4. company name and address of the hirer.

§ 1b
Einschränkungen im Baugewerbe

[1]Arbeitnehmerüberlassung nach § 1 in Betriebe des Baugewerbes für Arbeiten, die üblicherweise von Arbeitern verrichtet werden, ist unzulässig. [2]Sie ist gestattet

(a) zwischen Betrieben des Baugewerbes und anderen Betrieben, wenn diese Betriebe erfassende, für allgemeinverbindlich erklärte Tarifverträge dies bestimmen,

(b) zwischen Betrieben des Baugewerbes, wenn der verleihende Betrieb nachweislich seit mindestens drei Jahren von denselben Rahmen- und Sozialkassentarifverträgen oder von deren Allgemeinverbindlichkeit erfasst wird.

[3]Abweichend von Satz 2 ist für Betriebe des Baugewerbes mit Geschäftssitz in einem anderen Mitgliedstaat des Europäischen Wirtschaftsraumes Arbeitnehmerüberlassung auch gestattet, wenn die ausländischen Betriebe nicht von deutschen Rahmen- und Sozialkassentarifverträgen oder für allgemeinverbindlich erklärten Tarifverträgen erfasst werden, sie aber nachweislich seit mindestens drei Jahren überwiegend Tätigkeiten ausüben, die unter den Geltungsbereich derselben Rahmen- und Sozialkassentarifverträge fallen, von denen der Betrieb des Entleihers erfasst wird.

§ 2
Erteilung und Erlöschen der Erlaubnis

(1) Die Erlaubnis wird auf schriftlichen Antrag erteilt.

(2) [1]Die Erlaubnis kann unter Bedingungen erteilt und mit Auflagen verbunden werden, um sicherzustellen, dass keine Tatsachen eintreten, die nach § 3 die Versagung der Erlaubnis rechtfertigen. [2]Die Aufnahme, Änderung oder Ergänzung von Auflagen sind auch nach Erteilung der Erlaubnis zulässig.

(3) Die Erlaubnis kann unter dem Vorbehalt des Widerrufs erteilt werden, wenn eine abschließende Beurteilung des Antrags noch nicht möglich ist.

(4) [1]Die Erlaubnis ist auf ein Jahr zu befristen. [2]Der Antrag auf Verlängerung der Erlaubnis ist spätestens drei Monate vor Ablauf des Jahres zu stellen. [3]Die Erlaubnis verlängert sich um ein weiteres Jahr, wenn die Erlaubnisbehörde die Verlängerung nicht vor Ablauf des Jahres ablehnt. [4]Im Fall der Ablehnung gilt die Erlaubnis für die Abwicklung der nach § 1 erlaubt abgeschlossenen Verträge als fortbestehend, jedoch nicht länger als zwölf Monate.

Section 1b
Restrictions in the Construction Sector

Temporary agency employment in accordance with section 1 to companies in the construction sector for work that is normally carried out by workers is not permitted. It is permitted

(a) between undertakings in the construction sector and other undertakings, if collective agreements covering these undertakings and declaring them universally applicable so provide,

(b) between establishments in the construction sector, if it can be proved that the temporary work agency has been covered by the same framework and social security collective agreements for at least three years, or that they are generally applicable.

Derogating from the second sentence, temporary agency employment is also permitted for companies in the construction industry with their registered office in another Member State of the European Economic Area if the foreign companies are not covered by German framework and collective agreements or collective agreements which have been declared universally applicable, but it can be proved that for at least three years they have predominantly been engaged in activities which fall within the scope of the same framework and collective agreements which apply to the hirer's company.

Section 2
Issue and expiry of the licence

(1) A permit shall be granted on written application.

(2) [1]Permission may be granted subject to conditions and obligations to ensure that no facts occur which, under Section 3, justify refusal of permission. [2]The inclusion, modification or amendment of conditions shall be permissible even after the permit has been granted.

(3) Permission may be granted subject to revocation if a final assessment of the application is not yet possible.

(4) [1]The permit shall be limited to one year. [2]The application for renewal of the licence shall be submitted at the latest three months before the end of the year. [3]The permit shall be extended for a further year if the licensing authority does not refuse the extension before the end of the year. [4]In the event of refusal, the permit shall be deemed to continue in force for the execution of the contracts concluded in accordance with Section 1, but for no longer than twelve months.

(5) ¹Die Erlaubnis kann unbefristet erteilt werden, wenn der Verleiher drei aufeinanderfolgende Jahre lang nach § 1 erlaubt tätig war. ²Sie erlischt, wenn der Verleiher von der Erlaubnis drei Jahre lang keinen Gebrauch gemacht hat.

(5) ¹The permit may be granted for an unlimited period of time if the temporary work agency has worked for three consecutive years as permitted under Section 1. ²It shall expire if the temporary work agency has not made use of the permit for three years.

§ 2a
Gebühren und Auslagen

(1) Für die Bearbeitung von Anträgen auf Erteilung und Verlängerung der Erlaubnis werden vom Antragsteller Gebühren und Auslagen erhoben.

(2) ¹Die Bundesregierung wird ermächtigt, durch Rechtsverordnung die gebührenpflichtigen Tatbestände näher zu bestimmen und dabei feste Sätze und Rahmensätze vorzusehen. ²Die Gebühr darf im Einzelfall 2.500 Euro nicht überschreiten.

Section 2a
Fees and Expenses

(1) Fees and expenses shall be charged to the applicant for the processing of applications for the issue and renewal of a permit.

(2) ¹The Federal Government shall be authorised to specify the facts subject to fees in more detail by statutory instrument and to provide for fixed rates and framework rates. ²The fee may not exceed EUR 2,500 in individual cases.

§ 3
Versagung

(1) Die Erlaubnis oder ihre Verlängerung ist zu versagen, wenn Tatsachen die Annahme rechtfertigen, dass der Antragsteller

1. die für die Ausübung der Tätigkeit nach § 1 erforderliche Zuverlässigkeit nicht besitzt, insbesondere weil er die Vorschriften des Sozialversicherungsrechts, über die Einbehaltung und Abführung der Lohnsteuer, über die Arbeitsvermittlung, über die Anwerbung im Ausland oder über die Ausländerbeschäftigung, über die Überlassungshöchstdauer nach § 1 Absatz 1b, die Vorschriften des Arbeitsschutzrechts oder die arbeitsrechtlichen Pflichten nicht einhält;

2. nach der Gestaltung seiner Betriebsorganisation nicht in der Lage ist, die üblichen Arbeitgeberpflichten ordnungsgemäß zu erfüllen;

3. dem Leiharbeitnehmer die ihm nach § 8 zustehenden Arbeitsbedingungen einschließlich des Arbeitsentgelts nicht gewährt.

(2) Die Erlaubnis oder ihre Verlängerung ist ferner zu versagen, wenn für die Ausübung der Tätigkeit nach § 1 Betriebe, Betriebsteile oder Nebenbetriebe vorgesehen sind, die nicht in einem Mitgliedstaat der Europäischen Wirtschaftsgemeinschaft oder einem anderen Vertragsstaat des Abkommens über den Europäischen Wirtschaftsraum liegen.

Section 3
Refusal

(1) The authorisation or its renewal shall be refused where facts give reason to believe that the applicant

1. does not possess the reliability required for the performance of the activity pursuant to section 1, in particular because he/she does not comply with the provisions of social security law, withholding and payment of wage tax, employment services, recruitment abroad or employment of foreign nationals, the maximum assignment length according to section 1(1b), the provisions of employment protection law or the obligations under employment law

2. is not in a position to properly fulfil the usual obligations of an employer according to the organisation of his business;

3. does not grant the temporary agency worker the working conditions, including remuneration, to which he is entitled under section 8.

(2) Permission or its extension shall also be refused if the activities referred to in section 1 are to be carried out in establishments, parts of establishments or ancillary establishments which are not located in a Member State of the European Economic Community or in another State party to the Agreement on the European Economic Area.

(3) Die Erlaubnis kann versagt werden, wenn der Antragsteller nicht Deutscher im Sinne des Artikels 116 des Grundgesetzes ist oder wenn eine Gesellschaft oder juristische Person den Antrag stellt, die entweder nicht nach deutschem Recht gegründet ist oder die weder ihren satzungsmäßigen Sitz noch ihre Hauptverwaltung noch ihre Hauptniederlassung im Geltungsbereich dieses Gesetzes hat.

(4) ¹Staatsangehörige der Mitgliedstaaten der Europäischen Wirtschaftsgemeinschaft oder eines anderen Vertragsstaates des Abkommens über den Europäischen Wirtschaftsraum erhalten die Erlaubnis unter den gleichen Voraussetzungen wie deutsche Staatsangehörige. ²Den Staatsangehörigen dieser Staaten stehen gleich Gesellschaften und juristische Personen, die nach den Rechtsvorschriften dieser Staaten gegründet sind und ihren satzungsgemäßen Sitz, ihre Hauptverwaltung oder ihre Hauptniederlassung innerhalb dieser Staaten haben. ³Soweit diese Gesellschaften oder juristische Personen zwar ihren satzungsmäßigen Sitz, jedoch weder ihre Hauptverwaltung noch ihre Hauptniederlassung innerhalb dieser Staaten haben, gilt Satz 2 nur, wenn ihre Tätigkeit in tatsächlicher und dauerhafter Verbindung mit der Wirtschaft eines Mitgliedstaates oder eines Vertragsstaates des Abkommens über den Europäischen Wirtschaftsraum steht.

(5) ¹Staatsangehörige anderer als der in Absatz 4 genannten Staaten, die sich aufgrund eines internationalen Abkommens im Geltungsbereich dieses Gesetzes niederlassen und hierbei sowie bei ihrer Geschäftstätigkeit nicht weniger günstig behandelt werden dürfen als deutsche Staatsangehörige, erhalten die Erlaubnis unter den gleichen Voraussetzungen wie deutsche Staatsangehörige. ²Den Staatsangehörigen nach Satz 1 stehen gleich Gesellschaften, die nach den Rechtsvorschriften des anderen Staates gegründet sind.

(3) Permission may be refused if the applicant is not German within the meaning of Article 116 of the Basic Law or if the application is submitted by a company or legal entity which is either not incorporated under German law or which has neither its registered office nor its central administration nor its principal place of business within the territory covered by this Act.

(4) ¹Nationals of Member States of the European Economic Community or of another State party to the Agreement on the European Economic Area shall be granted permission under the same conditions as German nationals. ²The nationals of these States shall be treated in the same way as companies and legal persons which are formed in accordance with the laws of these States and have their registered office, central administration or principal place of business within these States. ³Insofar as these companies or legal persons have their registered office under their articles of association but neither their central administration nor their principal place of business within these States, the second sentence applies only if their activities have a real and lasting link with the economy of a Member State or a State party to the Agreement on the European Economic Area.

(5) ¹Nationals of States other than those referred to in paragraph 4 who, on the basis of an international agreement, establish themselves within the scope of this Act and who, in so doing and in their business activities, may not be treated less favourably than German nationals shall be granted permission under the same conditions as German nationals. ²The nationals referred to in the first sentence are treated in the same way as companies established under the legislation of the other State.

§ 3a
Lohnuntergrenze

Section 3a
Lower Wage Limit

(1) ¹Gewerkschaften und Vereinigungen von Arbeitgebern, die zumindest auch für ihre jeweiligen in der Arbeitnehmerüberlassung tätigen Mitglieder zuständig sind (vorschlagsberechtigte Tarifvertragsparteien) und bundesweit tarifliche Mindeststundenentgelte im Bereich der Arbeitnehmerüberlassung miteinander vereinbart haben, können dem Bundesministerium für Arbeit und Soziales gemeinsam vorschlagen, diese als Lohnuntergrenze in einer Rechtsverordnung verbindlich festzusetzen; die Mindeststundenentgelte können nach dem jeweiligen Beschäftigungsort differenzieren und

(1) ¹Trade unions and employers' associations which are also responsible at least for their respective members engaged in temporary agency employment (parties to collective agreements with the right to propose) and which have agreed minimum hourly rates of pay in the field of temporary agency employment with one another in collective agreements throughout Germany may jointly propose to the Federal Ministry of Labour and Social Affairs that these be made binding as a lower wage limit in a statutory instrument; the minimum hourly rates of pay may vary according to the respective place

auch Regelungen zur Fälligkeit entsprechender Ansprüche einschließlich hierzu vereinbarter Ausnahmen und deren Voraussetzungen umfassen. [2]Der Vorschlag muss für Verleihzeiten und verleihfreie Zeiten einheitliche Mindeststundenentgelte sowie eine Laufzeit enthalten. [3]Der Vorschlag ist schriftlich zu begründen.

(2) [1]Das Bundesministerium für Arbeit und Soziales kann, wenn dies im öffentlichen Interesse geboten erscheint, in einer Rechtsverordnung ohne Zustimmung des Bundesrates bestimmen, dass die vorgeschlagenen tariflichen Mindeststundenentgelte nach Absatz 1 als verbindliche Lohnuntergrenze auf alle in den Geltungsbereich der Verordnung fallenden Arbeitgeber sowie Leiharbeitnehmer Anwendung findet. [2]Der Verordnungsgeber kann den Vorschlag nur inhaltlich unverändert in die Rechtsverordnung übernehmen.

(3) [1]Der Verordnungsgeber hat bei seiner Entscheidung nach Absatz 2 im Rahmen einer Gesamtabwägung neben den Zielen dieses Gesetzes zu prüfen, ob eine Rechtsverordnung nach Absatz 2 insbesondere geeignet ist, die finanzielle Stabilität der sozialen Sicherungssysteme zu gewährleisten. [2]Der Verordnungsgeber hat zu berücksichtigen

1. die bestehenden bundesweiten Tarifverträge in der Arbeitnehmerüberlassung und

2. die Repräsentativität der vorschlagenden Tarifvertragsparteien.

(4) [1]Liegen mehrere Vorschläge nach Absatz 1 vor, hat der Verordnungsgeber bei seiner Entscheidung nach Absatz 2 im Rahmen der nach Absatz 3 erforderlichen Gesamtabwägung die Repräsentativität der vorschlagenden Tarifvertragsparteien besonders zu berücksichtigen. [2]Bei der Feststellung der Repräsentativität ist vorrangig abzustellen auf

1. die Zahl der jeweils in den Geltungsbereich einer Rechtsverordnung nach Absatz 2 fallenden Arbeitnehmer, die bei Mitgliedern der vorschlagenden Arbeitgebervereinigung beschäftigt sind;

2. die Zahl der jeweils in den Geltungsbereich einer Rechtsverordnung nach Absatz 2 fallenden Mitglieder der vorschlagenden Gewerkschaften.

(5) [1]Vor Erlass ist ein Entwurf der Rechtsverordnung im Bundesanzeiger bekannt zu machen. [2]Das Bundesministerium für Arbeit und Soziales gibt Verleihern und Leiharbeitnehmern sowie den Gewerkschaften und Vereinigungen von Arbeitgebern, die im Geltungsbereich der

of employment and may also include provisions on the due date of corresponding claims, including any exceptions agreed for this purpose and the conditions under which they are to be met. [2]The proposal must include uniform minimum hourly rates for rental periods and non-rental periods and a duration. The proposal must be justified in writing.

(2) [1]If this appears necessary in the public interest, the Federal Ministry of Labour and Social Affairs may, without the consent of the Bundesrat, stipulate in a statutory ordinance that the proposed collectively agreed minimum hourly rates of pay pursuant to paragraph 1 shall apply as a binding lower wage limit to all employers and temporary agency workers falling within the scope of the ordinance. [2]The legislator can only incorporate the proposal into the ordinance unchanged in terms of content.

(3) [1]When taking its decision under subsection 2, the legislature shall, in addition to the objectives of this Act, examine in the context of an overall balancing exercise whether a statutory ordinance under subsection 2 is in particular suitable for ensuring the financial stability of social security systems. [2]The legislator shall take into account

1. the existing nationwide collective agreements in temporary agency employment and

2. the representativeness of the proposing parties to the collective bargaining agreement.

(4) [1]If there are several proposals under subsection 1, the legislator shall, when taking its decision under subsection 2, take particular account of the representativeness of the proposing parties to the collective agreement in the context of the overall balancing exercise required under subsection 3. [2]In determining representativeness, priority shall be given to

1. the number of employees falling within the scope of a statutory instrument pursuant to subsection 2 who are employed by members of the proposing employers' association

J. the number of members of the proposing trade unions falling within the scope of a statutory instrument pursuant to subsection 2.

(5) [1]Before adoption, a draft of the statutory instrument shall be published in the Federal Gazette. [2]The Federal Ministry of Labour and Social Affairs shall give temporary work agencies and temporary agency workers as well as the trade unions and associations of employers

Rechtsverordnung zumindest teilweise tarifzuständig sind, Gelegenheit zur schriftlichen Stellungnahme innerhalb von drei Wochen ab dem Tag der Bekanntmachung des Entwurfs der Rechtsverordnung im Bundesanzeiger. ³Nach Ablauf der Stellungnahmefrist wird der in § 5 Absatz 1 Satz 1 des Tarifvertragsgesetzes genannte Ausschuss mit dem Vorschlag befasst.

(6) ¹Nach Absatz 1 vorschlagsberechtigte Tarifvertragsparteien können gemeinsam die Änderung einer nach Absatz 2 erlassenen Rechtsverordnung vorschlagen. ²Die Absätze 1 bis 5 finden entsprechend Anwendung.

which have at least partial collective bargaining competence within the scope of application of the statutory instrument the opportunity to submit written comments within three weeks of the date of publication of the draft statutory instrument in the Federal Gazette. ³After expiry of the period for submitting comments, the committee referred to in section 5(1) first sentence of the Collective Bargaining Act shall be referred to the proposal.

(6) ¹The parties to a collective agreement entitled to make proposals under subsection 1 may jointly propose the amendment of a statutory instrument issued under subsection 2. ²Subsections 1 to 5 shall apply mutatis mutandis.

§ 4
Rücknahme

(1) ¹Eine rechtswidrige Erlaubnis kann mit Wirkung für die Zukunft zurückgenommen werden. ²§ 2 Abs. 4 Satz 4 gilt entsprechend.

(2) ¹Die Erlaubnisbehörde hat dem Verleiher auf Antrag den Vermögensnachteil auszugleichen, den dieser dadurch erleidet, dass er auf den Bestand der Erlaubnis vertraut hat, soweit sein Vertrauen unter Abwägung mit dem öffentlichen Interesse schutzwürdig ist. ²Auf Vertrauen kann sich der Verleiher nicht berufen, wenn er

1. die Erlaubnis durch arglistige Täuschung, Drohung oder eine strafbare Handlung erwirkt hat;
2. die Erlaubnis durch Angaben erwirkt hat, die in wesentlicher Beziehung unrichtig oder unvollständig waren, oder
3. die Rechtswidrigkeit der Erlaubnis kannte oder infolge grober Fahrlässigkeit nicht kannte.

³Der Vermögensnachteil ist jedoch nicht über den Betrag des Interesses hinaus zu ersetzen, das der Verleiher an dem Bestand der Erlaubnis hat. Der auszugleichende Vermögensnachteil wird durch die Erlaubnisbehörde festgesetzt. Der Anspruch kann nur innerhalb eines Jahres geltend gemacht werden; die Frist beginnt, sobald die Erlaubnisbehörde den Verleiher auf sie hingewiesen hat.

(3) Die Rücknahme ist nur innerhalb eines Jahres seit dem Zeitpunkt zulässig, in dem die Erlaubnisbehörde von den Tatsachen Kenntnis erhalten hat, die die Rücknahme der Erlaubnis rechtfertigen.

Section 4
Withdrawal

(1) ¹An unlawful permit may be withdrawn with effect for the future. ²Section 2 (4) sentence 4 shall apply accordingly.

(2) ¹Upon application, the licensing autority shall compensate the temporary work agency for the pecuniary disadvantage suffered as a result of the fact that he had placed its trust in the existence of the licence to the extent that its trust is worthy of protection in consideration of the public interest. ²The temporary work agency may not invoke trust if it

1. has obtained permission by fraudulent deception, threat or a criminal offence
2. obtained the licence by providing information which was incorrect or incomplete in a material respect, or
3. was aware of the unlawfulness of the licence or was unaware of it due to gross negligence.

³However, the pecuniary disadvantage shall not be compensated for in excess of the amount of the interest the temporary work agency has in the stock of the licence. The financial disadvantage to be compensated shall be determined by the licensing authority. The claim may only be asserted within one year; the period begins as soon as the licensing authority has drawn the attention of the temporary work agency to it.

(3) Withdrawal shall only be permitted within one year of the date on which the licensing authority became aware of the facts justifying the withdrawal of the licence.

§5
Widerruf

(1) Die Erlaubnis kann mit Wirkung für die Zukunft widerrufen werden, wenn

1. der Widerruf bei ihrer Erteilung nach §2 Abs. 3 vorbehalten worden ist;

2. der Verleiher eine Auflage nach §2 nicht innerhalb einer ihm gesetzten Frist erfüllt hat;

3. die Erlaubnisbehörde aufgrund nachträglich eingetretener Tatsachen berechtigt wäre, die Erlaubnis zu versagen, oder

4. die Erlaubnisbehörde aufgrund einer geänderten Rechtslage berechtigt wäre, die Erlaubnis zu versagen; §4 Abs. 2 gilt entsprechend.

(2) ¹Die Erlaubnis wird mit dem Wirksamwerden des Widerrufs unwirksam. ²§2 Abs. 4 Satz 4 gilt entsprechend.

(3) Der Widerruf ist unzulässig, wenn eine Erlaubnis gleichen Inhalts erneut erteilt werden müsste.

(4) Der Widerruf ist nur innerhalb eines Jahres seit dem Zeitpunkt zulässig, in dem die Erlaubnisbehörde von den Tatsachen Kenntnis erhalten hat, die den Widerruf der Erlaubnis rechtfertigen.

§6
Verwaltungszwang

Werden Leiharbeitnehmer von einem Verleiher ohne die erforderliche Erlaubnis überlassen, so hat die Erlaubnisbehörde dem Verleiher dies zu untersagen und das weitere Überlassen nach den Vorschriften des Verwaltungsvollstreckungsgesetzes zu verhindern.

§7
Anzeigen und Auskünfte

(1) ¹Der Verleiher hat der Erlaubnisbehörde nach Erteilung der Erlaubnis unaufgefordert die Verlegung, Schließung und Errichtung von Betrieben, Betriebsteilen oder Nebenbetrieben vorher anzuzeigen, soweit diese die Ausübung der Arbeitnehmerüberlassung zum Gegenstand haben. ²Wenn die Erlaubnis Personengesamtheiten, Personengesellschaften oder juristischen Personen erteilt ist und nach ihrer Erteilung eine andere Person zur Geschäftsführung oder Vertretung nach Gesetz, Satzung oder Gesellschaftsvertrag berufen wird, ist auch dies unaufgefordert anzuzeigen.

Section 5
Revocation

(1) The licence may be revoked with effect for the future if

1. the right of revocation was reserved at the time of its issue in accordance with section 2 (3)

2. the temporary work agency has not fulfilled a condition pursuant to section 2 within a period of time set for it;

3. the licensing authority would be entitled to refuse the licence on the basis of facts that occurred subsequently, or

4. the licensing authority would be entitled to refuse the licence on the basis of a changed legal situation; section 4 subsection (2) shall apply mutatis mutandis.

(2) ¹The licence shall become invalid upon the effective date of revocation. ²Section 2 (4) sentence 4 shall apply accordingly.

(3) The revocation is inadmissible if a licence with the same content would have to be granted again.

(4) The revocation is only permissible within one year of the time at which the licensing authority has become aware of the facts justifying the revocation of the licence.

Section 6
Administrative Obligation

If temporary agency workers are provided by a temporary work agency without the required permit, the licensing authority shall prohibit the temporary work agency from doing so and prevent further assignment in accordance with the provisions of the Administrative Enforcement Act.

Section 7
Advertisements and Information

(1) ¹The temporary work agency shall notify the licensing authority in advance and without being asked of the relocation, closure and establishment of establishments, parts of establishments or ancillary establishments after the licence has been granted, insofar as these are concerned with the exercise of temporary agency employment. ²If the licence is granted to groups of persons, partnerships or legal entities and, after its granting, another person is appointed to manage or represent the company in accordance with the law, the articles of association or the articles of association, this must also be notified without being requested.

(2) [1]Der Verleiher hat der Erlaubnisbehörde auf Verlangen die Auskünfte zu erteilen, die zur Durchführung des Gesetzes erforderlich sind. [2]Die Auskünfte sind wahrheitsgemäß, vollständig, fristgemäß und unentgeltlich zu erteilen. [3]Auf Verlangen der Erlaubnisbehörde hat der Verleiher die geschäftlichen Unterlagen vorzulegen, aus denen sich die Richtigkeit seiner Angaben ergibt, oder seine Angaben auf sonstige Weise glaubhaft zu machen. [4]Der Verleiher hat seine Geschäftsunterlagen drei Jahre lang aufzubewahren.

(3) [1]In begründeten Einzelfällen sind die von der Erlaubnisbehörde beauftragten Personen befugt, Grundstücke und Geschäftsräume des Verleihers zu betreten und dort Prüfungen vorzunehmen. [2]Der Verleiher hat die Maßnahmen nach Satz 1 zu dulden. [3]Das Grundrecht der Unverletzlichkeit der Wohnung (Artikel 13 des Grundgesetzes) wird insoweit eingeschränkt.

(4) [1]Durchsuchungen können nur auf Anordnung des Richters bei dem Amtsgericht, in dessen Bezirk die Durchsuchung erfolgen soll, vorgenommen werden. [2]Auf die Anfechtung dieser Anordnung finden die §§ 304 bis 310 der Strafprozessordnung entsprechende Anwendung. [3]Bei Gefahr im Verzug können die von der Erlaubnisbehörde beauftragten Personen während der Geschäftszeit die erforderlichen Durchsuchungen ohne richterliche Anordnung vornehmen. [4]An Ort und Stelle ist eine Niederschrift über die Durchsuchung und ihr wesentliches Ergebnis aufzunehmen, aus der sich, falls keine richterliche Anordnung ergangen ist, auch die Tatsachen ergeben, die zur Annahme einer Gefahr im Verzug geführt haben.

(5) Der Verleiher kann die Auskunft auf solche Fragen verweigern, deren Beantwortung ihn selbst oder einen der in § 383 Abs. 1 Nr. 1 bis 3 der Zivilprozessordnung bezeichneten Angehörigen der Gefahr strafgerichtlicher Verfolgung oder eines Verfahrens nach dem Gesetz über Ordnungswidrigkeiten aussetzen würde.

(2) [1]On request, the temporary work agency shall provide the licensing authority with the information required to implement the Act. [2]The information shall be provided truthfully, completely, in due time and free of charge. [3]At the request of the licensing authority, the temporary work agency shall present the business documents from which the correctness of its information can be deduced or otherwise substantiate its information. [4]The temporary work agency shall keep its business documents for three years.

(3) [1]In justified individual cases the persons authorised by the licensing authority shall be authorised to enter the premises and business premises of the temporary work agency and to carry out inspections there. [2]The temporary work agency shall tolerate the measures pursuant to sentence 1. [3]The fundamental right of inviolability of the home (Article 13 of the Basic Law) is restricted in this respect.

(4) [1]Searches may only be carried out by order of the judge at the local court in whose district the search is to be carried out. [2]Sections 304 to 310 of the Code of Criminal Procedure shall apply mutatis mutandis to any challenge to this order. [3]In the event of imminent danger, the persons authorised by the licensing authority may carry out the necessary searches during business hours without a court order. [4]A record of the search and its main findings must be made on the spot, which, if no judicial order has been issued, must also indicate the facts that led to the assumption of imminent danger.

(5) The temporary work agency may refuse to provide information on questions the answer to which would expose him or one of the members referred to in Section 383(1) Nos 1 to 3 of the German Code of Civil Procedure to the risk of criminal prosecution or proceedings under the Act on Administrative Offences.

§ 8
Grundsatz der Gleichstellung

(1) [1]Der Verleiher ist verpflichtet, dem Leiharbeitnehmer für die Zeit der Überlassung an den Entleiher die im Betrieb des Entleihers für einen vergleichbaren Arbeitnehmer des Entleihers geltenden wesentlichen Arbeitsbedingungen einschließlich des Arbeitsentgelts zu gewähren (Gleichstellungsgrundsatz). [2]Erhält der Leiharbeitnehmer das für einen vergleichbaren Arbeitnehmer des Entleihers im Entleihbetrieb geschuldete tarifvertragliche Arbeits-

Section 8
The Principle of Equality

(1) [1]For the period of assignment to the hirer, the temporary work agency is obliged to provide the temporary agency worker with the essential working conditions, including pay, applicable in the hirer's business to a comparable worker of the hirer (principle of equality). [2]If the temporary worker receives the collective agreement remuneration owed for a comparable worker of the hirer in the user's business or, in the absence of such remuneration, a collective agreement

entgelt oder in Ermangelung eines solchen ein für vergleichbare Arbeitnehmer in der Einsatzbranche geltendes tarifvertragliches Arbeitsentgelt, wird vermutet, dass der Leiharbeitnehmer hinsichtlich des Arbeitsentgelts im Sinne von Satz 1 gleichgestellt ist. ³Werden im Betrieb des Entleihers Sachbezüge gewährt, kann ein Wertausgleich in Euro erfolgen.

(2) ¹Ein Tarifvertrag kann vom Gleichstellungsgrundsatz abweichen, soweit er nicht die in einer Rechtsverordnung nach § 3a Absatz 2 festgesetzten Mindeststundenentgelte unterschreitet. ²Soweit ein solcher Tarifvertrag vom Gleichstellungsgrundsatz abweicht, hat der Verleiher dem Leiharbeitnehmer die nach diesem Tarifvertrag geschuldeten Arbeitsbedingungen zu gewähren. ³Im Geltungsbereich eines solchen Tarifvertrages können nicht tarifgebundene Arbeitgeber und Arbeitnehmer die Anwendung des Tarifvertrages vereinbaren. ⁴Soweit ein solcher Tarifvertrag die in einer Rechtsverordnung nach § 3a Absatz 2 festgesetzten Mindeststundenentgelte unterschreitet, hat der Verleiher dem Leiharbeitnehmer für jede Arbeitsstunde das im Betrieb des Entleihers für einen vergleichbaren Arbeitnehmer des Entleihers für eine Arbeitsstunde zu zahlende Arbeitsentgelt zu gewähren.

(3) Eine abweichende tarifliche Regelung im Sinne von Absatz 2 gilt nicht für Leiharbeitnehmer, die in den letzten sechs Monaten vor der Überlassung an den Entleiher aus einem Arbeitsverhältnis bei diesem oder einem Arbeitgeber, der mit dem Entleiher einen Konzern im Sinne des § 18 des Aktiengesetzes bildet, ausgeschieden sind.

(4) ¹Ein Tarifvertrag im Sinne des Absatzes 2 kann hinsichtlich des Arbeitsentgelts vom Gleichstellungsgrundsatz für die ersten neun Monate einer Überlassung an einen Entleiher abweichen. ²Eine längere Abweichung durch Tarifvertrag ist nur zulässig, wenn

1. nach spätestens 15 Monaten einer Überlassung an einen Entleiher mindestens ein Arbeitsentgelt erreicht wird, das in dem Tarifvertrag als gleichwertig mit dem tarifvertraglichen Arbeitsentgelt vergleichbarer Arbeitnehmer in der Einsatzbranche festgelegt ist, und
2. nach einer Einarbeitungszeit von längstens sechs Wochen eine stufenweise Heranführung an dieses Arbeitsentgelt erfolgt.

remuneration applicable to comparable workers in the field of deployment, it is presumed that the temporary worker is treated equally with regard to remuneration within the meaning of the first sentence. ³If remuneration in kind is granted in the hirer's business, a value adjustment may be made in euros.

(2) ¹A collective agreement may derogate from the principle of equality of treatment insofar as it does not fall below the minimum hourly rates of pay laid down in a statutory instrument pursuant to section 3a(2). ²Where such a collective agreement derogates from the principle of equality of treatment, the temporary work agency must grant the temporary agency worker the working conditions owed under this collective agreement. ³Within the scope of such a collective agreement, employers and employees not bound by a collective agreement may agree on the application of the collective agreement. ⁴In so far as such a collective agreement falls below the minimum hourly rates of pay laid down in a statutory instrument under Section 3a(2), the temporary work agency must grant the temporary agency worker, for each hour of work, the remuneration payable for one hour of work in the hirer's business for a comparable employee of the hirer.

(3) A deviating collective agreement provision within the meaning of paragraph 2 shall not apply to temporary agency workers who, in the six months preceding assignment to the hirer, have left an employment relationship with the hirer or an employer which forms a group of companies with the hirer within the meaning of section 18 of the German Stock Corporation Act (Aktiengesetz).

(4) ¹A collective agreement within the meaning of subsection 2 may derogate from the principle of equality of treatment with regard to pay for the first nine months of assignment to a hirer. ²A longer derogation by collective agreement shall only be permitted if

1. after no more than 15 months of an assignment to a hirer, at least a level of remuneration is reached which is defined in the collective agreement as being equivalent to the collectively agreed remuneration of comparable workers in the assignment industry, and
2. after a training period of no more than six weeks, a gradual approach to this remuneration is made.

³Im Geltungsbereich eines solchen Tarifvertrages können nicht tarifgebundene Arbeitgeber und Arbeitnehmer die Anwendung der tariflichen Regelungen vereinbaren. ⁴Der Zeitraum vorheriger Überlassungen durch denselben oder einen anderen Verleiher an denselben Entleiher ist vollständig anzurechnen, wenn zwischen den Einsätzen jeweils nicht mehr als drei Monate liegen.

(5) Der Verleiher ist verpflichtet, dem Leiharbeitnehmer mindestens das in einer Rechtsverordnung nach § 3a Absatz 2 für die Zeit der Überlassung und für Zeiten ohne Überlassung festgesetzte Mindeststundenentgelt zu zahlen.

§ 9
Unwirksamkeit

(1) Unwirksam sind:

1. Verträge zwischen Verleihern und Entleihern sowie zwischen Verleihern und Leiharbeitnehmern, wenn der Verleiher nicht die nach § 1 erforderliche Erlaubnis hat; der Vertrag zwischen Verleiher und Leiharbeitnehmer wird nicht unwirksam, wenn der Leiharbeitnehmer schriftlich bis zum Ablauf eines Monats nach dem zwischen Verleiher und Entleiher für den Beginn der Überlassung vorgesehenen Zeitpunkt gegenüber dem Verleiher oder dem Entleiher erklärt, dass er an dem Arbeitsvertrag mit dem Verleiher festhält; tritt die Unwirksamkeit erst nach Aufnahme der Tätigkeit beim Entleiher ein, so beginnt die Frist mit Eintritt der Unwirksamkeit,

1a. Arbeitsverträge zwischen Verleihern und Leiharbeitnehmern, wenn entgegen § 1 Absatz 1 Satz 5 und 6 die Arbeitnehmerüberlassung nicht ausdrücklich als solche bezeichnet und die Person des Leiharbeitnehmers nicht konkretisiert worden ist, es sei denn, der Leiharbeitnehmer erklärt schriftlich bis zum Ablauf eines Monats nach dem zwischen Verleiher und Entleiher für den Beginn der Überlassung vorgesehenen Zeitpunkt gegenüber dem Verleiher oder dem Entleiher, dass er an dem Arbeitsvertrag mit dem Verleiher festhält,

³Within the scope of such a collective agreement, employers and employees not bound by collective agreements may agree to apply the provisions of such agreements. ⁴The period of previous assignments by the same or another temporary work agency to the same hirer is to be credited in full if no more than three months elapse between each assignment.

(5) The temporary work agency shall be obliged to pay the temporary agency worker at least the minimum hourly wage laid down in a statutory instrument pursuant to section 3a(2) for the period of assignment and for periods without assignment.

Section 9
Invalidity

(1) Ineffective are:

1. Contracts between temporary work agencies and hirers as well as between temporary agency workers and temporary work agencies if the temporary work agency does not have the permit required under § 1; the contract between the temporary work agency and the temporary agency worker shall not become invalid if the temporary agency worker declares in writing to the temporary work agency or the hirer by the end of one month after the point in time agreed between the temporary work agency and the hirer for the commencement of the assignment that he will adhere to the contract of employment with the temporary work agency; if the invalidity occurs only after the temporary agency worker's work commencement at the hirer, the period shall commence when the invalidity occurs,

1a. Employment contracts between temporary work agencies and temporary agency workers if, contrary to § 1 subsection (1), sentences 5 and 6, the temporary agency employment is not expressly designated as such and the person of the temporary agency worker has not been specified, unless the temporary agency worker declares in writing to the temporary work agency or the hirer by the end of one month after the point in time agreed between the temporary work agency and the hirer for the commencement of the assignment that he will adhere to the employment contract with the temporary work agency,

1b. Arbeitsverträge zwischen Verleihern und Leiharbeitnehmern mit dem Überschreiten der zulässigen Überlassungshöchstdauer nach § 1 Absatz 1b, es sei denn, der Leiharbeitnehmer erklärt schriftlich bis zum Ablauf eines Monats nach Überschreiten der zulässigen Überlassungshöchstdauer gegenüber dem Verleiher oder dem Entleiher, dass er an dem Arbeitsvertrag mit dem Verleiher festhält,

2. Vereinbarungen, die für den Leiharbeitnehmer schlechtere als die ihm nach § 8 zustehenden Arbeitsbedingungen einschließlich des Arbeitsentgelts vorsehen,

2a. Vereinbarungen, die den Zugang des Leiharbeitnehmers zu den Gemeinschaftseinrichtungen oder -diensten im Unternehmen des Entleihers entgegen § 13b beschränken,

3. Vereinbarungen, die dem Entleiher untersagen, den Leiharbeitnehmer zu einem Zeitpunkt einzustellen, in dem dessen Arbeitsverhältnis zum Verleiher nicht mehr besteht; dies schließt die Vereinbarung einer angemessenen Vergütung zwischen Verleiher und Entleiher für die nach vorangegangenem Verleih oder mittels vorangegangenem Verleih erfolgte Vermittlung nicht aus,

4. Vereinbarungen, die dem Leiharbeitnehmer untersagen, mit dem Entleiher zu einem Zeitpunkt, in dem das Arbeitsverhältnis zwischen Verleiher und Leiharbeitnehmer nicht mehr besteht, ein Arbeitsverhältnis einzugehen,

5. Vereinbarungen, nach denen der Leiharbeitnehmer eine Vermittlungsvergütung an den Verleiher zu zahlen hat.

(2) Die Erklärung nach Absatz 1 Nummer 1, 1a oder 1b (Festhaltenserklärung) ist nur wirksam, wenn

1. der Leiharbeitnehmer diese vor ihrer Abgabe persönlich in einer Agentur für Arbeit vorlegt,

2. die Agentur für Arbeit die abzugebende Erklärung mit dem Datum des Tages der Vorlage und dem Hinweis versieht, dass sie die Identität des Leiharbeitnehmers festgestellt hat, und

3. die Erklärung spätestens am dritten Tag nach der Vorlage in der Agentur für Arbeit dem Ver- oder Entleiher zugeht.

1b. Contracts of employment between temporary work agency and temporary work agencies with the exceeding of the permissible maximum assignment length pursuant to section 1, paragraph 1b, unless the temporary agency worker declares in writing to the temporarywork agency or the hirer by the end of one month after the permissible maximum assignment length has been exceeded that he will adhere to the contract of employment with the temporary work agencyr

2. agreements which provide for worse working conditions for the temporary agency worker than those to which he is entitled under Section 8, including pay,

2a. Agreements restricting the temporary agency worker's access to Community facilities or services in the hirer's undertaking contrary to Section 13b,

3. agreements prohibiting the hirer from hiring the temporary agency worker at a time when his employment relationship with the temporary work agency no longer exists; this does not preclude the agreement of an appropriate remuneration between the temporary work agency and the hirer for the placement carried out after or by means of previous hiring,

4. agreements prohibiting the temporary worker from entering into an employment relationship with the hirer at a time when the employment relationship between the temporary work agency and the temporary agency worker no longer exists,

5. agreements under which the temporary agency worker must pay a placement fee to the temporary work agency.

(2) The declaration referred to in paragraph 1, points 1, 1a or 1b (status quo declaration) shall be effective only if

1. the temporary agency worker presents them in person at an employment agency before handing them in

2. the Employment Agency provides the declaration to be made with the date of submission and with an indication that it has established the identity of the temporary agency worker, and

3. the declaration is received by the temporary work agency or the hirer no later than the third day after it is submitted to the Employment Agency.

(3) ¹Eine vor Beginn einer Frist nach Absatz 1 Nummer 1 bis 1b abgegebene Festhaltenserklärung ist unwirksam. ²Wird die Überlassung nach der Festhaltenserklärung fortgeführt, gilt Absatz 1 Nummer 1 bis 1b. ³Eine erneute Festhaltenserklärung ist unwirksam. ⁴§ 28e Absatz 2 Satz 4 des Vierten Buches Sozialgesetzbuch gilt unbeschadet der Festhaltenserklärung.

(3) ¹A status quo declaration made before the beginning of a period pursuant to paragraph 1, points 1 to 1b shall be invalid. ²If the assignment is continued after the status quo declaration, paragraph 1, points 1 to 1b shall apply. ³A new status quo declaration shall be invalid. ⁴Section 28e subsection 2 sentence 4 of Book 4 of the Social Code shall apply without prejudice to the status quo declaration.

§ 10
Rechtsfolgen bei Unwirksamkeit

(1) ¹Ist der Vertrag zwischen einem Verleiher und einem Leiharbeitnehmer nach § 9 unwirksam, so gilt ein Arbeitsverhältnis zwischen Entleiher und Leiharbeitnehmer zu dem zwischen dem Entleiher und dem Verleiher für den Beginn der Tätigkeit vorgesehenen Zeitpunkt als zustande gekommen; tritt die Unwirksamkeit erst nach Aufnahme der Tätigkeit beim Entleiher ein, so gilt das Arbeitsverhältnis zwischen Entleiher und Leiharbeitnehmer mit dem Eintritt der Unwirksamkeit als zustande gekommen. ²Das Arbeitsverhältnis nach Satz 1 gilt als befristet, wenn die Tätigkeit des Leiharbeitnehmers bei dem Entleiher nur befristet vorgesehen war und ein die Befristung des Arbeitsverhältnisses sachlich rechtfertigender Grund vorliegt. ³Für das Arbeitsverhältnis nach Satz 1 gilt die zwischen dem Verleiher und dem Entleiher vorgesehene Arbeitszeit als vereinbart. ⁴Im übrigen bestimmen sich Inhalt und Dauer dieses Arbeitsverhältnisses nach den für den Betrieb des Entleihers geltenden Vorschriften und sonstigen Regelungen; sind solche nicht vorhanden, gelten diejenigen vergleichbarer Betriebe. ⁵Der Leiharbeitnehmer hat gegen den Entleiher mindestens Anspruch auf das mit dem Verleiher vereinbarte Arbeitsentgelt.

Section 10
Legal Consequences in Case of Invalidity

(1) ¹If the contract between a hirer and a temporary work agency is ineffective in accordance with Section 9, an employment relationship between the hirer and the temporary agency worker shall be deemed to have come into existence at the point in time agreed between the hirer and the temporary work agency for the commencement of the activity; if the ineffectiveness occurs only after the commencement of the activity at the hirer, the employment relationship between the hirer and the temporary agency worker shall be deemed to have come into existence at the point in time of the ineffectiveness. ²The employment relationship in accordance with the first sentence above is deemed to be limited in time if the activity of the temporary agency worker at the hirer was only intended to be of limited duration and there is an objective reason justifying the limitation of the employment relationship. ³For the employment relationship in accordance with sentence 1, the working time envisaged between the temporary work agency and the hirer is deemed to be agreed. ⁴In all other respects, the content and duration of this employment relationship shall be determined by the provisions and other regulations applicable to the hirer's business; if no such regulations exist, those of comparable businesses shall apply. ⁵The temporary agency worker shall be entitled against the hirer at least to the remuneration agreed with the temporary work agency.

(2) ¹Der Leiharbeitnehmer kann im Fall der Unwirksamkeit seines Vertrags mit dem Verleiher nach § 9 von diesem Ersatz des Schadens verlangen, den er dadurch erleidet, dass er auf die Gültigkeit des Vertrags vertraut. ²Die Ersatzpflicht tritt nicht ein, wenn der Leiharbeitnehmer den Grund der Unwirksamkeit kannte.

(2) ¹If his contract with the temporary work agency is invalid, the temporary agency worker may, in accordance with Section 9, claim compensation from the latter for the damage he suffers because he trusts in the validity of the contract. ²The obligation to pay compensation does not apply if the temporary agency worker knew the reason for the invalidity.

(3) ¹Zahlt der Verleiher das vereinbarte Arbeitsentgelt oder Teile des Arbeitsentgelts an den Leiharbeitnehmer, obwohl der Vertrag nach § 9 unwirksam ist, so hat er auch sonstige Teile des Arbeitsentgelts, die bei einem wirksamen Arbeitsvertrag für den Leiharbeitnehmer an einen anderen zu zahlen wären, an den anderen zu zahlen. ²Hinsichtlich dieser Zahlungspflicht gilt der Verleiher neben dem Entleiher als Arbeitgeber; beide haften insoweit als Gesamtschuldner.

§ 10a
Rechtsfolgen bei Überlassung durch eine andere Person als den Arbeitgeber

Werden Arbeitnehmer entgegen § 1 Absatz 1 Satz 3 von einer anderen Person überlassen und verstößt diese Person hierbei gegen § 1 Absatz 1 Satz 1, 5 und 6 oder Absatz 1b, gelten für das Arbeitsverhältnis des Leiharbeitnehmers § 9 Absatz 1 Nummer 1 bis 1b und § 10 entsprechend.

§ 11
Sonstige Vorschriften über das Leiharbeitsverhältnis

(1) ¹Der Nachweis der wesentlichen Vertragsbedingungen des Leiharbeitsverhältnisses richtet sich nach den Bestimmungen des Nachweisgesetzes. ²Zusätzlich zu den in § 2 Abs. 1 des Nachweisgesetzes genannten Angaben sind in die Niederschrift aufzunehmen:

1. Firma und Anschrift des Verleihers, die Erlaubnisbehörde sowie Ort und Datum der Erteilung der Erlaubnis nach § 1,

2. Art und Höhe der Leistungen für Zeiten, in denen der Leiharbeitnehmer nicht verliehen ist.

(2) ¹Der Verleiher ist ferner verpflichtet, dem Leiharbeitnehmer bei Vertragsschluss ein Merkblatt der Erlaubnisbehörde über den wesentlichen Inhalt dieses Gesetzes auszuhändigen. ²Nichtdeutsche Leiharbeitnehmer erhalten das Merkblatt und den Nachweis nach Absatz 1 auf Verlangen in ihrer Muttersprache. ³Die Kosten des Merkblatts trägt der Verleiher. ⁴Der Verleiher hat den Leiharbeitnehmer vor jeder Überlassung darüber zu informieren, dass er als Leiharbeitnehmer tätig wird.

(3) ¹If the temporary work agency pays the agreed remuneration or parts of the remuneration to the temporary agency worker although the contract is invalid under Section 9, it must also pay to the other party any other parts of the remuneration which would have been payable to another party if the contract of employment for the temporary worker had been valid. ²With regard to this payment obligation, the temporary work agency is considered to be the employer alongside the hirer; both are jointly and severally liable debtors in this respect.

Section 10a
Legal Consequences of Assignment by a Person other than the Employer

If employees are assigned by another person in contravention of Section 1 (1) sentence 3 and this person violates Section 1 (1) sentences 1, 5 and 6 or (1b), Section 9 (1) nos. 1 to 1b and Section 10 apply accordingly to the employment relationship of the temporary agency worker.

Section 11
Other Rules on Temporary Employment Relationship

(1) ¹Evidence of the material contractual terms and conditions of the temporary employment relationship shall be provided in accordance with the provisions of the Act on the Proof of Substantial Conditions. ²In addition to the information specified in Section 2(1) of the Act on the Proof of Substatial Conditions, the minutes must contain the following information

1. The company name and address of the temporary work agency, the licensing authority and the place and date of issue of the licence under Article 1,

2. the nature and amount of benefits for periods during which the temporary work agency is not on loan

(2) ¹The temporary work agency is also obliged to provide the temporary agency worker with an information sheet from the licensing authority on the essential content of this Act when the contract is concluded. ²Non-German temporary agency workers shall receive the information sheet and the proof referred to in subsection 1 in their native language on request. ³The temporary work agency shall bear the costs of the information sheet. ⁴The temporary work agency must inform the temporary agency worker before each assignment that he is acting as a temporary agency worker.

(3) [1]Der Verleiher hat den Leiharbeitnehmer unverzüglich über den Zeitpunkt des Wegfalls der Erlaubnis zu unterrichten. [2]In den Fällen der Nichtverlängerung (§ 2 Abs. 4 Satz 3), der Rücknahme (§ 4) oder des Widerrufs (§ 5) hat er ihn ferner auf das voraussichtliche Ende der Abwicklung (§ 2 Abs. 4 Satz 4) und die gesetzliche Abwicklungsfrist (§ 2 Abs. 4 Satz 4 letzter Halbsatz) hinzuweisen.

(4) [1]§ 622 Abs. 5 Nr. 1 des Bürgerlichen Gesetzbuchs ist nicht auf Arbeitsverhältnisse zwischen Verleihern und Leiharbeitnehmern anzuwenden. [2]Das Recht des Leiharbeitnehmers auf Vergütung bei Annahmeverzug des Verleihers (§ 615 Satz 1 des Bürgerlichen Gesetzbuchs) kann nicht durch Vertrag aufgehoben oder beschränkt werden; § 615 Satz 2 des Bürgerlichen Gesetzbuchs bleibt unberührt. [3]Das Recht des Leiharbeitnehmers auf Vergütung kann durch Vereinbarung von Kurzarbeit für die Zeit aufgehoben werden, für die dem Leiharbeitnehmer Kurzarbeitergeld nach dem Dritten Buch Sozialgesetzbuch gezahlt wird; eine solche Vereinbarung kann das Recht des Leiharbeitnehmers auf Vergütung bis längstens zum 31. Dezember 2011 ausschließen.

(5) [1]Der Entleiher darf Leiharbeitnehmer nicht tätig werden lassen, wenn sein Betrieb unmittelbar durch einen Arbeitskampf betroffen ist. [2]Satz 1 gilt nicht, wenn der Entleiher sicherstellt, dass Leiharbeitnehmer keine Tätigkeiten übernehmen, die bisher von Arbeitnehmern erledigt wurden, die

1. sich im Arbeitskampf befinden oder

2. ihrerseits Tätigkeiten von Arbeitnehmern, die sich im Arbeitskampf befinden, übernommen haben.

[3]Der Leiharbeitnehmer ist nicht verpflichtet, bei einem Entleiher tätig zu sein, soweit dieser durch einen Arbeitskampf unmittelbar betroffen ist. [4]In den Fällen eines Arbeitskampfes hat der Verleiher den Leiharbeitnehmer auf das Recht, die Arbeitsleistung zu verweigern, hinzuweisen.

(6) [1]Die Tätigkeit des Leiharbeitnehmers bei dem Entleiher unterliegt den für den Betrieb des Entleihers geltenden öffentlich-rechtlichen Vorschriften des Arbeitsschutzrechts; die hieraus sich ergebenden Pflichten für den Arbeitgeber obliegen dem Entleiher unbeschadet der Pflichten des Verleihers. [2]Insbesondere hat der Entleiher den Leiharbeitnehmer vor Beginn der Beschäftigung und bei Veränderungen in seinem Arbeitsbereich über Gefahren für Sicherheit und Gesundheit, denen er bei der Arbeit ausgesetzt sein kann, sowie über die Maßnahmen und Einrichtungen zur Abwendung dieser

(3) [1]The temporary work agency must inform the temporary agency worker without delay of the date of expiry of the permit. [2]In cases of non-renewal (section 2, paragraph 4, sentence 3), withdrawal (section 4) or revocation (section 5), he must also inform him of the probable end of the processing (section 2, paragraph 4, sentence 4) and the statutory processing period (section 2, paragraph 4, sentence 4, last half-sentence).

(4) [1]Section 622 (5) No. 1 of the German Civil Code shall not apply to employment relationships between temporary work agencies and temporary agency workers. [2]The temporary agency worker's right to remuneration in the event of default of acceptance by the temporary work agency (section 615, first sentence, of the Civil Code) may not be cancelled or limited by contract; section 615, second sentence, of the Civil Code shall remain unaffected. [3]The temporary agency worker's right to remuneration may be revoked by agreement on short-time work for the period for which the temporary agency worker is paid short-time work compensation under Book Three of the Social Code; such an agreement may exclude the temporary agency worker's right to remuneration until 31th December 2011 at the latest.

(5) [1]The hirer may not allow temporary agency workers to work if his business is directly affected by industrial action. [2]Sentence 1 shall not apply if the hirer ensures that temporary agency workers do not take over activities which have previously been performed by workers who

1. are in industrial action or

2. for their part, have taken over activities of workers who are in industrial action.

[3]The temporary agency worker is not obliged to work for a hirer if the latter is directly affected by industrial action. In the event of industrial action, the temporary work agency must inform the temporary agency worker of his right to refuse to perform the work.

(6) [1]The activity of the temporary agency worker at the hirer's premises is subject to the public-law provisions of occupational health and safety law applicable to the operation of the hirer; the resulting obligations for the employer are incumbent on the hirer without prejudice to the obligations of the temporary work agency. [2]In particular, the hirer must inform the temporary agency worker, prior to the commencement of employment and in the event of changes in his field of work, of any hazards to safety and health to which he may be exposed at work and of the measures and facilities for averting such haz

Gefahren zu unterrichten. ³Der Entleiher hat den Leiharbeitnehmer zusätzlich über die Notwendigkeit besonderer Qualifikationen oder beruflicher Fähigkeiten oder einer besonderen ärztlichen Überwachung sowie über erhöhte besondere Gefahren des Arbeitsplatzes zu unterrichten.

(7) Hat der Leiharbeitnehmer während der Dauer der Tätigkeit bei dem Entleiher eine Erfindung oder einen technischen Verbesserungsvorschlag gemacht, so gilt der Entleiher als Arbeitgeber im Sinne des Gesetzes über Arbeitnehmererfindungen.

§ 12
Rechtsbeziehungen zwischen Verleiher und Entleiher

(1) ¹Der Vertrag zwischen dem Verleiher und dem Entleiher bedarf der Schriftform. ²Wenn der Vertrag und seine tatsächliche Durchführung einander widersprechen, ist für die rechtliche Einordnung des Vertrages die tatsächliche Durchführung maßgebend. ³In der Urkunde hat der Verleiher zu erklären, ob er die Erlaubnis nach § 1 besitzt. ⁴Der Entleiher hat in der Urkunde anzugeben, welche besonderen Merkmale die für den Leiharbeitnehmer vorgesehene Tätigkeit hat und welche berufliche Qualifikation dafür erforderlich ist sowie welche im Betrieb des Entleihers für einen vergleichbaren Arbeitnehmer des Entleihers wesentlichen Arbeitsbedingungen einschließlich des Arbeitsentgelts gelten; Letzteres gilt nicht, soweit die Voraussetzungen der in § 8 Absatz 2 und 4 Satz 2 genannten Ausnahme vorliegen.

(2) ¹Der Verleiher hat den Entleiher unverzüglich über den Zeitpunkt des Wegfalls der Erlaubnis zu unterrichten. ²In den Fällen der Nichtverlängerung (§ 2 Abs. 4 Satz 3), der Rücknahme (§ 4) oder des Widerrufs (§ 5) hat er ihn ferner auf das voraussichtliche Ende der Abwicklung (§ 2 Abs. 4 Satz 4) und die gesetzliche Abwicklungsfrist (§ 2 Abs. 4 Satz 4 letzter Halbsatz) hinzuweisen.

§ 13
Auskunftsanspruch des Leiharbeitnehmers

Der Leiharbeitnehmer kann im Falle der Überlassung von seinem Entleiher Auskunft über die im Betrieb des Entleihers für einen vergleichbaren Arbeitnehmer des Entleihers geltenden wesentlichen Arbeitsbedingungen einschließlich des Arbeitsentgelts verlangen; dies gilt nicht, soweit die Voraussetzungen der in § 8 Absatz 2 und 4 Satz 2 genannten Ausnahme vorliegen.

ards. ³In addition, the hirer must inform the temporary agency worker of the need for special qualifications or professional skills or special medical supervision and of any increased specific risks in the workplace.

(7) If the temporary agency worker has made an invention or a suggestion for technical improvement during the period of employment with the hirer, the hirer shall be deemed to be the employer within the meaning of the Law on Employees' Inventions.

Section 12
Legal Relations between Temporary Work Agency and Hirer

(1) ¹The contract between the temporary work agency and the hirer must be in writing. ²If the contract and its actual implementation contradict each other, the actual implementation shall be decisive for the legal classification of the contract. ³In the document, the temporary work agency must declare whether it has the permission according to Section 1. ⁴The hirer must state in the document the special characteristics of the activity envisaged for the temporary agency worker and the professional qualifications required for it, as well as the working conditions, including remuneration, which are essential in the hirer's business for a comparable worker of the hirer; the latter does not apply where the conditions of the exception referred to in Section 8 (2) and (4), second sentence, apply.

(2) ¹The temporary work agency shall inform the hirer without delay of the date of expiry of the licence. ²In cases of non-renewal (section 2, paragraph 4, sentence 3), withdrawal (section 4) or revocation (section 5), he shall also inform the hirer of the expected end of the winding-up (section 2, paragraph 4, sentence 4) and the statutory winding-up period (section 2, paragraph 4, sentence 4, last half-sentence).

Section 13
Temporary Agency Worker's Right to Information

In the event of assignment, the temporary agency worker may demand information from his hirer about the essential working conditions, including pay, applicable in the hirer's business to a comparable employee of the hirer; this does not apply if the conditions of the exception mentioned in Section 8 Paragraph 2 and 4 Sentence 2 are met.

§ 13a
Informationspflicht des Entleihers über freie Arbeitsplätze

[1]Der Entleiher hat den Leiharbeitnehmer über Arbeitsplätze des Entleihers, die besetzt werden sollen, zu informieren. [2]Die Information kann durch allgemeine Bekanntgabe an geeigncter, dem Leiharbeitnehmer zugänglicher Stelle im Betrieb und Unternehmen des Entleihers erfolgen.

Section 13a
Obligation of the Hirer to Inform about Vacant Jobs

[1]The hirer must inform the temporary agency worker of the workplaces of the hirer which are to be filled. [2]The information may be provided by general announcement at a suitable place in the hirer's business and enterprise which is accessible to the temporary agency worker.

§ 13b
Zugang des Leiharbeitnehmers zu Gemeinschaftseinrichtungen oder -diensten

[1]Der Entleiher hat dem Leiharbeitnehmer Zugang zu den Gemeinschaftseinrichtungen oder -diensten im Unternehmen unter den gleichen Bedingungen zu gewähren wie vergleichbaren Arbeitnehmern in dem Betrieb, in dem der Leiharbeitnehmer seine Arbeitsleistung erbringt, es sei denn, eine unterschiedliche Behandlung ist aus sachlichen Gründen gerechtfertigt. [2]Gemeinschaftseinrichtungen oder -dienste im Sinne des Satzes 1 sind insbesondere Kinderbetreuungseinrichtungen, Gemeinschaftsverpflegung und Beförderungsmittel.

Section 13b
Access by the Temporary Agency Worker to Community Bodies or Services

[1]The hirer must grant the temporary agency worker access to the Community facilities or services in the undertaking under the same conditions as those applicable to comparable workers in the undertaking where the temporary agency worker performs his work, unless a difference in treatment is justified on objective grounds. [2]Community facilities or services within the meaning of the first sentence are in particular childcare facilities, mass catering and means of transport.

§ 14
Mitwirkungs- und Mitbestimmungsrechte

(1) Leiharbeitnehmer bleiben auch während der Zeit ihrer Arbeitsleistung bei einem Entleiher Angehörige des entsendenden Betriebs des Verleihers.

(2) [1]Leiharbeitnehmer sind bei der Wahl der Arbeitnehmervertreter in den Aufsichtsrat im Entleiherunternehmen und bei der Wahl der betriebsverfassungsrechtlichen Arbeitnehmervertretungen im Entleiherbetrieb nicht wählbar. [2]Sie sind berechtigt, die Sprechstunden dieser Arbeitnehmervertretungen aufzusuchen und an den Betriebs- und Jugendversammlungen im Entleiherbetrieb teilzunehmen. [3]Die §§ 81, 82 Abs. 1 und die §§ 84 bis 86 des Betriebsverfassungsgesetzes gelten im Entleiherbetrieb auch in bezug auf die dort tätigen Leiharbeitnehmer. [4]Soweit Bestimmungen des Betriebsverfassungsgesetzes mit Ausnahme des § 112a, des Europäische Betriebsräte-Gesetzes oder der auf Grund der jeweiligen Gesetze erlassenen Wahlordnungen eine bestimmte Anzahl oder einen bestimmten Anteil von Arbeitnehmern voraussetzen, sind Leiharbeitnehmer auch im Entleiherbetrieb zu berücksichtigen. [5]Soweit Bestimmungen des Mitbestimmungsgesetzes, des Montan-Mitbestimmungsgesetzes, des Mit-

Section 14
Participation and Co-Determination Rights

(1) Temporary agency workers shall remain members of the posting company of the temporary work agency even during the period of their work for a hirer.

(2) [1]Temporary agency workers may not be elected to the supervisory board in the hirer's company or to the employee representative bodies under works constitution law in the company of the hirer. [2]They are entitled to attend the office hours of these employee representatives and to participate in the works and youth assemblies in the hirer's company. [3]Sections 81, 82 (1) and sections 84 to 86 of the Works Constitution Act also apply in the hirer's enterprise with regard to the temporary agency workers employed there. [4]Insofar as provisions of the Works Constitution Act, with the exception of section 112a, the European Works Councils Act or the electoral regulations issued on the basis of the respective laws, require a certain number or proportion of employees, temporary agency workers must also be taken into account in the hirer's company. [5]Insofar as provisions of the Co-Determination Act, the Coal and Steel Co-Determination Act, the Supplementary Co-Determination Act, the One-Third Partic-

bestimmungsergänzungsgesetzes, des Drittel-beteiligungsgesetzes, des Gesetzes über die Mitbestimmung der Arbeitnehmer bei einer grenzüberschreitenden Verschmelzung, des SE- und des SCE-Beteiligungsgesetzes oder der auf Grund der jeweiligen Gesetze erlassenen Wahl-ordnungen eine bestimmte Anzahl oder einen bestimmten Anteil von Arbeitnehmern voraus-setzen, sind Leiharbeitnehmer auch im Entlei-herunternehmen zu berücksichtigen. ⁶Soweit die Anwendung der in Satz 5 genannten Gesetze eine bestimmte Anzahl oder einen bestimmten Anteil von Arbeitnehmern erfordert, sind Leih-arbeitnehmer im Entleiherunternehmen nur zu berücksichtigen, wenn die Einsatzdauer sechs Monate übersteigt.

(3) ¹Vor der Übernahme eines Leiharbeitneh-mers zur Arbeitsleistung ist der Betriebsrat des Entleiherbetriebs nach § 99 des Betriebsver-fassungsgesetzes zu beteiligen. ²Dabei hat der Entleiher dem Betriebsrat auch die schriftliche Erklärung des Verleihers nach § 12 Abs. 1 Satz 2 vorzulegen. ³Er ist ferner verpflichtet, Mittei-lungen des Verleihers nach § 12 Abs. 2 unver-züglich dem Betriebsrat bekanntzugeben.

(4) Die Absätze 1 und 2 Satz 1 und 2 sowie Ab-satz 3 gelten für die Anwendung des Bundes-personalvertretungsgesetzes sinngemäß.

§ 15
Ausländische Leiharbeitnehmer ohne Genehmigung

(1) Wer als Verleiher einen Ausländer, der einen erforderlichen Aufenthaltstitel nach § 4 Abs. 3 des Aufenthaltsgesetzes, eine Aufenthaltsge-stattung oder eine Duldung, die zur Ausübung der Beschäftigung berechtigen, oder eine Ge-nehmigung nach § 284 Abs. 1 des Dritten Bu-ches Sozialgesetzbuch nicht besitzt, entgegen § 1 einem Dritten ohne Erlaubnis überlässt, wird mit Freiheitsstrafe bis zu drei Jahren oder mit Geldstrafe bestraft.

(2) ¹In besonders schweren Fällen ist die Strafe Freiheitsstrafe von sechs Monaten bis zu fünf Jahren. ²Ein besonders schwerer Fall liegt in der Regel vor, wenn der Täter gewerbsmäßig oder aus grobem Eigennutz handelt.

ipation Act, the Act on the Co-Determination of Employees in Cross-Border Mergers, the SE and SCE Participation Act or the electoral reg-ulations adopted on the basis of the respective laws require a certain number or proportion of employees, temporary agency workers must also be taken into account in the hirer's business. ⁶Insofar as the application of the laws referred to in the fifth sentence requires a certain number or proportion of employees, temporary agency workers are only to be taken into account in the hirer's undertaking if the period of employment exceeds six months.

(3) ¹Before a temporary agency worker is taken on to perform work, the works council of the hirer's enterprise must be involved in accord-ance with section 99 of the Works Constitution Act. ²At the same time, the hirer shall also sub-mit to the works council the written declaration of the temporary work agency pursuant to sec-tion 12(1) sentence 2. ³Furthermore, he shall be obliged to immediately notify the works coun-cil of any notifications of the temporary work agency pursuant to section 12, subsection 2.

(4) Paragraphs 1 and 2, sentences 1 and 2, and paragraph 3 shall apply mutatis mutandis to the application of the Federal Personnel Rep-resentation Act.

Section 15
Foreign Temporary Agency Workers without a Permit

(1) Any temporary work agency which, con-trary to Section 1, assigns a foreigner who does not possess a required residence title under Section 4(3) of the Residence Act, a residence permit or a toleration certificate entitling him/ her to take up employment, or a permit under Section 284(1) of Book Three of the Social Secu-rity Code, to a third party without permission, shall be punished with imprisonment for up to three years or a fine.

(2) ¹In particularly serious cases, the penalty shall be imprisonment of between six months and five years. ²As a rule, a particularly serious case is deemed to exist if the offender acts com-mercially or for gross self-interest.

§ 15a
Entleih von Ausländern ohne Genehmigung

(1) [1]Wer als Entleiher einen ihm überlassenen Ausländer, der einen erforderlichen Aufenthaltstitel nach § 4 Abs. 3 des Aufenthaltsgesetzes, eine Aufenthaltsgestattung oder eine Duldung, die zur Ausübung der Beschäftigung berechtigen, oder eine Genehmigung nach § 284 Abs. 1 des Dritten Buches Sozialgesetzbuch nicht besitzt, zu Arbeitsbedingungen des Leiharbeitsverhältnisses tätig werden lässt, die in einem auffälligen Missverhältnis zu den Arbeitsbedingungen deutscher Leiharbeitnehmer stehen, die die gleiche oder eine vergleichbare Tätigkeit ausüben, wird mit Freiheitsstrafe bis zu drei Jahren oder mit Geldstrafe bestraft. [2]In besonders schweren Fällen ist die Strafe Freiheitsstrafe von sechs Monaten bis zu fünf Jahren; ein besonders schwerer Fall liegt in der Regel vor, wenn der Täter gewerbsmäßig oder aus grobem Eigennutz handelt.

(2) [1]Wer als Entleiher

1. gleichzeitig mehr als fünf Ausländer, die einen erforderlichen Aufenthaltstitel nach § 4 Abs. 3 des Aufenthaltsgesetzes, eine Aufenthaltsgestattung oder eine Duldung, die zur Ausübung der Beschäftigung berechtigen, oder eine Genehmigung nach § 284 Abs. 1 des Dritten Buches Sozialgesetzbuch nicht besitzen, tätig werden läßt oder
2. eine in § 16 Abs. 1 Nr. 2 bezeichnete vorsätzliche Zuwiderhandlung beharrlich wiederholt,

wird mit Freiheitsstrafe bis zu einem Jahr oder mit Geldstrafe bestraft.

[2]Handelt der Täter aus grobem Eigennutz, ist die Strafe Freiheitsstrafe bis zu drei Jahren oder Geldstrafe.

§ 16
Ordnungswidrigkeiten

(1) Ordnungswidrig handelt, wer vorsätzlich oder fahrlässig

1. entgegen § 1 einen Leiharbeitnehmer einem Dritten ohne Erlaubnis überlässt,
1a. einen ihm von einem Verleiher ohne Erlaubnis überlassenen Leiharbeitnehmer tätig werden lässt,
1b. entgegen § 1 Absatz 1 Satz 3 einen Arbeitnehmer überlässt oder tätig werden lässt,

1c. entgegen § 1 Absatz 1 Satz 5 eine dort genannte Überlassung nicht, nicht richtig oder nicht rechtzeitig bezeichnet,

Section 15a
Hiring of Foreigners Without Authorisation

(1) [1]Any hirer who allows a foreigner assigned to him/her, who does not possess a required residence title pursuant to Section 4(3) of the Residence Act, a residence permit or a toleration certificate entitling him/her to take up employment, or a permit pursuant to Section 284(1) of Book Three of the Social Code, to work under temporary employment conditions which are conspicuously disproportionate to the working conditions of German temporary agency workers who are engaged in the same or a comparable occupation, shall be punished with imprisonment for up to three years or a fine. [2]In particularly serious cases, the penalty is imprisonment of between six months and five years; a particularly serious case is generally deemed to exist if the offender acts commercially or for gross self-interest.

(2) [1]Whoever as a hirer

1. simultaneously allows more than five foreigners who do not hold a required residence title under Section 4(3) of the Residence Act, a residence permit or a toleration certificate entitling them to take up employment, or a permit under Section 284(1) of Book Three of the Social Security Code to take up employment, or
2. persistently repeats an intentional infringement referred to in section 16(1)(2),

is punishable by imprisonment for up to one year or by a fine

[2]If the offender acts out of gross self-interest, the penalty is imprisonment for up to three years or a fine.

Section 16
Administrative Offences

(1) It is an administrative offence to deliberately or negligently

1. contrary to section 1, assigns a temporary worker to a third party without permission
1a. allows a temporary agency worker assigned to him by a temporary work agency without permission, to become active
1b. in contravention of section 1 subsection (1), third sentence, assigns or allows an employee to work,

1c. in contravention of section 1 (1) sentence 5, fails to designate, fails to designate correctly or fails to designate in good time an assignment mentioned therein,

1d. entgegen § 1 Absatz 1 Satz 6 die Person nicht, nicht richtig oder nicht rechtzeitig konkretisiert,

1e. entgegen § 1 Absatz 1b Satz 1 einen Leiharbeitnehmer überlässt,

1f. entgegen § 1b Satz 1 Arbeitnehmer überlässt oder tätig werden lässt,

2. einen ihm überlassenen ausländischen Leiharbeitnehmer, der einen erforderlichen Aufenthaltstitel nach § 4 Abs. 3 des Aufenthaltsgesetzes, eine Aufenthaltsgestattung oder eine Duldung, die zur Ausübung der Beschäftigung berechtigen, oder eine Genehmigung nach § 284 Abs. 1 des Dritten Buches Sozialgesetzbuch nicht besitzt, tätig werden lässt,

2a. eine Anzeige nach § 1a nicht richtig, nicht vollständig oder nicht rechtzeitig erstattet,

3. einer Auflage nach § 2 Abs. 2 nicht, nicht vollständig oder nicht rechtzeitig nachkommt,

4. eine Anzeige nach § 7 Abs. 1 nicht, nicht richtig, nicht vollständig oder nicht rechtzeitig erstattet,

5. eine Auskunft nach § 7 Abs. 2 Satz 1 nicht, nicht richtig, nicht vollständig oder nicht rechtzeitig erteilt,

6. seiner Aufbewahrungspflicht nach § 7 Abs. 2 Satz 4 nicht nachkommt,

6a. entgegen § 7 Abs. 3 Satz 2 eine dort genannte Maßnahme nicht duldet,

7. (weggefallen)

7a. entgegen § 8 Absatz 1 Satz 1 oder Absatz 2 Satz 2 oder 4 eine Arbeitsbedingung nicht gewährt,

7b. entgegen § 8 Absatz 5 in Verbindung mit einer Rechtsverordnung nach § 3a Absatz 2 Satz 1 das dort genannte Mindeststundenentgelt nicht oder nicht rechtzeitig zahlt,

8. einer Pflicht nach § 11 Abs. 1 oder Abs. 2 nicht nachkommt,

8a. entgegen § 11 Absatz 5 Satz 1 einen Leiharbeitnehmer tätig werden lässt,

9. entgegen § 13a Satz 1 den Leiharbeitnehmer nicht, nicht richtig oder nicht vollständig informiert,

10. entgegen § 13b Satz 1 Zugang nicht gewährt,

1d. contrary to section 1 subsection (1) sentence 6, fails to specify the person, fails to specify it correctly or fails to specify it in good time,

1e. assigns a temporary agency worker in breach of the first sentence of Paragraph 1(1b),

1f. in contravention of section 1b sentence 1, assigns employees or allows them to work,

2. has a foreign temporary agency worker assigned to him who does not possess the required residence title under Section 4(3) of the Residence Act, a residence permit or a toleration certificate entitling him to take up employment or a permit under Section 284(1) of Book Three of the Social Security Code,

2a. fails to make a notification in accordance with Section 1a correctly, completely or in time,

3. fails to comply with a condition pursuant to Section 2 (2) in whole or in part or does not comply in good time,

4. fails to make a report pursuant to Section 7 (1), or does not do so correctly, completely or in good time,

5. fails to provide information in accordance with section 7 (2) sentence 1, or provides it incorrectly, incompletely or in a timely manner,

6. fails to comply with its obligation to keep records in accordance with section 7 (2) sentence 4,

6a. contrary to the second sentence of section 7(3), does not tolerate a measure mentioned therein,

7. (omitted)

7a. contrary to section 8 subsection (1) sentence 1 or subsection (2) sentence 2 or 4, does not grant a working condition,

7b. in contravention of section 8(5) in conjunction with a statutory instrument under section 3a(2), first sentence, fails to pay the minimum hourly pay referred to therein or fails to pay it on time,

8. fails to comply with an obligation under section 11(1) or (2),

8a. allows a temporary agency worker to work in breach of section 11(5), first sentence,

9. contrary to section 13a sentence 1, fails to inform the temporary worker, or does not inform him correctly or completely,

10. contrary to section 13b sentence 1, access is not granted,

11. entgegen § 17a in Verbindung mit § 5 Absatz 1 Satz 1 Nummer 1 oder 3 des Schwarzarbeitsbekämpfungsgesetzes eine Prüfung nicht duldet oder bei dieser Prüfung nicht mitwirkt,

12. entgegen § 17a in Verbindung mit § 5 Absatz 1 Satz 1 Nummer 2 des Schwarzarbeitsbekämpfungsgesetzes das Betreten eines Grundstücks oder Geschäftsraums nicht duldet,

13. entgegen § 17a in Verbindung mit § 5 Absatz 5 Satz 1 des Schwarzarbeitsbekämpfungsgesetzes Daten nicht, nicht richtig, nicht vollständig, nicht in der vorgeschriebenen Weise oder nicht rechtzeitig übermittelt,

14. entgegen § 17b Absatz 1 Satz 1 eine Anmeldung nicht, nicht richtig, nicht vollständig, nicht in der vorgeschriebenen Weise oder nicht rechtzeitig zuleitet,

15. entgegen § 17b Absatz 1 Satz 2 eine Änderungsmeldung nicht, nicht richtig, nicht vollständig, nicht in der vorgeschriebenen Weise oder nicht rechtzeitig macht,

16. entgegen § 17b Absatz 2 eine Versicherung nicht beifügt,

17. entgegen § 17c Absatz 1 eine Aufzeichnung nicht, nicht richtig, nicht vollständig oder nicht rechtzeitig erstellt oder nicht oder nicht mindestens zwei Jahre aufbewahrt oder

18. entgegen § 17c Absatz 2 eine Unterlage nicht, nicht richtig, nicht vollständig oder nicht in der vorgeschriebenen Weise bereithält.

(2) Die Ordnungswidrigkeit nach Absatz 1 Nummer 1 bis 1f, 6 und 11 bis 18 kann mit einer Geldbuße bis zu dreißigtausend Euro, die Ordnungswidrigkeit nach Absatz 1 Nummer 2, 7a, 7b und 8a mit einer Geldbuße bis zu fünfhunderttausend Euro, die Ordnungswidrigkeit nach Absatz 1 Nummer 2a, 3, 9 und 10 mit einer Geldbuße bis zu zweitausendfünfhundert Euro, die Ordnungswidrigkeit nach Absatz 1 Nummer 4, 5, 6a und 8 mit einer Geldbuße bis zu tausend Euro geahndet werden.

(3) Verwaltungsbehörden im Sinne des § 36 Absatz 1 Nummer 1 des Gesetzes über Ordnungswidrigkeiten sind in den Fällen des Absatzes 1 Nummer 1, 1a, 1c, 1d, 1f, 2, 2a und 7b sowie 11 bis 18 die Behörden der Zollverwaltung jeweils für ihren Geschäftsbereich, in den Fällen des Absatzes 1 Nummer 1b, 1e, 3 bis 7a sowie 8 bis 10 die Bundesagentur für Arbeit.

11. contrary to section 17a in conjunction with section 5(1) sentence 1 number 1 or 3 of the Schwarzarbeitsbekämpfungsgesetz does not tolerate an examination or does not cooperate in such an examination,

12. contrary to section 17a in conjunction with section 5(1), first sentence, point 2 of the Schwarzarbeitsbekämpfungsgesetz, does not tolerate the entry into a property or business premises,

13. in contravention of section 17a in conjunction with the first sentence of section 5(5) of the Schwarzarbeitsbekämpfungsgesetz, fails to transmit data or to do so correctly, completely, in the prescribed manner or in good time,

14. in contravention of section 17b (1), first sentence, fails to submit a notification, fails to submit it correctly, fails to submit it in full, fails to submit it in the prescribed manner or fails to submit it in good time,

15. in contravention of section 17b (1) sentence 2, fails to make a notification of amendment, or fails to do so correctly, completely, in the prescribed manner or in good time,

16. contrary to section 17b (2) does not attach an insurance policy,

17. contrary to section 17c paragraph 1, fails to make a record, or fails to do so correctly, completely or on time, or fails to keep a record or does not keep it for at least two years, or

18. contrary to section 17c, paragraph 2, does not provide a document or does not provide it correctly, completely or in the prescribed manner.

(2) The administrative offence under subsection 1(1)(1) to (1f), (6) and (11) to (18) may be punishable by a fine of up to thirty thousand euro, and the administrative offence under subsection 1(2), (7a), (7b) and (8a) by a fine of up to five hundred thousand euro, the administrative offence referred to in paragraph 1, points 2a, 3, 9 and 10 shall be punishable by a fine of up to two thousand five hundred euros, and the administrative offence referred to in paragraph 1, points 4, 5, 6a and 8 shall be punishable by a fine of up to one thousand euros.

(3) Administrative authorities within the meaning of section 36(1)(1) of the Act on Administrative Offences shall be the customs administration authorities in the cases of subsection 1(1) (1), (1a), (1c), (1d), (1f), (2), (2a) and (7b) and (11) to (18), in each case for their area of activity, and in the cases of subsection 1(1b), (1e), (3) to (7a) and (8) to (10), the Federal Employment Agency.

(4) §§ 66 des Zehnten Buches Sozialgesetzbuch gilt entsprechend.

(5) ¹Die Geldbußen fließen in die Kasse der zuständigen Verwaltungsbehörde. ²Sie trägt abweichend von § 105 Abs. 2 des Gesetzes über Ordnungswidrigkeiten die notwendigen Auslagen und ist auch ersatzpflichtig im Sinne des § 110 Abs. 4 des Gesetzes über Ordnungswidrigkeiten.

§ 17
Durchführung

(1) ¹Die Bundesagentur für Arbeit führt dieses Gesetz nach fachlichen Weisungen des Bundesministeriums für Arbeit und Soziales durch. ²Verwaltungskosten werden nicht erstattet.

(2) Die Prüfung der Arbeitsbedingungen nach § 8 Absatz 5 obliegt zudem den Behörden der Zollverwaltung nach Maßgabe der §§ 17a bis 18a.

§ 17a
Befugnisse der Behörden der Zollverwaltung

Die §§ 2, 3 bis 6 und 14 bis 20, 22, 23 des Schwarzarbeitsbekämpfungsgesetzes sind entsprechend anzuwenden mit der Maßgabe, dass die dort genannten Behörden auch Einsicht in Arbeitsverträge, Niederschriften nach § 2 des Nachweisgesetzes und andere Geschäftsunterlagen nehmen können, die mittelbar oder unmittelbar Auskunft über die Einhaltung der Arbeitsbedingungen nach § 8 Absatz 5 geben.

§ 17b
Meldepflicht

(1) ¹Überlässt ein Verleiher mit Sitz im Ausland einen Leiharbeitnehmer zur Arbeitsleistung einem Entleiher, hat der Entleiher, sofern eine Rechtsverordnung nach § 3a auf das Arbeitsverhältnis Anwendung findet, vor Beginn jeder Überlassung der zuständigen Behörde der Zollverwaltung eine schriftliche Anmeldung in deutscher Sprache mit folgenden Angaben zuzuleiten:

1. Familienname, Vornamen und Geburtsdatum des überlassenen Leiharbeitnehmers,
2. Beginn und Dauer der Überlassung,
3. Ort der Beschäftigung,
4. Ort im Inland, an dem die nach § 17c erforderlichen Unterlagen bereitgehalten werden,
5. Familienname, Vornamen und Anschrift in Deutschland eines oder einer Zustellungsbevollmächtigten des Verleihers,

(4) Section 66 of Book 10 of the Social Code shall apply mutatis mutandis.

(5) The fines shall be paid into the treasury of the competent administrative authority. Notwithstanding section 105(2) of the Act on Administrative Offences, it shall bear the necessary expenses and shall also be liable to pay compensation within the meaning of section 110(4) of the Act on Administrative Offences.

Section 17
Implementation

(1) The Federal Employment Agency shall implement this Act in accordance with the technical instructions of the Federal Ministry of Labour and Social Affairs. Administrative costs shall not be reimbursed.

(2) In addition, the examination of the working conditions under section 8(5) is the responsibility of the customs authorities in accordance with sections 17a to 18a.

Section 17a
Powers of the Customs Authorities

Sections 2, 3 to 6 and 14 to 20, 22, 23 of the Act to Combat undeclared work shall apply mutatis mutandis, subject to the proviso that the authorities named therein may also inspect employment contracts, minutes pursuant to section 2 of the Evidence Act and other business documents which directly or indirectly provide information on compliance with the working conditions pursuant to section 8(5).

Section 17b
Obligation to Register

(1) ¹If a temporary work agency based abroad assigns a temporary agency worker at the disposal of a hirer for the purpose of performing work, the hirer shall, insofar as a statutory instrument pursuant to §3a applies to the employment relationship, submit a written declaration in German to the competent authority of the customs administration each assignment's commencement, containing the following information

1. surname, first name and date of birth of the temporary worker assigned,
2. beginning and duration of the assignment,
3. place of employment,
4. place in Germany where the documents required under § 17c are kept available,
5. the surname, first names and address in Germany of one or an authorised representative of the temporary work agency,

6. Branche, in die die Leiharbeitnehmer überlassen werden sollen, und

7. Familienname, Vornamen oder Firma sowie
Anschrift des Verleihers.

²Änderungen bezüglich dieser Angaben hat der
Entleiher unverzüglich zu melden.

(2) Der Entleiher hat der Anmeldung eine Versicherung des Verleihers beizufügen, dass dieser
seine Verpflichtungen nach § 8 Absatz 5 einhält.

(3) Das Bundesministerium der Finanzen kann
durch Rechtsverordnung im Einvernehmen
mit dem Bundesministerium für Arbeit und
Soziales ohne Zustimmung des Bundesrates
bestimmen,

1. dass, auf welche Weise und unter welchen
technischen und organisatorischen Voraussetzungen eine Anmeldung, Änderungsmeldung und Versicherung abweichend von
den Absätzen 1 und 2 elektronisch übermittelt werden kann,

2. unter welchen Voraussetzungen eine Änderungsmeldung ausnahmsweise entfallen
kann und

3. wie das Meldeverfahren vereinfacht oder abgewandelt werden kann.

(4) Das Bundesministerium der Finanzen kann
durch Rechtsverordnung ohne Zustimmung des
Bundesrates die zuständige Behörde nach Absatz 1 Satz 1 bestimmen.

§ 17c
Erstellen und Bereithalten von
Dokumenten

(1) Sofern eine Rechtsverordnung nach § 3a auf
ein Arbeitsverhältnis Anwendung findet, ist der
Entleiher verpflichtet, Beginn, Ende und Dauer
der täglichen Arbeitszeit des Leiharbeitnehmers
spätestens bis zum Ablauf des siebten auf den
Tag der Arbeitsleistung folgenden Kalendertages aufzuzeichnen und diese Aufzeichnungen
mindestens zwei Jahre beginnend ab dem für
die Aufzeichnung maßgeblichen Zeitpunkt aufzubewahren.

(2) ¹Jeder Verleiher ist verpflichtet, die für die
Kontrolle der Einhaltung einer Rechtsverordnung nach § 3a erforderlichen Unterlagen im
Inland für die gesamte Dauer der tatsächlichen
Beschäftigung des Leiharbeitnehmers im Geltungsbereich dieses Gesetzes, insgesamt jedoch
nicht länger als zwei Jahre, in deutscher Sprache
bereitzuhalten. ²Auf Verlangen der Prüfbehörde
sind die Unterlagen auch am Ort der Beschäftigung bereitzuhalten.

---

6. the sector to which the temporary agency
workers are to be assigned, and

7. surname, first name or company name and
address of the temporary work agency

²The hirer must report any changes to this information without delay.

(2) The hirer shall enclose with the notification
an assurance from the temporary work agency
that the latter will comply with its obligations
under Section 8, paragraph 5.

(3) The Federal Ministry of Finance may determine by statutory order in agreement with the
Federal Ministry of Labour and Social Affairs
without the consent of the Bundesrat,

1. that, by which means and under which
technical and organisational conditions a
notification, notification of change and insurance can be transmitted electronically in
derogation of paragraphs 1 and 2

2. under which conditions a notification of
change can exceptionally be omitted and

3. how the notification procedure can be simplified or modified.

(4) The Federal Ministry of Finance may, by
statutory ordinance and without the consent of
the Bundesrat, designate the competent authority pursuant to subsection 1 first sentence above.

Section 17c
Creating and Keeping Documents Ready

(1) If a statutory instrument pursuant to section 3a applies to an employment relationship,
the hirer is obliged to record the beginning,
end and duration of the daily working time of
the temporary agency worker at the latest by
the end of the seventh calendar day following
the day of performance of the work and to keep
these records for at least two years from the time
relevant for the recording.

(2) ¹Each temporary work agency is obliged to
keep the records required for checking compliance with a statutory instrument under section 3a in Germany in German for the entire
duration of the temporary agency worker's actual employment within the scope of this Act,
but for no longer than two years in total. ²At
the request of the audit authority, the documents must also be kept available at the place
of employment.

§ 18
Zusammenarbeit mit anderen Behörden

(1) Zur Verfolgung und Ahndung der Ordnungswidrigkeiten nach § 16 arbeiten die Bundesagentur für Arbeit und die Behörden der Zollverwaltung insbesondere mit folgenden Behörden zusammen:

1. den Trägern der Krankenversicherung als Einzugsstellen für die Sozialversicherungsbeiträge,
2. den in § 71 des Aufenthaltsgesetzes genannten Behörden,
3. den Finanzbehörden,
4. den nach Landesrecht für die Verfolgung und Ahndung von Ordnungswidrigkeiten nach dem Schwarzarbeitsbekämpfungsgesetz zuständigen Behörden,
5. den Trägern der Unfallversicherung,
6. den für den Arbeitsschutz zuständigen Landesbehörden,
7. den Rentenversicherungsträgern,
8. den Trägern der Sozialhilfe.

(2) Ergeben sich für die Bundesagentur für Arbeit oder die Behörden der Zollverwaltung bei der Durchführung dieses Gesetzes im Einzelfall konkrete Anhaltspunkte für

1. Verstöße gegen das Schwarzarbeitsbekämpfungsgesetz,
2. eine Beschäftigung oder Tätigkeit von Ausländern ohne erforderlichen Aufenthaltstitel nach § 4 Abs. 3 des Aufenthaltsgesetzes, eine Aufenthaltsgestattung oder eine Duldung, die zur Ausübung der Beschäftigung berechtigen, oder eine Genehmigung nach § 284 Abs. 1 des Dritten Buches Sozialgesetzbuch,
3. Verstöße gegen die Mitwirkungspflicht nach § 60 Abs. 1 Satz 1 Nr. 2 des Ersten Buches Sozialgesetzbuch gegenüber einer Dienststelle der Bundesagentur für Arbeit, einem Träger der gesetzlichen Kranken-, Pflege-, Unfall- oder Rentenversicherung oder einem Träger der Sozialhilfe oder gegen die Meldepflicht nach § 8a des Asylbewerberleistungsgesetzes,
4. Verstöße gegen die Vorschriften des Vierten und Siebten Buches Sozialgesetzbuch über die Verpflichtung zur Zahlung von Sozialversicherungsbeiträgen, soweit sie im Zusammenhang mit den in den Nummern 1 bis 3 genannten Verstößen sowie mit Arbeitnehmerüberlassung entgegen § 1 stehen,
5. Verstöße gegen die Steuergesetze,
6. Verstöße gegen das Aufenthaltsgesetz,

Section 18
Cooperation with other Authorities

(1) For the prosecution and punishment of the administrative offences under section 16, the Federal Employment Agency and the customs authorities shall cooperate in particular with the following authorities:

1. the health insurance institutions as collection points for social security contributions,
2. the authorities named in Section 71 of the Residence Act,
3. the tax authorities,
4. the authorities responsible under Land law for the prosecution and punishment of administrative offences in accordance with the Schwarzarbeitsbekämpfungsgesetz,
5. the institutions responsible for accident insurance,
6. the federal state authorities responsible for occupational health and safety,
7. the pension insurance institutions,
8. the providers of social assistance.

(2) If, in implementing this Act, the Federal Employment Agency or the authorities of the customs administration find concrete indications in individual cases of

1. infringements of the law on combating illegal employment,
2. an employment or activity of foreigners without the required residence title under Section 4(3) of the Residence Act, a residence permit or a toleration certificate entitling them to exercise employment, or a permit under Section 284(1) of Book Three of the Social Security Code,
3. violations of the duty to cooperate under Section 60 (1) sentence 1 no. 2 of Book One of the Social Security Code vis-à-vis an office of the Federal Employment Agency, a statutory health, nursing, accident or pension insurance institution or a social assistance institution, or of the obligation to register under Section 8a of the Asylum Seekers Benefits Act,
4. infringements of the provisions of Book 4 and Book 7 of the Social Security Code concerning the obligation to pay social security contributions, insofar as they are contrary to § 1 in connection with the infringements referred to in Nos. 1 to 3 and with temporary agency employment,
5. infringements of tax laws,
6. infringements of the Residence Act,

unterrichten sie die für die Verfolgung und Ahndung zuständigen Behörden, die Träger der Sozialhilfe sowie die Behörden nach § 71 des Aufenthaltsgesetzes.

(3) [1]In Strafsachen, die Straftaten nach den §§ 15 und 15a zum Gegenstand haben, sind der Bundesagentur für Arbeit und den Behörden der Zollverwaltung zur Verfolgung von Ordnungswidrigkeiten

1. bei Einleitung des Strafverfahrens die Personendaten des Beschuldigten, der Straftatbestand, die Tatzeit und der Tatort,
2. im Falle der Erhebung der öffentlichen Klage die das Verfahren abschließende Entscheidung mit Begründung

zu übermitteln. [2]Ist mit der in Nummer 2 genannten Entscheidung ein Rechtsmittel verworfen worden oder wird darin auf die angefochtene Entscheidung Bezug genommen, so ist auch die angefochtene Entscheidung zu übermitteln. [3]Die Übermittlung veranlasst die Strafvollstreckungs- oder die Strafverfolgungsbehörde. [4]Eine Verwendung

1. der Daten der Arbeitnehmer für Maßnahmen zu ihren Gunsten,
2. der Daten des Arbeitgebers zur Besetzung seiner offenen Arbeitsplätze, die im Zusammenhang mit dem Strafverfahren bekanntgeworden sind,
3. der in den Nummern 1 und 2 genannten Daten für Entscheidungen über die Einstellung oder Rückforderung von Leistungen der Bundesagentur für Arbeit

ist zulässig.

(4) (weggefallen)

(5) Die Behörden der Zollverwaltung unterrichten die zuständigen örtlichen Landesfinanzbehörden über den Inhalt von Meldungen nach § 17b.

(6) [1]Die Behörden der Zollverwaltung und die übrigen in § 2 des Schwarzarbeitsbekämpfungsgesetzes genannten Behörden dürfen nach Maßgabe der jeweils einschlägigen datenschutzrechtlichen Bestimmungen auch mit Behörden anderer Vertragsstaaten des Abkommens über den Europäischen Wirtschaftsraum zusammenarbeiten, die dem § 17 Absatz 2 entsprechende Aufgaben durchführen oder für die Bekämpfung illegaler Beschäftigung zuständig sind oder Auskünfte geben können, ob ein Arbeitgeber seine Verpflichtungen nach § 8 Absatz 5 erfüllt. [2]Die Regelungen über die internationale Rechtshilfe in Strafsachen bleiben hiervon unberührt.

inform the authorities responsible for prosecution and punishment, the social assistance institutions and the authorities under Section 71 of the Residence Act.

(3) [1]In criminal matters relating to offences under sections 15 and 15a, the Federal Employment Agency and the customs authorities shall, in order to prosecute administrative offences

1. when criminal proceedings are initiated, the personal data of the accused, the offence, the time and place of the offence
2. in the event of a public action being brought, the decision closing the proceedings, with reasons

to be transmitted. Where the decision referred to in point 2 dismisses an appeal or makes reference to the contested decision, the contested decision must also be notified. The transmission is to be made by the authority responsible for enforcement or prosecution. [4]A use of

1. the data of workers for measures in their favour
2. the employer's data on the filling of his vacancies which have become known in connection with the criminal proceedings
3. the data referred to in numbers 1 and 2 for decisions on the discontinuation or reclaiming of benefits from the Federal Employment Agency

is permissible.

(4) (omitted)

(5) The customs authorities shall inform the competent local state financial authorities of the content of declarations in accordance with section 17b.

(6) [1]The authorities of the customs administration and the other authorities mentioned in Section 2 of the Act to Combat Illegal Employment may, in accordance with the relevant provisions of data protection law, also cooperate with authorities of other states party to the Agreement on the European Economic Area which carry out tasks corresponding to Section 17(2) or are responsible for combating illegal employment or may provide information as to whether an employer fulfils its obligations under Section 8(5). [2]The provisions on international mutual assistance in criminal matters remain unaffected by this.

§ 18a
(Weggefallen)

Section 18a
(omitted)

§ 19
Übergangsvorschrift

(1) § 8 Absatz 3 findet keine Anwendung auf Leiharbeitsverhältnisse, die vor dem 15. Dezember 2010 begründet worden sind.

(2) Überlassungszeiten vor dem 1. April 2017 werden bei der Berechnung der Überlassungshöchstdauer nach § 1 Absatz 1b und der Berechnung der Überlassungszeiten nach § 8 Absatz 4 Satz 1 nicht berücksichtigt.

Section 19
Transitional Provision

(1) Section 8 subsection (3) shall not apply to temporary employment relationships which were established before 15 December 2010.

(2) Assignment periods prior to 1 April 2017 shall not be taken into account in calculating the maximum duration of hiring under section 1(1b) and in calculating the hiring periods under section 8(4) first sentence.

§ 20
Evaluation

Die Anwendung dieses Gesetzes ist im Jahr 2020 zu evaluieren.

Section 20
Evaluation

The application of this law is to be evaluated in 2020.

IV. Works Constitution Act (Excerpt)

Betriebsverfassungsgesetz – BetrVG (Auszug)

Stand: 18.12.2018

§ 1
Errichtung von Betriebsräten

(1) [1]In Betrieben mit in der Regel mindestens fünf ständigen wahlberechtigten Arbeitnehmern, von denen drei wählbar sind, werden Betriebsräte gewählt. [2]Dies gilt auch für gemeinsame Betriebe mehrerer Unternehmen.

(2) Ein gemeinsamer Betrieb mehrerer Unternehmen wird vermutet, wenn

1. zur Verfolgung arbeitstechnischer Zwecke die Betriebsmittel sowie die Arbeitnehmer von den Unternehmen gemeinsam eingesetzt werden oder

2. die Spaltung eines Unternehmens zur Folge hat, dass von einem Betrieb ein oder mehrere Betriebsteile einem an der Spaltung beteiligten anderen Unternehmen zugeordnet werden, ohne dass sich dabei die Organisation des betroffenen Betriebs wesentlich ändert.

§ 2
Stellung der Gewerkschaften und Vereinigungen der Arbeitgeber

(1) Arbeitgeber und Betriebsrat arbeiten unter Beachtung der geltenden Tarifverträge vertrauensvoll und im Zusammenwirken mit den im Betrieb vertretenen Gewerkschaften und Arbeitgebervereinigungen zum Wohl der Arbeitnehmer und des Betriebs zusammen.

(2) Zur Wahrnehmung der in diesem Gesetz genannten Aufgaben und Befugnisse der im Betrieb vertretenen Gewerkschaften ist deren Beauftragten nach Unterrichtung des Arbeitgebers oder seines Vertreters Zugang zum Betrieb zu gewähren, soweit dem nicht unumgängliche Notwendigkeiten des Betriebsablaufs, zwingende Sicherheitsvorschriften oder der Schutz von Betriebsgeheimnissen entgegenstehen.

(3) Die Aufgaben der Gewerkschaften und der Vereinigungen der Arbeitgeber, insbesondere die Wahrnehmung der Interessen ihrer Mitglieder, werden durch dieses Gesetz nicht berührt.

Section 1
Establishment of work councils

(1) [1]Works councils shall be elected in all establishments that normally have five or more permanent employees with voting rights, including three who are eligible. [2]The same shall apply to joint establishments of several companies.

(2) A joint establishment of several companies is assumed to exist if

1. the companies employ the equipment and workers jointly in order to pursue their working objectives, or

2. splitting a company would have the effect that one or several departments of an establishment would be allocated to another company that is involved in the split, without thereby fundamentally changing the organisation of the establishment concerned.

Section 2
Status of trade unions and employers' associations

(1) The employer and the works council shall work together in a spirit of mutual trust having regard to the applicable collective agreements and in co-operation with the trade unions and employers' associations represented in the establishment for the good of the employees and of the establishment.

(2) In order to permit the trade unions represented in the establishment to exercise the powers and duties established by this Act, their agents shall, after notification of the employer or his representative, be granted access to the establishment, in so far as this does not run counter to essential operational requirements, mandatory safety rules or the protection of trade secrets.

(3) This Act shall not affect the functions of trade unions and employers' associations and more particularly the representation of their members' interests.

§3
Abweichende Regelungen

(1) Durch Tarifvertrag können bestimmt werden:

1. für Unternehmen mit mehreren Betrieben

   (a) die Bildung eines unternehmenseinheitlichen Betriebsrats oder

   (b) die Zusammenfassung von Betrieben,

   wenn dies die Bildung von Betriebsräten erleichtert oder einer sachgerechten Wahrnehmung der Interessen der Arbeitnehmer dient;

2. für Unternehmen und Konzerne, soweit sie nach produkt- oder projektbezogenen Geschäftsbereichen (Sparten) organisiert sind und die Leitung der Sparte auch Entscheidungen in beteiligungspflichtigen Angelegenheiten trifft, die Bildung von Betriebsräten in den Sparten (Spartenbetriebsräte), wenn dies der sachgerechten Wahrnehmung der Aufgaben des Betriebsrats dient;

3. andere Arbeitnehmervertretungsstrukturen, soweit dies insbesondere aufgrund der Betriebs-, Unternehmens- oder Konzernorganisation oder aufgrund anderer Formen der Zusammenarbeit von Unternehmen einer wirksamen und zweckmäßigen Interessenvertretung der Arbeitnehmer dient;

4. zusätzliche betriebsverfassungsrechtliche Gremien (Arbeitsgemeinschaften), die der unternehmensübergreifenden Zusammenarbeit von Arbeitnehmervertretungen dienen;

5. zusätzliche betriebsverfassungsrechtliche Vertretungen der Arbeitnehmer, die die Zusammenarbeit zwischen Betriebsrat und Arbeitnehmern erleichtern.

(2) Besteht in den Fällen des Absatzes 1 Nr. 1, 2, 4 oder 5 keine tarifliche Regelung und gilt auch kein anderer Tarifvertrag, kann die Regelung durch Betriebsvereinbarung getroffen werden.

(3) ¹Besteht im Fall des Absatzes 1 Nr. 1 Buchstabe a keine tarifliche Regelung und besteht in dem Unternehmen kein Betriebsrat, können die Arbeitnehmer mit Stimmenmehrheit die Wahl eines unternehmenseinheitlichen Betriebsrats beschließen. ²Die Abstimmung kann von mindestens drei wahlberechtigten Arbeitnehmern des Unternehmens oder einer im Unternehmen vertretenen Gewerkschaft veranlasst werden.

Section 3
Different arrangements

(1) The following may be determined by collective agreements:

1. for companies comprising several establishments
   (a) the formation of a uniform works council for the company, or
   (b) the combination of companies or establishments
   if the formation of works councils is thereby facilitated, or if this combination serves the appropriate safeguarding of the workers' interests;

2. for companies and combines, to the extent that they have been organised according to product- or project-specific divisions (branches) and the branch management also makes decision concerning issues that require participation, the formation of works councils for the branches (branch works councils), if this arrangement serves to appropriately carry out the works council's duties;

3. other workers' representation structures to the extent that these structures serve an efficient and appropriate representation of workers' interests, in particular, because of the organisation of the establishment, company, or combine, or because of other types of cooperation between companies;

4. additional bodies under the Works Constitution Act (working groups) that serve for the inter-company co-operation of workers' representations;

5. additional workers' representations under the Works Constitution Act that facilitate cooperation between the works council and the workers.

(2) If no provisions are included in a collective agreement that cover the cases listed in subsection (1), clauses 1, 2, 4, or 5, and if no other collective agreement is available, such an arrangement can be agreed upon in a works agreement.

(3) ¹If no provisions are included in a collective agreement that cover the case described in subsection (1) clause 1 letter a), and if there is no works council in the establishment, a majority of workers can resolve to elect a uniform works council. ²This vote can be initiated by a minimum of three workers with voting rights employed by the establishment, or by a trade union represented in the establishment.

(4) ¹Sofern der Tarifvertrag oder die Betriebsvereinbarung nichts anderes bestimmt, sind Regelungen nach Absatz 1 Nr. 1 bis 3 erstmals bei der nächsten regelmäßigen Betriebsratswahl anzuwenden, es sei denn, es besteht kein Betriebsrat oder es ist aus anderen Gründen eine Neuwahl des Betriebsrats erforderlich. ²Sieht der Tarifvertrag oder die Betriebsvereinbarung einen anderen Wahlzeitpunkt vor, endet die Amtszeit bestehender Betriebsräte, die durch die Regelungen nach Absatz 1 Nr. 1 bis 3 entfallen, mit Bekanntgabe des Wahlergebnisses.

(5) ¹Die aufgrund eines Tarifvertrages oder einer Betriebsvereinbarung nach Absatz 1 Nr. 1 bis 3 gebildeten betriebsverfassungsrechtlichen Organisationseinheiten gelten als Betriebe im Sinne dieses Gesetzes. ²Auf die in ihnen gebildeten Arbeitnehmervertretungen finden die Vorschriften über die Rechte und Pflichten des Betriebsrats und die Rechtsstellung seiner Mitglieder Anwendung.

§4
Betriebsteile, Kleinstbetriebe

(1) ¹Betriebsteile gelten als selbständige Betriebe, wenn sie die Voraussetzungen des § 1 Abs. 1 Satz 1 erfüllen und

1. räumlich weit vom Hauptbetrieb entfernt oder
2. durch Aufgabenbereich und Organisation eigenständig sind.

²Die Arbeitnehmer eines Betriebsteils, in dem kein eigener Betriebsrat besteht, können mit Stimmenmehrheit formlos beschließen, an der Wahl des Betriebsrats im Hauptbetrieb teilzunehmen; § 3 Abs. 3 Satz 2 gilt entsprechend. ³Die Abstimmung kann auch vom Betriebsrat des Hauptbetriebs veranlasst werden. ⁴Der Beschluss ist dem Betriebsrat des Hauptbetriebs spätestens zehn Wochen vor Ablauf seiner Amtszeit mitzuteilen. ⁵Für den Widerruf des Beschlusses gelten die Sätze 2 bis 4 entsprechend.

(2) Betriebe, die die Voraussetzungen des § 1 Abs. 1 Satz 1 nicht erfüllen, sind dem Hauptbetrieb zuzuordnen.

(4) ¹Unless provided otherwise in the collective agreement or the works agreement, the arrangements specified in Subsection (1) clauses 1 to 3 shall be applied for the first time in the course of the next regular works council elections, unless no works council exists, or unless the works council has to be re-elected for other reasons. ²If the collective agreement or the works agreement provides for another voting time, the term of office of existing works councillors, which will become obsolete under the Subsection 1 clauses 1 to 3, shall terminate upon announcement of the election results.

(5) ¹The organisation units under the Works Constitution Act, which were established on the basis of a collective agreement or a plant-level agreement in accordance with Subsection 1 Clauses 1 to 3, are considered establishments for the purposes of this Act. ²The provisions concerning the rights and obligations of the works council and the legal position of its members shall be applicable to the workers' representations formed therein.

Section 4
Separate departments, very small establishments

(1) ¹Separate departments of establishments shall be regarded as independent establishments if they meet the conditions laid down in the first sentence of section 1 (1) and

1. are situated at a considerable distance from the principal establishment, or
2. are independent by reason of their function and organization.

²The employees of a separate department, in which no separate works council exists, may resolve by a simple majority of votes and without complying with a special form that they will participate in the works council elections of the principal establishment; the second sentence of section 3 (3) shall apply, mutatis mutandis. ³The vote may also be initiated by the works council of the principal establishment. ⁴The resolution shall be communicated to the works council of the principal establishment not later than ten weeks before expiry of its term of office. ⁵The second to fourth sentences of this subsection shall apply, mutatis mutandis, to the revocation of the resolution.

(2) Establishments that do not meet the conditions laid down in the first sentence of section 1 (1) shall be treated as part of the principal establishment.

| §5 | Section 5 |
| Arbeitnehmer | Employees |

(1) [1]Arbeitnehmer (Arbeitnehmerinnen und Arbeitnehmer) im Sinne dieses Gesetzes sind Arbeiter und Angestellte einschließlich der zu ihrer Berufsausbildung Beschäftigten, unabhängig davon, ob sie im Betrieb, im Außendienst oder mit Telearbeit beschäftigt werden. [2]Als Arbeitnehmer gelten auch die in Heimarbeit Beschäftigten, die in der Hauptsache für den Betrieb arbeiten. [3]Als Arbeitnehmer gelten ferner Beamte (Beamtinnen und Beamte), Soldaten (Soldatinnen und Soldaten) sowie Arbeitnehmer des öffentlichen Dienstes einschließlich der zu ihrer Berufsausbildung Beschäftigten, die in Betrieben privatrechtlich organisierter Unternehmen tätig sind.

(1) [1]In this Act the term "employee" (male and female) comprises wage earners and salaried employees including persons employed for the purpose of their vocational training, regardless of whether they are engaged in indoor work, in field service, or in tele-work. [2]The term includes persons engaged in home work who work principally for one and the same establishment. [3]Furthermore, (female and male) civil servants, (female and male) soldiers and employees of the public service, including persons employed for the purpose of their vocational training, are considered „employees" if they work in establishments organised under private law.

(2) Als Arbeitnehmer im Sinne dieses Gesetzes gelten nicht

(2) The following shall not be considered as employees for the purposes of this Act:

1. in Betrieben einer juristischen Person die Mitglieder des Organs, das zur gesetzlichen Vertretung der juristischen Person berufen ist;

1. in establishments belonging to a corporation, the members of the organs that are legally empowered to represent the corporation;

2. die Gesellschafter einer offenen Handelsgesellschaft oder die Mitglieder einer anderen Personengesamtheit, soweit sie durch Gesetz, Satzung oder Gesellschaftsvertrag zur Vertretung der Personengesamtheit oder zur Geschäftsführung berufen sind, in deren Betrieben;

2. partners in an ordinary commercial partnership or members of another association of persons in the establishment belonging to the partnership or association, in so far as they are empowered by law, its own by-laws or the articles of association to represent the association or to exercise management functions;

3. Personen, deren Beschäftigung nicht in erster Linie ihrem Erwerb dient, sondern vorwiegend durch Beweggründe karitativer oder religiöser Art bestimmt ist;

3. persons whose employment is not primarily for the purpose of earning their livelihood but is chiefly inspired by charitable or religious motives;

4. Personen, deren Beschäftigung nicht in erster Linie ihrem Erwerb dient und die vorwiegend zu ihrer Heilung, Wiedereingewöhnung, sittlichen Besserung oder Erziehung beschäftigt werden;

4. persons whose employment is not primarily for the purpose of earning their livelihood but principally for their cure or recovery, rehabilitation, moral improvement or education;

5. der Ehegatte, der Lebenspartner, Verwandte und Verschwägerte ersten Grades, die in häuslicher Gemeinschaft mit dem Arbeitgeber leben.

5. spouse, the life partner, as well as the relatives by blood or marriage of the first degree living with the employer.

(3) [1]Dieses Gesetz findet, soweit in ihm nicht ausdrücklich etwas anderes bestimmt ist, keine Anwendung auf leitende Angestellte. [2]Leitender Angestellter ist, wer nach Arbeitsvertrag und Stellung im Unternehmen oder im Betrieb

(3) [1]Unless this Act expressly provides to the contrary, it shall not apply to executive staff. [2]Executive staff are employees who, under their contract of employment and by their status in the company or establishment,

1. zur selbständigen Einstellung und Entlassung von im Betrieb oder in der Betriebsabteilung beschäftigten Arbeitnehmern berechtigt ist oder

1. are entitled on their own responsibility to engage and dismiss employees on behalf of the establishment or one of its departments; or

2. Generalvollmacht oder Prokura hat und die Prokura auch im Verhältnis zum Arbeitgeber nicht unbedeutend ist oder

2. are endowed with general authority (power of procuration) or full power of representation or power to sign, the latter also being important in relation to the employer; or

3. regelmäßig sonstige Aufgaben wahrnimmt, die für den Bestand und die Entwicklung des Unternehmens oder eines Betriebs von Bedeutung sind und deren Erfüllung besondere Erfahrungen und Kenntnisse voraussetzt, wenn er dabei entweder die Entscheidungen im Wesentlichen frei von Weisungen trifft oder sie maßgeblich beeinflusst; dies kann auch bei Vorgaben insbesondere auf Grund von Rechtsvorschriften, Plänen oder Richtlinien sowie bei Zusammenarbeit mit anderen leitenden Angestellten gegeben sein.

³Für die in Absatz 1 Satz 3 genannten Beamten und Soldaten gelten die Sätze 1 und 2 entsprechend.

(4) Leitender Angestellter nach Absatz 3 Nr. 3 ist im Zweifel, wer

1. aus Anlass der letzten Wahl des Betriebsrats, des Sprecherausschusses oder von Aufsichtsratsmitgliedern der Arbeitnehmer oder durch rechtskräftige gerichtliche Entscheidung den leitenden Angestellten zugeordnet worden ist oder

2. einer Leitungsebene angehört, auf der in dem Unternehmen überwiegend leitende Angestellte vertreten sind, oder

3. ein regelmäßiges Jahresarbeitsentgelt erhält, das für leitende Angestellte in dem Unternehmen üblich ist, oder

4. falls auch bei der Anwendung der Nummer 3 noch Zweifel bleiben, ein regelmäßiges Jahresarbeitsentgelt erhält, das das Dreifache der Bezugsgröße nach § 18 des Vierten Buches Sozialgesetzbuch überschreitet.

3. regularly carry out other duties which are important for the existence and development of the company or an establishment and fulfilment of which requires particular experience and knowledge, if, in doing so, they either essentially make decisions on their own responsibility or substantially influence these decisions; this may also be the case with stipulated procedures, particularly those based on legal provisions, plans or guidelines and when cooperating with other executive staff.

³The first and second sentences shall apply, mutatis mutandis, to the civil servants and soldiers referred to in subsection 1, sentence 3.

(4) In case of doubt, executive staff under subsection (3), clause 3, are employees who

1. have been assigned to the executive staff on the occasion of the last election of the works council, the executives' committee or of supervisory board members of the employees or by means of a final and conclusive legal decision; or

2. belong to a management level at which executive staff are predominantly represented in the company; or

3. regularly receive an annual salary which is customary for executive staff in the company; or

4. if there is still doubt on application of clause 3, regularly receive an annual salary which is three times greater than the reference figure as per section 18 of Book Four of the Social Code.

§ 7
Wahlberechtigung

¹Wahlberechtigt sind alle Arbeitnehmer des Betriebs, die das 18. Lebensjahr vollendet haben. ²Werden Arbeitnehmer eines anderen Arbeitgebers zur Arbeitsleistung überlassen, so sind diese wahlberechtigt, wenn sie länger als drei Monate im Betrieb eingesetzt werden.

Section 7
Voting rights

¹All employees of the establishment who are 18 years of age or over shall have voting rights. ²If employees of another employer are hired out for work, they are entitled to vote if they are working in the establishment for more than three months.

§ 8
Wählbarkeit

(1) ¹Wählbar sind alle Wahlberechtigten, die sechs Monate dem Betrieb angehören oder als in Heimarbeit Beschäftigte in der Hauptsache für den Betrieb gearbeitet haben. ²Auf diese sechsmonatige Betriebszugehörigkeit werden Zeiten angerechnet, in denen der Arbeitnehmer unmittelbar vorher einem anderen Betrieb desselben Unternehmens oder Konzerns (§ 18 Abs. 1 des Aktiengesetzes) angehört hat. ³Nicht wählbar ist, wer infolge strafgerichtlicher Verurteilung die Fähigkeit, Rechte aus öffentlichen Wahlen zu erlangen, nicht besitzt.

Section 8
Eligibility

(1) ¹All employees with voting rights who have been employed in or principally worked for the establishment as homeworkers for six months shall be eligible to the works council. ²The said period of six months shall be deemed to include any immediately preceding period during which the employee was employed in another establishment belonging to the same company or combine as defined in section 18 (1) of the Joint Stock Act. ³Persons who by court judgement have been declared ineligible or debarred from holding public office shall be ineligible to works councils.

(2) Besteht der Betrieb weniger als sechs Monate, so sind abweichend von der Vorschrift in Absatz 1 über die sechsmonatige Betriebszugehörigkeit diejenigen Arbeitnehmer wählbar, die bei der Einleitung der Betriebsratswahl im Betrieb beschäftigt sind und die übrigen Voraussetzungen für die Wählbarkeit erfüllen.

§9
Zahl der Betriebsratsmitglieder

¹Der Betriebsrat besteht in Betrieben mit in der Regel

5 bis 20 wahlberechtigten Arbeitnehmern aus einer Person,

21 bis 50 wahlberechtigten Arbeitnehmern aus 3 Mitgliedern,

51 wahlberechtigten Arbeitnehmern bis 100 Arbeitnehmern

101 bis 200 Arbeitnehmern aus 7 Mitgliedern,

201 bis 400 Arbeitnehmern aus 9 Mitgliedern,

401 bis 700 Arbeitnehmern aus 11 Mitgliedern,

701 bis 1 000 Arbeitnehmern aus 13 Mitgliedern,

1 001 bis 1 500 Arbeitnehmern aus 15 Mitgliedern,

1 501 bis 2 000 Arbeitnehmern aus 17 Mitgliedern,

2 001 bis 2 500 Arbeitnehmern aus 19 Mitgliedern,

2 501 bis 3 000 Arbeitnehmern aus 21 Mitgliedern,

3 001 bis 3 500 Arbeitnehmern aus 23 Mitgliedern,

3 501 bis 4 000 Arbeitnehmern aus 25 Mitgliedern,

4 001 bis 4 500 Arbeitnehmern aus 27 Mitgliedern,

4 501 bis 5 000 Arbeitnehmern aus 29 Mitgliedern,

5 001 bis 6 000 Arbeitnehmern aus 31 Mitgliedern,

6 001 bis 7 000 Arbeitnehmern aus 33 Mitgliedern,

7 001 bis 9 000 Arbeitnehmern aus 35 Mitgliedern.

²In Betrieben mit mehr als 9 000 Arbeitnehmern erhöht sich die Zahl der Mitglieder des Betriebsrats für je angefangene weitere 3.000 Arbeitnehmer um 2 Mitglieder.

(2) If the establishment has been in existence for less than six months, such employees as are employed in the establishment and fulfil the other conditions for eligibility at the announcement of the election for the works council shall be eligible notwithstanding the requirement of six months' service under subsection (1).

Section 9
Number of members of the works council

¹The membership of the works council shall be as follows, according to the number of employees with voting rights normally employed in the establishment:

5 to 20 employees entitled to vote: 1 person,

21 to 50 employees entitled to vote: 3 members,

51 to 100 employees entitled to vote: 5 members,

101 to 200 employees: 7 members,

201 to 400 employees: 9 members,

401 to 700 employees: 11 members

701 to 1000 employees: 13 members,

1001 to 1500 employees: 15 members,

1501 to 2000 employees: 17 members,

2001 to 2500 employees: 19 members,

2501 to 3000 employees: 21 members,

3001 to 3500 employees: 23 members,

3501 to 4000 employees: 25 members,

4001 to 4500 employees: 27 members,

4501 to 5000 employees: 29 members,

5001 to 6000 employees: 31 members,

6001 to 7000 employees: 33 members,

7001 to 9000 employees: 35 members.

²In establishments employing more than 9,000 employees the number of members of the works council shall be increased by two members for every additional fraction of 3,000 employees.

§ 11
Ermäßigte Zahl der Betriebsratsmitglieder

Hat ein Betrieb nicht die ausreichende Zahl von wählbaren Arbeitnehmern, so ist die Zahl der Betriebsratsmitglieder der nächstniedrigeren Betriebsgröße zugrunde zu legen.

§ 13
Zeitpunkt der Betriebsratswahlen

(1) ¹Die regelmäßigen Betriebsratswahlen finden alle vier Jahre in der Zeit vom 1. März bis 31. Mai statt. ²Sie sind zeitgleich mit den regelmäßigen Wahlen nach § 5 Abs. 1 des Sprecherausschussgesetzes einzuleiten.

(2) Außerhalb dieser Zeit ist der Betriebsrat zu wählen, wenn

1. mit Ablauf von 24 Monaten, vom Tage der Wahl an gerechnet, die Zahl der regelmäßig beschäftigten Arbeitnehmer um die Hälfte, mindestens aber um fünfzig, gestiegen oder gesunken ist,
2. die Gesamtzahl der Betriebsratsmitglieder nach Eintreten sämtlicher Ersatzmitglieder unter die vorgeschriebene Zahl der Betriebsratsmitglieder gesunken ist,
3. der Betriebsrat mit der Mehrheit seiner Mitglieder seinen Rücktritt beschlossen hat,
4. die Betriebsratswahl mit Erfolg angefochten worden ist,
5. der Betriebsrat durch eine gerichtliche Entscheidung aufgelöst ist oder
6. im Betrieb ein Betriebsrat nicht besteht.

(3) ¹Hat außerhalb des für die regelmäßigen Betriebsratswahlen festgelegten Zeitraums eine Betriebsratswahl stattgefunden, so ist der Betriebsrat in dem auf die Wahl folgenden nächsten Zeitraum der regelmäßigen Betriebsratswahlen neu zu wählen. ²Hat die Amtszeit des Betriebsrats zu Beginn des für die regelmäßigen Betriebsratswahlen festgelegten Zeitraums noch nicht ein Jahr betragen, so ist der Betriebsrat in dem übernächsten Zeitraum der regelmäßigen Betriebsratswahlen neu zu wählen.

Section 11
Reduction in the number of works council members

If the number of eligible employees in an establishment is insufficient, the number of members in the works council shall be the one specified for the next lower size of establishment.

Section 13
Time of elections to the works council

(1) ¹Regular elections to the works council shall be held every four years at some time between 1 March and 31 May. ²They shall be held at the same time as the regular elections in accordance with section 5 (1) of the Executives' Committee Act.

(2) Elections to the works council shall be held outside this period whenever –

1. by the end of twenty-four months from the date of the last election, the number of employees regularly employed has increased or decreased by one half but by not less than fifty in any case;
2. the total membership of the works council, after all the substitutes have been called upon, has fallen below the prescribed number;
3. the works council decides to resign by the vote of a majority of its members;
4. the works council election results are successfully contested;
5. the works council is dissolved by court order; or
6. there is no works council in the establishment.

(3) ¹If an election for a works council has been held outside the period set aside for regular works council elections, a new election shall be held in the next immediately following period for regular elections for the works council. ²If at the beginning of the period fixed for regular elections the works council has been in office for less than a year, the new works council elections shall be held in the regular election period that follows.

§ 14
Wahlvorschriften

(1) Der Betriebsrat wird in geheimer und unmittelbarer Wahl gewählt.

(2) ¹Die Wahl erfolgt nach den Grundsätzen der Verhältniswahl. ²Sie erfolgt nach den Grundsätzen der Mehrheitswahl, wenn nur ein Wahlvorschlag eingereicht wird oder wenn der Betriebsrat im vereinfachten Wahlverfahren nach § 14a zu wählen ist.

(3) Zur Wahl des Betriebsrats können die wahlberechtigten Arbeitnehmer und die im Betrieb vertretenen Gewerkschaften Wahlvorschläge machen.

(4) ¹Jeder Wahlvorschlag der Arbeitnehmer muss von mindestens einem Zwanzigstel der wahlberechtigten Arbeitnehmer, mindestens jedoch von drei Wahlberechtigten unterzeichnet sein; in Betrieben mit in der Regel bis zu zwanzig wahlberechtigten Arbeitnehmern genügt die Unterzeichnung durch zwei Wahlberechtigte. ²In jedem Fall genügt die Unterzeichnung durch fünfzig wahlberechtigte Arbeitnehmer.

(5) Jeder Wahlvorschlag einer Gewerkschaft muss von zwei Beauftragten unterzeichnet sein.

§ 14a
Vereinfachtes Wahlverfahren für Kleinbetriebe

(1) ¹In Betrieben mit in der Regel fünf bis fünfzig wahlberechtigten Arbeitnehmern wird der Betriebsrat in einem zweistufigen Verfahren gewählt. ²Auf einer ersten Wahlversammlung wird der Wahlvorstand nach § 17a Nr. 3 gewählt. ³Auf einer zweiten Wahlversammlung wird der Betriebsrat in geheimer und unmittelbarer Wahl gewählt. ⁴Diese Wahlversammlung findet eine Woche nach der Wahlversammlung zur Wahl des Wahlvorstands statt.

(2) Wahlvorschläge können bis zum Ende der Wahlversammlung zur Wahl des Wahlvorstands nach § 17a Nr. 3 gemacht werden; für Wahlvorschläge der Arbeitnehmer gilt § 14 Abs. 4 mit der Maßgabe, dass für Wahlvorschläge, die erst auf dieser Wahlversammlung gemacht werden, keine Schriftform erforderlich ist.

Section 14
Election rules

(1) The works council shall be elected directly by secret ballot.

(2) ¹The election shall be conducted according to the principles of proportional representation. ²If only one list of candidates is submitted, or if the works council is to be elected according to the simplified electoral procedure specified in Section 14a, the election shall be conducted according to the principles of majority representation.

(3) Employees with voting rights and trade unions represented in the establishment shall be entitled to submit lists of candidates for the works council elections.

(4) ¹Each list of candidates submitted by the employees shall be signed by not less than one-twentieth of the employees entitled to vote, but by not less than three employees with voting rights; in establishments with up to twenty voting employees, as a rule, the signatures of two employees with voting rights shall suffice. ²The signatures of fifty voting employees shall suffice in all cases.

(5) Each list of candidates from a trade union must be signed by two representatives.

Section 14a
Simplified electoral procedure for small establishments

(1) ¹Works councils shall be elected in a two-step process in establishments that normally have five to fifty employees with voting rights. ²The electoral board pursuant to section 17a clause 3 is elected at an initial election meeting. ³The works council shall be elected directly by secret ballot at a second election meeting. ⁴This election meeting shall take place one week after the election meeting in which the electoral board was elected.

(2) Lists of candidates may be submitted until the end of the election assembly in which the electoral board is elected pursuant to section 17a clause 3, and section 14 (4) shall be applicable to employees' lists of candidates with the proviso that lists of candidates submitted at this election meeting need not be submitted in writing.

(3) ¹Ist der Wahlvorstand in Betrieben mit in der Regel fünf bis fünfzig wahlberechtigten Arbeitnehmern nach § 17a Nr. 1 in Verbindung mit § 16 vom Betriebsrat, Gesamtbetriebsrat oder Konzernbetriebsrat oder nach § 17a Nr. 4 vom Arbeitsgericht bestellt, wird der Betriebsrat abweichend von Absatz 1 Satz 1 und 2 auf nur einer Wahlversammlung in geheimer und unmittelbarer Wahl gewählt. ²Wahlvorschläge können bis eine Woche vor der Wahlversammlung zur Wahl des Betriebsrats gemacht werden; § 14 Abs. 4 gilt unverändert.

(4) Wahlberechtigten Arbeitnehmern, die an der Wahlversammlung zur Wahl des Betriebsrats nicht teilnehmen können, ist Gelegenheit zur schriftlichen Stimmabgabe zu geben.

(5) In Betrieben mit in der Regel 51 bis 100 wahlberechtigten Arbeitnehmern können der Wahlvorstand und der Arbeitgeber die Anwendung des vereinfachten Wahlverfahrens vereinbaren.

§ 15
Zusammensetzung nach Beschäftigungsarten und Geschlechter

(1) Der Betriebsrat soll sich möglichst aus Arbeitnehmern der einzelnen Organisationsbereiche und der verschiedenen Beschäftigungsarten der im Betrieb tätigen Arbeitnehmer zusammensetzen.

(2) Das Geschlecht, das in der Belegschaft in der Minderheit ist, muss mindestens entsprechend seinem zahlenmäßigen Verhältnis im Betriebsrat vertreten sein, wenn dieser aus mindestens drei Mitgliedern besteht.

§ 16
Bestellung des Wahlvorstands

(1) ¹Spätestens zehn Wochen vor Ablauf seiner Amtszeit bestellt der Betriebsrat einen aus drei Wahlberechtigten bestehenden Wahlvorstand und einen von ihnen als Vorsitzenden. ²Der Betriebsrat kann die Zahl der Wahlvorstandsmitglieder erhöhen, wenn dies zur ordnungsgemäßen Durchführung der Wahl erforderlich ist. ³Der Wahlvorstand muss in jedem Fall aus einer ungeraden Zahl von Mitgliedern bestehen. ⁴Für jedes Mitglied des Wahlvorstands kann für den Fall seiner Verhinderung ein Ersatzmitglied bestellt werden. ⁵In Betrieben mit weiblichen und männlichen Arbeitnehmern sollen dem Wahlvorstand Frauen und Männer angehören. ⁶Jede im Betrieb vertretene Gewerkschaft kann zusätzlich einen dem Betrieb angehörenden Beauftragten als nicht stimmberechtigtes Mit-

(3) ¹Notwithstanding the first and second sentence of subsection (1) hereof, if the electoral board of establishments that normally have five to fifty voting employees has been appointed by the works council, the central works council or the combine works council pursuant to section 17a clause 1 in conjunction with section 16 or by the labour court pursuant to section 17a clause 4, the works council shall be elected directly by secret ballot at a single election meeting only. ²Lists of candidates may be submitted not later than one week before the election meeting in which the works council is elected; section 14 (4) shall not be affected.

(4) Those employees with voting rights who cannot participate in the election meeting in which the works council is elected shall be given the opportunity to cast their votes in writing.

(5) In establishments that normally have fifty-one to one-hundred employees with voting rights the electoral board and the employer may agree on the application of the simplified electoral procedure.

Section 15
Representation of employment categories and of male and female employees

(1) The works council should be composed as far as possible of employees of the various organisation units and the different employment categories of the workers employed in the establishment.

(2) The gender that accounts for a minority of staff shall at least be represented according to its relative numerical strength whenever the works council consists of three or more members.

Section 16
Appointment of the electoral board

(1) ¹Not less than ten weeks before the end of its term of office, the works council shall appoint an electoral board of three persons with voting rights, one of whom shall be the chairperson. ²The works council may increase the number of members on the electoral board if the proper conduct of the election so requires. ³In all cases the electoral board shall consist of an odd number of members. ⁴A substitute may be appointed for each member of the electoral board in order to replace him in his absence. ⁵In establishments with male and female employees, the electoral board shall comprise women and men. ⁶Each trade union represented in the establishment may, in addition, delegate a representative belonging to the establishment to the electoral board as a non-voting member, inasmuch as no

glied in den Wahlvorstand entsenden, sofern ihr nicht ein stimmberechtigtes Wahlvorstandsmitglied angehört.

(2) ¹Besteht acht Wochen vor Ablauf der Amtszeit des Betriebsrats kein Wahlvorstand, so bestellt ihn das Arbeitsgericht auf Antrag von mindestens drei Wahlberechtigten oder einer im Betrieb vertretenen Gewerkschaft; Absatz 1 gilt entsprechend. ²In dem Antrag können Vorschläge für die Zusammensetzung des Wahlvorstands gemacht werden. ³Das Arbeitsgericht kann für Betriebe mit in der Regel mehr als zwanzig wahlberechtigten Arbeitnehmern auch Mitglieder einer im Betrieb vertretenen Gewerkschaft, die nicht Arbeitnehmer des Betriebs sind, zu Mitgliedern des Wahlvorstands bestellen, wenn dies zur ordnungsgemäßen Durchführung der Wahl erforderlich ist.

(3) ¹Besteht acht Wochen vor Ablauf der Amtszeit des Betriebsrats kein Wahlvorstand, kann auch der Gesamtbetriebsrat oder, falls ein solcher nicht besteht, der Konzernbetriebsrat den Wahlvorstand bestellen. ²Absatz 1 gilt entsprechend.

§ 17
Bestellung des Wahlvorstands in Betrieben ohne Betriebsrat

(1) ¹Besteht in einem Betrieb, der die Voraussetzungen des § 1 Abs. 1 Satz 1 erfüllt, kein Betriebsrat, so bestellt der Gesamtbetriebsrat oder, falls ein solcher nicht besteht, der Konzernbetriebsrat einen Wahlvorstand. ²§ 16 Abs. 1 gilt entsprechend.

(2) ¹Besteht weder ein Gesamtbetriebsrat noch ein Konzernbetriebsrat, so wird in einer Betriebsversammlung von der Mehrheit der anwesenden Arbeitnehmer ein Wahlvorstand gewählt; § 16 Abs. 1 gilt entsprechend. ²Gleiches gilt, wenn der Gesamtbetriebsrat oder Konzernbetriebsrat die Bestellung des Wahlvorstands nach Absatz 1 unterlässt.

(3) Zu dieser Betriebsversammlung können drei wahlberechtigte Arbeitnehmer des Betriebs oder eine im Betrieb vertretene Gewerkschaft einladen und Vorschläge für die Zusammensetzung des Wahlvorstands machen.

(4) ¹Findet trotz Einladung keine Betriebsversammlung statt oder wählt die Betriebsversammlung keinen Wahlvorstand, so bestellt ihn das Arbeitsgericht auf Antrag von mindestens drei wahlberechtigten Arbeitnehmern oder einer im Betrieb vertretenen Gewerkschaft. ²§ 16 Abs. 2 gilt entsprechend.

voting member of the electoral board belongs to the trade union involved.

(2) ¹If no electoral board has been appointed by the beginning of the eighth week before the end of the term of office of the works council, it shall be appointed by the labour court on application from three or more persons with voting rights or a trade union represented in the establishment; the preceding subsection shall apply, mutatis mutandis. ²The application may contain proposals as to the composition of the electoral board. ³In the case of establishments that normally employ more than twenty employees with voting rights the labour court may also appoint as members of the electoral board persons who are not employed in the establishment but belong to a trade union represented in the establishment, if the proper conduct of the election so requires.

(3) ¹If no electoral board has been appointed by the beginning of the eighth week before the end of the term of office of the works council, the central works council or, in the absence of the latter, the combine works council may appoint the electoral board. ²Subsection (1), above, shall apply, mutatis mutandis.

Section 17
Appointment of the electoral board in establishments without a works council

(1) ¹If an establishment that fulfils the conditions of the first sentence of section 1 (1) has no works council, an electoral board shall be appointed by the central works council or, in the absence of the latter, the combine works council. ²Section 16 (1) shall apply, mutatis mutandis

(2) ¹If there is neither a central works council nor combine works council, an electoral board shall be elected at a works meeting of the employees on a majority vote of those present; Section 16 (1) shall apply, mutatis mutandis. ²The same applies if the central works council or combine works council fails to appoint the electoral board as stipulated in subsection (1).)

(3) Such works meeting may be called by three employees of the establishment with voting rights or a trade union represented in the establishment; in doing so, the said employees or trade union may make proposals as to the composition of the electoral board.

(4) ¹If a works meeting thus called is not held or fails to elect an electoral board, the board shall be appointed by the labour court on application from three or more persons with voting rights or a trade union represented in the establishment. ²Section 16 (2) shall apply, mutatis mutandis.

§ 17a
Bestellung des Wahlvorstands im vereinfachten Wahlverfahren

Im Fall des § 14a finden die §§ 16 und 17 mit folgender Maßgabe Anwendung:

1. Die Frist des § 16 Abs. 1 Satz 1 wird auf vier Wochen und die des § 16 Abs. 2 Satz 1, Abs. 3 Satz 1 auf drei Wochen verkürzt.

2. § 16 Abs. 1 Satz 2 und 3 findet keine Anwendung.

3. In den Fällen des § 17 Abs. 2 wird der Wahlvorstand in einer Wahlversammlung von der Mehrheit der anwesenden Arbeitnehmer gewählt. Für die Einladung zu der Wahlversammlung gilt § 17 Abs. 3 entsprechend.

4. § 17 Abs. 4 gilt entsprechend, wenn trotz Einladung keine Wahlversammlung stattfindet oder auf der Wahlversammlung kein Wahlvorstand gewählt wird.

§ 18
Vorbereitung und Durchführung der Wahl

(1) ¹Der Wahlvorstand hat die Wahl unverzüglich einzuleiten, sie durchzuführen und das Wahlergebnis festzustellen. ²Kommt der Wahlvorstand dieser Verpflichtung nicht nach, so ersetzt ihn das Arbeitsgericht auf Antrag des Betriebsrats, von mindestens drei wahlberechtigten Arbeitnehmern oder einer im Betrieb vertretenen Gewerkschaft. ³§ 16 Abs. 2 gilt entsprechend.

(2) Ist zweifelhaft, ob eine betriebsratsfähige Organisationseinheit vorliegt, so können der Arbeitgeber, jeder beteiligte Betriebsrat, jeder beteiligte Wahlvorstand oder eine im Betrieb vertretene Gewerkschaft eine Entscheidung des Arbeitsgerichts beantragen.

(3) ¹Unverzüglich nach Abschluss der Wahl nimmt der Wahlvorstand öffentlich die Auszählung der Stimmen vor, stellt deren Ergebnis in einer Niederschrift fest und gibt es den Arbeitnehmern des Betriebs bekannt. ²Dem Arbeitgeber und den im Betrieb vertretenen Gewerkschaften ist eine Abschrift der Wahlniederschrift zu übersenden.

Section 17a
Appointment of the electoral board in the simplified electoral procedure

If section 14a is applicable, sections 16 and 17 shall apply with the following modifications:

1. The period referred to in the first sentence of section 16 (1) shall be reduced to four weeks and the period referred to in the first sentences of section 16 (2) and (3) to three weeks.

2. The second and third sentences of section 16 (1) shall not apply.

3. If section 17 (2) is applicable, the electoral board shall be elected at an election meeting by the majority of the workers present. Section 17 (3) shall apply, mutatis mutandis, to the calling of the election meeting.

4. Section 17 (4) shall apply, mutatis mutandis, if no election meeting takes place although it has been properly convened, or if no electoral board was elected at the election meeting.

Section 18
Preparation and conduct of the election

(1) ¹The electoral board shall without delay call the election, carry it out and announce the results. ²If the electoral board fails to carry out this duty, the labour court shall act in its place on application of the works council, of three or more employees with voting rights or a trade union represented in the establishment. ³Section 16 (2) shall apply, mutatis mutandis.

(2) If there is any doubt as to whether an organisation unit qualifies for having a works council, the employer, any interested electoral board member or a trade union represented in the establishment shall be entitled to apply to the labour court for a decision.

(3) ¹Directly after termination of the election the electoral board shall count the votes in public, record the results in writing and announce them to the employees of the establishment. ²The employer and the trade unions represented in the establishment shall each be sent a copy of the election records.

§ 18a
Zuordnung der leitenden Angestellten bei Wahlen

(1) ¹Sind die Wahlen nach § 13 Abs. 1 und nach § 5 Abs. 1 des Sprecherausschussgesetzes zeitgleich einzuleiten, so haben sich die Wahlvorstände unverzüglich nach Aufstellung der Wählerlisten, spätestens jedoch zwei Wochen vor Einleitung der Wahlen, gegenseitig darüber zu unterrichten, welche Angestellten sie den leitenden Angestellten zugeordnet haben; dies gilt auch, wenn die Wahlen ohne Bestehen einer gesetzlichen Verpflichtung zeitgleich eingeleitet werden. ²Soweit zwischen den Wahlvorständen kein Einvernehmen über die Zuordnung besteht, haben sie in gemeinsamer Sitzung eine Einigung zu versuchen. ³Soweit eine Einigung zustande kommt, sind die Angestellten entsprechend ihrer Zuordnung in die jeweilige Wählerliste einzutragen.

(2) ¹Soweit eine Einigung nicht zustande kommt, hat ein Vermittler spätestens eine Woche vor Einleitung der Wahlen erneut eine Verständigung der Wahlvorstände über die Zuordnung zu versuchen. ²Der Arbeitgeber hat den Vermittler auf dessen Verlangen zu unterstützen, insbesondere die erforderlichen Auskünfte zu erteilen und die erforderlichen Unterlagen zur Verfügung zu stellen. ³Bleibt der Verständigungsversuch erfolglos, so entscheidet der Vermittler nach Beratung mit dem Arbeitgeber. ⁴Absatz 1 Satz 3 gilt entsprechend.

(3) ¹Auf die Person des Vermittlers müssen sich die Wahlvorstände einigen. ²Zum Vermittler kann nur ein Beschäftigter des Betriebs oder eines anderen Betriebs des Unternehmens oder Konzerns oder der Arbeitgeber bestellt werden. ³Kommt eine Einigung nicht zustande, so schlagen die Wahlvorstände je eine Person als Vermittler vor; durch Los wird entschieden, wer als Vermittler tätig wird.

(4) ¹Wird mit der Wahl nach § 13 Abs. 1 oder 2 nicht zeitgleich eine Wahl nach dem Sprecherausschussgesetz eingeleitet, so hat der Wahlvorstand den Sprecherausschuss entsprechend Absatz 1 Satz 1 erster Halbsatz zu unterrichten. ²Soweit kein Einvernehmen über die Zuordnung besteht, hat der Sprecherausschuss Mitglieder zu benennen, die anstelle des Wahlvorstands an dem Zuordnungsverfahren teilnehmen. ³Wird mit der Wahl nach § 5 Abs. 1 oder 2 des Sprecherausschussgesetzes nicht zeitgleich eine Wahl nach diesem Gesetz eingeleitet, so gelten die Sätze 1 und 2 für den Betriebsrat entsprechend.

Section 18a
Allocation of executive staff for elections

(1) ¹If the elections are to be held at the same time in accordance with section 13 (1) and section 5 (1) of the Executives' Committee Act, the electoral boards shall notify each other immediately after preparation of the voters' lists, but not later than two weeks prior to the start of the elections, which salaried employees have been allocated to the executive staff, this shall also apply if the elections are held at the same time without the existence of a legal obligation. ²Insofar as there is no agreement between the electoral boards regarding this allocation, an attempt must be made to reach an agreement in a joint meeting. ³Insofar as agreement is reached, the salaried employees shall be entered in the appropriate voters' list in accordance with their allocation.

(2) ¹Insofar as no agreement is reached, a mediator shall make a renewed attempt to achieve agreement between the electoral boards regarding allocation, this occurring not less than one week before the start of the elections. ²The employer shall support the mediator at his request, particularly by providing the necessary information and documentation. ³If this attempt to reach agreement fails, the mediator shall decide after consultation with the employer. ⁴The third sentence of subsection (1), above, shall apply, mutatis mutandis.

(3) ¹The electoral boards must agree on the mediator. ²Only an employee of the establishment or of another establishment of the company or combine, or the employer may be appointed as mediator. ³If no agreement is reached, the electoral boards shall each propose one person as a mediator; the casting of lots shall decide who will act as mediator.

(4) ¹If an election in accordance with the Executives' Committee Act is not held at the same time as the election in accordance with section 13 (1) or (2), the electoral board shall notify the executives' committee in accordance with the first phrase of the first sentence of subsection (1). ²If there is disagreement regarding allocation, the executives' committee shall appoint members to participate in the allocation procedure in lieu of the electoral board. ³If an election in accordance with this Act is not held at the same time as the election in accordance with section 5 (1) or (2) of the Executives' Committee Act, the first and second sentences of this subsection shall apply to the works council, mutatis mutandis.

(5) ¹Durch die Zuordnung wird der Rechtsweg nicht ausgeschlossen. ²Die Anfechtung der Betriebsratswahl oder der Wahl nach dem Sprecherausschussgesetz ist ausgeschlossen, soweit sie darauf gestützt wird, die Zuordnung sei fehlerhaft erfolgt. ³Satz 2 gilt nicht, soweit die Zuordnung offensichtlich fehlerhaft ist.

(5) ¹Recourse to the courts of law shall not be excluded by the allocation. ²Contestation of the works council election or the election in accordance with the Executives' Committee Act shall be excluded, insofar as it is based on the claim that the allocation was incorrect. ³The second sentence of this subsection shall not apply if the allocation is patently incorrect.

§ 19
Wahlanfechtung

Section 19
Contesting of elections

(1) Die Wahl kann beim Arbeitsgericht angefochten werden, wenn gegen wesentliche Vorschriften über das Wahlrecht, die Wählbarkeit oder das Wahlverfahren verstoßen worden ist und eine Berichtigung nicht erfolgt ist, es sei denn, dass durch den Verstoß das Wahlergebnis nicht geändert oder beeinflusst werden konnte.

(1) An election may be contested before the labour court, if any of the essential rules respecting the right to vote, eligibility or electoral procedure have been infringed and no subsequent correction has been made, unless the infringement could not have altered or influenced the election results.

(2) ¹Zur Anfechtung berechtigt sind mindestens drei Wahlberechtigte, eine im Betrieb vertretene Gewerkschaft oder der Arbeitgeber. ²Die Wahlanfechtung ist nur binnen einer Frist von zwei Wochen, vom Tage der Bekanntgabe des Wahlergebnisses an gerechnet, zulässig.

(2) ¹Such contestation may be made by any three or more persons with voting rights, a trade union represented in the establishment or the employer. ²To be receivable the action must be brought within two weeks of the announcement of the election results.

§ 20
Wahlschutz und Wahlkosten

Section 20
Protection against obstruction and costs of the election

(1) ¹Niemand darf die Wahl des Betriebsrats behindern. ²Insbesondere darf kein Arbeitnehmer in der Ausübung des aktiven und passiven Wahlrechts beschränkt werden.

(1) ¹No person shall obstruct the election of a works council. ²In particular, no employee shall be restricted in his right to vote or to stand for election.

(2) Niemand darf die Wahl des Betriebsrats durch Zufügung oder Androhung von Nachteilen oder durch Gewährung oder Versprechen von Vorteilen beeinflussen.

(2) Any attempt to influence a works council election by inflicting or threatening any unfavourable treatment or by granting or promising any advantage shall be unlawful.

(3) ¹Die Kosten der Wahl trägt der Arbeitgeber. ²Versäumnis von Arbeitszeit, die zur Ausübung des Wahlrechts, zur Betätigung im Wahlvorstand oder zur Tätigkeit als Vermittler (§ 18a) erforderlich ist, berechtigt den Arbeitgeber nicht zur Minderung des Arbeitsentgelts.

(3) ¹The costs of the election shall be borne by the employer. ²Any loss of working time entailed by voting, performance of duties on the electoral board or activity as a mediator (section 18a) shall not give the employer a right to reduce the remuneration.

§ 77
Durchführung gemeinsamer Beschlüsse, Betriebsvereinbarungen

Section 77
Execution of joint decisions, works agreements

(1) ¹Vereinbarungen zwischen Betriebsrat und Arbeitgeber, auch soweit sie auf einem Spruch der Einigungsstelle beruhen, führt der Arbeitgeber durch, es sei denn, dass im Einzelfall etwas anderes vereinbart ist. ²Der Betriebsrat darf nicht durch einseitige Handlungen in die Leitung des Betriebs eingreifen.

(1) ¹Agreements between the works council and the employer including those based on an award of the conciliation committee shall be executed by the employer save where otherwise agreed in particular cases. ²The works council shall not interfere with the management of the establishment by any unilateral action.

(2) ¹Betriebsvereinbarungen sind von Betriebsrat und Arbeitgeber gemeinsam zu beschließen und schriftlich niederzulegen. ²Sie sind von beiden Seiten zu unterzeichnen; dies gilt nicht, soweit Betriebsvereinbarungen auf einem Spruch der Einigungsstelle beruhen. ³Der Arbeitgeber hat die Betriebsvereinbarungen an geeigneter Stelle im Betrieb auszulegen.

(3) ¹Arbeitsentgelte und sonstige Arbeitsbedingungen, die durch Tarifvertrag geregelt sind oder üblicherweise geregelt werden, können nicht Gegenstand einer Betriebsvereinbarung sein. ²Dies gilt nicht, wenn ein Tarifvertrag den Abschluss ergänzender Betriebsvereinbarungen ausdrücklich zulässt.

(4) ¹Betriebsvereinbarungen gelten unmittelbar und zwingend. ²Werden Arbeitnehmern durch die Betriebsvereinbarung Rechte eingeräumt, so ist ein Verzicht auf sie nur mit Zustimmung des Betriebsrats zulässig. ³Die Verwirkung dieser Rechte ist ausgeschlossen. ⁴Ausschlussfristen für ihre Geltendmachung sind nur insoweit zulässig, als sie in einem Tarifvertrag oder einer Betriebsvereinbarung vereinbart werden; dasselbe gilt für die Abkürzung der Verjährungsfristen.

(5) Betriebsvereinbarungen können, soweit nichts anderes vereinbart ist, mit einer Frist von drei Monaten gekündigt werden.

(6) Nach Ablauf einer Betriebsvereinbarung gelten ihre Regelungen in Angelegenheiten, in denen ein Spruch der Einigungsstelle die Einigung zwischen Arbeitgeber und Betriebsrat ersetzen kann, weiter, bis sie durch eine andere Abmachung ersetzt werden.

§ 78
Schutzbestimmungen

¹Die Mitglieder des Betriebsrats, des Gesamtbetriebsrats, des Konzernbetriebsrats, der Jugend- und Auszubildendenvertretung, der Gesamt-Jugend- und Auszubildendenvertretung, der Konzern-Jugend- und Auszubildendenvertretung, des Wirtschaftsausschusses, der Bordvertretung, des Seebetriebsrats, der in § 3 Abs. 1 genannten Vertretungen der Arbeitnehmer, der Einigungsstelle, einer tariflichen Schlichtungsstelle (§ 76 Abs. 8) und einer betrieblichen Beschwerdestelle (§ 86) sowie Auskunftspersonen (§ 80 Absatz 2 Satz 4) dürfen in der Ausübung ihrer Tätigkeit nicht gestört oder behindert werden. ²Sie dürfen wegen ihrer Tätigkeit nicht benachteiligt oder begünstigt werden; dies gilt auch für ihre berufliche Entwicklung.

(2) ¹Works agreements shall be negotiated by the works council and the employer and recorded in writing. ²They shall be signed by both sides, except where they are based on an award of the conciliation committee. ³The employer shall display the works agreements in a suitable place in the establishment.

(3) ¹Works agreements shall not deal with remuneration and other conditions of employment that have been fixed or are normally fixed by collective agreement. ²The foregoing shall not apply where a collective agreement expressly authorises the making of supplementary works agreements.

(4) ¹Works agreements shall be mandatory and directly applicable. ²Any rights granted to employees under a works agreement cannot be waived except with the agreement of the works council. ³Such rights cannot be forfeited. ⁴Any time limits for invoking these rights shall be valid only in so far as they are laid down by collective or works agreement; the same shall apply to any reduction of the periods provided for the lapsing of rights.

(5) Unless otherwise agreed, works agreements may be terminated at three months' notice.

(6) After the expiry of a works agreement its provisions shall continue to apply until a fresh agreement is made in respect of all matters in which an award of the conciliation committee may take the place of an agreement between the employer and the works council.

Section 78
Protective provisions

¹Members of the works council, the central works council, the combine works council, the youth and trainee delegation, the central youth and trainee delegation, the combine youth and trainee delegation, the finance committee, the ship's committee, the fleet works council, the representative bodies of the employees referred to in section 3 (1), the conciliation committee, an arbitration board set up by collective agreement (section 76 (8)) a grievance committee (section 86), or personnel providing information (fourth sentence of section 80 (2)) shall not be interfered with or obstructed in the discharge of their duties. ²They shall not be prejudiced or favoured by reason of their office; this principle shall also apply to their vocational development.

§ 78a
Schutz Auszubildender in besonderen Fällen

(1) Beabsichtigt der Arbeitgeber, einen Auszubildenden, der Mitglied der Jugend- und Auszubildendenvertretung, des Betriebsrats, der Bordvertretung oder des Seebetriebsrats ist, nach Beendigung des Berufsausbildungsverhältnisses nicht in ein Arbeitsverhältnis auf unbestimmte Zeit zu übernehmen, so hat er dies drei Monate vor Beendigung des Berufsausbildungsverhältnisses dem Auszubildenden schriftlich mitzuteilen.

(3) Die Absätze 1 und 2 gelten auch, wenn das Berufsausbildungsverhältnis vor Ablauf eines Jahres nach Beendigung der Amtszeit der Jugend- und Auszubildendenvertretung, des Betriebsrats, der Bordvertretung oder des Seebetriebsrats endet.

(4) ¹Der Arbeitgeber kann spätestens bis zum Ablauf von zwei Wochen nach Beendigung des Berufsausbildungsverhältnisses beim Arbeitsgericht beantragen,

1. festzustellen, dass ein Arbeitsverhältnis nach Absatz 2 oder 3 nicht begründet wird, oder
2. das bereits nach Absatz 2 oder 3 begründete Arbeitsverhältnis aufzulösen,

wenn Tatsachen vorliegen, aufgrund derer dem Arbeitgeber unter Berücksichtigung aller Umstände die Weiterbeschäftigung nicht zugemutet werden kann. ²In dem Verfahren vor dem Arbeitsgericht sind der Betriebsrat, die Bordvertretung, der Seebetriebsrat, bei Mitgliedern der Jugend- und Auszubildendenvertretung auch diese Beteiligte.

(5) Die Absätze 2 bis 4 finden unabhängig davon Anwendung, ob der Arbeitgeber seiner Mitteilungspflicht nach Absatz 1 nachgekommen ist.

§ 79
Geheimhaltungspflicht

(1) ¹Die Mitglieder und Ersatzmitglieder des Betriebsrats sind verpflichtet, Betriebs- oder Geschäftsgeheimnisse, die ihnen wegen ihrer Zugehörigkeit zum Betriebsrat bekannt geworden und vom Arbeitgeber ausdrücklich als geheimhaltungsbedürftig bezeichnet worden sind, nicht zu offenbaren und nicht zu verwerten. ²Dies gilt auch nach dem Ausscheiden aus dem Betriebsrat. ³Die Verpflichtung gilt nicht gegenüber Mitgliedern des Betriebsrats. ⁴Sie gilt ferner nicht gegenüber dem Gesamtbetriebsrat, dem Konzernbetriebsrat, der Bordvertretung, dem Seebetriebsrat und den Arbeitnehmerver-

Section 78a
Protection of trainees in special cases

(1) Where the employer does not intend to offer a trainee who is a member of the youth and trainee delegation, the works council, the ship's committee or the fleet works council permanent employment after completion of vocational training, he shall notify the trainee of this fact in writing three months before completion of the vocational training.

(3) Subsections (1) and (2) shall also apply where the vocational training ends less than one year after the end of the term of office of the youth and trainee delegation, the works council, the ship's committee or the fleet works council.

(4) ¹The employer may apply to the labour court not more than two weeks after completion of the vocational training

1. to establish that an employment contract in accordance with subsection (2) or (3) has not been established, or
2. to dissolve an employment contract which has already been established in accordance with subsection (2) or (3),

if facts exist which indicate that, in view of all the circumstances, continued employment may not be reasonably expected of the employer. ²The works council, the ship's committee, the fleet works council and the youth and trainee delegation, if one of its members is concerned, are also involved in the proceedings before the labour court as interested parties.

(5) Subsections (2) to (4) shall apply, irrespective of whether the employer has observed his obligation to notify in pursuance of subsection (1).

Section 79
Secrecy

(1) ¹Members and substitute members of the works council shall be bound to refrain from divulging or making use of trade or business secrets that have come to their knowledge as a result of their membership on the works council and which the employer has expressly stated to be confidential. ²This obligation shall be maintained even after they have ceased to belong to the works council. ³It shall not apply as between members of the works council. ⁴Moreover it shall not apply as regards dealings with members of the central works council, the combine works council, the ship's committee,

tretern im Aufsichtsrat sowie im Verfahren vor der Einigungsstelle, der tariflichen Schlichtungsstelle (§ 76 Abs. 8) oder einer betrieblichen Beschwerdestelle (§ 86).

(2) Absatz 1 gilt sinngemäß für die Mitglieder und Ersatzmitglieder des Gesamtbetriebsrats, des Konzernbetriebsrats, der Jugend- und Auszubildendenvertretung, der Gesamt-Jugend- und Auszubildendenvertretung, der Konzern-Jugend- und Auszubildendenvertretung, des Wirtschaftsausschusses, der Bordvertretung, des Seebetriebsrats, der gemäß § 3 Abs. 1 gebildeten Vertretungen der Arbeitnehmer, der Einigungsstelle, der tariflichen Schlichtungsstelle (§ 76 Abs. 8) und einer betrieblichen Beschwerdestelle (§ 86) sowie für die Vertreter von Gewerkschaften oder von Arbeitgebervereinigungen.

§ 80
Allgemeine Aufgaben

(1) Der Betriebsrat hat folgende allgemeine Aufgaben:

1. darüber zu wachen, dass die zugunsten der Arbeitnehmer geltenden Gesetze, Verordnungen, Unfallverhütungsvorschriften, Tarifverträge und Betriebsvereinbarungen durchgeführt werden;
2. Maßnahmen, die dem Betrieb und der Belegschaft dienen, beim Arbeitgeber zu beantragen;
2a. die Durchsetzung der tatsächlichen Gleichstellung von Frauen und Männern, insbesondere bei der Einstellung, Beschäftigung, Aus-, Fort- und Weiterbildung und dem beruflichen Aufstieg, zu fördern;
2b. die Vereinbarkeit von Familie und Erwerbstätigkeit zu fördern;
3. Anregungen von Arbeitnehmern und der Jugend- und Auszubildendenvertretung entgegenzunehmen und, falls sie berechtigt erscheinen, durch Verhandlungen mit dem Arbeitgeber auf eine Erledigung hinzuwirken; er hat die betreffenden Arbeitnehmer über den Stand und das Ergebnis der Verhandlungen zu unterrichten;
4. die Eingliederung schwerbehinderter Menschen einschließlich der Forderung des Abschlusses von Inklusionsvereinbarungen nach § 166 des Neunten Buches Sozialgesetzbuch und sonstiger besonders schutzbedürftiger Personen zu fördern;

the fleet works council and the employees' representatives on the supervisory board or in the proceedings of the conciliation committee, the arbitration body set up by collective agreement (section 76 (8)) or a grievance committee (section 86).

(2) Subsection (1) shall apply, mutatis mutandis, to the members and substitute members of the central works council, the combine works council, the youth and trainee delegation, the central youth and trainee delegation, the combine youth and trainee delegation, the financial committee, the ship's committee, the fleet works council, the representative bodies of the employees established under section 3 (1), the conciliation committee, the arbitration body set up by collective agreement (section 76 (8)) and a grievance committee (section 86), as well as to the representatives of trade unions or employers' associations.

Section 80
General duties

(1) The works council shall have the following general duties:

1. to see that effect is given to Acts, ordinances, safety regulations, collective agreements and works agreements for the benefit of the employees;
2. to apply to the employer for measures that serve the establishment and the staff;
2a. to promote the implementation of actual equality between women and men, in particular, as regards recruitment, employment, training, further training and additional training and vocational advancement;
2b. to promote reconciliation of family and work;
3. to receive suggestions from employees and the youth and trainee delegation and, if they are found to be justified, to negotiate with the employer for their implementation; it shall inform the employees concerned of the state of the negotiations and their results;
4. to promote the integration of persons with severe disabilities including the adoption of integration agreements according to section 166 of Book Nine of the Social Code and of other persons in particular need of assistance;

5. die Wahl einer Jugend- und Auszubildendenvertretung vorzubereiten und durchzuführen und mit dieser zur Förderung der Belange der in § 60 Abs. 1 genannten Arbeitnehmer eng zusammenzuarbeiten; er kann von der Jugend- und Auszubildendenvertretung Vorschläge und Stellungnahmen anfordern;

6. die Beschäftigung älterer Arbeitnehmer im Betrieb zu fördern;

7. die Integration ausländischer Arbeitnehmer im Betrieb und das Verständnis zwischen ihnen und den deutschen Arbeitnehmern zu fördern sowie Maßnahmen zur Bekämpfung von Rassismus und Fremdenfeindlichkeit im Betrieb zu beantragen;

8. die Beschäftigung im Betrieb zu fördern und zu sichern;

9. Maßnahmen des Arbeitsschutzes und des betrieblichen Umweltschutzes zu fördern.

(2) ¹Zur Durchführung seiner Aufgaben nach diesem Gesetz ist der Betriebsrat rechtzeitig und umfassend vom Arbeitgeber zu unterrichten; die Unterrichtung erstreckt sich auch auf die Beschäftigung von Personen, die nicht in einem Arbeitsverhältnis zum Arbeitgeber stehen, und umfasst insbesondere den zeitlichen Umfang des Einsatzes, den Einsatzort und die Arbeitsaufgaben dieser Personen. ²Dem Betriebsrat sind auf Verlangen jederzeit die zur Durchführung seiner Aufgaben erforderlichen Unterlagen zur Verfügung zu stellen; in diesem Rahmen ist der Betriebsausschuss oder ein nach § 28 gebildeter Ausschuss berechtigt, in die Listen über die Bruttolöhne und -gehälter Einblick zu nehmen. ³Zu den erforderlichen Unterlagen gehören auch die Verträge, die der Beschäftigung der in Satz 1 genannten Personen zugrunde liegen. ⁴Soweit es zur ordnungsgemäßen Erfüllung der Aufgaben des Betriebsrats erforderlich ist, hat der Arbeitgeber ihm sachkundige Arbeitnehmer als Auskunftspersonen zur Verfügung zu stellen; er hat hierbei die Vorschläge des Betriebsrats zu berücksichtigen, soweit betriebliche Notwendigkeiten nicht entgegenstehen.

(3) Der Betriebsrat kann bei der Durchführung seiner Aufgaben nach näherer Vereinbarung mit dem Arbeitgeber Sachverständige hinzuziehen, soweit dies zur ordnungsgemäßen Erfüllung seiner Aufgaben erforderlich ist.

(4) Für die Geheimhaltungspflicht der Auskunftspersonen und der Sachverständigen gilt § 79 entsprechend.

5. to prepare and organise the election of a youth and trainee delegation and to collaborate closely with said delegation in promoting the interests of the employees referred to in section 60 (1); it may invite the youth and trainee delegation to make suggestions and to state its view on various matters;

6. to promote the employment of elderly workers in the establishment;

7. to promote the integration of foreign workers in the establishment and to further understanding between them and their German colleagues, and to request activities to combat racism and xenophobia in the establishment;

8. to promote and safeguard employment in the establishment;

9. to promote health and safety at work and the protection of the environment in the establishment.

(2) ¹The employer shall supply comprehensive information to the works council in good time to enable it to discharge its duties under this Act; such information shall also refer to the employment of persons who have not entered into a contract of employment with the employer and includes in particular the duration and place of the work assignment and the tasks to be performed by these persons. ²The works council shall, if it so requests, be granted access at any time to any documentation it may require for the discharge of its duties; in this connection the works committee or a committee set up in pursuance of section 28 shall be entitled to inspect the payroll showing the gross wages and salaries of the employees. ³The required documentation shall also include the contracts on which the employment of the persons referred to in the first sentence is based. ⁴The employer shall provide knowledgeable personnel as informers to the works council, if necessary for the proper discharge of its functions, having due regard to the suggestions of the works council, except where this is precluded by imperative operational requirements.

(3) In discharging its duties the works council may, after making a more detailed agreement with the employer, call on the advice of experts in as far as the proper discharge of its duties so requires.

(4) The informers and experts shall be bound to observe secrecy as prescribed in section 79, mutatis mutandis.

§ 81
Unterrichtungs- und Erörterungspflicht des Arbeitgebers

(1) ¹Der Arbeitgeber hat den Arbeitnehmer über dessen Aufgabe und Verantwortung sowie über die Art seiner Tätigkeit und ihre Einordnung in den Arbeitsablauf des Betriebs zu unterrichten. ²Er hat den Arbeitnehmer vor Beginn der Beschäftigung über die Unfall- und Gesundheitsgefahren, denen dieser bei der Beschäftigung ausgesetzt ist, sowie über die Maßnahmen und Einrichtungen zur Abwendung dieser Gefahren und die nach § 10 Abs. 2 des Arbeitsschutzgesetzes getroffenen Maßnahmen zu belehren.

(2) ¹Über Veränderungen in seinem Arbeitsbereich ist der Arbeitnehmer rechtzeitig zu unterrichten. ²Absatz 1 gilt entsprechend.

(3) In Betrieben, in denen kein Betriebsrat besteht, hat der Arbeitgeber die Arbeitnehmer zu allen Maßnahmen zu hören, die Auswirkungen auf Sicherheit und Gesundheit der Arbeitnehmer haben können.

(4) ¹Der Arbeitgeber hat den Arbeitnehmer über die aufgrund einer Planung von technischen Anlagen, von Arbeitsverfahren und Arbeitsabläufen oder der Arbeitsplätze vorgesehenen Maßnahmen und ihre Auswirkungen auf seinen Arbeitsplatz, die Arbeitsumgebung sowie auf Inhalt und Art seiner Tätigkeit zu unterrichten. ²Sobald feststeht, dass sich die Tätigkeit des Arbeitnehmers ändern wird und seine beruflichen Kenntnisse und Fähigkeiten zur Erfüllung seiner Aufgaben nicht ausreichen, hat der Arbeitgeber mit dem Arbeitnehmer zu erörtern, wie dessen berufliche Kenntnisse und Fähigkeiten im Rahmen der betrieblichen Möglichkeiten den künftigen Anforderungen angepasst werden können. ³Der Arbeitnehmer kann bei der Erörterung ein Mitglied des Betriebsrats hinzuziehen.

Section 81
Employer's obligation to inform and discuss

(1) ¹The employer shall inform the employee of his tasks and responsibilities, the nature of his activity and how it fits into the operations of the establishment. ²Before the employee takes up his employment, the employer shall instruct him on the safety and health hazards to which he will be exposed in his employment as well as on the measures and devices for the prevention of the said hazards and on the measures taken pursuant to section 10 (2) of the Health and Safety Act.

(2) ¹Any changes within the area of an employee's activities shall be brought to his notice in good time. ²Subsection (1) shall apply, mutatis mutandis.

(3) In those establishments which have no works council, the employer shall consult the employees concerning all measures that might affect the health and safety of the employees.

(4) ¹The employer shall inform the employee about measures envisaged due to plans concerning technical plants, works procedures and operations or jobs and their effects on his job, the working environment as well as the contents and nature of his activity. ²As soon as it is known that the activity of the employee will change and his professional knowledge and skills are no longer sufficient to fulfil his duties, the employer shall discuss with the employee how the latter's professional knowledge and skills can be adapted to the future requirements within the framework of the in-house possibilities. ³The employee may call in a member of the works council to the discussion.

§ 82
Anhörungs- und Erörterungsrecht des Arbeitnehmers

(1) ¹Der Arbeitnehmer hat das Recht, in betrieblichen Angelegenheiten, die seine Person betreffen, von den nach Maßgabe des organisatorischen Aufbaus des Betriebs hierfür zuständigen Personen gehört zu werden. ²Er ist berechtigt, zu Maßnahmen des Arbeitgebers, die ihn betreffen, Stellung zu nehmen sowie Vorschläge für die Gestaltung des Arbeitsplatzes und des Arbeitsablaufs zu machen.

Section 82
Employee's right to be heard and request explanations

(1) ¹The employee shall be entitled to obtain a hearing from the persons who are competent according to the organisational structure of the establishment on any operational matter concerning his own person. ²He shall be entitled to state his case on any measure taken by the employer concerning him and to make suggestions on the design of his workplace and the organization of operations.

(2) [1]Der Arbeitnehmer kann verlangen, dass ihm die Berechnung und Zusammensetzung seines Arbeitsentgelts erläutert und dass mit ihm die Beurteilung seiner Leistungen sowie die Möglichkeiten seiner beruflichen Entwicklung im Betrieb erörtert werden. [2]Er kann ein Mitglied des Betriebsrats hinzuziehen. [3]Das Mitglied des Betriebsrats hat über den Inhalt dieser Verhandlungen Stillschweigen zu bewahren, soweit es vom Arbeitnehmer im Einzelfall nicht von dieser Verpflichtung entbunden wird.

(2) [1]The employee shall be entitled to an explanation of how his remuneration is calculated and the elements of which it is composed and to apply for an interview on the assessment of his performance and his career possibilities in the establishment. [2]He may be accompanied by a member of the works council. [3]The member of the works council shall be bound to observe secrecy with respect to the contents of these discussions except where the employee releases him from this obligation in his particular case.

§83
Einsicht in die Personalakten

(1) [1]Der Arbeitnehmer hat das Recht, in die über ihn geführten Personalakten Einsicht zu nehmen. [2]Er kann hierzu ein Mitglied des Betriebsrats hinzuziehen. [3]Das Mitglied des Betriebsrats hat über den Inhalt der Personalakte Stillschweigen zu bewahren, soweit es vom Arbeitnehmer im Einzelfall nicht von dieser Verpflichtung entbunden wird.

(2) Erklärungen des Arbeitnehmers zum Inhalt der Personalakte sind dieser auf sein Verlangen beizufügen.

Section 83
Access to personal files

(1) [1]The employee shall have access to his personal file. [2]In this connection he may call in a member of the works council. [3]The member of the works council shall be bound to observe secrecy with respect to the contents of the personal file except where the employee releases him from this obligation in his particular case.

(2) Erklärungen des Arbeitnehmers zum Inhalt der Personalakte sind dieser auf sein Verlangen beizufügen.

§84
Beschwerderecht

(1) [1]Jeder Arbeitnehmer hat das Recht, sich bei den zuständigen Stellen des Betriebs zu beschweren, wenn er sich vom Arbeitgeber oder von Arbeitnehmern des Betriebs benachteiligt oder ungerecht behandelt oder in sonstiger Weise beeinträchtigt fühlt. [2]Er kann ein Mitglied des Betriebsrats zur Unterstützung oder Vermittlung hinzuziehen.

(2) Der Arbeitgeber hat den Arbeitnehmer über die Behandlung der Beschwerde zu bescheiden und, soweit er die Beschwerde für berechtigt erachtet, ihr abzuhelfen.

(3) Wegen der Erhebung einer Beschwerde dürfen dem Arbeitnehmer keine Nachteile entstehen.

Section 84
Right to make complaints

(1) [1]Every employee shall be entitled to make a complaint to the competent bodies in the establishment if he feels that he has been discriminated against or treated unfairly or otherwise put at a disadvantage by the employer or by other employees of the establishment. [2]He may call on a member of the works council for assistance or mediation.

(2) The employer shall inform the employee on how his complaint will be dealt with and, if he considers the complaint justified, remedy his grievance.

(3) The employee shall not suffer any prejudice as a result of having made a complaint.

§85
Behandlung von Beschwerden durch den Betriebsrat

(1) Der Betriebsrat hat Beschwerden von Arbeitnehmern entgegenzunehmen und, falls er sie für berechtigt erachtet, beim Arbeitgeber auf Abhilfe hinzuwirken.

(2) [1]Bestehen zwischen Betriebsrat und Arbeitgeber Meinungsverschiedenheiten über die Berechtigung der Beschwerde, so kann der Betriebsrat die Einigungsstelle anrufen. [2]Der Spruch der Einigungsstelle ersetzt die Einigung

Section 85
Works council's role in dealing with grievances

(1) The works council shall hear employees' grievances and, if they appear justified, induce the employer to remedy them.

(2) [1]If there are any differences of opinion between the works council and the employer as to whether the complaint is well-founded, the works council may appeal to the conciliation committee. [2]The award of the conciliation

zwischen Arbeitgeber und Betriebsrat. ³Dies gilt nicht, soweit Gegenstand der Beschwerde ein Rechtsanspruch ist.

(3) ¹Der Arbeitgeber hat den Betriebsrat über die Behandlung der Beschwerde zu unterrichten. ²§ 84 Abs. 2 bleibt unberührt.

§ 86
Ergänzende Vereinbarungen

¹Durch Tarifvertrag oder Betriebsvereinbarung können die Einzelheiten des Beschwerdeverfahrens geregelt werden. ²Hierbei kann bestimmt werden, dass in den Fällen des § 85 Abs. 2 an die Stelle der Einigungsstelle eine betriebliche Beschwerdestelle tritt.

§ 86a
Vorschlagsrecht der Arbeitnehmer

¹Jeder Arbeitnehmer hat das Recht, dem Betriebsrat Themen zur Beratung vorzuschlagen. ²Wird ein Vorschlag von mindestens 5 vom Hundert der Arbeitnehmer des Betriebs unterstützt, hat der Betriebsrat diesen innerhalb von zwei Monaten auf die Tagesordnung einer Betriebsratssitzung zu setzen.

§ 87
Mitbestimmungsrechte

(1) Der Betriebsrat hat, soweit eine gesetzliche oder tarifliche Regelung nicht besteht, in folgenden Angelegenheiten mitzubestimmen:

1. Fragen der Ordnung des Betriebs und des Verhaltens der Arbeitnehmer im Betrieb;

2. Beginn und Ende der täglichen Arbeitszeit einschließlich der Pausen sowie Verteilung der Arbeitszeit auf die einzelnen Wochentage;
3. vorübergehende Verkürzung oder Verlängerung der betriebsüblichen Arbeitszeit;

4. Zeit, Ort und Art der Auszahlung der Arbeitsentgelte;
5. Aufstellung allgemeiner Urlaubsgrundsätze und des Urlaubsplans sowie die Festsetzung der zeitlichen Lage des Urlaubs für einzelne Arbeitnehmer, wenn zwischen dem Arbeitgeber und den beteiligten Arbeitnehmern kein Einverständnis erzielt wird;

committee shall take the place of an agreement between the employer and the works council. ³The foregoing shall not apply in as far as the grievance relates to a legal entitlement.

(3) ¹The employer shall inform the works council on how the grievance is dealt with. ²The foregoing shall be without prejudice to section 84 (2).

Section 86
Supplementary agreements

¹The details of the grievance procedure may be fixed by collective agreement or works agreement. ²In this connection provision may be made for the conciliation committee to be replaced in cases covered by section 85 (2) by a grievance committee at the level of the establishment.

Section 86a
Employees' right of proposal

¹Each employee shall have the right to propose issues to be discussed by the works council. ²If a proposal is seconded by at least 5 per cent of the employees in the establishment, the works council shall place it on the agenda of a works council meeting within two months.

Section 87
Co-determination rights

(1) The works council shall have a right of co-determination in the following matters in so far as they are not prescribed by legislation or collective agreement:

1. matters relating to the rules of operation of the establishment and the conduct of employees in the establishment;

2. the commencement and termination of the daily working hours including breaks and the distribution of working hours among the days of the week;
3. any temporary reduction or extension of the hours normally worked in the establishment;

4. the time and place for and the form of payment of remuneration;
5. the establishment of general principles for leave arrangements and the preparation of the leave schedule as well as fixing the time at which the leave is to be taken by individual employees, if no agreement is reached between the employer and the employees concerned;

6. Einführung und Anwendung von technischen Einrichtungen, die dazu bestimmt sind, das Verhalten oder die Leistung der Arbeitnehmer zu überwachen;
7. Regelungen über die Verhütung von Arbeitsunfällen und Berufskrankheiten sowie über den Gesundheitsschutz im Rahmen der gesetzlichen Vorschriften oder der Unfallverhütungsvorschriften;
8. Form, Ausgestaltung und Verwaltung von Sozialeinrichtungen, deren Wirkungsbereich auf den Betrieb, das Unternehmen oder den Konzern beschränkt ist;
9. Zuweisung und Kündigung von Wohnräumen, die den Arbeitnehmern mit Rücksicht auf das Bestehen eines Arbeitsverhältnisses vermietet werden, sowie die allgemeine Festlegung der Nutzungsbedingungen;
10. Fragen der betrieblichen Lohngestaltung, insbesondere die Aufstellung von Entlohnungsgrundsätzen und die Einführung und Anwendung von neuen Entlohnungsmethoden sowie deren Änderung;

11. Festsetzung der Akkord- und Prämiensätze und vergleichbarer leistungsbezogener Entgelte, einschließlich der Geldfaktoren;
12. Grundsätze über das betriebliche Vorschlagswesen;
13. Grundsätze über die Durchführung von Gruppenarbeit; Gruppenarbeit im Sinne dieser Vorschrift liegt vor, wenn im Rahmen des betrieblichen Arbeitsablaufs eine Gruppe von Arbeitnehmern eine ihr übertragene Gesamtaufgabe im Wesentlichen eigenverantwortlich erledigt.

(2) ¹Kommt eine Einigung über eine Angelegenheit nach Absatz 1 nicht zustande, so entscheidet die Einigungsstelle. ²Der Spruch der Einigungsstelle ersetzt die Einigung zwischen Arbeitgeber und Betriebsrat.

§ 88
Freiwillige Betriebsvereinbarungen

Durch Betriebsvereinbarung können insbesondere geregelt werden

1. zusätzliche Maßnahmen zur Verhütung von Arbeitsunfällen und Gesundheitsschädigungen;
1a. Maßnahmen des betrieblichen Umweltschutzes;
2. die Errichtung von Sozialeinrichtungen, deren Wirkungsbereich auf den Betrieb, das Unternehmen oder den Konzern beschränkt ist;

---

6. the introduction and use of technical devices designed to monitor the behaviour or performance of the employees;
7. arrangements for the prevention of accidents at work and occupational diseases and for the protection of health on the basis of legislation or safety regulations;
8. the form, structuring and administration of social services whose scope is limited to the establishment, company or combine;
9. the assignment of and notice to vacate accommodation that is rented to employees in view of their employment relationship as well as the general fixing of the conditions for the use of such accommodation;
10. questions related to remuneration arrangements in the establishment, including in particular the establishment of principles of remuneration and the introduction and application of new remuneration methods or modification of existing methods;

11. the fixing of job and bonus rates and comparable performance-related remuneration including cash coefficients;
12. principles for suggestion schemes in the establishment;
13. principles governing the performance of group work; group work within the meaning of this provision is defined as a group of employees performing a complex task within the establishment's workflows, which has been assigned to it and is executed in a largely autonomous way.

(2) ¹If no agreement can be reached on a matter covered by the preceding subsection, the conciliation committee shall make a decision. ²The award of the conciliation committee shall take the place of an agreement between the employer and the works council.

Section 88
Works agreements on a voluntary basis

The following, in particular, may be determined by works agreements:

1. additional measures to prevent accidents at work and health damages;
1a. measures concerning the establishment's environmental policy;
2. the establishment of social services whose scope is limited to the establishment, company or combine;

3. Maßnahmen zur Förderung der Vermögensbildung;
4. Maßnahmen zur Integration ausländischer Arbeitnehmer sowie zur Bekämpfung von Rassismus und Fremdenfeindlichkeit im Betrieb;
5. Maßnahmen zur Eingliederung schwerbehinderter Menschen.

3. measures to promote capital formation;
4. measures to promote the integration of foreign employees and to combat racism and xenophobia in the establishment.;
5. measures to include persons with severe disabilities.

§ 89
Arbeits- und betrieblicher Umweltschutz

(1) ¹Der Betriebsrat hat sich dafür einzusetzen, dass die Vorschriften über den Arbeitsschutz und die Unfallverhütung im Betrieb sowie über den betrieblichen Umweltschutz durchgeführt werden. ²Er hat bei der Bekämpfung von Unfall- und Gesundheitsgefahren die für den Arbeitsschutz zuständigen Behörden, die Träger der gesetzlichen Unfallversicherung und die sonstigen in Betracht kommenden Stellen durch Anregung, Beratung und Auskunft zu unterstützen.

(2) ¹Der Arbeitgeber und die in Absatz 1 Satz 2 genannten Stellen sind verpflichtet, den Betriebsrat oder die von ihm bestimmten Mitglieder des Betriebsrats bei allen im Zusammenhang mit dem Arbeitsschutz oder der Unfallverhütung stehenden Besichtigungen und Fragen und bei Unfalluntersuchungen hinzuzuziehen. ²Der Arbeitgeber hat den Betriebsrat auch bei allen im Zusammenhang mit dem betrieblichen Umweltschutz stehenden Besichtigungen und Fragen hinzuzuziehen und ihm unverzüglich die den Arbeitsschutz, die Unfallverhütung und den betrieblichen Umweltschutz betreffenden Auflagen und Anordnungen der zuständigen Stellen mitzuteilen.

(3) Als betrieblicher Umweltschutz im Sinne dieses Gesetzes sind alle personellen und organisatorischen Maßnahmen sowie alle die betrieblichen Bauten, Räume, technische Anlagen, Arbeitsverfahren, Arbeitsabläufe und Arbeitsplätze betreffenden Maßnahmen zu verstehen, die dem Umweltschutz dienen.

(4) An Besprechungen des Arbeitgebers mit den Sicherheitsbeauftragten im Rahmen des § 22 Abs. 2 des Siebten Buches Sozialgesetzbuch nehmen vom Betriebsrat beauftragte Betriebsratsmitglieder teil.

(5) Der Betriebsrat erhält vom Arbeitgeber die Niederschriften über Untersuchungen, Besichtigungen und Besprechungen, zu denen er nach den Absätzen 2 und 4 hinzuzuziehen ist.

(6) Der Arbeitgeber hat dem Betriebsrat eine Durchschrift der nach § 193 Abs. 5 des Siebten Buches Sozialgesetzbuch vom Betriebsrat zu unterschreibenden Unfallanzeige auszuhändigen.

Section 89
Health and safety as well as environmental protection at work

(1) ¹The works council shall endeavour to ensure that the provisions on safety and health at work and accident prevention as well as environmental protection are observed in the establishment. ²It shall support the competent occupational safety and health authorities, the statutory accident insurance institutions and other relevant bodies in their efforts to eliminate safety and health hazards by offering suggestions, advice and information.

(2) ¹The employer and the bodies referred to in the second sentence of subsection (1) shall be obliged to invite the works council or the members it delegates for that purpose to participate in all inspections and issues relating to safety and health at work or the prevention of accidents and inquiries into accidents. ²The employer shall also consult the works council concerning all inspections and issues relating to environmental protection in the company, and shall immediately inform it of any conditions imposed and instructions given by the competent bodies relating to safety and health at work, the prevention of accidents, or environmental protection in the establishment.

(3) For the purposes of this Act, environmental protection in the establishment comprises all personnel and organisational measures as well as all measures relating to the establishment's buildings, rooms, technical equipment, working methods, working processes and work places that serve the protection of the environment.

(4) Members delegated by the works council shall take part in discussions between the employer and the safety delegates within the context of section 22 (2) of the Seventh Book of the Social Code.

(5) The works council shall receive from the employer the minutes of inquiries, inspections and discussions in respect of which subsections (2) and (4) provide for its participation.

(6) The employer shall supply the works council with a copy of the accident notification to be signed by the works council under section 193 (5) of the Seventh Book of the Social Code.

§90
Unterrichtungs- und Beratungsrechte

(1) Der Arbeitgeber hat den Betriebsrat über die Planung

1. von Neu-, Um- und Erweiterungsbauten von Fabrikations-, Verwaltungs- und sonstigen betrieblichen Räumcn,
2. von technischen Anlagen,
3. von Arbeitsverfahren und Arbeitsabläufen oder
4. der Arbeitsplätze

(2) ¹Der Arbeitgeber hat mit dem Betriebsrat die vorgesehenen Maßnahmen und ihre Auswirkungen auf die Arbeitnehmer, insbesondere auf die Art ihrer Arbeit sowie die sich daraus ergebenden Anforderungen an die Arbeitnehmer so rechtzeitig zu beraten, dass Vorschläge und Bedenken des Betriebsrats bei der Planung berücksichtigt werden können. ²Arbeitgeber und Betriebsrat sollen dabei auch die gesicherten arbeitswissenschaftlichen Erkenntnisse über die menschengerechte Gestaltung der Arbeit berücksichtigen.

§91
Mitbestimmungsrecht

¹Werden die Arbeitnehmer durch Änderungen der Arbeitsplätze, des Arbeitsablaufs oder der Arbeitsumgebung, die den gesicherten arbeitswissenschaftlichen Erkenntnissen über die menschengerechte Gestaltung der Arbeit offensichtlich widersprechen, in besonderer Weise belastet, so kann der Betriebsrat angemessene Maßnahmen zur Abwendung, Milderung oder zum Ausgleich der Belastung verlangen. ²Kommt eine Einigung nicht zustande, so entscheidet die Einigungsstelle. ³Der Spruch der Einigungsstelle ersetzt die Einigung zwischen Arbeitgeber und Betriebsrat.

§92
Personalplanung

(1) ¹Der Arbeitgeber hat den Betriebsrat über die Personalplanung, insbesondere über den gegenwärtigen und künftigen Personalbedarf sowie über die sich daraus ergebenden personellen Maßnahmen einschließlich der geplanten Beschäftigung von Personen, die nicht in einem Arbeitsverhältnis zum Arbeitgeber stehen, und Maßnahmen der Berufsbildung an Hand von Unterlagen rechtzeitig und umfassend zu unterrichten. ²Er hat mit dem Betriebsrat über Art und Umfang der erforderlichen Maßnahmen und über die Vermeidung von Härten zu beraten.

Section 90
Information and consultation rights

(1) The employer shall inform the works council in due time of any plans concerning

1. the construction, alteration or extension of works, offices and other premises belonging to the establishment,
2. technical plants,
3. working procedures and operations or
4. jobs and submit the necessary documents.

(2) ¹The employer shall consult the works council in good time on the action envisaged and its effects on the employees, taking particular account of its impact on the nature of their work and the resultant demands on the employees so that suggestions and objections on the part of the works council can be taken into account in the plans. ²In their consultations, the employer and the works council shall bear in mind the established findings of ergonomics relating to the tailoring of jobs to meet human requirements.

Section 91
Right of co-determination

¹Where a special burden is imposed on the employees as a result of changes in jobs, operations or the working environment that are in obvious contradiction to the established findings of ergonomics relating to the tailoring of jobs to meet human requirements, the works council may request appropriate action to obviate, relieve or compensate for the additional stress thus imposed. ²If no agreement is reached the matter shall be decided by the conciliation committee. ³The award of the conciliation committee shall take the place of an agreement between the employer and the works council.

Section 92
Manpower planning

(1) ¹The employer shall inform the works council in full and in good time of matters relating to manpower planning including in particular present and future manpower needs and the resulting staff measures including the planned employment of persons who are not in an employment relationship with the employer, and vocational training measures on the basis of documents. ²He shall consult the works council on the nature and extent of the action required and means of avoiding hardship.

(2) Der Betriebsrat kann dem Arbeitgeber Vorschläge für die Einführung einer Personalplanung und ihre Durchführung machen.

(3) ¹Die Absätze 1 und 2 gelten entsprechend für Maßnahmen im Sinne des § 80 Abs. 1 Nr. 2a und 2b, insbesondere für die Aufstellung und Durchführung von Maßnahmen zur Förderung der Gleichstellung von Frauen und Männern. ²Gleiches gilt für die Eingliederung schwerbehinderter Menschen nach § 80 Absatz 1 Nummer 4.

§ 99
Mitbestimmung bei personellen Einzelmaßnahmen

(1) ¹In Unternehmen mit in der Regel mehr als zwanzig wahlberechtigten Arbeitnehmern hat der Arbeitgeber den Betriebsrat vor jeder Einstellung, Eingruppierung, Umgruppierung und Versetzung zu unterrichten, ihm die erforderlichen Bewerbungsunterlagen vorzulegen und Auskunft über die Person der Beteiligten zu geben; er hat dem Betriebsrat unter Vorlage der erforderlichen Unterlagen Auskunft über die Auswirkungen der geplanten Maßnahme zu geben und die Zustimmung des Betriebsrats zu der geplanten Maßnahme einzuholen. ²Bei Einstellungen und Versetzungen hat der Arbeitgeber insbesondere den in Aussicht genommenen Arbeitsplatz und die vorgesehene Eingruppierung mitzuteilen. ³Die Mitglieder des Betriebsrats sind verpflichtet, über die ihnen im Rahmen der personellen Maßnahmen nach den Sätzen 1 und 2 bekannt gewordenen persönlichen Verhältnisse und Angelegenheiten der Arbeitnehmer, die ihrer Bedeutung oder ihrem Inhalt nach einer vertraulichen Behandlung bedürfen, Stillschweigen zu bewahren; § 79 Abs. 1 Satz 2 bis 4 gilt entsprechend.

(2) Der Betriebsrat kann die Zustimmung verweigern, wenn

1. die personelle Maßnahme gegen ein Gesetz, eine Verordnung, eine Unfallverhütungsvorschrift oder gegen eine Bestimmung in einem Tarifvertrag oder in einer Betriebsvereinbarung oder gegen eine gerichtliche Entscheidung oder eine behördliche Anordnung verstoßen würde,

2. die personelle Maßnahme gegen eine Richtlinie nach § 95 verstoßen würde,

3. die durch Tatsachen begründete Besorgnis besteht, dass infolge der personellen Maßnahme im Betrieb beschäftigte Arbeitnehmer gekündigt werden oder sonstige Nachteile erleiden, ohne dass dies aus betrieblichen oder persönlichen Gründen

(2) The works council may make recommendations to the employer relating to the introduction and implementation of manpower planning.

(3) ¹Subsections (1) and (2), above, shall apply, mutatis mutandis, to measures under section 80 (1) clauses 2a and 2b, in particular, the adoption and implementation of measures to promote equality between women and men. ²This shall also apply to the integration of persons with severe disabilities in accordance with section 80 (1) clause 4.

Section 99
Co-determination in individual staff measures

(1) ¹In companies normally employing more than twenty employees with voting rights the employer shall notify the works council in advance of any recruitment, grading, regrading and transfer, submit to it the appropriate recruitment documents and in particular supply information on the persons concerned; he shall inform the works council of the implications of the measure envisaged, supply it with the necessary supporting documentation and obtain its consent to the measure envisaged. ²In the case of recruitments and transfers the employer shall in particular supply information on the job and grading envisaged. ³Members of the works council shall refrain from divulging any information relating to the personal circumstances and private affairs of the employees concerned that has come to their knowledge in connection with the staff movements referred to in the first and second sentences, where such information is of a confidential nature by reason of its implications or contents; the second to fourth sentences of section 79 (1) shall apply, mutatis mutandis.

(2) The works council may refuse its consent in the following cases:

1. if the staff measure constitutes a breach of any Act, ordinance, safety regulation or stipulation of a collective agreement or works agreement, or of a court order or official instruction;

2. if the staff movement violates a guideline within the meaning of section 95;

3. if there is factual reason to assume that the staff measure is likely to result in the dismissal of or other prejudice to employees of the establishment not warranted by operational or personal reasons; in cases of permanent recruitment non-consideration of

gerechtfertigt ist; als Nachteil gilt bei unbefristeter Einstellung auch die Nichtberücksichtigung eines gleich geeigneten befristet Beschäftigten,

4. der betroffene Arbeitnehmer durch die personelle Maßnahme benachteiligt wird, ohne dass dies aus betrieblichen oder in der Person des Arbeitnehmers liegenden Gründen gerechtfertigt ist,

5. eine nach § 93 erforderliche Ausschreibung im Betrieb unterblieben ist oder

6. die durch Tatsachen begründete Besorgnis besteht, dass der für die personelle Maßnahme in Aussicht genommene Bewerber oder Arbeitnehmer den Betriebsfrieden durch gesetzwidriges Verhalten oder durch grobe Verletzung der in § 75 Abs. 1 enthaltenen Grundsätze, insbesondere durch rassische oder fremdenfeindliche Betätigung, stören werde.

(3) ¹Verweigert der Betriebsrat seine Zustimmung, so hat er dies unter Angabe von Gründen innerhalb einer Woche nach Unterrichtung durch den Arbeitgeber diesem schriftlich mitzuteilen. ² Teilt der Betriebsrat dem Arbeitgeber die Verweigerung seiner Zustimmung nicht innerhalb der Frist schriftlich mit, so gilt die Zustimmung als erteilt.

(4) Verweigert der Betriebsrat seine Zustimmung, so kann der Arbeitgeber beim Arbeitsgericht beantragen, die Zustimmung zu ersetzen.

§ 100
Vorläufige personelle Maßnahmen

(1) ¹Der Arbeitgeber kann, wenn dies aus sachlichen Gründen dringend erforderlich ist, die personelle Maßnahme im Sinne des § 99 Abs. 1 Satz 1 vorläufig durchführen, bevor der Betriebsrat sich geäußert oder wenn er die Zustimmung verweigert hat. ²Der Arbeitgeber hat den Arbeitnehmer über die Sach- und Rechtslage aufzuklären.

(2) ¹Der Arbeitgeber hat den Betriebsrat unverzüglich von der vorläufigen personellen Maßnahme zu unterrichten. ²Bestreitet der Betriebsrat, dass die Maßnahme aus sachlichen Gründen dringend erforderlich ist, so hat er dies dem Arbeitgeber unverzüglich mitzuteilen. ³In diesem Fall darf der Arbeitgeber die vorläufige personelle Maßnahme nur aufrechterhalten, wenn er innerhalb von drei Tagen beim Arbeitsgericht die Ersetzung der Zustimmung des Betriebsrats und die Feststellung beantragt, dass die Maßnahme aus sachlichen Gründen dringend erforderlich war.

an equally suitable employee on a fixed term contract shall also be considered a prejudice to that employee;

4. if the employee concerned suffers prejudice through the staff measure although this is not warranted by operational or personal reasons;

5. if the vacancy has not been notified in the establishment as required under section 93; or

6. if there is reason based on facts to assume that the applicant or employee envisaged for the staff movement would cause trouble in the establishment through unlawful conduct or gross violation of the principles laid down in section 75 (1), in particular through racist or xenophobic activities.

(3) ¹If the works council refuses its consent, it shall notify the employer in writing, giving its reasons, within one week of being informed by the employer. ²If the works council fails to do so within the said time limit it shall be deemed to have given its consent.

(4) If the works council refuses its consent, the employer may apply to the labour court for a decision in lieu of consent.

Section 100
Temporary staff measures

(1) ¹The employer may, if this is urgently required for reasons based on facts, make a staff measure within the meaning of the first sentence of section 99 (1) on a temporary basis before the works council takes a stand or if it has refused its consent. ²In such cases the employer shall inform the employee concerned of the position in fact and in law.

(2) ¹The employer shall immediately notify the works council of the temporary staff measure. ²If the works council contends the urgency of the action taken on grounds based on facts, it shall immediately report its objection to the employer. ³In such cases the employer shall be allowed to maintain the temporary staff measure only on condition that within three days he applies to the labour court for a decision in lieu of the consent of the works council and for a declaration stating that the action taken was urgently required for reasons based on facts.

(3) ¹Lehnt das Gericht durch rechtskräftige Entscheidung die Ersetzung der Zustimmung des Betriebsrats ab oder stellt es rechtskräftig fest, dass offensichtlich die Maßnahme aus sachlichen Gründen nicht dringend erforderlich war, so endet die vorläufige personelle Maßnahme mit Ablauf von zwei Wochen nach Rechtskraft der Entscheidung. ²Von diesem Zeitpunkt an darf die personelle Maßnahme nicht aufrechterhalten werden.

(3) ¹If the labour court by mandatory decision refuses to issue a decision in lieu of the works council's consent or if it hands down a final mandatory judgement to the effect that the action taken was manifestly not urgently required by reasons based on facts, the temporary staff measure shall be cancelled on the expiry of two weeks after the date on which the decision or judgement becomes operative. ²After that date it shall be unlawful to maintain the staff movement.

§ 101
Zwangsgeld

¹Führt der Arbeitgeber eine personelle Maßnahme im Sinne des § 99 Abs. 1 Satz 1 ohne Zustimmung des Betriebsrats durch oder hält er eine vorläufige personelle Maßnahme entgegen § 100 Abs. 2 Satz 3 oder Abs. 3 aufrecht, so kann der Betriebsrat beim Arbeitsgericht beantragen, dem Arbeitgeber aufzugeben, die personelle Maßnahme aufzuheben. ²Hebt der Arbeitgeber entgegen einer rechtskräftigen gerichtlichen Entscheidung die personelle Maßnahme nicht auf, so ist auf Antrag des Betriebsrats vom Arbeitsgericht zu erkennen, dass der Arbeitgeber zur Aufhebung der Maßnahme durch Zwangsgeld anzuhalten sei. ³Das Höchstmaß des Zwangsgeldes beträgt für jeden Tag der Zuwiderhandlung 250 Euro.

Section 101
Fines

¹If the employer carries out a staff measure within the meaning of the first sentence of section 99 (1) without the works council's consent or if he maintains a temporary staff measure in violation of section 100 (2), third sentence, or (3) the works council may request the labour court to order the employer to rescind the staff measure. ²If the employer fails to rescind the staff measure in violation of a mandatory court order, the labour court shall, on application by the works council, compel the employer to cancel the change by the imposition of fines. ³The maximum fine shall be EUR 250 in respect of each day on which the violation continues.

§ 102
Mitbestimmung bei Kündigungen

(1) ¹Der Betriebsrat ist vor jeder Kündigung zu hören. ²Der Arbeitgeber hat ihm die Gründe für die Kündigung mitzuteilen. ³Eine ohne Anhörung des Betriebsrats ausgesprochene Kündigung ist unwirksam.

(2) ¹Hat der Betriebsrat gegen eine ordentliche Kündigung Bedenken, so hat er diese unter Angabe der Gründe dem Arbeitgeber spätestens innerhalb einer Woche schriftlich mitzuteilen. ²Äußert er sich innerhalb dieser Frist nicht, gilt seine Zustimmung zur Kündigung als erteilt. ³Hat der Betriebsrat gegen eine außerordentliche Kündigung Bedenken, so hat er diese unter Angabe der Gründe dem Arbeitgeber unverzüglich, spätestens jedoch innerhalb von drei Tagen, schriftlich mitzuteilen. ⁴Der Betriebsrat soll, soweit dies erforderlich erscheint, vor seiner Stellungnahme den betroffenen Arbeitnehmer hören. ⁵§ 99 Abs. 1 Satz 3 gilt entsprechend.

Section 102
Co-determination in the case of dismissal

(1) ¹The works council shall be consulted before every dismissal. ²The employer shall indicate to the works council the reasons for dismissal. ³Any notice of dismissal that is given without consulting the works council shall be null and void.

(2) ¹If the works council has objections to a dismissal with due notice, it shall notify the employer in writing within a week giving its reasons. ²If it does not report its objections within the said time limit, it shall be deemed to have given its consent to the dismissal. ³If the works council has objections against a dismissal without notice, it shall notify the employer in writing immediately and at any rate not later than within three days, giving its reasons. ⁴The works council shall consult the employee concerned before it takes a stand, in so far as this appears necessary. ⁵The third sentence of section 99 (1) shall apply, mutatis mutandis

(3) Der Betriebsrat kann innerhalb der Frist des Absatzes 2 Satz 1 der ordentlichen Kündigung widersprechen, wenn

1. der Arbeitgeber bei der Auswahl des zu kündigenden Arbeitnehmers soziale Gesichtspunkte nicht oder nicht ausreichend berücksichtigt hat,
2. die Kündigung gegen eine Richtlinie nach § 95 verstößt,
3. der zu kündigende Arbeitnehmer an einem anderen Arbeitsplatz im selben Betrieb oder in einem anderen Betrieb des Unternehmens weiterbeschäftigt werden kann,
4. die Weiterbeschäftigung des Arbeitnehmers nach zumutbaren Umschulungs- oder Fortbildungsmaßnahmen möglich ist oder
5. eine Weiterbeschäftigung des Arbeitnehmers unter geänderten Vertragsbedingungen möglich ist und der Arbeitnehmer sein Einverständnis hiermit erklärt hat.

(4) Kündigt der Arbeitgeber, obwohl der Betriebsrat nach Absatz 3 der Kündigung widersprochen hat, so hat er dem Arbeitnehmer mit der Kündigung eine Abschrift der Stellungnahme des Betriebsrats zuzuleiten.

(5) [1]Hat der Betriebsrat einer ordentlichen Kündigung frist- und ordnungsgemäß widersprochen und hat der Arbeitnehmer nach dem Kündigungsschutzgesetz Klage auf Feststellung erhoben, dass das Arbeitsverhältnis durch die Kündigung nicht aufgelöst ist, so muss der Arbeitgeber auf Verlangen des Arbeitnehmers diesen nach Ablauf der Kündigungsfrist bis zum rechtskräftigen Abschluss des Rechtsstreits bei unveränderten Arbeitsbedingungen weiterbeschäftigen. [2]Auf Antrag des Arbeitgebers kann das Gericht ihn durch einstweilige Verfügung von der Verpflichtung zur Weiterbeschäftigung nach Satz 1 entbinden, wenn

1. die Klage des Arbeitnehmers keine hinreichende Aussicht auf Erfolg bietet oder mutwillig erscheint oder
2. die Weiterbeschäftigung des Arbeitnehmers zu einer unzumutbaren wirtschaftlichen Belastung des Arbeitgebers führen würde oder
3. der Widerspruch des Betriebsrats offensichtlich unbegründet war.

(3) The works council may oppose a dismissal with due notice within the time limit specified in the first sentence of subsection (2) in the following cases:

1. if the employer in selecting the employee to be dismissed disregarded or did not take sufficient account of social aspects;
2. if the dismissal amounted to non-observance of a guideline covered by section 95;
3. if the employee whose dismissal is being envisaged could be kept on at another job in the same establishment or in another establishment of the same company;,
4. if the employee could be kept on after a reasonable amount of retraining or further training; or
5. if the employee could be kept on after a change in the terms of his contract and he has indicated his agreement to such change.

(4) If the employer gives notice of dismissal although the works council has lodged objections to such dismissal under subsection (3), he shall append a copy of the works council's point of view to the notice of dismissal sent to the employee.

(5) [1]If the works council has lodged an objection to a routine dismissal within the period and in the manner prescribed and if the employee has brought an action under the Protection against Dismissal Act for a declaration that the employment relationship has not been dissolved by the notice of dismissal, the employer shall be bound to keep the employee in his employment at the latter's request after expiry of the term of notice until a final decision is given on the case at issue; during such period he shall not make any change in his conditions of work. [2]On application by the employer the court may issue an interim order releasing him from his obligation under the first sentence of this subsection to maintain the employment relationship in the following cases:

1. if the action brought by the employee is not reasonably likely to succeed or appears abusive; or
2. if the continuation of the employment relationship imposes an unreasonable financial burden on the employer; or
3. if the objection raised by the works council is manifestly unfounded.

(6) Arbeitgeber und Betriebsrat können vereinbaren, dass Kündigungen der Zustimmung des Betriebsrats bedürfen und dass bei Meinungsverschiedenheiten über die Berechtigung der Nichterteilung der Zustimmung die Einigungsstelle entscheidet.

(7) Die Vorschriften über die Beteiligung des Betriebsrats nach dem Kündigungsschutzgesetz bleiben unberührt.

(6) The employer and the works council may make an agreement to the effect that any notice of dismissal requires the approval of the works council and that differences of opinion on whether a refusal of consent is justified are to be submitted to the decision of the conciliation committee.

(7) The foregoing shall be without prejudice to the regulations relating to the participation of the works council made under the Protection against Dismissal Act.

V. Part-Time and Limited Term Employment Act (Excerpt)

Gesetz über Teilzeitarbeit und befristete Arbeitsverträge (Teilzeit- und Befristungsgesetz – TzBfG)

Stand: 31.12.2020

§ 14
Zulässigkeit der Befristung

(1) [1]Die Befristung eines Arbeitsvertrages ist zulässig, wenn sie durch einen sachlichen Grund gerechtfertigt ist. [2]Ein sachlicher Grund liegt insbesondere vor, wenn

1. der betriebliche Bedarf an der Arbeitsleistung nur vorübergehend besteht,
2. die Befristung im Anschluss an eine Ausbildung oder ein Studium erfolgt, um den Übergang des Arbeitnehmers in eine Anschlussbeschäftigung zu erleichtern,
3. der Arbeitnehmer zur Vertretung eines anderen Arbeitnehmers beschäftigt wird,
4. die Eigenart der Arbeitsleistung die Befristung rechtfertigt,
5. die Befristung zur Erprobung erfolgt,
6. in der Person des Arbeitnehmers liegende Gründe die Befristung rechtfertigen,
7. der Arbeitnehmer aus Haushaltmitteln vergütet wird, die haushaltsrechtlich für eine befristete Beschäftigung bestimmt sind, und er entsprechend beschäftigt wird oder
8. die Befristung auf einem gerichtlichen Vergleich beruht.

(2) [1]Die kalendermäßige Befristung eines Arbeitsvertrages ohne Vorliegen eines sachlichen Grundes ist bis zur Dauer von zwei Jahren zulässig; bis zu dieser Gesamtdauer von zwei Jahren ist auch die höchstens dreimalige Verlängerung eines kalendermäßig befristeten Arbeitsvertrages zulässig. [2]Eine Befristung nach Satz 1 ist nicht zulässig, wenn mit demselben Arbeitgeber bereits zuvor ein befristetes oder unbefristetes Arbeitsverhältnis bestanden hat. [3]Durch Tarifvertrag kann die Anzahl der Verlängerungen oder die Höchstdauer der Befristung abweichend von Satz 1 festgelegt werden. [4]Im Geltungsbereich eines solchen Tarifvertrages können nicht tarifgebundene Arbeitgeber und Arbeitnehmer die Anwendung der tariflichen Regelungen vereinbaren.

Section 14
Permissibility of Fixing Terms

(1) [1]The term of an employment agreement may be fixed if this is justified on objective grounds. [2]Such objective grounds exist in particular if

1. the operational need for the work performance is only temporary
2. the fixed-term contract is concluded following training or studies, in order to facilitate the worker's transition to subsequent employment,
3. the employee is employed to represent another employee
4. the specific nature of the work justifies the fixed term,
5. the time limit for testing is set,
6. reasons inherent in the person of the employee justify the time limit,
7. the worker is remunerated from budgetary resources earmarked for fixed-term employment under budgetary law and is employed accordingly, or
8. the time limit is based on a court settlement.

(2) [1]The limitation of the term of an employment agreement according to the calendar to up to two years where no objective grounds exist is permissible; moreover, a term fixed according to the calendar may be extended no more than three times up to a total term of two years. [2]A fixed term pursuant to sen-tence 1 is not permissible if a fixed or unlimited term employment relationship had previously existed with the same employer. [3]It is possible to stipulate the number of extensions or the maximum duration of the fixed term in deviation from sentence 1 in a collective bargaining agreement. [4]Within the scope of such a collective bargaining agreement, employers and employees not bound to such agreements may agree on the application of the contractual provisions.

(2a) ¹In den ersten vier Jahren nach der Gründung eines Unternehmens ist die kalendermäßige Befristung eines Arbeitsvertrages ohne Vorliegen eines sachlichen Grundes bis zur Dauer von vier Jahren zulässig; bis zu dieser Gesamtdauer von vier Jahren ist auch die mehrfache Verlängerung eines kalendermäßig befristeten Arbeitsvertrages zulässig. ²Dies gilt nicht für Neugründungen im Zusammenhang mit der rechtlichen Umstrukturierung von Unternehmen und Konzernen. ³Maßgebend für den Zeitpunkt der Gründung des Unternehmens ist die Aufnahme einer Erwerbstätigkeit, die nach § 138 der Abgabenordnung der Gemeinde oder dem Finanzamt mitzuteilen ist. ⁴Auf die Befristung eines Arbeitsvertrages nach Satz 1 findet Absatz 2 Satz 2 bis 4 entsprechende Anwendung.

(3) ¹Die kalendermäßige Befristung eines Arbeitsvertrages ohne Vorliegen eines sachlichen Grundes ist bis zu einer Dauer von fünf Jahren zulässig, wenn der Arbeitnehmer bei Beginn des befristeten Arbeitsverhältnisses das 52. Lebensjahr vollendet hat und unmittelbar vor Beginn des befristeten Arbeitsverhältnisses mindestens vier Monate beschäftigungslos im Sinne des § 138 Absatz 1 Nummer 1 des Dritten Buches Sozialgesetzbuch gewesen ist, Transferkurzarbeitergeld bezogen oder an einer öffentlich geförderten Beschäftigungsmaßnahme nach dem Zweiten oder Dritten Buch Sozialgesetzbuch teilgenommen hat. ²Bis zu der Gesamtdauer von fünf Jahren ist auch die mehrfache Verlängerung des Arbeitsvertrages zulässig.

(4) Die Befristung eines Arbeitsvertrages bedarf zu ihrer Wirksamkeit der Schriftform.

(2a) ¹In the first four years after the formation of a company, the limitation of the term of an employment agree-ment according to the calendar where no objective grounds exist is permissi-ble; moreover, a term fixed according to the calendar may be extended several times up to the expiration of this four-year period. ²This shall not apply to new formations in connection with thelegal restructuring of companies and corporate groups. ³Decisive for the time of formation of a company shall be the assumption of a business activity which must be reported to the municipality or the tax authority pursuant to section 138 of the German Tax Code (Abgabenordnung). ⁴With respect to the limitation of the term of an employment agreement pursuant to sentence 1, subsection (2) sentences 2 to 4 shall apply mutatis mutandis.

(3) ¹The limitation of the term of an employment agreement according to the calendar to up to five years where no objective grounds exist is permissible if the employee is 52 years of age and was unemployed within the meaning of section 138 (1) number 1 of the Third Book of the Social Security Code for at least four months immediately prior to the commencement of the fixed term employment agreement, received transfer short-time allowances or took part in a publicly subsidized employment measure pursuant to the Second or Third Book of the Social Security Code. ²The employment agreement may also be extended two or more times for up to a total period of five years.

(4) In order to be effective, a fixed term to an employment agreement must be in written form.

VI. Act on the Posting of Workers

Gesetz über zwingende Arbeitsbedingungen für grenzüberschreitend entsandte und für regelmäßig im Inland beschäftigte Arbeitnehmer und Arbeitnehmerinnen (Arbeitnehmer-Entsendegesetz – AEntG)

Stand: 22.11.2019

§ 1
Zielsetzung

[1]Ziele des Gesetzes sind die Schaffung und Durchsetzung angemessener Mindestarbeitsbedingungen für grenzüberschreitend entsandte und für regelmäßig im Inland beschäftigte Arbeitnehmer und Arbeitnehmerinnen sowie die Gewährleistung fairer und funktionierender Wettbewerbsbedingungen durch die Erstreckung der Rechtsnormen von Branchentarifverträgen. [2]Dadurch sollen zugleich sozialversicherungspflichtige Beschäftigung erhalten und die Ordnungs- und Befriedungsfunktion der Tarifautonomie gewahrt werden.

Section 1
Objective

[1]The aims of the law are to create and enforce adequate minimum working conditions for cross-border posted workers and for workers regularly employed in the country, and to ensure fair and effective competition by extending the legal provisions of sectoral collective agreements. [2]This should at the same time maintain employment subject to social security contributions and safeguard the regulatory and pacification function of collective bargaining autonomy.

§ 2
Allgemeine Arbeitsbedingungen

Die in Rechts- oder Verwaltungsvorschriften enthaltenen Regelungen über

1. die Mindestentgeltsätze einschließlich der Überstundensätze,
2. den bezahlten Mindestjahresurlaub,
3. die Höchstarbeitszeiten und Mindestruhezeiten,
4. die Bedingungen für die Überlassung von Arbeitskräften, insbesondere durch Leiharbeitsunternehmen,
5. die Sicherheit, den Gesundheitsschutz und die Hygiene am Arbeitsplatz,
6. die Schutzmaßnahmen im Zusammenhang mit den Arbeits- und Beschäftigungsbedingungen von Schwangeren und Wöchnerinnen, Kindern und Jugendlichen und
7. die Gleichbehandlung von Männern und Frauen sowie andere Nichtdiskriminierungsbestimmungen

finden auch auf Arbeitsverhältnisse zwischen einem im Ausland ansässigen Arbeitgeber und seinen im Inland beschäftigten Arbeitnehmern und Arbeitnehmerinnen zwingend Anwendung.

Section 2
General Working Conditions

The provisions contained in laws, regulations or administrative provisions concerning

1. the minimum wage rates, including overtime rates,
2. the minimum paid annual leave,
3. maximum working hours and minimum rest periods,
4. the conditions for the hiring of workers, in particular by temporary employment agencies,
5. safety, health and hygiene at work,
6. the protective measures relating to the terms and conditions of employment of pregnant women and women who have recently given birth, children and young people, and
7. equal treatment between men and women and other non-discrimination provisions

also apply mandatorily to employment relationships between an employer domiciled abroad and its employees employed in Germany.

§3
Tarifvertragliche Arbeitsbedingungen

¹Die Rechtsnormen eines bundesweiten Tarifvertrages finden unter den Voraussetzungen der §§ 4 bis 6 auch auf Arbeitsverhältnisse zwischen einem Arbeitgeber mit Sitz im Ausland und seinen im räumlichen Geltungsbereich dieses Tarifvertrages beschäftigten Arbeitnehmern und Arbeitnehmerinnen zwingend Anwendung, wenn der Tarifvertrag als Tarifvertrag nach § 4 Absatz 1 Nummer 1 für allgemeinverbindlich erklärt ist oder eine Rechtsverordnung nach § 7 oder § 7a vorliegt. ²Eines bundesweiten Tarifvertrages bedarf es nicht, soweit Arbeitsbedingungen im Sinne des § 5 Nummer 2, 3 oder 4 Gegenstand tarifvertraglicher Regelungen sind, die zusammengefasst räumlich den gesamten Geltungsbereich dieses Gesetzes abdecken.

§4
Branchen

(1) § 3 gilt für Tarifverträge

1. des Bauhauptgewerbes oder des Baunebengewerbes im Sinne der Baubetriebe-Verordnung vom 28. Oktober 1980 (BGBl. I S. 2033), zuletzt geändert durch die Verordnung vom 26. April 2006 (BGBl. I S. 1085), in der jeweils geltenden Fassung einschließlich der Erbringung von Montageleistungen auf Baustellen außerhalb des Betriebssitzes,

2. der Gebäudereinigung,
3. für Briefdienstleistungen,
4. für Sicherheitsdienstleistungen,
5. für Bergbauspezialarbeiten auf Steinkohlebergwerken,
6. für Wäschereidienstleistungen im Objektkundengeschäft,
7. der Abfallwirtschaft einschließlich Straßenreinigung und Winterdienst,
8. für Aus- und Weiterbildungsdienstleistungen nach dem Zweiten oder Dritten Buch Sozialgesetzbuch und
9. für Schlachten und Fleischverarbeitung.

(2) § 3 gilt darüber hinaus für Tarifverträge aller anderen als der in Absatz 1 genannten Branchen, wenn die Erstreckung der Rechtsnormen des Tarifvertrages im öffentlichen Interesse geboten erscheint, um die in § 1 genannten Gesetzesziele zu erreichen und dabei insbesondere einem Verdrängungswettbewerb über die Lohnkosten entgegen zu wirken.

Section 3
Working conditions under collective bargaining agreements

¹The legal provisions of a nationwide collective agreement shall, subject to the conditions set out in sections 4 to 6, also apply on a mandatory basis to employment relationships between an employer domiciled abroad and its employees employed within the territorial scope of this collective agreement if the collective agreement has been declared generally binding as a collective agreement under section 4(1)(1) or a statutory instrument under section 7 or section 7a exists. ²There is no need for a nationwide collective agreement if working conditions within the meaning of section 5 no. 2, 3 or 4 are the subject of collective agreement provisions which, taken together, cover the entire territorial scope of this Act.

Section 4
Industries

(1) Section 3 shall apply to collective agreements

1. the main construction trade or ancillary construction trade within the meaning of the Construction Businesses Ordinance of 28 October 1980 (Federal Law Gazette I p. 2033), last amended by the Ordinance of 26 April 2006 (Federal Law Gazette I p. 1085), as amended, including the provision of assembly services on construction sites outside the company's headquarters

2. the cleaning of buildings,
3. for mail services,
4. for security services,
5. for special mining work on hard coal mines,
6. for laundry services in the contract customer business,
7. waste management, including street cleaning and winter maintenance
8. for education and training services according to the Second or Third Book of the Social Code and
9. for slaughter and meat processing.

(2) In addition, section 3 shall apply to collective agreements in all sectors other than those referred to in subsection 1 if the extension of the legal provisions of the collective agreement appears necessary in the public interest in order to achieve the statutory objectives referred to in section 1 and, in particular, to counteract predatory competition via wage costs.

§ 5
Arbeitsbedingungen

[1]Gegenstand eines Tarifvertrages nach § 3 können sein

1. Mindestentgeltsätze, die nach Art der Tätigkeit, Qualifikation der Arbeitnehmer und Arbeitnehmerinnen und Regionen differieren können, einschließlich der Überstundensätze,
2. die Dauer des Erholungsurlaubs, das Urlaubsentgelt oder ein zusätzliches Urlaubsgeld,
3. die Einziehung von Beiträgen und die Gewährung von Leistungen im Zusammenhang mit Urlaubsansprüchen nach Nummer 2 durch eine gemeinsame Einrichtung der Tarifvertragsparteien, wenn sichergestellt ist, dass der ausländische Arbeitgeber nicht gleichzeitig zu Beiträgen zu der gemeinsamen Einrichtung der Tarifvertragsparteien und zu einer vergleichbaren Einrichtung im Staat seines Sitzes herangezogen wird und das Verfahren der gemeinsamen Einrichtung der Tarifvertragsparteien eine Anrechnung derjenigen Leistungen vorsieht, die der ausländische Arbeitgeber zur Erfüllung des gesetzlichen, tarifvertraglichen oder einzelvertraglichen Urlaubsanspruchs seines Arbeitnehmers oder seiner Arbeitnehmerin bereits erbracht hat,
4. die Anforderungen an die Unterkünfte von Arbeitnehmern und Arbeitnehmerinnen, wenn sie vom Arbeitgeber für Arbeitnehmer und Arbeitnehmerinnen, die von ihrem regelmäßigen Arbeitsplatz entfernt eingesetzt werden, zur Verfügung gestellt werden, und
5. Arbeitsbedingungen im Sinne des § 2 Nr. 3 bis 7.

[2]Die Arbeitsbedingungen nach Satz 1 Nummer 1 bis 3 umfassen auch Regelungen zur Fälligkeit entsprechender Ansprüche einschließlich hierzu vereinbarter Ausnahmen und deren Voraussetzungen.

Section 5
Working Conditions

[1]The subject matter of a collective agreement under section 3 may be

1. minimum rates of pay, which may vary according to the type of work, qualifications of workers and regions, including overtime rates
2. the duration of the holiday, the holiday pay or an additional holiday allowance
3. the collection of contributions and the granting of benefits in connection with holiday entitlement in accordance with No. 2 by a joint institution of the parties to a collective agreement, if it is ensured that the foreign employer is not called upon to make contributions simultaneously to the joint institution of the parties to the collective agreement and to a comparable institution in the State in which he is domiciled and the procedure of the joint institution of the parties to the collective agreement provides for the crediting of those benefits which the foreign employer has already provided in order to satisfy the statutory, collectively agreed or individual holiday entitlement of his employee
4. the requirements concerning the accommodation of workers where it is provided by the employer for workers who are deployed remotely from their regular place of work, and
5. working conditions within the meaning of § 2 nos. 3 to 7.

[2]The working conditions in accordance with sentence 1, nos. 1 to 3 also include regulations on the due date of corresponding claims including any exceptions agreed for this purpose and the conditions for these.

§ 6
Besondere Regelungen

(1) [1]Dieser Abschnitt findet keine Anwendung auf Erstmontage- oder Einbauarbeiten, die Bestandteil eines Liefervertrages sind, für die Inbetriebnahme der gelieferten Güter unerlässlich sind und von Facharbeitern oder Facharbeiterinnen oder angelernten Arbeitern oder Arbeiterinnen des Lieferunternehmens ausgeführt werden, wenn die Dauer der Entsendung acht Tage nicht übersteigt. [2]Satz 1 gilt nicht für Bauleistungen im Sinne des § 101 Abs. 2 des Dritten Buches Sozialgesetzbuch und nicht für Arbeitsbedingungen nach § 5 Nummer 4 und 5.

Section 6
Special Arrangements

(1) [1]This section shall not apply to initial assembly or installation work which forms part of a supply contract, is essential for putting the supplied goods into operation and is carried out by skilled or semi-skilled workers or workers of the supplier company, if the duration of the posting does not exceed eight days. [2]Sentence 1 shall not apply to construction work within the meaning of section 101(2) of Book III of the Social Security Code and not to working conditions pursuant to section 5, points 4 and 5.

(2) Im Falle eines Tarifvertrages nach § 4 Absatz 1 Nr. 1 findet dieser Abschnitt Anwendung, wenn der Betrieb oder die selbstständige Betriebsabteilung im Sinne des fachlichen Geltungsbereichs des Tarifvertrages überwiegend Bauleistungen gemäß § 101 Abs. 2 des Dritten Buches Sozialgesetzbuch erbringt.

(3) Im Falle eines Tarifvertrages nach § 4 Absatz 1 Nr. 2 findet dieser Abschnitt Anwendung, wenn der Betrieb oder die selbstständige Betriebsabteilung überwiegend Gebäudereinigungsleistungen erbringt.

(4) Im Falle eines Tarifvertrages nach § 4 Absatz 1 Nr. 3 findet dieser Abschnitt Anwendung, wenn der Betrieb oder die selbstständige Betriebsabteilung überwiegend gewerbs- oder geschäftsmäßig Briefsendungen für Dritte befördert.

(5) Im Falle eines Tarifvertrages nach § 4 Absatz 1 Nr. 4 findet dieser Abschnitt Anwendung, wenn der Betrieb oder die selbstständige Betriebsabteilung überwiegend Dienstleistungen des Bewachungs- und Sicherheitsgewerbes oder Kontroll- und Ordnungsdienste erbringt, die dem Schutz von Rechtsgütern aller Art, insbesondere von Leben, Gesundheit oder Eigentum dienen.

(6) Im Falle eines Tarifvertrages nach § 4 Absatz 1 Nr. 5 findet dieser Abschnitt Anwendung, wenn der Betrieb oder die selbstständige Betriebsabteilung im Auftrag eines Dritten überwiegend auf inländischen Steinkohlebergwerken Grubenräume erstellt oder sonstige untertägige bergbauliche Spezialarbeiten ausführt.

(7) ¹Im Falle eines Tarifvertrages nach § 4 Absatz 1 Nr. 6 findet dieser Abschnitt Anwendung, wenn der Betrieb oder die selbstständige Betriebsabteilung gewerbsmäßig überwiegend Textilien für gewerbliche Kunden sowie öffentlich-rechtliche oder kirchliche Einrichtungen wäscht, unabhängig davon, ob die Wäsche im Eigentum der Wäscherei oder des Kunden steht. ²Dieser Abschnitt findet keine Anwendung auf Wäschereidienstleistungen, die von Werkstätten für behinderte Menschen im Sinne des § 219 des Neunten Buches Sozialgesetzbuch erbracht werden.

(8) Im Falle eines Tarifvertrages nach § 4 Absatz 1 Nr. 7 findet dieser Abschnitt Anwendung, wenn der Betrieb oder die selbstständige Betriebsabteilung überwiegend Abfälle im Sinne des § 3 Absatz 1 Satz 1 des Kreislaufwirtschaftsgesetzes sammelt, befördert, lagert, beseitigt oder verwertet oder Dienstleistungen des Kehrens und Reinigens öffentlicher Verkehrsflächen und Schnee- und Eisbeseitigung von öffentlichen Verkehrsflächen einschließlich Streudienste erbringt.

(2) In the case of a collective agreement pursuant to section 4(1) No. 1, this section shall apply if the business or independent business department within the meaning of the technical scope of the collective agreement predominantly provides construction services within the meaning of section 101(2) of the Third Book of the Social Code.

(3) In the case of a collective agreement under Section 4(1) No. 2, this section shall apply if the establishment or independent operational department predominantly provides building cleaning services.

(4) In the case of a collective agreement pursuant to section 4(1) No. 3, this section shall apply if the establishment or the independent operational department mainly transports letters for third parties on a commercial or business basis.

(5) In the case of a collective agreement under Section 4(1) No 4, this section shall apply if the establishment or the independent operational department mainly provides services in the security and surveillance industry or control and order services which serve to protect legal interests of all kinds, in particular life, health or property.

(6) In the case of a collective agreement pursuant to Section 4(1) No. 5, this section shall apply if the establishment or the independent works department mainly constructs mine workings on behalf of a third party at domestic coal mines or carries out other underground special mining work.

(7) ¹In the case of a collective agreement under Section 4(1)(6), this section shall apply if the business or independent department of the business washes commercially predominantly textiles for commercial customers and public or church institutions, irrespective of whether the laundry is owned by the laundry or the customer. ²This section does not apply to laundry services provided by workshops for disabled persons within the meaning of § 219 of Book 9 of the Social Security Code.

(8) In the case of a collective agreement under section 4(1) No 7, this section shall apply if the business or independent business department mainly collects, transports, stores, disposes of or recycles waste within the meaning of section 3(1) first sentence of the Closed Substance Cycle and Waste Management Act or provides services of sweeping and cleaning public traffic areas and removing snow and ice from public traffic areas, including gritting services.

(9) ¹Im Falle eines Tarifvertrages nach § 4 Absatz 1 Nr. 8 findet dieser Abschnitt Anwendung, wenn der Betrieb oder die selbstständige Betriebsabteilung überwiegend Aus- und Weiterbildungsmaßnahmen nach dem Zweiten oder Dritten Buch Sozialgesetzbuch durchführt. ²Ausgenommen sind Einrichtungen der beruflichen Rehabilitation im Sinne des § 51 Absatz 1 Satz 1 des Neunten Buches Sozialgesetzbuch.

(10) ¹Im Falle eines Tarifvertrages nach § 4 Absatz 1 Nr. 9 findet dieser Abschnitt Anwendung in Betrieben und selbstständigen Betriebsabteilungen, in denen überwiegend geschlachtet oder Fleisch verarbeitet wird (Betriebe der Fleischwirtschaft) sowie in Betrieben und selbstständigen Betriebsabteilungen, die ihre Arbeitnehmer und Arbeitnehmerinnen überwiegend in Betrieben der Fleischwirtschaft einsetzen. ²Das Schlachten umfasst dabei alle Tätigkeiten des Schlachtens und Zerlegens von Tieren mit Ausnahme von Fischen. ³Die Verarbeitung umfasst alle Tätigkeiten der Weiterverarbeitung von beim Schlachten gewonnenen Fleischprodukten zur Herstellung von Nahrungsmitteln sowie deren Portionierung und Verpackung. ⁴Nicht erfasst ist die Verarbeitung, wenn die Behandlung, die Portionierung oder die Verpackung beim Schlachten gewonnener Fleischprodukte direkt auf Anforderung des Endverbrauchers erfolgt.

§ 7
Rechtsverordnung für die Fälle des § 4 Absatz 1

(1) Auf gemeinsamen Antrag der Parteien eines Tarifvertrages im Sinne von § 4 Absatz 1 sowie §§ 5 und 6 kann das Bundesministerium für Arbeit und Soziales durch Rechtsverordnung ohne Zustimmung des Bundesrates bestimmen, dass die Rechtsnormen dieses Tarifvertrages auf alle unter seinen Geltungsbereich fallenden und nicht an ihn gebundenen Arbeitgeber sowie Arbeitnehmer und Arbeitnehmerinnen Anwendung finden, wenn dies im öffentlichen Interesse geboten erscheint, um die in § 1 genannten Gesetzesziele zu erreichen.

(2) ¹Kommen in einer Branche mehrere Tarifverträge mit zumindest teilweise demselben fachlichen Geltungsbereich zur Anwendung, hat der Verordnungsgeber bei seiner Entscheidung nach Absatz 1 im Rahmen einer Gesamtabwägung ergänzend zu den in § 1 genannten Gesetzeszielen die Repräsentativität der jeweiligen Tarifverträge zu berücksichtigen. ²Bei der Feststellung der Repräsentativität ist vorrangig abzustellen auf

(9) ¹In the case of a collective agreement pursuant to Section 4(1) No 8, this section shall apply if the establishment or independent operational department mainly carries out initial and further training measures in accordance with Book II or Book III of the Social Code. ²This excludes vocational rehabilitation facilities within the meaning of Article 51(1), first sentence, of Book Nine of the Social Code.

(10) ¹In the case of a collective agreement under Section 4(1) No 9, this section shall apply in establishments and independent departments of establishments in which slaughtering or meat processing is predominantly carried out (establishments in the meat industry) and in establishments and independent departments of establishments which employ their workers predominantly in establishments in the meat industry. ²Slaughter includes all activities of slaughtering and cutting up animals with the exception of fish. ³Processing includes all activities of further processing of meat products obtained from slaughtering for the production of food, as well as portioning and packaging. ⁴It does not include processing where the handling, portioning or packaging of meat products obtained at slaughter is carried out directly at the request of the final consumer.

Section 7
Legal Regulation for the Cases of Section 4 Paragraph 1

(1) At the joint request of the parties to a collective agreement within the meaning of section 4(1) and sections 5 and 6, the Federal Ministry of Labour and Social Affairs may, by statutory instrument and without the consent of the Bundesrat, determine that the legal provisions of this collective agreement shall apply to all employers and employees falling within its scope and not bound by it if this appears necessary in the public interest in order to achieve the objectives of the Act referred to in section 1.

(2) ¹If several collective agreements with at least partly the same technical scope are applicable in a given industry, the legislator shall, when making its decision under subsection 1, take into account the representativeness of the respective collective agreements in addition to the statutory objectives set out in section 1 within the framework of an overall balancing exercise. ²In determining representativeness, priority shall be given to

1. die Zahl der von den jeweils tarifgebundenen Arbeitgebern beschäftigten unter den Geltungsbereich des Tarifvertrages fallenden Arbeitnehmer und Arbeitnehmerinnen,
2. die Zahl der jeweils unter den Geltungsbereich des Tarifvertrages fallenden Mitglieder der Gewerkschaft, die den Tarifvertrag geschlossen hat.

(3) Liegen für mehrere Tarifverträge Anträge auf Allgemeinverbindlicherklärung vor, hat der Verordnungsgeber mit besonderer Sorgfalt die von einer Auswahlentscheidung betroffenen Güter von Verfassungsrang abzuwägen und die widerstreitenden Grundrechtsinteressen zu einem schonenden Ausgleich zu bringen.

(4) Vor Erlass der Rechtsverordnung gibt das Bundesministerium für Arbeit und Soziales den in den Geltungsbereich der Rechtsverordnung fallenden Arbeitgebern sowie Arbeitnehmern und Arbeitnehmerinnen, den Parteien des Tarifvertrages sowie in den Fällen des Absatzes 2 den Parteien anderer Tarifverträge und paritätisch besetzten Kommissionen, die auf der Grundlage kirchlichen Rechts Arbeitsbedingungen für den Bereich kirchlicher Arbeit geber zumindest teilweise im Geltungsbereich der Rechtsverordnung festlegen, Gelegenheit zur schriftlichen Stellungnahme innerhalb von drei Wochen ab dem Tag der Bekanntmachung des Entwurfs der Rechtsverordnung.

(5) ¹Wird in einer Branche nach § 4 Absatz 1 erstmals ein Antrag nach Absatz 1 gestellt, wird nach Ablauf der Frist nach Absatz 4 der Ausschuss nach § 5 Absatz 1 Satz 1 des Tarifvertragsgesetzes (Tarifausschuss) befasst. ²Stimmen mindestens vier Ausschussmitglieder für den Antrag oder gibt der Tarifausschuss innerhalb von zwei Monaten keine Stellungnahme ab, kann eine Rechtsverordnung nach Absatz 1 erlassen werden. ³Stimmen zwei oder drei Ausschussmitglieder für den Antrag, kann eine Rechtsverordnung nur von der Bundesregierung erlassen werden. ⁴Die Sätze 1 bis 3 gelten nicht für Tarifverträge nach § 4 Absatz 1 Nummer 1 bis 8.

1. the number of employees employed by the respective employers bound by collective agreements and falling within the scope of the collective agreement
2. the number of members covered by the collective agreement of the trade union which has concluded the collective agreement

(3) If there are applications for a declaration of general applicability for several collective agreements, the legislator shall weigh up with particular care the constitutional goods affected by a selection decision and bring the conflicting fundamental rights interests into a careful balance.

(4) Before issuing the statutory order, the Federal Ministry of Labour and Social Affairs shall give employers and employees falling within the scope of the statutory order, the parties to the collective agreement and, in the cases referred to in subsection 2, the parties to other collective agreements and commissions with equal representation which, on the basis of church law, lay down working conditions for the area of church employers at least partly within the scope of the statutory order, the opportunity to submit written comments within three weeks of the date of publication of the draft statutory order.

(5) ¹If an application under subsection 1 is made for the first time in a sector under section 4(1), the matter shall be referred to the committee under section 5(1) first sentence of the Collective Bargaining Act (bargaining committee) after expiry of the period under subsection 4. ²If at least four members of the committee vote in favour of the motion or if the bargaining committee does not issue an opinion within two months, a statutory instrument may be issued in accordance with subsection 1. ³If two or three members of the committee vote in favour of the motion, a statutory ordinance may be issued only by the Federal Government. ⁴Sentences 1 to 3 shall not apply to collective agreements under section 4(1) Nos 1 to 8.

§ 7a
Rechtsverordnung für die Fälle des § 4 Absatz 2

(1) [1]Auf gemeinsamen Antrag der Parteien eines Tarifvertrages im Sinne von § 4 Absatz 2 sowie §§ 5 und 6 Absatz 1 kann das Bundesministerium für Arbeit und Soziales durch Rechtsverordnung ohne Zustimmung des Bundesrates bestimmen, dass die Rechtsnormen dieses Tarifvertrages auf alle unter seinen Geltungsbereich fallenden und nicht an ihn gebundenen Arbeitgeber sowie Arbeitnehmer und Arbeitnehmerinnen Anwendung finden, wenn dies im öffentlichen Interesse geboten erscheint, um die in § 1 genannten Gesetzesziele zu erreichen und dabei insbesondere einem Verdrängungswettbewerb über die Lohnkosten entgegenzuwirken. [2]Eine Rechtsverordnung, deren Geltungsbereich die Pflegebranche (§ 10) erfasst, erlässt das Bundesministerium für Arbeit und Soziales im Einvernehmen mit dem Bundesministerium für Gesundheit ohne Zustimmung des Bundesrates. [3]Im Fall einer Rechtsverordnung nach Satz 2 sind auch die in Absatz 1a genannten Voraussetzungen zu erfüllen und die in § 11 Absatz 2 genannten Gesetzesziele zu berücksichtigen.

(1a) [1]Vor Abschluss eines Tarifvertrages nach Absatz 1, dessen Geltungsbereich die Pflegebranche erfasst, gibt das Bundesministerium für Arbeit und Soziales auf gemeinsame Mitteilung der Tarifvertragsparteien bekannt, dass Verhandlungen über einen derartigen Tarifvertrag aufgenommen worden sind. [2]Religionsgesellschaften, in deren Bereichen paritätisch besetzte Kommissionen zur Festlegung von Arbeitsbedingungen auf der Grundlage kirchlichen Rechts für den Bereich kirchlicher Arbeitgeber in der Pflegebranche gebildet sind, können dem Bundesministerium für Arbeit und Soziales innerhalb von drei Wochen ab der Bekanntmachung jeweils eine in ihrem Bereich gebildete Kommission benennen, die von den Tarifvertragsparteien zu dem voraussichtlichen Inhalt des Tarifvertrages angehört wird. [3]Die Anhörung erfolgt mündlich, wenn dies die jeweilige Kommission verlangt oder die Tarifvertragsparteien verlangen. [4]Der Antrag nach Absatz 1 erfordert die schriftliche Zustimmung von mindestens zwei nach Satz 2 benannten Kommissionen. [5]Diese Kommissionen müssen in den Bereichen von Religionsgesellschaften gebildet sein, in deren Bereichen insgesamt mindestens zwei Drittel aller in der Pflegebranche im Bereich von Religionsgesellschaften beschäftigten Arbeitnehmer beschäftigt sind. [6]Mit der Zustimmung einer Kommission werden etwaige Mängel im Zusammenhang mit deren Anhörung geheilt.

Section 7a
Legal Eegulation for the Cases of Section 4 Paragraph 2

(1) [1]At the joint request of the parties to a collective bargaining agreement within the meaning of section 4(2) and sections 5 and 6(1), the Federal Ministry of Labour and Social Affairs may, by statutory instrument and without the consent of the Bundesrat, determine that the legal provisions of this collective bargaining agreement shall apply to all employers and employees covered by and not bound by it if this appears necessary in the public interest in order to achieve the statutory objectives set out in section 1 and, in particular, to counteract predatory competition by means of wage costs. [2]The Federal Ministry of Labour and Social Affairs issues a statutory ordinance whose scope covers the care sector (Article 10) in agreement with the Federal Ministry of Health without the consent of the Bundesrat. [3]In the case of a statutory ordinance pursuant to the second sentence above, the conditions specified in paragraph 1a must also be met and the statutory objectives specified in Article 11 paragraph 2 must be taken into account.

(1a) [1]Prior to the conclusion of a collective agreement under subsection 1, the scope of which covers the care sector, the Federal Ministry of Labour and Social Affairs shall, upon joint notification by the parties to the collective agreement, announce that negotiations on such an agreement have been commenced. [2]Religious organisations in whose areas commissions with equal representation have been formed to determine working conditions on the basis of church law for the area of church employers in the care sector may, within three weeks of the announcement, nominate to the Federal Ministry of Labour and Social Affairs a commission formed in their area, which is consulted by the parties to the collective agreement on the probable content of the collective agreement. [3]The hearing shall take place orally if the respective commission so requests or the parties to the collective agreement so request. [4]The request under subsection 1 shall require the written consent of at least two commissions appointed under the second sentence. [5]These commissions must be formed in the areas of religious communities in whose areas a total of at least two thirds of all workers employed in the care sector in the area of religious communities are employed. [6]With the approval of a commission, any shortcomings in connection with its consultation shall be remedied.

(2) § 7 Absatz 2 und 3 findet entsprechende Anwendung.

(3) ¹Vor Erlass der Rechtsverordnung gibt das Bundesministerium für Arbeit und Soziales den in den Geltungsbereich der Rechtsverordnung fallenden und den möglicherweise von ihr betroffenen Arbeitgebern sowie Arbeitnehmern und Arbeitnehmerinnen, den Parteien des Tarifvertrages sowie allen am Ausgang des Verfahrens interessierten Gewerkschaften, Vereinigungen der Arbeitgeber und paritätisch besetzten Kommissionen, die auf der Grundlage kirchlichen Rechts Arbeitsbedingungen für den Bereich kirchlicher Arbeitgeber festlegen, Gelegenheit zur schriftlichen Stellungnahme innerhalb von drei Wochen ab dem Tag der Bekanntmachung des Entwurfs der Rechtsverordnung. ²Die Gelegenheit zur Stellungnahme umfasst insbesondere auch die Frage, inwieweit eine Erstreckung der Rechtsnormen des Tarifvertrages geeignet ist, die in § 1 genannten Gesetzesziele zu erfüllen und dabei insbesondere einem Verdrängungswettbewerb über die Lohnkosten entgegenzuwirken. ³Soweit der Geltungsbereich der Rechtsverordnung die Pflegebranche erfasst, umfasst die Gelegenheit zur Stellungnahme insbesondere auch die Frage, inwieweit eine Erstreckung der Rechtsnormen des Tarifvertrages geeignet ist, die in § 11 Absatz 2 genannten Gesetzesziele zu erfüllen.

(4) ¹Wird ein Antrag nach Absatz 1 gestellt, wird nach Ablauf der Frist nach Absatz 3 der Ausschuss nach § 5 Absatz 1 Satz 1 des Tarifvertragsgesetzes (Tarifausschuss) befasst. ²Stimmen mindestens vier Ausschussmitglieder für den Antrag oder gibt der Tarifausschuss innerhalb von zwei Monaten keine Stellungnahme ab, kann eine Rechtsverordnung nach Absatz 1 erlassen werden. ³Stimmen zwei oder drei Ausschussmitglieder für den Antrag, kann eine Rechtsverordnung nur von der Bundesregierung erlassen werden.

(2) Section 7 paragraphs 2 and 3 shall apply mutatis mutandis.

(3) ¹Before issuing the statutory order, the Federal Ministry of Labour and Social Affairs shall give the employers and employees falling within the scope of the statutory order and those possibly affected by it, the parties to the collective agreement and all trade unions, employers' associations and commissions with equal representation which are interested in the outcome of the proceedings and which, on the basis of church law, lay down working conditions for the area of church employers, the opportunity to submit written comments within three weeks of the date of announcement of the draft statutory order. ²The opportunity to submit comments includes in particular the question of the extent to which an extension of the legal provisions of the collective agreement is suitable for fulfilling the statutory objectives set out in section 1 and, in particular, for counteracting predatory competition via wage costs. Insofar as the scope of the statutory order covers the care sector, the opportunity to comment also includes in particular the question of the extent to which an extension of the legal norms of the collective agreement is suitable for fulfilling the statutory objectives listed in Section 11 (2).

(4) ¹If an application is made under subsection 1, the matter shall be referred to the committee under section 5(1) first sentence of the Collective Bargaining Act (bargaining committee) after expiry of the period under subsection 3. ²If at least four committee members vote in favour of the motion or if the bargaining committee does not issue an opinion within two months, a statutory instrument may be issued under subsection 1. ³If two or three members of the committee vote in favour of the application, a statutory ordinance may be issued only by the Federal Government.

§ 8
Pflichten des Arbeitgebers zur Gewährung von Arbeitsbedingungen

(1) [1]Arbeitgeber mit Sitz im In- oder Ausland, die unter den Geltungsbereich eines für allgemeinverbindlich erklärten Tarifvertrages nach § 4 Absatz 1 Nummer 1 sowie §§ 5 und 6 Absatz 2 oder einer Rechtsverordnung nach § 7 oder § 7a fallen, sind verpflichtet, ihren Arbeitnehmern und Arbeitnehmerinnen mindestens die in dem Tarifvertrag für den Beschäftigungsort vorgeschriebenen Arbeitsbedingungen zu gewähren sowie einer gemeinsamen Einrichtung der Tarifvertragsparteien die ihr nach § 5 Nr. 3 zustehenden Beiträge zu leisten. [2]Satz 1 gilt unabhängig davon, ob die entsprechende Verpflichtung kraft Tarifbindung nach § 3 des Tarifvertragsgesetzes oder kraft Allgemeinverbindlicherklärung nach § 5 des Tarifvertragsgesetzes oder aufgrund einer Rechtsverordnung nach § 7 oder § 7a besteht.

(2) Ein Arbeitgeber ist verpflichtet, einen Tarifvertrag nach § 4 Absatz 1 Nummer 1 sowie §§ 5 und 6 Absatz 2, der durch Allgemeinverbindlicherklärung sowie einen Tarifvertrag nach §§ 4 bis 6, der durch Rechtsverordnung nach § 7 oder § 7a auf nicht an ihn gebundene Arbeitgeber sowie Arbeitnehmer und Arbeitnehmerinnen erstreckt wird, auch dann einzuhalten, wenn er nach § 3 des Tarifvertragsgesetzes oder kraft Allgemeinverbindlicherklärung nach § 5 des Tarifvertragsgesetzes an einen anderen Tarifvertrag gebunden ist.

(3) Wird ein Leiharbeitnehmer oder eine Leiharbeitnehmerin vom Entleiher mit Tätigkeiten beschäftigt, die in den Geltungsbereich eines für allgemeinverbindlich erklärten Tarifvertrages nach § 4 Absatz 1 Nummer 1 sowie §§ 5 und 6 Absatz 2 oder einer Rechtsverordnung nach § 7 oder § 7a fallen, hat der Verleiher zumindest die in diesem Tarifvertrag oder in dieser Rechtsverordnung vorgeschriebenen Arbeitsbedingungen zu gewähren sowie die der gemeinsamen Einrichtung nach diesem Tarifvertrag zustehenden Beiträge zu leisten; dies gilt auch dann, wenn der Betrieb des Entleihers nicht in den fachlichen Geltungsbereich dieses Tarifvertrages oder dieser Rechtsverordnung fällt.

Section 8
Obligations of the Employer to Provide Working Conditions

(1) [1]Employers domiciled in Germany or abroad who fall within the scope of a collective agreement which has been declared universally applicable under section 4(1)(1) and sections 5 and 6(2) or a statutory instrument under section 7 or section 7a shall be obliged to grant their employees at least the working conditions prescribed by the collective agreement for the place of employment and to pay a joint body of the parties to the collective agreement the contributions to which it is entitled under section 5(3). [2]The first sentence applies irrespective of whether the corresponding obligation exists by virtue of a collective agreement pursuant to section 3 of the Collective Bargaining Act or by virtue of a declaration of general applicability pursuant to section 5 of the Collective Bargaining Act or by virtue of a statutory instrument pursuant to section 7 or section 7a.

(2) An employer shall be obliged to comply with a collective agreement under section 4(1), point 1, and sections 5 and 6(2), which is made universally applicable and a collective agreement under sections 4 to 6, which is extended by statutory instrument under section 7 or section 7a to employers and employees not bound by it, even if it is bound by another collective agreement under section 3 of the Collective Bargaining Act or by virtue of a declaration of universality under section 5 of the Collective Bargaining Act.

(3) If a temporary worker is employed by the hirer in activities which fall within the scope of a collective agreement declared universally applicable under section 4(1)(1) and sections 5 and 6(2) or a statutory instrument pursuant to section 7 or section 7a, the temporary employment agency must at least grant the working conditions prescribed in that collective agreement or statutory instrument and pay the contributions due to the joint establishment under that collective agreement; this shall also apply if the business of the hirer does not fall within the professional scope of this collective agreement or statutory instrument.

§9
Verzicht, Verwirkung

[1]Ein Verzicht auf den entstandenen Anspruch auf das Mindestentgelt nach § 8 ist nur durch gerichtlichen Vergleich zulässig; im Übrigen ist ein Verzicht ausgeschlossen. [2]Die Verwirkung des Anspruchs der Arbeitnehmer und Arbeitnehmerinnen auf das Mindestentgelt nach § 8 ist ausgeschlossen. [3]Ausschlussfristen für die Geltendmachung des Anspruchs können ausschließlich in dem für allgemeinverbindlich erklärten Tarifvertrag nach den §§ 4 bis 6 oder dem der Rechtsverordnung nach § 7 zugrunde liegenden Tarifvertrag geregelt werden; die Frist muss mindestens sechs Monate betragen.

§10
Anwendungsbereich

[1]Dieser Abschnitt findet Anwendung auf die Pflegebranche. [2]Diese umfasst Betriebe und selbstständige Betriebsabteilungen, die überwiegend ambulante, teilstationäre oder stationäre Pflegeleistungen oder ambulante Krankenpflegeleistungen für Pflegebedürftige erbringen (Pflegebetriebe). [3]Pflegebedürftig sind Personen, die gesundheitlich bedingte Beeinträchtigungen der Selbständigkeit oder der Fähigkeiten aufweisen, deshalb vorübergehend oder auf Dauer der Hilfe durch andere bedürfen und körperliche, kognitive oder psychische Beeinträchtigungen oder gesundheitlich bedingte Belastungen oder Anforderungen nicht selbständig kompensieren oder bewältigen können. [4]Keine Pflegebetriebe im Sinne des Satzes 2 sind Einrichtungen, in denen die Leistungen zur medizinischen Vorsorge, zur medizinischen Rehabilitation, zur Teilhabe am Arbeitsleben oder am Leben in der Gemeinschaft, die schulische Ausbildung oder die Erziehung kranker oder behinderter Menschen im Vordergrund des Zweckes der Einrichtung stehen, sowie Krankenhäuser.

§11
Rechtsverordnung

(1) Das Bundesministerium für Arbeit und Soziales kann durch Rechtsverordnung ohne Zustimmung des Bundesrates bestimmen, dass die von der nach § 12 errichteten Kommission vorgeschlagenen Arbeitsbedingungen nach § 5 Nr. 1 und 2 auf alle Arbeitgeber sowie Arbeitnehmer und Arbeitnehmerinnen, die unter den Geltungsbereich einer Empfehlung nach § 12a Absatz 2 fallen, Anwendung finden.

Section 9
Waiver, Forfeiture

[1]A waiver of the accrued claim to the minimum remuneration pursuant to section 8 is only permissible by court settlement; otherwise a waiver is excluded. [2]The forfeiture of the employees' claim to the minimum remuneration under section 8 is excluded. [3]Limitation periods for the assertion of the claim may be regulated exclusively in the collective agreement declared generally binding pursuant to sections 4 to 6 or the collective agreement underlying the statutory instrument pursuant to section 7; the period must be at least six months.

Section 10
Scope of Application

[1]This section applies to the care sector. [2]This includes companies and independent company departments that predominantly provide outpatient, semi-inpatient or inpatient care services or outpatient nursing services for people in need of care (care companies). [3]Persons in need of care are those who have health-related impairments of independence or abilities, therefore require temporary or permanent assistance from others and who are unable to independently compensate for or cope with physical, cognitive or psychological impairments or health-related burdens or demands. [4]No care facilities within the meaning of sentence 2 are facilities in which the services of medical prevention, medical rehabilitation, participation in working life or life in the community, school education or the education of sick or disabled persons are at the forefront of the facility's purpose, as are hospitals.

Section 11
Statutory Instrument

(1) The Federal Ministry of Labour and Social Affairs may, by statutory order without the consent of the Bundesrat, determine that the working conditions pursuant to section 5 nos. 1 and 2 proposed by the Commission established under section 12 shall apply to all employers and employees falling within the scope of a recommendation under section 12a(2).

(2) Das Bundesministerium für Arbeit und Soziales hat bei seiner Entscheidung nach Absatz 1 neben den in § 1 genannten Gesetzeszielen die Sicherstellung der Qualität der Pflegeleistung sowie den Auftrag kirchlicher und sonstiger Träger der freien Wohlfahrtspflege nach § 11 Abs. 2 des Elften Buches Sozialgesetzbuch zu berücksichtigen.

(3) Vor Erlass einer Rechtsverordnung gibt das Bundesministerium für Arbeit und Soziales den in den Geltungsbereich der Rechtsverordnung fallenden Arbeitgebern und Arbeitnehmern und Arbeitnehmerinnen sowie den Parteien von Tarifverträgen, die zumindest teilweise in den fachlichen Geltungsbereich der Rechtsverordnung fallen, und paritätisch besetzten Kommissionen, die auf der Grundlage kirchlichen Rechts Arbeitsbedingungen für den Bereich kirchlicher Arbeitgeber in der Pflegebranche festlegen, Gelegenheit zur schriftlichen Stellungnahme innerhalb von drei Wochen ab dem Tag der Bekanntmachung des Entwurfs der Rechtsverordnung.

§ 12
Berufung der Kommission

(1) Das Bundesministerium für Arbeit und Soziales beruft eine ständige Kommission, die über Empfehlungen zur Festlegung von Arbeitsbedingungen nach § 12a Absatz 2 beschließt.

(2) ¹Die Kommission wird für die Dauer von fünf Jahren berufen. ²Das Bundesministerium für Arbeit und Soziales kann die Dauer der Berufung verlängern, wenn die Kommission bereits Beratungen über neue Empfehlungen begonnen, jedoch noch keinen Beschluss über diese Empfehlungen gefasst hat. ³Die neue Berufung erfolgt in diesem Fall unverzüglich nach der Beschlussfassung, spätestens jedoch drei Monate nach Ablauf der fünfjährigen Dauer der Berufung.

(3) ¹Die Kommission besteht aus acht Mitgliedern. ²Die Mitglieder nehmen ihre Tätigkeit in der Kommission ehrenamtlich wahr. ³Sie sind an Weisungen nicht gebunden.

(4) ¹Das Bundesministerium für Arbeit und Soziales benennt acht geeignete Personen als ordentliche Mitglieder sowie acht geeignete Personen als deren Stellvertreter unter Berücksichtigung von Vorschlägen vorschlagsberechtigter Stellen. ²Vorschlagsberechtigte Stellen sind

1. Tarifvertragsparteien in der Pflegebranche, wobei
    (a) in der Pflegebranche tarifzuständige Gewerkschaften oder Zusammenschlüsse von Gewerkschaften sowie

(2) In making its decision under subsection 1, the Federal Ministry of Labour and Social Affairs must take account not only of the statutory objectives set out in Article 1 but also of the need to ensure the quality of care services and of the mandate of church and other voluntary welfare organisations under Article 11(2) of Book Eleven of the Social Code.

(3) Before issuing a statutory order, the Federal Ministry of Labour and Social Affairs shall give employers and employees who fall within the scope of the statutory order, as well as the parties to collective agreements which fall at least in part within the technical scope of the statutory order, and commissions with equal representation which, on the basis of church law, lay down working conditions for church employers in the care sector, the opportunity to submit written comments within three weeks of the date of publication of the draft statutory order.

Section 12
Appeals by the Commission

(1) The Federal Ministry of Labour and Social Affairs appoints a standing commission which decides on recommendations for the establishment of working conditions in accordance with section 12a, paragraph 2.

(2) ¹The Commission shall be appointed for a period of five years. ²The Federal Ministry of Labour and Social Affairs may extend the duration of the appointment if the Commission has already begun deliberations on new recommendations but has not yet taken a decision on these recommendations. ³In this case, the new appointment is made immediately after the decision has been taken, but no later than three months after the expiry of the five-year period of the appointment.

(3) ¹The Commission shall consist of eight members. ²The members perform their duties in the Commission on an honorary basis. ³They are not bound by instructions.

(4) ¹The Federal Ministry of Labour and Social Affairs appoints eight suitable persons as full members and eight suitable persons as their deputies, taking into account proposals by bodies entitled to make proposals. ²Authorised to propose bodies are

1. parties to collective bargaining agreements in the care sector, whereby
    (a) trade unions or associations of trade unions with collective bargaining powers in the care sector; and

(b) in der Pflegebranche tarifzuständige Vereinigungen von Arbeitgebern oder Zusammenschlüsse von Vereinigungen von Arbeitgebern

jeweils für zwei ordentliche Mitglieder und zwei Stellvertreter vorschlagsberechtigt sind, und

2. die Dienstnehmerseite und die Dienstgeberseite paritätisch besetzter Kommissionen, die auf der Grundlage kirchlichen Rechts Arbeitsbedingungen für den Bereich kirchlicher Arbeitgeber in der Pflegebranche festlegen, wobei
(a) die Dienstnehmerseite sowie
(b) die Dienstgeberseite
jeweils für zwei ordentliche Mitglieder und zwei Stellvertreter vorschlagsberechtigt sind.

[3]Vorschlagsberechtigte Stellen, die derselben der in Satz 2 Nummer 1 Buchstabe a bis Nummer 2 Buchstabe b genannten Gruppen angehören, können gemeinsame Vorschläge abgeben.

(5) [1]Das Bundesministerium für Arbeit und Soziales fordert innerhalb einer von ihm zu bestimmenden angemessenen Frist zur Abgabe von Vorschlägen auf. [2]Nach Fristablauf zugehende Vorschläge sind nicht zu berücksichtigen. [3]Das Bundesministerium für Arbeit und Soziales prüft die Vorschläge und kann verlangen, dass für die Prüfung relevante Umstände innerhalb einer von ihm zu bestimmenden angemessenen Frist mitgeteilt und glaubhaft gemacht werden. [4]Nach Fristablauf mitgeteilte oder glaubhaft gemachte Umstände sind nicht zu berücksichtigen.

(6) [1]Überschreitet die Zahl der Vorschläge die Zahl der auf die jeweilige in Absatz 4 Satz 2 genannte Gruppe entfallenden Sitze in der Kommission, entscheidet das Bundesministerium für Arbeit und Soziales, welchen Vorschlägen zu folgen ist. [2]Bei dieser Entscheidung sind zu berücksichtigen

1. im Falle mehrerer Vorschläge von in der Pflegebranche tarifzuständigen Gewerkschaften oder Zusammenschlüssen von Gewerkschaften: deren Repräsentativität,
2. im Falle mehrerer Vorschläge von in der Pflegebranche tarifzuständigen Vereinigungen von Arbeitgebern oder Zusammenschlüssen von Vereinigungen von Arbeitgebern: die Abbildung der Vielfalt von freigemeinnützigen, öffentlichen und privaten Trägern sowie gleichermaßen die Repräsentativität der jeweiligen Vereinigung bzw. des jeweiligen Zusammenschlusses.

(b) employers' associations or federations of employers' associations with collective bargaining powers in the care sector

are each entitled to propose two full members and two alternates, and

2. commissions with equal representation of employees and employers, which, on the basis of church law, lay down working conditions for church employers in the care sector, whereby

(a) the employee side; and
(b) the employer side
are each entitled to propose two full members and two alternates.

[3]Eligible proposers belonging to the same group as those referred to in the second sentence, points 1(a) to 2(b), may submit joint proposals.

(5) [1]The Federal Ministry of Labour and Social Affairs shall call for proposals within a reasonable period to be determined by it. [2]Proposals received after expiry of the deadline shall not be taken into consideration. [3]The Federal Ministry of Labour and Social Affairs shall examine the proposals and may demand that circumstances relevant to the examination be communicated and substantiated within a reasonable period to be determined by it. [4]Circumstances notified or substantiated after expiry of the deadline are not to be taken into account.

(6) [1]If the number of proposals exceeds the number of seats in the Commission allocated to the respective group referred to in paragraph 4, second sentence, the Federal Ministry of Labour and Social Affairs shall decide which proposals are to be followed. [2]The following shall be taken into account in this decision

1. in the case of several proposals from trade unions with collective bargaining powers in the care sector or associations of trade unions: their representativeness,
2. in the case of several proposals from employers' associations or federations of employers' associations with collective bargaining responsibility in the care sector: the illustration of the diversity of non-profit, public and private institutions and equally the representativeness of the respective association or federation.

³Die Repräsentativität einer Gewerkschaft oder eines Zusammenschlusses von Gewerkschaften beurteilt sich nach der Zahl der als Arbeitnehmer in der Pflegebranche beschäftigten Mitglieder der jeweiligen Gewerkschaft oder des jeweiligen Zusammenschlusses und der diesem Zusammenschluss angehörenden Gewerkschaften. ⁴Die Repräsentativität einer Vereinigung von Arbeitgebern beurteilt sich nach der Zahl der in der Pflegebranche beschäftigten Arbeitnehmer, deren Arbeitgeber Mitglieder der jeweiligen Vereinigung von Arbeitgebern sind und nach der Art ihrer Mitgliedschaft tarifgebunden sein können. ⁵Die Repräsentativität eines Zusammenschlusses von Vereinigungen von Arbeitgebern beurteilt sich nach der Zahl der in der Pflegebranche beschäftigten Arbeitnehmer, deren Arbeitgeber

1. Mitglieder des Zusammenschlusses sind und nach der Art ihrer Mitgliedschaft tarifgebunden sein können oder

2. Mitglieder der diesem Zusammenschluss angehörenden Vereinigungen von Arbeitgebern sind und nach der Art ihrer Mitgliedschaft sowie der Mitgliedschaft der jeweiligen Vereinigung von Arbeitgebern tarifgebunden sein können.

⁶Bei gemeinsamen Vorschlägen im Sinne des Absatzes 4 Satz 3 sind die auf die vorschlagsberechtigten Stellen entfallenden maßgeblichen Arbeitnehmerzahlen zu addieren.

(7) ¹Scheidet ein ordentliches Mitglied oder ein Stellvertreter aus, benennt das Bundesministerium für Arbeit und Soziales eine andere geeignete Person. ²War das Bundesministerium für Arbeit und Soziales mit der Benennung des ausgeschiedenen ordentlichen Mitglieds oder des Stellvertreters dem Vorschlag einer vorschlagsberechtigten Stelle oder, im Falle eines gemeinsamen Vorschlags nach Absatz 4 Satz 3, vorschlagsberechtigter Stellen gefolgt, so erfolgt auch die neue Benennung unter Berücksichtigung deren Vorschlags. ³Schlägt die Stelle oder schlagen die Stellen innerhalb einer von dem Bundesministerium für Arbeit und Soziales zu bestimmenden angemessenen Frist keine geeignete Person vor, so entscheidet das Bundesministerium für Arbeit und Soziales über die Benennung. ⁴Absatz 5 Satz 3 und 4 gilt entsprechend.

(8) Klagen gegen die Benennung von Mitgliedern durch das Bundesministerium für Arbeit und Soziales haben keine aufschiebende Wirkung.

³The representativeness of a trade union or association of trade unions is assessed on the basis of the number of members employed as workers in the care sector in the trade union or association concerned and the trade unions belonging to that association. ⁴The representativeness of an association of employers shall be determined by the number of employees employed in the care sector whose employers are members of the respective association of employers and may be bound by collective agreements according to the nature of their membership. ⁵The representativeness of an association of employers' associations is assessed by the number of employees employed in the care sector whose employers

1. are members of the association and may be bound by collective bargaining agreements according to the nature of their membership or

2. are members of the associations of employers belonging to this association and may be bound by collective agreements according to the nature of their membership and the membership of the respective association of employers.

⁶In the case of joint proposals within the meaning of subsection (4), third sentence, the relevant numbers of employees attributable to the bodies entitled to make proposals shall be added together.

(7) ¹If a full member or a deputy member resigns, the BMU shall appoint another suitable person. ²If, in appointing the full member or deputy who has resigned, the BMU had followed the proposal of a body entitled to propose or, in the case of a joint proposal pursuant to paragraph 4, sentence 3, of bodies entitled to propose, the new appointment shall also be made in consideration of their proposal. ³If the body or the bodies do not propose a suitable person within a reasonable period to be determined by the Federal Ministry of Labour and Social Affairs, the Federal Ministry of Labour and Social Affairs shall decide on the appointment. ⁴Section 5, sentences 3 and 4 shall apply accordingly.

(8) Actions against the appointment of members by the Federal Ministry of Labour and Social Affairs shall not have a suspensive effect.

§ 12a
Empfehlung von Arbeitsbedingungen

(1) ¹Auf Antrag einer vorschlagsberechtigten Stelle im Sinne des § 12 Absatz 4 Satz 2 nimmt die Kommission Beratungen auf. ²Hat das Bundesministerium für Arbeit und Soziales bekannt gegeben, dass Verhandlungen über einen Tarifvertrag im Sinne des § 7a Absatz 1a Satz 1 aufgenommen worden sind, so können drei Viertel der Mitglieder der Gruppen nach § 12 Absatz 4 Satz 2 Nummer 2 Buchstabe a und b gemeinsam verlangen, dass Beratungen über neue Empfehlungen frühestens vier Monate nach Ablauf der Frist für die Benennung von Kommissionen nach § 7a Absatz 1a Satz 2 aufgenommen oder fortgesetzt werden.

(2) ¹Die Kommission beschließt Empfehlungen zur Festlegung von Arbeitsbedingungen nach § 5 Satz 1 Nummer 1 oder 2. ²Dabei berücksichtigt die Kommission die in den §§ 1 und 11 Absatz 2 genannten Ziele. ³Empfohlene Mindestentgeltsätze sollen nach der Art der Tätigkeit oder der Qualifikation der Arbeitnehmer differenzieren. ⁴Empfehlungen sollen sich auf eine Dauer von mindestens 24 Monaten beziehen. ⁵Die Kommission kann eine Ausschlussfrist empfehlen, die den Anforderungen des § 9 Satz 3 entspricht. ⁶Empfehlungen sind schriftlich zu begründen.

(3) ¹Ein Beschluss der Kommission kommt zustande, wenn mindestens drei Viertel der Mitglieder

1. der Gruppen nach § 12 Absatz 4 Satz 2 Nummer 1 Buchstabe a und b,
2. der Gruppen nach § 12 Absatz 4 Satz 2 Nummer 2 Buchstabe a und b,
3. der Gruppen nach § 12 Absatz 4 Satz 2 Nummer 1 Buchstabe a und Nummer 2 Buchstabe a sowie
4. der Gruppen nach § 12 Absatz 4 Satz 2 Nummer 1 Buchstabe b und Nummer 2 Buchstabe b

anwesend sind und zustimmen. ²Ordentliche Mitglieder können durch ihre jeweiligen Stellvertreter vertreten werden.

(4) ¹Die Sitzungen der Kommission werden von einem oder einer nicht stimmberechtigten Beauftragten des Bundesministeriums für Arbeit und Soziales geleitet. ²Sie sind nicht öffentlich. ³Der Inhalt ihrer Beratungen ist vertraulich. ⁴Die Kommission zieht regelmäßig nicht stimmberechtigte Vertreter des Bundesministeriums für Arbeit und Soziales und des Bundesministeriums für Gesundheit zu den Sitzungen hinzu. ⁵Näheres ist in der Geschäftsordnung der Kommission zu regeln.

Section 12a
Recommendation of Working Conditions

(1) ¹At the request of a body entitled to make a proposal within the meaning of Section 12 (4) sentence 2, the Commission shall enter into consultations. ²If the Federal Ministry of Labour and Social Affairs has announced that negotiations on a collective agreement within the meaning of Article 7a (1a), first sentence, have been commenced, three-quarters of the members of the groups pursuant to Article 12 (4), second sentence, number 2 (a) and (b) may jointly request that deliberations on new recommendations be commenced or continued at the earliest four months after expiry of the deadline for the appointment of commissions pursuant to Article 7a (1a), second sentence.

(2) ¹The Commission shall adopt recommendations for the establishment of working conditions under section 5, first sentence, number 1 or 2, ²taking into account the objectives set out in sections 1 and 11(2). ³Recommended minimum rates of pay shall differentiate according to the type of activity or the qualifications of the employees. ⁴Recommendations should refer to a period of at least 24 months. ⁵The Commission may recommend a cut-off period that meets the requirements of section 9, third sentence. ⁶Recommendations shall be justified in writing.

(3) ¹A Commission decision shall be adopted if at least three quarters of the members

1. the groups pursuant to section 12(4), second sentence, point 1(a) and (b)
2. the groups pursuant to section 12(4), second sentence, point 2(a) and (b),
3. the groups pursuant to section 12 (4) sentence 2 number 1 letter a and number 2 letter a, and
4. the groups referred to in section 12 (4) sentence 2 number 1 letter b and number 2 letter b

are present and agree. ²Full members may be represented by their respective deputies.

(4) ¹The meetings of the Commission shall be chaired by a representative of the Federal Ministry of Labour and Social Affairs who is not entitled to vote. ²They are not public. ³The content of its deliberations is confidential. ⁴The Commission regularly involves non-voting representatives of the Federal Ministry of Labour and Social Affairs and the Federal Ministry of Health in its meetings. ⁵Further details are to be laid down in the Commission's rules of procedure.

§ 13
Rechtsfolgen

[1]Die Regelungen einer Rechtsverordnung nach § 7a gehen den Regelungen einer Rechtsverordnung nach § 11 vor, soweit sich die Geltungsbereiche der Rechtsverordnungen überschneiden. [2]Unbeschadet des Satzes 1 steht eine Rechtsverordnung nach § 11 für die Anwendung der §§ 8 und 9 sowie der Abschnitte 5 und 6 einer Rechtsverordnung nach § 7 gleich.

Section 13
Legal Consequences

[1]The provisions of a statutory instrument pursuant to section 7a shall take precedence over the provisions of a statutory instrument pursuant to section 11 insofar as the scopes of the statutory instruments overlap. [2]Notwithstanding the first sentence above, a statutory instrument pursuant to section 11 shall, for the application of sections 8 and 9 and sections 5 and 6, be deemed equivalent to a statutory instrument pursuant to section 7.

§ 13a
Gleichstellung

Die Verordnung (EU) Nr. 1214/2011 des Europäischen Parlaments und des Rates vom 16. November 2011 über den gewerbsmäßig grenzüberschreitenden Straßentransport von Euro-Bargeld zwischen den Mitgliedstaaten des Euroraums (ABl. L 316 vom 29.11.2011, S. 1) steht für die Anwendung der §§ 8 und 9 sowie der Abschnitte 5 und 6 einer Rechtsverordnung nach § 7 gleich.

Section 13a
Equality

Regulation (EU) No 1214/2011 of the European Parliament and of the Council of 16 November 2011 on the professional cross-border transportation of euro cash by road between euro-area Member States (OJ L 316, 29.11.2011, p. 1) shall, for the purposes of applying Sections 8 and 9 and Sections 5 and 6, be deemed equivalent to a statutory instrument pursuant to Section 7.

§ 14
Haftung des Auftraggebers

[1]Ein Unternehmer, der einen anderen Unternehmer mit der Erbringung von Werk- oder Dienstleistungen beauftragt, haftet für die Verpflichtungen dieses Unternehmers, eines Nachunternehmers oder eines von dem Unternehmer oder einem Nachunternehmer beauftragten Verleihers zur Zahlung des Mindestentgelts an Arbeitnehmer oder Arbeitnehmerinnen oder zur Zahlung von Beiträgen an eine gemeinsame Einrichtung der Tarifvertragsparteien nach § 8 wie ein Bürge, der auf die Einrede der Vorausklage verzichtet hat. [2]Das Mindestentgelt im Sinne des Satzes 1 umfasst nur den Betrag, der nach Abzug der Steuern und der Beiträge zur Sozialversicherung und zur Arbeitsförderung oder entsprechender Aufwendungen zur sozialen Sicherung an Arbeitnehmer oder Arbeitnehmerinnen auszuzahlen ist (Nettoentgelt).

Section 14
Liability of the Client

[1]A contractor who commissions another contractor to provide work or services is liable for the obligations of this contractor, a subcontractor or a lender commissioned by the contractor or a subcontractor to pay the minimum wage to employees or to pay contributions to a joint institution of the parties to a collective agreement in accordance with § 8, like a guarantor who has waived the defence of advance action. [2]The minimum wage within the meaning of sentence 1 shall comprise only the amount which is to be paid to employees after deduction of taxes and contributions to social security and employment promotion or corresponding social security expenses (net wage).

§ 15
Gerichtsstand

[1]Arbeitnehmer und Arbeitnehmerinnen, die in den Geltungsbereich dieses Gesetzes entsandt sind oder waren, können vor den Zeitraum der Entsendung bezogene Klage auf Erfüllung der Verpflichtungen nach den §§ 2, 8 oder 14 auch vor einem deutschen Gericht für Arbeitssachen erheben. [2]Diese Klagemöglichkeit besteht auch für eine gemeinsame Einrichtung der Tarifvertragsparteien nach § 5 Nr. 3 in Bezug auf die ihr zustehenden Beiträge.

Section 15
Place of Jurisdiction

[1]Employees who are or have been posted within the scope of this Act may also bring an action before a German court for employment matters in respect of the period of posting for fulfilment of the obligations under Sections 2, 8 or 14. [2]This possibility of bringing an action also exists for a joint institution of the parties to a collective agreement under Section 5 No. 3 in respect of the contributions due to it.

§ 16
Zuständigkeit

Für die Prüfung der Einhaltung der Pflichten eines Arbeitgebers nach § 8, soweit sie sich auf die Gewährung von Arbeitsbedingungen nach § 5 Satz 1 Nummer 1 bis 4 beziehen, sind die Behörden der Zollverwaltung zuständig.

Section 16
Responsibility

The authorities of the customs administration are responsible for examining whether an employer's obligations under Section 8 have been complied with in so far as they relate to the granting of working conditions under Section 5, first sentence, numbers 1 to 4.

§ 17
Befugnisse der Behörden der Zollverwaltung und anderer Behörden

[1]Die §§ 2 bis 6, 14, 15, 20, 22 und 23 des Schwarzarbeitsbekämpfungsgesetzes sind entsprechend anzuwenden mit der Maßgabe, dass

1. die dort genannten Behörden auch Einsicht in Arbeitsverträge, Niederschriften nach § 2 des Nachweisgesetzes und andere Geschäftsunterlagen nehmen können, die mittelbar oder unmittelbar Auskunft über die Einhaltung der Arbeitsbedingungen nach § 8 geben,

2. die nach § 5 Abs. 1 des Schwarzarbeitsbekämpfungsgesetzes zur Mitwirkung Verpflichteten diese Unterlagen vorzulegen haben, und

3. die Behörden der Zollverwaltung zur Prüfung von Arbeitsbedingungen nach § 5 Satz 1 Nummer 4 befugt sind, bei einer dringenden Gefahr für die öffentliche Sicherheit und Ordnung die vom Arbeitgeber zur Verfügung gestellten Unterkünfte für Arbeitnehmer und Arbeitnehmerinnen zu jeder Tages- und Nachtzeit zu betreten.

[2]Die §§ 16 bis 19 des Schwarzarbeitsbekämpfungsgesetzes finden Anwendung. [3]§ 6 Absatz 4 des Schwarzarbeitsbekämpfungsgesetzes findet entsprechende Anwendung. [4]Für die Datenverarbeitung, die dem in § 16 genannten Zweck oder der Zusammenarbeit mit den Behörden des Europäischen Wirtschaftsraums nach § 20 Abs. 2 dient, findet § 67 Absatz 3 Nummer 4 des Zehnten Buches Sozialgesetzbuch keine Anwendung. [5]Das Grundrecht der Unverletzlichkeit der Wohnung (Artikel 13 des Grundgesetzes) wird durch Satz 1 Nummer 3 eingeschränkt.

Section 17
Powers of the Customs Authorities and other Authorities

[1]Sections 2 to 6, 14, 15, 20, 22 and 23 of the Act to Combat undeclared work shall apply mutatis mutandis, provided that

1. the authorities named therein may also inspect employment contracts, minutes in accordance with section 2 of the Evidence Act and other business documents which directly or indirectly provide information on compliance with the working conditions in accordance with section 8

2. those obliged to cooperate under section 5(1) of the Illegal Employment Act must submit these documents, and

3. the customs administration authorities are authorised to inspect working conditions in accordance with § 5 sentence 1 number 4, in the event of an urgent danger to public safety and order, to enter the accommodation for employees provided by the employer at any time of day or night.

[2]Sections 16 to 19 of the Schwarzarbeitsbekämpfungsgesetz (Act to Combat undeclared work) shall apply. [3]Section 6 paragraph 4 of the Act to Combat undeclared work shall apply mutatis mutandis. [4]Section 67(3)(4) of Book Ten of the Social Security Code shall not apply to data processing serving the purpose referred to in section 16 or for cooperation with the authorities of the European Economic Area pursuant to section 20(2). [5]The fundamental right of inviolability of the home (Article 13 of the Basic Law) is restricted by sentence 1 number 3.

§ 18
Meldepflicht

(1) [1]Soweit die Rechtsnormen eines für allgemeinverbindlich erklärten Tarifvertrages nach § 4 Absatz 1 Nummer 1, § 5 Satz 1 Nummer 1 bis 4 und § 6 Absatz 2 oder einer Rechtsverordnung nach § 7 oder § 7a, soweit sie Arbeitsbedingungen nach § 5 Satz 1 Nummer 1 bis 4 vorschreibt, auf das Arbeitsverhältnis Anwendung finden, ist

Section 18
Obligation to Report

(1) [1]Insofar as the legal provisions of a collective agreement which has been declared universally applicable pursuant to section 4(1)(1), section 5, first sentence, numbers 1 to 4 and section 6(2) or a statutory instrument pursuant to section 7 or section 7a, insofar as it prescribes working conditions pursuant to section 5, first sentence,

ein Arbeitgeber mit Sitz im Ausland, der einen Arbeitnehmer oder eine Arbeitnehmerin oder mehrere Arbeitnehmer oder Arbeitnehmerinnen innerhalb des Geltungsbereichs dieses Gesetzes beschäftigt, verpflichtet, vor Beginn jeder Werk- oder Dienstleistung eine schriftliche Anmeldung in deutscher Sprache bei der zuständigen Behörde der Zollverwaltung vorzulegen, die die für die Prüfung wesentlichen Angaben enthält. ²Wesentlich sind die Angaben über

1. Familienname, Vornamen und Geburtsdatum der von ihm im Geltungsbereich dieses Gesetzes beschäftigten Arbeitnehmer und Arbeitnehmerinnen,
2. Beginn und voraussichtliche Dauer der Beschäftigung,
3. Ort der Beschäftigung, bei Bauleistungen die Baustelle,
4. Ort im Inland, an dem die nach § 19 erforderlichen Unterlagen bereitgehalten werden,
5. Familienname, Vornamen, Geburtsdatum und Anschrift in Deutschland des oder der verantwortlich Handelnden,
6. Branche, in die die Arbeitnehmer und Arbeitnehmerinnen entsandt werden sollen, und
7. Familienname, Vornamen und Anschrift in Deutschland eines oder einer Zustellungsbevollmächtigten, soweit dieser oder diese nicht mit dem oder der in Nummer 5 genannten verantwortlich Handelnden identisch ist.

³Änderungen bezüglich dieser Angaben hat der Arbeitgeber im Sinne des Satzes 1 unverzüglich zu melden.

(2) Der Arbeitgeber hat der Anmeldung eine Versicherung beizufügen, dass er seine Verpflichtungen nach § 8 einhält.

(3) ¹Überlässt ein Verleiher mit Sitz im Ausland einen Arbeitnehmer oder eine Arbeitnehmerin oder mehrere Arbeitnehmer oder Arbeitnehmerinnen zur Arbeitsleistung einem Entleiher, hat der Entleiher unter den Voraussetzungen des Absatzes 1 Satz 1 vor Beginn jeder Werk- oder Dienstleistung der zuständigen Behörde der Zollverwaltung eine schriftliche Anmeldung in deutscher Sprache mit folgenden Angaben zuzuleiten:

1. Familienname, Vornamen und Geburtsdatum der überlassenen Arbeitnehmer und Arbeitnehmerinnen,
2. Beginn und Dauer der Überlassung,
3. Ort der Beschäftigung, bei Bauleistungen die Baustelle,
4. Ort im Inland, an dem die nach § 19 erforderlichen Unterlagen bereitgehalten werden,

numbers 1 to 4, apply to the employment relationship, an employer domiciled abroad who employs one or more workers within the scope of this Act, shall be obliged to submit a written declaration in German to the competent authority of the customs administration prior to the commencement of each work or service, which contains the information essential for the examination. ²Essential information is the information on

1. the surname, first names and date of birth of the employees he/she employs within the scope of this Act
2. the starting date and probable duration of employment,
3. place of employment, in the case of construction services the construction site,
4. place in Germany where the documents required under section 19 are kept available,
5. surname, first name, date of birth and address in Germany of the person or persons responsible,
6. the sector to which the workers are to be posted, and
7. the surname, forenames and address in Germany of an authorised person or person authorised to accept service, unless this person or this person is identical to the responsible person or persons referred to in point 5

³The employer within the meaning of sentence 1 must notify any changes to this information without delay.

(2) The employer shall attach to the notification an assurance that it will comply with its obligations under section 8.

(3) ¹If a lender based abroad provides an employee or employees to a hirer for the performance of work, the hirer shall, subject to the conditions of subsection 1 first sentence, submit a written declaration in German to the competent authority of the customs administration prior to the commencement of each work or service, containing the following information:

1. 1surname, first names and date of birth of the temporary workers,
2. beginning and duration of the transfer,
3. place of employment, in the case of construction work the building site,
4. place in Germany where the documents required under section 19 are kept available,

5. Familienname, Vornamen und Anschrift in Deutschland eines oder einer Zustellungsbevollmächtigten des Verleihers,

6. Branche, in die die Arbeitnehmer und Arbeitnehmerinnen entsandt werden sollen, und

7. Familienname, Vornamen oder Firma sowie Anschrift des Verleihers.

²Absatz 1 Satz 3 gilt entsprechend.

(4) Der Entleiher hat der Anmeldung eine Versicherung des Verleihers beizufügen, dass dieser seine Verpflichtungen nach § 8 einhält.

(5) Das Bundesministerium der Finanzen kann durch Rechtsverordnung im Einvernehmen mit dem Bundesministerium für Arbeit und Soziales ohne Zustimmung des Bundesrates bestimmen,

1. dass, auf welche Weise und unter welchen technischen und organisatorischen Voraussetzungen eine Anmeldung, Änderungsmeldung und Versicherung abweichend von Absatz 1 Satz 1 und 3, Absatz 2 und 3 Satz 1 und 2 und Absatz 4 elektronisch übermittelt werden kann,

2. unter welchen Voraussetzungen eine Änderungsmeldung ausnahmsweise entfallen kann, und

3. wie das Meldeverfahren vereinfacht oder abgewandelt werden kann, sofern die entsandten Arbeitnehmer und Arbeitnehmerinnen im Rahmen einer regelmäßig wiederkehrenden Werk- oder Dienstleistung eingesetzt werden oder sonstige Besonderheiten der zu erbringenden Werk- oder Dienstleistungen dies erfordern.

(6) Das Bundesministerium der Finanzen kann durch Rechtsverordnung ohne Zustimmung des Bundesrates die zuständige Behörde nach Absatz 1 Satz 1 und Absatz 3 Satz 1 bestimmen.

§ 19
Erstellen und Bereithalten von Dokumenten

(1) ¹Soweit die Rechtsnormen eines für allgemeinverbindlich erklärten Tarifvertrages nach § 4 Absatz 1 Nummer 1, § 5 Satz 1 Nummer 1 bis 4 und § 6 Absatz 2 oder einer entsprechenden Rechtsverordnung nach § 7 oder § 7a über die Zahlung eines Mindestentgelts oder die Einziehung von Beiträgen und die Gewährung von Leistungen im Zusammenhang mit Urlaubsansprüchen auf das Arbeitsverhältnis Anwendung finden, ist der Arbeitgeber verpflichtet, Beginn, Ende und Dauer der täglichen Arbeits-

5. the surname, first names and address in Germany of one or an authorised representative of the lender for service of process,

6. the sector to which the workers are to be posted, and

7. surname, first name or company name and address of the lender

²Paragraph 1 sentence 3 shall apply accordingly.

(4) The borrower shall enclose with the application an assurance by the lender that the latter will comply with his obligations under Section 8.

(5) The Federal Ministry of Finance may, by statutory order, in agreement with the Federal Ministry of Labour and Social Affairs, determine, without the consent of the Bundesrat

1. that, by what means and under what technical and organisational conditions a notification, notification of change and insurance can be transmitted electronically in derogation of paragraph 1, sentences 1 and 3, paragraphs 2 and 3, sentences 1 and 2 and paragraph 4

2. under which conditions a notification of change can exceptionally be omitted, and

3. how the notification procedure can be simplified or modified if the posted workers are to be used in the context of a regularly recurring work or service or if other specific features of the work or services to be provided require this.

(6) The Federal Ministry of Finance may, by statutory order without the consent of the Bundesrat, designate the competent authority under subsection 1, first sentence, and subsection 3, first sentence.

Section 19
Creating and Keeping Documents Ready

(1) ¹Insofar as the legal provisions of a collective agreement which has been declared universally applicable under section 4(1)(1), the first sentence of section 5(1)(1) to (4) and section 6(2) or a corresponding statutory instrument under section 7 or section 7a concerning the payment of a minimum wage or the collection of contributions and the granting of benefits in connection with holiday entitlements apply to the employment relationship the employer is obliged to record the beginning, end and dura-

zeit der Arbeitnehmer und Arbeitnehmerinnen spätestens bis zum Ablauf des siebten auf den Tag der Arbeitsleistung folgenden Kalendertages aufzuzeichnen und diese Aufzeichnungen mindestens zwei Jahre beginnend ab dem für die Aufzeichnung maßgeblichen Zeitpunkt aufzubewahren. [2]Satz 1 gilt entsprechend für einen Entleiher, dem ein Verleiher einen Arbeitnehmer oder eine Arbeitnehmerin oder mehrere Arbeitnehmer oder Arbeitnehmerinnen zur Arbeitsleistung überlässt.

(2) [1]Jeder Arbeitgeber ist verpflichtet, die für die Kontrolle der Einhaltung eines für allgemeinverbindlich erklärten Tarifvertrages nach § 4 Absatz 1 Nummer 1, § 5 Satz 1 Nummer 1 bis 4 und § 6 Absatz 2 oder einer entsprechenden Rechtsverordnung nach § 7 oder § 7a erforderlichen Unterlagen im Inland für die gesamte Dauer der tatsächlichen Beschäftigung der Arbeitnehmer und Arbeitnehmerinnen im Geltungsbereich dieses Gesetzes, mindestens für die Dauer der gesamten Werk- oder Dienstleistung, insgesamt jedoch nicht länger als zwei Jahre in deutscher Sprache bereitzuhalten. [2]Auf Verlangen der Prüfbehörde sind die Unterlagen auch am Ort der Beschäftigung bereitzuhalten, bei Bauleistungen auf der Baustelle.

(3) Das Bundesministerium für Arbeit und Soziales kann durch Rechtsverordnung ohne Zustimmung des Bundesrates die Verpflichtungen des Arbeitgebers oder eines Entleihers nach § 18 und den Absätzen 1 und 2 hinsichtlich einzelner Branchen oder Gruppen von Arbeitnehmern und Arbeitnehmerinnen einschränken.

(4) Das Bundesministerium der Finanzen kann durch Rechtsverordnung im Einvernehmen mit dem Bundesministerium für Arbeit und Soziales ohne Zustimmung des Bundesrates bestimmen, wie die Verpflichtung des Arbeitgebers, die tägliche Arbeitszeit bei ihm beschäftigter Arbeitnehmer und Arbeitnehmerinnen aufzuzeichnen und diese Aufzeichnungen aufzubewahren, vereinfacht oder abgewandelt werden kann, sofern Besonderheiten der zu erbringenden Werk- oder Dienstleistungen oder Besonderheiten der Branche dies erfordern.

§ 20
Zusammenarbeit der in- und ausländischen Behörden

(1) Die Behörden der Zollverwaltung unterrichten die zuständigen örtlichen Landesfinanzbehörden über Meldungen nach § 18 Abs. 1 und 3.

tion of the daily working time of employees no later than the end of the seventh calendar day following the day of performance of work, and to keep these records for at least two years from the date relevant for the recording. [2]Sentence 1 shall apply mutatis mutandis to a hirer to whom a lender provides one or more workers for the performance of work.

(2) [1]Every employer shall be obliged to keep available in German the documents necessary for checking compliance with a collective agreement declared universally applicable under section 4(1), point 1, section 5, first sentence, points 1 to 4 and section 6(2) or a corresponding statutory instrument under section 7 or section 7a for the entire duration of the actual employment of the employees within the scope of this Act, at least for the duration of the entire work or service, but not more than two years in total. [2]At the request of the inspection authority, the documents shall also be kept available at the place of employment, in the case of construction work on the construction site.

(3) The Federal Ministry of Labour and Social Affairs may by statutory order without the consent of the Bundesrat restrict the obligations of the employer or a hirer under section 18 and subsections 1 and 2 with regard to individual sectors or groups of employees.

(4) The Federal Ministry of Finance may determine by statutory instrument, in agreement with the Federal Ministry of Labour and Social Affairs and without the consent of the Bundesrat, how the employer's obligation to record the daily working hours of employees employed by it and to keep such records may be simplified or modified, if special features of the work or services to be provided or special features of the industry so require.

Section 20
Cooperation between Domestic and Foreign Authorities

(1) The customs authorities shall inform the competent local state financial authorities of notifications under section 18(1) and (3).

(2) ¹Die Behörden der Zollverwaltung und die übrigen in § 2 des Schwarzarbeitsbekämpfungsgesetzes genannten Behörden dürfen nach Maßgabe der datenschutzrechtlichen Vorschriften auch mit Behörden anderer Vertragsstaaten des Abkommens über den Europäischen Wirtschaftsraum zusammenarbeiten, die diesem Gesetz entsprechende Aufgaben durchführen oder für die Bekämpfung illegaler Beschäftigung zuständig sind oder Auskünfte geben können, ob ein Arbeitgeber seine Verpflichtungen nach § 8 erfüllt. ²Die Regelungen über die internationale Rechtshilfe in Strafsachen bleiben hiervon unberührt.

(3) Die Behörden der Zollverwaltung unterrichten das Gewerbezentralregister über rechtskräftige Bußgeldentscheidungen nach § 23 Abs. 1 bis 3, sofern die Geldbuße mehr als zweihundert Euro beträgt.

§ 21
Ausschluss von der Vergabe öffentlicher Aufträge

(1) ¹Von der Teilnahme an einem Wettbewerb um einen Liefer-, Bau- oder Dienstleistungsauftrag der in §§ 99 und 100 des Gesetzes gegen Wettbewerbsbeschränkungen genannten Auftraggeber sollen Bewerber oder Bewerberinnen für eine angemessene Zeit bis zur nachgewiesenen Wiederherstellung ihrer Zuverlässigkeit ausgeschlossen werden, die wegen eines Verstoßes nach § 23 mit einer Geldbuße von wenigstens zweitausendfünfhundert Euro belegt worden sind. ²Das Gleiche gilt auch schon vor Durchführung eines Bußgeldverfahrens, wenn im Einzelfall angesichts der Beweislage kein vernünftiger Zweifel an einer schwerwiegenden Verfehlung im Sinne des Satzes 1 besteht.

(2) Die für die Verfolgung oder Ahndung der Ordnungswidrigkeiten nach § 23 zuständigen Behörden dürfen öffentlichen Auftraggebern nach § 99 des Gesetzes gegen Wettbewerbsbeschränkungen und solchen Stellen, die von öffentlichen Auftraggebern zugelassene Präqualifikationsverzeichnisse oder Unternehmer- und Lieferantenverzeichnisse führen, auf Verlangen die erforderlichen Auskünfte geben.

(3) ¹Öffentliche Auftraggeber nach Absatz 2 fordern im Rahmen ihrer Tätigkeit beim Gewerbezentralregister Auskünfte über rechtskräftige Bußgeldentscheidungen wegen einer Ordnungswidrigkeit nach § 23 Abs. 1 oder 2 an oder verlangen von Bewerbern oder Bewerberinnen eine Erklärung, dass die Voraussetzungen für einen Ausschluss nach Absatz 1 nicht vorliegen. ²Im Falle einer Erklärung des Bewerbers oder der Bewerberin können öffentliche

(2) ¹The authorities of the customs administration and the other authorities referred to in section 2 of the Act to Combat Illegal Employment may, in accordance with the provisions of data protection law, also cooperate with authorities of other states party to the Agreement on the European Economic Area which carry out tasks corresponding to this Act or which are responsible for combating illegal employment or may provide information as to whether an employer is fulfilling its obligations under section 8. ²The provisions on international mutual assistance in criminal matters shall remain unaffected by this.

(3) The authorities of the customs administration shall inform the Central Trade Register of legally binding decisions on fines in accordance with Section 23 (1) to (3) if the fine is more than two hundred euros.

Section 21
Exclusion from the Award of Public Contracts

(1) ¹Candidates who have been fined at least two thousand five hundred euros for an infringement under section 23 shall be excluded from participation in a competition for a supply, works or service contract of the contracting entities referred to in sections 99 and 100 of the Act against Restraints of Competition for a reasonable period of time until proven good repute has been restored. ²The same applies even before fine proceedings are conducted if, in the individual case, there is no reasonable doubt in the light of the evidence as to serious misconduct within the meaning of the first sentence.

(2) The authorities responsible for the prosecution or punishment of administrative offences under section 23 may, on request, provide the necessary information to public contracting authorities under section 99 of the Act against Restraints of Competition and to such bodies which maintain prequalification lists or lists of contractors and suppliers approved by public contracting authorities.

(3) ¹Contracting authorities under subsection (2) shall, within the scope of their activities, request information from the central trade register on final and absolute decisions imposing fines for an administrative offence under section 23(1) or (2) or require candidates to declare that the conditions for exclusion under subsection (1) are not met. ²In the event of a declaration by the applicant, contracting authorities under subsection 2 may at any time request

Auftraggeber nach Absatz 2 jederzeit zusätzlich Auskünfte des Gewerbezentralregisters nach § 150a der Gewerbeordnung anfordern.

(4) Bei Aufträgen ab einer Höhe von 30 000 Euro fordert der öffentliche Auftraggeber nach Absatz 2 für den Bewerber oder die Bewerberin, der oder die den Zuschlag erhalten soll, vor der Zuschlagserteilung eine Auskunft aus dem Gewerbezentralregister nach § 150a der Gewerbeordnung an.

(5) Vor der Entscheidung über den Ausschluss ist der Bewerber oder die Bewerberin zu hören.

additional information from the Central Trade Register under section 150a of the Trade Code.

(4) In the case of contracts with a value of EUR 30,000 or more, the contracting authority under subsection 2 shall request information from the central trade register under section 150a of the Gewerbeordnung on behalf of the candidate who is to be awarded the contract before the contract is awarded.

(5) The candidate shall be heard before the decision on exclusion.

§ 22
[aufgehoben]

Section 22
[omitted]

§ 23
Bußgeldvorschriften

(1) Ordnungswidrig handelt, wer vorsätzlich oder fahrlässig

1. entgegen § 8 Abs. 1 Satz 1 oder Abs. 3 eine dort genannte Arbeitsbedingung nicht oder nicht rechtzeitig gewährt oder einen Beitrag nicht oder nicht rechtzeitig leistet,

2. entgegen § 17 Satz 1 in Verbindung mit § 5 Abs. 1 Satz 1 Nummer 1 oder 3 des Schwarzarbeitsbekämpfungsgesetzes eine Prüfung nicht duldet oder bei einer Prüfung nicht mitwirkt,

3. entgegen § 17 Satz 1 in Verbindung mit § 5 Abs. 1 Satz 1 Nummer 2 des Schwarzarbeitsbekämpfungsgesetzes das Betreten eines Grundstücks oder Geschäftsraums nicht duldet,

4. entgegen § 17 Satz 1 in Verbindung mit § 5 Absatz 5 Satz 1 des Schwarzarbeitsbekämpfungsgesetzes Daten nicht, nicht richtig, nicht vollständig, nicht in der vorgeschriebenen Weise oder nicht rechtzeitig übermittelt,

5. entgegen § 18 Abs. 1 Satz 1 oder Abs. 3 Satz 1 eine Anmeldung nicht, nicht richtig, nicht vollständig, nicht in der vorgeschriebenen Weise oder nicht rechtzeitig vorlegt oder nicht, nicht richtig, nicht vollständig, nicht in der vorgeschriebenen Weise oder nicht rechtzeitig zuleitet,

Section 23
Fines regulations

(1) It is an administrative offence to deliberately or negligently

1. in contravention of section 8 (1), first sentence, or (3), fails to grant a working condition specified therein or fails to grant it in time or fails to pay a contribution in time or at all

2. in contravention of section 17, first sentence, in conjunction with section 5(1), first sentence, points 1 or 3 of the Schwarzarbeitsbekämpfungsgesetz (Law to Combat undeclared work), does not tolerate an examination or does not cooperate in an examination

3. contrary to section 17, first sentence, in conjunction with section 5(1), first sentence, no. 2 of the Schwarzarbeitsbekämpfungsgesetz (Law to Combat undeclared work), does not tolerate the entry into a property or business premises

4. in contravention of section 17, first sentence, in conjunction with section 5(5), first sentence, of the Schwarzarbeitsbekämpfungsgesetz, fails to transmit data or to do so correctly, completely, in the prescribed manner or in good time

5. in contravention of section 18(1), first sentence, or (3), first sentence, fails to submit an application, fails to submit it correctly, fails to submit it completely, fails to submit it in the prescribed manner or fails to submit it in time, or fails to submit it correctly, fails to submit it completely, fails to submit it in the prescribed manner or fails to submit it in time

6. entgegen § 18 Abs. 1 Satz 3, auch in Verbindung mit Absatz 3 Satz 2, eine Änderungsmeldung nicht, nicht richtig, nicht vollständig, nicht in der vorgeschriebenen Weise oder nicht rechtzeitig macht,

7. entgegen § 18 Abs. 2 oder 4 eine Versicherung nicht, nicht richtig oder nicht rechtzeitig beifügt,

8. entgegen § 19 Absatz 1 Satz 1, auch in Verbindung mit Satz 2, eine Aufzeichnung nicht, nicht richtig, nicht vollständig oder nicht rechtzeitig erstellt oder nicht oder nicht mindestens zwei Jahre aufbewahrt oder

9. entgegen § 19 Abs. 2 eine Unterlage nicht, nicht richtig, nicht vollständig oder nicht in der vorgeschriebenen Weise bereithält.

(2) Ordnungswidrig handelt, wer Werk- oder Dienstleistungen in erheblichem Umfang ausführen lässt, indem er als Unternehmer einen anderen Unternehmer beauftragt, von dem er weiß oder fahrlässig nicht weiß, dass dieser bei der Erfüllung dieses Auftrags

1. entgegen § 8 Abs. 1 Satz 1 oder Abs. 3 eine dort genannte Arbeitsbedingung nicht oder nicht rechtzeitig gewährt oder einen Beitrag nicht oder nicht rechtzeitig leistet oder

2. einen Nachunternehmer einsetzt oder zulässt, dass ein Nachunternehmer tätig wird, der entgegen § 8 Abs. 1 Satz 1 oder Abs. 3 eine dort genannte Arbeitsbedingung nicht oder nicht rechtzeitig gewährt oder einen Beitrag nicht oder nicht rechtzeitig leistet.

(3) Die Ordnungswidrigkeit kann in den Fällen des Absatzes 1 Nr. 1 und des Absatzes 2 mit einer Geldbuße bis zu fünfhunderttausend Euro, in den übrigen Fällen mit einer Geldbuße bis zu dreißigtausend Euro geahndet werden.

(4) Verwaltungsbehörden im Sinne des § 36 Abs. 1 Nr. 1 des Gesetzes über Ordnungswidrigkeiten sind die in § 16 genannten Behörden jeweils für ihren Geschäftsbereich.

(5) Für die Vollstreckung zugunsten der Behörden des Bundes und der bundesunmittelbaren juristischen Personen des öffentlichen Rechts sowie für die Vollziehung des Vermögensarrestes nach § 111e der Strafprozessordnung in Verbindung mit § 46 des Gesetzes über Ordnungswidrigkeiten durch die in § 16 genannten Behörden gilt das Verwaltungs-Vollstreckungsgesetz des Bundes.

6. contrary to section 18 subsection (1), third sentence, also in conjunction with subsection (3), second sentence, fails to make a notification of amendment, or fails to do so correctly, completely, in the prescribed manner or in good time

7. contrary to § 18 (2) or (4), fails to attach an insurance policy, fails to attach it correctly or does not attach it in time,

8. in contravention of section 19 subsection (1) first sentence, also in conjunction with sentence 2, fails to make a recording or to do so correctly, completely or in good time or fails to retain it or retain it for at least two years or

9. contrary to section 19 subsection (2), fails to provide a document, or provides it incorrectly, incompletely or not in the prescribed manner

(2) Acts in an administrative offence, has work or services carried out to a considerable extent by commissioning another contractor of whom he knows or negligently does not know that this contractor, in the performance of this contract

1. contrary to section 8 subsection (1), first sentence, or subsection (3), fails to grant a condition of employment specified therein or fails to grant it in time or fails to pay a contribution in time, or

2. employs or permits a subcontractor to employ a subcontractor who, contrary to section 8 (1) sentence 1 or (3), does not grant a working condition specified therein or does not grant it in time or does not make a contribution or does not do so in time

(3) The administrative offence may be punishable by a fine of up to five hundred thousand euros in the cases of subsection 1 No. 1 and subsection 2 and by a fine of up to thirty thousand euros in the other cases.

(4) Administrative authorities within the meaning of section 36(1)(1) of the Administrative Offences Act shall be the authorities referred to in section 16, each for its area of responsibility.

(5) Enforcement for the benefit of the authorities of the Federation and the federal direct legal entities under public law as well as the enforcement of property arrest pursuant to section 111e of the Code of Criminal Procedure in conjunction with section 46 of the Act on Administrative Offences by the authorities named in section 16 shall be governed by the Federal Administrative Enforcement Act.

§ 24
Evaluation

Die nach § 7 festgesetzten Mindestentgeltsätze sind im Hinblick auf ihre Beschäftigungswirkungen, insbesondere auf sozialversicherungspflichtige Beschäftigung sowie die Schaffung angemessener Mindestarbeitsbedingungen, fünf Jahre nach Inkrafttreten des Gesetzes zu überprüfen.

§ 24a
[aufgehoben]

§ 25
Übergangsregelung

[1]Auf eine vor dem 29. November 2019 berufene Kommission sind § 11 Absatz 1, § 12 Absatz 1 bis 6 und § 12a nicht anwendbar. [2]§ 12 Absatz 8 ist nur insoweit anwendbar, als die jeweiligen Mitglieder ab dem 29. November 2019 ausscheiden und nach § 12 Absatz 7 benannt werden. [3]Auf diese Kommission sind § 11 Absatz 1 und § 12 in der bis zum Ablauf des 28. November 2019 geltenden Fassung anwendbar.

Section 24
Evaluation

The minimum wage rates set in accordance with section 7 shall be reviewed five years after the Act enters into force with regard to their effects on employment, in particular on employment subject to social security contributions and the creation of appropriate minimum working conditions.

Section 24a
[omitted]

Section 25
Transitional Arrangements

[1]Sections 11(1), 12(1) to (6) and 12a shall not apply to a commission appointed before 29 November 2019. [2]Section 12(8) shall apply only to the extent that the respective members resign from 29 November 2019 and are appointed in accordance with section 12(7). [3]Sections 11(1) and 12 shall apply to this Commission in the version in force until the end of 28 November 2019.

VII. Home Employment Act

Heimarbeitsgesetz (HAG)

Stand: 20.11.2019

§ 1
Geltungsbereich

(1) In Heimarbeit Beschäftigte sind

(a) die Heimarbeiter (§ 2 Abs. 1);
(b) die Hausgewerbetreibenden (§ 2 Abs. 2).

(2) ¹Ihnen können, wenn dieses wegen ihrer Schutzbedürftigkeit gerechtfertigt erscheint, gleichgestellt werden

(a) Personen, die in der Regel allein oder mit ihren Familienangehörigen (§ 2 Abs. 5) in eigener Wohnung oder selbstgewählter Betriebsstätte eine sich in regelmäßigen Arbeitsvorgängen wiederholende Arbeit im Auftrage eines anderen gegen Entgelt ausüben, ohne daß ihre Tätigkeit als gewerblich anzusehen oder daß der Auftraggeber ein Gewerbetreibender oder Zwischenmeister (§ 2 Abs. 3) ist;
(b) Hausgewerbetreibende, die mit mehr als zwei fremden Hilfskräften (§ 2 Abs. 6) oder Heimarbeitern (§ 2 Abs. 1) arbeiten;

(c) andere im Lohnauftrag arbeitende Gewerbetreibende, die infolge ihrer wirtschaftlichen Abhängigkeit eine ähnliche Stellung wie Hausgewerbetreibende einnehmen;
(d) Zwischenmeister (§ 2 Abs. 3).

²Für die Feststellung der Schutzbedürftigkeit ist das Ausmaß der wirtschaftlichen Abhängigkeit maßgebend. ³Dabei sind insbesondere die Zahl der fremden Hilfskräfte, die Abhängigkeit von einem oder mehreren Auftraggebern, die Möglichkeiten des unmittelbaren Zugangs zum Absatzmarkt, die Höhe und die Art der Eigeninvestitionen sowie der Umsatz zu berücksichtigen.

Section 1
Scope of Application

(1) Employees working from home are

(a) home workers (section 2 (1));
(b) the home-based tradesmen (section 2 subsection 2).

(2) ¹The following may be treated in the same way as home workers if this appears justified by their need for protection

(a) Persons who, as a rule, alone or with members of their family (section 2, Subsection 5), in their own home or self-chosen place of business, carry out work which is repeated in regular work processes on behalf of another person for remuneration, without their activity being regarded as commercial or without the principal being a trader or intermediate master (Section 2, Subsection 3);
(b) domestic craftsmen who work with more than two external auxiliary workers (section 2, subsection 6) or home workers (section 2, subsection 1);

(c) other professionals working on a subcontracting basis who, because of their economic dependence, occupy a position similar to that of home-based professionals;
(d) intermediate master craftsmen (section 2, paragraph 3).

²The extent of economic dependence is decisive for determining the need for protection. In particular, the number of external auxiliary staff, the dependence on one or more clients, the possibilities of direct access to the sales market, the amount and type of own investments and turnover must be taken into account.

(3) ¹Die Gleichstellung erstreckt sich, wenn in ihr nichts anderes bestimmt ist, auf die allgemeinen Schutzvorschriften und die Vorschriften über die Entgeltregelung, den Entgeltschutz und die Auskunftspflicht über Entgelte (Dritter, Sechster, Siebenter und Achter Abschnitt). ²Die Gleichstellung kann auf einzelne dieser Vorschriften beschränkt oder auf weitere Vorschriften des Gesetzes ausgedehnt werden. ³Sie kann für bestimmte Personengruppen oder Gewerbezweige oder Beschäftigungsarten allgemein oder räumlich begrenzt ergehen; auch bestimmte einzelne Personen können gleichgestellt werden.

(4) ¹Die Gleichstellung erfolgt durch widerrufliche Entscheidung des zuständigen Heimarbeitsausschusses (§ 4) nach Anhörung der Beteiligten. ²Sie ist vom Vorsitzenden zu unterschreiben und bedarf der Zustimmung der zuständigen Arbeitsbehörde (§ 3 Abs. 1) und der Veröffentlichung im Wortlaut an der von der zuständigen Arbeitsbehörde bestimmten Stelle. ³Sie tritt am Tage nach der Veröffentlichung in Kraft, wenn in ihr nicht ein anderer Zeitpunkt bestimmt ist. ⁴Die Veröffentlichung kann unterbleiben, wenn die Gleichstellung nur bestimmte einzelne Personen betrifft; in diesem Falle ist in der Gleichstellung der Zeitpunkt ihres Inkrafttretens festzusetzen.

(5) ¹Besteht ein Heimarbeitsausschuß für den Gewerbezweig oder die Beschäftigungsart nicht, so entscheidet über die Gleichstellung die zuständige Arbeitsbehörde nach Anhörung der Beteiligten. ²Die Entscheidung ergeht unter Mitwirkung der zuständigen Gewerkschaften und Vereinigungen der Auftraggeber, soweit diese zur Mitwirkung bereit sind. ³Die Vorschriften des Absatzes 4 über die Veröffentlichung und das Inkrafttreten finden entsprechende Anwendung.

(6) Gleichgestellte haben bei Entgegennahme von Heimarbeit auf Befragen des Auftraggebers ihre Gleichstellung bekanntzugeben.

§ 2
Begriffe

(2) ¹Hausgewerbetreibender im Sinne dieses Gesetzes ist, wer in eigener Arbeitsstätte (eigener Wohnung oder Betriebsstätte) mit nicht mehr als zwei fremden Hilfskräften (Absatz 6) oder Heimarbeitern (Absatz 1) im Auftrag von Gewerbetreibenden oder Zwischenmeistern Waren herstellt, bearbeitet oder verpackt, wobei er selbst wesentlich am Stück mitarbeitet, jedoch die Verwertung der Arbeitsergebnisse dem unmittelbar oder mittelbar auftraggebenden Gewerbetreibenden überläßt. ²Beschafft der Hausgewerbetreibende

(3) ¹Unless otherwise provided for, equality of treatment shall extend to the general rules on protection and the rules on remuneration, protection of remuneration and the obligation to provide information on remuneration (sections three, six, seven and eight). ²Equal treatment may be limited to some of these provisions or extended to other provisions of the Act. ³It may be general or geographically limited to certain groups of persons or branches of industry or types of employment; certain individual persons may also be treated equally.

(4) ¹Equality shall be achieved by revocable decision of the competent homework committee (section 4) after hearing the parties involved. ²It shall be signed by the chairperson and shall require the approval of the competent employment authority (section 3 subsection (1)) and publication in the wording at the place determined by the competent employment authority. ³It shall enter into force on the day following publication, unless it specifies a different date. ⁴Publication may be omitted if the equivalence only affects certain individual persons; in this case, the date of its entry into force shall be specified in the equivalence.

(5) ¹In the absence of a homeworking committee for the branch of industry or type of employment, the competent labour authority shall decide on equal treatment after consulting the parties concerned. ²The decision shall be taken with the participation of the competent trade unions and associations of the contracting authorities, insofar as they are prepared to participate. ³The provisions of paragraph 4 on publication and entry into force shall apply accordingly.

(6) Persons of equal standing must, on receipt of homework, make known their equal status when questioned by the employer.

Section 2
Terms

(2) ¹A cottage industry operator within the meaning of this Act is someone who manufactures, processes or packages goods in his own place of work (his own home or business premises) with no more than two external auxiliary workers (subsection 6) or home workers (subsection 1) on behalf of tradesmen or intermediate master craftsmen, whereby he himself contributes substantially to the work, but leaves the exploitation of the results of the work to the tradesman who directly or indirectly places the order.

die Roh- und Hilfsstoffe selbst oder arbeitet er vorübergehend unmittelbar für den Absatzmarkt, so wird hierdurch seine Eigenschaft als Hausgewerbetreibender nicht beeinträchtigt.

(3) Zwischenmeister im Sinne dieses Gesetzes ist, wer, ohne Arbeitnehmer zu sein, die ihm von Gewerbetreibenden übertragene Arbeit an Heimarbeiter oder Hausgewerbetreibende weitergibt.

(4) Die Eigenschaft als Heimarbeiter, Hausgewerbetreibender und Zwischenmeister ist auch dann gegeben, wenn Personen, Personenvereinigungen oder Körperschaften des privaten oder öffentlichen Rechts, welche die Herstellung, Bearbeitung oder Verpackung von Waren nicht zum Zwecke der Gewinnerzielung betreiben, die Auftraggeber sind.

(5) Als Familienangehörige im Sinne dieses Gesetzes gelten, wenn sie Mitglieder der häuslichen Gemeinschaft sind:

(a) Ehegatten und Lebenspartner der in Heimarbeit Beschäftigten (§ 1 Abs. 1) oder der nach § 1 Abs. 2 Buchstabe a Gleichgestellten;

(b) Personen, die mit dem in Heimarbeit Beschäftigten oder nach § 1 Abs. 2 Buchstabe a Gleichgestellten oder deren Ehegatten oder Lebenspartner bis zum dritten Grade verwandt oder verschwägert sind;

(c) Mündel, Betreute und Pflegekinder des in Heimarbeit Beschäftigten oder nach § 1 Absatz 2 Buchstabe a Gleichgestellten oder deren Ehegatten oder Lebenspartner sowie Mündel, Betreute und Pflegekinder des Ehegatten oder Lebenspartners des in Heimarbeit Beschäftigten oder nach § 1 Absatz 2 Buchstabe a Gleichgestellten.

(6) Fremde Hilfskraft im Sinne dieses Gesetzes ist, wer als Arbeitnehmer eines Hausgewerbetreibenden oder nach § 1 Abs. 2 Buchstaben b und c Gleichgestellten in deren Arbeitsstätte beschäftigt ist.

§ 3
Zuständige Arbeitsbehhörde

(1) [1]Zuständige Arbeitsbehörde im Sinne dieses Gesetzes ist die Oberste Arbeitsbehörde des Landes. [2]Für Angelegenheiten (§§ 1, 4, 5, 11, 19 und 22), die nach Umfang, Auswirkung oder Bedeutung den Zuständigkeitsbereich mehrerer Länder umfassen, wird die Zuständigkeit durch die Obersten Arbeitsbehörden der beteiligten Länder nach näherer Vereinbarung gemeinsam im Einvernehmen mit dem Bundesministerium für Arbeit und Soziales wahrgenommen. [3]Be-

[2]If the cottage industry trader procures the raw materials and supplies himself or temporarily works directly for the sales market, this does not affect his status as a cottage industry trader.

(3) An intermediate master within the meaning of this Act is anyone who, without being an employee, passes on the work entrusted to him by tradesmen to homeworkers or cottage industries.

(4) The status of homeworker, cottage trader and intermediate master shall also be deemed to exist where persons, associations of persons or bodies governed by private or public law which do not engage in the manufacture, processing or packaging of goods for profit are the contracting authorities.

(5) Family members within the meaning of this Act shall be deemed to be family members if they are members of the domestic community:

(a) Spouses and life partners of persons employed in homework (section 1 subsection 1) or of persons treated as such pursuant to section 1 subsection 2 letter a;

(b) Persons who are related or in-lawed up to the third degree to the homeworker or person treated as equivalent under section 1 subsection 2 letter a or their spouse or partner;

(c) wards, foster children and foster children of the home-based employee or persons treated as such in accordance with section 1 subsection 2 letter a or their spouses or life partners as well as wards, foster children and foster children of the spouse or life partner of the home-based employee or persons treated as such in accordance with section 1 subsection 2 letter a.

(6) Within the meaning of this Act, a foreign auxiliary staff member shall be deemed to be a person employed as an employee of a domestic craftsman or persons treated as such pursuant to section 1 subsection 2 letters b and c in their place of work.

Section 3
Competent Labour Authority

(1) [1]The competent labour authority within the meaning of this Act shall be the Supreme Labour Authority of the country. [2]For matters (Sections 1, 4, 5, 11, 19 and 22) which, in terms of their scope, impact or significance, cover the area of responsibility of several Länder, responsibility is exercised by the supreme labour authorities of the Länder involved, after closer agreement, jointly in agreement with the Federal Ministry of Labour and Social Affairs. [3]If

trifft eine Angelegenheit nach Umfang, Auswirkung oder Bedeutung das gesamte Bundesgebiet oder kommt eine Vereinbarung nach Satz 2 nicht zustande, so ist das Bundesministerium für Arbeit und Soziales zuständig.

(2) ¹Den Obersten Arbeitsbehörden der Länder und den von ihnen bestimmten Stellen obliegt die Aufsicht über die Durchführung dieses Gesetzes. ²Die Vorschriften des § 139b der Gewerbordnung über die Aufsicht gelten für die Befugnisse der mit der Aufsicht über die Durchführung dieses Gesetzes beauftragten Stellen auch hinsichtlich der Arbeitsstätten der in Heimarbeit Beschäftigten entsprechend.

§ 4
Heimarbeitsausschüsse

(1) ¹Die zuständige Arbeitsbehörde errichtet zur Wahrnehmung der in den §§ 1, 10, 11, 18 und 19 genannten Aufgaben Heimarbeitsausschüsse für die Gewerbezweige und Beschäftigungsarten, in denen Heimarbeit in nennenswertem Umfang geleistet wird. ²Erfordern die unterschiedlichen Verhältnisse innerhalb eines Gewerbezweiges gesonderte Regelungen auf einzelnen Gebieten, so sind zu diesem Zweck jeweils besondere Heimarbeitsausschüsse zu errichten. ³Die Heimarbeitsausschüsse können innerhalb ihres sachlichen Zuständigkeitsbereichs Unterausschüsse bilden, wenn dies erforderlich erscheint. ⁴Für Heimarbeit, für die nach den Sätzen 1 und 2 dieses Absatzes Heimarbeitsausschüsse nicht errichtet werden, ist ein gemeinsamer Heimarbeitsausschuß zu errichten.

(2) ¹Der Heimarbeitsausschuß besteht aus je drei Beisitzern aus Kreisen der Auftraggeber und Beschäftigten seines Zuständigkeitsbereichs und einem von der zuständigen Arbeitsbehörde bestimmten Vorsitzenden. ²Weitere sachkundige Personen können zugezogen werden; sie haben kein Stimmrecht. ³Die Beisitzer haben Stellvertreter, für die Satz 1 entsprechend gilt.

(3) ¹Der Heimarbeitsausschuß ist beschlußfähig, wenn außer dem Vorsitzenden mindestens mehr als die Hälfte der Beisitzer anwesend sind. ²Die Beschlüsse des Heimarbeitsausschusses bedürfen der Mehrheit der Stimmen seiner anwesenden Mitglieder. ³Bei der Beschlußfassung hat sich der Vorsitzende zunächst der Stimme zu enthalten; kommt eine Stimmenmehrheit nicht zustande, so übt nach weiterer Beratung der Vorsitzende sein Stimmrecht aus.

a matter concerns the entire Federal Republic of Germany in terms of its scope, impact or significance, or if an agreement pursuant to sentence 2 is not reached, the Federal Ministry of Labour and Social Affairs is responsible.

(2) ¹The supreme labour authorities of the Länder and the bodies designated by them shall be responsible for supervising the implementation of this Act. ²The provisions of section 139b of the Trade and Industry Code on supervision shall apply mutatis mutandis to the powers of the bodies entrusted with the supervision of the implementation of this Act, including those relating to the workplaces of homeworkers.

Section 4
Home Employment Committees

(1) ¹The competent employment authority shall set up homework committees for the branches of trade and types of employment in which homework is carried out to a considerable extent in order to perform the tasks specified in sections 1, 10, 11, 18 and 19. ²If the different conditions within a branch of industry require separate regulations in individual areas, special homework committees must be set up for this purpose. ³The homeworking committees may form subcommittees within their area of responsibility if this appears necessary. ⁴For home work for which home work committees are not established in accordance with the first and second sentences of this paragraph, a joint home work committee shall be established.

(2) ¹The homeworking committee shall consist of three assessors from each of the contracting authorities and employees in its area of responsibility and a chairman appointed by the competent labour authority. ²Other competent persons may be called in; they shall not have the right to vote. ³The assessors shall have deputies to whom sentence 1 shall apply mutatis mutandis.

(3) ¹The homeworking committee shall have a quorum if at least more than half of the assessors are present in addition to the chairman. ²The decisions of the homeworking committee require a majority of the votes of its members present. ³When passing resolutions, the chairman must initially abstain from voting; if a majority of votes is not achieved, the chairman shall exercise his voting right after further discussion.

(4) ¹Der Heimarbeitsausschuß kann sonstige Bestimmungen über die Geschäftsführung in einer schriftlichen Geschäftsordnung treffen. ²Für die Beschlußfassung über die Geschäftsordnung gilt Absatz 3.

§ 5
Beisitzer

(1) ¹Als Beisitzer oder Stellvertreter werden von der zuständigen Arbeitsbehörde geeignete Personen unter Berücksichtigung der Gruppen der Beschäftigten (§ 1 Abs. 1 und 2) auf Grund von Vorschlägen der fachlich und räumlich zuständigen Gewerkschaften und Vereinigungen der Auftraggeber oder, soweit solche nicht bestehen oder keine Vorschläge einreichen, auf Grund von Vorschlägen der Zusammenschlüsse von Gewerkschaften und von Vereinigungen von Arbeitgebern (Spitzenorganisationen) für die Dauer von drei Jahren berufen. ²Soweit eine Spitzenorganisation keine Vorschläge einreicht, werden die Beisitzer oder Stellvertreter dieser Seite nach Anhörung geeigneter Personen aus den Kreisen der Auftraggeber oder Beschäftigten des Zuständigkeitsbereichs, für den der Heimarbeitsausschuß errichtet ist, berufen.

(2) Auf die Voraussetzungen für das Beisitzeramt, die Besonderheiten für Beisitzer aus Kreisen der Auftraggeber und der Beschäftigten, die Ablehnung des Beisitzeramtes und den Schutz der Beschäftigtenbeisitzer finden die für die ehrenamtlichen Richter der Arbeitsgerichte geltenden Vorschriften mit den sich aus Absatz 3 ergebenden Abweichungen entsprechend Anwendung.

(3) ¹Wird das Fehlen einer Voraussetzung für die Berufung nachträglich bekannt oder fällt eine Voraussetzung nachträglich fort oder verletzt ein Beisitzer gröblich seine Amtspflichten, so kann ihn die zuständige Arbeitsbehörde seines Amtes entheben. ²Über die Berechtigung zur Ablehnung des Beisitzeramtes entscheidet die zuständige Arbeitsbehörde.

(4) ¹Das Amt des Beisitzers ist ein Ehrenamt. ²Die Beisitzer erhalten eine angemessene Entschädigung für den ihnen aus der Wahrnehmung ihrer Tätigkeit erwachsenden Verdienstausfall und Aufwand sowie Ersatz der Fahrkosten entsprechend den für die ehrenamtlichen Richter der Arbeitsgerichte geltenden Vorschriften. ³Die Entschädigung und die erstattungsfähigen Fahrkosten setzt im Einzelfall der Vorsitzende des Heimarbeitsausschusses fest.

(4) ¹The homework committee may make other provisions concerning the management of the business in written rules of procedure. ²Paragraph 3 applies to the adoption of decisions on the rules of procedure.

Section 5
Assessor

(1) ¹Suitable persons shall be appointed as assessors or deputies by the competent labour authority for a period of three years, taking into account the groups of employees (section 1 subsections 1 and 2), on the basis of proposals from the trade unions and associations of employers with technical and geographical responsibility or, where these do not exist or do not submit proposals, on the basis of proposals from the unions and associations of employers (umbrella organisations). ²If an umbrella organisation does not submit proposals, the assessors or deputies of this side will be appointed after hearing suitable persons from the circles of the contracting authorities or employees in the area of competence for which the homeworking committee is established.

(2) The provisions applicable to honorary judges of labour courts shall apply mutatis mutandis to the requirements for the office of assessor, the special features for assessors from circles of the clients and employees, the refusal of the office of assessor and the protection of employee assessors, with the deviations resulting from subsection 3.

(3) ¹If the absence of a prerequisite for the appointment becomes known subsequently or if a prerequisite subsequently ceases to apply or if an assessor grossly violates his official duties, the competent labour authority may relieve him of his office. ²The competent labour authority shall decide on the entitlement to refuse the assessor's office.

(4) ¹The office of observer is an honorary office. ²The assessors shall receive appropriate compensation for the loss of earnings and expenses incurred in the performance of their duties as well as reimbursement of travel expenses in accordance with the provisions applicable to honorary judges of the labour courts. ³The compensation and the reimbursable travel costs shall be determined in each individual case by the chairman of the homework committee.

§ 6
Listenführung

[1]Wer Heimarbeit ausgibt oder weitergibt, hat jeden, den er mit Heimarbeit beschäftigt oder dessen er sich zur Weitergabe von Heimarbeit bedient, in Listen auszuweisen. [2]Je drei Abschriften sind halbjährlich der Obersten Arbeitsbehörde des Landes oder der von ihr bestimmten Stelle einzusenden.

§ 7
Mitteilungspflicht

Wer erstmalig Personen mit Heimarbeit beschäftigen will, hat dies der Obersten Arbeitsbehörde des Landes oder der von ihr bestimmten Stelle mitzuteilen.

§ 7a
Unterrichtungspflicht

[1]Wer Heimarbeit ausgibt oder weitergibt, hat die Personen, die die Arbeit entgegennehmen, vor Aufnahme der Beschäftigung über die Art und Weise der zu verrichtenden Arbeit, die Unfall- und Gesundheitsgefahren, denen diese bei der Beschäftigung ausgesetzt sind, sowie über die Maßnahmen und Einrichtungen zur Abwendung dieser Gefahren zu unterrichten. [2]Der Auftraggeber hat sich von der Person, die von ihm Arbeit entgegennimmt, schriftlich bestätigen zu lassen, daß sie entsprechend dieser Vorschrift unterrichtet worden ist.

§ 8
Entgeltverzeichnisse

(1) [1]Wer Heimarbeit ausgibt oder abnimmt, hat in den Räumen der Ausgabe und Abnahme Entgeltverzeichnisse und Nachweise über die sonstigen Vertragsbedingungen offen auszulegen. [2]Soweit Musterbücher Verwendung finden, sind sie den Entgeltverzeichnissen beizufügen. [3]Wird Heimarbeit den Beschäftigten in die Wohnung oder Betriebsstätte gebracht, so hat der Auftraggeber dafür zu sorgen, daß das Entgeltverzeichnis zur Einsichtnahme vorgelegt wird.

(2) [1]Die Entgeltverzeichnisse müssen die Entgelte für jedes einzelne Arbeitsstück enthalten. [2]Die Preise für mitzuliefernde Roh- und Hilfsstoffe sind besonders auszuweisen. [3]Können die Entgelte für das einzelne Arbeitsstück nicht aufgeführt werden, so ist eine zuverlässige und klare Berechnungsgrundlage einzutragen.

Section 6
List Management

[1]Anyone who spends or passes on homework must identify in lists everyone whom he employs to work from home or whom he uses to pass on homework. [2]Three copies of each list must be sent to the Supreme Labour Authority of the country or to the body designated by it every six months.

Section 7
Notification Obligation

Anyone wishing to employ people working from home for the first time must notify the Supreme Labour Authority of the country or the body designated by it.

Section 7a
Information Obligation

[1]Anyone who dispenses or subcontracts home work must, before taking up employment, inform the persons who receive the work of the nature and type of work to be done, the accident and health risks to which they are exposed during employment and the measures and facilities to prevent these risks. [2]The contracting authority must obtain written confirmation from the person who takes up work from him that he has been informed in accordance with this provision.

Section 8
List of Remuneration

(1) [1]Anyone who dispenses or accepts homework must openly display lists of fees and proof of other contractual conditions on the premises where it is dispensed and accepted. [2]If sample books are used, they shall be attached to the payroll. [3]If home work is brought to the home or business premises of the employees, the customer shall ensure that the payroll is presented for inspection.

(2) [1]The payroll must contain the remuneration for each individual piece of work. [2]The prices of raw and auxiliary materials to be supplied must be shown separately. [3]If the charges for the individual piece of work cannot be listed, a reliable and clear basis for calculation shall be entered.

(3) ¹Bei Vorliegen einer Entgeltregelung gemäß den §§ 17 bis 19 ist diese auszulegen. ²Hierbei ist für die Übersichtlichkeit dadurch zu sorgen, daß nur der Teil der Entgeltregelung ausgelegt wird, der für die Beschäftigten in Betracht kommt.

(4) Die Vorschriften der Absätze 1 bis 3 gelten nicht für neue Muster, die als Einzelstücke erst auszuarbeiten sind.

§9
Entgeltbelege

(1) ¹Wer Heimarbeit ausgibt oder weitergibt, hat den Personen, welche die Arbeit entgegennehmen, auf seine Kosten Entgeltbücher für jeden Beschäftigten (§ 1 Abs. 1 und 2) auszuhändigen. ²In die Entgeltbücher, die bei den Beschäftigten verbleiben, sind bei jeder Ausgabe und Abnahme von Arbeit ihre Art und ihr Umfang, die Entgelte und die Tage der Ausgabe und der Lieferung einzutragen. ³Diese Vorschrift gilt nicht für neue Muster, die als Einzelstücke erst auszuarbeiten sind.

(2) An Stelle von Entgeltbüchern (Absatz 1) können auch Entgelt- oder Arbeitszettel mit den zu einer ordnungsmäßigen Sammlung geeigneten Heften ausgegeben werden, falls die Oberste Arbeitsbehörde des Landes oder die von ihr bestimmte Stelle dieses genehmigt hat.

(3) ¹Die in Heimarbeit Beschäftigten haben für die ordnungsmäßige Aufbewahrung der Entgeltbelege zu sorgen. ²Sie haben sie den von der Obersten Arbeitsbehörde des Landes bestimmten Stellen auf Verlangen vorzulegen. ³Diese Verpflichtung gilt auch für die Auftraggeber, in deren Händen sich die Entgeltbelege befinden.

§10
Schutz vor Zeitversäumnis

¹Wer Heimarbeit ausgibt oder abnimmt, hat dafür zu sorgen, daß unnötige Zeitversäumnis bei der Ausgabe oder Abnahme vermieden wird. ²Die Oberste Arbeitsbehörde des Landes oder die von ihr bestimmte Stelle kann im Benehmen mit dem Heimarbeitsausschuß die zur Vermeidung unnötiger Zeitversäumnis bei der Abfertigung erforderlichen Maßnahmen anordnen. ³Bei Anordnungen gegenüber einem einzelnen Auftraggeber kann die Beteiligung des Heimarbeitsausschusses unterbleiben.

§11
Verteilung der Heimarbeit

(1) Wer Heimarbeit an mehrere in Heimarbeit Beschäftigte ausgibt, soll die Arbeitsmenge auf die Beschäftigten gleichmäßig unter Berücksichtigung ihrer und ihrer Mitarbeiter Leistungsfähigkeit verteilen.

(3) ¹Where a fee regulation pursuant to sections 17 to 19 exists, it shall be interpreted. ²In this context, clarity shall be ensured by interpreting only that part of the remuneration scheme which is applicable to the employees.

(4) The provisions of subsections 1 to 3 shall not apply to new designs which are still to be developed as individual items.

Section 9
Remuneration Receipt

(1) ¹Anyone who dispenses or passes on homework shall, at his own expense, hand over pay books for each employee (section 1 (1) and (2)) to the persons who receive the work. ²In the pay books, which shall remain with the employees, the nature and extent of each issue and acceptance of work, the remuneration and the days of issue and delivery shall be entered. ³This provision does not apply to new samples which have to be prepared as individual items.

(2) Instead of pay books (paragraph 1), pay or work slips containing the booklets suitable for proper collection may also be issued if the Supreme Labour Authority of the Land or the body designated by it has approved this.

(3) ¹The homeworkers must ensure that the pay slips are properly stored. ²They must present them on request to the bodies designated by the supreme employment authority of the Land. ³This obligation shall also apply to the contracting authorities in whose hands the remuneration slips are kept.

Section 10
Protection against Time-Failure

¹Anyone who dispenses or accepts homework must ensure that unnecessary delays in dispensing or accepting it are avoided. ²The Supreme Labour Authority of the country or the body designated by it may, in consultation with the Homework Committee, order the necessary measures to avoid unnecessary delays in check-in. ³In the case of orders issued to a single client, the home work committee may not be involved.

Section 11
Distribution of Home-Employment

(1) Whoever distributes homework to several homeworkers shall distribute the workload equally among the employees, taking into account their and their employees' performance.

(2) [1]Der Heimarbeitsausschuß kann zur Beseitigung von Mißständen, die durch ungleichmäßige Verteilung der Heimarbeit entstehen, für einzelne Gewerbezweige oder Arten von Heimarbeit die Arbeitsmenge festsetzen, die für einen bestimmten Zeitraum auf einen Entgeltbeleg (§ 9) ausgegeben werden darf. [2]Die Arbeitsmenge ist so zu bemessen, daß sie durch eine vollwertige Arbeitskraft ohne Hilfskräfte in der für vergleichbare Betriebsarbeiter üblichen Arbeitszeit bewältigt werden kann. [3]Für jugendliche Heimarbeiter ist eine Arbeitsmenge festzusetzen, die von vergleichbaren jugendlichen Betriebsarbeitern in der für sie üblichen Arbeitszeit bewältigt werden kann. [4]Die Festsetzung erfolgt durch widerrufliche Entscheidung nach Anhörung der Beteiligten. [5]Sie ist vom Vorsitzenden zu unterschreiben und bedarf der Zustimmung der zuständigen Arbeitsbehörde und der Veröffentlichung im Wortlaut an der von der zuständigen Arbeitsbehörde bestimmten Stelle. [6]Sie tritt am Tage nach der Veröffentlichung in Kraft, wenn in ihr nicht ein anderer Zeitpunkt bestimmt ist. [7]Die Vorschriften des § 8 Abs. 1 über die Auslegung und Vorlegung von Entgeltverzeichnissen gelten entsprechend.

(3) [1]Soweit für einzelne Gewerbezweige oder Arten von Heimarbeit Bestimmungen nach Absatz 2 getroffen sind, darf an einen in Heimarbeit Beschäftigten eine größere Menge nicht ausgegeben werden. [2]Die Ausgabe einer größeren Menge ist zulässig, wenn Hilfskräfte (Familienangehörige oder fremde Hilfskräfte) zur Mitarbeit herangezogen werden. [3]Für diese Hilfskräfte sind dann weitere Entgeltbelege nach § 9 auszustellen.

(4) [1]Aus wichtigen Gründen, insbesondere wenn nach Auskunft der Agentur für Arbeit geeignete unbeschäftigte Heimarbeiter und Hausgewerbetreibende nicht oder nicht in ausreichender Zahl vorhanden sind oder wenn besondere persönliche Verhältnisse eines in Heimarbeit Beschäftigten es rechtfertigen, kann der Vorsitzende des Heimarbeitsausschusses einem Auftraggeber die Ausgabe größerer Arbeitsmengen auf einen Entgeltbeleg gestatten. [2]Die Erlaubnis kann jeweils nur für einen bestimmten Zeitraum, der sechs Monate nicht überschreiten darf, erteilt werden.

(2) [1]The homeworking committee may, in order to remedy abuses arising from the uneven distribution of homework, determine for individual branches of industry or types of homework the quantity of work which may be issued on a remuneration statement (section 9) for a certain period of time. [2]The amount of work is to be calculated in such a way that it can be performed by a full-time worker without auxiliaries during the working hours normally worked by comparable company workers. [3]For young homeworkers, a quantity of work shall be determined which can be performed by comparable young workers in the company in the normal working hours. [4]The determination is made by revocable decision after hearing the parties involved. [5]It is to be signed by the chairman and requires the approval of the competent labour authority and publication in the wording at the place determined by the competent labour authority. [6]It shall enter into force on the day following publication, unless it specifies a different date. [7]The provisions of section 8 subsection (1) on the interpretation and presentation of lists of wages and salaries shall apply accordingly.

(3) [1]Insofar as provisions have been made for individual branches of industry or types of homework pursuant to subsection 2, a larger quantity may not be issued to a person employed in homework. [2]The issue of a larger quantity is permissible if auxiliary staff (family members or external auxiliary staff) are called in to assist. [3]Further remuneration slips must then be issued for these auxiliary staff in accordance with § 9.

(4) [1]For important reasons, in particular if, according to information provided by the employment agency, suitable unemployed homeworkers and home-based tradesmen are not available or not available in sufficient numbers or if special personal circumstances of a person employed in homework justify it, the chairman of the homework committee may permit a client to issue larger quantities of work on a pay slip. [2]Such permission may only be granted for a specific period, which may not exceed six months.

§ 12
Grundsätze des Gefahrenschutzes

(1) Die Arbeitsstätten der in Heimarbeit Beschäftigten einschließlich der Maschinen, Werkzeuge und Geräte müssen so beschaffen, eingerichtet und unterhalten und Heimarbeit muß so ausgeführt werden, daß keine Gefahren für Leben, Gesundheit und Sittlichkeit der Beschäftigten und ihrer Mitarbeiter sowie für die öffentliche Gesundheit im Sinne des § 14 entstehen.

(2) Werden von Hausgewerbetreibenden oder Gleichgestellten fremde Hilfskräfte beschäftigt, so gelten auch die sonstigen Vorschriften über den Betriebsschutz und die sich daraus ergebenden Verpflichtungen des Arbeitgebers seinen Arbeitnehmern gegenüber.

§ 13
Arbeitsschutz

(1) Die Bundesregierung kann mit Zustimmung des Bundesrates für einzelne Gewerbezweige oder bestimmte Artcn von Beschäftigungen oder Arbeitsstätten Rechtsverordnungen zur Durchführung des Arbeitsschutzes durch die in Heimarbeit Beschäftigten und ihre Auftraggeber erlassen.

(2) Die Bundesregierung kann mit Zustimmung des Bundesrates Heimarbeit, die mit erheblichen Gefahren für Leben, Gesundheit oder Sittlichkeit der Beschäftigten verbunden ist, durch Rechtsverordnung verbieten.

§ 14
Schutz der öffentlichen Gesundheit

(1) Die Bundesregierung kann mit Zustimmung des Bundesrates für einzelne Gewerbezweige oder bestimmte Arten von Beschäftigungen oder Arbeitsstätten Rechtsverordnungen zum Schutze der Öffentlichkeit gegen gemeingefährliche und übertragbare Krankheiten und gegen Gefahren, die beim Verkehr mit Arznei-, Heil- und Betäubungsmitteln, Giften, Lebens- und Genußmitteln sowie Bedarfsgegenständen entstehen können, erlassen.

(2) Die Polizeibehörde kann im Benehmen mit dem Gewerbeaufsichtsamt und dem Gesundheitsamt für einzelne Arbeitsstätten Verfügungen zur Durchführung des öffentlichen Gesundheitsschutzes im Sinne des Absatzes 1 treffen, insbesondere zur Verhütung von Gefahren für die öffentliche Gesundheit, die sich bei der Herstellung, Verarbeitung oder Verpackung von Lebens- und Genußmitteln ergeben.

Section 12
Principles of Hazard Protection

(1) The workplaces of homeworkers, including the machines, tools and equipment, must be procured, set up and maintained in such a way, and homework must be carried out in such a way that there is no danger to the life, health and morals of the employees and their staff, or to public health within the meaning of section 14.

(2) If external auxiliary staff are employed by home-based tradesmen or persons of equivalent status, the other regulations on the protection of the workplace and the employer's obligations towards his employees arising therefrom shall also apply.

Section 13
Industrial Safety

(1) The Federal Government may, with the consent of the Bundesrat, issue statutory orders for the implementation of occupational health and safety by homeworkers and their employers in individual branches of industry or certain types of employment or workplaces.

(2) With the consent of the Bundesrat, the Federal Government may, by statutory order, prohibit home work that involves considerable risk to the life, health or morals of employees.

Section 14
Protection of Public Health

(1) The Federal Government may, with the consent of the Bundesrat, issue statutory orders for individual branches of industry or certain types of employment or workplaces to protect the general public against dangerous and transmissible diseases and against dangers which may arise from the trade in drugs, medicines, narcotics, poisons, foodstuffs, luxury foods and consumer goods.

(2) The police authority may, in consultation with the labour inspectorate and the public health department, issue orders for individual workplaces for the purpose of implementing public health protection within the meaning of subsection 1, in particular for the prevention of risks to public health arising from the production, processing or packaging of foodstuffs and luxury items.

(3) Die Bundesregierung kann mit Zustimmung des Bundesrates Heimarbeit, die mit erheblichen Gefahren für die öffentliche Gesundheit im Sinne des Absatzes 1 verbunden ist, durch Rechtsverordnung verbieten.

(3) The Federal Government may, with the consent of the Bundesrat, prohibit by statutory order home work that involves substantial risks to public health within the meaning of subsection 1.

§ 15
Anzeigepflicht

Section 15
Duty of Disclosure

Wer Heimarbeit ausgibt, für die zur Durchführung des Gefahrenschutzes besondere Vorschriften gelten, hat dem Gewerbeaufsichtsamt und der Polizeibehörde Namen und Arbeitsstätte der von ihm mit Heimarbeit Beschäftigten anzuzeigen.

Whoever issues homework to which special regulations apply for the implementation of hazard protection must notify the trade supervisory authority and the police authority of the names and places of work of the persons he employs to work from home.

§ 16
Durchführungspflicht

Section 16
Compulsory Implementation

(1) Wer Heimarbeit ausgibt oder weitergibt, hat dafür zu sorgen, daß Leben oder Gesundheit der in der Heimarbeit Beschäftigten durch technische Arbeitsmittel und Arbeitsstoffe, die er ihnen zur Verwendung überläßt, nicht gefährdet werden.

(1) Anyone who dispenses or passes on homework shall ensure that the lives or health of the persons employed in the homework are not endangered by technical equipment and working materials which he provides for their use.

(2) Die zur Durchführung des Gefahrenschutzes erforderlichen Maßnahmen, die sich auf Räume oder Betriebseinrichtungen beziehen, hat der zu treffen, der die Räume und Betriebseinrichtungen unterhält.

(2) The measures necessary for the implementation of hazard protection which relate to rooms or operating facilities shall be taken by the person who maintains the rooms and operating facilities.

§ 16a
Anordnungen

Section 16a
Orders

[1]Das Gewerbeaufsichtsamt kann in Einzelfällen anordnen, welche Maßnahmen zur Durchführung der §§ 12, 13 und 16 sowie der auf § 13 und § 34 Abs. 2 gestützten Rechtsverordnungen zu treffen sind. [2]Neben den auf Grund von § 3 Abs. 2 bestimmten Stellen nimmt das Gewerbeaufsichtsamt die Aufsichtsbefugnisse nach § 139b der Gewerbeordnung wahr.

[1]In individual cases, the labour inspectorate may order which measures are to be taken for the implementation of sections 12, 13 and 16 as well as the statutory orders based on sections 13 and § 34 (2). [2]In addition to the bodies determined on the basis of Article 3, paragraph 2, the labour inspectorate exercises the supervisory powers under Article 139b of the Trade Licensing Act.

§ 17
Tarifverträge, Entgeltregelungen

Section 17
Collectiv Bargaining Agreements, Remuneration Regulations

(1) Als Tarifverträge gelten auch schriftliche Vereinbarungen zwischen Gewerkschaften einerseits und Auftraggebern oder deren Vereinigungen andererseits über Inhalt, Abschluß oder Beendigung von Vertragsverhältnissen der in Heimarbeit Beschäftigten oder Gleichgestellten mit ihren Auftraggebern.

(1) Written agreements between trade unions, on the one hand, and clients or their associations, on the other hand, concerning the content, conclusion or termination of contractual relationships of homeworkers or persons treated as such with their clients shall also be deemed to be collective agreements.

(2) Entgeltregelungen im Sinne dieses Gesetzes sind Tarifverträge, bindende Festsetzungen von Entgelten und sonstigen Vertragsbedingungen (§ 19) und von Mindestarbeitsbedingungen für fremde Hilfskräfte (§ 22).

(2) Remuneration provisions within the meaning of this Act are collective agreements, binding definitions of remuneration and other contractual conditions (section 19) and of minimum working conditions for external auxiliary staff (section 22).

§ 18
Aufgaben des Heimarbeitsausschusses auf dem Gebiete der Entgeltregelung

Der Heimarbeitsausschuß hat die Aufgaben:

(a) auf das Zustandekommen von Tarifverträgen hinzuwirken;

(b) zur Vermeidung und Beendigung von Gesamtstreitigkeiten zwischen den in § 17 Abs. 1 genannten Parteien diesen auf Antrag einer Partei Vorschläge für den Abschluß eines Tarifvertrages zu unterbreiten; wird ein schriftlich abgefaßter Vorschlag von allen Parteien durch Erklärung gegenüber dem Heimarbeitsausschuß angenommen, so hat er die Wirkung eines Tarifvertrages;

(c) bindende Festsetzungen für Entgelte und sonstige Vertragsbedingungen nach Maßgabe des § 19 zu treffen.

§ 19
Bindende Festsetzungen

(1) ¹Bestehen Gewerkschaften oder Vereinigungen der Auftraggeber für den Zuständigkeitsbereich eines Heimarbeitsausschusses nicht oder umfassen sie nur eine Minderheit der Auftraggeber oder Beschäftigten, so kann der Heimarbeitsausschuß nach Anhörung der Auftraggeber und Beschäftigten, für die eine Regelung getroffen werden soll, Entgelte und sonstige Vertragsbedingungen mit bindender Wirkung für alle Auftraggeber und Beschäftigten seines Zuständigkeitsbereichs festsetzen, wenn unzulängliche Entgelte gezahlt werden oder die sonstigen Vertragsbedingungen unzulänglich sind. ²Als unzulänglich sind insbesondere Entgelte und sonstige Vertragsbedingungen anzusehen, die unter Berücksichtigung der sozialen und wirtschaftlichen Eigenart der Heimarbeit unter den tarifvertraglichen Löhnen oder sonstigen durch Tarifvertrag festgelegten Arbeitsbedingungen für gleiche oder gleichwertige Betriebsarbeit liegen. ³Soweit im Zuständigkeitsbereich eines Heimarbeitsausschusses Entgelte und sonstige Vertragsbedingungen für Heimarbeit derselben Art tarifvertraglich vereinbart sind, sollen in der bindenden Festsetzung keine für die Beschäftigten günstigeren Entgelte oder sonstigen Vertragsbedingungen festgesetzt werden.

(2) ¹Die bindende Festsetzung bedarf der Zustimmung der zuständigen Arbeitsbehörde und der Veröffentlichung im Wortlaut an der von der zuständigen Arbeitsbehörde bestimmten Stelle. ²Der persönliche Geltungsbereich der bindenden Festsetzung ist unter Berücksichtigung der Vorschriften des § 1 zu bestimmen. ³Sie tritt am

Section 18
Tasks of the Homework Committee in the field of Remuneration Regulations

The homework committee has the tasks:

(a) encourage the emergence of collective agreements;

(b) to submit to the parties referred to in section 17, subsection 1, at the request of any one of them proposals for the conclusion of a collective agreement in order to prevent and end collective disputes between the parties referred to in section 17, subsection 1; if a proposal made in writing is accepted by all parties by declaration to the homeworkers' committee, it shall have the effect of a collective agreement;

(c) to make binding determinations of remuneration and other contractual conditions in accordance with section 19.

Section 19
Binding Provisions

(1) ¹If trade unions or associations of the contracting authorities do not exist for the area of responsibility of a home work committee or if they only cover a minority of the contracting authorities or employees, the home work committee may, after consulting the contracting authorities and employees for whom regulation is to be made, fix remuneration and other contractual conditions with binding effect for all contracting authorities and employees in its area of responsibility if inadequate remuneration is paid or the other contractual conditions are inadequate. ²In particular, pay and other contractual conditions are deemed to be inadequate if they are lower than collectively agreed wages or other working conditions for the same or equivalent work in the undertaking, taking into account the social and economic nature of homework. ³Where, within the area of competence of a homeworking committee, remuneration and other contractual conditions for homeworking of the same kind are agreed by collective agreement, the binding determination should not set remuneration or other contractual conditions which are more favourable to the employees.

(2) ¹The binding determination shall require the consent of the competent labour authority and shall be published in the text at the place determined by the competent labour authority. ²The personal scope of the binding assessment shall be determined taking into account the provisions of section 1. ³It shall enter into force on the

Tage nach der Veröffentlichung in Kraft, wenn in ihr nicht ein anderer Zeitpunkt bestimmt ist. [4]Beabsichtigt die zuständige Arbeitsbehörde die Zustimmung zu einer bindenden Festsetzung insbesondere wegen Unzulänglichkeit der Entgelte oder der sonstigen Vertragsbedingungen (Absatz 1 Satz 2) zu versagen, so hat sie dies dem Heimarbeitsausschuß unter Angabe von Gründen mitzuteilen und ihm vor ihre Entscheidung über die Zustimmung Gelegenheit zu geben, die bindende Festsetzung zu ändern.

(3) [1]Die bindende Festsetzung hat die Wirkung eines allgemeinverbindlichen Tarifvertrages und ist in das beim Bundesministerium für Arbeit und Soziales geführte Tarifregister einzutragen. [2]Von den Vorschriften einer bindenden Festsetzung kann nur zugunsten des Beschäftigten abgewichen werden. [3]Ein Verzicht auf Rechte, die auf Grund einer bindenden Festsetzung eines Beschäftigten entstanden sind, ist nur in einem von der Obersten Arbeitsbehörde des Landes oder der von ihr bestimmten Stelle gebilligten Vergleich zulässig. [4]Die Verwirkung solcher Rechte ist ausgeschlossen. [5]Ausschlußfristen für ihre Geltendmachung können nur durch eine bindende Festsetzung vorgesehen werden; das gleiche gilt für die Abkürzung von Verjährungsfristen. [6]Im übrigen gelten für die bindende Festsetzung die gesetzlichen Vorschriften über den Tarifvertrag sinngemäß, soweit sich aus dem Fehlen der Vertragsparteien nicht etwas anderes ergibt.

(4) [1]Der Heimarbeitsausschuß kann nach Anhörung der Auftraggeber und Beschäftigten bindende Festsetzungen ändern oder aufheben. [2]Die Absätze 1 bis 3 gelten entsprechend.

(5) Die Absätze 1 bis 4 gelten entsprechend für die Festsetzung von vermögenswirksamen Leistungen im Sinne des Fünften Vermögensbildungsgesetzes.

§ 20
Art der Entgelte

[1]Die Entgelte für Heimarbeit sind in der Regel als Stückentgelte, und zwar möglichst auf der Grundlage von Stückzeiten zu regeln. [2]Ist dieses nicht möglich, so sind Zeitentgelte festzusetzen, die der Stückentgeltberechnung im Einzelfall zugrunde gelegt werden können.

day following publication unless another date is specified in it. [4]If the competent employment authority intends to refuse consent to a binding assessment, in particular because of inadequate remuneration or other contractual conditions (subsection 1, second sentence), it must notify the homework committee of this, stating reasons, and give it the opportunity to amend the binding assessment before deciding on consent.

(3) [1]The binding determination has the effect of a generally binding collective agreement and must be entered in the collective agreement register kept by the Federal Ministry of Labour and Social Affairs. [2]Deviations from the provisions of a binding agreement may only be made in favour of the employee. [3]A waiver of rights which have arisen on the basis of a binding determination of an employee is only permissible in a settlement approved by the supreme labour authority of the Land or the body designated by it. [4]The forfeiture of such rights is excluded. [5]Exclusion periods for their assertion may be provided for only by a binding determination; the same applies to the shortening of limitation periods. [6]In all other respects, the statutory provisions on collective agreements shall apply mutatis mutandis to the binding determination, unless the absence of the contracting parties indicates otherwise.

(4) [1]The homeworking committee may, after hearing the contracting authorities and employees, amend or repeal binding provisions. [2]Paragraphs 1 to 3 shall apply accordingly.

(5) Paragraphs 1 to 4 shall apply mutatis mutandis to the determination of capital-forming benefits within the meaning of the Fifth Capital Formation Act.

Section 20
Type of Remuneration

[1]Remuneration for homework is to be regulated as a rule in the form of piecework payments, if possible on the basis of piecework times. [2]If this is not possible, time rates are to be set which can be used as a basis for calculating the unit rate in individual cases.

§ 21
Entgeltregelung für Zwischenmeister, Mithaftung des Auftraggebers

(1) Für Zwischenmeister, die nach § 1 Abs. 2 Buchstabe d den in Heimarbeit Beschäftigten gleichgestellt sind, können im Verhältnis zu ihren Auftraggebern durch Entgeltregelungen gemäß den §§ 17 bis 19 Zuschläge festgelegt werden.

(2) Zahlt ein Auftraggeber an einen Zwischenmeister ein Entgelt, von dem er weiß oder den Umständen nach wissen muß, daß es zur Zahlung der in der Entgeltregelung festgelegten Entgelte an die Beschäftigten nicht ausreicht, oder zahlt er an einen Zwischenmeister, dessen Unzuverlässigkeit er kennt oder kennen muß, so haftet er neben dem Zwischenmeister für diese Entgelte.

§ 22
Mindestarbeitsbedingungen für fremde Hilfskräfte

(1) ¹Für fremde Hilfskräfte, die von Hausgewerbetreibenden oder Gleichgestellten beschäftigt werden, können Mindestarbeitsbedingungen festgesetzt werden. ²Voraussetzung ist, daß die Entgelte der Hausgewerbetreibenden oder Gleichgestellten durch eine Entgeltregelung (§§ 17 bis 19) festgelegt sind.

(2) ¹Für die Festsetzung gilt § 19 entsprechend mit der Maßgabe, daß an die Stelle der Heimarbeitsausschüsse Entgeltausschüsse für fremde Hilfskräfte der Heimarbeit treten. ²Für die Auslegung der Mindestarbeitsbedingungen gilt § 8 Abs. 3 entsprechend.

(3) ¹Die Entgeltausschüsse werden im Bedarfsfall durch die zuständige Arbeitsbehörde errichtet. ²Für ihre Zusammensetzung und das Verfahren vor ihnen gelten § 4 Absätze 2 bis 4 und § 5 entsprechend. ³Die Beisitzer und Stellvertreter sind aus Kreisen der beteiligten Arbeitnehmer einerseits sowie der Hausgewerbetreibenden und Gleichgestellten andererseits auf Grund von Vorschlägen der fachlich und räumlich zuständigen Gewerkschaften und Vereinigungen der Hausgewerbetreibenden oder Gleichgestellten, soweit solche nicht bestehen oder keine Vorschläge einreichen, nach Anhörung der Beteiligten jeweils zu berufen.

Section 21
Remuneration Regulations for Intermediate Masters, Joint Liability of the Client

(1) Intermediate masters who, pursuant to section 1(2)(d), are treated in the same way as homeworkers, may be subject to surcharges in relation to their clients by means of remuneration arrangements in accordance with sections 17 to 19.

(2) If a client pays a fee to an intermediate master of which he knows or must know under the circumstances that it is not sufficient to pay the employees the fees laid down in the remuneration scheme, or if he pays to an intermediate master whose unreliability he knows or must know, he shall be liable for these fees alongside the intermediate master.

Section 22
Minimum Working Conditions for Foreign Auxiliary Staff

(1) ¹Minimum working conditions may be laid down for outside auxiliary staff employed by persons engaged in the household trade or persons treated as such. ²A precondition is that the remuneration of the cottage industry operators or persons of equivalent status is laid down by a remuneration regulation (sections 17 to 19).

(2) ¹Section 19 shall apply mutatis mutandis to the fixing, subject to the proviso that the homework committees are replaced by remuneration committees for external auxiliary staff for homework. ²8(3) shall apply mutatis mutandis to the interpretation of the minimum working conditions.

(3) ¹The remuneration committees shall be set up by the competent labour authority if necessary. ²Section 4(2) to (4) and section 5 shall apply mutatis mutandis to their composition and the procedure before them. ³The assessors and deputies shall be appointed from among the participating employees on the one hand and the home-trade operators and persons treated as equals on the other hand on the basis of proposals made by the trade unions and associations of home-trade operators or persons treated as equals which are competent in terms of subject matter and geographical area, insofar as such do not exist or do not submit any proposals, in each case after hearing the parties concerned.

§ 23
Entgeltprüfung

(1) Die Oberste Arbeitsbehörde des Landes hat für eine wirksame Überwachung der Entgelte und sonstigen Vertragsbedingungen durch Entgeltprüfer Sorge zu tragen.

(2) Die Entgeltprüfer haben die Innehaltung der Vorschriften des Dritten Abschnittes dieses Gesetzes und der gemäß den §§ 17 bis 19, 21 und 22 geregelten Entgelte und sonstigen Vertragsbedingungen zu überwachen sowie auf Antrag bei der Errechnung der Stückentgelte Berechnungshilfe zu leisten.

(3) Die Oberste Arbeitsbehörde des Landes kann die Aufgaben der Entgeltprüfer anderen Stellen übertragen, insbesondere für Bezirke, in denen Heimarbeit nur in geringem Umfange geleistet wird.

§ 24
Aufforderung zur Nachzahlung der Minderbeträge

¹Hat ein Auftraggeber oder Zwischenmeister einem in Heimarbeit Beschäftigten oder einem Gleichgestellten ein Entgelt gezahlt, das niedriger ist als das in einer Entgeltregelung gemäß den §§ 17 bis 19 festgesetzte oder das in § 29 Abs. 5 oder 6 bestimmte, so kann ihn die Oberste Arbeitsbehörde des Landes oder die von ihr bestimmte Stelle auffordern, innerhalb einer in der Aufforderung festzusetzenden Frist den Minderbetrag nachzuzahlen und den Zahlungsnachweis vorzulegen. ²Satz 1 gilt entsprechend für sonstige Vertragsbedingungen, die gemäß den §§ 17 bis 19 festgesetzt sind und die Geldleistungen an einen in Heimarbeit Beschäftigten oder einen Gleichgestellten zum Inhalt haben. ³Die Oberste Arbeitsbehörde des Landes soll von einer Maßnahme nach Satz 1 absehen, wenn glaubhaft gemacht worden ist, daß ein Gleichgestellter im Falle des § 1 Abs. 6 nicht oder wahrheitswidrig geantwortet hat.

§ 25
Klagebefugnis der Länder

¹Das Land, vertreten durch die Oberste Arbeitsbehörde oder die von ihr bestimmte Stelle, kann im eigenen Namen den Anspruch auf Nachzahlung des Minderbetrages an den Berechtigten gerichtlich geltend machen. ²Das Urteil wirkt auch für und gegen den in Heimarbeit Beschäftigten oder den Gleichgestellten. ³§ 24 Satz 3 gilt entsprechend.

Section 23
Examination of Remuneration

(1) The Supreme Labour Authority of the Land shall ensure effective monitoring of remuneration and other contractual conditions by remuneration auditors.

(2) The remuneration auditors shall monitor compliance with the provisions of Section 3 of this Act and with the remuneration and other contractual terms and conditions regulated under Sections 17 to 19, 21 and 22 and, upon request, provide calculation assistance in the calculation of unit rates.

(3) The supreme employment authority of the Land may delegate the tasks of the remuneration auditors to other bodies, in particular for districts in which home work is performed only to a limited extent.

Section 24
Resquest for Subsequent Payment of the Reduced Amounts

¹If a principal or intermediate master has paid a homeworker or equivalent a remuneration which is lower than that set out in a remuneration scheme pursuant to sections 17 to 19 or that set out in section 29(5) or (6), the supreme employment authority of the Land or the body designated by it may request him to pay the reduced amount within a period to be specified in the request and to submit proof of payment. ²Sentence 1 shall apply mutatis mutandis to other contractual terms and conditions which are determined in accordance with §§ 17 to 19 and which relate to cash payments to a homeworker or equivalent. ³The supreme employment authority of the Land shall refrain from taking a measure pursuant to sentence 1 if it has been demonstrated that a person treated as an equal in the case of § 1, subsection 6, did not reply or did not reply truthfully.

Section 25
Legal Actions of the Federal States

¹The State, represented by the Supreme Labour Authority or the body designated by it, may, in its own name, assert in court the claim for subsequent payment of the reduced amount to the person entitled. ²The judgment also has effect for and against the homeworker or equivalent. Section 24, third sentence, shall apply mutatis mutandis.

§ 26
Entgeltschutz für fremde Hilfskräfte

(1) Hat ein Hausgewerbetreibender oder Gleichgestellter einer fremden Hilfskraft ein Entgelt gezahlt, das niedriger ist als das durch Mindestarbeitsbedingungen (§ 22) festgesetzte, so gelten die Vorschriften der §§ 24 und 25 über die Aufforderung zur Nachzahlung der Minderbeträge und über die Klagebefugnis der Länder sinngemäß.

(2) ¹Das gleiche gilt, wenn ein Hausgewerbetreibender oder Gleichgestellter eine fremde Hilfskraft nicht nach der einschlägigen tariflichen Regelung entlohnt. ²Voraussetzung ist, daß die Entgelte des Hausgewerbetreibenden oder Gleichgestellten durch eine Entgeltregelung (§§ 17 bis 19) festgelegt sind.

§ 27
Pfändungsschutz

Für das Entgelt, das den in Heimarbeit Beschäftigten oder den Gleichgestellten gewährt wird, gelten die Vorschriften über den Pfändungsschutz für Vergütungen, die auf Grund eines Arbeits- oder Dienstverhältnisses geschuldet werden, entsprechend.

§ 28

(1) ¹Auftraggeber, Zwischenmeister, Beschäftigte und fremde Hilfskräfte haben den mit der Entgeltfestsetzung oder Entgeltprüfung beauftragten Stellen auf Verlangen Auskunft über alle die Entgelte berührenden Fragen zu erteilen und hierbei auch außer den Entgeltbelegen (§ 9) Arbeitsstücke, Stoffproben und sonstige Unterlagen für die Entgeltfestsetzung oder Entgeltprüfung vorzulegen. ²Die mit der Entgeltfestsetzung oder Entgeltprüfung beauftragten Stellen können Erhebungen über Arbeitszeiten für einzelne Arbeitsstücke anstellen oder anstellen lassen.

(2) Der in Heimarbeit Beschäftigte und Gleichgestellte kann von seinem Auftraggeber verlangen, daß ihm die Berechnung und Zusammensetzung seines Entgelts erläutert wird.

§ 29
Allgemeiner Kündigungsschutz

(1) Das Beschäftigungsverhältnis eines in Heimarbeit Beschäftigten kann beiderseits an jedem Tag für den Ablauf des folgenden Tages gekündigt werden.

(2) Wird ein in Heimarbeit Beschäftigter von einem Auftraggeber oder Zwischenmeister länger als vier Wochen beschäftigt, so kann das Beschäftigungsverhältnis beiderseits nur mit einer Frist von zwei Wochen gekündigt werden.

Section 26
Protection of Remuneration for Foreign Auxiliary Staff

(1) If a cottage industry operator or assimilator of a foreign auxiliary staff has paid remuneration which is lower than that laid down by minimum working conditions (section 22), the provisions of sections 24 and 25 on the demand for subsequent payment of the reduced amounts and on the right of action of the Länder shall apply mutatis mutandis.

(2) ¹The same shall apply if a cottage industry operator or equivalent does not remunerate a foreign auxiliary staff in accordance with the relevant collective agreement. ²This shall be subject to the condition that the remuneration of the cottage industry operator or equivalent is determined by a remuneration scheme (sections 17 to 19).

Section 27
Seizure Protection

The rules on protection against attachment of remuneration due on the basis of an employment relationship shall apply mutatis mutandis to remuneration paid to homeworkers or persons treated as such.

Section 28

(1) ¹On request, the customer, intermediate master craftsmen, employees and external assistants must provide the bodies charged with determining or checking the fees with information on all questions relating to the fees and, in addition to the fee vouchers (section 9), must submit work pieces, fabric samples and other documents for determining or checking the fees. ²The bodies charged with determining or reviewing fees may conduct or arrange for surveys of working hours for individual items of work.

(2) The homeworker and equivalent may require his principal to explain to him the calculation and composition of his remuneration.

Section 29
General Protection Against Dismissal

(1) The employment relationship of an employee working from home may be terminated by either party on any day for the end of the following day.

(2) If a homeworker is employed by a principal or intermediate foreman for more than four weeks, the employment relationship may be terminated by either party only with two weeks' notice.

(3) ¹Wird ein in Heimarbeit Beschäftigter überwiegend von einem Auftraggeber oder Zwischenmeister beschäftigt, so kann das Beschäftigungsverhältnis mit einer Frist von vier Wochen zum Fünfzehnten oder zum Ende eines Kalendermonats gekündigt werden. ²Während einer vereinbarten Probezeit, längstens für die Dauer von sechs Monaten, beträgt die Kündigungsfrist zwei Wochen.

(4) Unter der in Absatz 3 Satz 1 genannten Voraussetzung beträgt die Frist für eine Kündigung durch den Auftraggeber oder Zwischenmeister, wenn das Beschäftigungsverhältnis

1. zwei Jahre bestanden hat, einen Monat zum Ende eines Kalendermonats,
2. fünf Jahre bestanden hat, zwei Monate zum Ende eines Kalendermonats,
3. acht Jahre bestanden hat, drei Monate zum Ende eines Kalendermonats,
4. zehn Jahre bestanden hat, vier Monate zum Ende eines Kalendermonats,
5. zwölf Jahre bestanden hat, fünf Monate zum Ende eines Kalendermonats,
6. fünfzehn Jahre bestanden hat, sechs Monate zum Ende eines Kalendermonats,
7. zwanzig Jahre bestanden hat, sieben Monate zum Ende eines Kalendermonats.

(5) § 622 Abs. 4 bis 6 des Bürgerlichen Gesetzbuches gilt entsprechend.

(6) Für die Kündigung aus wichtigem Grund gilt § 626 des Bürgerlichen Gesetzbuches entsprechend.

(7) ¹Für die Dauer der Kündigungsfrist nach den Absätzen 2 bis 5 hat der Beschäftigte auch bei Ausgabe einer geringeren Arbeitsmenge Anspruch auf Arbeitsentgelt in Höhe von einem Zwölftel bei einer Kündigungsfrist von zwei Wochen, zwei Zwölfteln bei einer Kündigungsfrist von vier Wochen, drei Zwölfteln bei einer Kündigungsfrist von einem Monat, vier Zwölfteln bei einer Kündigungsfrist von zwei Monaten, sechs Zwölfteln bei einer Kündigungsfrist von drei Monaten, acht Zwölfteln bei einer Kündigungsfrist von vier Monaten, zehn Zwölfteln bei einer Kündigungsfrist von fünf Monaten, zwölf Zwölfteln bei einer Kündigungsfrist von sechs Monaten und vierzehn Zwölfteln bei einer Kündigungsfrist von sieben Monaten des Gesamtbetrages, den er in den dem Zugang der Kündigung vorausgegangenen 24 Wochen als Entgelt erhalten hat. ²Bei Entgelterhöhungen während des Berechnungszeitraums oder der Kündigungsfrist ist von dem erhöhten Entgelt auszugehen. ³Zeiten des Bezugs von Krankengeld oder Kurzarbeitergeld sind in den Berechnungszeitraum nicht mit einzubeziehen.

(3) ¹If a homeworker is predominantly employed by a principal or an intermediate master craftsman, the employment relationship may be terminated with four weeks' notice with effect from the fifteenth day of the month or at the end of a calendar month. ²During an agreed probationary period, for a maximum of six months, the notice period shall be two weeks.

(4) Subject to the condition set out in paragraph 3 sentence 1, the period of notice for termination by the client or intermediate master if the employment relationship

1. has existed for two years, one month at the end of a calendar month,
2. has existed for five years, two months at the end of a calendar month,
3. has existed for eight years, three months at the end of a calendar month,
4. has existed for ten years, four months at the end of a calendar month,
5. has existed for twelve years, five months at the end of a calendar month,
6. has existed for fifteen years, six months to the end of a calendar month,
7. has existed for twenty years, seven months to the end of a calendar month.

(5) Section 622 (4) to (6) of the German Civil Code shall apply accordingly.

(6) Section 626 of the German Civil Code shall apply mutatis mutandis to termination for good cause.

(7) ¹For the duration of the period of notice under subsections 2 to 5, the employee shall be entitled to remuneration of one twelfth in the case of a two-week period of notice, two twelfths in the case of a four-week period of notice, three twelfths in the case of a one-month period of notice, four twelfths in the case of a two-month period of notice, even if a smaller quantity of work is performed, six-twelfths at three months' notice, eight-twelfths at four months' notice, ten-twelfths at five months' notice, twelve-twelfths at six months' notice and fourteen-twelfths at seven months' notice of the total amount of remuneration received in the 24 weeks preceding receipt of the notice. ²In the event of an increase in remuneration during the calculation period or the period of notice, the increased remuneration shall be assumed. ³Periods of receipt of sickness benefit or short-time working allowance are not to be included in the calculation period.

(8) ¹Absatz 7 gilt entsprechend, wenn ein Auftraggeber oder Zwischenmeister die Arbeitsmenge, die er mindestens ein Jahr regelmäßig an einen Beschäftigten, auf den die Voraussetzungen der Absätze 2, 3, 4 oder 5 zutreffen, ausgegeben hat, um mindestens ein Viertel verringert, es sei denn, daß die Verringerung auf einer Festsetzung gemäß § 11 Abs. 2 beruht. ²Hat das Beschäftigungsverhältnis im Falle des Absatzes 2 ein Jahr noch nicht erreicht, so ist von der während der Dauer des Beschäftigungsverhältnisses ausgegebenen Arbeitsmenge auszugehen. ³Die Sätze 1 und 2 finden keine Anwendung, wenn die Verringerung der Arbeitsmenge auf rechtswirksam eingeführter Kurzarbeit beruht.

(9) Teilt ein Auftraggeber einem Zwischenmeister, der überwiegend für ihn Arbeit weitergibt, eine künftige Herabminderung der regelmäßig zu verteilenden Arbeitsmenge nicht rechtzeitig mit, so kann dieser vom Auftraggeber Ersatz der durch Einhaltung der Kündigungsfrist verursachten Aufwendungen insoweit verlangen, als während der Kündigungsfrist die Beschäftigung wegen des Verhaltens des Auftraggebers nicht möglich war.

§ 29a
Kündigungsschutz im Rahmen der Betriebsverfassung

(1) ¹Die Kündigung des Beschäftigungsverhältnisses eines in Heimarbeit beschäftigten Mitglieds eines Betriebsrats oder einer Jugend- und Auszubildendenvertretung ist unzulässig, es sei denn, daß Tatsachen vorliegen, die einen Arbeitgeber zur Kündigung eines Arbeitsverhältnisses aus wichtigem Grund ohne Einhaltung einer Kündigungsfrist berechtigen würden, und daß die nach § 103 des Betriebsverfassungsgesetzes erforderliche Zustimmung vorliegt oder durch gerichtliche Entscheidung ersetzt ist. ²Nach Beendigung der Amtszeit ist die Kündigung innerhalb eines Jahres, jeweils vom Zeitpunkt der Beendigung der Amtszeit an gerechnet, unzulässig, es sei denn, daß Tatsachen vorliegen, die einen Arbeitgeber zur Kündigung eines Arbeitsverhältnisses aus wichtigem Grund ohne Einhaltung einer Kündigungsfrist berechtigen würden; dies gilt nicht, wenn die Beendigung der Mitgliedschaft auf einer gerichtlichen Entscheidung beruht.

(2) ¹Die Kündigung eines in Heimarbeit beschäftigten Mitglieds eines Wahlvorstands ist vom Zeitpunkt seiner Bestellung an, die Kündigung eines in Heimarbeit beschäftigten Wahlbewerbers vom Zeitpunkt der Aufstellung des Wahlvorschlags an jeweils bis zur Bekanntgabe des Wahlergebnisses unzulässig, es sei denn,

(8) ¹Sub-Clause 7 shall apply mutatis mutandis if a principal or intermediate master reduces the quantity of work which he has regularly issued for at least one year to an employee to whom the requirements of Sub-Clause 2, 3, 4 or 5 apply by at least one quarter, unless the reduction is based on a determination in accordance with section 11(2). ²If, in the case of subsection (2) above, the employment relationship has not yet lasted one year, the amount of work spent during the period of employment shall be taken as a basis. Sentences 1 and 2 shall not apply if the reduction in the quantity of work is based on legally effective short-time working.

(9) If a client does not inform an intermediate foreman, who mainly subcontracts work for him, in good time of a future reduction in the quantity of work to be regularly distributed, the latter may demand compensation from the client for the expenses caused by compliance with the period of notice to the extent that employment was not possible during the period of notice due to the client's conduct.

Section 29a
Protection Agains Dismissal under the Works Constitution

(1) ¹The termination of the employment relationship of a member of a works council or a youth and trainee representative body employed in homework is inadmissible unless there are facts which would entitle an employer to terminate an employment relationship for good cause without notice and unless the consent required under section 103 of the Works Constitution Act has been obtained or has been replaced by a court decision. ²After termination of the term of office, termination within one year, in each case calculated from the date of termination of the term of office, is inadmissible unless there are facts which would entitle an employer to terminate an employment relationship for good cause without notice; this does not apply if the termination is based on a court decision.

(2) ¹The termination of a member of an election board employed in homework is inadmissible from the time of his appointment, the termination of an election candidate employed in homework from the time of the preparation of the election proposal until the announcement of the election result in each case, unless facts

daß Tatsachen vorliegen, die einen Arbeitgeber zur Kündigung eines Arbeitsverhältnisses aus wichtigem Grund ohne Einhaltung einer Kündigungsfrist berechtigen würden, und daß die nach § 103 des Betriebsverfassungsgesetzes erforderliche Zustimmung vorliegt oder durch eine gerichtliche Entscheidung ersetzt ist. ²Innerhalb von sechs Monaten nach Bekanntgabe des Wahlergebnisses ist die Kündigung unzulässig, es sei denn, daß Tatsachen vorliegen, die einen Arbeitgeber zur Kündigung eines Arbeitsverhältnisses aus wichtigem Grund ohne Einhaltung einer Kündigungsfrist berechtigen würden; dies gilt nicht für Mitglieder des Wahlvorstands, wenn dieser nach § 18 Abs. 1 des Betriebsverfassungsgesetzes durch gerichtliche Entscheidung durch einen anderen Wahlvorstand ersetzt worden ist.

(3) Wird die Vergabe von Heimarbeit eingestellt, so ist die Kündigung des Beschäftigungsverhältnisses der in den Absätzen 1 und 2 genannten Personen frühestens zum Zeitpunkt der Einstellung der Vergabe zulässig, es sei denn, daß die Kündigung zu einem früheren Zeitpunkt durch zwingende betriebliche Erfordernisse bedingt ist.

exist which would entitle an employer to terminate an employment relationship for good cause without observing a period of notice, and the consent required under § 103 of the Works Constitution Act is available or has been replaced by a court decision. ²Within six months of the announcement of the election results, the notice of termination is inadmissible unless there are facts which would entitle an employer to terminate an employment relationship for good cause without notice; this does not apply to members of the election board if the board has been replaced by another election board by court decision in accordance with section 18 (1) of the Works Constitution Act.

(3) Where the provision of home work is discontinued, the employment of the persons referred to in paragraphs 1 and 2 may be terminated at the earliest at the time when the provision of home work is discontinued, unless the termination is earlier due to overriding operational requirements.

§ 30
Verbot der Ausgabe von Heimarbeit

Die Oberste Arbeitsbehörde des Landes oder die von ihr bestimmte Stelle kann einer Person, die

1. in den letzten fünf Jahren wiederholt wegen eines Verstoßes gegen die Vorschriften dieses Gesetzes rechtskräftig verurteilt oder mit Geldbuße belegt worden ist,
2. der Obersten Arbeitsbehörde des Landes oder der von ihr bestimmten Stelle falsche Angaben gemacht oder falsche Unterlagen vorgelegt hat, um sich der Pflicht zur Nachzahlung von Minderbeträgen (§ 24) zu entziehen, oder
3. der Aufforderung der Obersten Arbeitsbehörde des Landes oder der von ihr bestimmten Stelle zur Nachzahlung von Minderbeträgen (§ 24) wiederholt nicht nachgekommen ist oder die Minderbeträge nach Aufforderung zwar nachgezahlt, jedoch weiter zu niedrige Entgelte gezahlt hat,

die Aus- und Weitergabe von Heimarbeit verbieten.

Section 30
Prohibition to Order Homework

The Supreme Labour Authority of the country or the body designated by it may grant a person who

1. has been convicted or fined repeatedly within the last five years for an infringement of the provisions of this Act and has been convicted by a final judgment or a fine
2. has given false information or submitted false documents to the Supreme Labour Authority of the Land or to the body designated by it in order to evade the obligation to make subsequent payments of reduced amounts (section 24), or
3. repeatedly failed to comply with the request of the Supreme Labour Authority of the Land or the body appointed by it for the subsequent payment of reduced amounts (section 24) or repeatedly failed to pay the reduced amounts after the request for subsequent payment, but continued to pay insufficient remuneration,

prohibit the export and transfer of home work.

§ 31
Ausgabe verbotener Heimarbeit

(1) Wer Heimarbeit, die nach einer zur Durchführung des Gefahrenschutzes erlassenen Rechtsvorschrift (§ 13 Abs. 2, § 14 Abs. 3, § 34 Abs. 2 Satz 2) verboten ist, ausgibt oder weitergibt, wird mit Freiheitsstrafe bis zu einem Jahr oder mit Geldstrafe bestraft.

(2) Handelt der Täter fahrlässig, so ist die Strafe Freiheitsstrafe bis zu sechs Monaten oder Geldstrafe bis zu einhundertachtzig Tagessätzen.

§ 32
Straftaten und Ordnungswidrigkeiten im Bereich des Arbeits- und Gefahrenschutzes

(1) [1]Ordnungswidrig handelt, wer, abgesehen von den Fällen des § 31, vorsätzlich oder fahrlässig

1. einer zur Durchführung des Gefahrenschutzes erlassenen Rechtsvorschrift (§§ 13, 14 Abs. 1, 3, § 34 Abs. 2 Satz 2), soweit sie für einen bestimmten Tatbestand auf diese Bußgeldvorschrift verweist, oder
2. einer vollziehbaren Verfügung nach § 14 Abs. 2 oder § 16a

zuwiderhandelt. [2]Die in Satz 1 Nr. 1 vorgeschriebene Verweisung ist nicht erforderlich, soweit die dort genannten Rechtsvorschriften vor Inkrafttreten dieses Gesetzes erlassen sind.

(2) Die Ordnungswidrigkeit kann mit einer Geldbuße bis zu zehntausend Euro geahndet werden.

(3) Wer vorsätzlich eine der in Absatz 1 bezeichneten Handlungen begeht und dadurch in Heimarbeit Beschäftigte in ihrer Arbeitskraft oder Gesundheit gefährdet, wird mit Freiheitsstrafe bis zu einem Jahr oder mit Geldstrafe bestraft.

(4) Wer in den Fällen des Absatzes 3 die Gefahr fahrlässig verursacht, wird mit Freiheitsstrafe bis zu sechs Monaten oder mit Geldstrafe bis zu einhundertachtzig Tagessätzen bestraft.

§ 32a
Sonstige Ordnungswidrigkeiten

(1) Ordnungswidrig handelt, wer vorsätzlich oder fahrlässig einem nach § 30 ergangenen vollziehbaren Verbot der Ausgabe oder Weitergabe von Heimarbeit zuwiderhandelt.

(2) Ordnungswidrig handelt auch, wer vorsätzlich oder fahrlässig

Section 31
Order of Prohibited Homework

(1) Anyone who spends or passes on homework which is prohibited under a legal provision enacted to implement hazard protection (section 13 (2), section 14 (3), section 34 (2), second sentence) shall be punished with imprisonment for up to one year or with a fine.

(2) If the offender acts negligently, the penalty shall be imprisonment for up to six months or a fine of up to one hundred and eighty daily rates.

Section 32
Criminal Offences and Administrative Offences in the Field of Occupational Health and Safety

(1) [1]An administrative offence shall be deemed to have been committed by any person who, except in the cases of section 31, wilfully or negligently

1. a legal provision enacted to implement hazard protection (sections 13, 14 (1), (3), 34 (2), second sentence), insofar as it refers to this provision on fines for a specific offence, or
2. an enforceable ruling pursuant to section 14 subsection (2) or section 16a

is contravened. [2]The referral prescribed in sentence 1 no. 1 is not necessary if the legal provisions referred to therein were enacted before the entry into force of this Act.

(2) The administrative offence may be punishable by a fine of up to ten thousand euros.

(3) Anyone who intentionally commits one of the acts referred to in subsection 1 and thereby endangers the manpower or health of homeworkers shall be punished by imprisonment for up to one year or by a fine.

(4) Anyone who negligently causes the risk in the cases of paragraph 3 shall be punished with imprisonment for up to six months or a fine of up to one hundred and eighty daily rates.

Section 32a
Other Administrative Offences

(1) It is an administrative offence to deliberately or negligently contravene an enforceable prohibition of the issue or transfer of homework issued in accordance with section 30.

(2) It is also an administrative offence to deliberately or negligently

1. einer Vorschrift über die Listenführung (§ 6), die Mitteilung oder Anzeige von Heimarbeit (§§ 7, 15), die Unterrichtungspflicht (§ 7a), die Offenlegung der Entgeltverzeichnisse (§ 8), die Entgeltbelege (§ 9) oder die Auskunftspflicht über die Entgelte (§ 28 Abs. 1) zuwiderhandelt,

2. einer vollziehbaren Anordnung zum Schutze der Heimarbeiter vor Zeitversäumnis (§ 10) zuwiderhandelt,

3. einer Regelung zur Verteilung der Heimarbeit nach § 11 Abs. 2 zuwiderhandelt, soweit sie für einen bestimmten Tatbestand auf diese Bußgeldvorschrift verweist oder

4. als in Heimarbeit Beschäftigter (§ 1 Abs. 1) oder diesem Gleichgestellter (§ 1 Abs. 2) duldet, daß ein mitarbeitender Familienangehöriger eine Zuwiderhandlung nach § 32 begeht.

(3) Die Ordnungswidrigkeit nach Absatz 1 kann mit einer Geldbuße bis zu zehntausend Euro, die Ordnungswidrigkeit nach Absatz 2 mit einer Geldbuße bis zu zweitausendfünfhundert Euro geahndet werden.

§ 33
Durchführungsvorschriften

(1) Das Bundesministerium für Arbeit und Soziales wird ermächtigt, mit Zustimmung des Bundesrates und nach Anhörung der Spitzenverbände der Gewerkschaften und der Vereinigungen der Arbeitgeber die zur Durchführung dieses Gesetzes erforderlichen Rechtsverordnungen zu erlassen über

(a) das Verfahren bei der Gleichstellung (§ 1 Abs. 2 bis 5);

(b) die Errichtung von Heimarbeitsausschüssen und von Entgeltausschüssen für fremde Hilfskräfte der Heimarbeit und das Verfahren vor ihnen (§§ 4, 5, 11, 18 bis 22);

(c) Form, Inhalt und Einsendung der Listen und der Anzeige bei erstmaliger Ausgabe von Heimarbeit (§§ 6 und 7);

(d) Form, Inhalt, Ausgabe und Aufbewahrung von Entgeltbelegen (§ 9).

(2) Das Bundesministerium für Arbeit und Soziales kann mit Zustimmung des Bundesrates und nach Anhörung der Spitzenverbände der Gewerkschaften und der Vereinigung der Arbeitgeber allgemeine Verwaltungsvorschriften für die Durchführung dieses Gesetzes erlassen

1. contravenes a regulation on the keeping of lists (section 6), the notification or advertisement of homework (sections 7, 15), the obligation to provide information (section 7a), the disclosure of the payroll (section 8), the pay slips (section 9) or the obligation to provide information on the remuneration (section 28 (1))

2. contravenes an enforceable order to protect home workers from missed time (section 10)

3. contravenes a regulation on the distribution of homework in accordance with § 11 (2), insofar as it refers to this provision on fines for a specific offence, or

4. as a homeworker (section 1 (1)) or equivalent (section 1 (2)), tolerates the fact that a family member working in the home labour force commits an offence under section 32

(3) The administrative offence referred to in subsection 1 may be punishable by a fine of up to ten thousand euros, and the administrative offence referred to in subsection 2 by a fine of up to two thousand five hundred euros.

Section 33
Implementing Rules

(1) The Federal Ministry of Labour and Social Affairs shall be authorised, with the consent of the Bundesrat and after hearing the leading trade union organisations and employers' associations, to issue the statutory ordinances necessary for the implementation of this Act on

(a) the procedure in the case of equality (section 1 (2) to (5));

(b) the establishment of homework committees and of remuneration committees for external homework assistants and the procedure before them (sections 4, 5, 11, 18 to 22);

(c) the form, content and submission of the lists and the notification when homework is first issued (sections 6 and 7);

(d) Form, content, issue and storage of pay slips (section 9).

(2) The Federal Ministry of Labour and Social Affairs may, with the consent of the Bundesrat and after hearing the central organisations of the trade unions and the employers' association, issue general administrative provisions for the implementation of this Act

§ 34
Inkrafttreten

(1) Das Gesetz tritt einen Monat nach seiner Verkündung, der § 33 am Tage nach der Verkündung in Kraft.

(2) [1]Mit dem Inkrafttreten dieses Gesetzes treten das Gesetz über die Heimarbeit in der Fassung der Bekanntmachung vom 30. Oktober 1939 (Reichsgesetzbl. I S. 2145) und die Verordnung zur Durchführung des Gesetzes über die Heimarbeit vom 30. Oktober 1939 (Reichsgesetzbl. I S. 2152) außer Kraft. [2]Die auf Grund der bisherigen gesetzlichen Vorschriften zur Durchführung des Gefahrenschutzes erlassenen Verordnungen bleiben mit der Maßgabe in Kraft, daß anstelle der in ihnen erwähnten Vorschriften des Gesetzes über die Heimarbeit in der Fassung vom 30. Oktober 1939 und des Hausarbeitsgesetzes in der Fassung vom 30. Juni 1923 (Reichsgesetzbl. S. 472/730) die entsprechenden Vorschriften dieses Gesetzes treten.

Section 34
Coming into Force

(1) The Act shall enter into force one month after its promulgation, section 33 on the day after promulgation.

(2) [1]On entry into force of this Act, the Act on Home Work in the version promulgated on 30 October 1939 (Reich Law Gazette I p. 2145) and the Ordinance on the Implementation of the Act on Home Work of 30 October 1939 (Reich Law Gazette I p. 2152) shall cease to have effect. [2]The ordinances issued on the basis of the previous statutory provisions for the implementation of hazard protection shall remain in force subject to the proviso that the corresponding provisions of this Act shall replace the provisions of the Act on Home Work in the version of 30 October 1939 and the Domestic Work Act in the version of 30 June 1923 (Reichsgesetzbl. p. 472/730) mentioned therein.

VIII. Law on Documenting Essential Applicable Conditions for Employment Relationships (Excerpt)

Nachweisgesetz – NachwG

Stand: 11.08.2014

§ 2
Nachweispflicht

(1) [1]Der Arbeitgeber hat spätestens einen Monat nach dem vereinbarten Beginn des Arbeitsverhältnisses die wesentlichen Vertragsbedingungen schriftlich niederzulegen, die Niederschrift zu unterzeichnen und dem Arbeitnehmer auszuhändigen. [2]In die Niederschrift sind mindestens aufzunehmen:

1. der Name und die Anschrift der Vertragsparteien,
2. der Zeitpunkt des Beginns des Arbeitsverhältnisses,
3. bei befristeten Arbeitsverhältnissen: die vorhersehbare Dauer des Arbeitsverhältnisses,
4. der Arbeitsort oder, falls der Arbeitnehmer nicht nur an einem bestimmten Arbeitsort tätig sein soll, ein Hinweis darauf, daß der Arbeitnehmer an verschiedenen Orten beschäftigt werden kann,
5. eine kurze Charakterisierung oder Beschreibung der vom Arbeitnehmer zu leistenden Tätigkeit,
6. die Zusammensetzung und die Höhe des Arbeitsentgelts einschließlich der Zuschläge, der Zulagen, Prämien und Sonderzahlungen sowie anderer Bestandteile des Arbeitsentgelts und deren Fälligkeit,
7. die vereinbarte Arbeitszeit,
8. die Dauer des jährlichen Erholungsurlaubs,
9. die Fristen für die Kündigung des Arbeitsverhältnisses,
10. ein in allgemeiner Form gehaltener Hinweis auf die Tarifverträge, Betriebs- oder Dienstvereinbarungen, die auf das Arbeitsverhältnis anzuwenden sind.

[3]Der Nachweis der wesentlichen Vertragsbedingungen in elektronischer Form ist ausgeschlossen.

(1a) [1]Wer einen Praktikanten einstellt, hat unverzüglich nach Abschluss des Praktikumsvertrages, spätestens vor Aufnahme der Praktikantentätigkeit, die wesentlichen Ver-

Section 2
Obligation to provide proof

(1) [1]The employer shall, no later than one month after the agreed commencement of the employment relationship, record the essential terms of the contract in writing, sign the record and hand it over to the employee. [2]The record must at least include the following information:

1. the name and address of the contracting parties,
2. the date of commencement of the employment relationship,
3. in case of fixed-term employment: the foreseeable duration of the employment relationship,
4. the place of work or, if the employee is to work not only at a specific place of work, an indication that the employee can be employed at different places,
5. a brief characterization or description of the activities to be performed by the employee
6. the composition and the amount of the remuneration including surcharges, supplements, premiums and special payments as well as other components of the remuneration and their maturity,
7. the agreed working time,
8. the duration of the annual recovery leave
9. the deadlines for terminating the employment relationship,
10. a general reference to the collective agreements, works or Service agreements applicable to the employment relationship.

[3]The essential contractual terms cannot be documented in electronic form.

(1a) [1]Whoever hires an intern must immediately after the conclusion of the internship contract, at the latest before starting the internship, put down the essential contractual conditions in

tragsbedingungen schriftlich niederzulegen, die Niederschrift zu unterzeichnen und dem Praktikanten auszuhändigen. ²In die Niederschrift sind mindestens aufzunehmen:

1. der Name und die Anschrift der Vertragsparteien,
2. die mit dem Praktikum verfolgten Lern- und Ausbildungsziele,
3. Beginn und Dauer des Praktikums,
4. Dauer der regelmäßigen täglichen Praktikumszeit,
5. Zahlung und Höhe der Vergütung,
6. Dauer des Urlaubs,
7. ein in allgemeiner Form gehaltener Hinweis auf die Tarifverträge, Betriebs- oder Dienstvereinbarungen, die auf das Praktikumsverhältnis anzuwenden sind.

³Absatz 1 Satz 3 gilt entsprechend.

(2) Hat der Arbeitnehmer seine Arbeitsleistung länger als einen Monat außerhalb der Bundesrepublik Deutschland zu erbringen, so muß die Niederschrift dem Arbeitnehmer vor seiner Abreise ausgehändigt werden und folgende zusätzliche Angaben enthalten:

1. die Dauer der im Ausland auszuübenden Tätigkeit,
2. die Währung, in der das Arbeitsentgelt ausgezahlt wird,
3. ein zusätzliches mit dem Auslandsaufenthalt verbundenes Arbeitsentgelt und damit verbundene zusätzliche Sachleistungen,
4. die vereinbarten Bedingungen für die Rückkehr des Arbeitnehmers.

(3) ¹Die Angaben nach Absatz 1 Satz 2 Nr. 6 bis 9 und Absatz 2 Nr. 2 und 3 können ersetzt werden durch einen Hinweis auf die einschlägigen Tarifverträge, Betriebs- oder Dienstvereinbarungen und ähnlichen Regelungen, die für das Arbeitsverhältnis gelten. ²Ist in den Fällen des Absatzes 1 Satz 2 Nr. 8 und 9 die jeweilige gesetzliche Regelung maßgebend, so kann hierauf verwiesen werden.

(4) Wenn dem Arbeitnehmer ein schriftlicher Arbeitsvertrag ausgehändigt worden ist, entfällt die Verpflichtung nach den Absätzen 1 und 2, soweit der Vertrag die in den Absätzen 1 bis 3 geforderten Angaben enthält.

§5
Unabdingbarkeit

Von den Vorschriften dieses Gesetzes kann nicht zuungunsten des Arbeitnehmers abgewichen werden.

writing, sign the written document and hand it over to the intern. ²The written document shall include at least the following

1. the name and address of the parties to the contract,
2. the learning and training objectives pursued with the internship,
3. start and duration of the internship,
4. duration of the regular daily work placement,
5. payment and amount of the remuneration,
6. duration of the vacation,
7. a general reference to the collective bargaining agreements, company or service agreements which are applicable to the internship relationship.

³Paragraph 1 sentence 3 shall apply accordingly.

(2) If the employee is to perform his/ her activities outside of the Federal Republic of Germany for more than one month, the record must be handed over to the employee before his/her departure and contain the following additional information:

1. the duration of the activity abroad to be exercised,
2. the currency in which the remuneration is paid,
3. an additional salary related to the stay abroad and additional benefits in kind,
4. the agreed conditions for the employee's return.

(3) ¹The information in accordance with paragraph 1 sentence 2 Nukbers 6 to 9 and paragraph 2 Numbers 2 and 3 may be replaced by a reference to the relevant collective agreements, operating or service agreements and similar regulations which apply to the employment relationship. ²If in the cases of paragraph 1 sentence 2 numbers 8 and 9 the respective legal regulation is decisive, reference may be made to it.

(4) If a written employment contract has been handed over to the employee, the obligation according to paragraphs 1 and 2 shall not apply if the contract contains the information required in paragraphs 1 to 3.

Section 5
Indispensability (Mandatory Nature)

No deviation from this statute may be made to the detriment of the employee.

IX. Administrative Offences Act (Excerpt)

Gesetz über Ordnungswidrigkeiten – OWiG (Auszug)

Stand: 09.12.2019

§ 9	Section 9
Handeln für einen anderen	**Acting for another**

(1) Handelt jemand

1. als vertretungsberechtigtes Organ einer juristischen Person oder als Mitglied eines solchen Organs,
2. als vertretungsberechtigter Gesellschafter einer rechtsfähigen Personengesellschaft oder
3. als gesetzlicher Vertreter eines anderen,

so ist ein Gesetz, nach dem besondere persönliche Eigenschaften, Verhältnisse oder Umstände (besondere persönliche Merkmale) die Möglichkeit der Ahndung begründen, auch auf den Vertreter anzuwenden, wenn diese Merkmale zwar nicht bei ihm, aber bei dem Vertretenen vorliegen.

(2) ¹Ist jemand von dem Inhaber eines Betriebes oder einem sonst dazu Befugten

1. beauftragt, den Betrieb ganz oder zum Teil zu leiten, oder
2. ausdrücklich beauftragt, in eigener Verantwortung Aufgaben wahrzunehmen, die dem Inhaber des Betriebes obliegen,

und handelt er auf Grund dieses Auftrages, so ist ein Gesetz, nach dem besondere persönliche Merkmale die Möglichkeit der Ahndung begründen, auch auf den Beauftragten anzuwenden, wenn diese Merkmale zwar nicht bei ihm, aber bei dem Inhaber des Betriebes vorliegen. ²Dem Betrieb im Sinne des Satzes 1 steht das Unternehmen gleich. ³Handelt jemand auf Grund eines entsprechenden Auftrages für eine Stelle, die Aufgaben der öffentlichen Verwaltung wahrnimmt, so ist Satz 1 sinngemäß anzuwenden.

(3) Die Absätze 1 und 2 sind auch dann anzuwenden, wenn die Rechtshandlung, welche die Vertretungsbefugnis oder das Auftragsverhältnis begründen sollte, unwirksam ist.

(1) If someone acts

1. as an entity authorised to represent a legal person or as a member of such an entity,
2. as a partner authorised to represent a commercial partnership, or
3. as a statutory representative of another,

then a statute, in accordance with which special personal attributes, relationships or circumstances (special personal characteristics) form the basis of sanctioning, shall also be applicable to the representative if these characteristics do not indeed pertain to him, but to the person represented.

(2) ¹If the owner of a business or someone otherwise so authorised

1. commissions a person to manage a business, in whole or in part, or
2. expressly commissions a person to perform on his own responsibility duties which are incumbent on the owner of the business,

and if this person acts on the basis of this commission, then a statute in accordance with which special personal characteristics are the basis of sanctioning shall also be applicable to the person commissioned if these characteristics do not indeed pertain to him, but to the owner of the business. ²Within the meaning of the first sentence, an enterprise shall be the equivalent of a business. ³If someone acts on the basis of a corresponding commission for an agency which performs duties of public administration, then the first sentence shall apply mutatis mutandis.

(3) Subsections 1 and 2 shall also apply if the legal act which was intended to form the basis of the power of representation or the agency is void.

§ 17
Höhe der Geldbuße

(1) Die Geldbuße beträgt mindestens fünf Euro und, wenn das Gesetz nichts anderes bestimmt, höchstens eintausend Euro.

(2) Droht das Gesetz für vorsätzliches und fahrlässiges Handeln Geldbuße an, ohne im Höchstmaß zu unterscheiden, so kann fahrlässiges Handeln im Höchstmaß nur mit der Hälfte des angedrohten Höchstbetrages der Geldbuße geahndet werden.

(3) ¹Grundlage für die Zumessung der Geldbuße sind die Bedeutung der Ordnungswidrigkeit und der Vorwurf, der den Täter trifft. ²Auch die wirtschaftlichen Verhältnisse des Täters kommen in Betracht; bei geringfügigen Ordnungswidrigkeiten bleiben sie jedoch in der Regel unberücksichtigt.

(4) ¹Die Geldbuße soll den wirtschaftlichen Vorteil, den der Täter aus der Ordnungswidrigkeit gezogen hat, übersteigen. ²Reicht das gesetzliche Höchstmaß hierzu nicht aus, so kann es überschritten werden.

§ 29
Sondervorschrift für Organe und Vertreter

(1) Hat jemand

1. als vertretungsberechtigtes Organ einer juristischen Person oder als Mitglied eines solchen Organs,
2. als Vorstand eines nicht rechtsfähigen Vereins oder als Mitglied eines solchen Vorstandes,
3. als vertretungsberechtigter Gesellschafter einer rechtsfähigen Personengesellschaft,
4. als Generalbevollmächtigter oder in leitender Stellung als Prokurist oder Handlungsbevollmächtigter einer juristischen Person oder einer in Nummer 2 oder 3 genannten Personenvereinigung oder
5. als sonstige Person, die für die Leitung des Betriebs oder Unternehmens einer juristischen Person oder einer in Nummer 2 oder 3 genannten Personenvereinigung verantwortlich handelt, wozu auch die Überwachung der Geschäftsführung oder die sonstige Ausübung von Kontrollbefugnissen in leitender Stellung gehört,

Section 17
Amount of regulatory fine

(1) The amount of the regulatory fine shall not be less than five Euros and unless otherwise provided by statute shall not exceed one thousand Euros.

(2) If the law threatens to impose a regulatory fine for intentional and negligent action without distinction as to the maximum regulatory fine, the maximum sanction for a negligent action shall not exceed half of the maximum regulatory fine imposable.

(3) ¹The significance of the regulatory offence and the charge faced by the perpetrator shall form the basis for the assessment of the regulatory fine. ²The perpetrator's financial circumstances shall also be taken into account; however, they shall, as a rule, be disregarded in cases involving negligible regulatory offences.

(4) ¹The regulatory fine shall exceed the financial benefit that the perpetrator has obtained from commission of the regulatory offence. ²If the statutory maximum does not suffice for that purpose, it may be exceeded.

Section 29
Special Provision for Entities and Representatives

(1) If someone has committed an act:

1. as an entity authorised to represent a legal person or as a member of such an entity,
2. as chairman of the executive committee of an association without legal capacity or as a member of such committee,
3. as a partner authorised to represent a commercial partnership, or
4. as authorised representative with full power of attorney or in a managerial position as procura-holder or authorised representative with a commercial power of attorney of a legal person or an association of persons named in numbers 2 or 3, or
5. as another person acting with responsibility for managing the operation or enterprise of a legal person or of an association of persons named in numbers 2 or 3, also including the monitoring of the management or the other exercise of monitoring activities in a managerial position

eine Handlung vorgenommen, die ihm gegenüber unter den übrigen Voraussetzungen der §§ 22 bis 25 und § 28 die Einziehung eines Gegenstandes oder des Wertersatzes zulassen oder den Ausschluß der Entschädigung begründen würde, so wird seine Handlung bei Anwendung dieser Vorschriften dem Vertretenen zugerechnet.

(2) § 9 Abs. 3 gilt entsprechend.

which in relation to him and under the other prerequisites of sections 22 to 25 and 28 would permit the confiscation of an object or of its replacement value or justify the exclusion of compensation, then his act shall be attributed by application of these provisions to the person represented.

(2) Section 9 subsection 3 shall apply mutatis mutandis.

§ 29a
Einziehung des Wertes von Taterträgen

Section 29a
Confiscation of the Value of the Proceeds of an Offence

(1) Hat der Täter durch eine mit Geldbuße bedrohte Handlung oder für sie etwas erlangt und wird gegen ihn wegen der Handlung eine Geldbuße nicht festgesetzt, so kann gegen ihn die Einziehung eines Geldbetrages bis zu der Höhe angeordnet werden, die dem Wert des Erlangten entspricht.

(1) If the perpetrator has gained something by means of or for an act which may be sanctioned by a regulatory fine, and if a regulatory fine has not been assessed against him for the act, the confiscation of a sum up to the amount of the pecuniary advantage gained may be ordered.

(2) [1]Die Anordnung der Einziehung eines Geldbetrages bis zu der in Absatz 1 genannten Höhe kann sich gegen einen anderen, der nicht Täter ist, richten, wenn

(2) [1]The ordering of the confiscation of a sum up to the amount stated in subsection 1 may be directed against another party who is not the offender if

1. er durch eine mit Geldbuße bedrohte Handlung etwas erlangt hat und der Täter für ihn gehandelt hat,
2. ihm das Erlangte
   a) unentgeltlich oder ohne rechtlichen Grund übertragen wurde oder
   b) übertragen wurde und er erkannt hat oder hätte erkennen müssen, dass das Erlangte aus einer mit Geldbuße bedrohten Handlung herrührt, oder
3. das Erlangte auf ihn
   a) als Erbe übergegangen ist oder
   b) als Pflichtteilsberechtigter oder Vermächtnisnehmer übertragen worden ist.

1. he has obtained something by means of an act which may be sanctioned by a regulatory fine and the offender acted for him,
2. what has been acquired
   a) was transferred to him free of charge or without lawful reason, or
   b) was transferred, and he recognised or should have recognised that what has been acquired originates from an act which may be sanctioned by a regulatory fine, or
3. what has been acquired
   a) has passed to him as an inheritance, or
   b) was transferred to him as a person entitled to a compulsory portion or a legatee.

[2]Satz 1 Nummer 2 und 3 findet keine Anwendung, wenn das Erlangte zuvor einem Dritten, der nicht erkannt hat oder hätte erkennen müssen, dass das Erlangte aus einer mit Geldbuße bedrohten Handlung herrührt, entgeltlich und mit rechtlichem Grund übertragen wurde.

[2]The first sentence numbers 2 and 3 shall not apply if what has been acquired was previously transferred to a third party who did not recognise or could not be expected to recognise that what has been acquired originates from an act which may be sanctioned by a regulatory fine, for a fee and with a lawful reason.

(3) [1]Bei der Bestimmung des Wertes des Erlangten sind die Aufwendungen des Täters oder des anderen abzuziehen. [2]Außer Betracht bleibt jedoch das, was für die Begehung der Tat oder für ihre Vorbereitung aufgewendet oder eingesetzt worden ist.

(3) [1]The expenditure of the offender or of the third party shall be deducted when determining the value of what has been acquired. [2]What was expended or used for the commission of the offence or its preparation shall however not be allowed.

(4) [1]Umfang und Wert des Erlangten einschließlich der abzuziehenden Aufwendungen können geschätzt werden. [2]§ 18 gilt entsprechend.

(4) [1]The extent and value of what has been acquired, including the deductible expenditure, may be estimated. [2]Section 18 shall apply mutatis mutandis.

(5) Wird gegen den Täter ein Bußgeldverfahren nicht eingeleitet oder wird es eingestellt, so kann die Einziehung selbständig angeordnet werden.

(5) If no regulatory fining proceedings are initiated against the perpetrator, or if they are discontinued, confiscation may be ordered in its own right.

§ 30
Geldbuße gegen juristische Personen und Personenvereinigungen

(1) Hat jemand

1. als vertretungsberechtigtes Organ einer juristischen Person oder als Mitglied eines solchen Organs,

2. als Vorstand eines nicht rechtsfähigen Vereins oder als Mitglied eines solchen Vorstandes,

3. als vertretungsberechtigter Gesellschafter einer rechtsfähigen Personengesellschaft,

4. als Generalbevollmächtigter oder in leitender Stellung als Prokurist oder Handlungsbevollmächtigter einer juristischen Person oder einer in Nummer 2 oder 3 genannten Personenvereinigung oder

5. als sonstige Person, die für die Leitung des Betriebs oder Unternehmens einer juristischen Person oder einer in Nummer 2 oder 3 genannten Personenvereinigung verantwortlich handelt, wozu auch die Überwachung der Geschäftsführung oder die sonstige Ausübung von Kontrollbefugnissen in leitender Stellung gehört,

eine Straftat oder Ordnungswidrigkeit begangen, durch die Pflichten, welche die juristische Person oder die Personenvereinigung treffen, verletzt worden sind oder die juristische Person oder die Personenvereinigung bereichert worden ist oder werden sollte, so kann gegen diese eine Geldbuße festgesetzt werden.

(2) ^{1}Die Geldbuße beträgt

im Falle einer vorsätzlichen Straftat bis zu zehn Millionen Euro,

im Falle einer fahrlässigen Straftat bis zu fünf Millionen Euro.

Section 30
Regulatory Fine Imposed on Legal Persons and on Associations of Persons

(1) Where someone acting

1. as an entity authorised to represent a legal person or as a member of such an entity,

2. as chairman of the executive committee of an association without legal capacity or as a member of such committee,

3. as a partner authorised to represent a partnership with legal capacity, or

4. as the authorised representative with full power of attorney or in a managerial position as procura-holder or the authorised representative with a commercial power of attorney of a legal person or of an association of persons referred to in numbers 2 or 3,

5. as another person responsible on behalf of the management of the operation or enterprise forming part of a legal person, or of an association of persons referred to in numbers 2 or 3, also covering supervision of the conduct of business or other exercise of controlling powers in a managerial position,

has committed a criminal offence or a regulatory offence as a result of which duties incumbent on the legal person or on the association of persons have been violated, or where the legal person or the association of persons has been enriched or was intended to be enriched, a regulatory fine may be imposed on such person or association

(2) ^{1}The regulatory fine shall amount

in the case of a criminal offence committed with intent, to not more than ten million Euros,

in the case of a criminal offence committed negligently, to not more than five million Euros.

²Im Falle einer Ordnungswidrigkeit bestimmt sich das Höchstmaß der Geldbuße nach dem für die Ordnungswidrigkeit angedrohten Höchstmaß der Geldbuße. ³Verweist das Gesetz auf diese Vorschrift, so verzehnfacht sich das Höchstmaß der Geldbuße nach Satz 2 für die im Gesetz bezeichneten Tatbestände. ⁴Satz 2 gilt auch im Falle einer Tat, die gleichzeitig Straftat und Ordnungswidrigkeit ist, wenn das für die Ordnungswidrigkeit angedrohte Höchstmaß der Geldbuße das Höchstmaß nach Satz 1 übersteigt.

(2a) ¹Im Falle einer Gesamtrechtsnachfolge oder einer partiellen Gesamtrechtsnachfolge durch Aufspaltung (§ 123 Absatz 1 des Umwandlungsgesetzes) kann die Geldbuße nach Absatz 1 und 2 gegen den oder die Rechtsnachfolger festgesetzt werden. ²Die Geldbuße darf in diesen Fällen den Wert des übernommenen Vermögens sowie die Höhe der gegenüber dem Rechtsvorgänger angemessenen Geldbuße nicht übersteigen. ³Im Bußgeldverfahren tritt der Rechtsnachfolger oder treten die Rechtsnachfolger in die Verfahrensstellung ein, in der sich der Rechtsvorgänger zum Zeitpunkt des Wirksamwerdens der Rechtsnachfolge befunden hat.

(3) § 17 Abs. 4 und § 18 gelten entsprechend.

(4) ¹Wird wegen der Straftat oder Ordnungswidrigkeit ein Straf- oder Bußgeldverfahren nicht eingeleitet oder wird es eingestellt oder wird von Strafe abgesehen, so kann die Geldbuße selbständig festgesetzt werden. ²Durch Gesetz kann bestimmt werden, daß die Geldbuße auch in weiteren Fällen selbständig festgesetzt werden kann. ³Die selbständige Festsetzung einer Geldbuße gegen die juristische Person oder Personenvereinigung ist jedoch ausgeschlossen, wenn die Straftat oder Ordnungswidrigkeit aus rechtlichen Gründen nicht verfolgt werden kann; § 33 Abs. 1 Satz 2 bleibt unberührt.

(5) Die Festsetzung einer Geldbuße gegen die juristische Person oder Personenvereinigung schließt es aus, gegen sie wegen derselben Tat die Einziehung nach den §§ 73 oder 73c des Strafgesetzbuches oder nach § 29a anzuordnen.

²Where there has been commission of a regulatory offence, the maximum regulatory fine that can be imposed shall be determined by the maximum regulatory fine imposable for the regulatory offence concerned. ³If the Act refers to this provision, the maximum amount of the regulatory fine in accordance with the second sentence shall be multiplied by ten for the offences referred to in the Act. ⁴The second sentence shall also apply where there has been commission of an act simultaneously constituting a criminal offence and a regulatory offence, provided that the maximum regulatory fine imposable for the regulatory offence exceeds the maximum in accordance with the first sentence.

(2a) ¹In the event of a universal succession or of a partial universal succession by means of splitting (section 123 subsection 1 of the Reorganisation Act [Umwandlungsgesetz]), the regulatory fine in accordance with subsections 1 and 2 may be imposed on the legal successor(s). ²In such cases, the regulatory fine may not exceed the value of the assets which have been assumed, as well as the amount of the regulatory fine which is suitable against the legal successor. ³The legal successor(s) shall take up the procedural position in the regulatory fine proceedings in which the legal predecessor was at the time when the legal succession became effective.

(3) Section 17 subsection 4 and section 18 shall apply mutatis mutandis.

(4) ¹If criminal proceedings or regulatory fining proceedings are not commenced on account of the criminal offence or of the regulatory offence, or if such proceedings are discontinued, or if imposition of a criminal penalty is dispensed with, the regulatory fine may be assessed independently. ²Statutory provision may be made to the effect that a regulatory fine may be imposed in its own right in further cases as well. ³Independent assessment of a regulatory fine against the legal person or association of persons shall however be precluded where the criminal offence or the regulatory offence cannot be prosecuted for legal reasons; section 33 subsection 1 second sentence shall remain unaffected.

(5) Assessment of a regulatory fine incurred by the legal person or association of persons shall, in respect of one and the same offence, preclude a confiscation order, in accordance with sections 73 or 73c of the Penal Code or in accordance with section 29a, against such person or association of persons.

(6) Bei Erlass eines Bußgeldbescheids ist zur Sicherung der Geldbuße § 111e Absatz 2 der Strafprozessordnung mit der Maßgabe anzuwenden, dass an die Stelle des Urteils der Bußgeldbescheid tritt.

(6) On issuance of a regulatory fining notice, in order to secure the regulatory fine, section 111e subsection 2 of the Code of Criminal Procedure shall be applied on proviso that the judgment is substituted by the regulatory fining notice.

§ 31
Verfolgungsverjährung

(1) ¹Durch die Verjährung werden die Verfolgung von Ordnungswidrigkeiten und die Anordnung von Nebenfolgen ausgeschlossen. ²§ 27 Abs. 2 Satz 1 Nr. 1 bleibt unberührt.

(2) Die Verfolgung von Ordnungswidrigkeiten verjährt, wenn das Gesetz nichts anderes bestimmt,

1. in drei Jahren bei Ordnungswidrigkeiten, die mit Geldbuße im Höchstmaß von mehr als fünfzehntausend Euro bedroht sind,

2. in zwei Jahren bei Ordnungswidrigkeiten, die mit Geldbuße im Höchstmaß von mehr als zweitausendfünfhundert bis zu fünfzehntausend Euro bedroht sind,

3. in zwei Jahren bei Ordnungswidrigkeiten, die mit Geldbuße im Höchstmaß von mehr als zweitausendfünfhundert bis zu fünfzehntausend Euro bedroht sind,

4. in zwei Jahren bei Ordnungswidrigkeiten, die mit Geldbuße im Höchstmaß von mehr als zweitausendfünfhundert bis zu fünfzehntausend Euro bedroht sind,

5. in zwei Jahren bei Ordnungswidrigkeiten, die mit Geldbuße im Höchstmaß von mehr als zweitausendfünfhundert bis zu fünfzehntausend Euro bedroht sind,

6. in zwei Jahren bei Ordnungswidrigkeiten, die mit Geldbuße im Höchstmaß von mehr als zweitausendfünfhundert bis zu fünfzehntausend Euro bedroht sind,

7. in einem Jahr bei Ordnungswidrigkeiten, die mit Geldbuße im Höchstmaß von mehr als eintausend bis zu zweitausendfünfhundert Euro bedroht sind,

8. in sechs Monaten bei den übrigen Ordnungswidrigkeiten.

(3) ¹Die Verjährung beginnt, sobald die Handlung beendet ist. ²Tritt ein zum Tatbestand gehörender Erfolg erst später ein, so beginnt die Verjährung mit diesem Zeitpunkt.

Section 31
Prosecution Barred by the Statute of Limitation

(1) ¹Prosecution of regulatory offences and the ordering of incidental consequences shall be barred after the period of limitation has expired. ²Section 27 subsection 2 first sentence number 1 shall remain unaffected.

(2) If not otherwise provided by statute, the period of limitation for the prosecution of regulatory offences shall expire:

1. after three years in the case of regulatory offences for which a maximum regulatory fine of more than fifteen thousand Euros may be imposed,

2. after two years in the case of regulatory offences for which a maximum regulatory fine is imposable ranging from more than two thousand five hundred to fifteen thousand Euros,

3. after two years in the case of regulatory offences for which a maximum regulatory fine is imposable ranging from more than two thousand five hundred to fifteen thousand Euros,

4. after two years in the case of regulatory offences for which a maximum regulatory fine is imposable ranging from more than two thousand five hundred to fifteen thousand Euros,

5. after one year in the case of regulatory offences for which a maximum regulatory fine is imposable ranging from more than one thousand Euros to two thousand five hundred Euros,

6. after six months in all other cases involving regulatory offences.

7. in one year for administrative offences punishable by a fine of a maximum of more than one thousand up to two thousand five hundred euros

8. in six months for the remaining administrative offences

(3) ¹The statute of limitation shall begin to run as soon as the act is completed. ²If a result constituting a factual element of the offence occurs only later, the period of limitation shall begin to run at that time.

§ 130
Verletzung der Aufsichtspflicht in Betrieben und Unternehmen

(1) ¹Wer als Inhaber eines Betriebes oder Unternehmens vorsätzlich oder fahrlässig die Aufsichtsmaßnahmen unterläßt, die erforderlich sind, um in dem Betrieb oder Unternehmen Zuwiderhandlungen gegen Pflichten zu verhindern, die den Inhaber treffen und deren Verletzung mit Strafe oder Geldbuße bedroht ist, handelt ordnungswidrig, wenn eine solche Zuwiderhandlung begangen wird, die durch gehörige Aufsicht verhindert oder wesentlich erschwert worden wäre. ²Zu den erforderlichen Aufsichtsmaßnahmen gehören auch die Bestellung, sorgfältige Auswahl und Überwachung von Aufsichtspersonen.

(2) Betrieb oder Unternehmen im Sinne des Absatzes 1 ist auch das öffentliche Unternehmen.

(3) ¹Die Ordnungswidrigkeit kann, wenn die Pflichtverletzung mit Strafe bedroht ist, mit einer Geldbuße bis zu einer Million Euro geahndet werden. ²§ 30 Absatz 2 Satz 3 ist anzuwenden. ³Ist die Pflichtverletzung mit Geldbuße bedroht, so bestimmt sich das Höchstmaß der Geldbuße wegen der Aufsichtspflichtverletzung nach dem für die Pflichtverletzung angedrohten Höchstmaß der Geldbuße. ⁴Satz 3 gilt auch im Falle einer Pflichtverletzung, die gleichzeitig mit Strafe und Geldbuße bedroht ist, wenn das für die Pflichtverletzung angedrohte Höchstmaß der Geldbuße das Höchstmaß nach Satz 1 übersteigt.

Section 130
Violation of obligtory supervision in operations and enterprises

(1) ¹Whoever, as the owner of an operation or undertaking, intentionally or negligently omits to take the supervisory measures required to prevent contraventions, within the operation or undertaking, of duties incumbent on the owner and the violation of which carries a criminal penalty or a regulatory fine, shall be deemed to have committed a regulatory offence in a case where such contravention has been committed as would have been prevented, or made much more difficult, if there had been proper supervision. ²The required supervisory measures shall also comprise appointment, careful selection and surveillance of supervisory personnel.

(2) An operation or undertaking within the meaning of subsection 1 shall include a public enterprise.

(3) ¹Where the breach of duty carries a criminal penalty, the regulatory offence may carry a regulatory fine not exceeding one million Euros. ²Section 30 subsection 2 third sentence shall be applicable. ³Where the breach of duty carries a regulatory fine, the maximum regulatory fine for breach of the duty of supervision shall be determined by the maximum regulatory fine imposable for the breach of duty. ⁴The third sentence shall also apply in the case of a breach of duty carrying simultaneously a criminal penalty and a regulatory fine, provided that the maximum regulatory fine imposable for the breach of duty exceeds the maximum in accordance with the first sentence.

X. Criminal Code (Excerpt)

Strafgesetzbuch – StGB (Auszug)

Stand: 20.11.2019

§ 9
Ort der Tat

(1) Eine Tat ist an jedem Ort begangen, an dem der Täter gehandelt hat oder im Falle des Unterlassens hätte handeln müssen oder an dem der zum Tatbestand gehörende Erfolg eingetreten ist oder nach der Vorstellung des Täters eintreten sollte.

(2) ¹Die Teilnahme ist sowohl an dem Ort begangen, an dem die Tat begangen ist, als auch an jedem Ort, an dem der Teilnehmer gehandelt hat oder im Falle des Unterlassens hätte handeln müssen oder an dem nach seiner Vorstellung die Tat begangen werden sollte. ²Hat der Teilnehmer an einer Auslandstat im Inland gehandelt, so gilt für die Teilnahme das deutsche Strafrecht, auch wenn die Tat nach dem Recht des Tatorts nicht mit Strafe bedroht ist.

§ 14
Handeln für einen anderen

(1) Handelt jemand

1. als vertretungsberechtigtes Organ einer juristischen Person oder als Mitglied eines solchen Organs,
2. als vertretungsberechtigter Gesellschafter einer rechtsfähigen Personengesellschaft oder
3. als gesetzlicher Vertreter eines anderen,

so ist ein Gesetz, nach dem besondere persönliche Eigenschaften, Verhältnisse oder Umstände (besondere persönliche Merkmale) die Strafbarkeit begründen, auch auf den Vertreter anzuwenden, wenn diese Merkmale zwar nicht bei ihm, aber bei dem Vertretenen vorliegen.

(2) ¹Ist jemand von dem Inhaber eines Betriebs oder einem sonst dazu Befugten

1. beauftragt, den Betrieb ganz oder zum Teil zu leiten, oder

Section 9
Place of commission of offence

(1) An offence is deemed to have been committed at every place where the offender acted or, in the case of an omission, was required to act or in which the result, if it is an element of the offence, occurs or was to have occurred as envisaged by the offender.

(2) ¹Acts of participation are not only committed at the place where the offence was committed, but also at every place where the participant acted or, in the case of an omission, was required to act or where, as envisaged by the participant, the offence was to have been committed. ²If the participant to an offence committed abroad acted within the territory of the Federal Republic of Germany, German criminal law applies to the participation even if the act is not a criminal offence according to the law of the place of its commission.

Section 14
Acting as agent

(1) If a person acts

1. in the capacity as an organ which is authorised to represent a legal entity or as a member of such an organ,
2. in the capacity as a partner who is authorised to represent a partnership with legal capacity or
3. in the capacity as statutory representative of another,

then any law under which special personal attributes, relationships or circumstances (special personal characteristics) give rise to criminal liability also applies to the representative if these characteristics do not exist in the person of that representative but in the entity, partnership or person represented.

(2) ¹If a person, whether by the owner of a business or somebody delegated by the owner to do so,

1. has been commissioned to manage the business in whole or in part or

2. ausdrücklich beauftragt, in eigener Verantwortung Aufgaben wahrzunehmen, die dem Inhaber des Betriebs obliegen,

und handelt er auf Grund dieses Auftrags, so ist ein Gesetz, nach dem besondere persönliche Merkmale die Strafbarkeit begründen, auch auf den Beauftragten anzuwenden, wenn diese Merkmale zwar nicht bei ihm, aber bei dem Inhaber des Betriebs vorliegen. ²Dem Betrieb im Sinne des Satzes 1 steht das Unternehmen gleich. ³Handelt jemand auf Grund eines entsprechenden Auftrags für eine Stelle, die Aufgaben der öffentlichen Verwaltung wahrnimmt, so ist Satz 1 sinngemäß anzuwenden.

(3) Die Absätze 1 und 2 sind auch dann anzuwenden, wenn die Rechtshandlung, welche die Vertretungsbefugnis oder das Auftragsverhältnis begründen sollte, unwirksam ist.

2. has been expressly commissioned to perform autonomous duties which are incumbent upon the owner of the business

and that person acts on the basis of this commission, then any law under which special personal characteristics give rise to criminal liability also applies to the person commissioned if these characteristics do not exist in the person commissioned but in the person of the owner of the business. ²An enterprise is equal to a business within the meaning of sentence 1. ³If a person acts on the basis of a similar commission for an agency performing public administrative services, sentence 1 applies analogously.

(3) Subsections (1) and (2) apply even if the act of commission intended to create the power of representation or the agency is void.

§ 16
Irrtum über Tatumstände

(1) ¹Wer bei Begehung der Tat einen Umstand nicht kennt, der zum gesetzlichen Tatbestand gehört, handelt nicht vorsätzlich. ²Die Strafbarkeit wegen fahrlässiger Begehung bleibt unberührt.

(2) Wer bei Begehung der Tat irrig Umstände annimmt, welche den Tatbestand eines milderen Gesetzes verwirklichen würden, kann wegen vorsätzlicher Begehung nur nach dem milderen Gesetz bestraft werden.

Section 16
Mistake of fact

(1) ¹Whoever, at the time of the commission of the offence, is unaware of a fact which is a statutory element of the offence is deemed to lack intention. ²Any criminal liability for negligence remains unaffected.

(2) Whoever, at the time of commission of the offence, mistakenly assumes the existence of facts which would satisfy the elements of a more lenient provision may only be punished for the intentional commission of the offence under the more lenient provision.

§ 27
Beihilfe

(1) Als Gehilfe wird bestraft, wer vorsätzlich einem anderen zu dessen vorsätzlich begangener rechtswidriger Tat Hilfe geleistet hat.

(2) ¹Die Strafe für den Gehilfen richtet sich nach der Strafdrohung für den Täter. ²Sie ist nach § 49 Abs. 1 zu mildern.

Section 27
Aiding

(1) Whoever intentionally assists another in the intentional commission of an unlawful act incurs a penalty as an aider.

(2) ¹The penalty for the aider is determined in accordance with the penalty threatened for the offender. ²It must be mitigated pursuant to section 49 (1).

§ 73
Einziehung von Taterträgen bei Tätern und Teilnehmern

(1) Hat der Täter oder Teilnehmer durch eine rechtswidrige Tat oder für sie etwas erlangt, so ordnet das Gericht dessen Einziehung an.

(2) Hat der Täter oder Teilnehmer Nutzungen aus dem Erlangten gezogen, so ordnet das Gericht auch deren Einziehung an.

Section 73
Confiscation of proceeds of crime from offenders and participants

(1) If the offender or participant has obtained anything by or for an unlawful act, the court orders the confiscation of that which was obtained.

(2) If the offender or participant has derived any benefits from the proceeds, the court also orders the confiscation of the benefits.

(3) Das Gericht kann auch die Einziehung der Gegenstände anordnen, die der Täter oder Teilnehmer erworben hat

1. durch Veräußerung des Erlangten oder als Ersatz für dessen Zerstörung, Beschädigung oder Entziehung oder
2. auf Grund eines erlangten Rechts.

(3) The court may also order confiscation of objects which the offender or participant has obtained

1. by way of sale of the object obtained or as compensation for its destruction, damage or confiscation or
2. on the basis of a right obtained.

§ 73c
Einziehung des Wertes von Taterträgen

¹Ist die Einziehung eines Gegenstandes wegen der Beschaffenheit des Erlangten oder aus einem anderen Grund nicht möglich oder wird von der Einziehung eines Ersatzgegenstandes nach § 73 Absatz 3 oder nach § 73b Absatz 3 abgesehen, so ordnet das Gericht die Einziehung eines Geldbetrages an, der dem Wert des Erlangten entspricht. ²Eine solche Anordnung trifft das Gericht auch neben der Einziehung eines Gegenstandes, soweit dessen Wert hinter dem Wert des zunächst Erlangten zurückbleibt.

Section 73c
Confiscation of value of proceeds of crime

¹If the confiscation of a particular object is impossible due to the nature of that which was obtained or for some other reason or because confiscation of a surrogate object has not been ordered as required by section 73 (3) or section 73b (3), the court orders the confiscation of a sum of money equal to the value of that which was obtained. ²The court also makes such an order in addition to confiscating an object to the extent that its value falls short of the value of that which was originally obtained.

§ 74e
Sondervorschrift für Organe und Vertreter

¹Hat jemand

1. als vertretungsberechtigtes Organ einer juristischen Person oder als Mitglied eines solchen Organs,
2. als Vorstand eines nicht rechtsfähigen Vereins oder als Mitglied eines solchen Vorstandes,
3. als vertretungsberechtigter Gesellschafter einer rechtsfähigen Personengesellschaft,
4. als Generalbevollmächtigter oder in leitender Stellung als Prokurist oder Handlungsbevollmächtigter einer juristischen Person oder einer in Nummer 2 oder 3 genannten Personenvereinigung oder
5. als sonstige Person, die für die Leitung des Betriebs oder Unternehmens einer juristischen Person oder einer in Nummer 2 oder 3 genannten Personenvereinigung verantwortlich handelt, wozu auch die Überwachung der Geschäftsführung oder die sonstige Ausübung von Kontrollbefugnissen in leitender Stellung gehört,

Section 74e
Special provision applicable to organs and representatives

¹Whoever commits an act

1. in the capacity as an organ authorised to represent a legal entity or as a member of such an organ,
2. in the capacity as a director of an association lacking independent legal capacity or as a member of the board of directors of such an association,
3. in the capacity as a partner authorised to represent a partnership with independent legal capacity,
4. in the capacity as a general agent (Generalbevollmächtigter) or, in a management position, with general power of representation (Prokurist) or with commercial power of attorney (Handlungsbevollmächtigter) of a legal entity or of one of the associations referred to in nos. 2 or 3 or
5. as another person acting in a responsible capacity for the management of the business or enterprise of a legal entity or association referred to in no. 2 or 3, including oversight of the management of the business or other exercise of controlling powers in a senior management position,

eine Handlung vorgenommen, die ihm gegenüber unter den übrigen Voraussetzungen der §§ 74 bis 74c die Einziehung eines Gegenstandes oder des Wertersatzes zulassen oder den Ausschluss der Entschädigung begründen würde, wird seine Handlung bei Anwendung dieser Vorschriften dem Vertretenen zugerechnet. ²§ 14 Absatz 3 gilt entsprechend.

which in relation to them and under the other conditions of sections 74 to 74c would allow the confiscation of an object or of its equivalent value or justify the denial of compensation, has this act attributed and these provisions applied to the person or entity represented. ²Section 14 (3) applies accordingly.

§ 78
Verjährungsfrist

(1) ¹Die Verjährung schließt die Ahndung der Tat und die Anordnung von Maßnahmen (§ 11 Abs. 1 Nr. 8) aus. ²§ 76a Absatz 2 bleibt unberührt.

(2) Verbrechen nach § 211 (Mord) verjähren nicht.

(3) Soweit die Verfolgung verjährt, beträgt die Verjährungsfrist

1. dreißig Jahre bei Taten, die mit lebenslanger Freiheitsstrafe bedroht sind,
2. zwanzig Jahre bei Taten, die im Höchstmaß mit Freiheitsstrafen von mehr als zehn Jahren bedroht sind,
3. zehn Jahre bei Taten, die im Höchstmaß mit Freiheitsstrafen von mehr als fünf Jahren bis zu zehn Jahren bedroht sind,
4. fünf Jahre bei Taten, die im Höchstmaß mit Freiheitsstrafen von mehr als einem Jahr bis zu fünf Jahren bedroht sind,
5. drei Jahre bei den übrigen Taten

(4) Die Frist richtet sich nach der Strafdrohung des Gesetzes, dessen Tatbestand die Tat verwirklicht, ohne Rücksicht auf Schärfungen oder Milderungen, die nach den Vorschriften des Allgemeinen Teils oder für besonders schwere oder minder schwere Fälle vorgesehen sind.

Section 78
Limitation period

(1) ¹The imposition of a penalty and the ordering of measures (section 11 (1) no. 8) are ruled out following expiry of the limitation period. ²Section 76a (2) remains unaffected.

(2) Serious criminal offences under section 211 (murder under specific aggravating circumstances) are not subject to the statute of limitations.

(3) Where prosecution is subject to the statute of limitations, the limitation period is

1. 30 years in the case of offences which are punishable by imprisonment for life
2. 20 years in the case of offences which are punishable by a maximum sentence of imprisonment of more than 10 years,
3. 10 years in the case of offences which are punishable by a maximum sentence of imprisonment of more than five years but no more than 10 years,
4. five years in the case of offences which are punishable by a maximum sentence of imprisonment of more than one year but no more than five years,
5. three years in the case of other offences.

(4) The period is determined in accordance with the penalty threatened under the law which defines the elements of the offence realised, irrespective of aggravating or mitigating circumstances provided for in the provisions of the General Part or of aggravated or less serious cases under the Special Part.

§ 78a
Beginn

¹Die Verjährung beginnt, sobald die Tat beendet ist. ²Tritt ein zum Tatbestand gehörender Erfolg erst später ein, so beginnt die Verjährung mit diesem Zeitpunkt.

Section 78a
Commencement

¹The limitation period begins to run as soon as the offence is completed. ²If a result constituting an element of the offence occurs later, the limitation period begins to run as of that time.

§ 263
Betrug

(1) Wer in der Absicht, sich oder einem Dritten einen rechtswidrigen Vermögensvorteil zu verschaffen, das Vermögen eines anderen dadurch beschädigt, daß er durch Vorspiegelung falscher oder durch Entstellung oder Unterdrückung wahrer Tatsachen einen Irrtum erregt oder unterhält, wird mit Freiheitsstrafe bis zu fünf Jahren oder mit Geldstrafe bestraft.

(2) Der Versuch ist strafbar

(3) [1]In besonders schweren Fällen ist die Strafe Freiheitsstrafe von sechs Monaten bis zu zehn Jahren. [2]Ein besonders schwerer Fall liegt in der Regel vor, wenn der Täter

1. gewerbsmäßig oder als Mitglied einer Bande handelt, die sich zur fortgesetzten Begehung von Urkundenfälschung oder Betrug verbunden hat,
2. einen Vermögensverlust großen Ausmaßes herbeiführt oder in der Absicht handelt, durch die fortgesetzte Begehung von Betrug eine große Zahl von Menschen in die Gefahr des Verlustes von Vermögenswerten zu bringen,
3. eine andere Person in wirtschaftliche Not bringt,
4. seine Befugnisse oder seine Stellung als Amtsträger oder Europäischer Amtsträger mißbraucht oder
5. einen Versicherungsfall vortäuscht, nachdem er oder ein anderer zu diesem Zweck eine Sache von bedeutendem Wert in Brand gesetzt oder durch eine Brandlegung ganz oder teilweise zerstört oder ein Schiff zum Sinken oder Stranden gebracht hat.

(4) § 243 Abs. 2 sowie die §§ 247 und 248a gelten entsprechend.

(5) Mit Freiheitsstrafe von einem Jahr bis zu zehn Jahren, in minder schweren Fällen mit Freiheitsstrafe von sechs Monaten bis zu fünf Jahren wird bestraft, wer den Betrug als Mitglied einer Bande, die sich zur fortgesetzten Begehung von Straftaten nach den §§ 263 bis 264 oder 267 bis 269 verbunden hat, gewerbsmäßig begeht.

(6) Das Gericht kann Führungsaufsicht anordnen (§ 68 Abs. 1).

Section 263
Fraud

(1) Whoever, with the intention of obtaining an unlawful pecuniary benefit for themselves or a third party, damages the assets of another by causing or maintaining an error under false pretences or distorting or suppressing true facts incurs a penalty of imprisonment for a term not exceeding five years or a fine.

(2) The attempt is punishable.

(3) [1]In especially serious cases, the penalty is imprisonment for a term of between six months and 10 years. [2]An especially serious case typically occurs where the offender

1. gang whose purpose is the continued commission of forgery of documents or fraud, acts on a commercial basis or as a member of a
2. causes a major financial loss to or acts with the intention of placing a large number of persons in danger of financial loss by the continued commission of fraud,
3. places another person in financial hardship,
4. abuses his or her powers or position as a public official or European official or
5. pretends that an insured event has happened after they or another person have set fire to an object of significant value or destroyed it, in whole or in part, by setting fire to it or caused the sinking or grounding of a ship.

(4) Section 243 (2) and sections 247 and 248a apply accordingly.

(5) Whoever commits fraud on a commercial basis as a member of a gang whose purpose is the continued commission of offences under sections 263 to 264 or sections 267 to 269 incurs a penalty of imprisonment for a term of between one year and 10 years, in less serious cases imprisonment for a term of between six months and five years.

(6) The court may make an order for the supervision of conduct (section 68 (1)).

§ 266a
Vorenthalten und Veruntreuen von Arbeitsentgelt

(1) Wer als Arbeitgeber der Einzugsstelle Beiträge des Arbeitnehmers zur Sozialversicherung einschließlich der Arbeitsförderung, unabhängig davon, ob Arbeitsentgelt gezahlt wird, vorenthält, wird mit Freiheitsstrafe bis zu fünf Jahren oder mit Geldstrafe bestraft.

(2) Ebenso wird bestraft, wer als Arbeitgeber

1. der für den Einzug der Beiträge zuständigen Stelle über sozialversicherungsrechtlich erhebliche Tatsachen unrichtige oder unvollständige Angaben macht oder
2. die für den Einzug der Beiträge zuständige Stelle pflichtwidrig über sozialversicherungsrechtlich erhebliche Tatsachen in Unkenntnis lässt

und dadurch dieser Stelle vom Arbeitgeber zu tragende Beiträge zur Sozialversicherung einschließlich der Arbeitsförderung, unabhängig davon, ob Arbeitsentgelt gezahlt wird, vorenthält.

(3) ¹Wer als Arbeitgeber sonst Teile des Arbeitsentgelts, die er für den Arbeitnehmer an einen anderen zu zahlen hat, dem Arbeitnehmer einbehält, sie jedoch an den anderen nicht zahlt und es unterlässt, den Arbeitnehmer spätestens im Zeitpunkt der Fälligkeit oder unverzüglich danach über das Unterlassen der Zahlung an den anderen zu unterrichten, wird mit Freiheitsstrafe bis zu fünf Jahren oder mit Geldstrafe bestraft. ²Satz 1 gilt nicht für Teile des Arbeitsentgelts, die als Lohnsteuer einbehalten werden.

(4) ¹In besonders schweren Fällen der Absätze 1 und 2 ist die Strafe Freiheitsstrafe von sechs Monaten bis zu zehn Jahren. ²Ein besonders schwerer Fall liegt in der Regel vor, wenn der Täter

1. aus grobem Eigennutz in großem Ausmaß Beiträge vorenthält,
2. unter Verwendung nachgemachter oder verfälschter Belege fortgesetzt Beiträge vorenthält,
3. fortgesetzt Beiträge vorenthält und sich zur Verschleierung der tatsächlichen Beschäftigungsverhältnisse unrichtige, nachgemachte oder verfälschte Belege von einem Dritten verschafft, der diese gewerbsmäßig anbietet,

Section 266a
Withholding wages and salaries

(1) Whoever, in the capacity as an employer, withholds an employee's contributions to the social security system, including employment promotion, regardless of whether wages or salaries are actually being paid, incurs a penalty of imprisonment for a term not exceeding five years or a fine.

(2) Whoever, in the capacity as an employer

1. supplies, to the agency responsible for collecting contributions, incorrect or incomplete particulars regarding facts which are relevant under social insurance law or
2. contrary to their duty, withholds from the agency responsible for collecting contributions facts which are relevant to the social insurance system,

and thereby withholds the contributions to be paid by the employer to social insurance, including employment promotion, regardless of whether salary or wages are actually being paid, incurs the same penalty

(3) ¹Whoever, in the capacity as an employer, otherwise withholds parts of wages or salaries which they are under a duty to pay to another on behalf of the employee but does not pay them to the other party and omits to inform the employee about the failure to make the payment at the latest on the due date or promptly thereafter incurs a penalty of imprisonment for a term not exceeding five years or a fine. ²Sentence 1 does not apply to those parts of the wages or salary which are deducted as income tax on wages and salaries.

(4) ¹In especially serious cases under subsections (1) and (2), the penalty is imprisonment for a term of between six months and 10 years. ²An especially serious case typically occurs where the offender

1. withholds, out of gross self-interest, contributions on a large scale,
2. by using counterfeit or falsified supporting documentation continually withholds contributions,
3. continually withholds contributions and procures incorrect, counterfeit or falsified supporting documentation from a third party for the purpose of concealing the true employment relationship, that third party offering such supporting documentation on a commercial basis,

4. als Mitglied einer Bande handelt, die sich zum fortgesetzten Vorenthalten von Beiträgen zusammengeschlossen hat und die zur Verschleierung der tatsächlichen Beschäftigungsverhältnisse unrichtige, nachgemachte oder verfälschte Belege vorhält, oder

5. die Mithilfe eines Amtsträgers ausnutzt, der seine Befugnisse oder seine Stellung missbraucht.

(5) Dem Arbeitgeber stehen der Auftraggeber eines Heimarbeiters, Hausgewerbetreibenden oder einer Person, die im Sinne des Heimarbeitsgesetzes diesen gleichgestellt ist, sowie der Zwischenmeister gleich.

(6) ¹In den Fällen der Absätze 1 und 2 kann das Gericht von einer Bestrafung nach dieser Vorschrift absehen, wenn der Arbeitgeber spätestens im Zeitpunkt der Fälligkeit oder unverzüglich danach der Einzugsstelle schriftlich

1. die Höhe der vorenthaltenen Beiträge mitteilt und

2. darlegt, warum die fristgemäße Zahlung nicht möglich ist, obwohl er sich darum ernsthaft bemüht hat.

²Liegen die Voraussetzungen des Satzes 1 vor und werden die Beiträge dann nachträglich innerhalb der von der Einzugsstelle bestimmten angemessenen Frist entrichtet, wird der Täter insoweit nicht bestraft. ³In den Fällen des Absatzes 3 gelten die Sätze 1 und 2 entsprechend.

4. acts as a member of a gang whose purpose is the continued withholding of contributions and which presents incorrect, counterfeit or falsified supporting documentation for the purpose of concealing the true employment relationship or

5. takes advantage of the assistance of a public official who abuses his or her powers or position.

(5) A person who hires people who work or conduct a trade at home or who are equal to them within the meaning of the Home Work Act (*Heimarbeitsgesetz*) as well as the intermediary are equal to an employer.

(6) ¹In the cases under subsections (1) and (2), the court may dispense with imposing a penalty pursuant to this provision if the employer, at the latest on the due date or promptly thereafter,

1. informs the collecting agency in writing of the amount of the withheld contributions and

2. explains in writing why it is not possible to make the payment on time although the employer has made earnest efforts to do so.

²If the conditions of sentence 1 are met and the contributions are subsequently paid within the appropriate period determined by the collecting agency, the offender incurs not penalty. ³In the cases under subsection (3), sentences 1 and 2 apply accordingly.

XI. Act to Combat Illegal Employment

Schwarzarbeitsbekämpfungsgesetz (SchwarzArbG)

Stand: 21.12.2019

§ 1
Zweck des Gesetzes

(1) Zweck des Gesetzes ist die Bekämpfung der Schwarzarbeit und illegalen Beschäftigung.

(2) [1]Schwarzarbeit leistet, wer Dienst- oder Werkleistungen erbringt oder ausführen lässt und dabei

1. als Arbeitgeber, Unternehmer oder versicherungspflichtiger Selbstständiger seine sich auf Grund der Dienst- oder Werkleistungen ergebenden sozialversicherungsrechtlichen Melde-, Beitrags- oder Aufzeichnungspflichten nicht erfüllt,
2. als Steuerpflichtiger seine sich auf Grund der Dienst- oder Werkleistungen ergebenden steuerlichen Pflichten nicht erfüllt,
3. als Empfänger von Sozialleistungen seine sich auf Grund der Dienst- oder Werkleistungen ergebenden Mitteilungspflichten gegenüber dem Sozialleistungsträger nicht erfüllt,
4. als Erbringer von Dienst- oder Werkleistungen seiner sich daraus ergebenden Verpflichtung zur Anzeige vom Beginn des selbstständigen Betriebes eines stehenden Gewerbes (§ 14 der Gewerbeordnung) nicht nachgekommen ist oder die erforderliche Reisegewerbekarte (§ 55 der Gewerbeordnung) nicht erworben hat oder
5. als Erbringer von Dienst- oder Werkleistungen ein zulassungspflichtiges Handwerk als stehendes Gewerbe selbstständig betreibt, ohne in der Handwerksrolle eingetragen zu sein (§ 1 der Handwerksordnung).

[2]Schwarzarbeit leistet auch, wer vortäuscht, eine Dienst- oder Werkleistung zu erbringen oder ausführen zu lassen, und wenn er selbst oder ein Dritter dadurch Sozialleistungen nach dem Zweiten oder Dritten Buch Sozialgesetzbuch zu Unrecht bezieht.

(3) Illegale Beschäftigung übt aus, wer

Section 1
Purpose of this act

(1) The purpose of this Act is to intensify the fight against undeclared work.

(2) [1]Undeclared work is deemed to have been engaged in by any persons who, in performing or commissioning work or services,

1. fail, in their capacity as an employer, business, or self-employed person subject to social security contributions, to fulfil the reporting, contribution, or record-keeping duties required of them under social security legislation,
2. fail, in their capacity as a taxpayer, to fulfil the tax obligations that arise from the work or services,
3. are in receipt of social benefits and fail to fulfil the reporting duties towards their benefits provider that arise from the work or services,
4. perform the work or services themselves and fail to fulfil their duty to report the opening of an independent business operating from a fixed location (section 14 of the Trade Regulation Code) or to obtain the required itinerant trader's licence (section 15 of the Trade Regulation Code) or
5. perform the work or services themselves in the form of a craft or trade for which a licence is required as an independent business operating from a fixed location without being enrolled in the trade and craft register (section 1 of the Trade and Crafts Code).

[2]Undeclared work is also performed by anyone who pretends to provide a service or work or to have a service or work performed, and if he himself or a third party thereby wrongfully receives social benefits under the Second or Third Book of Social Law.

(3) Illegal employment shall be deemed to be held by

1. Ausländer und Ausländerinnen als Arbeitgeber unerlaubt beschäftigt oder als Entleiher unerlaubt tätig werden lässt,
2. als Ausländer oder Ausländerin unerlaubt eine Erwerbstätigkeit ausübt,
3. als Arbeitgeber Arbeitnehmer und Arbeitnehmerinnen
   a) ohne erforderliche Erlaubnis nach § 1 Absatz 1 Satz 1 des Arbeitnehmerüberlassungsgesetzes oder
   b) entgegen den Bestimmungen nach § 1 Absatz 1 Satz 5 und 6, § 1a oder § 1b des Arbeitnehmerüberlassungsgesetzes

   überlässt oder für sich tätig werden lässt,
4. als Arbeitgeber Arbeitnehmer und Arbeitnehmerinnen beschäftigt, ohne dass die Arbeitsbedingungen nach Maßgabe des Mindestlohngesetzes, des Arbeitnehmer-Entsendegesetzes oder des § 8 Absatz 5 des Arbeitnehmerüberlassungsgesetzes in Verbindung mit einer Rechtsverordnung nach § 3a Absatz 2 Satz 1 des Arbeitnehmerüberlassungsgesetzes eingehalten werden, oder
5. als Arbeitgeber Arbeitnehmer und Arbeitnehmerinnen zu ausbeuterischen Arbeitsbedingungen beschäftigt.

(4) ¹Die Absätze 2 und 3 finden keine Anwendung für nicht nachhaltig auf Gewinn gerichtete Dienst- oder Werkleistungen, die

1. von Angehörigen im Sinne des § 15 der Abgabenordnung oder Lebenspartnern,
2. aus Gefälligkeit,
3. im Wege der Nachbarschaftshilfe oder
4. im Wege der Selbsthilfe im Sinne des § 36 Abs. 2 und 4 des Zweiten Wohnungsbaugesetzes in der Fassung der Bekanntmachung vom 19. August 1994 (BGBl. I S. 2137) oder als Selbsthilfe im Sinne des § 12 Abs. 1 Satz 2 des Wohnraumförderungsgesetzes vom 13. September 2001 (BGBl. I S. 2376), zuletzt geändert durch Artikel 7 des Gesetzes vom 29. Dezember 2003 (BGBl. I S. 3076),

erbracht werden. ²Als nicht nachhaltig auf Gewinn gerichtet gilt insbesondere eine Tätigkeit, die gegen geringes Entgelt erbracht wird.

§ 2
Prüfungsaufgaben

(1) ¹Die Behörden der Zollverwaltung prüfen, ob

1. die sich aus den Dienst- oder Werkleistungen ergebenden Pflichten nach § 28a des Vierten Buches Sozialgesetzbuch erfüllt werden oder wurden,

1. employs foreign nationals illegally as employers or allows them to work illegally as borrowers,
2. performs an illicit gainful activity as a foreigner,
3. as employers employees
   a) without the required permission pursuant to Section 1 (1) sentence 1 of the German Act on the Provision of Temporary Workers or
   b) contrary to the provisions of Section 1 (1) sentences 5 and 6, Section 1a or Section 1b of the German Act on the Provision of Temporary Workers
   or has them act on his behalf,
4. employs employees as an employer without complying with the working conditions pursuant to the Minimum Wages Act, the Posting of Workers Act or Section 8 (5) of the Temporary Employment Act in conjunction with a statutory instrument pursuant to Section 3a (2) sentence 1 of the Temporary Employment Act, or
5. as employer, employs workers under exploitative working conditions.

(4) ¹Paragraphs 2 and 3 do not apply to services or works which are not profit-oriented on a sustained basis and which

1. of relatives within the meaning of § 15 of the German Tax Code or life partners
2. As a courtesy,
3. by way of neighbourhood assistance, or
4. by way of self-help in the sense of section 36 (2) and (4) of the Second Housing Act in the version of the announcement of 19 August 1994 (Federal Law Gazette I p. 2137) or as self-help in the sense of section 12 (1) sentence 2 of the Housing Promotion Act of 13 September 2001 (Federal Law Gazette I p. 2376), last amended by section 7 of the Act of 29 December 2003 (Federal Law Gazette I p. 3076)

can be provided. ²In particular, an activity that is performed for a small fee is not considered to be sustainably profit-oriented.

Section 2
Matters for inspection

(1) The customs authorities inspect whether

1. the obligations arising from work or services under section 28a of Book IV of the Social Code are being, or were in the past, fulfilled,

2. auf Grund der Dienst- oder Werkleistungen oder der Vortäuschung von Dienst- oder Werkleistungen Sozialleistungen nach dem Zweiten oder Dritten Buch Sozialgesetzbuch zu Unrecht bezogen werden oder wurden,

3. die Angaben des Arbeitgebers, die für die Sozialleistungen nach dem Zweiten und Dritten Buch Sozialgesetzbuch erheblich sind, zutreffend bescheinigt wurden,

4. Ausländer und Ausländerinnen

    (a) entgegen § 4 Absatz 3 Satz 1 und 2 des Aufenthaltsgesetzes beschäftigt oder beauftragt werden oder wurden oder

    (b) entgegen § 284 Absatz 1 des Dritten Buches Sozialgesetzbuch beschäftigt werden oder wurden,

5. Arbeitnehmer und Arbeitnehmerinnen
    (a) ohne erforderliche Erlaubnis nach § 1 Absatz 1 Satz 1 des Arbeitnehmerüberlassungsgesetzes ver- oder entliehen werden oder wurden und

    (b) entgegen den Bestimmungen nach § 1 Absatz 1 Satz 5 und 6, § 1a oder § 1b des Arbeitnehmerüberlassungsgesetzes ver- oder entliehen werden oder wurden,

6. die Arbeitsbedingungen nach Maßgabe des Mindestlohngesetzes, des Arbeitnehmer-Entsendegesetzes und des § 8 Absatz 5 des Arbeitnehmerüberlassungsgesetzes in Verbindung mit einer Rechtsverordnung nach § 3a Absatz 2 Satz 1 des Arbeitnehmerüberlassungsgesetzes eingehalten werden oder wurden,

7. Arbeitnehmer und Arbeitnehmerinnen zu ausbeuterischen Arbeitsbedingungen beschäftigt werden oder wurden und

8. die Arbeitskraft im öffentlichen Raum entgegen § 5a angeboten oder nachgefragt wird oder wurde.

[2]Zur Erfüllung ihrer Mitteilungspflicht nach § 6 Absatz 1 Satz 1 in Verbindung mit § 6 Absatz 4 Nummer 4 prüfen die Behörden der Zollverwaltung im Rahmen ihrer Prüfungen nach Satz 1 auch, ob Anhaltspunkte dafür bestehen, dass Steuerpflichtige den sich aus den Dienst- oder Werkleistungen ergebenden steuerlichen Pflichten im Sinne von § 1 Absatz 2 Satz 1 Nummer 2 nicht nachgekommen sind. [3]Zur Erfüllung ihrer Mitteilungspflicht nach § 6 Absatz 1 Satz 1 in Verbindung mit § 6 Absatz 4 Nummer 4 und 7 prüfen die Behörden der Zollverwaltung im Rahmen ihrer Prüfungen nach Satz 1 auch, ob Anhaltspunkte dafür bestehen, dass Kindergeldempfänger ihren Mitwirkungspflichten nicht nachgekommen sind.

2. benefits under Books II and III of the Social Code or benefits under the Partial Retirement Act are being, or were in the past, unlawfully claimed in connection with the work or services,

3. information submitted by the employer that is relevant for benefits under Book III of the Social Code was sufficiently substantiated,

4. foreign nationals are not being and were not, in the past,
    (a) employed in contravention of section 4 (3) sentences 1 and 2 of the Residence Act

    (b) employed in contravention of section 284 (1) of Book III of the Social Code

5. employees
    (a) are or have been contracted or borrowed without the required permission pursuant to section 1, Subsection 1, Sentence 1, of the German Law on Temporary Employment and

    (b) are or have been contracted or borrowed contrary to the provisions of Section 1 (1), sentences 5 and 6, Section 1a or Section 1b of the German Act on the Provision of Temporary Workers,

6. the working conditions pursuant to the Minimum Wages Act, the Posting of Workers Act and Section 8 (5) of the Temporary Employment Act in conjunction with a statutory order pursuant to Section 3a (2) sentence 1 of the Temporary Employment Act are or have been complied with,

7. employees are or have been employed under exploitative working conditions, and

8. the worker is or was offered or demanded in public space contrary to section 5a.

[2]In order to fulfil their duty of notification under section 6 (1) sentence 1 in conjunction with section 6 (4) number 4, the Customs Administration authorities shall also examine, as part of their audits under sentence 1, whether there are indications that taxpayers have not complied with the tax obligations within the meaning of section 1 (2) sentence 1 number 2 arising from the services or works. [3]In order to fulfil their duty of notification under section 6 (1) sentence 1 in conjunction with section 6 (4) numbers 4 and 7, the customs authorities shall also examine, in the context of their audits under sentence 1, whether there are indications that child benefit recipients have not fulfilled their duties to cooperate.

(2) ¹Die Prüfung der Erfüllung steuerlicher Pflichten nach § 1 Absatz 2 Satz 1 Nummer 2 obliegt den zuständigen Landesfinanzbehörden und die Prüfung der Erfüllung kindergeldrechtlicher Mitwirkungspflichten den zuständigen Familienkassen. ²Die Behörden der Zollverwaltung sind zur Mitwirkung an Prüfungen der Landesfinanzbehörden und der Familienkassen bei der Bundesagentur für Arbeit berechtigt. ³Grundsätze der Zusammenarbeit der Behörden der Zollverwaltung mit den Landesfinanzbehörden werden von den obersten Finanzbehörden des Bundes und der Länder im gegenseitigen Einvernehmen geregelt. ⁴Grundsätze der Zusammenarbeit der Behörden der Zollverwaltung mit den Familienkassen bei der Bundesagentur für Arbeit werden von den Behörden der Zollverwaltung und den Familienkassen bei der Bundesagentur für Arbeit im Einvernehmen mit den Fachaufsichtsbehörden geregelt.

(3) Die nach Landesrecht für die Verfolgung und Ahndung von Ordnungswidrigkeiten nach diesem Gesetz zuständigen Behörden prüfen, ob

1. der Verpflichtung zur Anzeige vom Beginn des selbstständigen Betriebes eines stehenden Gewerbes (§ 14 der Gewerbeordnung) nachgekommen oder die erforderliche Reisegewerbekarte (§ 55 der Gewerbeordnung) erworben wurde,
2. ein zulassungspflichtiges Handwerk als stehendes Gewerbe selbstständig betrieben wird und die Eintragung in die Handwerksrolle vorliegt.

(4) ¹Die Behörden der Zollverwaltung werden bei den Prüfungen nach Absatz 1 unterstützt von

1. den Finanzbehörden,
2. der Bundesagentur für Arbeit, auch in ihrer Funktion als Familienkasse,
3. der Bundesnetzagentur für Elektrizität, Gas, Telekommunikation, Post und Eisenbahnen,
4. den Einzugsstellen (§ 28i des Vierten Buches Sozialgesetzbuch),
5. den Trägern der Rentenversicherung,
6. den Trägern der Unfallversicherung,
7. den gemeinsamen Einrichtungen und den zugelassenen kommunalen Trägern nach dem Zweiten Buch Sozialgesetzbuch sowie der Bundesagentur für Arbeit als verantwortliche Stelle für die zentral verwalteten IT-Verfahren nach § 50 Absatz 3 des Zweiten Buches Sozialgesetzbuch,

(2) ¹The examination of the fulfilment of tax obligations in accordance with section 1 (2) sentence 1 number 2 is the responsibility of the competent regional tax authorities and the examination of the fulfilment of the obligations to cooperate under child benefit law is the responsibility of the competent family offices. ²Customs administration authorities are entitled to participate in audits of the regional financial authorities and the company funds at the Federal Employment Agency. ³Principles of cooperation between the customs administration authorities and the state financial authorities are regulated by the supreme financial authorities of the Federation and the states by mutual agreement. ⁴Principles of cooperation between the authorities of the customs administration and the family funds at the Federal Employment Agency are regulated by the authorities of the customs administration and the family funds at the Federal Employment Agency in consultation with the specialist supervisory authorities.

(3) The authorities responsible under Land law for the prosecution and punishment of administrative offences under this Act shall examine whether

1. the obligation to report the commencement of independent operation of a standing trade (section 14 of the Trade Regulation Act) has been fulfilled or the required travel trade card section 55 of the Trade Regulation Act) has been acquired
2. a craft that requires a licence is operated independently as a standing trade and is registered in the register of craftsmen.

(4) ¹The customs authorities shall be assisted in the checks referred to in paragraph 1 by

1. the tax authorities,
2. the Federal Employment Agency, also in its function as family fund,
3. the Federal Network Agency for Electricity, Gas, Telecommunications, Post and Railway
4. the collection agencies (Section 28i of Book IV of the Social Code),
5. the pension insurance institutions,
6. the institutions responsible for accident insurance,
7. the joint institutions and the approved local authority institutions pursuant to Book II of the Social Security Code and the Federal Employment Agency as the body responsible for the centrally administered IT procedures pursuant to section 50 (3) of Book II of the Social Security Code

8. den nach dem Asylbewerberleistungsgesetz zuständigen Behörden,
9. den in § 71 Abs. 1 bis 3 des Aufenthaltsgesetzes genannten Behörden,
10. dem Bundesamt für Güterverkehr,
11. den nach Landesrecht für die Genehmigung und Überwachung des Gelegenheitsverkehrs mit Kraftfahrzeugen nach § 46 des Personenbeförderungsgesetzes zuständigen Behörden,
12. den nach Landesrecht für die Genehmigung und Überwachung des gewerblichen Güterkraftverkehrs zuständigen Behörden,
13. den für den Arbeitsschutz zuständigen Landesbehörden,
14. den Polizeivollzugsbehörden des Bundes und der Länder auf Ersuchen im Einzelfall,
15. den nach Landesrecht für die Verfolgung und Ahndung von Ordnungswidrigkeiten nach diesem Gesetz zuständigen Behörden,
16. den nach § 14 der Gewerbeordnung für die Entgegennahme der Gewerbeanzeigen zuständigen Stellen,
17. den nach Landesrecht für die Überprüfung der Einhaltung der Vergabe- und Tariftreuegesetze der Länder zuständigen Prüfungs- oder Kontrollstellen,
18. den nach Landesrecht für die Entgegennahme der Anmeldung von Prostituierten nach § 3 des Prostituiertenschutzgesetzes und für die Erlaubniserteilung an Prostitutionsgewerbetreibende nach § 12 des Prostituiertenschutzgesetzes zuständigen Behörden,
19. den nach Landesrecht für die Erlaubniserteilung nach § 34a der Gewerbeordnung zuständigen Behörden und
20. den gemeinsamen Einrichtungen der Tarifvertragsparteien im Sinne des § 4 Absatz 2 des Tarifvertragsgesetzes.

²Die Aufgaben dieser Stellen nach anderen Rechtsvorschriften bleiben unberührt. ³Die Prüfungen können mit anderen Prüfungen der in diesem Absatz genannten Stellen verbunden werden; die Vorschriften über die Unterrichtung und Zusammenarbeit bleiben hiervon unberührt. ⁴Verwaltungskosten der unterstützenden Stellen werden nicht erstattet.

8. the authorities responsible under the Asylum Seeker Benefits Act,
9. the authorities referred to in section 71 (1) to (3) of the Residence Act,
10. the Federal Office for Goods Transport,
11. the authorities responsible under Land law for the approval and supervision of occasional services by motor vehicles pursuant to section 46 of the Passenger Transport Act,
12. the authorities responsible under national law for the authorisation and supervision of commercial road haulage,
13. the state authorities responsible for occupational health and safety,
14. the federal and state police enforcement authorities on request in individual cases
15. the authorities responsible under Land law for the prosecution and punishment of administrative offences under this Act,
16. the offices responsible for receiving trade notifications in accordance with section 14 of the Trade, Commerce and Industry Regulation Act,
17. the audit or control bodies responsible under Land law for verifying compliance with the public procurement and tariff laws of the Länder,
18. the authorities responsible under provincial law for receiving the registration of prostitutes under section 3 of the Prostitute Protection Act and for granting permits to prostitutes under section 12 of the Prostitute Protection Act,
19. the authorities responsible under Land law for issuing permits in accordance with section 34a of the Gewerbeordnung (German Trade Regulation Act) and
20. the joint institutions of the parties to collective agreements within the meaning of section 4 (2) of the Collective Agreement Act

² The tasks of these bodies under other legal provisions remain unaffected. ³The audits may be combined with other audits of the bodies referred to in this paragraph; this shall not affect the provisions on information and cooperation. ⁴Administrative costs of the supporting bodies shall not be reimbursed.

§ 2a
Mitführungs- und Vorlagepflicht von Ausweispapieren

(1) Bei der Erbringung von Dienst- oder Werkleistungen sind die in folgenden Wirtschaftsbereichen oder Wirtschaftszweigen tätigen Personen verpflichtet, ihren Personalausweis, Pass, Passersatz oder Ausweisersatz mitzuführen und den Behörden der Zollverwaltung auf Verlangen vorzulegen:

1. im Baugewerbe,
2. im Gaststätten- und Beherbergungsgewerbe,
3. im Personenbeförderungsgewerbe,
4. im Speditions-, Transport- und damit verbundenen Logistikgewerbe,
5. im Schaustellergewerbe,
6. bei Unternehmen der Forstwirtschaft,
7. im Gebäudereinigungsgewerbe,
8. bei Unternehmen, die sich am Auf- und Abbau von Messen und Ausstellungen beteiligen,
9. in der Fleischwirtschaft,
10. im Prostitutionsgewerbe,
11. im Wach- und Sicherheitsgewerbe.

(2) Der Arbeitgeber hat jeden und jede seiner Arbeitnehmer und Arbeitnehmerinnen nachweislich und schriftlich auf die Pflicht nach Absatz 1 hinzuweisen, diesen Hinweis für die Dauer der Erbringung der Dienst- oder Werkleistungen aufzubewahren und auf Verlangen bei den Prüfungen nach § 2 Abs. 1 vorzulegen.

(3) Die Vorlagepflichten nach den Absätzen 1 und 2 bestehen auch gegenüber den nach Landesrecht für die Verfolgung und Ahndung von Ordnungswidrigkeiten nach diesem Gesetz zuständigen Behörden in den Fällen des § 2 Absatz 3.

§ 3
Befugnisse bei der Prüfung von Personen

(1) ¹Zur Durchführung der Prüfungen nach § 2 Absatz 1 sind die Behörden der Zollverwaltung und die sie gemäß § 2 Absatz 4 unterstützenden Stellen befugt, Geschäftsräume, mit Ausnahme von Wohnungen, und Grundstücke des Arbeitgebers, des Auftraggebers von Dienst- oder Werkleistungen, des Entleihers sowie des Selbstständigen während der Arbeitszeiten der dort tätigen Personen oder während der Geschäftszeiten zu betreten. ²Dabei sind die Behörden der Zollverwaltung und die sie gemäß § 2 Absatz 4 unterstützenden Stellen befugt,

Section 2a
Obligation to carry and produce identification

(1) When performing work or services, persons working in the following sectors and industries are obliged to carry on their person their identity card, passport, travel document issued in lieu of a passport or document issued in lieu of an identity card and present it to the customs authorities upon request:

1. construction,
2. the catering and hotel business,
3. passenger transport,
4. the haulage, transport and associated logistics sectors,
5. the fairground and amusement sector,
6. forestry business,
7. industrial cleaning,
8. businesses engaged in setting up and dismantling at trade fairs and exhibitions,
9. the meat industry,
10. prostitution and
11. In the security business

(2) Employers must provide each of their workers with a written notification of the obligation set out in subsection (1), keep this notification on file for the duration of the work or service, and produce it upon request during inspections under section 2 (1).

(3) The submission obligations under subsections (1) and (2) shall also exist vis-à-vis the authorities responsible under Land law for the prosecution and punishment of administrative offences under this Act in the cases of section 2 (3).

Section 3
Powers during inspections of persons

(1) ¹In order to carry out the checks in accordance with section 2 (1), the Customs Administration authorities and the bodies supporting them in accordance with section 2 (4) are authorised to enter business premises, with the exception of homes, and land belonging to the employer, the client of services or work, the hirer and the self-employed person during the working hours of the persons working there or during business hours. ²The authorities of the customs administration and the agencies supporting them in accordance with section 2 (4) are authorised to do so,

289

1. von den Personen, die in den Geschäftsräumen und auf den Grundstücken tätig sind, Auskünfte über ihre Beschäftigungsverhältnisse oder ihre tatsächlichen oder scheinbaren Tätigkeiten einzuholen und
2. Einsicht in Unterlagen zu nehmen, die von diesen Personen mitgeführt werden und von denen anzunehmen ist, dass aus ihnen Umfang, Art oder Dauer ihrer Beschäftigungsverhältnisse oder ihrer tatsächlichen oder scheinbaren Tätigkeiten hervorgehen oder abgeleitet werden können.

(2) ¹Ist eine Person zur Ausführung von Dienst- oder Werkleistungen bei Dritten tätig, gilt Absatz 1 entsprechend. ²Bietet eine Person im öffentlichen Raum Dienst- oder Werkleistungen an, gilt Absatz 1 Satz 2 entsprechend.

(3) ¹Zur Durchführung der Prüfungen nach § 2 Absatz 1 sind die Behörden der Zollverwaltung und die sie gemäß § 2 Absatz 4 unterstützenden Stellen befugt, die Personalien zu überprüfen

1. der Personen, die in den Geschäftsräumen oder auf dem Grundstück des Arbeitgebers, des Auftraggebers von Dienst- oder Werkleistungen und des Entleihers tätig sind, und
2. des Selbstständigen.

²Sie können zu diesem Zweck die in Satz 1 genannten Personen anhalten, sie nach ihren Personalien (Vor-, Familien- und Geburtsnamen, Ort und Tag der Geburt, Beruf, Wohnort, Wohnung und Staatsangehörigkeit) befragen und verlangen, dass sie mitgeführte Ausweispapiere zur Prüfung aushändigen.

(4) Im Verteidigungsbereich darf ein Betretensrecht nur im Einvernehmen mit dem Bundesministerium der Verteidigung ausgeübt werden.

(5) ¹Die Bediensteten der Zollverwaltung dürfen Beförderungsmittel anhalten. ²Führer von Beförderungsmitteln haben auf Verlangen zu halten und den Zollbediensteten zu ermöglichen, in das Beförderungsmittel zu gelangen und es wieder zu verlassen. ³Die Zollverwaltung unterrichtet die Polizeivollzugsbehörden der Länder über groß angelegte Kontrollen.

(6) Die Absätze 1 bis 4 gelten entsprechend für die nach Landesrecht für die Verfolgung und Ahndung von Ordnungswidrigkeiten nach diesem Gesetz zuständigen Behörden zur Durchführung von Prüfungen nach § 2 Absatz 3, sofern Anhaltspunkte dafür vorliegen, dass Schwarzarbeit im Sinne des § 1 Absatz 2 Nummer 4 und 5 geleistet wird.

1. obtain information from the persons working in the business premises and on the land about their employment relationships or their actual or apparent activities and
2. inspect any documents which are carried by such persons and which are likely to reveal or be likely to reveal the scope, nature or duration of their employment or their actual or apparent activities.

(2) ¹If a person is employed by third parties to perform services or work, paragraph 1 applies accordingly. ²If a person offers services or works in public places, subsection 1 sentence 2 shall apply mutatis mutandis.

(3) ¹In order to carry out the checks in accordance with section 2 (1), the Customs Administration authorities and the bodies assisting them in accordance with section 2 (4) shall be authorised

1. persons working in the business premises or on the premises of the employer, the party commissioning services or work and the hirer, and
2. the self-employed person.

²For this purpose they may stop the persons mentioned in sentence 1, question them about their personal data (first name, surname and maiden name, place and date of birth, occupation, place of residence, apartment and nationality) and request that they hand over any identity papers they may have carried for examination.

(4) In the defence sector, the right to enter premises may be exercised only with the agreement of the Federal Ministry of Defence.

(5) ¹Customs officials are authorised to stop vehicles. ²Drivers of vehicles must stop upon request and allow customs officials to enter and leave the vehicle. ³The customs administration must inform the police authorities of the Länder of any large-scale operations.

(6) Subsections (1) to (4) apply mutatis mutandis to the authorities responsible under the legislation of the respective Land for prosecuting and punishing administrative offences as described in this Act for the purposes of conducting inspections under section 2 (3), provided that there are indications of undeclared work as defined in section 1 (2) nos 4 and 5.

§ 4
Befugnisse bei der Prüfung von Geschäftsunterlagen

(1) Zur Durchführung der Prüfungen nach § 2 Absatz 1 sind die Behörden der Zollverwaltung und die sie gemäß § 2 Absatz 4 unterstützenden Stellen befugt, Geschäftsräume, mit Ausnahme von Wohnungen, und Grundstücke des Arbeitgebers, des Auftraggebers von Dienst- oder Werkleistungen, des Entleihers sowie des Selbstständigen während der Geschäftszeiten zu betreten und dort Einsicht in die Lohn- und Meldeunterlagen, Bücher und andere Geschäftsunterlagen zu nehmen, aus denen Umfang, Art oder Dauer von tatsächlich bestehenden oder vorgespiegelten Beschäftigungsverhältnissen oder Tätigkeiten hervorgehen oder abgeleitet werden können.

(2) Zur Durchführung der Prüfungen nach § 2 Absatz 3 sind die nach Landesrecht für die Verfolgung und Ahndung von Ordnungswidrigkeiten nach diesem Gesetz zuständigen Behörden befugt, Geschäftsräume und Grundstücke einer selbstständig tätigen Person, des Arbeitgebers und des Auftraggebers während der Arbeitszeit der dort tätigen Personen zu betreten und dort Einsicht in Unterlagen zu nehmen, von denen anzunehmen ist, dass aus ihnen Umfang, Art oder Dauer der Ausübung eines Gewerbes, eines Reisegewerbes oder eines zulassungspflichtigen Handwerks oder der Beschäftigungsverhältnisse hervorgehen oder abgeleitet werden können, sofern Anhaltspunkte dafür vorliegen, dass Schwarzarbeit im Sinne des § 1 Absatz 2 Nummer 4 und 5 geleistet wird.

(3) ¹Die Behörden der Zollverwaltung sind zur Durchführung der Prüfungen nach § 2 Abs. 1 befugt, Einsicht in die Unterlagen zu nehmen, aus denen die Vergütung der tatsächlich erbrachten oder vorgetäuschten Dienst- oder Werkleistungen hervorgeht, die natürliche oder juristische Personen oder Personenvereinigungen in Auftrag gegeben haben. ²Satz 1 gilt im Rahmen der Durchführung der Prüfung nach § 2 Absatz 1 Nummer 4, 5 und 6 entsprechend für Unterlagen, aus denen die Vergütung des Leiharbeitsverhältnisses hervorgeht.

(4) Die Behörden der Zollverwaltung sind zur Durchführung der Prüfungen nach § 2 Abs. 1 befugt, bei dem Auftraggeber, der nicht Unternehmer im Sinne des § 2 des Umsatzsteuergesetzes 1999 ist, Einsicht in die Rechnungen, einen Zahlungsbeleg oder eine andere beweiskräftige Unterlage über ausgeführte Werklieferungen oder sonstige Leistungen im Zusammenhang mit einem Grundstück zu nehmen.

Section 4
Powers during inspections of business documents

(1) In order to carry out the inspections referred to in section 2 (1), the Customs Administration authorities and the bodies supporting them in accordance with section 2 (4) shall be authorised to enter business premises, with the exception of dwellings, and land belonging to the employer, the customer for services or work, the hirer and the self-employed person during business hours and to inspect there the wage and registration documents, books and other business records from which the extent, nature or duration of actual or simulated employment relationships or activities can be ascertained or derived.

(2) For the purposes of conducting an inspection under section 2 (3), the authorities responsible under the legislation of the respective Land for prosecuting and punishing administrative offences as described in this Act are authorised to enter, during the working hours of the persons employed in these places, the business premises and properties of the self-employed person, the employer and the party contracting self-employed persons and check documents where it may be assumed that the scope, type or duration of the operation of a business, an itinerant trade, a craft or trade for which a licence is required, or of employment can be obtained or deduced from these documents, provided that there are indications of undeclared work as defined in section 1 (2) nos 4 and 5.

(3) ¹The customs administration authorities are authorised to carry out the audits in accordance with section 2 (1) and to inspect documents showing the remuneration for services or work actually performed or simulated which natural or legal persons or associations of persons have commissioned. ²Sentence 1 shall apply mutatis mutandis within the scope of the audit under section 2 (1) Nos. 4, 5 and 6 to documents showing the remuneration of the temporary employment relationship.

(4) For the purposes of conducting an inspection under section 2 (1), the customs authorities are authorised to check, at the premises of contracting parties that are not traders as defined in section 2 of the VAT Act of 1999, invoices, payment vouchers or other substantiating documents about supplies of work (including materials) and other services in connection with real estate.

§ 5
Duldungs- und Mitwirkungspflichten

(1) ¹Arbeitgeber, tatsächlich oder scheinbar beschäftigte Arbeitnehmer und Arbeitnehmerinnen, Auftraggeber von Dienst- oder Werkleistungen, tatsächlich oder scheinbar selbstständig tätige Personen und Dritte, die bei einer Prüfung nach § 2 Absatz 1 und 3 angetroffen werden, sowie Entleiher, die bei einer Prüfung nach § 2 Absatz 1 Satz 1 Nummer 5 und 6 angetroffen werden, haben

1. die Prüfung zu dulden und dabei mitzuwirken, insbesondere für die Prüfung erhebliche Auskünfte zu erteilen und die in den §§ 3 und 4 genannten Unterlagen vorzulegen,
2. in den Fällen des § 3 Absatz 1, 2 und 6 sowie des § 4 Absatz 1, 2 und 3 auch das Betreten der Grundstücke und der Geschäftsräume zu dulden und
3. in den Fällen des § 2 Absatz 1 auf Verlangen der Behörden der Zollverwaltung schriftlich oder an Amtsstelle mündlich Auskünfte zu erteilen oder die in den §§ 3 und 4 genannten Unterlagen vorzulegen.

²Auskünfte, die die verpflichtete Person oder einen ihrer in § 15 der Abgabenordnung bezeichneten Angehörigen der Gefahr aussetzen würden, wegen einer Straftat oder Ordnungswidrigkeit verfolgt zu werden, können verweigert werden.

(2) ¹Die Behörden der Zollverwaltung sind insbesondere dann befugt, eine mündliche Auskunft an Amtsstelle zu verlangen, wenn trotz Aufforderung keine schriftliche Auskunft erteilt worden ist oder wenn eine schriftliche Auskunft nicht zu einer Klärung des Sachverhalts geführt hat. ²Über die mündliche Auskunft an Amtsstelle ist auf Antrag des Auskunftspflichtigen eine Niederschrift aufzunehmen. ³Die Niederschrift soll den Namen der anwesenden Personen, den Ort, den Tag und den wesentlichen Inhalt der Auskunft enthalten. ⁴Sie soll von dem Amtsträger, dem die mündliche Auskunft erteilt wird, und dem Auskunftspflichtigen unterschrieben werden. ⁵Den Beteiligten ist eine Abschrift der Niederschrift zu überlassen.

(3) ¹Ausländer sind ferner verpflichtet, ihren Pass, Passersatz oder Ausweisersatz und ihren Aufenthaltstitel, ihre Duldung oder ihre Aufenthaltsgestattung den Behörden der Zollverwaltung auf Verlangen vorzulegen und, sofern sich Anhaltspunkte für einen Verstoß gegen ausländerrechtliche Vorschriften ergeben, zur

Section 5
Duty to submit to and cooperate with inspections

(1) ¹Employers, employees actually or apparently employed, clients of services or works, persons actually or apparently self-employed and third parties encountered during an examination in accordance with section 2 (1) and (3), as well as borrowers encountered during an examination in accordance with section 2 (1) sentence 1 numbers 5 and 6, shall

1. tolerate the audit and to cooperate in it, in particular to provide information relevant to the audit and to submit the documents mentioned in sections 3 and 4
2. in the cases of section 3 paras. 1, 2 and 6 and section 4 paras. 1, 2 and 3, also tolerate the entering of the property and business premises and
3. in the cases referred to in section 2 (1), to provide information to the Customs Administration at the request of the authorities in writing or orally at an official office or to submit the documents referred to in sections 3 and 4.

²Information which would expose the obliged person or one of his relatives referred to in section 15 of the Tax Code to the risk of prosecution for a criminal offence or administrative offence may be refused.

(2) ¹In particular, the customs administration authorities are authorised to request oral information at their office if no written information has been provided despite a request or if written information has not led to a clarification of the facts. ²At the request of the person responsible for providing information, minutes shall be taken of the oral information provided at the office. ³The minutes shall contain the names of the persons present, the place, the date and the essential content of the information. ⁴The minutes shall be signed by the official to whom the oral information is given and by the person responsible for providing the information. ⁵A copy of the minutes shall be given to the parties involved.

(3) ¹Foreigners are also obliged to present their passport, passport replacement or identity card replacement and their residence permit, toleration or residence permit to the customs authorities on request and, if there are indications of a violation of provisions under the law on foreign nationals, to hand them over to the

Weiterleitung an die zuständige Ausländerbehörde zu überlassen. ²Werden die Dokumente einbehalten, erhält der betroffene Ausländer eine Bescheinigung, welche die einbehaltenen Dokumente und die Ausländerbehörde bezeichnet, an die die Dokumente weitergeleitet werden. ³Der Ausländer ist verpflichtet, unverzüglich mit der Bescheinigung bei der Ausländerbehörde zu erscheinen. ⁴Darauf ist in der Bescheinigung hinzuweisen. ⁵Gibt die Ausländerbehörde die einbehaltenen Dokumente zurück oder werden Ersatzdokumente ausgestellt oder vorgelegt, behält die Ausländerbehörde die Bescheinigung ein.

(4) ¹In Fällen des § 4 Absatz 4 haben die Auftraggeber, die nicht Unternehmer im Sinne des § 2 des Umsatzsteuergesetzes 1999 sind, eine Prüfung nach § 2 Abs. 1 zu dulden und dabei mitzuwirken, insbesondere die für die Prüfung erheblichen Auskünfte zu erteilen und die in § 4 Absatz 4 genannten Unterlagen vorzulegen. ²Absatz 1 Satz 3 gilt entsprechend.

(5) ¹In Datenverarbeitungsanlagen gespeicherte Daten haben der Arbeitgeber und der Auftraggeber sowie der Entleiher im Rahmen einer Prüfung nach § 2 Absatz 1 Nummer 4, 5 und 6 auszusondern und den Behörden der Zollverwaltung auf deren Verlangen auf automatisiert verarbeitbaren Datenträgern oder in Listen zu übermitteln. ²Der Arbeitgeber und der Auftraggeber sowie der Entleiher im Rahmen einer Prüfung nach § 2 Absatz 1 Nummer 4, 5 und 6 dürfen automatisiert verarbeitbare Datenträger oder Datenlisten, die die erforderlichen Daten enthalten, ungesondert zur Verfügung stellen, wenn die Aussonderung mit einem unverhältnismäßigen Aufwand verbunden wäre und überwiegende schutzwürdige Interessen des Betroffenen nicht entgegenstehen. ³In diesem Fall haben die Behörden der Zollverwaltung die Daten zu trennen und die nicht nach Satz 1 zu übermittelnden Daten zu löschen. ⁴Soweit die übermittelten Daten für Zwecke der Ermittlung von Straftaten oder Ordnungswidrigkeiten, der Ermittlung von steuerlich erheblichen Sachverhalten oder der Festsetzung von Sozialversicherungsbeiträgen oder Sozialleistungen nicht benötigt werden, sind die Datenträger oder Listen nach Abschluss der Prüfungen nach § 2 Abs. 1 auf Verlangen des Arbeitgebers oder des Auftraggebers zurückzugeben oder die Daten unverzüglich zu löschen.

competent foreigners authority for forwarding. ²If the documents are withheld, the foreigner concerned shall receive a certificate identifying the documents withheld and the aliens authority to which the documents are forwarded. ³The foreigner is obliged to appear at the aliens authority immediately with the certificate. ⁴Reference to this must be made in the certificate. ⁵If the aliens authority returns the retained documents or if replacement documents are issued or submitted, the aliens authority shall retain the certificate.

(4) In cases covered by section 4 (4), contracting parties that are not traders as defined in section 2 of the VAT Act of 1999 must submit to and cooperate with inspections under section 2 (1); in particular, they must provide information relevant to the inspection and present the documents specified in section 4 (4). Subsection (1) sentence 3 applies mutatis mutandis.

(5) ¹Data stored in data processing systems must be separated by the employer, the client and the hirer within the framework of an inspection in accordance with section 2 (1) Nos. 4, 5 and 6 and transmitted to the customs authorities at their request on automatically processable data carriers or in lists. ²The employer and the client as well as the hirer within the scope of an inspection in accordance with section 2 (1) Nos. 4, 5 and 6 may make available automatically processable data carriers or data lists containing the required data without separation if the separation would involve disproportionate expense and there are no overriding interests of the person concerned worthy of protection that would conflict with this. ³In this case, the Customs Administration authorities shall separate the data and delete the data not to be transferred in accordance with sentence 1. ⁴In so far as the data transmitted are not required for the purposes of investigating criminal offences or administrative offences, determining facts relevant for tax purposes or setting social security contributions or social benefits, the data carriers or lists must be returned at the request of the employer or the client after completion of the checks in accordance with section 2 (1) or the data must be deleted immediately.

§ 5a
Unzulässiges Anbieten und Nachfragen der Arbeitskraft

(1) ¹Es ist einer Person verboten, ihre Arbeitskraft als Tagelöhner im öffentlichen Raum aus einer Gruppe heraus in einer Weise anzubieten, die geeignet ist, Schwarzarbeit oder illegale Beschäftigung zu ermöglichen. ²Ebenso ist es einer Person verboten, ein unzulässiges Anbieten der Arbeitskraft dadurch nachzufragen, dass sie ein solches Angebot einholt oder annimmt.

(2) Die Behörden der Zollverwaltung können eine Person, die gegen das Verbot des unzulässigen Anbietens und Nachfragens der Arbeitskraft verstößt, vorübergehend von einem Ort verweisen oder ihr vorübergehend das Betreten eines Ortes verbieten.

§ 6
Unterrichtung von und Zusammenarbeit mit Behörden im Inland und in der Europäischen Union sowie im Europäischen Wirtschaftsraum

(1) ¹Die Behörden der Zollverwaltung und die sie gemäß § 2 Absatz 4 unterstützenden Stellen sind verpflichtet, einander die für deren Prüfungen erforderlichen Informationen einschließlich personenbezogener Daten und die Ergebnisse der Prüfungen zu übermitteln, soweit deren Kenntnis für die Erfüllung der Aufgaben der Behörden oder Stellen erforderlich ist. ²Die Behörden der Zollverwaltung einerseits und die Strafverfolgungsbehörden und die Polizeivollzugsbehörden andererseits sind verpflichtet, einander die erforderlichen Informationen, einschließlich personenbezogener Daten, für die Verhütung und Verfolgung von Straftaten und Ordnungswidrigkeiten, die in Zusammenhang mit einem der in § 2 Abs. 1 genannten Prüfgegenstände stehen, zu übermitteln. ³An Strafverfolgungsbehörden und Polizeivollzugsbehörden sind darüber hinaus Informationen einschließlich personenbezogener Daten zu übermitteln, sofern tatsächliche Anhaltspunkte dafür vorliegen, dass diese Informationen für die Verhütung und Verfolgung von Straftaten oder Ordnungswidrigkeiten, die nicht in Zusammenhang mit einem der in § 2 Abs. 1 genannten Prüfgegenstände stehen, erforderlich sind.

Section 5a
Improper supply and demand of labour

(1) ¹It is forbidden for a person to offer his or her labour as a day labourer in public space from within a group in a way that is likely to facilitate illegal work or illegal employment. ²It is also forbidden for a person to ask for an illegal offer of labour by soliciting or accepting such an offer.

(2) The authorities of the customs administration may temporarily expel a person who violates the prohibition of unlawful offer and demand of labour from a place or temporarily forbid him to enter a place.

Section 6
Information to and cooperation among authorities at home and in the European Union and the European Economic Area

(1) ¹The customs authorities and the cooperating bodies specified in section 2 (4) have a duty to share with each other any information necessary for inspections, including personal data and the results of inspections, to the extent that the authorities and bodies need these to perform their tasks. ²The customs authorities on the one hand and the law enforcement authorities and police authorities on the other hand must share with each other any information necessary for the prevention and prosecution of criminal and administrative offences related to one of the matters for inspection specified in section 2 (1). ³Personal data may be transmitted to law enforcement authorities and police authorities only if there are actual indications that the data are necessary for the prevention and prosecution of criminal or administrative offences related to one of the matters for inspection specified in section 2 (1).

(2) ¹Die Behörden der Zollverwaltung dürfen zur Wahrnehmung ihrer Aufgaben nach § 2 Abs. 1 sowie zur Verfolgung von Straftaten oder Ordnungswidrigkeiten die Dateisysteme der Bundesagentur für Arbeit über erteilte Arbeitsgenehmigungen-EU und Zustimmungen zur Beschäftigung, über im Rahmen von Werkvertragskontingenten beschäftigte ausländische Arbeitnehmer und Arbeitnehmerinnen sowie über Leistungsempfänger nach dem Dritten Buch Sozialgesetzbuch automatisiert abrufen, die Strafverfolgungsbehörden sind zum automatisierten Abruf nur berechtigt, soweit dies zur Verfolgung von Straftaten oder Ordnungswidrigkeiten erforderlich ist. ²§ 79 Abs. 2 bis 4 des Zehnten Buches Sozialgesetzbuch gilt entsprechend. ³Die Behörden der Zollverwaltung dürfen, soweit dies zur Verfolgung von Straftaten oder Ordnungswidrigkeiten erforderlich ist, Daten aus den Datenbeständen der Träger der Rentenversicherung automatisiert abrufen; § 150 Absatz 5 Satz 1 des Sechsten Buches Sozialgesetzbuch bleibt unberührt. ⁴Die Behörden der Zollverwaltung dürfen, soweit dies zur Vorbereitung und Durchführung von Prüfungen nach § 2 Absatz 1 Satz 1 Nummer 2 und 3 und zur Verhütung und Verfolgung von Straftaten und Ordnungswidrigkeiten, die mit dieser Prüfungsaufgabe zusammenhängen, erforderlich ist, Daten aus folgenden Datenbeständen automatisiert abrufen:

1. die Datenbestände der gemeinsamen Einrichtungen und der zugelassenen kommunalen Träger nach dem Zweiten Buch Sozialgesetzbuch und
2. die Datenbestände der Bundesagentur für Arbeit als verantwortliche Stelle für die zentral verwalteten IT-Verfahren nach § 50 Absatz 3 des Zweiten Buches Sozialgesetzbuch über Leistungsempfänger nach dem Zweiten Buch Sozialgesetzbuch.

⁵Das Bundesministerium für Arbeit und Soziales wird ermächtigt, durch Rechtsverordnung mit Zustimmung des Bundesrates die Voraussetzungen für das Abrufverfahren nach Satz 4 sowie die Durchführung des Abrufverfahrens festzulegen.

(3) ¹Die Behörden der Zollverwaltung dürfen die beim Bundeszentralamt für Steuern nach § 5 Absatz 1 Nummer 13 des Finanzverwaltungsgesetzes vorgehaltenen Daten abrufen, soweit dies zur Wahrnehmung ihrer Prüfungsaufgaben nach § 2 Absatz 1 oder für die damit unmittelbar zusammenhängenden Bußgeld- und Strafverfahren erforderlich ist. ²Für den Abruf der nach § 30 der Abgabenordnung dem Steuergeheimnis unterliegenden Daten ist ein automatisiertes Verfahren auf Abruf einzurichten. ³Die Verantwortung für die Zulässig-

(2) ¹In order to fulfil their tasks as set out in section 2 (1) and for the purpose of prosecuting criminal and administrative offences, the customs authorities may electronically retrieve the Federal Employment Agency's data records on EU work permits and authorisations to take up employment issued as well as on foreign nationals employed under works and services contract quotas; law enforcement authorities may retrieve such data records by automated means only to the extent that this is necessary for the prosecution of criminal and administrative offences. ²Section 79 (2) to (4) of Book X of the Social Code applies mutatis mutandis. ³The customs authorities may, insofar as this is necessary for the prosecution of criminal offences or administrative offences, automatically retrieve data from the databases of the pension insurance institutions; section 150 (5) sentence 1 of Book 6 of the Social Security Code remains unaffected. ⁴The Customs Administration authorities may, insofar as this is necessary for the preparation and performance of audits in accordance with section 2 (1) sentence 1 Nos. 2 and 3 and for the prevention and prosecution of criminal offences and administrative offences connected with this audit task, retrieve data from the following data files automatically

1. the databases of the joint institutions and the approved local authority bodies in accordance with Book II of the Social Code, and
2. the data stocks of the Federal Employment Agency as the body responsible for the centrally administered IT procedures pursuant to section 50 (3) of the Second Book of the Social Code on benefit recipients under the Second Book of the Social Code.

⁵The Federal Ministry of Labour and Social Affairs is authorised to determine by statutory order, with the consent of the Bundesrat, the requirements for the retrieval procedure in accordance with sentence 4 and the implementation of the retrieval procedure.

(3) ¹The customs authorities may retrieve the data held by the Federal Central Tax Office in accordance with section 5 (1) No. 13 of the Tax Administration Act to the extent that this is necessary for the performance of their auditing duties in accordance with section 2 (1) or for the directly related administrative fine and criminal proceedings. ²For the retrieval of the data subject to tax secrecy according to section 30 of the Tax Code, an automated procedure shall be set up on demand. ³Responsibility for the admissibility of the individual retrieval

keit des einzelnen Abrufs trägt die Behörde der Zollverwaltung, die die Daten abruft. ⁴Die abrufende Stelle darf die Daten nach Satz 1 zu dem Zweck verarbeiten, zu dem sie die Daten abgerufen hat. ⁵Ist zu befürchten, dass ein Datenabruf nach Satz 1 den Untersuchungszweck eines Ermittlungsverfahrens im Sinne des § 30 Absatz 2 Nummer 1 Buchstabe b der Abgabenordnung gefährdet, so kann die für dieses Verfahren zuständige Finanzbehörde oder die zuständige Staatsanwaltschaft anordnen, dass kein Datenabruf erfolgen darf. ⁶§ 478 Absatz 1 Satz 1 und 2 der Strafprozessordnung findet Anwendung, wenn die Daten Verfahren betreffen, die zu einem Strafverfahren geführt haben. ⁷Weitere Einzelheiten insbesondere zum automatischen Verfahren auf Abruf einschließlich der Protokollierung sowie zum Nachweis der aus den Artikeln 24, 25 und 32 der Verordnung (EU) 2016/679 des Europäischen Parlaments und des Rates vom 27. April 2016 zum Schutz natürlicher Personen bei der Verarbeitung personenbezogener Daten, zum freien Datenverkehr und zur Aufhebung der Richtlinie 95/46/EG (Datenschutz Grundverordnung; ABl. L 119 vom 4.5.2016, S. 1; L 314 vom 22.11.2016, S. 72; L 127 vom 23.5.2018, S. 2) oder § 64 des Bundesdatenschutzgesetzes erforderlichen technischen und organisatorischen Maßnahmen regelt eine Rechtsverordnung des Bundesministeriums der Finanzen, die der Zustimmung des Bundesrates bedarf.

(4) ¹Die Behörden der Zollverwaltung unterrichten die jeweils zuständigen Stellen, wenn sich bei der Durchführung ihrer Aufgaben nach diesem Gesetz Anhaltspunkte ergeben für Verstöße gegen

1. dieses Gesetz,
2. das Arbeitnehmerüberlassungsgesetz,
3. Bestimmungen des Vierten und Siebten Buches Sozialgesetzbuch zur Zahlung von Beiträgen,
4. die Steuergesetze,
5. das Aufenthaltsgesetz,
6. die Mitwirkungspflicht nach § 60 Abs. 1 Satz 1 Nr. 1 und 2 des Ersten Buches Sozialgesetzbuch oder die Meldepflicht nach § 8a des Asylbewerberleistungsgesetzes,
7. das Bundeskindergeldgesetz,
8. die Handwerks- oder Gewerbeordnung,
9. das Güterkraftverkehrsgesetz,
10. das Personenbeförderungsgesetz,
11. sonstige Strafgesetze,
12. das Arbeitnehmer-Entsendegesetz,
13. das Mindestlohngesetz,

shall be borne by the authority of the Customs Administration which retrieves the data. ⁴The retrieving authority may process the data in accordance with sentence 1 for the purpose for which it has retrieved the data. ⁵If there is reason to fear that a data retrieval in accordance with sentence 1 will jeopardise the purpose of an investigation in terms of section 30 (2) number 1 letter b of the Tax Code, the tax authority responsible for this procedure or the competent public prosecutor's office may order that no data retrieval may take place. ⁶Section 478 (1) sentences 1 and 2 of the Code of Criminal Procedure shall apply if the data relate to proceedings that have led to criminal proceedings. ⁷Further details, in particular on the automatic procedure on demand, including logging, as well as on the proof of the data obtained from Sections 24, 25 and 32 of Regulation (EU) 2016/679 of the European Parliament and of the Council of 27 April 2016 on the protection of individuals with regard to the processing of personal data, on the free movement of such data and on the repeal of Directive 95/46/EC (Basic Regulation on data protection; OJ L 241, 30.12.201, p. 1), shall be provided by the competent public prosecutor's office. The technical and organisational measures required under Article 119 of 4.5.2016, p. 1; Article L 314 of 22.11.2016, p. 72; Article L 127 of 23.5.2018, p. 2) or Article 64 of the Federal Data Protection Act shall be regulated by a statutory order of the Federal Ministry of Finance, which shall require the consent of the Bundesrat.

(4) ¹The customs authorities must inform the relevant authorities if, in fulfilling their responsibilities as set out in this Act, they find any indications of violations of

1. this Act,
2. the Temporary Employment Act,
3. provisions of Books IV and VII of the Social Code on the payment of contributions,,
4. tax laws,
5. the Residence Act,
6. the duty to cooperate as set out in section 60 (1), sentence 1, nos 1 and 2 of Book I of the Social Code or the reporting obligation as set out in section 8a of the Asylum Seekers Benefit Act,
7. Federal Child Benefits Act,
8. the Trade and Crafts Code or the Trade Regulation Code,
9. the Road Haulage Act,
10. the Passenger Transport Act,
11. other criminal laws,
12. the Posted Workers Act
13. the Minimum Wage Act,

14. die Arbeitsschutzgesetze oder

15. die Vergabe- und Tariftreuegesetze der Länder.

²Nach § 5 Absatz 3 Satz 1 in Verwahrung genommene Urkunden sind der Ausländerbehörde unverzüglich zu übermitteln.

(5) Bestehen Anhaltspunkte dafür, dass eine nach § 5 Absatz 3 Satz 1 in Verwahrung genommene Urkunde unecht oder verfälscht ist, ist sie an die zuständige Polizeivollzugsbehörde zu übermitteln.

(6) Auf die Zusammenarbeit der Behörden der Zollverwaltung mit Behörden anderer Mitgliedstaaten der Europäischen Union und mit Behörden anderer Vertragsstaaten des Abkommens über den Europäischen Wirtschaftsraum gemäß § 20 Absatz 2 des Arbeitnehmer-Entsendegesetzes, § 18 Absatz 2 des Mindestlohngesetzes und § 18 Absatz 6 des Arbeitnehmerüberlassungsgesetzes finden die §§ 8a bis 8e des Verwaltungsverfahrensgesetzes in Verbindung mit Artikel 6 Absatz 1, 2 und 4 bis 9, den Artikeln 7 und 21 der Richtlinie 2014/67/EU des Europäischen Parlaments und des Rates vom 15. Mai 2014 zur Durchsetzung der Richtlinie 96/71/EG über die Entsendung von Arbeitnehmern im Rahmen der Erbringung von Dienstleistungen und zur Änderung der Verordnung (EU) Nr. 1024/2012 über die Verwaltungszusammenarbeit mit Hilfe des Binnenmarkt-Informationssystems („IMI-Verordnung") (ABl. L 159 vom 28.5.2014, S. 11) Anwendung.

14. the labour protection laws or

15. the public procurement and collective bargaining laws of the Länder.

²Documents seized under section 5 (3) sentence 1 must be transmitted to the authority responsible for foreign nationals without delay.

(5) If there are indications that a document seized under section 5 (3) is forged or has been tampered with, it must be transmitted to the police authority responsible.

(6) Sections 8a to 8e of the Administrative Procedure Act in conjunction with sections 6 (1), 2 and 4 to 9, sections 7 and 21 of Directive 2014/67/EU of the European Parliament and of the Council of 15 December 2014 and section 20 (2) of the Law on the Posting of Workers, section 18 (2) of the Minimum Wage Act and Article 18 (6) of the Law on the Provision of Temporary Workers shall apply to the cooperation of the customs authorities with the authorities of other Member States of the European Union and with the authorities of other States party to the Agreement on the European Economic Area. (1) OJ L 159, 28.5.2014, p. 11. Application of Directive 2014/67/EC of the European Parliament and of the Council of 15 May 2014 concerning the enforcement of Directive 96/71/EC on the posting of workers in the framework of the provision of services and amending Regulation (EU) No 1024/2012 on administrative cooperation in the Internal Market Information System (IMI Regulation).

§ 6a
Übermittlung personenbezogener Daten an Mitgliedstaaten der Europäischen Union

(1) ¹Die Behörden der Zollverwaltung können personenbezogene Daten, die in Zusammenhang mit einem der in § 2 Absatz 1 genannten Prüfgegenstände stehen, zum Zweck der Verhütung von Straftaten an eine für die Verhütung und Verfolgung zuständige Behörde eines Mitgliedstaates der Europäischen Union übermitteln. ²Dabei ist eine Übermittlung personenbezogener Daten ohne Ersuchen nur zulässig, wenn im Einzelfall die Gefahr der Begehung einer Straftat im Sinne des Artikels 2 Absatz 2 des Rahmenbeschlusses 2002/584/JI des Rates vom 13. Juni 2002 über den Europäischen Haftbefehl und die Übergabeverfahren zwischen den Mitgliedstaaten (ABl. L 190 vom 18.7.2002, S. 1), der zuletzt durch den Rahmenbeschluss 2009/299/JI (ABl. L 81 vom 27.3.2009, S. 24) geändert worden ist, besteht und konkrete Anhaltspunkte dafür vorliegen, dass die Übermittlung dieser personenbezogenen Daten dazu beitragen könnte, eine solche Straftat zu verhindern.

Section 6a
Transmission of personal data to member states of the European Union

(1) ¹The customs authorities may transmit personal data related to one of the matters for inspection specified in section 2 (1) to an authority of a European Union member state competent for the prevention and prosecution of crimes. ²In this context, the transmission of personal data without a request is permissible only if, in the case in question, there is a risk of the commission of a crime as defined in Article 2 (2) of Council Framework Decision 2002/584/JHA of 13 June 2002 on the European arrest warrant and the surrender procedures between Member States (OJ L 190, 18/07/2002, p. 1), most recently amended by Framework Decision 2009/299/JHA (OJ L 81, 27/02/2009, p. 24), and there are specific indications that the transmission of this personal data could contribute to preventing such a crime.

(2) Die Übermittlung personenbezogener Daten nach Absatz 1 ist nur zulässig, wenn das Ersuchen mindestens folgende Angaben enthält:

1. die Bezeichnung und die Anschrift der ersuchenden Behörde,
2. die Bezeichnung der Straftat, zu deren Verhütung die Daten benötigt werden,
3. die Beschreibung des Sachverhalts, der dem Ersuchen zugrunde liegt,
4. die Benennung des Zwecks, zu dem die Daten erbeten werden,
5. der Zusammenhang zwischen dem Zweck, zu dem die Informationen oder Erkenntnisse erbeten werden, und der Person, auf die sich diese Informationen beziehen,
6. Einzelheiten zur Identität der betroffenen Person, sofern sich das Ersuchen auf eine bekannte Person bezieht, und
7. Gründe für die Annahme, dass sachdienliche Informationen und Erkenntnisse im Inland vorliegen.

(3) Die Datenübermittlung nach Absatz 1 unterbleibt, wenn

1. hierdurch wesentliche Sicherheitsinteressen des Bundes oder der Länder beeinträchtigt würden,
2. die Übermittlung der Daten unverhältnismäßig wäre oder die Daten für die Zwecke, für die sie übermittelt werden sollen, nicht erforderlich sind,
3. die zu übermittelnden Daten bei der ersuchten Behörde nicht vorhanden sind und nur durchdas Ergreifen von Zwangsmaßnahmen erlangt werden können oder
4. besondere bundesgesetzliche Verwendungsregelungen entgegenstehen; die Verpflichtung zur Wahrung gesetzlicher Geheimhaltungspflichten oder von Berufs- oder besonderen Amtsgeheimnissen, die nicht auf gesetzlichen Vorschriften beruhen, bleibt unberührt.

(4) Die Übermittlung kann unterbleiben, wenn

1. die Tat, zu deren Verhütung die Daten übermittelt werden sollen, nach deutschem Recht mit einer Freiheitsstrafe von im Höchstmaß einem Jahr oder weniger bedroht ist,
2. die übermittelten Daten als Beweismittel vor einer Justizbehörde verwendet werden sollen,
3. die zu übermittelnden Daten bei der ersuchten Behörde nicht vorhanden sind, jedoch ohne das Ergreifen von Zwangsmaßnahmen erlangt werden können, oder
4. der Erfolg laufender Ermittlungen oder Leib, Leben oder Freiheit einer Person gefährdet würde.

(2) The transmission of personal data under subsection (1) is permissible only if the request contains at least the following details:

1. name and address of the requesting authority,
2. designation of the crime that is to be prevented with the help of the requested data,
3. description of the case on which the request is based,
4. purpose for which the data are requested,
5. connection between the purpose for which the information or intelligence is requested and the person who is the subject of the information,
6. details about the identity of the person concerned, if the request relates to a known person and
7. reasons for believing the relevant information and intelligence are available in Germany.

(3) Data must not be transmitted under subsection (1) if

1. doing so would impair core security interests of the Federation or the Länder,
2. the transmission of the data would be disproportionate or the data are not required for the purposes for which they are to be transmitted,
3. the data to be transmitted are not held by the requested authority and can only be obtained by taking coercive measures or
4. doing so would contravene special federal utilisation provisions; the duty to observe statutory secrecy obligations and professional or special official secrets that are not based on legal provisions remains unaffected.

(4) Transmission is not required if

1. the maximum penalty under German law for the act that is to be prevented is one year's imprisonment or less,
2. the transmitted data are to be used as evidence before a judicial authority,
3. the data to be transmitted are not held by the requested authority but could be obtained without taking coercive measures or
4. transmission would present a risk to the success of ongoing investigations or to a person's body, life or freedom.

(5) ¹Personenbezogene Daten, die nach dem Rahmenbeschluss 2006/960/JI des Rates vom 18. Dezember 2006 über die Vereinfachung des Austauschs von Informationen und Erkenntnissen zwischen den Strafverfolgungsbehörden der Mitgliedstaaten der Europäischen Union (ABl. L 386 vom 29.12.2006, S. 89, L 75 vom 15.3.2007, S. 26) an die Behörden der Zollverwaltung übermittelt worden sind, dürfen ohne Zustimmung des übermittelnden Staates nur für die Zwecke, für die sie übermittelt wurden, oder zur Abwehr einer gegenwärtigen und erheblichen Gefahr für die öffentliche Sicherheit verarbeitet werden. ²Für einen anderen Zweck oder als Beweismittel in einem gerichtlichen Verfahren dürfen sie nur verarbeitet werden, wenn der übermittelnde Staat zugestimmt hat. ³Bedingungen, die der übermittelnde Staat für die Verarbeitung der Daten stellt, sind zu beachten.

(6) Die Behörden der Zollverwaltung erteilen dem übermittelnden Staat auf dessen Ersuchen zu Zwecken der Datenschutzkontrolle Auskunft darüber, wie die übermittelten Daten verarbeitet wurden.

(7) Die Absätze 1 bis 6 finden auch Anwendung auf die Übermittlung von personenbezogenen Daten an für die Verhütung und Verfolgung von Straftaten zuständige Behörden eines Schengenassoziierten Staates im Sinne von § 91 Absatz 3 des Gesetzes über die internationale Rechtshilfe in Strafsachen.

§ 7
Auskunftsansprüche bei anonymen Angeboten und Werbemaßnahmen

¹Wurden Angebote oder Werbemaßnahmen ohne Angabe von Name und Anschrift veröffentlicht und bestehen in diesem Zusammenhang Anhaltspunkte für Schwarzarbeit oder illegale Beschäftigung nach § 1, so ist derjenige, der das Angebot oder die Werbemaßnahme veröffentlicht hat, verpflichtet, den Behörden der Zollverwaltung Namen und Anschrift des Auftraggebers des Angebots oder der Werbemaßnahme auf Verlangen unentgeltlich mitzuteilen. ²Soweit Name und Anschrift nicht vorliegen, sind die Daten mitzuteilen, die eine Identifizierung des Auftraggebers ermöglichen. ³Bei Anhaltspunkten nach § 1 Absatz 2 Satz 1 Nummer 4 oder 5 besteht diese Verpflichtung gegenüber den nach Landesrecht für die Verfolgung und Ahndung von Ordnungswidrigkeiten nach diesem Gesetz zuständigen Behörden.

(5) ¹Without the consent of the transmitting state, personal data transmitted to the customs authorities under Council Framework Decision 2006/960/JHA of 18 December 2006 on simplifying the exchange of information and intelligence between law enforcement authorities of the Member States of the European Union (OJ L 386 of 29/12/2006, p. 89, OJ L 75 of 15/3/2007, p. 26) may be used only for the purposes for which they were transmitted or to avert a present and substantial threat to public security ²The data may be used for other purposes or as evidence in judicial proceedings only if the transmitting state has given its consent. ³The conditions set by the transmitting state for the use of the data must be observed.

(6) For the purposes of monitoring data protection, the customs authorities must provide information to the transmitting state upon request about how the transmitted data were used.

(7) Subsections (1) to (6) also apply to the transmission of personal data to authorities of a Schengen associated state that are responsible for the prevention and prosecution of crimes as described in section 91 (3) of the International Assistance in Criminal Matters Act.

Section 7
Right to information in cases of anonymous advertising

¹If advertising is published without a name and address under a box number, and if there are indications of undeclared work under section 1, the person who published the box number advertisement must inform the customs authorities of the name and address of the client of the advertisement free of charge. ²If name and address are not available, the data that enable the identification of the client must be provided. ³In the event of indications under section 1 (2) sentence 1 nos. 4 or 5, this obligation is towards the authorities responsible under Land law for the prosecution and punishment of administrative offences under this Act.

§ 8
Bußgeldvorschriften

(1) Ordnungswidrig handelt, wer

1. (a)–(c) [aufgehoben]
    (d) der Verpflichtung zur Anzeige vom Beginn des selbstständigen Betriebes eines stehenden Gewerbes (§ 14 der Gewerbeordnung) nicht nachgekommen ist oder die erforderliche Reisegewerbekarte (§ 55 der Gewerbeordnung) nicht erworben hat oder
    (e) ein zulassungspflichtiges Handwerk als stehendes Gewerbe selbstständig betreibt, ohne in die Handwerksrolle eingetragen zu sein (§ 1 der Handwerksordnung)

    und Dienst- oder Werkleistungen in erheblichem Umfang erbringt oder
2. Dienst- oder Werkleistungen in erheblichem Umfang ausführen lässt, indem er eine oder mehrere Personen beauftragt, von der oder denen er weiß oder fahrlässig nicht weiß, dass diese Leistungen unter vorsätzlichem Verstoß gegen eine in Nummer 1 genannte Vorschrift erbringen.

(2) Ordnungswidrig handelt, wer vorsätzlich oder fahrlässig

1. entgegen § 2a Abs. 1 ein dort genanntes Dokument nicht mitführt oder nicht oder nicht rechtzeitig vorlegt,

2. entgegen § 2a Abs. 2 den schriftlichen Hinweis nicht oder nicht für die vorgeschriebene Dauer aufbewahrt oder nicht oder nicht rechtzeitig vorlegt,

3. entgegen
    a) § 5 Absatz 1 Satz 1 Nummer 1, 2 oder 3 oder
    b) § 5 Absatz 4 Satz 1

eine Prüfung oder das Betreten eines Grundstücks oder eines Geschäftsraumes nicht duldet oder bei einer Prüfung nicht mitwirkt,

4. entgegen § 5 Absatz 3 Satz 1 ein dort genanntes Dokument nicht oder nicht rechtzeitig vorlegt,

5. entgegen § 5 Absatz 5 Satz 1 Daten nicht, nicht richtig, nicht vollständig, nicht in der vorgeschriebenen Weise oder nicht rechtzeitig übermittelt,

6. entgegen § 5a Absatz 1 Satz 1 seine Arbeitskraft anbietet oder

Section 8
Administrative fines

(1) An administrative offence is deemed to have been committed by any persons who

1. (a)–(c) [rescinded]
    (d) fail to fulfil their duty to report the opening of an independent business operating from a fixed location (section 14 of the Trade Regulation Code) or to obtain the required itinerant trader's licence (section 15 of the Trade Regulation Code) or
    (e) carry out a craft or trade for which a licence is required as an independent business operating from a fixed location without being enrolled in the trade and craft register (section 1 of the Trade and Crafts Code)

    and perform a substantial volume of work or services or
2. arrange for a substantial volume of work or services to be carried out by commissioning one or more persons to perform such work or services in intentional violation of one of the provisions specified in no 1.

(2) An administrative offence is deemed to have been committed by any persons who, either intentionally or negligently,

1. in violation of section 2a (1), fail to carry on their person one of the documents specified therein or fail to produce such document either at all or within the prescribed period,

2. in violation of section 2a (2), fail to keep the notification on file either at all or for the prescribed period, or fail to produce such notification either at all or within the prescribed period,

3. in violation of
    a) section 5 (1) sentence 1, 2 or 3 or
    b) section 5 (4) sentence 1,

refuse to submit to an inspection or to the entering of a property or business premises or refuse to cooperate with an inspection,

4. in violation of section 5 (3) sentence 1, fail to produce one of the documents specified therein either at all or within the prescribed period or

5. in violation of section 5 (3) sentence 1, fail to transmit data, or fail to do so correctly, completely, in the prescribed manner or within the prescribed period.

6. in violation of section 5a (1) sentence 1 offers his employee, or

7. entgegen § 5a Absatz 1 Satz 2 eine Arbeitskraft nachfragt.

(3) Ordnungswidrig handelt, wer als Arbeitgeber eine in § 266a Absatz 2 Nummer 1 oder 2 des Strafgesetzbuches bezeichnete Handlung leichtfertig begeht und dadurch der Einzugsstelle Beiträge des Arbeitnehmers oder der Arbeitnehmerin zur Sozialversicherung einschließlich der Arbeitsförderung oder vom Arbeitgeber zu tragende Beiträge zur Sozialversicherung einschließlich der Arbeitsförderung, unabhängig davon, ob Arbeitsentgelt gezahlt wird, leichtfertig vorenthält.

(4) Ordnungswidrig handelt, wer

1. einen Beleg ausstellt, der in tatsächlicher Hinsicht nicht richtig ist und das Erbringen oder Ausführenlassen einer Dienst- oder Werkleistung vorspiegelt, oder

2. einen in Nummer 1 genannten Beleg in den Verkehr bringt

und dadurch Schwarzarbeit im Sinne des § 1 Absatz 2 oder illegale Beschäftigung im Sinne des § 1 Absatz 3 ermöglicht.

(5) Ordnungswidrig handelt, wer eine in Absatz 4 genannte Handlung begeht und

1. aus grobem Eigennutz für sich oder einen anderen Vermögensvorteile großen Ausmaßes erlangt oder

2. als Mitglied einer Bande handelt, die sich zur fortgesetzten Begehung solcher Taten verbunden hat.

(6) Die Ordnungswidrigkeit kann in den Fällen des Absatzes 5 mit einer Geldbuße bis zu fünfhunderttausend Euro, in den Fällen des Absatzes 4 mit einer Geldbuße bis zu einhunderttausend Euro, in den Fällen des Absatzes 1 Nummer 1 Buchstabe d und e, Nummer 2 in Verbindung mit Nummer 1 Buchstabe d und e sowie in den Fällen des Absatzes 3 mit einer Geldbuße bis zu fünfzigtausend Euro, in den Fällen des Absatzes 2 Nummer 3 Buchstabe a, Nummer 5 und 7 mit einer Geldbuße bis zu dreißigtausend Euro, in den Fällen des Absatzes 2 Nummer 1 und 6 mit einer Geldbuße bis zu

fünftausend Euro und in den übrigen Fällen mit einer Geldbuße bis zu tausend Euro geahndet werden.

(7) ¹Absatz 1 findet keine Anwendung für nicht nachhaltig auf Gewinn gerichtete Dienst- oder Werkleistungen, die

1. von Angehörigen im Sinne des § 15 der Abgabenordnung oder Lebenspartnern,

2. aus Gefälligkeit,

7. in violation of section 5a (1) sentence 1 requires a worker.

(3) An administrative offence is deemed to have been committed by any persons who commit recklessly an act described in section 266a (2) nos. 1 or 2 of the Criminal Code and thereby recklessly withhold from the collection agency the employee's social insurance contributions, including the promotion of employment, or social insurance contributions to be borne by the employer, including the promotion of employment, irrespective of whether remuneration is paid.

(4) An administrative offence is deemed to have been committed by any persons who

1. issues a document which is not correct in fact and pretends that a service or work has been performed or not performed, or

2. places on the market a document referred to in no. 1

and thereby enables undeclared work within the meaning of section 1 (2) or illegal employment within the meaning of section 1 (3).

(5) An administrative offence is deemed to have been committed by any persons who commits an act referred to in (4), and

1. obtains a large amount of property for his own benefit or for another pecuniary advantage of great magnitude, or

2. acts as a member of a gang which has joined together for the purpose of committing such acts.

(6) The administrative offence may be punishable by a fine of up to five hundred thousand euro in the cases referred to in subsection 5, by a fine of up to one hundred thousand euro in the cases referred to in subsection 4, by a fine of up to one hundred thousand euro in the cases referred to in subsection 1 no. 1 (d) and (e), no. 2 in conjunction with (1) (d) and (e) and by a fine of up to fifty thousand euro in the cases referred to in subsection 3, in the cases referred to in subsection 2 no. 3(a), nos. 5 and 7 shall be punishable by a fine not exceeding thirty thousand euro, in the cases referred to in subsection 2 nos. 1 and 6 by a fine not exceeding five thousand euro and in the other cases by a fine not exceeding one thousand euro.

(7) Subsection (1) does not apply to work or services that are not intended to produce sustainable profits and which are performed

1. by relatives as defined in section 15 of the Fiscal Code or by civil partners,

2. as a favour,

3. im Wege der Nachbarschaftshilfe oder

4. im Wege der Selbsthilfe im Sinne des § 36 Abs. 2 und 4 des Zweiten Wohnungsbaugesetzes in der Fassung der Bekanntmachung vom 19. August 1994 (BGBl. I S. 2137) oder als Selbsthilfe im Sinne des § 12 Abs. 1 Satz 2 des Wohnraumförderungsgesetzes vom 13. September 2001 (BGBl. I S. 2376), zuletzt geändert durch Artikel 7 des Gesetzes vom 29. Dezember 2003 (BGBl. I S. 3076), erbracht werden.

²Als nicht nachhaltig auf Gewinn gerichtet gilt insbesondere eine Tätigkeit, die gegen geringes Entgelt erbracht wird.

(8) Das Bundesministerium der Finanzen wird ermächtigt, durch Rechtsverordnung mit Zustimmung des Bundesrates Vorschriften über Regelsätze für Geldbußen wegen einer Ordnungswidrigkeit nach Absatz 1 oder 2 zu erlassen.

(9) Eine Geldbuße wird in den Fällen des Absatzes 3 nicht festgesetzt, wenn der Arbeitgeber spätestens im Zeitpunkt der Fälligkeit oder unverzüglich danach gegenüber der Einzugsstelle

1. schriftlich die Höhe der vorenthaltenen Beiträge mitteilt,

2. schriftlich darlegt, warum die fristgemäße Zahlung nicht möglich ist, obwohl er sich darum ernsthaft bemüht hat, und

3. die vorenthaltenen Beiträge nachträglich innerhalb der von der Einzugsstelle bestimmten angemessenen Frist entrichtet.

§ 9
[aufgehoben]

§ 10
Beschäftigung von Ausländern ohne Genehmigung oder ohne Aufenthaltstitel und zu ungünstigen Arbeitsbedingungen

(1) Wer vorsätzlich eine in § 404 Abs. 2 Nr. 3 des Dritten Buches Sozialgesetzbuch bezeichnete Handlung begeht und den Ausländer zu Arbeitsbedingungen beschäftigt, die in einem auffälligen Missverhältnis zu den Arbeitsbedingungen deutscher Arbeitnehmer und Arbeitnehmerinnen stehen, die die gleiche oder eine vergleichbare Tätigkeit ausüben, wird mit Freiheitsstrafe bis zu drei Jahren oder mit Geldstrafe bestraft.

(2) ¹In besonders schweren Fällen des Absatzes 1 ist die Strafe Freiheitsstrafe von sechs Monaten bis zu fünf Jahren. ²Ein besonders schwerer Fall liegt in der Regel vor, wenn der Täter gewerbsmäßig oder aus grobem Eigennutz handelt.

3. as a form of help among neighbours or

4. as a form of own labour as defined in section 36 (2) and (4) of the Second Housing Act as published on 19 August 1994 (Federal Law Gazette I, p. 2137), or as a form of own labour as defined in section 12 (1) sentence 2 of the Housing Subsidisation Act of 13 September 2001 (Federal Law Gazette I, p. 2376), last amended by Article 7 of the Act of 29 December 2003 (Federal Law Gazette I, p. 3076).

An activity that is not intended to produce sustainable profits is deemed to exist, in particular, if it is performed for a small fee.

(8) The Federal Ministry of Finance is authorised to adopt, by way of ordinances issued with the consent of the Bundesrat, rules on standard administrative fine amounts for administrative offences under subsections (1) and (2).

(9) In the cases referred to in paragraph 3, no fine shall be imposed if, at the latest on the due date or without undue delay thereafter, the employer

1. notifies in writing the amount of the withheld contributions

2. states in writing why payment within the time limit is not possible, although he has made a serious effort to do so, and

3. subsequently pays the withheld contributions within a reasonable period determined by the collection agency.

Section 9
[rescinded]

Section 10
Employment of foreign nationals who lack a work permit or residence permit under unfavourable working conditions

(1) Any person who intentionally commits one of the acts specified in section 404 (2) no 3 of Book III of the Social Code and employs a foreign national under conditions that are clearly less favourable than those of German workers who carry out the same or a similar activity is punished with imprisonment for up to three years or with a criminal fine.

(2) ¹In particularly serious cases, a penalty of between six months and ten years' imprisonment is imposed. ²As a rule, a particularly serious case is one in which the offender acts on a commercial basis or out of gross self-interest.

§ 10a
Beschäftigung von Ausländern ohne Aufenthaltstitel, die Opfer von Menschenhandel sind

Mit Freiheitsstrafe bis zu drei Jahren oder mit Geldstrafe wird bestraft, wer entgegen § 4 Absatz 3 Satz 2 des Aufenthaltsgesetzes einen Ausländer beschäftigt und hierbei eine Lage ausnutzt, in der sich der Ausländer durch eine gegen ihn gerichtete Tat eines Dritten nach § 232a Absatz 1 bis 5 oder § 232b des Strafgesetzbuchs befindet.

Section 10a
Employment of foreign nationals who lack a residence permit and who are victims of human trafficking

Any person who, in violation of section 4 (3) sentence 2 of the Residence Act, employs a foreign national and, in doing so, exploits a situation in which the foreign national finds him-/herself as a result of an act committed against him/her by a third party under section 232a (1) to (5) or section 232b of the Criminal Code is punished with imprisonment for up to three years or with a criminal fine.

§ 11
Erwerbstätigkeit von Ausländern ohne Genehmigung oder ohne Aufenthaltstitel in größerem Umfang oder von minderjährigen Ausländern

(1) Wer

1. gleichzeitig mehr als fünf Ausländer entgegen § 284 Abs. 1 des Dritten Buches Sozialgesetzbuch beschäftigt oder entgegen § 4 Abs. 3 Satz 2 des Aufenthaltsgesetzes beschäftigt oder mit Dienst- oder Werkleistungen beauftragt,

2. eine in

   (a) § 404 Abs. 2 Nr. 3 des Dritten Buches Sozialgesetzbuch,

   (b) § 404 Abs. 2 Nr. 4 des Dritten Buches Sozialgesetzbuch,

   (c) § 98 Absatz 2a Nummer 1 des Aufenthaltsgesetzes oder

   (d) § 98 Abs. 3 Nr. 1 des Aufenthaltsgesetzes

   bezeichnete vorsätzliche Handlung beharrlich wiederholt oder

3. entgegen § 4 Absatz 3 Satz 2 des Aufenthaltsgesetzes eine Person unter 18 Jahren beschäftigt,

wird mit Freiheitsstrafe bis zu einem Jahr oder mit Geldstrafe bestraft.

(2) Handelt der Täter in den Fällen des Absatzes 1 Nummer 1, Nummer 2 Buchstabe a oder Buchstabe c oder Nummer 3 aus grobem Eigennutz, ist die Strafe Freiheitsstrafe bis zu drei Jahren oder Geldstrafe.

Section 11
Larger-scale employment of foreign nationals who lack a work permit or residence permit and employment of underage foreign nationals

(1) Any person who

1. simultaneously employs more than five foreign nationals in violation of section 284 (1) of Book III of the Social Code or in violation of section 4 (3) sentence 2 of the Residence Act or commissions them to perform work or services,

2. repeatedly commits an intentional act specified in

   (a) section 404 (2) no 3 of the Social Code,

   (b) section 404 (2) no 4 of the Social Code,

   (c) section 98 (2a) of the Residence Act or

   (d) section 98 (3) no 1 of the Residence Act or

3. employs a person under the age of 18 in violation of section 4 (3) sentence 2 of the Residence Act

will be punished with imprisonment for up to one year or with a criminal fine.

(2) If, in the cases described in subsection (1) no 1, no 2 a) or c), or no 3, the offender acts out of gross self-interest, a penalty of up to three years' imprisonment or a criminal fine will be imposed.

§ 12
Allgemeines zu den Ordnungswidrigkeiten

(1) Verwaltungsbehörden im Sinne des § 36 Abs. 1 Nr. 1 des Gesetzes über Ordnungswidrigkeiten sind

1. [aufgehoben]

Section 12
General provisions on administrative offences

(1) The administrative authorities as described in section 36 (1) no 1 of the Administrative Offences Act are

1. [rescinded]

2. in den Fällen des § 8 Abs. 1 Nr. 1 Buchstabe d und e und Nr. 2 in Verbindung mit Nr. 1 Buchstabe d und e die nach Landesrecht zuständige Behörde,
3. in den Fällen des § 8 Abs. 2 die Behörden der Zollverwaltung sowie die nach Landesrecht zuständige Behörde jeweils für ihren Geschäftsbereich,
4. in den Fällen des § 8 Absatz 3 bis 5 die Behörden der Zollverwaltung.

(2) Die Geldbußen fließen in die Kasse der Verwaltungsbehörde, die den Bußgeldbescheid erlassen hat.

(3) ¹Die nach Absatz 2 zuständige Kasse trägt abweichend von § 105 Abs. 2 des Gesetzes über Ordnungswidrigkeiten die notwendigen Auslagen. ²Sie ist auch ersatzpflichtig im Sinne des § 110 Abs. 4 des Gesetzes über Ordnungswidrigkeiten.

(4) Die Behörden der Zollverwaltung unterrichten das Gewerbezentralregister über rechtskräftige Bußgeldbescheide nach § 8 Absatz 2 Nummer 3 Buchstabe a und Nummer 5 sowie Absatz 3 bis 5, sofern die Geldbuße mehr als zweihundert Euro beträgt.

(5) ¹Nimmt die Staatsanwaltschaft an der Hauptverhandlung nach § 75 Absatz 2 des Gesetzes über Ordnungswidrigkeiten nicht teil, so gibt das Gericht den Behörden der Zollverwaltung Gelegenheit, die Gründe vorzubringen, die aus ihrer Sicht für die Entscheidung von Bedeutung sind. ²Dies gilt auch, wenn das Gericht erwägt, das Verfahren einzustellen. ³Der Vertreter der Behörden der Zollverwaltung erhält in der Hauptverhandlung auf Verlangen das Wort. ⁴Ihm ist zu gestatten, Fragen an Betroffene, Zeugen und Sachverständige zu richten.

§ 13
Zusammenarbeit in Bußgeldverfahren

(1) Die Behörden der Zollverwaltung arbeiten insbesondere mit den in § 2 Absatz 4 genannten unterstützenden Stellen zusammen.

(2) ¹Ergeben sich für die in § 2 Absatz 4 Nummer 2 bis 20 genannten unterstützenden Stellen im Zusammenhang mit der Erfüllung ihrer gesetzlichen Aufgaben Anhaltspunkte für in § 8 genannte Verstöße, unterrichten sie die für die Verfolgung und Ahndung von Ordnungswidrigkeiten nach diesem Gesetz zuständigen Behörden. ²§ 31a der Abgabenordnung bleibt unberührt.

2. in the cases described in section 8 (1) no 1 d) and e) as well as no 2 in conjunction with no 1 d) and e), the authority responsible under the legislation of the respective Land,
3. in the cases described in section 8 (2), the customs authorities as well as the authority responsible under the legislation of the respective Land, each for its area of responsibility,
4. in the cases described in section 8 (3) to (5), the authorities of the customs administration.

(2) Administrative fines accrue to the cash office of the administrative authority that issued the fine notice.

(3) Notwithstanding section 105 (2) of the Administrative Offences Act, the cash office responsible under subsection (2) bears the necessary expenses. It is also liable to pay compensation as described in section 110 (4) of the Administrative Offences Act.

(4) The customs authorities notify the central register of trade and industry of final administrative fine notices under section 8 (2) no 3 a) and no 5 if the administrative fine exceeds two hundred euros.

(5) ¹If the Public Prosecutor's Office does not attend the main hearing in accordance with section 75 (2) of the Administrative Offences Act, the court shall give the Customs Administration authorities the opportunity to state the reasons which in their view are of significance for the decision. ²This also applies if the court considers discontinuing the proceedings. ³The representative of the Customs Administration authorities shall be given the floor at the main hearing on request. ⁴He shall be permitted to put questions to interested parties, witnesses and experts.

Section 13
Cooperation in administrative fine proceedings

(1) The customs authorities must work together with the cooperating bodies specified in section 2 (2) in particular.

(2) ¹If, in performing their statutory tasks, the cooperating bodies specified in section 2 (2) nos 2 to 11 find indications of offences specified in section 8, they must notify the authorities responsible for prosecuting and punishing administrative offences as described in this Act. ²Section 31a of the Fiscal Code remains unaffected.

(3) ¹Gerichte und Staatsanwaltschaften sollen den nach diesem Gesetz zuständigen Stellen Erkenntnisse übermitteln, die aus ihrer Sicht zur Verfolgung von Ordnungswidrigkeiten nach § 8 erforderlich sind, soweit nicht für das Gericht oder die Staatsanwaltschaft erkennbar ist, dass schutzwürdige Interessen der betroffenen Person oder anderer Verfahrensbeteiligter an dem Ausschluss der Übermittlung überwiegen. ²Dabei ist zu berücksichtigen, wie gesichert die zu übermittelnden Erkenntnisse sind.

§ 14
Ermittlungsbefugnisse

(1) ¹Die Behörden der Zollverwaltung haben bei der Verfolgung von Straftaten und Ordnungswidrigkeiten, die mit einem der in § 2 Abs. 1 genannten Prüfgegenstände unmittelbar zusammenhängen, die gleichen Befugnisse wie die Polizeivollzugsbehörden nach der Strafprozessordnung und dem Gesetz über Ordnungswidrigkeiten. ²Ihre Beamten sind insoweit Ermittlungspersonen der Staatsanwaltschaft. ³In den Dienst der Zollverwaltung übergeleitete Angestellte nehmen die Befugnisse nach Satz 1 wahr und sind insoweit Ermittlungspersonen der Staatsanwaltschaft, wenn sie

1. das 21. Lebensjahr vollendet haben,
2. am 31. Dezember 2003 im Dienst der Bundesanstalt für Arbeit gestanden haben und
3. dort mindestens zwei Jahre lang zur Bekämpfung der Schwarzarbeit oder der illegalen Beschäftigung eingesetzt waren.

(2) Zur Bekämpfung von Schwarzarbeit und illegaler Beschäftigung können die Behörden der Zollverwaltung, die Polizeibehörden und die Landesfinanzbehörden in Abstimmung mit der Staatsanwaltschaft gemeinsame Ermittlungsgruppen bilden.

(3) Die Behörden der Zollverwaltung dürfen bei der Verfolgung von Straftaten nach Absatz 1 erkennungsdienstliche Maßnahmen nach § 81b der Strafprozessordnung auch zur Vorsorge für künftige Strafverfahren durchführen.

(3) ¹Courts and public prosecutors should transmit to the authorities responsible under this Act any intelligence that they deem necessary to prosecute administrative offences under section 8, unless the court or public prosecutor has evidence that the person affected or another party has an overriding legitimate interest in non-transmission. ²In this context, due consideration must be given to how solid the intelligence to be transmitted is.

Section 14
Powers of investigations

(1) When prosecuting criminal and administrative offences directly related to one of the matters for inspection specified in section 2 (1), the customs authorities have the same powers as the police authorities under the Code of Criminal Procedure and the Administrative Offences Act. In this respect, their officials are investigators of the public prosecutor. Employees transferred to the customs administration exercise the powers under sentence 1 and are, in this respect, investigators of the public prosecutor if they

1. have reached the age of 21,
2. were in the employ of the Federal Employment Agency on 31 December 2003 and
3. were engaged in combating undeclared work and unlawful employment at the Federal Employment Agency for at least two years.

(2) The customs authorities, the police and the revenue authorities of the respective Land may form joint investigation teams in consultation with the public prosecutor.

(3) The authorities of the customs administration may, in the prosecution of offences under subsection 1, carry out identification measures in accordance with Section 81b of the Code of Criminal Procedure, also as a precaution for future criminal proceedings.

§ 14a
Selbstständige Durchführung von Ermittlungsverfahren

(1) [1]Die Behörden der Zollverwaltung führen in den Fällen, in denen ihnen die Befugnisse nach § 14 zustehen, die Ermittlungsverfahren nach Maßgabe dieser Vorschrift und in den Grenzen des § 14b selbstständig durch, wenn die Tat ausschließlich eine Straftat nach § 266a des Strafgesetzbuches darstellt und die Staatsanwaltschaft die Strafsache an die Behörden der Zollverwaltung abgegeben hat. [2]Die allgemeinen Gesetze über das Strafverfahren sind anzuwenden.

(2) [1]Eine Abgabe durch die Staatsanwaltschaft nach Absatz 1 erfolgt nicht, wenn besondere Umstände es angezeigt erscheinen lassen, dass das Ermittlungsverfahren unter der Verantwortung der Staatsanwaltschaft fortzuführen ist. [2]Dies ist insbesondere der Fall, wenn

1. eine Maßnahme nach den §§ 99, 102, 103 oder 104 der Strafprozessordnung beantragt worden ist,
2. eine Maßnahme nach § 100a der Strafprozessordnung beantragt worden ist,
3. die Anordnung der Untersuchungshaft nach § 112 der Strafprozessordnung beantragt worden ist,
4. die Strafsache besondere Schwierigkeiten aufweist,
5. der Beschuldigte außer dieser Tat noch einer anderen, prozessual selbstständigen Straftat beschuldigt wird und die Taten in einem einheitlichen Ermittlungsverfahren verfolgt werden sollen,
6. eine Freiheitsstrafe zu erwarten ist, die nicht im Strafbefehlsverfahren festgesetzt werden kann,
7. gegen die folgenden Personen ermittelt wird:
   a) Mitglieder des Europäischen Parlaments, des Deutschen Bundestages oder einer gesetzgebenden Körperschaft eines Landes,
   b) Mitglieder diplomatischer Vertretung und andere von der inländischen Gerichtsbarkeit befreite Personen,
   c) Mitglieder einer Truppe oder eines zivilen Gefolges eines NATO-Staates oder deren Angehörige,
   d) Personen, die in den Anwendungsbereich des Jugendgerichtsgesetzes fallen, oder

Section 14a
Independent conduct of preliminary proceedings

(1) [1]In cases where they have the powers under Section 14, the authorities of the Customs Administration shall conduct investigations independently in accordance with this provision and within the limits of Section 14b if the act constitutes exclusively a criminal offence under Section 266a of the Criminal Code and the public prosecutor's office has handed over the criminal case to the authorities of the Customs Administration. [2]The general laws on criminal procedure shall apply.

(2) [1]The Public Prosecutor's Office shall not hand the case over to the Customs Administration under subsection 1 if special circumstances make it seem appropriate that the investigation proceedings be continued under the responsibility of the Public Prosecutor's Office. [2]This is in particular the case if

1. a measure has been applied for under sections 99, 102, 103 or 104 of the Code of Criminal Procedure
2. a measure under section 100a of the Code of Criminal Procedure has been applied for,
3. an application has been made for the order of detention pending trial pursuant to section 112 of the Code of Criminal Procedure,
4. the criminal case presents particular difficulties,
5. the accused is accused of another, procedurally independent, criminal offence in addition to this act and the acts are to be prosecuted in a uniform investigation procedure
6. a custodial sentence is to be expected which cannot be determined in the criminal proceedings,
7. the following persons are under investigation:
   a) Members of the European Parliament, the German Bundestag or a legislative body of a Land
   b) members of diplomatic missions and other persons exempt from domestic jurisdiction
   c) members of a force or civilian staff of a NATO State or their dependants
   d) persons falling within the scope of the Juvenile Courts Act, or

e) Personen, bei denen Anhaltspunkte dafür vorliegen, dass sie vermindert schuldfähig (§ 21 des Strafgesetzbuches) oder aus psychischen Gründen in ihrer Verteidigung behindert sind, oder

8. ein Amtsträger der Zollverwaltung der Beteiligung verdächtig ist.

(3) ¹Soll nach Abgabe durch die Staatsanwaltschaft nach Absatz 1 eine Maßnahme nach Absatz 2 Satz 2 Nummer 1 oder 2 beantragt werden, so haben die Behörden der Zollverwaltung nicht die Befugnis, bei Gefahr im Verzug selbst Anordnungen vorzunehmen. ²Soll nach einer Abgabe durch die Staatsanwaltschaft nach Absatz 1 eine Maßnahme nach Absatz 2 Satz 2 Nummer 2 oder 3 beantragt werden oder ergibt sich nachträglich, dass ein Fall des Absatzes 2 Satz 2 Nummer 4 bis 8 vorliegt, geben die Behörden der Zollverwaltung die Strafsache an die Staatsanwaltschaft zurück.

(4) Im Übrigen können die Behörden der Zollverwaltung die Strafsache jederzeit an die Staatsanwaltschaft zurückgeben, die Staatsanwaltschaft kann die Strafsache jederzeit wieder an sich ziehen.

§ 14b
Rechte und Pflichten bei der selbstständigen Durchführung von Ermittlungsverfahren

(1) Führen die Behörden der Zollverwaltung das Ermittlungsverfahren nach § 14a selbstständig durch, so nehmen sie die Rechte und Pflichten wahr, die der Staatsanwaltschaft im Ermittlungsverfahren zustehen.

(2) Sie haben nicht die Befugnis, Ermittlungen durch die Behörden und Beamten des Polizeidienstes vornehmen zu lassen.

(3) Bieten die Ermittlungen genügenden Anlass zur Erhebung der öffentlichen Klage, so beantragt die Behörde der Zollverwaltung über die Staatsanwaltschaft bei dem zuständigen Gericht den Erlass eines Strafbefehls, wenn die Strafsache zur Behandlung im Strafbefehlsverfahren geeignet erscheint; andernfalls legt die Behörde der Zollverwaltung die Akten der Staatsanwaltschaft vor.

(4) Hat die Behörde der Zollverwaltung den Erlass eines Strafbefehls beantragt, so nimmt sie die Rechte und Pflichten der Staatsanwaltschaft wahr, solange nach § 408 Absatz 3 Satz 2 der Strafprozessordnung die Hauptverhandlung anberaumt oder Einspruch gegen den Strafbefehl erhoben ist.

e) Persons with indications that they are less culpable (section 21 of the German Criminal Code) or that they are hindered in their defence for psychological reasons, or

8. an official of the customs administration is suspected of involvement

(3) ¹If, after submission by the public prosecutor's office in accordance with subsection 1, an application is made for a measure in accordance with subsection 2 sentence 2 nos. 1 or 2, the authorities of the Customs Administration shall not have the power to issue orders themselves in the event of imminent danger. ²If, after a submission by the public prosecutor's office in accordance with subsection 1, an application is made for a measure in accordance with subsection 2, second sentence, nos. 2 or 3, or if it subsequently emerges that a case in accordance with subsection 2, second sentence, nos. 4 to 8 exists, the Customs Administration authorities shall return the criminal case to the public prosecutor's office.

(4) Otherwise, the Customs Administration authorities may return the criminal case to the Public Prosecutor's Office at any time; the Public Prosecutor's Office may at any time take back the criminal case.

Section 14b
Rights and obligations in the independent conduct of pre-trial procedures

(1) If the Customs Administration authorities conduct the investigation procedure pursuant to Section 14a independently, they shall exercise the rights and duties to which the public prosecutor's office is entitled in the investigation procedure.

(2) They do not have the authority to have investigations conducted by the authorities and officials of the police service.

(3) If the investigations provide sufficient grounds for bringing a public prosecution, the authority of the Customs Administration, through the Public Prosecutor's Office, shall apply to the competent court for the issue of a penalty order if the criminal case appears to be suitable for consideration in the penalty order proceedings; otherwise the authority shall submit the files to the Public Prosecutor's Office.

(4) If the authority of the Customs Administration has applied for the issue of a criminal order, it shall exercise the rights and duties of the Public Prosecutor's Office until the main hearing has been scheduled in accordance with section 408 (3), second sentence, of the Code of Criminal Procedure or an objection to the criminal order has been raised.

(5) Hat die Behörde der Zollverwaltung den Antrag gestellt, eine Einziehung gemäß § 435 der Strafprozessordnung selbstständig anzuordnen oder eine Geldbuße gegen eine juristische Person oder eine Personenvereinigung gemäß § 444 Absatz 3 der Strafprozessordnung selbstständig festzusetzen, so nimmt sie die Rechte und Pflichten der Staatsanwaltschaft wahr, solange die mündliche Verhandlung nicht beantragt oder vom Gericht angeordnet ist.

§ 14c
Sachliche und örtliche Zuständigkeit bei der selbstständigen Durchführung von Ermittlungsverfahren

(1) Sachlich zuständig für die Durchführung des selbstständigen Ermittlungsverfahrens nach § 14a ist das Hauptzollamt.

(2) ¹Örtlich zuständig für die Durchführung des selbstständigen Ermittlungsverfahrens ist das Hauptzollamt,

1. in dessen Bezirk die Straftat begangen oder entdeckt worden ist,
2. das zum Zeitpunkt der Abgabe des Ermittlungsverfahrens durch die Staatsanwaltschaft für die Prüfung gemäß § 2 Absatz 1 zuständig ist oder
3. in dessen Bezirk der Beschuldigte zum Zeitpunkt der Abgabe des Ermittlungsverfahrens seinen Wohnsitz hat; hat der Beschuldigte im räumlichen Geltungsbereich dieses Gesetzes keinen Wohnsitz, so wird die Zuständigkeit durch den Ort des gewöhnlichen Aufenthalts bestimmt.

²Sind nach Satz 1 mehrere Hauptzollämter zuständig, so ist das Hauptzollamt örtlich zuständig, an das die Staatsanwaltschaft das Ermittlungsverfahren abgegeben hat.

(3) ¹Ändert sich in den Fällen des Absatzes 2 Satz 1 Nummer 3 der Wohnsitz oder der Ort des gewöhnlichen Aufenthalts des Beschuldigten nach Abgabe des Ermittlungsverfahrens, so ist auch das Hauptzollamt örtlich zuständig, in dessen Bezirk der neue Wohnsitz oder Ort des gewöhnlichen Aufenthalts liegt. ²Übergibt das nach Absatz 2 örtlich zuständige Hauptzollamt das Ermittlungsverfahren an das nach Satz 1 auch örtlich zuständige Hauptzollamt, so hat es die Staatsanwaltschaft davon in Kenntnis zu setzen.

(5) If the authority has submitted an application to the Customs Administration to independently order confiscation pursuant to section 435 of the Code of Criminal Procedure or to independently fix a fine against a legal person or an association of persons pursuant to section 444 (3) of the Code of Criminal Procedure, it shall exercise the rights and duties of the Public Prosecutor's Office as long as the oral hearing has not been requested or ordered by the court.

Section 14c
Substantive and local jurisdiction in the independent conduct of investigations

(1) The Principal Customs Office shall be responsible for conducting the independent investigation procedure in accordance with section 14a.

(2) ¹Locally responsible for conducting the independent investigation procedure is the Main Customs Office,

1. in whose district the offence has been committed or discovered
2. which at the time of the submission of the preliminary investigation by the public prosecutor's office is responsible for the examination pursuant to section 2 (1) or
3. in whose district the suspect is domiciled at the time of the submission of the preliminary investigation; if the suspect is not domiciled within the territorial scope of this Act, jurisdiction shall be determined by the place of habitual residence.

²If several main customs offices have jurisdiction in accordance with the first sentence, the main customs office to which the public prosecutor's office has handed over the investigation procedure shall have local jurisdiction.

(3) ¹If the domicile or the place of habitual residence of the accused changes in the cases of paragraph 2 sentence 1 number 3 after the investigation procedure has been surrendered, the main customs office in whose district the new domicile or place of habitual residence is located shall also have local jurisdiction. ²If the main customs office that is locally competent in accordance with subsection 2 transfers the investigation procedure to the main customs office that is also locally competent in accordance with sentence 1, it must inform the public prosecutor's office thereof.

§ 15
Allgemeines

[1]Für die Wahrnehmung der Aufgaben nach diesem Gesetz durch die Behörden der Zollverwaltung gelten hinsichtlich der Sozialdaten die Vorschriften des Zweiten Kapitels des Zehnten Buches Sozialgesetzbuch. [2]Diese Aufgaben gelten in datenschutzrechtlicher Hinsicht auch als Aufgaben nach dem Sozialgesetzbuch. [3]Die Vorschriften des Vierten Abschnitts des Ersten Teils der Abgabenordnung zum Steuergeheimnis bleiben unberührt.

§ 16
Zentrales Informationssystem für die Finanzkontrolle Schwarzarbeit

(1) Die Behörden der Zollverwaltung führen ein zentrales Informationssystem für die Finanzkontrolle Schwarzarbeit, in dem die zur Aufgabenerfüllung nach diesem Gesetz erhobenen und übermittelten Daten automatisiert verarbeitet werden.

(2) [1]Im zentralen Informationssystem für die Finanzkontrolle Schwarzarbeit werden folgende Daten gespeichert:

1. Familienname, frühere Namen, Vornamen, Tag und Ort der Geburt einschließlich Bezirk, Geburtsland, Geschlecht, Staatsangehörigkeiten, Wohnanschriften, Familienstand, Berufsbezeichnung, Steuernummer, Personalausweis- und Reisepassnummer, Kontodaten, Sozialversicherungsnummer, bei Unternehmen Name, Sitz, Rechtsform, Registernummer und -ort, Vertretungsverhältnisse des Unternehmens, Adressdaten, Steuernummer, Betriebsnummer, Kontodaten,

2. die Bezeichnung der aktenführenden Dienststelle der Zollverwaltung und das Aktenzeichen und

3. der Zeitpunkt der Einleitung des Verfahrens, der Zeitpunkt der letzten Verfahrenshandlung und der Zeitpunkt der Erledigung des Verfahrens, jeweils durch die Behörden der Zollverwaltung, sowie der Zeitpunkt und die Art der Erledigung durch das Gericht oder die Staatsanwaltschaft.

[2]Das Bundesministerium der Finanzen kann durch Rechtsverordnung ergänzend weitere Daten bestimmen, soweit diese für die Finanzkontrolle Schwarzarbeit im Rahmen ihrer Aufgaben

1. zur Vorbereitung und Durchführung von Prüfungen nach § 2 Absatz 1, oder

Section 15
General provisions

[1]With regard to social data, the provisions of the Second Chapter of Book X of the Social Code apply to the customs authorities in performing their tasks under this Act. [2]In terms of data protection, these tasks are deemed to be tasks pursuant to the Social Code. [3]The tax secrecy provisions set out in the Fourth Chapter of the First Part of the Fiscal Code remain unaffected.

Section 16
Central information system for the financial control of undeclared work

(1) The customs authorities maintain a central information system for the financial control of undeclared work in which the data required to perform the tasks set out in this Act are processed by automated means.

(2) [1]The following data are stored in the central information system for the financial control of undeclared work:

1. surname, former names, given names, date and place of birth (including district), country of birth, sex, nationalities, addresses, marital status, occupation, tax number, identity card and passport number, bank details, social security number; in the case of companies: name, headquarters, legal form, registration number and place, agency relationships, address data, tax number, establishment number, bank details,

2. the name of the customs authority handling the case and the file number and

3. the time of initiation of the proceedings, the time of the most recent procedural action and the time of resolution of the proceedings, in each case by the customs authorities, as well as the time and manner of resolution by the court or public prosecutor.

[2]The Federal Ministry of Finance may, by way of ordinances, designate further supplementary data insofar as these are necessary for the financial control of undeclared work in connection with its tasks of

1. preparing and conducting inspections under section 2 (1) or

2. zur Verhütung und Verfolgung von Straftaten und Ordnungswidrigkeiten, die mit einem der in § 2 Absatz 1 genannten Prüfgegenstände zusammenhängen,

erforderlich sind.

(3) Im zentralen Informationssystem für die Finanzkontrolle Schwarzarbeit dürfen personenbezogene Daten nur zu folgenden Zwecken verarbeitet werden:

1. zur Vorbereitung und Durchführung von Prüfungen nach § 2 Absatz 1,

2. zur Verhütung und Verfolgung von Straftaten und Ordnungswidrigkeiten, die mit einem der in § 2 Absatz 1 genannten Prüfgegenstände zusammenhängen,

3. zur Besteuerung, soweit sie im Zusammenhang mit der Erbringung von Dienst- oder Werkleistungen steht,

4. zur Erfüllung von Aufgaben, welche den Behörden der Zollverwaltung nach § 5a des Finanzverwaltungsgesetzes oder § 17a des Zollverwaltungsgesetzes zugewiesen sind, und

5. zur Fortbildung im Bereich der Finanzkontrolle Schwarzarbeit, soweit die Daten anonymisiert werden.

(4) ¹Die Generalzolldirektion erstellt für die automatisierte Verarbeitung nach Absatz 1 eine Errichtungsanordnung, die der Zustimmung des Bundesministeriums der Finanzen bedarf. ²In der Errichtungsanordnung sind festzulegen:

1. die Bezeichnung des Verantwortlichen,

2. die Rechtsgrundlage und der Zweck der Verarbeitung,

3. der Personenkreis, über den Daten gespeichert werden,

4. die Art und der Inhalt der gespeicherten personenbezogenen Daten,

5. die Arten der personenbezogenen Daten, die der Erschließung der Sammlung dienen,

6. die Anlieferung oder die Eingabe der gespeicherten Daten,

7. die Voraussetzungen, unter denen gespeicherte personenbezogene Daten an welche Empfänger und in welchen Verfahren übermittelt werden,

8. die Prüffristen und die Speicherungsdauer,

9. die Protokollierung sowie

10. die Verpflichtung zur Erstellung und zur Pflege eines Rollen- und Berechtigungskonzeptes.

³Die oder der Bundesbeauftragte für den Datenschutz und die Informationsfreiheit ist vor Erlass der Errichtungsanordnung anzuhören.

2. preventing and prosecuting criminal and administrative offences related to one of the matters for inspection specified in section 2 (1).

(3) Personal data may be processed and used in the central information system for the financial control of undeclared work for the following purposes only:

1. preparing and conducting inspections under section 2 (1),

2. preventing and prosecuting criminal and administrative offences related to one of the matters for inspection specified in section 2 (1),

3. taxation, insofar as it is related to the performance of work or services,

4. performing the tasks assigned to the customs authorities under section 5a of the Fiscal Administration Act or section 17a of the Customs Administration Act and

5. training in the area of the financial control of undeclared work, provided that the data are anonymised.

(4) ¹The Central Customs Authority must issue an opening order for automated processing under subsection (1) which requires the approval of the Federal Ministry of Finance. ²The opening order must specify:

1. the name of the responsible authority,

2. the legal basis and the purpose of processing the data,

3. the group of persons about whom data are stored,

4. the type and content of the personal data stored,

5. the types of personal data that serve to render the file accessible,

6. the supply or input of the data stored,

7. the conditions under which the personal data stored may be transmitted, the recipients to whom they may be transmitted and the procedures to be followed,

8. the time limits and storage duration,

9. the logging requirements and

10. the obligation to develop and maintain role and authorisation guidelines.

³The Federal Commissioner for Data Protection and Freedom of Information must be heard prior to an opening order being issued.

§ 17
**Übermittlung von Daten aus dem
zentralen Informationssystem**

Section 17
**Transmission of data to the police
authorities of the Federation and the
Länder, the revenue authorities and public
prosecutors**

(1) ¹Die Übermittlung von Daten aus dem zentralen Informationssystem für die Finanzkontrolle Schwarzarbeit erfolgt auf Ersuchen an

(1) ¹Upon request, data from the central information system for the financial control of undeclared work must be transmitted to

1. [aufgehoben]
2. die Staatsanwaltschaften für Zwecke der Strafverfolgung,
3. die Polizeivollzugsbehörden des Bundes und der Länder für die Verhütung und Verfolgung von Straftaten und Ordnungswidrigkeiten, die im Zusammenhang mit einem der in § 2 Abs. 1 genannten Prüfgegenstände stehen,
4. die Finanzbehörden der Länder zur Durchführung eines Steuerstraf- oder Steuerordnungswidrigkeitenverfahrens und für die Besteuerung, soweit die Besteuerung im Zusammenhang mit der Erbringung oder der Vortäuschung der Erbringung von Dienst- oder Werkleistungen steht,
5. die Zentralstelle für Finanztransaktionsuntersuchungen zur Erfüllung ihrer Aufgaben nach § 28 Absatz 1 Satz 2 Nummer 2 des Geldwäschegesetzes,
6. die Bundesagentur für Arbeit zur Durchführung von Ordnungswidrigkeitenverfahren wegen Leistungsmissbrauchs und für die damit zusammenhängende Einstellung der Gewährung von Leistungen nach dem Dritten Buch Sozialgesetzbuch,
7. die Bundesagentur für Arbeit zur Durchführung von Ordnungswidrigkeitenverfahren nach dem Arbeitnehmerüberlassungsgesetz sowie für den Widerruf, die Versagung oder die Versagung der Verlängerung der Erlaubnis im Sinne des § 1 Absatz 1 Satz 1 des Arbeitnehmerüberlassungsgesetzes,
8. die Bundesagentur für Arbeit in ihrer Funktion als Familienkasse zur Durchführung von Steuerstrafverfahren und Ordnungswidrigkeitenverfahren und für die damit zusammenhängende Einstellung der Gewährung von Kindergeldleistungen und des Kinderzuschlags,
9. die gemeinsamen Einrichtungen und die zugelassenen kommunalen Träger nach dem Zweiten Buch Sozialgesetzbuch zur Durchführung von Ordnungswidrigkeitenverfahren wegen Leistungsmissbrauchs und für die damit zusammenhängende Leistungsbearbeitung nach dem Zweiten Buch Sozialgesetzbuch oder

1. [rescinded]
2. public prosecutors for the purposes of criminal prosecution,
3. the police authorities of the Federation and the Länder for the prevention and prosecution of criminal and administrative offences related to one of the matters for inspection specified in section 2 (1),
4. the Länder revenue authorities for the purposes of conducting tax crime or tax offence proceedings and for the purposes of taxation, insofar as it is related to the performance of work or services or
5. the Financial Intelligence Unit for the performance of its tasks under section 28 (1) sentence 2 no 2 of the Money Laundering Act.
6. the Federal Employment Agency to conduct administrative offence proceedings for misuse of benefits and for the related discontinuation of the granting of benefits under Book Three of the Social Code,
7. the Federal Employment Agency to conduct administrative offence proceedings pursuant to the temporary employment act and to revoke, refuse to renew or refuse to renew the permit within the meaning of section 1 (1) sentence 1 of the Temporary Employment Act
8. the Federal Employment Agency in its function as a family fund for conducting criminal tax proceedings and administrative offence proceedings and for the related discontinuation of the granting of child benefits and the child supplement
9. the joint institutions and the approved municipal bodies pursuant to Book II of the Social Security Code for conducting administrative offence proceedings for misuse of benefits and for the related benefit processing pursuant to Book II of the Social Security Code, or

10. die Träger nach dem Zwölften Buch Sozialgesetzbuch zur Durchführung von
Ordnungswidrigkeitenverfahren wegen
Leistungsmissbrauchs und für die damit
zusammenhängende Leistungsbearbeitung
nach dem Zwölften Buch Sozialgesetzbuch.

²Soweit durch eine Übermittlung von Daten die
Gefährdung des Untersuchungszwecks eines
Ermittlungsverfahrens zu besorgen ist, kann
die für dieses Verfahren zuständige Behörde der
Zollverwaltung oder die zuständige Staatsanwaltschaft anordnen, dass keine Übermittlung
von Daten erfolgen darf. ³§ 480 Absatz 1 Satz 1
und 2 der Strafprozessordnung findet Anwendung, wenn die Daten Verfahren betreffen, die
zu einem Strafverfahren geführt haben.

(2) ¹Die Übermittlung der Daten erfolgt im
Wege eines automatisierten Abrufverfahrens
oder eines automatisierten Anfrage- und Aus-
kunftsverfahrens, im Fall einer Störung der
Datenfernübertragung oder bei außergewöhnli-
cher Dringlichkeit telefonisch oder durch Tele-
fax. ²Die beteiligten Stellen haben zu gewährleisten, dass dem jeweiligen Stand der Technik
entsprechende Maßnahmen zur Sicherstellung
von Datenschutz und Datensicherheit getroffen
werden, die insbesondere die Vertraulichkeit
und Unversehrtheit der Daten gewährleisten;
im Fall der Nutzung allgemein zugänglicher
Netze sind dem jeweiligen Stand der Technik
entsprechende Verschlüsselungsverfahren anzuwenden. ³Es gilt § 79 Abs. 2 bis 4 des Zehnten
Buches Sozialgesetzbuch.

§ 18
Auskunft an die betroffene Person

¹Für die Auskunft an die betroffene Person
gilt § 83 des Zehnten Buches Sozialgesetzbuch.
²Die Auskunft bedarf des Einvernehmens der
zuständigen Staatsanwaltschaft, wenn sie Daten aus einem Verfahren betrifft, das zu einem
Strafverfahren geführt hat.

§ 19
Löschung

Die Daten im zentralen Informationssystem
für die Finanzkontrolle Schwarzarbeit und die
dazugehörigen Verfahrensakten in Papierform
sind nach den Bestimmungen des § 489 der
Strafprozessordnung, des § 49c des Gesetzes
über Ordnungswidrigkeiten und des § 84 des
Zehnten Buches Sozialgesetzbuch zu löschen
und zu vernichten, spätestens jedoch

1. ein Jahr nach Ablauf des Kalenderjahres, in
dem eine Prüfung nach § 2 ohne Einleitung
eines Ermittlungsverfahrens abgeschlossen
worden ist,

10. the institutions pursuant to Book Twelfth of
the Social Security Code for conducting administrative offence proceedings for benefit
abuse and for the related benefit processing
pursuant to Book Twelfth of the Social Security Code.

²If the transmission of data might endanger
the purpose of an investigation, the customs
authority responsible for the investigation or
the public prosecutor responsible may order
that no transmission take place. ³Section 480
(1) sentences 1 and 2 of the Code of Criminal
Procedure apply if the data relate to cases that
resulted in criminal proceedings.

(2) ¹The data must be transmitted through an
automated retrieval procedure or an automated
query and information-sharing procedure or,
in the case of a disruption of data transmission
or in cases of exceptional urgency, by telephone
or fax. ²The authorities involved must ensure
that state-of-the-art measures to safeguard data
protection and data security are in place which,
in particular, guarantee the confidentiality and
integrity of the data; if generally accessible networks are used, state-of-the-art encryption procedures must be applied. ³Section 79 (2) to (4) of
Book X of the Social Code applies.

Section 18
Notification of the person concerned

¹Section 83 of Book X of the Social Code applies
when it comes to the notification of the person concerned. ²Such notification requires the
agreement of the public prosecutor responsible
if it relates to data from a case that resulted in
criminal proceedings.

Section 19
Deletion

The data contained in the central information
system for the financial control of undeclared
work and the corresponding case files in paper
form must be deleted and destroyed in accordance with the provisions of section 489 of the
Code of Criminal Procedure, section 49c of the
Administrative Offences Act and section 84 of
Boox X of the Social Code, but no later than

1. one year following the end of the calendar
year in which an inspection under section 2
was completed without an investigation being initiated,

2. fünf Jahre nach Ablauf des Kalenderjahres, in dem ein Ermittlungsverfahren rechtskräftig abgeschlossen worden ist, oder

3. zwei Jahre nach Ablauf des Kalenderjahres, in dem ein Strafverfahren abgeschlossen worden ist, wenn

   (a) die Person, über die Daten nach § 16 gespeichert wurden, von dem betreffenden Tatvorwurf rechtskräftig freigesprochen worden ist,

   (b) die Eröffnung des Hauptverfahrens unanfechtbar abgelehnt worden ist oder

   (c) das Verfahren nicht nur vorläufig eingestellt worden ist.

§ 20
Entschädigung der Zeugen und Sachverständigen

Werden Zeugen und Sachverständige von den Behörden der Zollverwaltung herangezogen, so erhalten sie auf Antrag in entsprechender Anwendung des Justizvergütungs- und Entschädigungsgesetzes eine Entschädigung oder Vergütung

§ 21
Ausschluss von öffentlichen Aufträgen

(1) ¹Von der Teilnahme an einem Wettbewerb um einen Liefer-, Bau- oder Dienstleistungsauftrag der in den §§ 99 und 100 des Gesetzes gegen Wettbewerbsbeschränkungen genannten Auftraggeber sollen Bewerber bis zu einer Dauer von drei Jahren ausgeschlossen werden, die oder deren nach Satzung oder Gesetz Vertretungsberechtigte nach

1. § 8 Abs. 1 Nr. 2, §§ 10 bis 11,

2. § 404 Abs. 1 oder 2 Nr. 3 des Dritten Buches Sozialgesetzbuch,

3. §§ 15, 15a, 16 Abs. 1 Nr. 1, 1c, 1d, 1f oder 2 des Arbeitnehmerüberlassungsgesetzes oder

4. § 266a Abs. 1 bis 4 des Strafgesetzbuches

2. five years following the end of the calendar year in which an investigation was concluded with binding legal effect or

3. two years following the end of the calendar year in which criminal proceedings were concluded if

   (a) the person about whom data were stored under section 16 was acquitted of the crime in question with binding legal effect,

   (b) the opening of the main proceedings was incontestably rejected or

   (c) the proceedings were discontinued more than just temporarily.

Section 20
Reimbursement for witnesses and experts

If the customs authorities consult witnesses and experts, these must, upon application, be compensated or remunerated by way of application mutatis mutandis of the Judicial Remuneration and Compensation Act.

Section 21
Exclusion from public contracts

(1) ¹Applicants should be excluded from competing for supply, works or service contracts of contracting authorities specified in section 99 and 100 of the Act against Restraints of Competition if they themselves or their authorised representatives as designated by law or articles of association have been sentenced to imprisonment for a period of more than three months or to a criminal fine exceeding 90 daily units or punished with an administrative fine of at least two thousand five hundred euros under

1. section 8 (1) no 2, sections 10 and 11 of this Act,

2. section 404 (1) or (2) no 3 of Book III of the Social Code,

3. section 15, 15a or 16 (1) nos 1, 1c, 1d, 1f or 2 of the Temporary Employment Act or

4. Section 266a (1) sentences 1 to 4 of the Criminal Code.

zu einer Freiheitsstrafe von mehr als drei Monaten oder einer Geldstrafe von mehr als neunzig Tagessätzen verurteilt oder mit einer Geldbuße von wenigstens zweitausendfünfhundert Euro belegt worden sind. ²Das Gleiche gilt auch schon vor Durchführung eines Straf- oder Bußgeldverfahrens, wenn im Einzelfall angesichts der Beweislage kein vernünftiger Zweifel an einer schwerwiegenden Verfehlung nach Satz 1 besteht. ³Die für die Verfolgung oder Ahndung zuständigen Behörden nach Satz 1 Nr. 1 bis 4 dürfen den öffentlichen Auftraggebern nach § 99 des Gesetzes gegen Wettbewerbsbeschränkungen und solchen Stellen, die von öffentlichen Auftraggebern zugelassene Präqualifikationsverzeichnisse oder Unternehmer- und Lieferantenverzeichnisse führen, auf Verlangen die erforderlichen Auskünfte geben. ⁴Öffentliche Auftraggeber nach Satz 3 fordern im Rahmen ihrer Tätigkeit Auskünfte des Gewerbezentralregisters nach § 150a der Gewerbeordnung an oder verlangen vom Bewerber eine Erklärung, dass die Voraussetzungen für einen Ausschluss nach Satz 1 oder 2 nicht vorliegen; auch im Falle einer Erklärung des Bewerbers können öffentliche Auftraggeber Auskünfte des Gewerbezentralregisters nach § 150a der Gewerbeordnung jederzeit anfordern. ⁵Für den Bewerber, der den Zuschlag erhalten soll, fordert der öffentliche Auftraggeber nach Satz 3 bei Aufträgen ab einer Höhe von 30 000 Euro vor Zuschlagserteilung eine Auskunft aus dem Gewerbezentralregister nach § 150a der Gewerbeordnung an. ⁶Der Bewerber ist vor der Entscheidung über den Ausschluss zu hören.

(2) Eine Verfehlung nach Absatz 1 steht einer Verletzung von Pflichten nach § 241 Abs. 2 des Bürgerlichen Gesetzbuchs gleich.

²The exclusion can be imposed prior to criminal or administrative proceedings if the evidence in the case in question leaves no reasonable doubt that a serious offence under sentence 1 has been committed. ³Upon request, the authorities responsible for prosecution and punishment under sentence 1 nos 1 to 4 may provide the required information to contracting authorities under section 99 of the Act against Restraints of Competition and to authorities that maintain preliminary qualification registers or registers of companies and suppliers approved by contracting authorities. ⁴As part of their duties, contracting authorities under sentence 3 must request information from the central register of trade and industry under section 150a of the Trade Regulation Code or require the applicant to submit a declaration stating that there are no grounds for an exclusion under sentences 1 or 2; contracting authorities may request information from the central register of trade and industry under section 150a of the Trade Regulation Code at any time even if such a declaration has been submitted. ⁵In the case of contracts exceeding 30,000 euros, the contracting authority under sentence 3 must request information about the successful applicant from the central register of trade and industry under section 150a of the Trade Regulation Code prior to awarding the contract. ⁶The applicant must be heard before a decision on exclusion is taken.

(2) An offence under subsection (1) is deemed equivalent to a breach of obligations under section 241 (2) of the Civil Code.

§ 22
Verwaltungsverfahren

Soweit dieses Gesetz nichts anderes bestimmt, gelten die Vorschriften der Abgabenordnung sinngemäß für das Verwaltungsverfahren der Behörden der Zollverwaltung nach diesem Gesetz.

Section 22
Administrative proceedings

Unless otherwise stipulated in this Act, the provisions of the Fiscal Code apply mutatis mutandis to administrative proceedings of customs authorities under this Act.

§ 23
Rechtsweg

In öffentlich-rechtlichen Streitigkeiten über Verwaltungshandeln der Behörden der Zollverwaltung nach diesem Gesetz ist der Finanzrechtsweg gegeben.

Section 23
Legal recourse

Recourse to the tax courts is possible in public-law disputes regarding the administrative actions of customs authorities under this Act.

XII. Social Security Code I – General Part (Excerpt)

Sozialgesetzbuch (SGB) Erstes Buch (I) – Allgemeiner Teil (Auszug)

Stand: 12.12.2019

§ 32
Verbot nachteiliger Vereinbarungen

Section 32
Prohibition of disadvantageous agreements

Privatrechtliche Vereinbarungen, die zum Nachteil des Sozialleistungsberechtigten von Vorschriften dieses Gesetzbuchs abweichen, sind nichtig.

Private law agreements that deviate from the provisions of this Code to the detriment of the person entitled to social benefits are invalid.

XIII. Social Security Code III – Employment Promotion (Excerpt)

Sozialgesetzbuch (SGB) Drittes Buch (III) – Arbeitsförderung (Auszug)

Stand: 22.11.2019

§ 35
Vermittlungsangebot

(1) ¹Die Agentur für Arbeit hat Ausbildungsuchenden, Arbeitsuchenden und Arbeitgebern Ausbildungsvermittlung und Arbeitsvermittlung (Vermittlung) anzubieten. ²Die Vermittlung umfasst alle Tätigkeiten, die darauf gerichtet sind, Ausbildungsuchende mit Arbeitgebern zur Begründung eines Ausbildungsverhältnisses und Arbeitsuchende mit Arbeitgebern zur Begründung eines Beschäftigungsverhältnisses zusammenzuführen. ³Die Agentur für Arbeit stellt sicher, dass Ausbildungsuchende und Arbeitslose, deren berufliche Eingliederung voraussichtlich erschwert sein wird, eine verstärkte vermittlerische Unterstützung erhalten.

(2) ¹Die Agentur für Arbeit hat durch Vermittlung darauf hinzuwirken, dass Ausbildungsuchende eine Ausbildungsstelle, Arbeitsuchende eine Arbeitsstelle und Arbeitgeber geeignete Auszubildende sowie geeignete Arbeitnehmerinnen und Arbeitnehmer erhalten. ²Sie hat dabei die Neigung, Eignung und Leistungsfähigkeit der Ausbildungsuchenden und Arbeitsuchenden sowie die Anforderungen der angebotenen Stellen zu berücksichtigen.

(3) ¹Die Agentur für Arbeit hat Vermittlung auch über die Selbstinformationseinrichtungen nach § 40 Absatz 2 im Internet durchzuführen. ²Soweit es für diesen Zweck erforderlich ist, darf sie die Daten aus den Selbstinformationseinrichtungen nutzen und übermitteln.

Section 35
Placement offer

(1) ¹The Federal Employment Agency shall offer training and employment services (placement) to persons seeking training, job seekers and employers. ²Placement includes all activities aimed at bringing together people seeking training with employers to establish a training relationship and job seekers with employers to establish an employment relationship. ³The Employment Agency shall ensure that those seeking training and unemployed persons whose occupational integration is likely to be difficult receive increased mediation support.

(2) ¹The Federal Employment Agency shall work towards ensuring, through placement, that persons seeking training receive a training place, job seekers a job and employers suitable trainees and suitable employees. ²In doing so, it shall take into account the inclination, aptitude and performance of trainees and job seekers as well as the requirements of the jobs on offer.

(3) ¹The Employment Agency shall also carry out placement via the self information facilities according to § 40 paragraph 2 on the Internet. ²In so far as it is necessary for this purpose, it may use and transmit the data from the self-information facilities.

§ 284
Arbeitsgenehmigung-EU für Staatsangehörige der neuen EU-Mitgliedstaaten

(1) Soweit nach Maßgabe des Beitrittsvertrages eines Mitgliedstaates zur Europäischen Union abweichende Regelungen als Übergangsregelungen von der Arbeitnehmerfreizügigkeit anzuwenden sind, dürfen Staatsangehörige dieses Mitgliedstaates und ihre freizügigkeitsberechtigten Familienangehörigen eine Beschäftigung nur mit Genehmigung der Bundesagentur ausüben sowie von Arbeitgebern nur beschäftigt werden, wenn sie eine solche Genehmigung besitzen.

(2) ¹Die Genehmigung wird befristet als Arbeitserlaubnis-EU erteilt, wenn nicht Anspruch auf die unbefristete Erteilung als Arbeitsberechtigung-EU besteht. ²Die Genehmigung ist vor Aufnahme der Beschäftigung einzuholen.

(3) Die Arbeitserlaubnis-EU kann nach Maßgabe des § 39 Abs. 2 bis 4 des Aufenthaltsgesetzes erteilt werden.

(4) ¹Unionsbürgerinnen und Unionsbürger nach Absatz 1 und ihre freizügigkeitsberechtigten Familienangehörigen, die ihren Wohnsitz oder gewöhnlichen Aufenthalt im Ausland haben und eine Beschäftigung im Bundesgebiet aufnehmen wollen, darf eine Arbeitserlaubnis-EU nur erteilt werden, wenn dies durch zwischenstaatliche Vereinbarung bestimmt oder aufgrund einer Rechtsverordnung zulässig ist. ²Für die Beschäftigungen, die durch Rechtsverordnung zugelassen werden, ist Staatsangehörigen aus den Mitgliedstaaten der Europäischen Union nach Absatz 1 gegenüber Staatsangehörigen aus Drittstaaten vorrangig eine Arbeitserlaubnis-EU zu erteilen, soweit dies der EU-Beitrittsvertrag vorsieht.

(5) Die Erteilung der Arbeitsberechtigung-EU bestimmt sich nach der aufgrund des § 288 erlassenen Rechtsverordnung.

(6) ¹Das Aufenthaltsgesetz und die aufgrund des § 42 des Aufenthaltsgesetzes erlassenen Rechtsverordnungen gelten entsprechend, soweit nicht eine aufgrund des § 288 erlassene Rechtsverordnung günstigere Regelungen enthält. ²Bei Anwendung der Vorschriften steht die Arbeitsgenehmigung-EU der Zustimmung zu einem Aufenthaltstitel nach § 4 Abs. 3 des Aufenthaltsgesetzes gleich.

Section 284
EU work permit for nationals of the new EU member states

(1) Insofar as, in accordance with the provisions of the Treaty of Accession of a Member State to the European Union, regulations deviating from the free movement of workers are to be applied as transitional regulations, nationals of this Member State and their family members entitled to freedom of movement may only take up employment with the approval of the Federal Agency and may only be employed by employers if they hold such an approval.

(2) 1The permit is issued for a limited period of time as an EU work permit, if there is no entitlement to an unlimited issue as an EU work permit. 2The permit must be obtained before taking up employment.

(3) The EU work permit can be issued in accordance with § 39 Paragraphs 2 to 4 of the Residence Act.

(4) ¹Union citizens in accordance with paragraph 1 and their family members entitled to freedom of movement who have their residence or habitual abode abroad and wish to take up employment in the Federal Republic of Germany may only be granted an EU work permit if this is determined by intergovernmental agreement or is permissible on the basis of a statutory instrument. ²For the employments which are permitted by legal regulation, nationals from the member states of the European Union in accordance with paragraph 1 are to be granted an EU work permit with priority over nationals from third countries, insofar as the EU accession treaty provides for this.

(5) The granting of the EU work permit is determined by the legal regulation issued on the basis of § 288.

(6) ¹The Residence Act and the ordinances issued on the basis of § 42 of the Residence Act shall apply accordingly, unless a ordinance issued on the basis of § 288 contains more favourable provisions. ²If the regulations are applied, the EU work permit is equivalent to the approval of a residence permit in accordance with § 4 paragraph 3 of the Residence Act.

(7) ¹Ein Aufenthaltstitel zur Ausübung einer Beschäftigung, der vor dem Tag, an dem der Beitrittsvertrag eines Mitgliedstaates zur Europäischen Union, der Übergangsregelungen hinsichtlich der Arbeitnehmerfreizügigkeit vorsieht, für die Bundesrepublik Deutschland in Kraft getreten ist, erteilt wurde, gilt als Arbeitserlaubnis-EU fort. ²Beschränkungen des Aufenthaltstitels hinsichtlich der Ausübung der Beschäftigung bleiben als Beschränkungen der Arbeitserlaubnis-EU bestehen. ³Ein vor diesem Zeitpunkt erteilter Aufenthaltstitel, der zur unbeschränkten Ausübung einer Beschäftigung berechtigt, gilt als Arbeitsberechtigung-EU fort.

(7) ¹A residence title for the purpose of employment which was issued for the Federal Republic of Germany prior to the date on which the Accession Treaty of a Member State to the European Union, which provides for transitional arrangements with regard to the free movement of workers, came into force for the Federal Republic of Germany, shall continue to be deemed an EU work permit. ²Restrictions of the residence title with regard to the exercise of employment remain in force as restrictions of the EU work permit. ³A residence title issued before this date that entitles the holder to unrestricted employment is still considered an EU work permit.

XIV. Social Security Code IV – Social Security (Excerpt)

Sozialgesetzbuch(SGB) Viertes Buch(IV) – Gemeinsame Vorschriften für die Sozialversicherung (Auszug)

Stand: 22.11.2019

§ 1
Sachlicher Geltungsbereich

(1) ¹Die Vorschriften dieses Buches gelten für die gesetzliche Kranken-, Unfall- und Rentenversicherung einschließlich der Alterssicherung der Landwirte sowie die soziale Pflegeversicherung (Versicherungszweige). ²Die Vorschriften dieses Buches gelten mit Ausnahme des Ersten und Zweiten Titels des Vierten Abschnitts und des Fünften Abschnitts auch für die Arbeitsförderung. ³Die Bundesagentur für Arbeit gilt im Sinne dieses Buches als Versicherungsträger.

(2) § 18h gilt auch für die Sozialhilfe und die Grundsicherung für Arbeitsuchende; außerdem gelten die §§ 18f, 18g und 19a für die Grundsicherung für Arbeitsuchende.

(3) Regelungen in den Sozialleistungsbereichen dieses Gesetzbuches, die in den Absätzen 1 und 2 genannt sind, bleiben unberührt, soweit sie von den Vorschriften dieses Buches abweichen.

§ 2
Versicherter Personenkreis

(1) Die Sozialversicherung umfasst Personen, die kraft Gesetzes oder Satzung (Versicherungspflicht) oder auf Grund freiwilligen Beitritts oder freiwilliger Fortsetzung der Versicherung (Versicherungsberechtigung) versichert sind.

(1a) Deutsche im Sinne der Vorschriften über die Sozialversicherung und die Arbeitsförderung sind Deutsche im Sinne des Artikels 116 des Grundgesetzes.

(2) In allen Zweigen der Sozialversicherung sind nach Maßgabe der besonderen Vorschriften für die einzelnen Versicherungszweige versichert

1. Personen, die gegen Arbeitsentgelt oder zu ihrer Berufsausbildung beschäftigt sind,
2. behinderte Menschen, die in geschützten Einrichtungen beschäftigt werden,
3. Landwirte.

Section 1
Material scope of application

(1) ¹The regulations of this book apply to the legal health, accident and pension insurance including the age security of the farmers as well as the social care insurance (insurance branches). ²The regulations of this book apply with exception of the first and second title of the fourth section and the fifth section also to the promotion of employment. ³The Federal Employment Agency shall be deemed to be the insurance carrier for the purposes of this book.

(2) Section 18h shall also apply to social assistance and basic support for job seekers; in addition, sections 18f, 18g and 19a shall apply to the basic support for job seekers.

(3) Regulations in the social service areas of this Code which are mentioned in paragraphs 1 and 2 shall remain unaffected insofar as they deviate from the provisions of this Book.

Section 2
Insured group of persons

(1) Social insurance covers persons who are insured by law or by the statutes (compulsory insurance) or who are insured on the basis of voluntary membership or voluntary continuation of insurance (entitlement to insurance).

(1a) Germans within the meaning of the provisions on social security and employment promotion are Germans within the meaning of Article 116 of the Basic Law.

(2) In all branches of social insurance, the following shall be insured in accordance with the special provisions for the individual branches of insurance

1. persons employed for remuneration or for the purpose of their vocational training
2. disabled people employed in sheltered accommodation,
3. farmers.

(3) ¹Deutsche Seeleute, die auf einem Seeschiff beschäftigt sind, das nicht berechtigt ist, die Bundesflagge zu führen, werden auf Antrag des Reeders

1. in der gesetzlichen Kranken-, Renten- und Pflegeversicherung versichert und in die Versicherungspflicht nach dem Dritten Buch einbezogen,
2. in der gesetzlichen Unfallversicherung versichert, wenn der Reeder das Seeschiff der Unfallverhütung und Schiffssicherheitsüberwachung durch die Berufsgenossenschaft Verkehrswirtschaft Post-Logistik Telekommunikation unterstellt hat und der Staat, dessen Flagge das Seeschiff führt, dem nicht widerspricht.

²Für deutsche Seeleute, die ihren Wohnsitz oder gewöhnlichen Aufenthalt im Inland haben und auf einem Seeschiff beschäftigt sind, das im überwiegenden wirtschaftlichen Eigentum eines deutschen Reeders mit Sitz im Inland steht, ist der Reeder verpflichtet, einen Antrag nach Satz 1 Nummer 1 und unter den Voraussetzungen des Satzes 1 Nummer 2 einen Antrag nach Satz 1 Nummer 2 zu stellen. ³Der Reeder hat auf Grund der Antragstellung gegenüber den Versicherungsträgern die Pflichten eines Arbeitgebers. ⁴Ein Reeder mit Sitz im Ausland hat für die Erfüllung seiner Verbindlichkeiten gegenüber den Versicherungsträgern einen Bevollmächtigten im Inland zu bestellen. ⁵Der Reeder und der Bevollmächtigte haften gegenüber den Versicherungsträgern als Gesamtschuldner; sie haben auf Verlangen entsprechende Sicherheit zu leisten.

(4) Die Versicherung weiterer Personengruppen in einzelnen Versicherungszweigen ergibt sich aus den für sie geltenden besonderen Vorschriften.

§ 3
Persönlicher und räumlicher Geltungsbereich

Die Vorschriften über die Versicherungspflicht und die Versicherungsberechtigung gelten,

1. soweit sie eine Beschäftigung oder eine selbständige Tätigkeit voraussetzen, für alle Personen, die im Geltungsbereich dieses Gesetzbuchs beschäftigt oder selbständig tätig sind,
2. soweit sie eine Beschäftigung oder eine selbständige Tätigkeit nicht voraussetzen, für alle Personen, die ihren Wohnsitz oder gewöhnlichen Aufenthalt im Geltungsbereich dieses Gesetzbuchs haben.

(3) ¹German seafarers who are employed on a seagoing vessel which is not entitled to fly the federal flag shall, at the request of the shipowner

1. be insured in the statutory health, pension and nursing care insurance and included in the compulsory insurance under the Third Book
2. be insured under the statutory accident insurance scheme if the shipowner has placed the ocean-going vessel under the accident prevention and ship safety monitoring by the Employer's Liability Insurance Association Transport Industry Postal Logistics Telecommunications and the state whose flag the ocean-going vessel flies does not object to this.

²For German seafarers who have their residence or habitual abode in Germany and are employed on a seagoing vessel which is predominantly beneficially owned by a German shipowner domiciled in Germany, the shipowner is obliged to submit an application in accordance with sentence 1 number 1 and, under the conditions of sentence 1 number 2, an application in accordance with sentence 1 number 2. ³On the basis of the application, the shipowner has the obligations of an employer towards the insurance carriers. ⁴A shipowner domiciled abroad must appoint an authorised representative in Germany to fulfil his obligations towards the insurance carriers. ⁵The shipowner and the authorised representative shall be jointly and severally liable to the insurance carriers; they shall provide appropriate security upon request.

(4) The insurance of other groups of persons in individual classes of insurance shall be governed by the special provisions applicable to them.

Section 3
Personal and territorial scope

The rules on compulsory insurance and eligibility for insurance apply,

1. in so far as they presuppose employment or self-employment, for all persons employed or self-employed within the scope of this Code
2. insofar as they do not require an employment or self-employment activity, for all persons who have their residence or habitual abode within the scope of this Code.

§ 4
Ausstrahlung

(1) Soweit die Vorschriften über die Versicherungspflicht und die Versicherungsberechtigung eine Beschäftigung voraussetzen, gelten sie auch für Personen, die im Rahmen eines im Geltungsbereich dieses Gesetzbuchs bestehenden Beschäftigungsverhältnisses in ein Gebiet außerhalb dieses Geltungsbereichs entsandt werden, wenn die Entsendung infolge der Eigenart der Beschäftigung oder vertraglich im Voraus zeitlich begrenzt ist.

(2) Für Personen, die eine selbständige Tätigkeit ausüben, gilt Absatz 1 entsprechend.

§ 5
Einstrahlung

(1) Soweit die Vorschriften über die Versicherungspflicht und die Versicherungsberechtigung eine Beschäftigung voraussetzen, gelten sie nicht für Personen, die im Rahmen eines außerhalb des Geltungsbereichs dieses Gesetzbuchs bestehenden Beschäftigungsverhältnisses in diesen Geltungsbereich entsandt werden, wenn die Entsendung infolge der Eigenart der Beschäftigung oder vertraglich im Voraus zeitlich begrenzt ist.

(2) Für Personen, die eine selbständige Tätigkeit ausüben, gilt Absatz 1 entsprechend.

§ 6
Vorbehalt abweichender Regelungen

Regelungen des über- und zwischenstaatlichen Rechts bleiben unberührt.

§ 7
Beschäftigung

(1) [1]Beschäftigung ist die nichtselbständige Arbeit, insbesondere in einem Arbeitsverhältnis. [2]Anhaltspunkte für eine Beschäftigung sind eine Tätigkeit nach Weisungen und eine Eingliederung in die Arbeitsorganisation des Weisungsgebers.

(1a) [1]Eine Beschäftigung besteht auch in Zeiten der Freistellung von der Arbeitsleistung von mehr als einem Monat, wenn

1. während der Freistellung Arbeitsentgelt aus einem Wertguthaben nach § 7b fällig ist und

2. das monatlich fällige Arbeitsentgelt in der Zeit der Freistellung nicht unangemessen von dem für die vorausgegangenen zwölf Kalendermonate abweicht, in denen Arbeitsentgelt bezogen wurde.

Section 4
Broadcast

(1) Insofar as the provisions on compulsory insurance and eligibility for insurance require employment, they shall also apply to persons who are posted to a territory outside the scope of this Code in the context of an employment relationship existing within the scope of this Code, if the posting is limited in time as a result of the nature of the employment or contractually in advance.

(2) Paragraph 1 shall apply accordingly to persons who are self-employed.

Section 5
Irradiation

(1) Insofar as the provisions on compulsory insurance and eligibility for insurance require employment, they shall not apply to persons who are posted to this area of application in the context of an employment relationship existing outside the scope of this Code, if the posting is limited in time as a result of the nature of the employment or contractually in advance.

(2) Paragraph 1 shall apply accordingly to persons who are self-employed.

Section 6
Subject to deviating regulations

Regulations of supranational and intergovernmental law remain unaffected.

Section 7
Employment

(1) [1]Employment means paid employment, particularly in an employment relationship. [2]Employment is work performed in accordance with instructions and integration into the employer's work organisation.

(1a) [1]Employment also exists in periods of release from work of more than one month if

1. during the release from work, remuneration is due from a credit balance in accordance with § 7b and

2. the monthly remuneration due in the period of exemption does not deviate unreasonably from that for the preceding twelve calendar months in which remuneration was received.

²Satz 1 gilt entsprechend, wenn während einer bis zu dreimonatigen Freistellung Arbeitsentgelt aus einer Vereinbarung zur flexiblen Gestaltung der werktäglichen oder wöchentlichen Arbeitszeit oder dem Ausgleich betrieblicher Produktions- und Arbeitszeitzyklen fällig ist. ³Beginnt ein Beschäftigungsverhältnis mit einer Zeit der Freistellung, gilt Satz 1 Nummer 2 mit der Maßgabe, dass das monatlich fällige Arbeitsentgelt in der Zeit der Freistellung nicht unangemessen von dem für die Zeit der Arbeitsleistung abweichen darf, mit der das Arbeitsentgelt später erzielt werden soll. ⁴Eine Beschäftigung gegen Arbeitsentgelt besteht während der Zeit der Freistellung auch, wenn die Arbeitsleistung, mit der das Arbeitsentgelt später erzielt werden soll, wegen einer im Zeitpunkt der Vereinbarung nicht vorhersehbaren vorzeitigen Beendigung des Beschäftigungsverhältnisses nicht mehr erbracht werden kann. ⁵Die Vertragsparteien können beim Abschluss der Vereinbarung nur für den Fall, dass Wertguthaben wegen der Beendigung der Beschäftigung auf Grund verminderter Erwerbsfähigkeit, des Erreichens einer Altersgrenze, zu der eine Rente wegen Alters beansprucht werden kann, oder des Todes des Beschäftigten nicht mehr für Zeiten einer Freistellung von der Arbeitsleistung verwendet werden können, einen anderen Verwendungszweck vereinbaren. ⁶Die Sätze 1 bis 4 gelten nicht für Beschäftigte, auf die Wertguthaben übertragen werden. ⁷Bis zum 31. Dezember 2024 werden Wertguthaben, die durch Arbeitsleistung im Beitrittsgebiet erzielt werden, getrennt erfasst; sind für die Beitrags- oder Leistungsberechnung im Beitrittsgebiet und im übrigen Bundesgebiet unterschiedliche Werte vorgeschrieben, sind die Werte maßgebend, die für den Teil des Inlandes gelten, in dem das Wertguthaben erzielt worden ist.

(1b) Die Möglichkeit eines Arbeitnehmers zur Vereinbarung flexibler Arbeitszeiten gilt nicht als eine die Kündigung des Arbeitsverhältnisses durch den Arbeitgeber begründende Tatsache im Sinne des § 1 Absatz 2 Satz 1 des Kündigungsschutzgesetzes.

(2) Als Beschäftigung gilt auch der Erwerb beruflicher Kenntnisse, Fertigkeiten oder Erfahrungen im Rahmen betrieblicher Berufsbildung.

²Sentence 1 shall apply accordingly if, during a period of up to three months' leave, remuneration is due under an agreement on the flexible organisation of working hours on a weekday or weekly basis or on the balancing of operational production and working time cycles. ³If an employment relationship begins with a period of time off, sentence 1 number 2 shall apply under the condition that the monthly remuneration due during the period of time off may not deviate unreasonably from that due for the period of work performance with which the remuneration is to be achieved later. ⁴Employment against remuneration shall also exist during the period of leave if the work with which the remuneration is to be subsequently earned can no longer be performed due to an early termination of the employment relationship which could not be foreseen at the time of the agreement. ⁵When concluding the agreement, the contracting parties may only agree on a different purpose of use in the event that credit balances can no longer be used for periods of leave from work due to the termination of employment due to reduced earning capacity, the reaching of an age limit at which an old-age pension can be claimed or the death of the employee. ⁶Sentences 1 to 4 do not apply to employees to whom credit balances are transferred. ⁷Until 31 December 2024, credit balances achieved through work performed in the territory of the Accession Region shall be recorded separately; if different values are prescribed for the calculation of contributions or benefits in the Accession Region and in the rest of the Federal Republic, the values that apply to the part of Germany in which the credit balance was achieved shall be decisive.

(1b) An employee's ability to agree flexible working hours shall not be regarded as a fact justifying termination of the employment relationship by the employer within the meaning of section 1(2) first sentence of the Act on Protection against Unfair Dismissal.

(2) The acquisition of vocational knowledge, skills or experience within the framework of in-company vocational training shall also be deemed to be employment.

(3) ¹Eine Beschäftigung gegen Arbeitsentgelt gilt als fortbestehend, solange das Beschäftigungsverhältnis ohne Anspruch auf Arbeitsentgelt fortdauert, jedoch nicht länger als einen Monat. ²Eine Beschäftigung gilt auch als fortbestehend, wenn Arbeitsentgelt aus einem der Deutschen Rentenversicherung Bund übertragenen Wertguthaben bezogen wird. ³Satz 1 gilt nicht, wenn Krankengeld, Krankentagegeld, Verletztengeld, Versorgungskrankengeld, Übergangsgeld, Pflegeunterstützungsgeld oder Mutterschaftsgeld oder nach gesetzlichen Vorschriften Erziehungsgeld oder Elterngeld bezogen oder Elternzeit in Anspruch genommen oder Wehrdienst oder Zivildienst geleistet wird. ⁴Satz 1 gilt auch nicht für die Freistellung nach § 3 des Pflegezeitgesetzes.

(4) Beschäftigt ein Arbeitgeber einen Ausländer ohne die nach § 284 Absatz 1 des Dritten Buches erforderliche Genehmigung oder ohne die nach § 4 Absatz 3 des Aufenthaltsgesetzes erforderliche Berechtigung zur Erwerbstätigkeit, wird vermutet, dass ein Beschäftigungsverhältnis gegen Arbeitsentgelt für den Zeitraum von drei Monaten bestanden hat.

§ 7a
Anfrageverfahren

(1) ¹Die Beteiligten können schriftlich oder elektronisch eine Entscheidung beantragen, ob eine Beschäftigung vorliegt, es sei denn, die Einzugsstelle oder ein anderer Versicherungsträger hatte im Zeitpunkt der Antragstellung bereits ein Verfahren zur Feststellung einer Beschäftigung eingeleitet. ²Die Einzugsstelle hat einen Antrag nach Satz 1 zu stellen, wenn sich aus der Meldung des Arbeitgebers (§ 28a) ergibt, dass der Beschäftigte Ehegatte, Lebenspartner oder Abkömmling des Arbeitgebers oder geschäftsführender Gesellschafter einer Gesellschaft mit beschränkter Haftung ist. ³Über den Antrag entscheidet abweichend von § 28h Absatz 2 die Deutsche Rentenversicherung Bund.

(2) Die Deutsche Rentenversicherung Bund entscheidet auf Grund einer Gesamtwürdigung aller Umstände des Einzelfalles, ob eine Beschäftigung vorliegt.

(3) ¹Die Deutsche Rentenversicherung Bund teilt den Beteiligten schriftlich oder elektronisch mit, welche Angaben und Unterlagen sie für ihre Entscheidung benötigt. ²Sie setzt den Beteiligten eine angemessene Frist, innerhalb der diese die Angaben zu machen und die Unterlagen vorzulegen haben.

(3) ¹Employment for pay is deemed to continue as long as the employment relationship continues without entitlement to pay, but not for longer than one month. ²Employment is also deemed to be continuing if remuneration is drawn from a credit balance transferred to the German Pension Insurance Fund of the Federation. ³Sentence 1 does not apply if sick pay, daily sickness benefit, injury benefit, sickness benefit for long-term care, transitional allowance, nursing care support allowance or maternity benefit or if the person concerned receives child-raising benefit or parental allowance in accordance with statutory provisions or takes parental leave or performs military or civilian service. ⁴Sentence 1 shall also not apply to the exemption pursuant to § 3 of the Care Leave Act.

(4) If an employer employs a foreigner without the permit required under Section 284(1) of Book Three or without the entitlement to gainful employment required under Section 4(3) of the Residence Act, it shall be presumed that an employment relationship has existed for a period of three months against remuneration.

Section 7a
Inquiry procedure

(1) ¹The parties concerned may request a decision on whether employment is involved, in writing or electronically, unless the collection agency or another insurance institution had already initiated a procedure to establish employment at the time of the request. ²The collection agency must file an application in accordance with sentence 1 if the employer's notification (Article 28a) shows that the employee is the spouse, life partner or descendant of the employer or managing partner of a limited liability company. ³In derogation of § 28h paragraph 2, the decision on the application shall be taken by the Deutsche Rentenversicherung Bund.

(2) The German Pension Insurance Federation decides on the basis of an overall assessment of all the circumstances of the individual case whether employment is involved.

(3) ¹The German Pension Insurance Federation shall inform the parties concerned in writing or electronically of the information and documents required for its decision. ²It shall set the parties concerned a reasonable period of time within which they must provide the information and submit the documents.

(4) Die Deutsche Rentenversicherung Bund teilt den Beteiligten mit, welche Entscheidung sie zu treffen beabsichtigt, bezeichnet die Tatsachen, auf die sie ihre Entscheidung stützen will, und gibt den Beteiligten Gelegenheit, sich zu der beabsichtigten Entscheidung zu äußern.

(5) Die Deutsche Rentenversicherung Bund fordert die Beteiligten auf, innerhalb einer angemessenen Frist die Tatsachen anzugeben, die eine Widerlegung begründen, wenn diese die Vermutung widerlegen wollen.

(6) ¹Wird der Antrag nach Absatz 1 innerhalb eines Monats nach Aufnahme der Tätigkeit gestellt und stellt die Deutsche Rentenversicherung Bund ein versicherungspflichtiges Beschäftigungsverhältnis fest, tritt die Versicherungspflicht mit der Bekanntgabe der Entscheidung ein, wenn der Beschäftigte

1. zustimmt und
2. er für den Zeitraum zwischen Aufnahme der Beschäftigung und der Entscheidung eine Absicherung gegen das finanzielle Risiko von Krankheit und zur Altersvorsorge vorgenommen hat, die der Art nach den Leistungen der gesetzlichen Krankenversicherung und der gesetzlichen Rentenversicherung entspricht.

²Der Gesamtsozialversicherungsbeitrag wird erst zu dem Zeitpunkt fällig, zu dem die Entscheidung, dass eine Beschäftigung vorliegt, unanfechtbar geworden ist.

(7) ¹Widerspruch und Klage gegen Entscheidungen, dass eine Beschäftigung vorliegt, haben aufschiebende Wirkung. ²Eine Klage auf Erlass der Entscheidung ist abweichend von § 88 Absatz 1 des Sozialgerichtsgesetzes nach Ablauf von drei Monaten zulässig.

§ 7b
Wertguthabenvereinbarung

Eine Wertguthabenvereinbarung liegt vor, wenn

1. der Aufbau des Wertguthabens auf Grund einer schriftlichen Vereinbarung erfolgt,
2. diese Vereinbarung nicht das Ziel der flexiblen Gestaltung der werktäglichen oder wöchentlichen Arbeitszeit oder den Ausgleich betrieblicher Produktions- und Arbeitszeitzyklen verfolgt,
3. Arbeitsentgelt in das Wertguthaben eingebracht wird, um es für Zeiten der Freistellung von der Arbeitsleistung oder der Verringerung der vertraglich vereinbarten Arbeitszeit zu entnehmen,

(4) The German Pension Insurance Federation shall notify the parties concerned of the decision it intends to take, indicate the facts on which it intends to base its decision and give the parties concerned the opportunity to comment on the intended decision.

(5) The German Pension Insurance Federation shall call upon the parties concerned to state within a reasonable period of time the facts giving rise to a rebuttal if they wish to rebut the presumption.

(6) ¹If the application referred to in paragraph 1 is filed within one month of taking up employment and if Deutsche Rentenversicherung Bund establishes that the employment relationship is subject to compulsory insurance, the obligation to insure shall take effect on notification of the decision if the employee

1. agrees, and
2. for the period between taking up employment and the decision, he has taken out insurance against the financial risk of sickness and for old-age provision which, by its nature, corresponds to the benefits provided by the statutory health insurance scheme and the statutory pension insurance scheme.

²The total social security contribution is due only at the time when the decision that there is employment has become final.

(7) ¹Oppositions and appeals against decisions that an employment exists shall have suspensive effect. 2In derogation of Article 88(1) of the Sozialgerichtsgesetz, an action for the adoption of a decision is admissible after a period of three months.

Section 7b
Value credit agreement

A value credit agreement exists if

1. the value credit is built up on the basis of a written agreement,
2. this agreement does not pursue the objective of flexible organisation of working time on a working day or week or of balancing operational production and working time cycles,
3. remuneration is included in the value credit in order to withdraw it for periods of release from work or reduction of the contractually agreed working time,

4. das aus dem Wertguthaben fällige Arbeitsentgelt mit einer vor oder nach der Freistellung von der Arbeitsleistung oder der Verringerung der vertraglich vereinbarten Arbeitszeit erbrachten Arbeitsleistung erzielt wird und

5. das fällige Arbeitsentgelt insgesamt 450 Euro monatlich übersteigt, es sei denn, die Beschäftigung wurde vor der Freistellung als geringfügige Beschäftigung ausgeübt.

§ 7c
Verwendung von Wertguthaben

(1) Das Wertguthaben auf Grund einer Vereinbarung nach § 7b kann in Anspruch genommen werden

1. für gesetzlich geregelte vollständige oder teilweise Freistellungen von der Arbeitsleistung oder gesetzlich geregelte Verringerungen der Arbeitszeit, insbesondere für Zeiten,
   (a) in denen der Beschäftigte eine Freistellung nach § 3 des Pflegezeitgesetzes oder nach § 2 des Familienpflegezeitgesetzes verlangen kann,
   (b) in denen der Beschäftigte nach § 15 des Bundeselterngeld- und Elternzeitgesetzes ein Kind selbst betreut und erzieht,

   (c) für die der Beschäftigte eine Verringerung seiner vertraglich vereinbarten Arbeitszeit nach § 8 oder § 9a des Teilzeit- und Befristungsgesetzes verlangen kann; § 8 des Teilzeit- und Befristungsgesetzes gilt mit der Maßgabe, dass die Verringerung der Arbeitszeit auf die Dauer der Entnahme aus dem Wertguthaben befristet werden kann,
2. für vertraglich vereinbarte vollständige oder teilweise Freistellungen von der Arbeitsleistung oder vertraglich vereinbarte Verringerungen der Arbeitszeit, insbesondere für Zeiten,
   (a) die unmittelbar vor dem Zeitpunkt liegen, zu dem der Beschäftigte eine Rente wegen Alters nach dem Sechsten Buch bezieht oder beziehen könnte oder
   (b) in denen der Beschäftigte an beruflichen Qualifizierungsmaßnahmen teilnimmt.

(2) Die Vertragsparteien können die Zwecke, für die das Wertguthaben in Anspruch genommen werden kann, in der Vereinbarung nach § 7b abweichend von Absatz 1 auf bestimmte Zwecke beschränken.

Section 7c
Use of credit balances

1) The value credit based on an agreement in accordance with § 7b may be used

1. for legally regulated complete or partial exemptions from work or legally regulated reductions in working hours, in particular for periods of time
   (a) in which the employee can demand release from work in accordance with § 3 of the Care Time Act or § 2 of the Family Care Time Act,
   (b) in which the employee looks after and brings up a child himself/herself in accordance with § 15 of the Federal Parental Benefits and Parental Leave Act,
   (c) for which the employee can demand a reduction in his contractually agreed working time in accordance with § 8 or § 9a of the Part-Time and Fixed-Term Act; § 8 of the Part-Time and Fixed-Term Act shall apply with the proviso that the reduction in working time can be limited to the duration of the withdrawal from the value credit,
2. for contractually agreed complete or partial releases from work or contractually agreed reductions in working hours, in particular for times

   (a) which are immediately prior to the date on which the worker receives or is likely to receive an old-age pension under the Sixth Book; or
   (b) in which the worker takes part in vocational training measures.

(2) In the agreement pursuant to § 7b, notwithstanding paragraph 1, the contracting parties may restrict the purposes for which the value credit may be used to specific purposes.

§ 7d
Führung und Verwaltung von Wertguthaben

(1) ¹Wertguthaben sind als Arbeitsentgeltguthaben einschließlich des darauf entfallenden Arbeitgeberanteils am Gesamtsozialversicherungsbeitrag zu führen. ²Die Arbeitszeitguthaben sind in Arbeitsentgelt umzurechnen.

(2) Arbeitgeber haben Beschäftigte mindestens einmal jährlich in Textform über die Höhe ihres im Wertguthaben enthaltenen Arbeitsentgeltguthabens zu unterrichten.

(3) ¹Für die Anlage von Wertguthaben gelten die Vorschriften über die Anlage der Mittel von Versicherungsträgern nach dem Vierten Titel des Vierten Abschnitts entsprechend, mit der Maßgabe, dass eine Anlage in Aktien oder Aktienfonds bis zu einer Höhe von 20 Prozent zulässig und ein Rückfluss zum Zeitpunkt der Inanspruchnahme des Wertguthabens mindestens in der Höhe des angelegten Betrages gewährleistet ist. ²Ein höherer Anlageanteil in Aktien oder Aktienfonds ist zulässig, wenn

1. dies in einem Tarifvertrag oder auf Grund eines Tarifvertrages in einer Betriebsvereinbarung vereinbart ist oder
2. das Wertguthaben nach der Wertguthabenvereinbarung ausschließlich für Freistellungen nach § 7c Absatz 1 Nummer 2 Buchstabe a in Anspruch genommen werden kann.

§ 7e
Insolvenzschutz

(1) ¹Die Vertragsparteien treffen im Rahmen ihrer Vereinbarung nach § 7b durch den Arbeitgeber zu erfüllende Vorkehrungen, um das Wertguthaben einschließlich des darin enthaltenen Gesamtsozialversicherungsbeitrages gegen das Risiko der Insolvenz des Arbeitgebers vollständig abzusichern, soweit

1. ein Anspruch auf Insolvenzgeld nicht besteht und wenn
2. das Wertguthaben des Beschäftigten einschließlich des darin enthaltenen Gesamtsozialversicherungsbeitrages einen Betrag in Höhe der monatlichen Bezugsgröße übersteigt.

²In einem Tarifvertrag oder auf Grund eines Tarifvertrages in einer Betriebsvereinbarung kann ein von Satz 1 Nummer 2 abweichender Betrag vereinbart werden.

Section 7d
Management and administration of assets

(1) ¹Value credit balances are to be managed as remuneration credit balances including the employer's share of the total social insurance contribution. ²The working time credits shall be converted into remuneration.

(2) Employers must inform employees at least once a year in text form of the amount of their remuneration credit contained in the value credit.

(3) ¹For the investment of credit balances, the regulations on the investment of the funds of insurance carriers in accordance with Title IV of Section 4 shall apply accordingly, subject to the proviso that an investment in shares or share funds up to an amount of 20 per cent is permitted and that a reflux at the time the credit balance is drawn down is guaranteed at least in the amount invested. ²A higher investment proportion in shares or equity funds is permitted if

1. this is agreed in a collective agreement or, on the basis of a collective agreement, in a works agreement, or
2. the value credit according to the value credit agreement can only be used for exemptions in accordance with § 7c paragraph 1 number 2 letter a.

Section 7e
Insolvency protection

(1) ¹The contracting parties shall take precautions within the scope of their agreement in accordance with § 7b to be fulfilled by the employer in order to fully protect the assets, including the total social security contribution contained therein, against the risk of insolvency of the employer, provided that

1. there is no claim to insolvency money and if
2. the value credit of the employee, including the total social security contribution included therein, exceeds an amount equal to the monthly reference value.

²An amount deviating from sentence 1 number 2 may be agreed in a collective agreement or on the basis of a collective agreement in a works agreement.

(2) ¹Zur Erfüllung der Verpflichtung nach Absatz 1 sind Wertguthaben unter Ausschluss der Rückführung durch einen Dritten zu führen, der im Fall der Insolvenz des Arbeitgebers für die Erfüllung der Ansprüche aus dem Wertguthaben für den Arbeitgeber einsteht, insbesondere in einem Treuhandverhältnis, das die unmittelbare Übertragung des Wertguthabens in das Vermögen des Dritten und die Anlage des Wertguthabens auf einem offenen Treuhandkonto oder in anderer geeigneter Weise sicherstellt. ²Die Vertragsparteien können in der Vereinbarung nach § 7b ein anderes, einem Treuhandverhältnis im Sinne des Satzes 1 gleichwertiges Sicherungsmittel vereinbaren, insbesondere ein Versicherungsmodell oder ein schuldrechtliches Verpfändungs- oder Bürgschaftsmodell mit ausreichender Sicherung gegen Kündigung.

(3) Keine geeigneten Vorkehrungen sind bilanzielle Rückstellungen sowie zwischen Konzernunternehmen (§ 18 des Aktiengesetzes) begründete Einstandspflichten, insbesondere Bürgschaften, Patronatserklärungen oder Schuldbeitritte.

(4) Der Arbeitgeber hat den Beschäftigten unverzüglich über die Vorkehrungen zum Insolvenzschutz in geeigneter Weise schriftlich zu unterrichten, wenn das Wertguthaben die in Absatz 1 Satz 1 Nummer 2 genannten Voraussetzungen erfüllt.

(5) Hat der Beschäftigte den Arbeitgeber schriftlich aufgefordert, seinen Verpflichtungen nach den Absätzen 1 bis 3 nachzukommen und weist der Arbeitgeber dem Beschäftigten nicht innerhalb von zwei Monaten nach der Aufforderung die Erfüllung seiner Verpflichtung zur Insolvenzsicherung des Wertguthabens nach, kann der Beschäftigte die Vereinbarung nach § 7b mit sofortiger Wirkung kündigen; das Wertguthaben ist nach Maßgabe des § 23b Absatz 2 aufzulösen.

(6) ¹Stellt der Träger der Rentenversicherung bei der Prüfung des Arbeitgebers nach § 28p fest, dass

1. für ein Wertguthaben keine Insolvenzschutzregelung getroffen worden ist,
2. die gewählten Sicherungsmittel nicht geeignet sind im Sinne des Absatzes 3,
3. die Sicherungsmittel in ihrem Umfang das Wertguthaben um mehr als 30 Prozent unterschreiten oder
4. die Sicherungsmittel den im Wertguthaben enthaltenen Gesamtsozialversicherungsbeitrag nicht umfassen,

(2) ¹In order to fulfil the obligation under subsection 1, value credit balances must be managed, excluding repatriation by a third party, who, in the event of the employer's insolvency, is responsible for the fulfilment of claims arising from the value credit balance on behalf of the employer, in particular in a fiduciary relationship which ensures the direct transfer of the value credit balance to the assets of the third party and the investment of the value credit balance in an open fiduciary account or in another suitable manner. ²In the agreement pursuant to § 7b, the contracting parties may agree on another means of security equivalent to a fiduciary relationship within the meaning of sentence 1, in particular an insurance model or a pledge or guarantee model under the law of obligations with sufficient security against termination.

(3) No suitable precautions are provisions in the balance sheet or obligations arising between group companies (Article 18 of the German Stock Corporation Act), in particular guarantees, letters of comfort or debt obligations.

(4) The employer shall immediately inform the employee in writing in a suitable manner about the precautions for insolvency protection if the credit balance meets the requirements set out in paragraph 1 sentence 1 number 2.

(5) If the employee has requested the employer in writing to fulfil its obligations under subsections 1 to 3 and the employer does not prove to the employee within two months of the request that it has fulfilled its obligation to provide insolvency protection for the assets, the employee may terminate the agreement under section 7b with immediate effect; the assets shall be dissolved in accordance with section 23b(2).

(6) ¹If the pension insurance institution, when examining the employer under section 28p, finds that

1. no insolvency protection regulation has been concluded for a credit balance
2. the chosen means of protection are not suitable within the meaning of paragraph 3,
3. the amount of the security funds is more than 30 per cent less than the value credit balance or
4. the security funds do not include the total social security contribution included in the value credit

weist er in dem Verwaltungsakt nach § 28p Absatz 1 Satz 5 den in dem Wertguthaben enthaltenen und vom Arbeitgeber zu zahlenden Gesamtsozialversicherungsbeitrag aus. [2]Weist der Arbeitgeber dem Träger der Rentenversicherung innerhalb von zwei Monaten nach der Feststellung nach Satz 1 nach, dass er seiner Verpflichtung nach Absatz 1 nachgekommen ist, entfällt die Verpflichtung zur sofortigen Zahlung des Gesamtsozialversicherungsbeitrages. [3]Hat der Arbeitgeber den Nachweis nach Satz 2 nicht innerhalb der dort vorgesehenen Frist erbracht, ist die Vereinbarung nach § 7b als von Anfang an unwirksam anzusehen; das Wertguthaben ist aufzulösen.

(7) [1]Kommt es wegen eines nicht geeigneten oder nicht ausreichenden Insolvenzschutzes zu einer Verringerung oder einem Verlust des Wertguthabens, haftet der Arbeitgeber für den entstandenen Schaden. [2]Ist der Arbeitgeber eine juristische Person oder eine Gesellschaft ohne Rechtspersönlichkeit haften auch die organschaftlichen Vertreter gesamtschuldnerisch für den Schaden. [3]Der Arbeitgeber oder ein organschaftlicher Vertreter haften nicht, wenn sie den Schaden nicht zu vertreten haben.

(8) Eine Beendigung, Auflösung oder Kündigung der Vorkehrungen zum Insolvenzschutz vor der bestimmungsgemäßen Auflösung des Wertguthabens ist unzulässig, es sei denn, die Vorkehrungen werden mit Zustimmung des Beschäftigten durch einen mindestens gleichwertigen Insolvenzschutz abgelöst.

(9) Die Absätze 1 bis 8 finden keine Anwendung gegenüber dem Bund, den Ländern, Gemeinden, Körperschaften, Stiftungen und Anstalten des öffentlichen Rechts, über deren Vermögen die Eröffnung des Insolvenzverfahrens nicht zulässig ist, sowie solchen juristischen Personen des öffentlichen Rechts, bei denen der Bund, ein Land oder eine Gemeinde kraft Gesetzes die Zahlungsfähigkeit sichert.

§ 7f
Übertragung von Wertguthaben

(1) [1]Bei Beendigung der Beschäftigung kann der Beschäftigte durch schriftliche Erklärung gegenüber dem bisherigen Arbeitgeber verlangen, dass das Wertguthaben nach § 7b

1. auf den neuen Arbeitgeber übertragen wird, wenn dieser mit dem Beschäftigten eine Wertguthabenvereinbarung nach § 7b abgeschlossen und der Übertragung zugestimmt hat,

in the administrative act pursuant to the fifth sentence of Paragraph 28p(1), it shall state the total social security contribution included in the value credit and payable by the employer. [2]If the employer proves to the pension insurance institution within two months of the determination in accordance with the first sentence above that it has fulfilled its obligation under subsection 1, the obligation to pay the total social security contribution immediately ceases to apply. [3]If the employer has not provided the proof in accordance with sentence 2 within the period provided for therein, the agreement under section 7b shall be deemed invalid from the outset; the value credit shall be cancelled.

(7) [1]If the value of assets is reduced or lost due to unsuitable or insufficient insolvency protection, the employer shall be liable for the loss incurred. [2]If the employer is a legal entity or a company without legal personality, the representatives of the executive bodies are also jointly and severally liable for the damage. [3]The employer or a representative of a corporate body shall not be liable if they are not responsible for the damage.

(8) Termination, dissolution or termination of the precautions for insolvency protection prior to the proper dissolution of the assets is not permitted unless the precautions are replaced by insolvency protection of at least equivalent value with the consent of the employee.

(9) Paragraphs 1 to 8 shall not apply to the Federal Government, the Länder, local authorities, corporations, foundations and public-law institutions in respect of whose assets the opening of insolvency proceedings is not permitted, nor to such legal entities under public law in respect of which the Federal Government, a Land or a local authority ensures solvency by operation of law.

Section 7f
Transfer of value credits

(1) [1] On termination of employment, the employee may demand in writing from his previous employer that the value credit in accordance with § 7b

1. is transferred to the new employer if the latter has concluded a value credit agreement with the employee in accordance with § 7b and has consented to the transfer

2. auf die Deutsche Rentenversicherung Bund übertragen wird, wenn das Wertguthaben einschließlich des Gesamtsozialversicherungsbeitrages einen Betrag in Höhe des Sechsfachen der monatlichen Bezugsgröße übersteigt; die Rückübertragung ist ausgeschlossen.

²Nach der Übertragung sind die mit dem Wertguthaben verbundenen Arbeitgeberpflichten vom neuen Arbeitgeber oder von der Deutschen Rentenversicherung Bund zu erfüllen.

(2) ¹Im Fall der Übertragung auf die Deutsche Rentenversicherung Bund kann der Beschäftigte das Wertguthaben für Zeiten der Freistellung von der Arbeitsleistung und Zeiten der Verringerung der vertraglich vereinbarten Arbeitszeit nach § 7c Absatz 1 sowie auch außerhalb eines Arbeitsverhältnisses für die in § 7c Absatz 1 Nummer 2 Buchstabe a genannten Zeiten in Anspruch nehmen. ²Der Antrag ist spätestens einen Monat vor der begehrten Freistellung schriftlich bei der Deutschen Rentenversicherung Bund zu stellen; in dem Antrag ist auch anzugeben, in welcher Höhe Arbeitsentgelt aus dem Wertguthaben entnommen werden soll; dabei ist § 7 Absatz 1a Satz 1 Nummer 2 zu berücksichtigen.

(3) ¹Die Deutsche Rentenversicherung Bund verwaltet die ihr übertragenen Wertguthaben einschließlich des darin enthaltenen Gesamtsozialversicherungsbeitrages als ihr übertragene Aufgabe bis zu deren endgültiger Auflösung getrennt von ihrem sonstigen Vermögen treuhänderisch. ²Die Wertguthaben sind nach den Vorschriften über die Anlage der Mittel von Versicherungsträgern nach dem Vierten Titel des Vierten Abschnitts anzulegen. ³Die der Deutschen Rentenversicherung Bund durch die Übertragung, Verwaltung und Verwendung von Wertguthaben entstehenden Kosten sind vollständig vom Wertguthaben in Abzug zu bringen und in der Mitteilung an den Beschäftigten nach § 7d Absatz 2 gesondert auszuweisen.

2. transferred to the German Pension Insurance Federation if the value credit including the total social security contribution exceeds an amount of six times the monthly reference value; retransfer is excluded.

²After the transfer, the employer obligations associated with the value credit must be fulfilled by the new employer or by the German Pension Insurance Federation.

(2) ¹In the event of a transfer to German Pension Insurance Federation, the employee may use the assets for periods of exemption from work and periods of reduction of the contractually agreed working time in accordance with Article 7c(1) and also outside an employment relationship for the periods referred to in Article 7c(1)(2)(a). ²The application must be submitted in writing to the German Pension Insurance Federation no later than one month before the requested exemption; the application must also state the amount of remuneration to be withdrawn from the value credit; in doing so, § 7 paragraph 1a sentence 1 number 2 must be taken into account.

(3) ¹German Pension Insurance Federation shall manage the assets transferred to it, including the total social security contribution contained therein, as a task entrusted to it, separately from its other assets in a fiduciary capacity until their final dissolution. ²The assets shall be invested in accordance with the provisions on the investment of funds of insurance institutions set out in Title IV of Section IV. ³The costs incurred by the German Pension Insurance Federation through the transfer, administration and use of assets are to be deducted in full from the assets and shown separately in the notification to the employee in accordance with Article 7d paragraph 2.

§ 8
Geringfügige Beschäftigung und geringfügige selbständige Tätigkeit

(1) Eine geringfügige Beschäftigung liegt vor, wenn

1. das Arbeitsentgelt aus dieser Beschäftigung regelmäßig im Monat 450 Euro nicht übersteigt,

Section 8
Marginal employment and minor self-employment

(1) A minor job is considered to be minor employment if

1. the remuneration from such employment does not regularly exceed EUR 450 per month,

2. die Beschäftigung innerhalb eines Kalenderjahres auf längstens drei Monate oder 70 Arbeitstage nach ihrer Eigenart begrenzt zu sein pflegt oder im Voraus vertraglich begrenzt ist, es sei denn, dass die Beschäftigung berufsmäßig ausgeübt wird und ihr Entgelt 450 Euro im Monat übersteigt.

(2) ¹Bei der Anwendung des Absatzes 1 sind mehrere geringfügige Beschäftigungen nach Nummer 1 oder Nummer 2 sowie geringfügige Beschäftigungen nach Nummer 1 mit Ausnahme einer geringfügigen Beschäftigung nach Nummer 1 und nicht geringfügige Beschäftigungen zusammenzurechnen. ²Eine geringfügige Beschäftigung liegt nicht mehr vor, sobald die Voraussetzungen des Absatzes 1 entfallen. ³Wird beim Zusammenrechnen nach Satz 1 festgestellt, dass die Voraussetzungen einer geringfügigen Beschäftigung nicht mehr vorliegen, tritt die Versicherungspflicht erst mit dem Tag ein, an dem die Entscheidung über die Versicherungspflicht nach § 37 des Zehnten Buches durch die Einzugsstelle nach § 28i Satz 5 oder einen anderen Träger der Rentenversicherung bekannt gegeben wird. ⁴Dies gilt nicht, wenn der Arbeitgeber vorsätzlich oder grob fahrlässig versäumt hat, den Sachverhalt für die versicherungsrechtliche Beurteilung der Beschäftigung aufzuklären.

(3) ¹Die Absätze 1 und 2 gelten entsprechend, soweit anstelle einer Beschäftigung eine selbständige Tätigkeit ausgeübt wird. ²Dies gilt nicht für das Recht der Arbeitsförderung.

§ 8a
Geringfügige Beschäftigung in Privathaushalten

¹Werden geringfügige Beschäftigungen ausschließlich in Privathaushalten ausgeübt, gilt § 8. ²Eine geringfügige Beschäftigung im Privathaushalt liegt vor, wenn diese durch einen privaten Haushalt begründet ist und die Tätigkeit sonst gewöhnlich durch Mitglieder des privaten Haushalts erledigt wird.

§ 9
Beschäftigungsort

(1) Beschäftigungsort ist der Ort, an dem die Beschäftigung tatsächlich ausgeübt wird.

(2) Als Beschäftigungsort gilt der Ort, an dem eine feste Arbeitsstätte errichtet ist, wenn Personen

1. von ihr aus mit einzelnen Arbeiten außerhalb der festen Arbeitsstätte beschäftigt werden oder

2. the employment within a calendar year is limited to a maximum of three months or 70 working days according to its nature or is contractually limited in advance, unless the employment is exercised professionally and the remuneration exceeds 450 euros per month.

(2) ¹For the purposes of applying paragraph 1, several minor employments as defined in paragraph 1 or paragraph 2 and minor employments as defined in paragraph 1, with the exception of a minor employment as defined in paragraph 1, and non-minor employments shall be added together. ²Minor employment ceases to exist as soon as the requirements of paragraph 1 cease to apply. ³If it is established when adding up in accordance with the first sentence above that the requirements for minor employment no longer apply, the obligation to pay insurance does not arise until the day on which the decision on the obligation to pay insurance in accordance with § 37 of the Tenth Book is announced by the collection agency in accordance with § 28i sentence 5 or another pension insurance institution. ⁴This does not apply if the employer has deliberately or through gross negligence failed to clarify the facts of the case for the purposes of assessing the employment under insurance law.

(3) ¹Paragraphs 1 and 2 shall apply mutatis mutandis where a self-employed activity is pursued instead of employment. ²This does not apply to the law on the promotion of employment.

Section 8a
Marginal employment in private households

¹If minor employment is carried out exclusively in private households, Article 8 shall apply. ²Minor employment in a private household is deemed to exist if the employment is in a private household and the activity is otherwise usually carried out by members of the private household.

Section 9
Place of employment

(1). The place of employment shall be the place where the employment is actually pursued.

(2) The place of employment shall be the place where a fixed place of work is established if persons

1. are employed by it with individual work outside the fixed place of work or

2. außerhalb der festen Arbeitsstätte beschäftigt werden und diese Arbeitsstätte sowie der Ort, an dem die Beschäftigung tatsächlich ausgeübt wird, im Bezirk desselben Versicherungsamts liegen.

(3) Sind Personen bei einem Arbeitgeber an mehreren festen Arbeitsstätten beschäftigt, gilt als Beschäftigungsort die Arbeitsstätte, in der sie überwiegend beschäftigt sind.

(4) Erstreckt sich eine feste Arbeitsstätte über den Bezirk mehrerer Gemeinden, gilt als Beschäftigungsort der Ort, an dem die Arbeitsstätte ihren wirtschaftlichen Schwerpunkt hat.

(5) ¹Ist eine feste Arbeitsstätte nicht vorhanden und wird die Beschäftigung an verschiedenen Orten ausgeübt, gilt als Beschäftigungsort der Ort, an dem der Betrieb seinen Sitz hat. ²Leitet eine Außenstelle des Betriebs die Arbeiten unmittelbar, ist der Sitz der Außenstelle maßgebend. ³Ist nach den Sätzen 1 und 2 ein Beschäftigungsort im Geltungsbereich dieses Gesetzbuchs nicht vorhanden, gilt als Beschäftigungsort der Ort, an dem die Beschäftigung erstmals im Geltungsbereich dieses Gesetzbuchs ausgeübt wird.

(6) ¹In den Fällen der Ausstrahlung gilt der bisherige Beschäftigungsort als fortbestehend. ²Ist ein solcher nicht vorhanden, gilt als Beschäftigungsort der Ort, an dem der Betrieb, von dem der Beschäftigte entsandt wird, seinen Sitz hat.

(7) ¹Gelten für einen Arbeitnehmer auf Grund über- oder zwischenstaatlichen Rechts die deutschen Rechtsvorschriften über soziale Sicherheit und übt der Arbeitnehmer die Beschäftigung nicht im Geltungsbereich dieses Buches aus, gilt Absatz 6 entsprechend. ²Ist auch danach kein Beschäftigungsort im Geltungsbereich dieses Buches gegeben, gilt der Arbeitnehmer als in Berlin (Ost) beschäftigt.

§ 10
Beschäftigungsort für besondere Personengruppen

(1) Für Personen, die ein freiwilliges soziales Jahr oder ein freiwilliges ökologisches Jahr im Sinne des Jugendfreiwilligendienstegesetzes leisten, gilt als Beschäftigungsort der Ort, an dem der Träger des freiwilligen sozialen Jahres oder des freiwilligen ökologischen Jahres seinen Sitz hat.

(2) ¹Für Entwicklungshelfer gilt als Beschäftigungsort der Sitz des Trägers des Entwicklungsdienstes. ²Für auf Antrag im Ausland versicherte Personen gilt als Beschäftigungsort der Sitz der antragstellenden Stelle.

2. are employed outside the permanent place of work and this place of work and the place where the employment is actually carried out are located in the district of the same insurance office.

(3) If persons are employed by an employer at several fixed places of work, the place of employment shall be deemed to be the place where they are predominantly employed.

(4) If a fixed place of work extends over the district of several municipalities, the place of employment shall be deemed to be the place where the place of work has its economic centre.

(5) ¹If there is no fixed place of work and the employment is carried out in different places, the place of employment shall be the place where the establishment is located. ²If a branch of the enterprise directly directs the work, the location of the branch shall be decisive. ³If, pursuant to the first and second sentences, there is no place of employment within the scope of this Code, the place of employment shall be the place where the employment is first exercised within the scope of this Code.

(6) ¹In cases of broadcasting, the previous place of employment shall be deemed to continue to exist. ²If no such place of employment exists, the place of employment shall be the place where the business from which the employee is seconded has its registered office.

(7) ¹If German social security legislation applies to an employee on the basis of supranational or intergovernmental law and the employee does not exercise the employment within the scope of this Book, paragraph 6 shall apply mutatis mutandis. ²If there is still no place of employment within the scope of this Book, the employee shall be deemed to be employed in Berlin (East).

Section 10
Place of employment for special categories of persons

(1) For persons who perform a voluntary social year or a voluntary ecological year within the meaning of the Youth Voluntary Service Act, the place of employment shall be the place where the institution responsible for the voluntary social year or voluntary ecological year is located.

(2) ¹For development workers, the place of employment shall be the place where the institution of the development service has its seat. ²For persons insured abroad on application, the place of employment shall be the seat of the applicant organisation.

(3) ¹Für Seeleute gilt als Beschäftigungsort der Heimathafen des Seeschiffs. ²Ist ein Heimathafen im Geltungsbereich dieses Gesetzbuchs nicht vorhanden, gilt als Beschäftigungsort Hamburg.

(3) ¹For seafarers, the place of employment shall be the home port of the seagoing vessel. ²If a home port does not exist within the scope of application of this Code, Hamburg shall be deemed the place of employment

§ 11
Tätigkeitsort

Section 11
Place of activity

(1) Die Vorschriften über den Beschftigungsort gelten für selbständige Tätigkeiten entsprechend, soweit sich nicht aus Absatz 2 Abweichendes ergibt.

(1) The provisions concerning the place of employment shall apply mutatis mutandis to self-employed activities, unless otherwise provided for in paragraph 2.

(2) Ist eine feste Arbeitsstätte nicht vorhanden und wird die selbständige Tätigkeit an verschiedenen Orten ausgeübt, gilt als Tätigkeitsort der Ort des Wohnsitzes oder des gewöhnlichen Aufenthalts.

(2) If there is no fixed place of work and the self-employed activity is carried out at different places, the place of activity shall be the place of residence or habitual abode.

§ 12
Hausgewerbetreibende, Heimarbeiter und Zwischenmeister

Section 12
Domestic craftsmen, home workers and intermediaries

(1) Hausgewerbetreibende sind selbständig Tätige, die in eigener Arbeitsstätte im Auftrag und für Rechnung von Gewerbetreibenden, gemeinnützigen Unternehmen oder öffentlich-rechtlichen Körperschaften gewerblich arbeiten, auch wenn sie Roh- oder Hilfsstoffe selbst beschaffen oder vorübergehend für eigene Rechnung tätig sind.

(1) Domestic craftsmen are self-employed persons who work commercially in their own place of work on behalf and for the account of tradesmen, non-profit-making enterprises or public-law corporations, even if they procure raw materials or auxiliary materials themselves or work temporarily for their own account.

(2) Heimarbeiter sind sonstige Personen, die in eigener Arbeitsstätte im Auftrag und für Rechnung von Gewerbetreibenden, gemeinnützigen Unternehmen oder öffentlich-rechtlichen Körperschaften erwerbsmäßig arbeiten, auch wenn sie Roh- oder Hilfsstoffe selbst beschaffen; sie gelten als Beschäftigte.

(2) Homeworkers are other persons who work commercially in their own place of work on behalf and for the account of traders, non-profit-making enterprises or public-law bodies, even if they procure raw materials or supplies themselves; they are considered to be employees.

(3) Als Arbeitgeber der Hausgewerbetreibenden oder Heimarbeiter gilt, wer die Arbeit unmittelbar an sie vergibt, als Auftraggeber der, in dessen Auftrag und für dessen Rechnung sie arbeiten.

(3) The employer of home-based tradesmen or homeworkers shall be deemed to be the person who directly contracts work out to them, and the principal shall be deemed to be the person on whose behalf and for whose account they work.

(4) Zwischenmeister ist, wer, ohne Arbeitnehmer zu sein, die ihm übertragene Arbeit an Hausgewerbetreibende oder Heimarbeiter weitergibt.

(4) An intermediate master is someone who, without being an employee, subcontracts the work assigned to him/her to cottage industries or homeworkers.

(5) ¹Als Hausgewerbetreibende, Heimarbeiter oder Zwischenmeister gelten auch die nach § 1 Absatz 2 Satz 1 Buchstaben a, c und d des Heimarbeitsgesetzes gleichgestellten Personen. ²Dies gilt nicht für das Recht der Arbeitsförderung.

(5) ¹Persons treated as home-based tradesmen, homeworkers or intermediate supervisors under Section 1 paragraph 2 sentence 1 letters a, c and d of the Home Work Act are also deemed to be equivalent to homeworkers. ²This does not apply to the law on the promotion of employment.

§ 13
Reeder, Seeleute und Deutsche Seeschiffe

(1) [1]Reeder sind die Eigentümer von Seeschiffen. [2]Seeleute sind alle abhängig beschäftigten Besatzungsmitglieder an Bord von Seeschiffen; Kanalsteurer auf dem Nord-Ostsee-Kanal stehen den Seeleuten gleich.

(2) Als deutsche Seeschiffe gelten alle zur Seefahrt bestimmten Schiffe, die berechtigt sind, die Bundesflagge zu führen.

§ 14
Arbeitsentgelt

(1) [1]Arbeitsentgelt sind alle laufenden oder einmaligen Einnahmen aus einer Beschäftigung, gleichgültig, ob ein Rechtsanspruch auf die Einnahmen besteht, unter welcher Bezeichnung oder in welcher Form sie geleistet werden und ob sie unmittelbar aus der Beschäftigung oder im Zusammenhang mit ihr erzielt werden. [2]Arbeitsentgelt sind auch Entgeltteile, die durch Entgeltumwandlung nach § 1 Absatz 2 Nummer 3 des Betriebsrentengesetzes für betriebliche Altersversorgung in den Durchführungswegen Direktzusage oder Unterstützungskasse verwendet werden, soweit sie 4 vom Hundert der jährlichen Beitragsbemessungsgrenze der allgemeinen Rentenversicherung übersteigen.

(2) [1]Ist ein Nettoarbeitsentgelt vereinbart, gelten als Arbeitsentgelt die Einnahmen des Beschäftigten einschließlich der darauf entfallenden Steuern und der seinem gesetzlichen Anteil entsprechenden Beiträge zur Sozialversicherung und zur Arbeitsförderung. [2]Sind bei illegalen Beschäftigungsverhältnissen Steuern und Beiträge zur Sozialversicherung und zur Arbeitsförderung nicht gezahlt worden, gilt ein Nettoarbeitsentgelt als vereinbart.

(3) Wird ein Haushaltsscheck (§ 28a Absatz 7) verwendet, bleiben Zuwendungen unberücksichtigt, die nicht in Geld gewährt worden sind.

§ 15
Arbeitseinkommen

(1) [1]Arbeitseinkommen ist der nach den allgemeinen Gewinnermittlungsvorschriften des Einkommensteuerrechts ermittelte Gewinn aus einer selbständigen Tätigkeit. [2]Einkommen ist als Arbeitseinkommen zu werten, wenn es als solches nach dem Einkommensteuerrecht zu bewerten ist.

Section 13
Shipowners, seafarers and German seagoing vessels

(1) [1]Shipowners are the owners of sea-going vessels. [2]Seafarers are all employed crew members on board seagoing vessels; canal helmsmen on the Kiel Canal are equal to seafarers.

(2) German seagoing vessels are all vessels intended for sea transport which are entitled to fly the German flag.

Section 14
Remuneration

(1) [1]Employment income means all current or non-recurrent income from employment, irrespective of whether there is a legal right to the income, under what title or in what form it is received and whether it is derived directly from employment or in connection therewith. [2]Employment income also includes income components that are used through deferred compensation in accordance with Article 1(2) (3) of the Betriebsrentengesetz für betriebliche Altersversorgung (Company Pensions Act) in the form of direct commitments or support funds, provided that they exceed 4 % of the annual contribution assessment ceiling for general pension insurance.

(2) [1]If net remuneration has been agreed, the employee's income, including the taxes payable thereon and the social security and employment promotion contributions corresponding to his statutory share, shall be deemed to be remuneration. [2]If taxes and social security and employment promotion contributions have not been paid in the case of illegal employment, net remuneration shall be deemed to have been agreed.

(3) If a household cheque (Article 28a(7)) is used, allowances which have not been granted in cash shall not be taken into account.

Section 15
Employment income

(1) [1]Employment income is the profit from self-employment calculated in accordance with the general rules for determining profits under income tax law. [2]Income is to be regarded as employment income if it is to be assessed as such under income tax law.

(2) Bei Landwirten, deren Gewinn aus Land- und Forstwirtschaft nach § 13a des Einkommensteuergesetzes ermittelt wird, ist als Arbeitseinkommen der sich aus § 32 Absatz 6 des Gesetzes über die Alterssicherung der Landwirte ergebende Wert anzusetzen.

(2) In the case of farmers whose profit from agriculture and forestry is determined in accordance with Section 13a of the Income Tax Act, the value resulting from Section 32(6) of the Act on Old-Age Provision for Farmers shall be taken as the income from work.

§ 16
Gesamteinkommen

Gesamteinkommen ist die Summe der Einkünfte im Sinne des Einkommensteuerrechts; es umfasst insbesondere das Arbeitsentgelt und das Arbeitseinkommen.

Section 16
Total income

Total income is the sum of income within the meaning of income tax law; it includes in particular pay for work and income from employment.

§ 17
Verordnungsermächtigung

(1) ¹Das Bundesministerium für Arbeit und Soziales wird ermächtigt, durch Rechtsverordnung mit Zustimmung des Bundesrates zur Wahrung der Belange der Sozialversicherung und der Arbeitsförderung, zur Förderung der betrieblichen Altersversorgung oder zur Vereinfachung des Beitragseinzugs zu bestimmen,

1. dass einmalige Einnahmen oder laufende Zulagen, Zuschläge, Zuschüsse oder ähnliche Einnahmen, die zusätzlich zu Löhnen oder Gehältern gewährt werden, und steuerfreie Einnahmen ganz oder teilweise nicht als Arbeitsentgelt gelten,
2. dass Beiträge an Direktversicherungen und Zuwendungen an Pensionskassen oder Pensionsfonds ganz oder teilweise nicht als Arbeitsentgelt gelten,
3. wie das Arbeitsentgelt, das Arbeitseinkommen und das Gesamteinkommen zu ermitteln und zeitlich zuzurechnen sind,
4. den Wert der Sachbezüge nach dem tatsächlichen Verkehrswert im Voraus für jedes Kalenderjahr.

²Dabei ist eine möglichst weitgehende Übereinstimmung mit den Regelungen des Steuerrechts sicherzustellen.

(2) ¹Das Bundesministerium für Arbeit und Soziales bestimmt im Voraus für jedes Kalenderjahr durch Rechtsverordnung mit Zustimmung des Bundesrates die Bezugsgröße (§ 18). ²Das Bundesministerium für Arbeit und Soziales wird ermächtigt, durch Rechtsverordnung mit Zustimmung des Bundesrates auch sonstige aus der Bezugsgröße abzuleitende Beträge zu bestimmen.

Section 17
Authorisation by decree

(1) ¹The Federal Ministry of Labour and Social Affairs shall be authorised to determine by statutory order, with the consent of the Bundesrat, how to safeguard the interests of social security and employment promotion, to promote occupational pension schemes or to simplify the collection of contributions,

1. that non-recurring income or current allowances, supplements, subsidies or similar income granted in addition to wages or salaries, and tax-free income, shall not be regarded, in whole or in part, as remuneration for work
2. that contributions to direct insurance schemes and contributions to pension funds or pension funds are not regarded in whole or in part as remuneration,
3. how pay, income from work and total income are to be determined and allocated over time,
4. the value of benefits in kind according to the actual market value in advance for each calendar year.

In this context, it must be ensured that the provisions of tax law are complied with as far as possible.

(2) ¹The Federal Ministry of Labour and Social Affairs shall determine the reference value for each calendar year in advance by statutory order with the consent of the Bundesrat (section 18). ²The Federal Ministry of Labour and Social Affairs is authorised to determine by statutory order, with the consent of the Bundesrat, other amounts to be derived from the reference value.

§ 17a	Section 17a
Umrechnung von ausländischem Einkommen	**Conversion of foreign income**

(1) [1]Ist Einkommen zu berücksichtigen, das in fremder Währung erzielt wird, wird es in Euro nach dem Referenzkurs umgerechnet, den die Europäische Zentralbank öffentlich bekannt gibt. [2]Wird für die fremde Währung von der Europäischen Zentralbank ein Referenzkurs nicht veröffentlicht, wird das Einkommen nach dem von der Deutschen Bundesbank ermittelten Mittelkurs für die Währung des betreffenden Landes umgerechnet; für Länder mit differenziertem Kurssystem ist der Kurs für den nichtkommerziellen Bereich zugrunde zu legen.

(2) [1]Bei Berücksichtigung von Einkommen ist in den Fällen, in denen der Beginn der Leistung oder der neu berechneten Leistung in der Vergangenheit liegt, der Umrechnungskurs für den Kalendermonat maßgebend, in dem die Anrechnung des Einkommens beginnt. [2]Bei Berücksichtigung von Einkommen ist in den Fällen, in denen der Beginn der Leistung oder der neu berechneten Leistung nicht in der Vergangenheit liegt, der Umrechnungskurs für den ersten Monat des Kalendervierteljahres maßgebend, das dem Beginn der Berücksichtigung von Einkommen vorausgeht. [3]Überstaatliches Recht bleibt unberührt.

(3) [1]Der angewandte Umrechnungskurs bleibt so lange maßgebend, bis

1. die Sozialleistung zu ändern ist,
2. sich das zu berücksichtigende Einkommen ändert oder
3. eine Kursveränderung von mehr als 10 vom Hundert gegenüber der letzten Umrechnung eintritt, jedoch nicht vor Ablauf von drei Kalendermonaten.

[2]Die Kursveränderung nach Nummer 3 sowie der neue Umrechnungskurs werden in entsprechender Anwendung von Absatz 2 ermittelt.

(4) [1]Die Absätze 1 bis 3 finden entsprechende Anwendung auf

1. Unterhaltsleistungen,
2. Prämien für eine Krankenversicherung.

[2]Sie finden keine Anwendung bei der Ermittlung von Bemessungsgrundlagen von Sozialleistungen.

(5) Die Absätze 1 bis 4 sind auch anzuwenden, wenn der Versicherungsfall vor dem 1. Juli 1985 eingetreten ist.

(1) [1]If income generated in foreign currency is to be taken into account, it shall be converted into euro at the reference rate publicly announced by the European Central Bank. [2]If a reference exchange rate for the foreign currency is not published by the European Central Bank, income shall be converted at the average exchange rate determined by the Deutsche Bundesbank for the currency of the country concerned; for countries with a differentiated exchange rate system, the rate for the non-commercial sector shall be used.

(2) [1]When taking income into account, in cases where the commencement of the benefit or the recalculated benefit is in the past, the conversion rate for the calendar month in which the income is credited shall apply. [2]When taking income into account, in cases where the commencement of the benefit or of the recalculated benefit is not in the past, the conversion rate for the first month of the calendar quarter preceding the commencement of the taking into account of income is decisive. 3National law remains unaffected.

(3) [1]The conversion rate applied shall remain applicable until

1. the social benefit is to be changed
2. the income to be taken into account changes or
3. there is a change in the exchange rate of more than 10 per cent compared with the last conversion, but not before the end of three calendar months.

[2]The change in exchange rate referred to in paragraph 3 and the new conversion rate shall be determined by applying paragraph 2 mutatis mutandis.

(4) [1] Paragraphs 1 to 3 shall apply mutatis mutandis to

1. maintenance payments,
2. premiums for health insurance.

[2]They do not apply to the determination of bases of assessment for social security benefits

(5) Paragraphs 1 to 4 shall also apply if the insured event occurred before 1 July 1985.

§ 18
Bezugsgröße

(1) Bezugsgröße im Sinne der Vorschriften für die Sozialversicherung ist, soweit in den besonderen Vorschriften für die einzelnen Versicherungszweige nichts Abweichendes bestimmt ist, das Durchschnittsentgelt der gesetzlichen Rentenversicherung im vorvergangenen Kalenderjahr, aufgerundet auf den nächsthöheren, durch 420 teilbaren Betrag.

(2) ¹Die Bezugsgröße für das Beitrittsgebiet (Bezugsgröße [Ost]) verändert sich zum 1. Januar eines jeden Kalenderjahres auf den Wert, der sich ergibt, wenn der für das vorvergangene Kalenderjahr geltende Wert der Anlage 1 zum Sechsten Buch durch den für das Kalenderjahr der Veränderung bestimmten Wert der Anlage 10 zum Sechsten Buch geteilt wird, aufgerundet auf den nächsthöheren, durch 420 teilbaren Betrag. ²Für die Zeit ab 1. Januar 2025 ist eine Bezugsgröße (Ost) nicht mehr zu bestimmen.

(3) Beitrittsgebiet ist das in Artikel 3 des Einigungsvertrages genannte Gebiet.

§ 18a
Art des zu berücksichtigenden Einkommens

(1) ¹Bei Renten wegen Todes sind als Einkommen zu berücksichtigen

1. Erwerbseinkommen,
2. Leistungen, die erbracht werden, um Erwerbseinkommen zu ersetzen (Erwerbsersatzeinkommen),
3. Vermögenseinkommen,
4. Elterngeld und
5. Aufstockungsbeträge und Zuschläge nach § 3 Nummer 28 des Einkommensteuergesetzes.

²Nicht zu berücksichtigen sind

1. Arbeitsentgelt, das eine Pflegeperson von dem Pflegebedürftigen erhält, wenn das Entgelt das dem Umfang der Pflegetätigkeit entsprechende Pflegegeld nach § 37 des Elften Buches nicht übersteigt,
2. Einnahmen aus Altersvorsorgeverträgen, soweit sie nach § 10a oder Abschnitt XI des Einkommensteuergesetzes gefördert worden sind,
3. Renten nach § 3 Nummer 8a des Einkommensteuergesetzes und
4. Arbeitsentgelt, das ein behinderter Mensch von einem Träger einer in § 1 Satz 1 Nummer 2 des Sechsten Buches genannten Einrichtung erhält.

Section 18
Reference value

(1) The reference value within the meaning of the provisions for social insurance is, unless otherwise specified in the special provisions for the individual classes of insurance, the average pay of the statutory pension insurance in the previous calendar year, rounded up to the next higher amount divisible by 420.

(2) ¹The reference value for the acceding territory (reference value (east)) shall be changed on 1 January of each calendar year to the value obtained by dividing the value in Annex 1 to Book 6 applicable in the preceding calendar year by the value in Annex 10 to Book 6 determined for the calendar year of the change, rounded up to the next higher amount divisible by 420. ²For the period from 1 January 2025, a reference value (East) is no longer to be determined.

(3) The acceding territory is the territory referred to in Article 3 of the Unification Treaty.

Section 18a
Type of income to be taken into account

(1) ¹In the case of pensions due to death, the following shall be taken into account as income

1. earned income,
2. services provided to replace earned income (replacement income),
3. property income,
4. parental allowance and
5. top-up amounts and surcharges under Section 3 No. 28 of the Income Tax Act.

²Not to be taken into account are

1. remuneration which a carer receives from the person in need of care if the remuneration does not exceed the care allowance corresponding to the scope of the care activity in accordance with § 37 of Book Eleven
2. income from old-age provision contracts, insofar as they have been subsidised under Section 10a or Section XI of the Income Tax Act,
3. pensions under Section 3 No. 8a of the Income Tax Act, and
4. remuneration received by a disabled person from an institution of an institution referred to in Section 1, first sentence, point 2 of Book Six.

³Die Sätze 1 und 2 gelten auch für vergleichbare ausländische Einkommen.

(2) Erwerbseinkommen im Sinne des Absatzes 1 Satz 1 Nummer 1 sind Arbeitsentgelt, Arbeitseinkommen und vergleichbares Einkommen.

(2a) Arbeitseinkommen im Sinne des Absatzes 2 Satz 1 ist die positive Summe der Gewinne oder Verluste aus folgenden Arbeitseinkommensarten:

1. Gewinne aus Land- und Forstwirtschaft im Sinne der §§ 13, 13a und 14 des Einkommensteuergesetzes in Verbindung mit § 15 Absatz 2,
2. Gewinne aus Gewerbebetrieb im Sinne der §§ 15, 16 und 17 des Einkommensteuergesetzes und
3. Gewinne aus selbständiger Arbeit im Sinne des § 18 des Einkommensteuergesetzes.

(3) ¹Erwerbsersatzeinkommen im Sinne des Absatzes 1 Satz 1 Nummer 2 sind

1. das Krankengeld, das Verletztengeld, das Versorgungskrankengeld, das Mutterschaftsgeld, das Übergangsgeld, das Pflegeunterstützungsgeld, das Kurzarbeitergeld, das Arbeitslosengeld, das Insolvenzgeld, das Krankentagegeld und vergleichbare Leistungen,
2. Renten der Rentenversicherung wegen Alters oder verminderter Erwerbsfähigkeit, die Erziehungsrente, die Knappschaftsausgleichsleistung, das Anpassungsgeld für entlassene Arbeitnehmer des Bergbaus und Leistungen nach den §§ 27 und 28 des Sozialversicherungs-Angleichungsgesetzes Saar,
3. Altersrenten und Renten wegen Erwerbsminderung der Alterssicherung der Landwirte, die an ehemalige Landwirte oder mitarbeitende Familienangehörige gezahlt werden,
4. die Verletztenrente der Unfallversicherung, soweit sie einen der Grundrente nach dem Bundesversorgungsgesetz entsprechenden Betrag übersteigt; eine Kürzung oder ein Wegfall der Verletztenrente wegen Anstaltspflege oder Aufnahme in ein Alters- oder Pflegeheim bleibt unberücksichtigt; bei einer Minderung der Erwerbsfähigkeit um 20 vom Hundert ist ein Betrag in Höhe von zwei Dritteln, bei einer Minderung der Erwerbsfähigkeit um 10 vom Hundert ist ein Betrag in Höhe von einem Drittel der Mindestgrundrente anzusetzen,

³The first and second sentences also apply to comparable foreign income.

(2) Earnings within the meaning of subsection (1), first sentence, no. 1 shall be deemed to be pay, income from work and comparable income.

(2a) Employment income within the meaning of subsection (2), first sentence, is the positive sum of the gains or losses from the following types of employment income:

1. profits from agriculture and forestry within the meaning of sections 13, 13a and 14 of the Income Tax Act in conjunction with section 15(2)
2. profits from commercial operations within the meaning of sections 15, 16 and 17 of the Income Tax Act, and
3. profits from self-employment within the meaning of Section 18 of the Income Tax Act.

(3) 1Substitute incomes from gainful employment within the meaning of subsection (1), first sentence, point 2 are

1. sickness benefit, injury benefit, sickness benefit, maternity benefit, transitional allowance, care support allowance, short-time working allowance, unemployment benefit, insolvency benefit, daily sickness benefit and comparable benefits
2. pensions paid by the pension insurance scheme on account of age or reduced earning capacity, the child-raising pension, the miners' compensation benefit, the adjustment allowance for laid-off mining workers and benefits under Sections 27 and 28 of the Saar Social Insurance Adjustment Act,
3. old-age pensions and pensions due to reduced earning capacity of the old-age pension scheme of farmers, paid to former farmers or family members assisting them
4. the injury pension under the accident insurance scheme, insofar as it exceeds an amount corresponding to the basic pension under the Federal Pensions Act; a reduction or discontinuation of the injury pension due to institutional care or admission to an old people's or nursing home shall not be taken into account; in the event of a reduction in earning capacity of 20 per cent, an amount equal to two thirds of the minimum basic pension shall be applied; in the event of a reduction in earning capacity of 10 per cent, an amount equal to one third of the minimum basic pension shall be applied,

5. das Ruhegehalt und vergleichbare Bezüge aus einem öffentlich-rechtlichen Dienst- oder Amtsverhältnis oder aus einem versicherungsfreien Arbeitsverhältnis mit Anspruch auf Versorgung nach beamtenrechtlichen Vorschriften oder Grundsätzen, Altersgeld oder vergleichbare Alterssicherungsleistungen sowie vergleichbare Bezüge aus der Versorgung der Abgeordneten, Leistungen nach dem Bundesversorgungsteilungsgesetz und vergleichbare Leistungen nach entsprechenden länderrechtlichen Regelungen,

6. das Unfallruhegehalt und vergleichbare Bezüge aus einem öffentlich-rechtlichen Dienst- oder Amtsverhältnis oder aus einem versicherungsfreien Arbeitsverhältnis mit Anspruch auf Versorgung nach beamtenrechtlichen Vorschriften oder Grundsätzen sowie vergleichbare Bezüge aus der Versorgung der Abgeordneten; wird daneben kein Unfallausgleich gezahlt, gilt Nummer 4 letzter Teilsatz entsprechend,

7. Renten der öffentlich-rechtlichen Versicherungs- oder Versorgungseinrichtungen bestimmter Berufsgruppen wegen Minderung der Erwerbsfähigkeit oder Alters,

8. der Berufsschadensausgleich nach § 30 Absatz 3 bis 11 des Bundesversorgungsgesetzes und anderen Gesetzen, die die entsprechende Anwendung der Leistungsvorschriften des Bundesversorgungsgesetzes vorsehen,

9. Renten wegen Alters oder verminderter Erwerbsfähigkeit, die aus Anlass eines Arbeitsverhältnisses zugesagt worden sind sowie Leistungen aus der Versorgungsausgleichskasse,

10. Renten wegen Alters oder verminderter Erwerbsfähigkeit aus privaten Lebens- und Rentenversicherungen, allgemeinen Unfallversicherungen sowie sonstige private Versorgungsrenten.

²Kinderzuschuss, Kinderzulage und vergleichbare kindbezogene Leistungen bleiben außer Betracht. ³Wird eine Kapitalleistung oder anstelle einer wiederkehrenden Leistung eine Abfindung gezahlt, ist der Betrag als Einkommen zu berücksichtigen, der bei einer Verrentung der Kapitalleistung oder als Rente ohne die Abfindung zu zahlen wäre.

5. the retirement pension and comparable remuneration from a public-law service or official relationship or from an insurance-free employment relationship with entitlement to pension benefits in accordance with civil service regulations or principles, old-age pension or comparable old age security benefits as well as comparable remuneration from the pension scheme for members of parliament, benefits in accordance with the Federal Pension Sharing Act (Bundesversorgungsteilungsgesetz) and comparable benefits in accordance with corresponding regulations of the Länder,

6. the accident rest allowance and comparable remuneration from a public-law service or official relationship or from an insurance-free employment relationship with entitlement to pension benefits in accordance with the provisions or principles of civil service law, as well as comparable remuneration from the pensions of Members; if no accident compensation is paid in addition, the last sub-sentence of point 4 shall apply mutatis mutandis,

7. pensions paid by the public insurance or pension institutions of certain occupational groups due to reduced earning capacity or old age,

8. the compensation for occupational injury under Section 30(3) to (11) of the Federal Pensions Act and other laws which provide for the corresponding application of the benefit provisions of the Federal Pensions Act,

9. pensions due to old age or reduced earning capacity which have been promised on the occasion of an employment relationship as well as benefits from the pension equalisation fund,

10. pensions due to old age or reduced earning capacity from private life and pension insurance, general accident insurance and other private pension schemes.

²Child allowance, child allowance and comparable child-related benefits are not taken into account. 3If a lump-sum benefit or, instead of a recurrent benefit, a lump-sum settlement is paid, the amount to be taken into account as income is that which would have been payable if the lump-sum benefit had been paid out in the form of an annuity or as a pension without the lump-sum settlement.

(4) Vermögenseinkommen im Sinne des Absatzes 1 Satz 1 Nummer 3 ist die positive Summe der positiven oder negativen Überschüsse, Gewinne oder Verluste aus folgenden Vermögenseinkommensarten:

1. a) Einnahmen aus Kapitalvermögen im Sinne des § 20 des Einkommensteuergesetzes; Einnahmen im Sinne des § 20 Absatz 1 Nummer 6 des Einkommensteuergesetzes in der ab dem 1. Januar 2005 geltenden Fassung sind auch bei einer nur teilweisen Steuerpflicht jeweils die vollen Unterschiedsbeträge zwischen den Versicherungsleistungen einerseits und den auf sie entrichteten Beiträgen oder den Anschaffungskosten bei entgeltlichem Erwerb des Anspruchs auf die Versicherungsleistung andererseits,

   b) Einnahmen aus Versicherungen auf den Erlebens- oder Todesfall im Sinne des § 10 Absatz 1 Nummer 2 Buchstabe b Doppelbuchstabe cc und dd des Einkommensteuergesetzes in der am 1. Januar 2004 geltenden Fassung, wenn die Laufzeit dieser Versicherungen vor dem 1. Januar 2005 begonnen hat und ein Versicherungsbeitrag bis zum 31. Dezember 2004 entrichtet wurde, es sei denn, sie werden wegen Todes geleistet; zu den Einnahmen gehören außerrechnungsmäßige und rechnungsmäßige Zinsen aus den Sparanteilen, die in den Beiträgen zu diesen Versicherungen enthalten sind, im Sinne des § 20 Absatz 1 Nummer 6 des Einkommensteuergesetzes in der am 21. September 2002 geltenden Fassung.

1. Bei der Ermittlung der Einnahmen ist als Werbungskostenpauschale der Sparer-Pauschbetrag abzuziehen,
2. Einnahmen aus Vermietung und Verpachtung im Sinne des § 21 des Einkommensteuergesetzes nach Abzug der Werbungskosten und
3. Gewinne aus privaten Veräußerungsgeschäften im Sinne des § 23 des Einkommensteuergesetzes, soweit sie mindestens 600 Euro im Kalenderjahr betragen.

(4) Property income within the meaning of paragraph 1, first sentence, point 3 is the positive sum of the positive or negative surpluses, gains or losses from the following types of property income

1. a) Income from capital assets within the meaning of section 20 of the Income Tax Act; income within the meaning of section 20(1)(6) of the Income Tax Act as amended on 1 January 2005 shall be the full difference between the insurance benefits on the one hand and the contributions paid on them or the acquisition costs in the case of acquisition of the right to insurance benefits against payment on the other hand, even in the case of only partial tax liability,

   b) income from insurance on survival or death within the meaning of Article 10(1)(2)(b), double letters (cc) and (dd) of the Income Tax Act in the version in force on 1 January 2004, if the term of such insurance began before 1 January 2005 and an insurance premium has been paid until 31 December 2005 The income includes extra-accounting and accounting interest on the savings portions included in the contributions to those insurance policies within the meaning of Section 20(1)(6) of the Income Tax Act as applicable on 21 September 2002.

1. When calculating the income, the flat-rate amount for income-related expenses is to be deducted from the savers' flat-rate amount,
2. income from letting and leasing within the meaning of § 21 of the Income Tax Act after deduction of income-related expenses, and
3. profits from private sales transactions within the meaning of Section 23 of the Income Tax Act, provided they amount to at least 600 euros per calendar year.

§ 18b
Höhe des zu berücksichtigenden Einkommens

(1) [1]Maßgebend ist das für denselben Zeitraum erzielte monatliche Einkommen. [2]Mehrere zu berücksichtigende Einkommen sind zusammenzurechnen. [3]Wird die Rente nur für einen Teil des Monats gezahlt, ist das entsprechend gekürzte monatliche Einkommen maßgebend. [4]Einmalig gezahltes Vermögenseinkommen gilt als für die dem Monat der Zahlung folgenden zwölf Kalendermonate als erzielt. [5]Einmalig gezahltes Vermögenseinkommen ist Einkommen, das einem bestimmten Zeitraum nicht zugeordnet werden kann oder in einem Betrag für mehr als zwölf Monate gezahlt wird.

(2) [1]Bei Erwerbseinkommen und Erwerbsersatzeinkommen nach § 18a Absatz 3 Satz 1 Nummer 1 gilt als monatliches Einkommen im Sinne von Absatz 1 Satz 1 das im letzten Kalenderjahr aus diesen Einkommensarten erzielte Einkommen, geteilt durch die Zahl der Kalendermonate, in denen es erzielt wurde. [2]Wurde Erwerbseinkommen neben Erwerbsersatzeinkommen nach § 18a Absatz 3 Satz 1 Nummer 1 erzielt, sind diese Einkommen zusammenzurechnen; wurden diese Einkommen zeitlich aufeinander folgend erzielt, ist das Erwerbseinkommen maßgebend. [3]Die für einmalig gezahltes Arbeitsentgelt in § 23a getroffene zeitliche Zuordnung gilt entsprechend. [4]Für die Zeiten des Bezugs von Kurzarbeitergeld ist das dem Versicherungsträger gemeldete Arbeitsentgelt maßgebend. [5]Bei Vermögenseinkommen gilt als monatliches Einkommen im Sinne von Absatz 1 Satz 1 ein Zwölftel dieses im letzten Kalenderjahr erzielten Einkommens; bei einmalig gezahltem Vermögenseinkommen gilt ein Zwölftel des gezahlten Betrages als monatliches Einkommen nach Absatz 1 Satz 1. [6]Steht das zu berücksichtigende Einkommen des vorigen Kalenderjahres noch nicht fest, so wird das voraussichtlich erzielte Einkommen zugrunde gelegt.

Section 18b
Level of income to be taken into account

(1) [1]The monthly income earned for the same period is decisive. [2]Multiple incomes to be taken into account shall be added together. [3]If the pension is paid for only part of the month, the correspondingly reduced monthly income is decisive. [4]Income from property paid once is deemed to have been earned for the twelve calendar months following the month of payment. [5]Non-recurrent property income is income which cannot be attributed to a specific period or is paid in one sum for more than twelve months.

(2) [1]In the case of income from gainful employment and income in lieu of gainful employment under Section 18a(3), first sentence, point 1, monthly income within the meaning of subsection (1), first sentence, shall be deemed to be the income earned from these types of income in the previous calendar year, divided by the number of calendar months in which it was earned. [2]If income from gainful employment was earned in addition to income from replacement employment under Article 18a paragraph 3 sentence 1 number 1, this income shall be added together; if this income was earned consecutively, the income from employment shall be decisive. [3]The temporal allocation made in section 23a for one-off remuneration shall apply accordingly. [4]For the periods during which short-time working allowance is received, the remuneration reported to the insurance institution shall be decisive. [5]In the case of income from property, one-twelfth of the income earned in the previous calendar year shall be deemed to be monthly income within the meaning of subsection (1), first sentence; in the case of income from property paid on a one-off basis, one-twelfth of the amount paid shall be deemed to be monthly income within the meaning of subsection (1), first sentence. [6]If the income to be taken into account for the previous calendar year has not yet been determined, the income likely to be earned shall be taken as the basis.

(3) ¹Ist im letzten Kalenderjahr Einkommen nach Absatz 2 nicht oder nur Erwerbsersatzeinkommen nach § 18a Absatz 3 Satz 1 Nummer 1 erzielt worden, gilt als monatliches Einkommen im Sinne von Absatz 1 Satz 1 das laufende Einkommen. ²Satz 1 gilt auch bei der erstmaligen Feststellung der Rente, wenn das laufende Einkommen im Durchschnitt voraussichtlich um wenigstens zehn vom Hundert geringer ist als das nach Absatz 2 maßgebende Einkommen; jährliche Sonderzuwendungen sind beim laufenden Einkommen mit einem Zwölftel zu berücksichtigen. ³Umfasst das laufende Einkommen Erwerbsersatzeinkommen im Sinne von § 18a Absatz 3 Satz 1 Nummer 1, ist dieses nur zu berücksichtigen, solange diese Leistung gezahlt wird.

(4) Bei Erwerbsersatzeinkommen nach § 18a Absatz 3 Satz 1 Nummer 2 bis 10 gilt als monatliches Einkommen im Sinne von Absatz 1 Satz 1 das laufende Einkommen; jährliche Sonderzuwendungen sind beim laufenden Einkommen mit einem Zwölftel zu berücksichtigen.

(5) ¹Das monatliche Einkommen ist zu kürzen

1. bei Arbeitsentgelt um 40 vom Hundert, jedoch bei
   a) Bezügen aus einem öffentlich-rechtlichen Dienst- oder Amtsverhältnis oder aus einem versicherungsfreien Arbeitsverhältnis mit Anwartschaft auf Versorgung nach beamtenrechtlichen Vorschriften oder Grundsätzen und bei Einkommen, das solchen Bezügen vergleichbar ist, um 27,5 vom Hundert,
   b) Beschäftigten, die die Voraussetzungen des § 172 Absatz 1 des Sechsten Buches erfüllen, um 30,5 vom Hundert; das Arbeitsentgelt von Beschäftigten, die die Voraussetzungen des § 172 Absatz 3 oder § 276a des Sechsten Buches erfüllen, und Aufstockungsbeträge nach § 3 Absatz 1 Satz 1 Nummer 1 Buchstabe a des Altersteilzeitgesetzes werden nicht gekürzt, Zuschläge nach § 6 Absatz 2 des Bundesbesoldungsgesetzes werden um 7,65 vom Hundert gekürzt,
2. bei Arbeitseinkommen um 39,8 vom Hundert, bei steuerfreien Einnahmen im Rahmen des Halbeinkünfteverfahrens oder des Teileinkünfteverfahrens um 24,8 vom Hundert,

(3) ¹If income pursuant to subsection (2) above has not been earned in the previous calendar year or only income in lieu of income pursuant to section 18a subsection (3), first sentence, number 1, the current income shall be deemed to be monthly income within the meaning of subsection (1), first sentence. ²Sentence 1 shall also apply when the pension is determined for the first time if the current income is likely to be at least ten per cent lower on average than the income referred to in subsection 2; one-twelfth of the current income shall be taken into account for special annual benefits. ³If current income includes income in lieu of employment within the meaning of Article 18a paragraph 3 sentence 1 number 1, it shall only be taken into account as long as this benefit is paid.

(4) In the case of income in lieu of gainful employment under section 18a(3), first sentence, nos. 2 to 10, monthly income within the meaning of subsection (1), first sentence, shall be deemed to be current income; one-twelfth of current income shall be accounted for in respect of special annual benefits.

(5) ¹Monthly income shall be reduced

1. in the case of pay at 40 per cent, but
   a) 27,5 % of the remuneration of civil servants in the case of remuneration from a public-law service or an official relationship or from an insurance-free employment relationship with a right to a pension in accordance with the provisions or principles of civil service law and with income comparable to such remuneration
   b) employees who satisfy the conditions laid down in Paragraph 172(1) of Book Six by 30.5 %; the remuneration of employees who satisfy the conditions laid down in section 172(3) or section 276a of Book Six and top-up amounts under section 3(1), first sentence, point 1(a) of the Partial Retirement Act shall not be reduced, and top-up amounts under section 6(2) of the Federal Salaries Act shall be reduced by 7.65 per cent,
2. 39.8 % for employment income and 24.8 % for tax-free income under the half-income system or the partial income system, 3. in

3. bei Leistungen nach § 18a Absatz 3 Satz 1 Nummer 7 um 27,5 vom Hundert bei Leistungsbeginn vor dem Jahre 2011 und um 29,6 vom Hundert bei Leistungsbeginn nach dem Jahre 2010,

4. bei Leistungen nach § 18a Absatz 3 Satz 1 Nummer 5 und 6 um 23,7 vom Hundert bei Leistungsbeginn vor dem Jahre 2011 und um 25 vom Hundert bei Leistungsbeginn nach dem Jahre 2010,

5. bei Leistungen nach § 18a Absatz 3 Satz 1 Nummer 9 um 17,5 vom Hundert; sofern es sich dabei um Leistungen handelt, die der nachgelagerten Besteuerung unterliegen, ist das monatliche Einkommen um 21,2 vom Hundert bei Leistungsbeginn vor dem Jahre 2011 und um 23 vom Hundert bei Leistungsbeginn nach dem Jahre 2010 zu kürzen,

6. bei Leistungen nach § 18a Absatz 3 Satz 1 Nummer 10 um 12,7 vom Hundert,

7. bei Vermögenseinkommen um 25 vom Hundert; bei steuerfreien Einnahmen nach dem Halbeinkünfteverfahren um 5 vom Hundert; bei Besteuerung nach dem gesonderten Steuertarif für Einkünfte aus Kapitalvermögen um 30 vom Hundert; Einnahmen aus Versicherungen nach § 18a Absatz 4 Nummer 1 werden nur gekürzt, soweit es sich um steuerpflichtige Kapitalerträge handelt,

8. bei Leistungen nach § 18a Absatz 3 Satz 1 Nummer 2 und 3 um 13 vom Hundert bei Leistungsbeginn vor dem Jahre 2011 und um 14 vom Hundert bei Leistungsbeginn nach dem Jahre 2010.

²Die Leistungen nach § 18a Absatz 3 Satz 1 Nummer 1 und 4 sind um den Anteil der vom Berechtigten zu tragenden Beiträge zur Bundesagentur für Arbeit und, soweit Beiträge zur sonstigen Sozialversicherung oder zu einem Krankenversicherungsunternehmen gezahlt werden, zusätzlich um 10 vom Hundert zu kürzen.

(5a) Elterngeld wird um den anrechnungsfreien Betrag nach § 10 des Bundeselterngeld- und Elternzeitgesetzes gekürzt.

(6) Soweit ein Versicherungsträger über die Höhe des zu berücksichtigenden Einkommens entschieden hat, ist diese Entscheidung auch für einen anderen Versicherungsträger bindend.

3. in the case of benefits under section 18a(3) sentence 1 number 7, by 27.5 % if the benefit commences before 2011 and by 29.6 % if the benefit commences after 2010,

4. in the case of benefits under section 18a(3) sentence 1 nos. 5 and 6, by 23.7 per cent if the benefit commences before 2011 and by 25 per cent if the benefit commences after 2010,

5. in the case of benefits under section 18a(3) first sentence no. 9 by 17.5 %; insofar as these benefits are subject to deferred taxation, the monthly income shall be reduced by 21.2 % if the benefits begin before 2011 and by 23 % if the benefits begin after 2010,

6. in the case of benefits under section 18a(3) sentence 1 number 10 by 12.7 per cent,

7. 25 per cent in the case of income from property; 5 per cent in the case of tax-free income under the half-income system; 30 per cent in the case of taxation under the separate tax scale for income from capital assets; income from insurance policies pursuant to Section 18a (4) No. 1 shall only be reduced if it is taxable capital income,

8. in the case of benefits under section 18a(3) sentence 1 numbers 2 and 3, by 13 per cent if the benefit commences before 2011 and by 14 per cent if the benefit commences after 2010.

²The benefits under Article 18a paragraph 3 sentence 1 Nos. 1 and 4 shall be reduced by the proportion of the contributions to the Federal Employment Agency to be borne by the beneficiary and, if contributions are paid to other social insurance or to a health insurance company, additionally by 10 per cent.

(5a) Parental allowance shall be reduced by the credit-free amount under section 10 of the Federal Parental Allowance and Parental Leave Act.

(6) Insofar as one insurance institution has decided on the amount of income to be taken into account, this decision shall also be binding on another insurance institution.

§ 18c
Erstmalige Ermittlung des Einkommens

(1) Der Berechtigte hat das zu berücksichtigende Einkommen nachzuweisen.

(2) ¹Beziher von Arbeitsentgelt und diesem vergleichbaren Einkommen können verlangen, dass ihnen der Arbeitgeber eine Bescheinigung über das von ihnen für das letzte Kalenderjahr erzielte Arbeitsentgelt oder vergleichbare Einkommen und den Zeitraum, für den es gezahlt wurde, ausstellt. ²Der Arbeitgeber ist zur Ausstellung der Bescheinigung nicht verpflichtet, wenn er der Sozialversicherung das Arbeitsentgelt gemäß den Vorschriften über die Erfassung von Daten und Datenübermittlung bereits gemeldet hat. ³Satz 2 gilt nicht, wenn das tatsächliche Entgelt die Beitragsbemessungsgrenze übersteigt oder die abgegebene Meldung nicht für die Rentenversicherung bestimmt war.

(3) Beziher von Erwerbsersatzeinkommen können verlangen, dass ihnen die Zahlstelle eine Bescheinigung über das von ihr im maßgebenden Zeitraum gezahlte Erwerbsersatzeinkommen und den Zeitraum, für den es gezahlt wurde, ausstellt.

(4) Beziher von Vermögenseinkommen können verlangen, dass ihnen die Kapitalerträge nach § 20 des Einkommensteuergesetzes auszahlende Stelle eine Bescheinigung über die von ihr im letzten Kalenderjahr gezahlten Erträge ausstellt.

§ 18d
Einkommensänderungen

(1) ¹Einkommensänderungen sind erst vom nächstfolgenden 1. Juli an zu berücksichtigen; einmalig gezahltes Vermögenseinkommen ist vom Beginn des Kalendermonats an zu berücksichtigen, für den es als erzielt gilt. ²Eine Änderung des Einkommens ist auch die Änderung des zu berücksichtigenden voraussichtlichen Einkommens oder die Feststellung des tatsächlichen Einkommens nach der Berücksichtigung voraussichtlichen Einkommens.

(2) ¹ Minderungen des berücksichtigten Einkommens können vom Zeitpunkt ihres Eintritts an berücksichtigt werden, wenn das laufende Einkommen im Durchschnitt voraussichtlich um wenigstens zehn vom Hundert geringer ist als das berücksichtigte Einkommen; Erwerbsersatzeinkommen im Sinne von § 18a Absatz 3 Satz 1 Nummer 1 ist zu berücksichtigen, solange diese Leistung gezahlt wird. ²Jährliche Sonderzuwendungen sind mit einem Zwölftel zu berücksichtigen.

Section 18c
Initial determination of income

(1) The beneficiary shall provide evidence of the income to be taken into account.

(2) ¹Drawers of remuneration and comparable income may request that their employer issue them with a certificate stating the remuneration or comparable income they received for the previous calendar year and the period for which it was paid. ²The employer is not obliged to issue the certificate if he has already declared the pay to the social security fund in accordance with the provisions on the recording of data and data transmission. 3Sentence 2 does not apply if the actual pay exceeds the contribution assessment ceiling or the submitted declaration was not intended for pension insurance.

(3) Recipients of replacement income may request that the paying agency issue them with a certificate stating the replacement income paid by it in the relevant period and the period for which it was paid.

(4) Recipients of income from property may demand that the office paying out investment income under section 20 of the Income Tax Act issue them with a certificate of the income it paid in the previous calendar year.

Section 18d
Changes in income

(1) ¹Income changes shall be taken into account only from the following 1 July; property income paid on a one-off basis shall be taken into account from the beginning of the calendar month for which it is deemed to have been received. ²A change in income is also a change in the foreseeable income to be taken into account or the determination of actual income after foreseeable income has been taken into account.

(2) ¹Decreases in the income taken into account may be taken into account from the time of their occurrence if the current income is likely to be at least ten per cent lower on average than the income taken into account, income in lieu of employment within the meaning of Section 18a(3) first sentence, point 1, shall be taken into account as long as this benefit is paid. 2Annual special allowances are to be taken into account with one twelfth.

§ 18e
Ermittlung von Einkommensänderungen

(1) ¹Für Bezieher von Arbeitsentgelt und diesem vergleichbaren Einkommen hat der Arbeitgeber auf Verlangen des Versicherungsträgers das von ihnen für das letzte Kalenderjahr erzielte Arbeitsentgelt und vergleichbare Einkommen und den Zeitraum, für den es gezahlt wurde, mitzuteilen. ²Der Arbeitgeber ist zur Mitteilung nicht verpflichtet, wenn er der Sozialversicherung das Arbeitsentgelt gemäß den Vorschriften über die Erfassung von Daten und Datenübermittlung bereits gemeldet hat. ³Satz 2 gilt nicht, wenn das tatsächliche Entgelt die Beitragsbemessungsgrenze übersteigt.

(2) Bezieher von Arbeitseinkommen haben auf Verlangen des Versicherungsträgers ihr im letzten Kalenderjahr erzieltes Arbeitseinkommen und den Zeitraum, in dem es erzielt wurde, bis zum 31. März des Folgejahres mitzuteilen.

(3) Für Bezieher von Erwerbsersatzeinkommen haben die Zahlstellen auf Verlangen des Versicherungsträgers das von ihnen im maßgebenden Zeitraum gezahlte Erwerbsersatzeinkommen und den Zeitraum, für den es gezahlt wurde, mitzuteilen.

(3a) ¹Bezieher von Vermögenseinkommen haben auf Verlangen des Versicherungsträgers ihr im letzten Kalenderjahr erzieltes Einkommen mitzuteilen. ²Für Bezieher von Kapitalerträgen nach § 20 des Einkommensteuergesetzes haben die auszahlenden Stellen eine Bescheinigung über die von ihr gezahlten Erträge auszustellen.

(4) [aufgehoben]

(5) Im Fall des § 18d Absatz 2 findet § 18c für den erforderlichen Nachweis der Einkommensminderung entsprechende Anwendung.

(6) Bei der Berücksichtigung von Einkommensänderungen bedarf es nicht der vorherigen Anhörung des Berechtigten.

(7) Wird eine Rente wegen Todes wegen der Höhe des zu berücksichtigenden Einkommens nach dem 1. Juli eines jeden Jahres weiterhin in vollem Umfang nicht gezahlt, ist der Erlass eines erneuten Verwaltungsaktes nicht erforderlich.

§ 18h
Ausstellung des Sozialversicherungsausweises

(1) ¹Die Datenstelle der Rentenversicherung stellt für jede Person, für die sie eine Versicherungsnummer vergibt, einen Sozialversicherungsausweis aus, der nur folgende personenbezogene Daten über die Inhaberin oder den Inhaber enthalten darf:

Section 18e
Determination of changes in income

(1) ¹For recipients of remuneration and comparable income, the employer must, at the request of the insurance institution, provide information on the remuneration and comparable income they received for the last calendar year and the period for which it was paid. ²The employer is not obliged to notify if it has already notified the social security institution of the pay in accordance with the provisions on the collection of data and the transmission of data. ³Sentence 2 does not apply if the actual pay exceeds the contribution assessment ceiling.

(2) At the request of the insurance institution, recipients of income from employment shall, by 31 March of the following year, disclose their income from employment earned in the previous calendar year and the period in which it was earned.

(3) For recipients of income in lieu of gainful employment, the paying agencies shall, at the request of the insurance institution, disclose the income in lieu of gainful employment paid by them during the relevant period and the period for which it was paid.

(3a) ¹Drawers of property income must, at the request of the insurance institution, declare their income earned in the previous calendar year. ²For recipients of investment income under Section 20 of the Income Tax Act, the paying agencies must issue a certificate of the income paid by them.

(4) [repealed].

(5) In the case of section 18d(2), section 18c shall apply mutatis mutandis to the required proof of reduced income.

(6) The taking into account of changes in income does not require prior consultation of the person entitled.

(7) If a pension on account of death continues not to be paid in full after 1 July of each year because of the amount of income to be taken into account, the issue of a new administrative act is not required.

Section 18h
Issue of the social security card

(1) ¹The data centre of the pension insurance scheme shall issue a social security card for each person for whom it issues an insurance number, which may only contain the following personal data on the holder

1. die Versicherungsnummer,
2. den Familiennamen und den Geburtsnamen und
3. den Vornamen,
4. das Ausstellungsdatum.

[2]Die Daten zu den Nummern 1 bis 4 sind außerdem codiert aufzubringen und digital zu signieren; § 95 gilt. [3]Die Gestaltung und das Verfahren zur Ausstellung des Sozialversicherungsausweises legt die Deutsche Rentenversicherung Bund in Grundsätzen fest, die vom Bundesministerium für Arbeit und Soziales zu genehmigen und im Bundesanzeiger zu veröffentlichen sind.

(2) [1]Beschäftigte sind verpflichtet, den Sozialversicherungsausweis bei Beginn einer Beschäftigung dem Arbeitgeber vorzulegen. [2]Kann der Beschäftigte dies nicht zum Zeitpunkt des Beschäftigungsbeginns, so hat er dies unverzüglich nachzuholen.

(3) [1]Die Inhaberin oder der Inhaber ist verpflichtet, der zuständigen Einzugsstelle (§ 28i) oder dem Rentenversicherungsträger den Verlust des Sozialversicherungsausweises oder sein Wiederauffinden unverzüglich anzuzeigen. [2]Ein neuer Sozialversicherungsausweis wird ausgestellt

1. auf Antrag bei der zuständigen Einzugsstelle oder beim Rentenversicherungsträger, wenn der Sozialversicherungsausweis zerstört worden, abhanden gekommen oder unbrauchbar geworden ist,
2. von Amts wegen, wenn sich die Versicherungsnummer, der Familienname oder der Vorname geändert hat.

[3]Eine Person darf nur einen auf ihren Namen ausgestellten Sozialversicherungsausweis besitzen; unbrauchbare und weitere Sozialversicherungsausweise sind an die zuständige Einzugsstelle oder den Rentenversicherungsträger zurückzugeben.

§ 18i
Betriebsnummer für Beschäftigungsbetriebe der Arbeitgeber

(1) Der Arbeitgeber hat zur Teilnahme an den Meldeverfahren zur Sozialversicherung bei der Bundesagentur für Arbeit eine Betriebsnummer für jeden seiner Beschäftigungsbetriebe elektronisch zu beantragen.

(2) Der Arbeitgeber hat zur Vergabe der Betriebsnummer der Bundesagentur für Arbeit die dazu notwendigen Angaben, insbesondere den Namen und die Anschrift des Beschäftigungsbetriebes, den Beschäftigungsort, die wirtschaftliche Tätigkeit des Beschäftigungsbetriebes und die Rechtsform des Betriebes elektronisch zu übermitteln.

1. the insurance number,
2. the surname and maiden name, and
3. the first name,
4. the date of issue.

[2]The data for numbers 1 to 4 must also be applied in code and digitally signed; § 95 applies. [3]The design and the procedure for issuing the social insurance card shall be laid down by the Deutsche Rentenversicherung Bund in principles to be approved by the Federal Ministry of Labour and Social Affairs and published in the Federal Gazette.

(2) [1]Employees are obliged to present the social security card to their employer at the start of employment. [2]If the employee is unable to do so at the time of commencement of employment, he shall do so without delay.

(3) [1]The holder is obliged to notify the competent collection agency (Section 28i) or the pension insurance institution immediately of the loss of the social security card or its retrieval. [2]A new social security card shall be issued

1. upon application to the competent collection agency or pension insurance institution, if the social security card has been destroyed, lost or rendered unusable
2. ex officio, if the insurance number, surname or first name has changed

[3]A person may only hold a social security card issued in his or her name; unusable and other social security cards must be returned to the competent collection agency or pension insurance institution.

Section 18i
Company number for employers' employment establishments

(1) In order to participate in the social security registration procedures, the employer shall apply electronically to the Federal Employment Agency for a company number for each of its employment enterprises.

(2) In order to assign the company number, the employer shall electronically transmit to the Federal Employment Agency the necessary information, in particular the name and address of the place of employment, the place of employment, the economic activity of the place of employment and the legal form of the company.

(3) ¹Der Beschäftigungsbetrieb ist eine nach der Gemeindegrenze und der wirtschaftlichen Betätigung abgegrenzte Einheit, in der Beschäftigte für einen Arbeitgeber tätig sind. ²Für einen Arbeitgeber kann es mehrere Beschäftigungsbetriebe in einer Gemeinde geben, sofern diese Beschäftigungsbetriebe eine jeweils eigene, wirtschaftliche Einheit bilden. ³Für Beschäftigungsbetriebe desselben Arbeitgebers mit unterschiedlicher wirtschaftlicher Betätigung oder in verschiedenen Gemeinden sind jeweils eigene Betriebsnummern zu vergeben.

(4) Änderungen zu den Angaben nach Absatz 2 sowie eine Meldung im Fall der vollständigen Beendigung der Betriebstätigkeit sind vom Arbeitgeber, nach Eröffnung des Insolvenzverfahrens vom Insolvenzverwalter, unverzüglich der Bundesagentur für Arbeit durch gesicherte und verschlüsselte Datenübertragung aus systemgeprüften Programmen oder mittels maschinell erstellter Ausfüllhilfen zu übermitteln.

(5) Das Nähere zum Verfahren und zum Inhalt der zu übermittelnden Angaben, insbesondere der Datensätze, regeln die Gemeinsamen Grundsätze nach § 28b Absatz 1 Satz 1 Nummer 1 bis 3.

(6) Die Betriebsnummern und alle Angaben nach den Absätzen 2 und 4 werden bei der Bundesagentur für Arbeit in einem elektronischen Dateisystem der Beschäftigungsbetriebe gespeichert.

§ 18k
Betriebsnummer für
Beschäftigungsbetriebe weiterer
Meldepflichtiger

(1) ¹Arbeitgeber von knappschaftlichen Beschäftigungsbetrieben und von Beschäftigungsbetrieben der Seefahrt haben abweichend von § 18i Absatz 1 die Betriebsnummer bei der Deutschen Rentenversicherung Knappschaft-Bahn-See zu beantragen, die diese im Auftrag der Bundesagentur für Arbeit vergibt. ²§ 18i Absatz 4 gilt entsprechend.

(2) Für Arbeitgeber von Beschäftigten in privaten Haushalten, die eine Meldung nach § 28a Absatz 7 abzugeben haben, vergibt die Deutsche Rentenversicherung Knappschaft-Bahn-See im Auftrag der Bundesagentur für Arbeit eine Betriebsnummer bei Eingang der ersten Meldung.

(3) ¹The place of employment is a unit, delimited by municipal boundaries and economic activity, in which employees work for an employer. ²An employer may have several employment enterprises in a commune, provided that each of these employment enterprises forms a separate economic unit. ³Separate business numbers must be assigned to employment enterprises of the same employer with different economic activities or in different communes.

(4) Amendments to the information under subsection 2 and a notification in the event of the complete termination of business activity must be submitted by the employer, after the opening of insolvency proceedings by the insolvency administrator, without delay to the Federal Employment Agency by means of secure and encrypted data transmission from system-checked programmes or by means of mechanically generated completion aids.

(5) The details of the procedure and the content of the information to be transmitted, in particular the data records, shall be governed by the common principles pursuant to section 28b(1), first sentence, points 1 to 3.

(6) The business numbers and all information under subsections (2) and (4) shall be stored by the Federal Employment Agency in an electronic file system of the employing enterprises.

Section 18k
Establishment number for employment
establishments of other declarants

(1) ¹Employers of miners' employment enterprises and of maritime employment enterprises must, notwithstanding Section 18i, paragraph 1, apply to the Deutsche Rentenversicherung Knappschaft-Bahn-See (German Pension Insurance Institution for Miners' and Railway-Sea Employees) for the company number which the latter allocates on behalf of the Federal Employment Agency. ²§ 18i, subsection 4 shall apply mutatis mutandis.

(2) For employers of employees in private households who are required to submit a notification in accordance with § 28a, paragraph 7, the Deutsche Rentenversicherung Knappschaft-Bahn-See shall assign a company number on receipt of the first notification on behalf of the Federal Employment Agency.

(3) Die Deutsche Rentenversicherung Knappschaft-Bahn-See übermittelt die vergebenen Betriebsnummern mit den nach § 18i Absatz 2 erforderlichen Angaben unverzüglich nach Vergabe oder Änderung an die Datei der Beschäftigungsbetriebe der Bundesagentur für Arbeit; § 18i Absatz 6 gilt entsprechend.

(3) The Deutsche Rentenversicherung Knappschaft-Bahn-See shall transmit the allocated business numbers with the information required under Section 18i (2) to the file of employment enterprises of the Federal Employment Agency immediately after allocation or amendment; Section 18i (6) shall apply accordingly.

§ 18l
Identifikation weiterer Verfahrensbeteiligter in elektronischen Meldeverfahren

Section 18l
Identification of further parties involved in electronic notification procedures

(1) ¹Beauftragt der Arbeitgeber einen Dritten mit der Durchführung der Meldeverfahren nach diesem Gesetzbuch, hat diese Stelle unverzüglich eine Betriebsnummer nach § 18i Absatz 1 zu beantragen, soweit sie nicht schon über eine eigene Betriebsnummer verfügt. ²§ 18i Absatz 2 bis 6 gilt entsprechend.

(1) ¹If the employer commissions a third party to carry out the notification procedures under this Act, that body shall apply for a company number under section 18i(1) without delay, unless it already has its own company number. ²Section 18i (2) to (6) shall apply mutatis mutandis.

(2) ¹Sonstige Verfahrensbeteiligte haben vor Teilnahme an den Meldeverfahren nach diesem Gesetzbuch eine Betriebsnummer nach § 18i Absatz 1 zu beantragen, soweit sie nicht schon über eine eigene Betriebsnummer verfügen. ²Diese Betriebsnummer gilt in den elektronischen Übertragungsverfahren als Kennzeichnung des Verfahrensbeteiligten. ²§ 18i Absatz 2 bis 6 gilt entsprechend.

(2) ¹Other parties to the proceedings must apply for an establishment number under section 18i(1) before participating in the notification procedures under this Act, unless they already have their own establishment number. ²In electronic transmission procedures, this establishment number shall be deemed to identify the party to the procedure. 2 Article 18i paragraphs 2 to 6 shall apply mutatis mutandis.

§ 18m
Verarbeitung der Betriebsnummer

Section 18m
Processing the farm number

(1) Die Bundesagentur für Arbeit übermittelt die Betriebsnummern und die Angaben nach § 18i Absatz 2 und 4 aus dem Dateisystem der Beschäftigungsbetriebe den Leistungsträgern nach den §§ 12 und 18 bis 29 des Ersten Buches, der Künstlersozialkasse, der Datenstelle der Rentenversicherung, den berufsständischen Versorgungseinrichtungen und deren Datenannahmestelle und der Deutschen Gesetzlichen Unfallversicherung e. V. zur weiteren Verarbeitung, soweit dies für die Erfüllung ihrer Aufgaben nach diesem Gesetzbuch erforderlich ist.

(1) The Federal Employment Agency shall transmit the business numbers and the information in accordance with Section 18i (2) and (4) from the file system of the employing enterprises to the service providers in accordance with Sections 12 and 18 to 29 of Book One, the artists' social insurance fund, the data centre of the pension insurance scheme, the occupational pension schemes and their data acceptance office and the Deutsche Gesetzliche Unfallversicherung e. V. for further processing, insofar as this is necessary for the fulfilment of its tasks in accordance with this Code of Law.

(2) ¹Die Sozialversicherungsträger, ihre Verbände und ihre Arbeitsgemeinschaften, die Künstlersozialkasse, die Behörden der Zollverwaltung, soweit sie Aufgaben nach § 2 des Schwarzarbeitsbekämpfungsgesetzes oder nach § 66 des Zehnten Buches wahrnehmen, sowie die zuständigen Aufsichtsbehörden und die Arbeitgeber dürfen die Betriebsnummern speichern, verändern, nutzen, übermitteln und in der Verarbeitung einschränken, soweit dies für die Erfüllung einer Aufgabe nach diesem Gesetzbuch oder dem Künstlersozialversiche-

(2) ¹The social insurance institutions, their associations and their working groups, the artists' social insurance fund, the customs authorities, insofar as they perform tasks under Section 2 of the Act to Combat Illegal Employment or under Section 66 of the Tenth Book, as well as the competent supervisory authorities and employers may store, modify, use, transmit and restrict the processing of company numbers insofar as this is necessary for the performance of a task under this Code or the Artists' Social Insurance Act. ²Other authorities, courts or third parties

rungsgesetz erforderlich ist. [2]Andere Behörden, Gerichte oder Dritte dürfen die Betriebsnummern speichern, verändern, nutzen, übermitteln oder in der Verarbeitung einschränken, soweit dies für die Erfüllung einer gesetzlichen Aufgabe einer der in Satz 1 genannten Stellen erforderlich ist.

may store, change, use, transmit or restrict the processing of the business numbers to the extent that this is necessary for the fulfilment of a statutory task of one of the bodies mentioned in sentence 1.

§ 18n
Absendernummer

(1) Eine meldende Stelle erhält auf elektronischen Antrag bei der Vergabe eines Zertifikates zur Sicherung der Datenübertragung von der das Zertifikat ausstellenden Stelle eine Absendernummer, die der Betriebsnummer der meldenden Stelle entspricht.

(2) [1]In den Fällen, in denen eine meldende Stelle für einen Beschäftigungsbetrieb für mehr als einen Abrechnungskreis Meldungen erstatten will, erhält sie auf elektronischen Antrag bei der Vergabe eines weiteren Zertifikates zur Sicherung der Datenübertragung von der das Zertifikat ausstellenden Stelle eine gesonderte Absendernummer. [2]Für diese gesonderte achtstellige Absendernummer ist ein festgelegter alphanumerischer Nummernkreis zu nutzen. [3]Das Nähere zum Aufbau der Nummer, zu den übermittelnden Angaben und zum Verfahren regeln die Gemeinsamen Grundsätze nach § 28b Absatz 1 Satz 1 Nummer 4.

Section 18n
Sender number

(1) A notifying authority shall, upon electronic request, receive a consignor number from the authority issuing the certificate, which shall be the same as the company number of the notifying authority, when issuing an allowance for the purpose of securing data transmission.

(2) [1]In those cases in which a reporting agency wishes to submit reports for an employment enterprise for more than one accounting area, it shall receive a separate sender number from the agency issuing the certificate upon electronic application when issuing a further certificate to secure data transmission. [2]A defined alphanumeric number range must be used for this separate eight-digit sender number. [3]Details on the structure of the number, the information to be transmitted and the procedure are governed by the Common Principles under Article 28b paragraph 1 sentence 1 number 4.

§ 19
Leistungen auf Antrag oder von Amts wegen

[1]Leistungen in der gesetzlichen Kranken- und Rentenversicherung, nach dem Recht der Arbeitsförderung sowie in der sozialen Pflegeversicherung werden auf Antrag erbracht, soweit sich aus den Vorschriften für die einzelnen Versicherungszweige nichts Abweichendes ergibt. [2]Leistungen in der gesetzlichen Unfallversicherung werden von Amts wegen erbracht, soweit sich aus den Vorschriften für die gesetzliche Unfallversicherung nichts Abweichendes ergibt.

Section 19
Services on request or ex officio

[1]Services in statutory health and pension insurance, under the law on employment promotion and in social long-term care insurance shall be provided on application, unless otherwise specified in the regulations for the individual classes of insurance. [2]Services in statutory accident insurance shall be provided ex officio, unless the regulations for statutory accident insurance provide otherwise.

§ 19a
Benachteiligungsverbot

[1]Bei der Inanspruchnahme von Leistungen, die den Zugang zu allen Formen und allen Ebenen der Berufsberatung, der Berufsbildung, der beruflichen Weiterbildung, der Umschulung einschließlich der praktischen Berufserfahrung betreffen, darf niemand aus Gründen der Rasse oder wegen der ethnischen Herkunft, des Geschlechts, der Religion oder Weltanschauung, einer Behinderung, des Alters oder der

Section 19a
Prohibition of discrimination

[1] In the use of services relating to access to all forms and all levels of vocational guidance, vocational training, further vocational training, retraining, including practical work experience, no one shall be disadvantaged on grounds of racial or ethnic origin, sex, religion or belief, disability, age or sexual identity. [2]Claims may only be asserted or derived to the extent that their conditions and content are determined

sexuellen Identität benachteiligt werden. ²Ansprüche können nur insoweit geltend gemacht oder hergeleitet werden, als deren Voraussetzungen und Inhalt durch die Vorschriften der besonderen Teile dieses Gesetzbuchs im Einzelnen bestimmt sind.

§ 20
Aufbringung der Mittel, Übergangsbereich

(1) Die Mittel der Sozialversicherung einschließlich der Arbeitsförderung werden nach Maßgabe der besonderen Vorschriften für die einzelnen Versicherungszweige durch Beiträge der Versicherten, der Arbeitgeber und Dritter, durch staatliche Zuschüsse und durch sonstige Einnahmen aufgebracht.

(2) Der Übergangsbereich im Sinne dieses Gesetzbuches umfasst Arbeitsentgelte aus mehr als geringfügigen Beschäftigungen nach § 8 Absatz 1 Nummer 1, die regelmäßig 1 300 Euro im Monat nicht übersteigen; bei mehreren Beschäftigungsverhältnissen ist das insgesamt erzielte Arbeitsentgelt maßgebend.

(3) ¹Der Arbeitgeber trägt abweichend von den besonderen Vorschriften für Beschäftigte für die einzelnen Versicherungszweige den Gesamtsozialversicherungsbeitrag allein, wenn

1. Versicherte, die zu ihrer Berufsausbildung beschäftigt sind, ein Arbeitsentgelt erzielen, das auf den Monat bezogen 325 Euro nicht übersteigt, oder
2. Versicherte ein freiwilliges soziales Jahr oder ein freiwilliges ökologisches Jahr im Sinne des Jugendfreiwilligendienstegesetzes oder einen Bundesfreiwilligendienst nach dem Bundesfreiwilligendienstgesetz leisten.

²Wird infolge einmalig gezahlten Arbeitsentgelts die in Satz 1 genannte Grenze überschritten, tragen die Versicherten und die Arbeitgeber den Gesamtsozialversicherungsbeitrag von dem diese Grenze übersteigenden Teil des Arbeitsentgelts jeweils zur Hälfte; in der gesetzlichen Krankenversicherung gilt dies nur für den um den Beitragsanteil, der allein vom Arbeitnehmer zu tragen ist, reduzierten Beitrag.

§ 21
Bemessung der Beiträge

Die Versicherungsträger haben die Beiträge, soweit diese von ihnen festzusetzen sind, so zu bemessen, dass die Beiträge zusammen mit den anderen Einnahmen

1. die gesetzlich vorgeschriebenen und zugelassenen Ausgaben des Versicherungsträgers decken und

in detail by the provisions of the special parts of this Code.

Section 20
Raising of funds, transitional area

(1) Social security resources, including employment promotion, shall be provided, in accordance with the specific provisions for each class of insurance, by contributions from insured persons, employers and third parties, by State subsidies and by other revenue.

(2) The transitional area within the meaning of this Act shall include remuneration from more than marginal employment under section 8(1) (1) which does not regularly exceed EUR 1 300 per month; in the case of more than one employment relationship, the total remuneration received shall be decisive.

(3) ¹Notwithstanding the special provisions for employees for the individual classes of insurance, the employer alone shall pay the total social security contribution if

1. insured persons who are employed for the purpose of their vocational training earn a salary which does not exceed EUR 325 per month, or
2. insured persons perform a voluntary social year or a voluntary ecological year within the meaning of the Youth Voluntary Service Act or a federal voluntary service under the Federal Voluntary Service Act.

²If the limit referred to in the first sentence above is exceeded as a result of one-off pay, the insured persons and the employers shall each pay half of the total social security contribution on that part of the pay exceeding that limit; in the case of statutory health insurance, this shall apply only to the contribution reduced by the contribution share to be borne solely by the employee.

Section 21
Assessment of contributions

The insurance institutions shall set the contributions, in so far as they are to be fixed by them, in such a way that the contributions, together with other revenue

1. cover the statutory and authorised expenditure of the insurance institution, and

2. sicherstellen, dass die gesetzlich vorgeschriebenen oder zugelassenen Betriebsmittel und Rücklagen bereitgehalten werden
können.

2. ensure that the legally prescribed or approved operating resources and reserves can
be kept available.

§ 22
Entstehen der Beitragsansprüche, Zusammentreffen mehrerer Versicherungsverhältnisse

(1) [1]Die Beitragsansprüche der Versicherungsträger entstehen, sobald ihre im Gesetz oder
auf Grund eines Gesetzes bestimmten Voraussetzungen vorliegen. [2]Bei einmalig gezahltem
Arbeitsentgelt sowie bei Arbeitsentgelt, das aus
Arbeitszeitguthaben abgeleiteten Entgeltguthaben errechnet wird, entstehen die Beitragsansprüche, sobald dieses ausgezahlt worden ist.
[3]Satz 2 gilt nicht, soweit das einmalig gezahlte
Arbeitsentgelt nur wegen eines Insolvenzereignisses im Sinne des § 165 des Dritten Buches
vom Arbeitgeber nicht ausgezahlt worden ist
oder die Beiträge für aus Arbeitszeitguthaben
abgeleiteten Entgeltguthaben schon aus laufendem Arbeitsentgelt gezahlt wurden.

(2) [1]Treffen beitragspflichtige Einnahmen aus
mehreren Versicherungsverhältnissen zusammen und übersteigen sie die für das jeweilige
Versicherungsverhältnis maßgebliche Beitragsbemessungsgrenze, so vermindern sie sich zum
Zwecke der Beitragsberechnung nach dem
Verhältnis ihrer Höhe so zueinander, dass sie
zusammen höchstens die Beitragsbemessungsgrenze erreichen. [2]Die beitragspflichtigen Einnahmen aus dem jeweiligen Versicherungsverhältnis sind vor der Verhältnisrechnung nach
Satz 1 auf die maßgebliche Beitragsbemessungsgrenze zu reduzieren. [3]Für die knappschaftliche
Rentenversicherung und die allgemeine Rentenversicherung sind die Berechnungen nach Satz 1
getrennt durchzuführen.

Section 22
Arising of contribution claims, coincidence of several insurance relationships

(1) [1]The insurance institutions' contribution
claims shall arise as soon as the conditions laid
down by or pursuant to a law are met. [2]In the
case of remuneration paid on a one-off basis and
remuneration calculated on the basis of credit
balances for working hours, contribution entitlements shall arise as soon as these have been
paid out. [3]Sentence 2 does not apply if the employer has not paid the one-off remuneration
only because of an insolvency event within the
meaning of § 165 of the Third Book or if the
contributions for remuneration credit balances
derived from working time credit have already
been paid from current remuneration.

(2) [1]If income subject to contributions from
several insurance relationships comes together
and exceeds the income ceiling applicable to
the respective insurance relationship, then for
the purpose of calculating contributions it shall
be reduced in proportion to each other so that
together it does not exceed the income ceiling.
[2]The income from the respective insurance relationship that is subject to contributions shall
be reduced to the relevant income ceiling before
the ratio calculation in accordance with sentence 1. [3]The calculations in accordance with
sentence 1 must be carried out separately for
miners' pension insurance and general pension
insurance.

§ 23
Fälligkeit

(1) [1]Laufende Beiträge, die geschuldet werden, werden entsprechend den Regelungen
der Satzung der Krankenkasse und den Entscheidungen des Spitzenverbandes Bund der
Krankenkassen fällig. [2]Beiträge, die nach dem
Arbeitsentgelt oder dem Arbeitseinkommen zu
bemessen sind, sind in voraussichtlicher Höhe
der Beitragsschuld spätestens am drittletzten Bankarbeitstag des Monats fällig, in dem
die Beschäftigung oder Tätigkeit, mit der das
Arbeitsentgelt oder Arbeitseinkommen erzielt
wird, ausgeübt worden ist oder als ausgeübt gilt;
ein verbleibender Restbeitrag wird zum drittletzten Bankarbeitstag des Folgemonats fällig.

Section 23
Due date

(1) [1]Ongoing contributions that are owed are
due in accordance with the provisions of the
health insurance fund's statutes and the decisions of the central association, the Federal
Association of Health Insurance Funds. [2]Con-
tributions that are to be calculated on the basis
of salary or earned income are due in the antic-
ipated amount of the contribution debt no later
than on the third-last banking day of the month
in which the employment or activity with which
the salary or earned income is earned was or is
deemed to have been performed; any remaining
contribution is due on the third-last banking
day of the following month. [3]Notwithstanding

³Der Arbeitgeber kann abweichend von Satz 2 den Betrag in Höhe der Beiträge des Vormonats zahlen; für einen verbleibenden Restbetrag bleibt es bei der Fälligkeit zum drittletzten Bankarbeitstag des Folgemonats. ⁴Sonstige Beiträge werden spätestens am Fünfzehnten des Monats fällig, der auf den Monat folgt, für den sie zu entrichten sind. ⁵Die erstmalige Fälligkeit der Beiträge für die nach § 3 Satz 1 Nummer 1a des Sechsten Buches versicherten Pflegepersonen ist abhängig von dem Zeitpunkt, zu dem die Pflegekasse, das private Versicherungsunternehmen, die Festsetzungsstelle für die Beihilfe oder der Dienstherr bei Heilfürsorgeberechtigten die Versicherungspflicht der Pflegeperson festgestellt hat oder ohne Verschulden hätte feststellen können. ⁶Wird die Feststellung in der Zeit vom Ersten bis zum Fünfzehnten eines Monats getroffen, werden die Beiträge erstmals spätestens am Fünfzehnten des folgenden Monats fällig; wird die Feststellung in der Zeit vom Sechzehnten bis zum Ende eines Monats getroffen, werden die Beiträge erstmals am Fünfzehnten des zweiten darauffolgenden Monats fällig; das Nähere vereinbaren die Spitzenverbände der beteiligten Träger der Sozialversicherung, der Verband der privaten Krankenversicherung e. V. und die Festsetzungsstellen für die Beihilfe.

(2) ¹Die Beiträge für eine Sozialleistung im Sinne des § 3 Satz 1 Nummer 3 des Sechsten Buches einschließlich Sozialleistungen, auf die die Vorschriften des Fünften und des Sechsten Buches über die Kranken- und Rentenversicherung der Bezieher von Arbeitslosengeld oder die Krankenversicherung der Bezieher von Arbeitslosengeld II entsprechend anzuwenden sind, werden am Achten des auf die Zahlung der Sozialleistung folgenden Monats fällig. ²Die Träger der Rentenversicherung und die Bundesagentur für Arbeit können unbeschadet des Satzes 1 vereinbaren, dass die Beiträge zur Rentenversicherung aus Sozialleistungen der Bundesagentur für Arbeit zu den vom Bundesamt für Soziale Sicherung festgelegten Fälligkeitsterminen für die Rentenzahlungen im Inland gezahlt werden. ³Die Träger der Rentenversicherung mit Ausnahme der Deutschen Rentenversicherung Knappschaft-Bahn-See als Träger der knappschaftlichen Rentenversicherung, die Bundesagentur für Arbeit und die Behörden des sozialen Entschädigungsrechts können unbeschadet des Satzes 1 vereinbaren, dass die Beiträge zur Rentenversicherung und nach dem Recht der Arbeitsförderung aus Sozialleistungen nach dem sozialen Entschädigungsrecht in voraussichtlicher Höhe der Beitragsschuld spätestens zum 30. Juni des laufenden Jahres und ein verbleibender Restbetrag zum nächsten Fälligkeitstermin gezahlt werden.

sentence 2, the employer may pay the amount equal to the previous month's contributions; any remaining amount shall remain due on the third-last banking day of the following month. ⁴Other contributions shall be due no later than the fifteenth day of the month following the month for which they are due. ⁵The first due date of the contributions for carers insured in accordance with § 3 sentence 1 number 1a of Book 6 depends on the point in time at which the care insurance fund, the private insurance company, the assessment office for the allowance or the employer in the case of persons entitled to care has established the carer's obligation to be insured or could have established this without fault. ⁶If the determination is made in the period from the first to the fifteenth of a month, the contributions shall be due for the first time no later than the fifteenth of the following month; if the determination is made in the period from the sixteenth to the end of a month, the contributions shall be due for the first time on the fifteenth of the second month following; the details shall be agreed by the umbrella organisations of the participating social insurance institutions, the Verband der privaten Krankenversicherung e. V. (Association of Private Health Insurance Companies) and the assessment authorities for the allowance.

(2) ¹The contributions for a social benefit within the meaning of Section 3, first sentence, point 3 of Book Six, including social benefits to which the provisions of the Fifth and Sixth Books on health and pension insurance for recipients of unemployment benefit or health insurance for recipients of unemployment benefit II are to be applied mutatis mutandis, shall become due on the eighth day of the month following payment of the social benefit. ²The pension insurance institutions and the Federal Employment Agency may, notwithstanding the first sentence above, agree that pension insurance contributions from social benefits paid by the Federal Employment Agency shall be paid on the due dates laid down by the Federal Social Security Office for pension payments in Germany. 3The pension insurance institutions, with the exception of the Deutsche Rentenversicherung Knappschaft-Bahn-See as the institution responsible for miners' pension insurance, the Federal Employment Agency and the authorities responsible for social compensation law may, notwithstanding the first sentence, agree that the contributions to pension insurance and under the law on the promotion of employment from social benefits under social compensation law shall be paid in the expected amount of the contribution debt by 30 June of the current year at the latest and any remaining balance by the next due date.

(2a) Bei Verwendung eines Haushaltsschecks (§ 28a Absatz 7) sind die Beiträge für das in den Monaten Januar bis Juni erzielte Arbeitsentgelt am 31. Juli des laufenden Jahres und für das in den Monaten Juli bis Dezember erzielte Arbeitsentgelt am 31. Januar des folgenden Jahres fällig.

(3) ¹Geschuldete Beiträge der Unfallversicherung werden am Fünfzehnten des Monats fällig, der dem Monat folgt, in dem der Beitragsbescheid dem Zahlungspflichtigen bekannt gegeben worden ist; Entsprechendes gilt für Beitragsvorschüsse, wenn der Bescheid hierüber keinen anderen Fälligkeitstermin bestimmt. ²Die landwirtschaftliche Berufsgenossenschaft kann in ihrer Satzung von Satz 1 abweichende Fälligkeitstermine bestimmen. ³Für den Tag der Zahlung und die zulässigen Zahlungsmittel gelten die für den Gesamtsozialversicherungsbeitrag geltenden Bestimmungen entsprechend. ⁴Die Fälligkeit von Beiträgen für geringfügig Beschäftigte in Privathaushalten, die nach § 28a Absatz 7 der Einzugsstelle gemeldet worden sind, richtet sich abweichend von Satz 1 nach Absatz 2a.

(4) Besondere Vorschriften für einzelne Versicherungszweige, die von den Absätzen 1 bis 3 abweichen oder abweichende Bestimmungen zulassen, bleiben unberührt.

§ 23a
Einmalig gezahltes Arbeitsentgelt als beitragspflichtige Einnahmen

(1) ¹Einmalig gezahltes Arbeitsentgelt sind Zuwendungen, die dem Arbeitsentgelt zuzurechnen sind und nicht für die Arbeit in einem einzelnen Entgeltabrechnungszeitraum gezahlt werden. ²Als einmalig gezahltes Arbeitsentgelt gelten nicht Zuwendungen nach Satz 1, wenn sie

1. üblicherweise zur Abgeltung bestimmter Aufwendungen des Beschäftigten, die auch im Zusammenhang mit der Beschäftigung stehen,
2. als Waren oder Dienstleistungen, die vom Arbeitgeber nicht überwiegend für den Bedarf seiner Beschäftigten hergestellt, vertrieben oder erbracht werden und monatlich in Anspruch genommen werden können,
3. als sonstige Sachbezüge, die monatlich gewährt werden, oder
4. als vermögenswirksame Leistungen vom Arbeitgeber erbracht werden.

³Einmalig gezahltes Arbeitsentgelt ist dem Entgeltabrechnungszeitraum zuzuordnen, in dem es gezahlt wird, soweit die Absätze 2 und 4 nichts Abweichendes bestimmen.

(2a) If a budget cheque is used (Section 28a(7)), contributions shall be due on 31 July of the current year for pay earned in the months of January to June and on 31 January of the following year for pay earned in the months of July to December.

(3) ¹Accident insurance contributions due shall be due on the fifteenth day of the month following the month in which the party liable to pay the contributions is notified of the notice of assessment; the same shall apply mutatis mutandis to advance contributions if the notice of assessment does not specify any other due date. ²The agricultural employers' liability insurance association may specify in its statutes due dates that differ from those in sentence 1. ³The provisions applicable to the total social security contribution shall apply mutatis mutandis to the date of payment and the means of payment permitted. ⁴The due date for contributions for marginally employed persons in private households who have been registered with the collection agency in accordance with Article 28a paragraph 7 shall be determined in accordance with paragraph 2a, notwithstanding sentence 1.

(4) Special provisions for individual classes of insurance which deviate from subsections 1 to 3 or permit different provisions shall remain unaffected.

Section 23a
One-off payments as income subject to contributions

(1) ¹Salary paid in a single payment is a benefit which is part of the salary and is not paid for work done in a single pay period. ²Benefits in accordance with sentence 1 shall not be deemed to be one-off pay if they

1. usually to compensate for certain expenses of the employee, which are also related to employment
2. as goods or services which are not produced, distributed or provided by the employer predominantly for the needs of his employees and which can be consumed on a monthly basis
3. as other benefits in kind granted monthly, or
4. are provided as capital-forming benefits by the employer.

³Salary paid in a single payment shall be allocated to the payroll period in which it is paid, unless paragraphs 2 and 4 provide otherwise.

(2) Einmalig gezahltes Arbeitsentgelt, das nach Beendigung oder bei Ruhen des Beschäftigungsverhältnisses gezahlt wird, ist dem letzten Entgeltabrechnungszeitraum des laufenden Kalenderjahres zuzuordnen, auch wenn dieser nicht mit Arbeitsentgelt belegt ist.

(3) ¹Das einmalig gezahlte Arbeitsentgelt ist bei der Feststellung des beitragspflichtigen Arbeitsentgelts für Beschäftigte zu berücksichtigen, soweit das bisher gezahlte beitragspflichtige Arbeitsentgelt die anteilige Beitragsbemessungsgrenze nicht erreicht. ²Die anteilige Beitragsbemessungsgrenze ist der Teil der Beitragsbemessungsgrenze, der der Dauer aller Beschäftigungsverhältnisse bei demselben Arbeitgeber im laufenden Kalenderjahr bis zum Ablauf des Entgeltabrechnungszeitraumes entspricht, dem einmalig gezahltes Arbeitsentgelt zuzuordnen ist; auszunehmen sind Zeiten, die nicht mit Beiträgen aus laufendem (nicht einmalig gezahltem) Arbeitsentgelt belegt sind.

(4) ¹In der Zeit vom 1. Januar bis zum 31. März einmalig gezahltes Arbeitsentgelt ist dem letzten Entgeltabrechnungszeitraum des vergangenen Kalenderjahres zuzuordnen, wenn es vom Arbeitgeber dieses Entgeltabrechnungszeitraumes gezahlt wird und zusammen mit dem sonstigen für das laufende Kalenderjahr festgestellten beitragspflichtigen Arbeitsentgelt die anteilige Beitragsbemessungsgrenze nach Absatz 3 Satz 2 übersteigt. ²Satz 1 gilt nicht für nach dem 31. März einmalig gezahltes Arbeitsentgelt, das nach Absatz 2 einem in der Zeit vom 1. Januar bis zum 31. März liegenden Entgeltabrechnungszeitraum zuzuordnen ist.

(5) Ist der Beschäftigte in der gesetzlichen Krankenversicherung pflichtversichert, ist für die Zuordnung des einmalig gezahlten Arbeitsentgelts nach Absatz 4 Satz 1 allein die Beitragsbemessungsgrenze der gesetzlichen Krankenversicherung maßgebend.

(2) Non-recurring remuneration paid after termination or suspension of the employment relationship shall be allocated to the last payroll period of the current calendar year, even if it is not subject to remuneration.

(3) ¹The one-off pay is to be taken into account when determining the contributory pay for employees if the contributory pay paid to date does not reach the pro rata income threshold. ²The pro rata income threshold is that part of the income threshold which corresponds to the duration of all employment relationships with the same employer in the current calendar year until the end of the payroll period to which one-off pay is to be allocated; periods which are not covered by contributions from current (non one-off) pay are excluded.

(4) ¹Earnings paid once in the period from 1 January to 31 March are to be assigned to the last payroll period of the previous calendar year if they are paid by the employer in this payroll period and, together with the other earnings subject to contributions determined for the current calendar year, exceed the pro rata income threshold in accordance with paragraph 3 sentence 2. ²Sentence 1 shall not apply to remuneration paid once after 31 March which, in accordance with paragraph 2, is to be allocated to a payroll period between 1 January and 31 March

(5) If the employee is compulsorily insured in the statutory health insurance scheme, only the contribution assessment ceiling of the statutory health insurance scheme shall be decisive for the allocation of the one-off remuneration paid under subsection 4, first sentence.

§ 23b
Beitragspflichtige Einnahmen bei flexiblen Arbeitszeitregelungen

(1) ¹Bei Vereinbarungen nach § 7b ist für Zeiten der tatsächlichen Arbeitsleistung und für Zeiten der Inanspruchnahme des Wertguthabens nach § 7c das in dem jeweiligen Zeitraum fällige Arbeitsentgelt als Arbeitsentgelt im Sinne des § 23 Absatz 1 maßgebend. ²Im Falle des § 23a Absatz 3 und 4 gilt das in dem jeweils maßgebenden Zeitraum erzielte Arbeitsentgelt bis zu einem Betrag in Höhe der Beitragsbemessungsgrenze als bisher gezahltes beitragspflichtiges Arbeitsentgelt; in Zeiten einer Freistellung von der Arbeitsleistung tritt an die Stelle des erzielten Arbeitsentgelts das fällige Arbeitsentgelt.

Section 23b
Contributable income under flexible working time arrangements

(1) ¹In the case of agreements under Section 7b, the remuneration due in the respective period shall be deemed to be the remuneration within the meaning of Section 23(1) for periods of actual work performance and for periods of use of the credit balance under Section 7c. ²In the case of § 23a paragraphs 3 and 4, the pay earned in the relevant period shall be deemed to be the pay subject to contribution payment up to an amount equal to the income threshold; in periods of exemption from work, the pay due shall replace the pay earned.

(2) [1]Soweit das Wertguthaben nicht gemäß § 7c verwendet wird, insbesondere

1. nicht laufend für eine Zeit der Freistellung von der Arbeitsleistung oder der Verringerung der vertraglich vereinbarten Arbeitszeit in Anspruch genommen wird oder

2. nicht mehr für solche Zeiten gezahlt werden kann, da das Beschäftigungsverhältnis vorzeitig beendet wurde,

ist als Arbeitsentgelt im Sinne des § 23 Absatz 1 ohne Berücksichtigung einer Beitragsbemessungsgrenze die Summe der Arbeitsentgelte maßgebend, die zum Zeitpunkt der tatsächlichen Arbeitsleistung ohne Berücksichtigung der Vereinbarung nach § 7b beitragspflichtig gewesen wäre. [2]Maßgebend ist jedoch höchstens der Betrag des Wertguthabens aus diesen Arbeitsentgelten zum Zeitpunkt der nicht zweckentsprechenden Verwendung des Arbeitsentgelts. [3]Zugrunde zu legen ist der Zeitraum ab dem Abrechnungsmonat der ersten Gutschrift auf einem Wertguthaben bis zum Zeitpunkt der nicht zweckentsprechenden Verwendung des Arbeitsentgelts. [4]Bei einem nach § 7f Absatz 1 Satz 1 Nummer 2 auf die Deutsche Rentenversicherung Bund übertragenen Wertguthaben gelten die Sätze 1 bis 3 entsprechend, soweit das Wertguthaben wegen der Inanspruchnahme einer Rente wegen verminderter Erwerbsfähigkeit, einer Rente wegen Alters oder wegen des Todes des Versicherten nicht mehr in Anspruch genommen werden kann. [5]Wird das Wertguthaben vereinbarungsgemäß an einen bestimmten Wertmaßstab gebunden, ist der im Zeitpunkt der nicht zweckentsprechenden Verwendung des Arbeitsentgelts maßgebende angepasste Betrag als Höchstbetrag der Berechnung zugrunde zu legen. [6]Im Falle der Insolvenz des Arbeitgebers gilt auch als beitragspflichtiges Arbeitsentgelt höchstens der Betrag, der als Arbeitsentgelt den gezahlten Beiträgen zugrunde liegt. [7]Für die Berechnung der Beiträge sind der für den Entgeltabrechnungszeitraum nach den Sätzen 8 und 9 für den einzelnen Versicherungszweig geltende Beitragssatz und die für diesen Zeitraum für den Einzug des Gesamtsozialversicherungsbeitrags zuständige Einzugsstelle maßgebend; für Beschäftigte, die bei keiner Krankenkasse versichert sind, gilt § 28i Satz 2 entsprechend. [8]Die Beiträge sind mit den Beiträgen der Entgeltabrechnung für den Kalendermonat fällig, der dem Kalendermonat folgt, in dem

1. im Fall der Insolvenz die Mittel für die Beitragszahlung verfügbar sind,

2. das Arbeitsentgelt nicht zweckentsprechend verwendet wird.

(2) [1]Insofar as the credit balance is not used in accordance with § 7c, in particular

1. is not continuously used for a period of time off work or a reduction of the contractually agreed working time or

2. can no longer be paid for such periods because the employment relationship was terminated prematurely,

the pay within the meaning of section 23(1) without taking into account an assessment ceiling shall be the sum of the earnings which, at the time of actual performance of work, would have been subject to contributions under section 7b without taking into account the agreement under section 7b. [2]However, no more than the amount of the credit balance from this pay at the time of the improper use of the pay shall be decisive. [3]The period from the month of settlement of the first credit to a credit balance until the time of the improper use of the remuneration shall be taken as the basis. [4]In the case of a credit balance transferred to the Deutsche Rentenversicherung Bund in accordance with § 7f paragraph 1 sentence 1 number 2, sentences 1 to 3 shall apply mutatis mutandis if the credit balance can no longer be used because the insured person is drawing a pension due to reduced earning capacity, a pension due to old age or due to his death. [5]If, as agreed, the credit balance is tied to a certain value standard, the adjusted amount applicable at the time of the inappropriate use of the salary is to be taken as the maximum amount for the calculation. [6]In the event of the employer's insolvency, the maximum amount of remuneration subject to contributions shall also be the amount on which the contributions paid are based as remuneration. [7]For the calculation of contributions, the contribution rate applicable for the payroll period in accordance with sentences 8 and 9 for the individual insurance branch and the collection agency responsible for collecting the total social security contribution for this period shall be decisive; Section 28i sentence 2 shall apply mutatis mutandis to employees who are not insured with any health insurance fund. [8]Contributions shall be due with the contributions in the pay slip for the calendar month following the calendar month in which

1. in the event of insolvency, the funds are available for the payment of contributions

2. the remuneration is not used for the intended purpose.

[9]Wird durch einen Bescheid eines Trägers der Rentenversicherung der Eintritt von verminderter Erwerbsfähigkeit festgestellt, gilt der Zeitpunkt des Eintritts der verminderten Erwerbsfähigkeit als Zeitpunkt der nicht zweckentsprechenden Verwendung des bis dahin erzielten Wertguthabens; in diesem Fall sind die Beiträge mit den Beiträgen der auf das Ende des Beschäftigungsverhältnisses folgenden Entgeltabrechnung fällig. [10]Wird eine Rente wegen verminderter Erwerbsfähigkeit in Anspruch genommen und besteht ein nach § 7f Absatz 1 Satz 1 Nummer 2 an die Deutsche Rentenversicherung Bund übertragenes Wertguthaben, kann der Versicherte der Auflösung dieses Wertguthabens widersprechen. [11]Ist für den Fall der Insolvenz des Arbeitgebers ein Dritter Schuldner des Arbeitsentgelts, erfüllt dieser insoweit die Pflichten des Arbeitgebers.

(2a) [1]Als Arbeitsentgelt im Sinne des § 23 Absatz 1 gilt im Falle des Absatzes 2 auch der positive Betrag, der sich ergibt, wenn die Summe der ab dem Abrechnungsmonat der ersten Gutschrift auf ein Wertguthaben für die Zeit der Arbeitsleistung maßgebenden Beträge der jeweiligen Beitragsbemessungsgrenze um die Summe der in dieser Zeit der Arbeitsleistung abgerechneten beitragspflichtigen Arbeitsentgelte gemindert wird, höchstens der Betrag des Wertguthabens im Zeitpunkt der nicht zweckentsprechenden Verwendung des Arbeitsentgelts. [2]Absatz 2 Satz 5 bis 11 findet Anwendung, Absatz 1 Satz 2 findet keine Anwendung.

(3) Kann das Wertguthaben wegen Beendigung des Beschäftigungsverhältnisses nicht mehr nach § 7c oder § 7f Absatz 2 Satz 1 verwendet werden und ist der Versicherte unmittelbar anschließend wegen Arbeitslosigkeit bei einer deutschen Agentur für Arbeit als Arbeitsuchender gemeldet und bezieht eine öffentlich-rechtliche Leistung oder nur wegen des zu berücksichtigenden Einkommens oder Vermögens nicht, sind die Beiträge spätestens sieben Kalendermonate nach dem Kalendermonat, in dem das Arbeitsentgelt nicht zweckentsprechend verwendet worden ist, oder bei Aufnahme einer Beschäftigung in diesem Zeitraum zum Zeitpunkt des Beschäftigungsbeginns fällig, es sei denn, eine zweckentsprechende Verwendung wird vereinbart; beginnt in diesem Zeitraum eine Rente wegen Alters oder Todes oder tritt verminderte Erwerbsfähigkeit ein, gelten diese Zeitpunkte als Zeitpunkt der nicht zweckentsprechenden Verwendung.

[9]If a decision by a pension insurance institution establishes the occurrence of reduced earning capacity, the date of occurrence of the reduced earning capacity shall be deemed to be the date of the inappropriate use of the credit balance achieved up to that point; in this case, the contributions shall be due together with the contributions to the payroll statement following the end of the employment relationship. [10]If a pension is claimed due to reduced earning capacity and if a credit balance transferred to the Deutsche Rentenversicherung Bund in accordance with § 7f paragraph 1 sentence 1 number 2 exists, the insured person may object to the dissolution of this credit balance. [11]If, in the event of the employer's insolvency, a third party is the debtor of the salary, this third party shall fulfil the employer's obligations in this respect.

(2a) [1]In the case of subsection (2), pay within the meaning of section 23(1) is also deemed to be the positive amount that results if the sum of the amounts of the respective income threshold applicable from the accounting month in which the first credit balance is credited to a credit balance for the period in which the work is performed is reduced by the sum of the earnings subject to compulsory contributions that are accounted for during this period in which the work is performed, up to a maximum of the amount of the credit balance at the time of the improper use of the pay. [2]Sentences 5 to 11 of subsection 2 shall apply; subsection 1 sentence 2 shall not apply.

(3) If the value credit can no longer be used in accordance with § 7c or § 7f paragraph 2 sentence 1 due to termination of the employment relationship and if the insured person is immediately afterwards registered as a jobseeker with a German employment agency due to unemployment and does not receive a benefit under public law or only because of the income or assets to be taken into account, the contributions shall be due at the latest seven calendar months after the calendar month in which the remuneration was not used for the intended purpose or, if employment is taken up during this period, at the time of commencement of employment, unless an appropriate use is agreed; If a pension due to old age or death or reduced earning capacity commences during this period, these dates shall be deemed to be the date of the inappropriate use.

(3a) ¹Sieht die Vereinbarung nach § 7b bereits bei ihrem Abschluss für den Fall, dass Wertguthaben wegen der Beendigung der Beschäftigung auf Grund verminderter Erwerbsfähigkeit, des Erreichens einer Altersgrenze, zu der eine Rente wegen Alters beansprucht werden kann, oder des Todes des Beschäftigten nicht mehr für Zeiten einer Freistellung von der Arbeitsleistung oder der Verringerung der vertraglich vereinbarten Arbeitszeit verwendet werden können, deren Verwendung für Zwecke der betrieblichen Altersversorgung vor, gilt das bei Eintritt dieser Fälle für Zwecke der betrieblichen Altersversorgung verwendete Wertguthaben nicht als beitragspflichtiges Arbeitsentgelt; dies gilt nicht,

1. wenn die Vereinbarung über die betriebliche Altersversorgung eine Abfindung vorsieht oder zulässt oder Leistungen im Falle des Todes, der Invalidität und des Erreichens einer Altersgrenze, zu der eine Rente wegen Alters beansprucht werden kann, nicht gewährleistet sind oder
2. soweit bereits im Zeitpunkt der Ansammlung des Wertguthabens vorhersehbar ist, dass es nicht für Zwecke nach § 7c oder § 7f Absatz 2 Satz 1 verwendet werden kann.

²Die Bestimmungen dieses Absatzes finden keine Anwendung auf Vereinbarungen, die nach dem 13. November 2008 geschlossen worden sind.

(4) Werden Wertguthaben auf Dritte übertragen, gelten die Absätze 2 bis 3a nur für den Übertragenden, der die Arbeitsleistung tatsächlich erbringt.

§ 23c
Sonstige nicht beitragspflichtige Einnahmen

(1) ¹Zuschüsse des Arbeitgebers zum Krankengeld, Verletztengeld, Übergangsgeld, Pflegeunterstützungsgeld oder Krankentagegeld und sonstige Einnahmen aus einer Beschäftigung, die für die Zeit des Bezuges von Krankengeld, Krankentagegeld, Versorgungskrankengeld, Verletztengeld, Übergangsgeld, Pflegeunterstützungsgeld, Mutterschaftsgeld, Erziehungsgeld oder Elterngeld weiter erzielt werden, gelten nicht als beitragspflichtiges Arbeitsentgelt, wenn die Einnahmen zusammen mit den genannten Sozialleistungen das Nettoarbeitsentgelt (§ 47 des Fünften Buches) nicht um mehr als 50 Euro im Monat übersteigen. ²Zur Berechnung des Nettoarbeitsentgelts bei freiwilligen Mitgliedern der gesetzlichen Krankenversicherung ist der um den Beitragszuschuss für Beschäftigte verminderte Beitrag des Ver-

(3a) ¹If the agreement pursuant to § 7b already provides at the time of its conclusion for the use of credit balances for the purposes of occupational pension schemes in the event that credit balances can no longer be used for periods of exemption from work or reduction of the contractually agreed working time due to the termination of employment on account of reduced earning capacity, the reaching of an age limit at which a pension on account of old age can be claimed or the death of the employee, the credit balances used for the purposes of occupational pension schemes at the time of the occurrence of these cases shall not be regarded as remuneration subject to contributions; this shall not apply,

1. if the agreement on occupational pension schemes provides for or allows for a severance payment or if benefits in the event of death, disability or the reaching of an age limit at which an old-age pension can be claimed are not guaranteed, or
2. f it is already foreseeable at the time of accumulation of the credit balance that it cannot be used for purposes pursuant to section 7c or section 7f (2) sentence 1.

²The provisions of this paragraph do not apply to agreements concluded after 13 November 2008.

(4) If assets are transferred to third parties, subsections 2 to 3a shall apply only to the transferor who actually performs the work.

Section 23c
Other revenue not subject to contributions

(1) ¹Subsidies paid by the employer towards sickness benefit, injury benefit, transitional allowance, care allowance or daily sickness benefit and other income from employment which is received for the period of receipt of sickness benefit, daily sickness benefit, care allowance, injury benefit, transitional allowance, Nursing care allowance, maternity allowance, child-raising allowance or parental allowance are not regarded as earnings subject to contributions if the income, together with the above-mentioned social benefits, does not exceed net earnings (§ 47 of Book 5) by more than 50 euros per month. ²For the purpose of calculating net pay in the case of voluntary members of the statutory health insurance scheme, the insured person's contribution to health and long-term care insurance, reduced by the contribution al-

sicherten zur Kranken- und Pflegeversicherung abzuziehen; dies gilt entsprechend für Personen und für ihre nicht selbstversicherten Angehörigen, die bei einem privaten Krankenversicherungsunternehmen versichert sind einschließlich der Versicherung für das Krankentagegeld. [3]Für Beschäftigte, die nach § 6 Absatz 1 Satz 1 Nummer 1 des Sechsten Buches von der Versicherungspflicht befreit sind und Pflichtbeiträge an eine berufsständische Versorgungseinrichtung entrichten, sind bei der Ermittlung des Nettoentgeltes die um den Arbeitgeberzuschuss nach § 172a des Sechsten Buches verminderten Pflichtbeiträge des Beschäftigten entsprechend abzuziehen.

(2) [1]Einnahmen aus Tätigkeiten als Notärztin oder Notarzt im Rettungsdienst sind nicht beitragspflichtig, wenn diese Tätigkeiten neben

1. einer Beschäftigung mit einem Umfang von regelmäßig mindestens 15 Stunden wöchentlich außerhalb des Rettungsdienstes oder
2. einer Tätigkeit als zugelassener Vertragsarzt oder als Arzt in privater Niederlassung

[2]Für Tätigkeiten, bei denen die Einnahmen nach Satz 1 nicht beitragspflichtig sind, bestehen keine Meldepflichten nach diesem Buch.

§ 24
Säumniszuschlag

(1) [1]Für Beiträge und Beitragsvorschüsse, die der Zahlungspflichtige nicht bis zum Ablauf des Fälligkeitstages gezahlt hat, ist für jeden angefangenen Monat der Säumnis ein Säumniszuschlag von eins vom Hundert des rückständigen, auf 50 Euro nach unten abgerundeten Betrages zu zahlen. [2]Bei einem rückständigen Betrag unter 100 Euro ist der Säumniszuschlag nicht zu erheben, wenn dieser gesondert schriftlich anzufordern wäre.

(2) Wird eine Beitragsforderung durch Bescheid mit Wirkung für die Vergangenheit festgestellt, ist ein darauf entfallender Säumniszuschlag nicht zu erheben, soweit der Beitragsschuldner glaubhaft macht, dass er unverschuldet keine Kenntnis von der Zahlungspflicht hatte.

(3) [1]Hat der Zahlungspflichtige ein Lastschriftmandat zum Einzug der Beiträge erteilt, so sind Säumniszuschläge zu erheben, wenn der Beitragseinzug aus Gründen, die vom Zahlungspflichtigen zu vertreten sind, nicht ausgeführt werden kann oder zurückgerufen wird. [2]Zusätzlich zum Säumniszuschlag soll der Gläubiger vom Zahlungspflichtigen den Ersatz der von einem Geldinstitut erhobenen Entgelte für Rück-

lowance for employees, shall be deducted; this shall apply mutatis mutandis to persons and their non-self-insured dependants who are insured with a private health insurance company, including insurance for daily sickness benefit. [3]For employees who are exempt from compulsory insurance under Article 6 paragraph 1 sentence 1 number 1 of Book 6 and who pay compulsory contributions to a professional pension scheme, the employee's compulsory contributions reduced by the employer's allowance under Article 172a of Book 6 shall be deducted accordingly when calculating net pay.

(2) [1]Earnings from activities as an emergency physician in the emergency services are not subject to contributions if these activities are carried out in addition

1. a job involving at least 15 hours of regular work per week outside the emergency services, or
2. an activity as an authorised panel doctor or as a doctor in private practice

[2]For activities for which the income in accordance with sentence 1 is not subject to contributions, there is no obligation to report under this book.

Section 24
Late fee

(1) [1]For contributions and contribution advances not paid by the payer by the end of the due date, a late payment surcharge of one percent of the amount in arrears, rounded down to the nearest 50 euros, shall be payable for each month or part thereof. [2]For an amount in arrears of less than EUR 100, the late payment surcharge shall not be levied if it would have to be requested separately in writing.

(2) If a claim for contributions is established by notice with effect for the past, no surcharge for late payment shall be levied if the party liable to pay the contributions substantiates that he had no knowledge of the payment obligation through no fault of his own.

(3) [1]If the debtor has issued a direct debit mandate for the collection of contributions, surcharges for late payment shall be levied if the collection of contributions cannot be executed or is recalled for reasons for which the debtor is responsible. [2]In addition to the surcharge for late payment, the creditor shall require the debtor to reimburse the fees charged by a financial institution for returned direct debits; this

lastschriften verlangen; dieser Kostenersatz ist wie die Gebühren, die im Zusammenhang mit der Durchsetzung von Beitragsansprüchen erhoben werden, zu behandeln.

reimbursement of costs shall be treated in the same way as fees charged in connection with the enforcement of contribution claims.

§ 25
Verjährung

(1) ¹Ansprüche auf Beiträge verjähren in vier Jahren nach Ablauf des Kalenderjahrs, in dem sie fällig geworden sind. ²Ansprüche auf vorsätzlich vorenthaltene Beiträge verjähren in dreißig Jahren nach Ablauf des Kalenderjahrs, in dem sie fällig geworden sind.

(2) ¹Für die Hemmung, die Ablaufhemmung, den Neubeginn und die Wirkung der Verjährung gelten die Vorschriften des Bürgerlichen Gesetzbuchs sinngemäß. ²Die Verjährung ist für die Dauer einer Prüfung beim Arbeitgeber gehemmt; diese Hemmung der Verjährung bei einer Prüfung gilt auch gegenüber den auf Grund eines Werkvertrages für den Arbeitgeber tätigen Nachunternehmern und deren weiteren Nachunternehmern. ³Satz 2 gilt nicht, wenn die Prüfung unmittelbar nach ihrem Beginn für die Dauer von mehr als sechs Monaten aus Gründen unterbrochen wird, die die prüfende Stelle zu vertreten hat. ⁴Die Hemmung beginnt mit dem Tag des Beginns der Prüfung beim Arbeitgeber oder bei der vom Arbeitgeber mit der Lohn- und Gehaltsabrechnung beauftragten Stelle und endet mit der Bekanntgabe des Beitragsbescheides, spätestens nach Ablauf von sechs Kalendermonaten nach Abschluss der Prüfung. ⁵Kommt es aus Gründen, die die prüfende Stelle nicht zu vertreten hat, zu einem späteren Beginn der Prüfung, beginnt die Hemmung mit dem von dem Versicherungsträger in seiner Prüfungsankündigung ursprünglich bestimmten Tag. ⁶Die Sätze 2 bis 5 gelten für Prüfungen der Beitragszahlung bei sonstigen Versicherten, in Fällen der Nachversicherung und bei versicherungspflichtigen Selbständigen entsprechend. ⁷Die Sätze 1 bis 5 gelten entsprechend für Prüfungen im Bereich der Bemessung, Entrichtung und Weiterleitung von Beiträgen zur gesetzlichen Krankenversicherung.

Section 25
Limitation period

(1) ¹Claims for contributions shall lapse four years after the end of the calendar year in which they became due. ²Claims for intentionally withheld contributions shall lapse thirty years after the end of the calendar year in which they became due.

(2) ¹For the suspension of expiration, the recommencement and the effect of the cimitation period the provitions of the German Civil Code shall apply. ²The statute of limitations is suspended for the duration of an audit at the employer's premises; this suspension of the statute of limitations during an audit also applies to subcontractors and their further subcontractors working for the employer on the basis of a contract for work and services. ³Sentence 2 shall not apply if the audit is interrupted immediately after its commencement for a period of more than six months for reasons for which the auditing agency is responsible. ⁴The suspension shall begin on the day the audit begins at the employer or at the office commissioned by the employer with payroll accounting and shall end on notification of the notice of contribution, at the latest six calendar months after the audit has been completed. ⁵If the examination is commenced at a later date for reasons for which the examining agency is not responsible, the suspension shall begin on the date originally specified by the insurer in its announcement of the examination. ⁶Sentences 2 to 5 shall apply mutatis mutandis to examinations of the payment of contributions for other insured persons, in cases of supplementary insurance and for self-employed persons subject to compulsory insurance. ⁷Sentences 1 to 5 shall apply mutatis mutandis to examinations in the area of assessment, payment and forwarding of contributions to statutory health insurance.

§ 26
Beanstandung und Erstattung zu Unrecht entrichteter Beiträge

(1) ¹Sind Pflichtbeiträge in der Rentenversicherung für Zeiten nach dem 31. Dezember 1972 trotz Fehlens der Versicherungspflicht nicht spätestens bei der nächsten Prüfung beim Arbeitgeber beanstandet worden, gilt § 45 Absatz 2 des Zehnten Buches entsprechend. ²Beiträge, die nicht mehr beanstandet werden dürfen,

Section 26
Complaints and reimbursement of unduly paid contributions

(1) ¹If compulsory contributions to the pension insurance scheme for periods after 31 December 1972 have not been objected to by the employer at the latest at the next examination despite the absence of compulsory insurance, Section 45(2) of Book 10 shall apply mutatis mutandis. ²Contributions that may no longer be objected to are

gelten als zu Recht entrichtete Pflichtbeiträge. ³Gleiches gilt für zu Unrecht entrichtete Beiträge nach Ablauf der in § 27 Absatz 2 Satz 1 bestimmten Frist.

(2) Zu Unrecht entrichtete Beiträge sind zu erstatten, es sei denn, dass der Versicherungsträger bis zur Geltendmachung des Erstattungsanspruchs auf Grund dieser Beiträge oder für den Zeitraum, für den die Beiträge zu Unrecht entrichtet worden sind, Leistungen erbracht oder zu erbringen hat; Beiträge, die für Zeiten entrichtet worden sind, die während des Bezugs von Leistungen beitragsfrei sind, sind jedoch zu erstatten.

(3) ¹Der Erstattungsanspruch steht dem zu, der die Beiträge getragen hat. ²Soweit dem Arbeitgeber Beiträge, die er getragen hat, von einem Dritten ersetzt worden sind, entfällt sein Erstattungsanspruch.

(4) ¹In den Fällen, in denen eine Mehrfachbeschäftigung vorliegt und nicht auszuschließen ist, dass die Voraussetzungen des § 22 Absatz 2 vorliegen, hat die Einzugsstelle nach Eingang der Entgeltmeldungen von Amts wegen die Ermittlung einzuleiten, ob Beiträge zu Unrecht entrichtet wurden. ²Die Einzugsstelle kann weitere Angaben zur Ermittlung der zugrunde zu legenden Entgelte von den Meldepflichtigen anfordern. ³Die elektronische Anforderung hat durch gesicherte und verschlüsselte Datenübertragung zu erfolgen. ⁴Dies gilt auch für die Rückübermittlung der ermittelten Gesamtentgelte an die Meldepflichtigen. ⁵Die Einzugsstelle hat das Verfahren innerhalb von zwei Monaten nach Vorliegen aller insoweit erforderlichen Meldungen abzuschließen. ⁶Das Verfahren gilt für Abrechnungszeiträume ab dem 1. Januar 2015. ⁷Das Nähere zum Verfahren, zu den zu übermittelnden Daten sowie den Datensätzen regeln die Gemeinsamen Grundsätze nach § 28b Absatz 1.

§ 27
Verzinsung und Verjährung des Erstattungsanspruchs

(1) ¹Der Erstattungsanspruch ist nach Ablauf eines Kalendermonats nach Eingang des vollständigen Erstattungsantrags, beim Fehlen eines Antrags nach der Bekanntgabe der Entscheidung über die Erstattung bis zum Ablauf des Kalendermonats vor der Zahlung mit vier vom Hundert zu verzinsen. ²Verzinst werden volle Euro-Beträge. ³Dabei ist der Kalendermonat mit dreißig Tagen zugrunde zu legen.

deemed to be compulsory contributions that have been rightly paid. ³The same shall apply to contributions paid unjustly after expiry of the period specified in Article 27 paragraph 2 sentence 1.

(2) Unjustified contributions shall be reimbursed unless the insurer has paid or is required to pay benefits on the basis of such contributions or for the period for which the contributions were unjustifiably paid until the claim for reimbursement is asserted; however, contributions paid for periods which are non-contributory while benefits are being received shall be reimbursed.

(3) ¹The right to reimbursement is vested in the person who has paid the contributions. ²If the employer has been reimbursed by a third party for contributions paid by him, his right to reimbursement shall cease.

(4) ¹In cases of multiple employment, where it cannot be excluded that the conditions set out in Section 22(2) are met, the collection agency shall, after receipt of the salary notifications, initiate an ex officio investigation into whether contributions have been paid unlawfully. ²The collection agency may request further information from the persons obliged to report in order to determine the charges to be taken as a basis. ³The electronic request must be made by means of secure and encrypted data transmission. ⁴This also applies to the return transmission of the total charges determined to the parties required to register. ⁵The collection agency must complete the procedure within two months of all the notifications required in this respect. ⁶The procedure shall apply to accounting periods from 1 January 2015. 7 Details of the procedure, the data to be transmitted and the data records shall be governed by the common principles under Article 28b paragraph 1.

Section 27
Interest and limitation of the right to reimbursement

(1) ¹ Interest at the rate of four percent shall be payable on the refund claim at the end of one calendar month following receipt of the complete refund application, or, in the absence of an application following notification of the decision on the refund, at the end of the calendar month preceding payment. ²Interest shall be paid on full amounts in euro. ³The calendar month is to be taken as the basis for this calculation, with thirty days.

(2) ¹Der Erstattungsanspruch verjährt in vier Jahren nach Ablauf des Kalenderjahrs, in dem die Beiträge entrichtet worden sind. ²Beanstandet der Versicherungsträger die Rechtswirksamkeit von Beiträgen, beginnt die Verjährung mit dem Ablauf des Kalenderjahrs der Beanstandung.

(3) ¹Für die Hemmung, die Ablaufhemmung, den Neubeginn und die Wirkung der Verjährung gelten die Vorschriften des Bürgerlichen Gesetzbuchs sinngemäß. ²Die Verjährung wird auch durch schriftlichen Antrag auf die Erstattung oder durch Erhebung eines Widerspruchs gehemmt. ³Die Hemmung endet sechs Monate nach Bekanntgabe der Entscheidung über den Antrag oder den Widerspruch.

§ 28
Verrechnung und Aufrechnung des Erstattungsanspruchs

Der für die Erstattung zuständige Leistungsträger kann

1. mit Ermächtigung eines anderen Leistungsträgers dessen Ansprüche gegen den Berechtigten mit dem ihm obliegenden Erstattungsbetrag verrechnen,
2. mit Zustimmung des Berechtigten die zu Unrecht entrichteten Beiträge mit künftigen Beitragsansprüchen aufrechnen.

§ 28a
Meldepflicht

(1) ¹Der Arbeitgeber oder ein anderer Meldepflichtiger hat der Einzugsstelle für jeden in der Kranken-, Pflege-, Rentenversicherung oder nach dem Recht der Arbeitsförderung kraft Gesetzes Versicherten

1. bei Beginn der versicherungspflichtigen Beschäftigung,
2. bei Ende der versicherungspflichtigen Beschäftigung,
3. bei Eintritt eines Insolvenzereignisses,
4. (weggefallen)
5. bei Änderungen in der Beitragspflicht,

6. bei Wechsel der Einzugsstelle,
7. bei Anträgen auf Altersrenten oder Auskunftsersuchen des Familiengerichts in Versorgungsausgleichsverfahren,

8. bei Unterbrechung der Entgeltzahlung,

9. bei Auflösung des Arbeitsverhältnisses,

(2) ¹The claim for reimbursement shall become time-barred four years after the end of the calendar year in which the contributions were paid. ²If the insurer objects to the legal validity of premiums, the limitation period begins at the end of the calendar year in which the objection is raised.

(3) ¹The provisions of the German Civil Code shall apply mutatis mutandis to the suspension, suspension of expiry, recommencement and effect of the limitation period. ²The limitation period is also suspended by a written application for reimbursement or by the filing of an objection. ³Suspension shall end six months after notification of the decision on the application or objection.

Section 28
Offsetting and set-off of the right to reimbursement

The service provider responsible for reimbursement may

1. with the authorisation of another service provider, offset its claims against the beneficiary against the reimbursement amount incumbent on it
2. with the consent of the beneficiary, offset the unjustifiably paid contributions against future contribution claims.

Section 28a
Registration Requirement

(1) ¹The employer or any other person obliged to register must inform the collecting agency of the following for each person insured by law in health insurance, nursing care insurance, pension insurance or under the law on employment promotion

1. at the start of employment subject to compulsory insurance
2. at the end of employment subject to compulsory insurance,
3. upon the occurrence of an insolvency event,
4. (omitted)
5. in the event of changes in the obligation to pay contributions,

6. if the feed point is changed,
7. in the case of applications for old-age pensions or requests for information from the Family Court in pension equalisation proceedings,

8. in case of interruption of the payment of remuneration,

9. upon termination of the employment relationship,

10. auf Anforderung der Einzugsstelle nach § 26 Absatz 4 Satz 2,
11. bei Antrag des geringfügig Beschäftigten nach § 6 Absatz 1b des Sechsten Buches auf Befreiung von der Versicherungspflicht,

12. bei einmalig gezahltem Arbeitsentgelt,

13. bei Beginn der Berufsausbildung,

14. bei Ende der Berufsausbildung,
15. bei Wechsel im Zeitraum bis zum 31. Dezember 2024 von einem Beschäftigungsbetrieb im Beitrittsgebiet zu einem Beschäftigungsbetrieb im übrigen Bundesgebiet oder umgekehrt,
16. bei Beginn der Altersteilzeitarbeit,
17. bei Ende der Altersteilzeitarbeit,

18. bei Änderung des Arbeitsentgelts, wenn die in § 8 Absatz 1 Nummer 1 genannte Grenze über- oder unterschritten wird,
19. bei nach § 23b Absatz 2 bis 3 gezahltem Arbeitsentgelt oder
20. bei Wechsel im Zeitraum bis zum 31. Dezember 2024 von einem Wertguthaben, das im Beitrittsgebiet und einem Wertguthaben, das im übrigen Bundesgebiet erzielt wurde,

eine Meldung zu erstatten. ²Jede Meldung sowie die darin enthaltenen Datensätze sind mit einem eindeutigen Kennzeichen zur Identifizierung zu versehen. ³Meldungen nach diesem Buch erfolgen, soweit nichts Abweichendes geregelt ist, durch elektronische Datenübermittlung (Datenübertragung); dabei sind Datenschutz und Datensicherheit nach dem jeweiligen Stand der Technik sicherzustellen und bei Nutzung allgemein zugänglicher Netze Verschlüsselungsverfahren zu verwenden. ⁴Arbeitgeber oder andere Meldepflichtige haben ihre Meldungen durch Datenübertragung aus systemgeprüften Programmen oder mittels maschinell erstellter Ausfüllhilfen zu erstatten.

(2) Der Arbeitgeber hat jeden am 31. Dezember des Vorjahres Beschäftigten nach Absatz 1 zu melden (Jahresmeldung).

(2a) ¹Der Arbeitgeber hat für jeden in einem Kalenderjahr Beschäftigten, der in der Unfallversicherung versichert ist, zum 16. Februar des Folgejahres eine besondere Jahresmeldung zur Unfallversicherung zu erstatten. ²Diese Meldung enthält über die Angaben nach Absatz 3 Satz 1 Nummer 1 bis 3, 6 und 9 hinaus folgende Angaben:

10. at the request of the collection agency in accordance with § 26 paragraph 4 sentence 2,
11. in the case of an application for exemption from compulsory insurance by a marginally employed person under section 6(1b) of Book Six,

12. in the case of a one-off payment,

13. at the start of vocational training,

14. at the end of vocational training,
15. in the event of a change in the period up to 31 December 2024 from an employment enterprise in the territory of the acceding territory to an employment enterprise in the rest of the Federal Republic or vice versa,
16. at the start of partial retirement,
17. at the end of part-time work for older workers,
18. in the event of a change in remuneration, if the limit specified in section 8 paragraph 1 number 1 is exceeded or undercut,
19. in the case of remuneration paid under section 23b(2) to (3), or
20. in the case of bills of exchange in the period until 31 December 2024, from a value credit balance achieved in the territory of the Accession Area and a value credit balance achieved in the rest of the Federal Republic of Germany,

to make a report. ²Each report and the data records it contains must be provided with a unique identification mark. ³Unless otherwise provided, reports under this Book shall be made by electronic data transmission (data transmission); data protection and data security shall be ensured in accordance with the current state of the art and encryption procedures shall be used when using generally accessible networks. ⁴Employers or other persons subject to the obligation to register must submit their reports by data transmission from system-checked programmes or by means of mechanically generated completion aids.

(2) The employer must report every employee employed on 31 December of the previous year in accordance with paragraph 1 (annual report).

(2a) ¹The employer shall submit a special annual report on accident insurance by 16 February of the following year for each employee insured under the accident insurance scheme in a calendar year. ²In addition to the information specified in paragraph 3 sentence 1 numbers 1 to 3, 6 and 9, this report shall contain the following information:

1. die Mitgliedsnummer des Unternehmers;
2. die Betriebsnummer des zuständigen Unfallversicherungsträgers;
3. das in der Unfallversicherung beitragspflichtige Arbeitsentgelt in Euro und seine Zuordnung zur jeweilig anzuwendenden Gefahrtarifstelle.

[3]Arbeitgeber, die Mitglied der landwirtschaftlichen Berufsgenossenschaft sind und für deren Beitragsberechnung der Arbeitswert keine Anwendung findet, haben Meldungen nach Satz 2 Nummer 1 bis 3 nicht zu erstatten. [4]Abweichend von Satz 1 ist die Meldung bei Eintritt eines Insolvenzereignisses, bei einer endgültigen Einstellung des Unternehmens oder bei der Beendigung aller Beschäftigungsverhältnisse mit der nächsten Entgeltabrechnung, spätestens innerhalb von sechs Wochen, abzugeben.

(3) [1]Die Meldungen enthalten für jeden Versicherten insbesondere

1. seine Versicherungsnummer, soweit bekannt,
2. seinen Familien- und Vornamen,
3. sein Geburtsdatum,
4. seine Staatsangehörigkeit,
5. Angaben über seine Tätigkeit nach dem Schlüsselverzeichnis der Bundesagentur für Arbeit,
6. die Betriebsnummer seines Beschäftigungsbetriebes,
7. die Beitragsgruppen,
8. die zuständige Einzugsstelle und
9. den Arbeitgeber.

[2]Zusätzlich sind anzugeben

1. bei der Anmeldung
   (a) die Anschrift,
   (b) der Beginn der Beschäftigung,
   (c) sonstige für die Vergabe der Versicherungsnummer erforderliche Angaben,
   (d) die Angabe, ob zum Arbeitgeber eine Beziehung als Ehegatte, Lebenspartner oder Abkömmling besteht,
   (e) die Angabe, ob es sich um eine Tätigkeit als geschäftsführender Gesellschafter einer Gesellschaft mit beschränkter Haftung handelt,
   (f) die Angabe der Staatsangehörigkeit,
2. bei allen Entgeltmeldungen
   (a) eine Namens-, Anschriften- oder Staatsangehörigkeitsänderung, soweit diese Änderung nicht schon anderweitig gemeldet ist,
   (b) das in der Rentenversicherung oder nach dem Recht der Arbeitsförderung beitragspflichtige Arbeitsentgelt in Euro,

1. the membership number of the employer;
2. the company number of the competent accident insurance institution;
3. the pay in euros which is subject to contributions under the accident insurance scheme and its allocation to the respective applicable dangerous goods tariff point.

[3]Employers who are members of the agricultural employers' liability insurance association and whose contributions are not calculated on the basis of the work value do not have to submit reports in accordance with sentence 2 numbers 1 to 3. [4]Deviating from sentence 1, the report must be submitted when an insolvency event occurs, when the company is definitively discontinued or when all employment relationships are terminated with the next pay

(3) [1]For each insured person, the notifications shall contain in particular

1. his insurance number, if known

2. his surname and first name,
3. his date of birth,
4. his nationality,
5. information on his or her activity according to the key list of the Federal Employment Agency,
6. the business number of his employing enterprise,
7. the contribution groups,
8. the competent collection agency, and
9. the employer.

[2]The following must also be stated

1. at registration
   (a) the address,
   (b) the start of employment,
   (c) other information required for the allocation of the insurance number,
   (d) whether there is a relationship with the employer as a spouse, partner or descendant,
   (e) an indication whether the activity in question is that of a managing partner of a limited liability company,
   (f) the indication of nationality,
2. for all charge notifications
   (a) a change of name, address or nationality, unless the change is already covered by other provisions
   (b) the amount in euro of the salary liable to contribute to the pension scheme or to the employment promotion scheme,

(c) in Fällen, in denen die beitragspflichtige Einnahme in der gesetzlichen Rentenversicherung nach § 163 Absatz 10 des Sechsten Buches bemessen wird, das Arbeitsentgelt, das ohne Anwendung dieser Regelung zu berücksichtigen wäre,

(d) der Zeitraum, in dem das angegebene Arbeitsentgelt erzielt wurde,

(e) Wertguthaben, die auf die Zeit nach Eintritt der Erwerbsminderung entfallen,

3. [aufgehoben]

4. bei der Meldung nach Absatz 1 Satz 1 Nummer 19

(a) das Arbeitsentgelt in Euro, für das Beiträge gezahlt worden sind,

(b) im Falle des § 23b Absatz 2 der Kalendermonat und das Jahr der nicht zweckentsprechenden Verwendung des Arbeitsentgelts, im Falle der Zahlungsunfähigkeit des Arbeitgebers jedoch der Kalendermonat und das Jahr der Beitragszahlung.

(3a) ¹Der Arbeitgeber oder eine Zahlstelle nach § 202 Absatz 2 des Fünften Buches kann in den Fällen, in denen für eine Meldung keine Versicherungsnummer des Beschäftigten oder Versorgungsempfängers vorliegt, im Verfahren nach Absatz 1 eine Meldung zur Abfrage der Versicherungsnummer an die Datenstelle der Rentenversicherung übermitteln; die weiteren Meldepflichten bleiben davon unberührt. ²Die Datenstelle der Rentenversicherung übermittelt dem Arbeitgeber oder der Zahlstelle unverzüglich durch Datenübertragung die Versicherungsnummer oder den Hinweis, dass die Vergabe der Versicherungsnummer mit der Anmeldung erfolgt.

(4) ¹Arbeitgeber haben den Tag des Beginns eines Beschäftigungsverhältnisses spätestens bei dessen Aufnahme an die Datenstelle der Rentenversicherung nach Satz 2 zu melden, sofern sie Personen in folgenden Wirtschaftsbereichen oder Wirtschaftszweigen beschäftigen:

1. im Baugewerbe,
2. im Gaststätten- und Beherbergungsgewerbe,
3. im Personenbeförderungsgewerbe,
4. im Speditions-, Transport- und damit verbundenen Logistikgewerbe,
5. im Schaustellergewerbe,
6. bei Unternehmen der Forstwirtschaft,
7. im Gebäudereinigungsgewerbe,
8. bei Unternehmen, die sich am Auf- und Abbau von Messen und Ausstellungen beteiligen,

(c) in cases where the contributory income in the statutory pension insurance scheme is assessed in accordance with Section 163(10) of Book Six, the remuneration which would have to be taken into account if that provision did not apply,

(d) the period during which the declared pay was earned,

(e) Value credit balances attributable to the period after the occurrence of the reduction in earning capacity,

3. [repealed].

4. in the case of the notification pursuant to paragraph 1 sentence 1 number 19

(a) the pay in euro for which contributions have been paid

(b) in the case of Section 23b (2), the calendar month and the year in which the salary was not used for the intended purpose, but in the event of the employer's insolvency, the calendar month and the year in which the contributions were paid.

(3a) ¹In cases where no insurance number of the employee or pension recipient is available for a report, the employer or a paying agent under Section 202(2) of Book 5 may, in the procedure under paragraph 1, submit a report to the data centre of the pension insurance scheme to query the insurance number; this shall not affect further reporting obligations. ²The data centre of the pension insurance fund shall immediately transmit the insurance number or the information that the insurance number is assigned to the employer or the paying agency by data transmission.

(4) ¹Employers must report the date of commencement of employment to the data centre of the pension insurance scheme in accordance with sentence 2 at the latest when they take up employment, provided that they employ persons in the following economic sectors or branches of the economy

1. in the construction industry,
2. in the restaurant and accommodation sector,
3. in the passenger transport sector,
4. in the forwarding, transport and related logistics business,
5. in the fairground trade,
6. for forestry undertakings,
7. in the building cleaning trade,
8. for companies participating in the construction and dismantling of trade fairs and exhibitions

9. in der Fleischwirtschaft,
10. im Prostitutionsgewerbe,
11. im Wach- und Sicherheitsgewerbe.

²Die Meldung enthält folgende Angaben über den Beschäftigten:

1. den Familien- und die Vornamen,
2. die Versicherungsnummer, soweit bekannt, ansonsten die zur Vergabe einer Versicherungsnummer notwendigen Angaben (Tag und Ort der Geburt, Anschrift),
3. die Betriebsnummer des Arbeitgebers und
4. den Tag der Beschäftigungsaufnahme.

³Die Meldung wird in der Stammsatzdatei nach § 150 Absatz 1 und 2 des Sechsten Buches gespeichert. ⁴Die Meldung gilt nicht als Meldung nach Absatz 1 Satz 1 Nummer 1.

(4a) ¹Der Meldepflichtige erstattet die Meldungen nach Absatz 1 Satz 1 Nummer 10 an die zuständige Einzugsstelle. ²In der Meldung sind insbesondere anzugeben:

1. die Versicherungsnummer des Beschäftigten,
2. die Betriebsnummer des Beschäftigungsbetriebes,
3. das monatliche laufende und einmalig gezahlte Arbeitsentgelt, von dem Beiträge zur Renten-, Arbeitslosen-, Kranken- und Pflegeversicherung für das der Ermittlung nach § 26 Absatz 4 zugrunde liegende Kalenderjahr berechnet wurden.

(5) Der Meldepflichtige hat der zu meldenden Person den Inhalt der Meldung in Textform mitzuteilen; dies gilt nicht, wenn die Meldung ausschließlich auf Grund einer Veränderung der Daten für die gesetzliche Unfallversicherung erfolgt.

(6) Soweit der Arbeitgeber eines Hausgewerbetreibenden Arbeitgeberpflichten erfüllt, gilt der Hausgewerbetreibende als Beschäftigter.

(6a) Beschäftigt ein Arbeitgeber, der

1. im privaten Bereich nichtgewerbliche Zwecke oder
2. mildtätige, kirchliche, religiöse, wissenschaftliche oder gemeinnützige Zwecke im Sinne des § 10b des Einkommensteuergesetzes

verfolgt, Personen geringfügig nach § 8, kann er auf Antrag abweichend von Absatz 1 Meldungen auf Vordrucken erstatten, wenn er glaubhaft macht, dass ihm eine Meldung auf maschinell verwertbaren Datenträgern oder durch Datenübertragung nicht möglich ist.

---

9 in the meat sector,
10. in prostitution,
11. in the security and surveillance sector.

² The notification shall contain the following information on the employee:

1. the surname and first names,
2. the insurance number, if known, otherwise the information necessary for the assignment of an insurance number (date and place of birth, address),
3. the company number of the employer and
4. the date of taking up employment.

³The notification shall be stored in the master data file in accordance with § 150 paragraphs 1 and 2 of Book Six. ⁴The notification shall not be deemed to be a notification under subsection 1 sentence 1 number 1.

(4a) ¹The notifier shall submit the notifications under paragraph 1 sentence 1 number 10 to the competent collection agency. ²In particular, the notification must specify

1. the insurance number of the employee,
2. the establishment number of the employing establishment,
3. the monthly current and one-off paid remuneration from which contributions to pension, unemployment, health and long-term care insurance were calculated for the calendar year on which the calculation pursuant to section 26(4) is based.

(5) The person obliged to register shall inform the person to be registered of the content of the registration in text form; this shall not apply if the registration is made solely on the basis of a change in the data for statutory accident insurance.

(6) Insofar as the employer of a domestic trader fulfils employer obligations, the domestic trader shall be deemed to be an employee.

(6a) If an employer who

1. in the private sector for non-commercial purposes, or
2. charitable, ecclesiastical, religious, scientific or charitable purposes within the meaning of § 10b of the Income Tax Act

persecuted persons, persons of minor importance pursuant to section 8, he may, in derogation of subsection (1) above, submit reports on forms if he substantiates that it is not possible for him to submit a report on machine-readable data carriers or by data transmission.

(7) ¹Der Arbeitgeber hat der Einzugsstelle für einen im privaten Haushalt Beschäftigten anstelle einer Meldung nach Absatz 1 unverzüglich eine vereinfachte Meldung (Haushaltsscheck) mit den Angaben nach Absatz 8 Satz 1 zu erstatten, wenn das Arbeitsentgelt (§ 14 Absatz 3) aus dieser Beschäftigung regelmäßig 450 Euro im Monat nicht übersteigt. ²Der Arbeitgeber kann die Meldung nach Satz 1 auch durch Datenübertragung aus systemgeprüften Programmen oder mit maschinell erstellten Ausfüllhilfen übermitteln. ³Der Arbeitgeber hat der Einzugsstelle gesondert schriftlich ein Lastschriftmandat zum Einzug des Gesamtsozialversicherungsbeitrags zu erteilen. ⁴Die Absätze 2 bis 5 gelten nicht.

(8) ¹Der Haushaltsscheck enthält

1. den Familiennamen, Vornamen, die Anschrift und die Betriebsnummer des Arbeitgebers,

2. den Familiennamen, Vornamen, die Anschrift und die Versicherungsnummer des Beschäftigten; kann die Versicherungsnummer nicht angegeben werden, ist das Geburtsdatum des Beschäftigten einzutragen,

3. die Angabe, ob der Beschäftigte im Zeitraum der Beschäftigung bei mehreren Arbeitgebern beschäftigt ist, und

   (a) bei einer Meldung bei jeder Lohn- oder Gehaltszahlung den Zeitraum der Beschäftigung, das Arbeitsentgelt (§ 14 Absatz 3) für diesen Zeitraum sowie am Ende der Beschäftigung den Zeitpunkt der Beendigung,

   (b) bei einer Meldung zu Beginn der Beschäftigung deren Beginn und das monatliche Arbeitsentgelt (§ 14 Absatz 3),

   (c) bei einer Meldung wegen Änderung des Arbeitsentgelts (§ 14 Absatz 3) den neuen Betrag und den Zeitpunkt der Änderung,

   (d) bei einer Meldung am Ende der Beschäftigung den Zeitpunkt der Beendigung,

   (e) bei Erklärung des Verzichts auf Versicherungsfreiheit nach § 230 Absatz 8 Satz 2 des Sechsten Buches den Zeitpunkt des Verzichts,

   (f) bei Antrag auf Befreiung von der Versicherungspflicht nach § 6 Absatz 1b des Sechsten Buches den Tag des Zugangs des Antrags beim Arbeitgeber.

²Bei sich anschließenden Meldungen kann von der Angabe der Anschrift des Arbeitgebers und des Beschäftigten abgesehen werden.

(7) ¹Instead of a declaration under subsection 1, the employer shall immediately submit a simplified declaration (household cheque) to the collection agency for a person employed in a private household, containing the information under subsection 8, first sentence, if the remuneration (section 14 subsection (3)) from this employment regularly does not exceed EUR 450 per month. ²The employer may also submit the report in accordance with sentence 1 by means of data transmission from system-checked programmes or with mechanically generated completion aids. ³The employer must separately issue a direct debit mandate in writing to the collection agency to collect the total social insurance contribution. ⁴Paragraphs 2 to 5 do not apply.

(8) ¹The household cheque shall contain

1. the surname, first name, address and business number of the employer

2. the surname, first name, address and insurance number of the employee; if the insurance number cannot be provided, the employee's date of birth must be entered

3. an indication of whether the employee is employed by several employers during the period of employment, and

   (a) in the case of a declaration, for each wage or salary payment, the period of employment, the remuneration (Article 14(3)) for that period and, at the end of employment, the date of termination,

   (b) in the case of a declaration at the start of employment, its start date and the monthly salary (§ 14(3)),

   (c) in the event of notification of a change in remuneration (§ 14 paragraph 3), the new amount and the date of the change,

   (d) in the case of registration at the end of employment, the date of termination,

   (e) in the case of a declaration of waiver of exemption from insurance pursuant to the second sentence of Article 230(8) of Book Six, the date of the waiver,

   (f) in the case of an application for exemption from compulsory insurance under Paragraph 6(1b) of Book Six, the date of receipt of the application by the employer.

²The address of the employer and the employee may be omitted from subsequent notifications.

(9) ¹Soweit nicht anders geregelt, gelten für versicherungsfrei oder von der Versicherungspflicht befreite geringfügig Beschäftigte die Absätze 1 bis 6 entsprechend. ²Eine Jahresmeldung nach Absatz 2 ist für geringfügig Beschäftigte nach § 8 Absatz 1 Nummer 2 nicht zu erstatten.

(10) ¹Der Arbeitgeber hat für Beschäftigte, die nach § 6 Absatz 1 Satz 1 Nummer 1 des Sechsten Buches von der Versicherungspflicht befreit und Mitglied einer berufsständischen Versorgungseinrichtung sind, die Meldungen nach den Absätzen 1, 2 und 9 zusätzlich an die Annahmestelle der berufsständischen Versorgungseinrichtungen zu erstatten; dies gilt nicht für Meldungen nach Absatz 1 Satz 1 Nummer 10. ²Die Datenübermittlung hat durch gesicherte und verschlüsselte Datenübertragung aus systemgeprüften Programmen oder mittels systemgeprüfter maschinell erstellter Ausfüllhilfen zu erfolgen. ³Zusätzlich zu den Angaben nach Absatz 3 enthalten die Meldungen die Mitgliedsnummer des Beschäftigten bei der Versorgungseinrichtung. ⁴Die Absätze 5 bis 6a gelten entsprechend.

(11) ¹Der Arbeitgeber hat für Beschäftigte, die nach § 6 Absatz 1 Satz 1 Nummer 1 des Sechsten Buches von der Versicherungspflicht befreit und Mitglied in einer berufsständischen Versorgungseinrichtung sind, der Annahmestelle der berufsständischen Versorgungseinrichtungen monatliche Meldungen zur Beitragserhebung zu erstatten. ²Absatz 10 Satz 2 gilt entsprechend. ³Diese Meldungen enthalten für den Beschäftigten

1. die Mitgliedsnummer bei der Versorgungseinrichtung oder, wenn die Mitgliedsnummer nicht bekannt ist, die Personalnummer beim Arbeitgeber, den Familien- und Vornamen, das Geschlecht und das Geburtsdatum,
2. den Zeitraum, für den das Arbeitsentgelt gezahlt wird,
3. das beitragspflichtige ungekürzte laufende Arbeitsentgelt für den Zahlungszeitraum,
4. das beitragspflichtige ungekürzte einmalig gezahlte Arbeitsentgelt im Monat der Abrechnung,
5. die Anzahl der Sozialversicherungstage im Zahlungszeitraum,
6. den Beitrag, der bei Firmenzahlern für das Arbeitsentgelt nach Nummer 3 und 4 anfällt,
7. die Betriebsnummer der Versorgungseinrichtung,
8. die Betriebsnummer des Beschäftigungsbetriebes,
9. den Arbeitgeber,

(9) ¹Unless otherwise provided, paragraphs 1 to 6 apply mutatis mutandis to marginally employed persons who are exempt from compulsory insurance or exempt from compulsory insurance. ²An annual declaration in accordance with paragraph 2 is not required for marginally employed persons under Article 8 paragraph 1 number 2.

(10) ¹The employer shall additionally submit the reports under subsections 1, 2 and 9 to the receiving office of the occupational pension schemes for employees who are exempt from compulsory insurance under Section 6(1), first sentence, no. 1 of Book 6 and are members of an occupational pension scheme; this does not apply to reports under subsection 1, first sentence, no. 10. ²The data must be transmitted by means of secure and encrypted data transmission from system-audited programmes or by means of system-audited, mechanically generated completion aids. ³In addition to the information specified in paragraph 3, the reports shall contain the membership number of the employee with the pension fund. ⁴Paragraphs 5 to 6a apply accordingly.

(11) ¹The employer shall submit monthly reports to the receiving office of the occupational pension scheme for the purpose of collecting contributions for employees who are exempt from compulsory insurance under Section 6(1) first sentence, number 1 of Book 6 and are members of a professional pension scheme. ²(10), second sentence, shall apply mutatis mutandis. ³These reports shall contain for the employee

1. the membership number at the pension institution or, if the membership number is not known, the personnel number at the employer, the family and first name, sex and date of birth
2. the period for which the remuneration is paid
3. the full current salary liable for contributions for the payment period,
4. the full, unreduced, non-recurring remuneration subject to contributions in the month of settlement,
5. the number of social security days in the payment period,
6. the contribution payable by company payers for the remuneration referred to in points 3 and 4,
7. the operating number of the supply facility,
8. the company number of the employing enterprise,
9. the employer,

10. den Ort des Beschäftigungsbetriebes,

11. den Monat der Abrechnung.

⁴Soweit nicht aus der Entgeltbescheinigung des Beschäftigten zu entnehmen ist, dass die Meldung erfolgt ist und welchen Inhalt sie hatte, gilt Absatz 5.

(12) Der Arbeitgeber hat auch für ausschließlich nach § 2 Absatz 1 Nummer 1 des Siebten Buches versicherte Beschäftigte mit beitragspflichtigem Entgelt Meldungen nach den Absätzen 1 und 3 Satz 2 Nummer 2 abzugeben.

(13) ¹Die Künstlersozialkasse hat für die nach dem Künstlersozialversicherungsgesetz krankenversicherungspflichtigen Mitglieder monatlich eine Meldung an die zuständige Krankenkasse (§ 28i) durch Datenübermittlung mit den für den Nachweis der Beitragspflicht notwendigen Angaben, insbesondere die Versicherungsnummer, den Namen und Vornamen, den beitragspflichtigen Zeitraum, die Höhe des der Beitragspflicht zu Grunde liegenden Arbeitseinkommens, ein Kennzeichen über die Ruhensanordnung gemäß § 16 Absatz 2 des Künstlersozialversicherungsgesetzes und den Verweis auf die Versicherungspflicht in der Rentenversicherung des Versicherten zu übermitteln. ²Den Übertragungsweg und die Einzelheiten des Verfahrens wie den Aufbau des Datensatzes regeln die Künstlersozialkasse und der Spitzenverband Bund der Krankenkassen in Gemeinsamen Grundsätzen entsprechend § 28b Absatz 1. ³Bei der Nutzung allgemein zugänglicher Netze sind dem jeweiligen Stand der Technik entsprechende Verschlüsselungsverfahren zu verwenden.

§ 28b
Inhalte und Verfahren für die Gemeinsamen Grundsätze und die Datenfeldbeschreibung

(1) ¹Der Spitzenverband Bund der Krankenkassen, die Deutsche Rentenversicherung Bund, die Deutsche Rentenversicherung Knappschaft-Bahn-See, die Bundesagentur für Arbeit und die Deutsche Gesetzliche Unfallversicherung e V bestimmen in Gemeinsamen Grundsätzen bundeseinheitlich:

1. die Schlüsselzahlen für Personengruppen, Beitragsgruppen und für Abgabegründe der Meldungen,

10. the location of the establishment of employment,

11. the month of settlement.

⁴Unless the employee's remuneration certificate indicates that the notification was made and what its content was, paragraph 5 applies.

(12) The employer shall also submit notifications in accordance with subsections 1 and 3, second sentence, number 2, for employees who are exclusively insured under Section 2(1)(1) of Book 7 and whose remuneration is subject to contributions.

(13) ¹The Artists' Social Security Fund shall submit a monthly report to the competent health insurance fund (section 28i) for members liable to contribute under the Artists' Social Security Act by means of data transmission containing the information necessary to prove the obligation to contribute, in particular the insurance number, surname and first name, the period of employment subject to contribution, the amount of the employment income on which the obligation to contribute is based, an indicator of the suspension order under section 16(2) of the Artists' Social Security Fund and a reference to the obligation to contribute to the pension insurance scheme of the insured person. The method of transmission and the details of the procedure, such as the structure of the data set, are regulated by the Artists' Social Security Fund and the Federal Association of Health Insurance Funds in Common Principles in accordance with section 28b(1). 3The use of generally accessible networks requires the use of encryption procedures which are state of the art.

Section 28b
Content and procedures for the Common Principles and the data field description

(1) ¹ The Federal Association of Health Insurance Funds, the German Pension Insurance Fund, the German Pension Insurance Fund Knappschaft-Bahn-See (pension for miners, railway workers and seamen), the Federal Employment Agency and the German Statutory Accident Insurance Fund shall determine uniformly throughout Germany in Common Principles:

1. the key figures for groups of persons, contribution groups and for reasons for submitting notifications

2. den Aufbau, den Inhalt und die Identifizierung der einzelnen Datensätze für die Übermittlung von Meldungen und Beitragsnachweisen durch den Arbeitgeber an die Sozialversicherungsträger, soweit nichts Abweichendes in diesem Buch geregelt ist,

3. den Aufbau und den Inhalt der einzelnen Datensätze für die Übermittlung von Eingangs- und Weiterleitungsbestätigungen, Fehlermeldungen und sonstigen Meldungen der Sozialversicherungsträger und anderer am Meldeverfahren beteiligter Stellen an die Arbeitgeber in den Verfahren nach Nummer 2,

4. gesondert den Aufbau und den Inhalt der Datensätze für die Kommunikationsdaten, die einheitlich am Beginn und am Ende jedes Dateisystems in den Verfahren nach Nummer 2 bei jeder Datenübertragung vom Arbeitgeber an die Sozialversicherung und bei Meldungen an den Arbeitgeber zu übermitteln sind,

5. gesondert den Aufbau und den Inhalt aller Bestandsprüfungen in den elektronischen Verfahren mit den Arbeitgebern sowie das Verfahren zur Weiterleitung der geänderten Meldung an die Empfänger der Meldung und den Meldepflichtigen.

²Satz 1 Nummer 3 bis 5 gilt auch für das Zahlstellenmeldeverfahren nach § 202 des Fünften Buches und für das Antragsverfahren nach § 2 Absatz 3 des Aufwendungsausgleichsgesetzes. ³Die Gemeinsamen Grundsätze bedürfen der Genehmigung des Bundesministeriums für Arbeit und Soziales, das vorher die Bundesvereinigung der Deutschen Arbeitgeberverbände anzuhören hat.

(2) ¹Der Spitzenverband Bund der Krankenkassen, die Deutsche Rentenversicherung Bund, die Deutsche Rentenversicherung Knappschaft-Bahn-See und die Deutsche Gesetzliche Unfallversicherung e.V. bestimmen bundeseinheitlich die Gestaltung des Haushaltsschecks nach § 28a Absatz 7 und das der Einzugsstelle in diesem Verfahren zu erteilende Lastschriftmandat durch Gemeinsame Grundsätze. ²Die Grundsätze bedürfen der Genehmigung des Bundesministeriums für Arbeit und Soziales, das vorher in Bezug auf die steuerrechtlichen Angaben das Bundesministerium der Finanzen anzuhören hat.

(3) Soweit Meldungen nach § 28a Absatz 10 oder 11 betroffen sind, gilt Absatz 1 entsprechend mit der Maßgabe, dass die Arbeitsgemeinschaft berufsständischer Versorgungseinrichtungen e.V. zu beteiligen ist.

2. the structure, content and identification of the individual data records for the transmission of notifications and statements of contributions by the employer to the social insurance institutions, unless otherwise provided for in this book,

3. the structure and content of the individual data records for the transmission of acknowledgements of receipt and forwarding, error messages and other messages from the social insurance institutions and other bodies involved in the notification procedure to the employers in the procedures referred to in point 2

4. separately, the structure and content of the data records for the communication data, which must be transmitted in a uniform manner at the beginning and end of each file system in the procedures referred to in point 2 for each data transmission from the employer to the social security and for notifications to the employer,

5. separately, the structure and content of all inventory checks in the electronic procedures with employers and the procedure for forwarding the amended notification to the recipients of the notification and the notifier

²Sentence 1 Nos. 3 to 5 shall also apply to the paying agent reporting procedure under section 202 of Book 5 and to the application procedure under section 2(3) of the Expenditure Compensation Act. ³The Common Principles require the approval of the Federal Ministry of Labour and Social Affairs, which must first consult the Federal Confederation of German Employers' Associations.

(2) ¹The Federal Association of Health Insurance Funds, the German Pension Insurance Fund Federation, the German Pension Insurance Fund Knappschaft-Bahn-See (pension for miners, railway workers and seamen), and the German Statutory Accident Insurance Fund shall determine, on a uniform nationwide basis, the format of the budget cheque in accordance with Article 28a(7) and the direct debit mandate to be issued to the collection agency in this procedure by means of Common Principles. ²The principles require the approval of the Federal Ministry of Labour and Social Affairs, which must first consult the Federal Ministry of Finance with regard to tax information.

(3) Insofar as notifications under Article 28a, paragraph 10 or 11 are concerned, paragraph 1 shall apply mutatis mutandis subject to the proviso that the Arbeitsgemeinschaft berufsständischer Versorgungseinrichtungen e.V. is to be involved.

(4) [1]Alle Datenfelder sind eindeutig zu beschreiben und in allen Verfahren, für die Grundsätze oder Gemeinsame Grundsätze nach diesem Gesetzbuch und für das Aufwendungsausgleichsgesetz gelten, verbindlich in der jeweils aktuellen Beschreibung zu verwenden. [2]Zur Sicherung der einheitlichen Verwendung hält der Spitzenverband Bund der Krankenkassen eine Datenbankanwendung vor, in der alle Datenfelder beschrieben sowie ihre Verwendung in Datensätzen und Datenbausteinen in historisierter wie auch in aktueller Form gespeichert sind und von den an den Meldeverfahren nach diesem Gesetzbuch Beteiligten ab dem 1. Juli 2017 automatisiert abgerufen werden können. [3]Das Nähere zur Darstellung, zur Aktualisierung und zum Abrufverfahren der Daten regeln die in Absatz 1 Satz 1 genannten Organisationen der Sozialversicherung in Gemeinsamen Grundsätzen; Absatz 3 gilt entsprechend. [4]Die Grundsätze bedürfen der Genehmigung des Bundesministeriums für Arbeit und Soziales.

(4) [1]All data fields must be clearly described and bindingly used in the respective current description in all procedures to which principles or common principles under this Code and the Expenditure Compensation Act apply. [2]To ensure uniform use, the National Association of Health Insurance Funds maintains a database application in which all data fields are described and their use in data records and data modules is stored in both historical and current form and can be automatically retrieved by those involved in the reporting procedures under this Code from 1 July 2017. [3]Details of the presentation, updating and retrieval procedure of the data are regulated by the social security organisations mentioned in paragraph 1 sentence 1 in Common Principles; paragraph 3 applies accordingly. [4]These principles require the approval of the Federal Ministry of Labour and Social Affairs.

§ 28c
Verordnungsermächtigung

Das Bundesministerium für Arbeit und Soziales wird ermächtigt, durch Rechtsverordnung mit Zustimmung des Bundesrates das Nähere über das Melde- und Beitragsnachweisverfahren zu bestimmen, insbesondere

1. die Frist der Meldungen und Beitragsnachweise,
2. (weggefallen)
3. welche zusätzlichen, für die Verarbeitung der Meldungen und Beitragsnachweise oder die Durchführung der Versicherung erforderlichen Angaben zu machen sind,
4. das Verfahren über die Prüfung, Sicherung und Weiterleitung der Daten,
5. unter welchen Voraussetzungen Systemprüfungen durchzuführen, Meldungen und Beitragsnachweise durch Datenübertragung zu erstatten sind,
6. in welchen Fällen auf einzelne Meldungen oder Angaben verzichtet wird,
7. in welcher Form und Frist der Arbeitgeber die Beschäftigten über die Meldungen zu unterrichten hat.

Section 28c
Authorisation by decree

The Federal Ministry of Labour and Social Affairs is authorised, with the consent of the Federal Council, to determine by statutory order the details of the registration and contribution statement procedure, in particular

1. the deadline for notifications and proof of contributions,
2. (omitted)
3. what additional information is to be provided which is necessary for the processing of the notifications and contribution statements or the implementation of the insurance,
4. the procedure for checking, securing and forwarding data,
5. under which conditions system checks are to be carried out, notifications and contribution statements are to be submitted by data transmission,
6. in which cases individual notifications or information is waived,
7. in what form and within what period of time the employer must inform the employees about the notifications.

§ 28d
Gesamtsozialversicherungsbeitrag

[1]Die Beiträge in der Kranken- oder Rentenversicherung für einen kraft Gesetzes versicherten Beschäftigten oder Hausgewerbetreibenden sowie der Beitrag aus Arbeitsentgelt aus einer versicherungspflichtigen Beschäftigung nach dem

Section 28d
Total social security contribution

[1]Contributions to health or pension insurance for an employee or domestic craftsman insured by law, as well as the contribution from earnings from employment subject to compulsory insurance under the law on employment pro-

Recht der Arbeitsförderung werden als Gesamtsozialversicherungsbeitrag gezahlt. ²Satz 1 gilt auch für den Beitrag zur Pflegeversicherung für einen in der Krankenversicherung kraft Gesetzes versicherten Beschäftigten. ³Die nicht nach dem Arbeitsentgelt zu bemessenden Beiträge in der landwirtschaftlichen Krankenversicherung für einen kraft Gesetzes versicherten Beschäftigten gelten zusammen mit den Beiträgen zur Rentenversicherung und Arbeitsförderung im Sinne des Satzes 1 ebenfalls als Gesamtsozialversicherungsbeitrag.

§ 28e
Zahlungspflicht, Vorschuss

(1) ¹Den Gesamtsozialversicherungsbeitrag hat der Arbeitgeber und in den Fällen der nach § 7f Absatz 1 Satz 1 Nummer 2 auf die Deutsche Rentenversicherung Bund übertragenen Wertguthaben die Deutsche Rentenversicherung Bund zu zahlen. ²Die Zahlung des vom Beschäftigten zu tragenden Teils des Gesamtsozialversicherungsbeitrags gilt als aus dem Vermögen des Beschäftigten erbracht. ³Ist ein Träger der Kranken- oder Rentenversicherung oder die Bundesagentur für Arbeit der Arbeitgeber, gilt der jeweils für diesen Leistungsträger oder, wenn eine Krankenkasse der Arbeitgeber ist, auch der für die Pflegekasse bestimmte Anteil am Gesamtsozialversicherungsbeitrag als gezahlt; dies gilt für die Beiträge zur Rentenversicherung auch im Verhältnis der Träger der Rentenversicherung untereinander.

(2) ¹Für die Erfüllung der Zahlungspflicht des Arbeitgebers haftet bei einem wirksamen Vertrag der Entleiher wie ein selbstschuldnerischer Bürge, soweit ihm Arbeitnehmer gegen Vergütung zur Arbeitsleistung überlassen worden sind. ²Er kann die Zahlung verweigern, solange die Einzugsstelle den Arbeitgeber nicht gemahnt hat und die Mahnfrist nicht abgelaufen ist. ³Zahlt der Verleiher das vereinbarte Arbeitsentgelt oder Teile des Arbeitsentgelts an den Leiharbeitnehmer, obwohl der Vertrag nach § 9 Absatz 1 Nummer 1 bis 1b des Arbeitnehmerüberlassungsgesetzes unwirksam ist, so hat er auch den hierauf entfallenden Gesamtsozialversicherungsbeitrag an die Einzugsstelle zu zahlen. 4Hinsichtlich der Zahlungspflicht nach Satz 3 gilt der Verleiher neben dem Entleiher als Arbeitgeber; beide haften insoweit als Gesamtschuldner.

motion, shall be paid as a total social security contribution. ²Sentence 1 shall also apply to the contribution to long-term care insurance for an employee insured under the sickness insurance scheme by operation of law. ³Contributions to the agricultural health insurance scheme for an employee insured under the law, which are not calculated on the basis of remuneration, together with contributions to pension insurance and employment promotion schemes within the meaning of sentence 1, shall also be regarded as a total social security contribution.

Section 28e
Payment obligation, advance payment

(1) ¹The total social security contribution shall be paid by the employer and, in the case of the assets transferred to the German Pension Insurance Federation in accordance with Article 7f paragraph 1 sentence 1 number 2, by the German Pension Insurance Federation. ²Payment of the part of the total social security contribution to be borne by the employee shall be deemed to be made from the employee's assets. ³If a health or pension insurance institution or the Federal Employment Agency is the employer, the part of the total social security contribution intended for that institution or, if a health insurance fund is the employer, also the part of the total social security contribution intended for the nursing care insurance fund shall be deemed to have been paid; this shall also apply to pension insurance contributions in the relationship between the pension insurance institutions.

(2) ¹For the fulfilment of the employer's obligation to pay, the hirer is liable, in the case of an effective contract, like a directly liable guarantor, insofar as employees have been made available to him in return for remuneration for work performance. ²He may refuse payment as long as the collection agency has not sent the employer a reminder and the reminder period has not expired. ³If the temporary employment agency pays the agreed remuneration or part of the remuneration to the temporary worker, although the contract is invalid under Section 9(1), Nos 1 to 1b of the Law on the Provision of Temporary Workers, it must also pay the total social security contribution due to the temporary worker to the collection agency. ⁴With regard to the payment obligation under sentence 3, the temporary employment agency is deemed to be the employer alongside the hirer; both are jointly and severally liable in this respect.

(2a) [1]Für die Erfüllung der Zahlungspflicht, die sich für den Arbeitgeber knappschaftlicher Arbeiten im Sinne von § 134 Absatz 4 des Sechsten Buches ergibt, haftet der Arbeitgeber des Bergwerksbetriebes, mit dem die Arbeiten räumlich und betrieblich zusammenhängen, wie ein selbstschuldnerischer Bürge. [2]Der Arbeitgeber des Bergwerksbetriebes kann die Befriedigung verweigern, solange die Einzugsstelle den Arbeitgeber der knappschaftlichen Arbeiten nicht gemahnt hat und die Mahnfrist nicht abgelaufen ist.

(3) Für die Erfüllung der Zahlungspflicht des Arbeitgebers von Seeleuten nach § 13 Absatz 1 Satz 2 haften Arbeitgeber und Reeder als Gesamtschuldner.

(3a) [1]Ein Unternehmer des Baugewerbes, der einen anderen Unternehmer mit der Erbringung von Bauleistungen im Sinne des § 101 Absatz 2 des Dritten Buches beauftragt, haftet für die Erfüllung der Zahlungspflicht dieses Unternehmers oder eines von diesem Unternehmer beauftragten Verleihers wie ein selbstschuldnerischer Bürge. [2]Satz 1 gilt entsprechend für die vom Nachunternehmer gegenüber ausländischen Sozialversicherungsträgern abzuführenden Beiträge. [3]Absatz 2 Satz 2 gilt entsprechend.

(3b) [1]Die Haftung nach Absatz 3a entfällt, wenn der Unternehmer nachweist, dass er ohne eigenes Verschulden davon ausgehen konnte, dass der Nachunternehmer oder ein von ihm beauftragter Verleiher seine Zahlungspflicht erfüllt. [2]Ein Verschulden des Unternehmers ist ausgeschlossen, soweit und solange er Fachkunde, Zuverlässigkeit und Leistungsfähigkeit des Nachunternehmers oder des von diesem beauftragten Verleihers durch eine Präqualifikation nachweist, die die Eignungsvoraussetzungen nach § 8 der Vergabe- und Vertragsordnung für Bauleistungen Teil A in der Fassung der Bekanntmachung vom 20. März 2006 (BAnz. Nr. 94a vom 18. Mai 2006) erfüllt.

(3c) [1]Ein Unternehmer, der Bauleistungen im Auftrag eines anderen Unternehmers erbringt, ist verpflichtet, auf Verlangen der Einzugsstelle Firma und Anschrift dieses Unternehmers mitzuteilen. [2]Kann der Auskunftsanspruch nach Satz 1 nicht durchgesetzt werden, hat ein Unternehmer, der einen Gesamtauftrag für die Erbringung von Bauleistungen für ein Bauwerk erhält, der Einzugsstelle auf Verlangen Firma und Anschrift aller Unternehmer, die von ihm mit der Erbringung von Bauleistungen beauftragt wurden, zu benennen.

(2a) [1]For the fulfilment of the payment obligation arising for the employer of miners' work within the meaning of Section 134(4) of Book Six, the employer of the mining company with which the work is spatially and operationally connected shall be liable as a directly liable guarantor. [2]The employer of the mining company may refuse to satisfy the claim as long as the collecting agency has not sent a reminder to the employer of the mineworker and the period for reminders has not expired.

(3) The employer and shipowner shall be jointly and severally liable for the fulfilment of the seafarer's employer's payment obligation under section 13(1) sentence 2.

(3a) [1]A contractor in the construction industry who commissions another contractor to carry out construction work within the meaning of section 101(2) of Book Three shall be liable as a joint and several guarantor for the fulfilment of the payment obligation of that contractor or of a lender commissioned by that contractor. [2]Sentence 1 shall apply accordingly to the contributions to be paid by the subcontractor to foreign social security institutions. [3]Paragraph 2 sentence 2 shall apply accordingly.

(3b) [1]The liability under paragraph 3a shall not apply if the contractor proves that he could have assumed, through no fault of his own, that the subcontractor or a lender commissioned by him would fulfil his payment obligation. [2]The Contractor shall not be at fault if and for as long as he can prove the expertise, reliability and efficiency of the subcontractor or of the lender commissioned by the subcontractor by means of a prequalification which meets the suitability requirements in accordance with § 8 of the Vergabe- und Vertragsordnung für Bauleistungen Teil A in the version published on 20 March 2006 (BAnz. No. 94a of 18 May 2006).

(3c) [1]A contractor who performs construction work on behalf of another contractor is obliged to inform the collection agency of the name and address of that contractor if so requested. [2]If the right to information pursuant to sentence 1 cannot be enforced, an entrepreneur who is awarded a general contract for the provision of construction services for a building must, on request, provide the collection agency with the name and address of all entrepreneurs who have been commissioned by him to provide construction services.

(3d) [1]Absatz 3a gilt ab einem geschätzten Gesamtwert aller für ein Bauwerk in Auftrag gegebenen Bauleistungen von 275 000 Euro. [2]Für die Schätzung gilt § 3 der Vergabeverordnung vom 9. Januar 2001 (BGBl. I S. 110), die zuletzt durch Artikel 3 Absatz 1 des Gesetzes vom 16. Mai 2001 (BGBl. I S. 876) geändert worden ist.

(3e) [1]Die Haftung des Unternehmers nach Absatz 3a erstreckt sich in Abweichung von der dort getroffenen Regelung auf das von dem Nachunternehmer beauftragte nächste Unternehmen, wenn die Beauftragung des unmittelbaren Nachunternehmers bei verständiger Würdigung der Gesamtumstände als ein Rechtsgeschäft anzusehen ist, dessen Ziel vor allem die Auflösung der Haftung nach Absatz 3a ist. [2]Maßgeblich für die Würdigung ist die Verkehrsanschauung im Baubereich. [3]Ein Rechtsgeschäft im Sinne dieser Vorschrift, das als Umgehungstatbestand anzusehen ist, ist in der Regel anzunehmen,

(a) wenn der unmittelbare Nachunternehmer weder selbst eigene Bauleistungen noch planerische oder kaufmännische Leistungen erbringt oder

(b) wenn der unmittelbare Nachunternehmer weder technisches noch planerisches oder kaufmännisches Fachpersonal in nennenswertem Umfang beschäftigt oder

(c) wenn der unmittelbare Nachunternehmer in einem gesellschaftsrechtlichen Abhängigkeitsverhältnis zum Hauptunternehmer steht.

[4]Besonderer Prüfung bedürfen die Umstände des Einzelfalles vor allem in den Fällen, in denen der unmittelbare Nachunternehmer seinen handelsrechtlichen Sitz außerhalb des Europäischen Wirtschaftsraums hat.

(3f) [1]Der Unternehmer kann den Nachweis nach Absatz 3b Satz 2 anstelle der Präqualifikation auch durch Vorlage einer Unbedenklichkeitsbescheinigung der zuständigen Einzugsstelle für den Nachunternehmer oder den von diesem beauftragten Verleiher erbringen. [2]Die Unbedenklichkeitsbescheinigung enthält Angaben über die ordnungsgemäße Zahlung der Sozialversicherungsbeiträge und die Zahl der gemeldeten Beschäftigten. [3]Die Bundesregierung berichtet unter Beteiligung des Normenkontrollrates über die Wirksamkeit und Reichweite der Generalunternehmerhaftung für Sozialversicherungsbeiträge im Baugewerbe, insbesondere über die Haftungsfreistellung nach Satz 1 und nach Absatz 3b, den gesetzgebenden Körperschaften im Jahr 2012.

(3d) [1](3a) shall apply where the total estimated value of all the works ordered for a construction project exceeds EUR 275 000. [2]The estimate is subject to Section 3 of the Public Tendering Regulation of 9 January 2001 (BGBl. I p. 110), last amended by Article 3(1) of the Act of 16 May 2001 (BGBl. I p. 876).

(3e) [1]The liability of the entrepreneur under subsection 3a shall, in derogation of the provision made therein, extend to the next enterprise commissioned by the subcontractor if, on a reasonable assessment of the overall circumstances, the commissioning of the direct subcontractor is to be regarded as a legal transaction whose primary aim is to dissolve the liability under subsection 3a. [2]The relevant factor for the assessment is the traffic view in the construction sector. [3]A legal transaction within the meaning of this provision, which is to be regarded as a circumvention, is generally to be assumed,

(a) if the direct subcontractor does not itself provide construction services or planning or commercial services, or

(b) if the direct subcontractor does not employ any technical, planning or commercial specialist staff to any significant extent or

(c) where the direct subcontractor is in a relationship of dependency with the main contractor under company law.

[4]Special examination of the circumstances of the individual case is required in particular in cases where the direct subcontractor has its commercial domicile outside the European Economic Area.

(3f) [1]Instead of prequalification, the Contractor may also provide proof in accordance with paragraph 3b sentence 2 by presenting a clearance certificate from the competent collection agency for the subcontractor or the lender commissioned by the latter. [2]The clearance certificate shall contain information on the proper payment of social security contributions and the number of registered employees. [3]The Federal Government, with the participation of the Normenkontrollrat, shall report to the legislative bodies on the effectiveness and scope of general contractor liability for social security contributions in the construction industry, in particular on the exemption from liability under sentence 1 and under paragraph 3b, in 2012.

(3g) [1]Für einen Unternehmer im Speditions-, Transport- und damit verbundenen Logistikgewerbe, der im Bereich der Kurier-, Express- und Paketdienste tätig ist und der einen anderen Unternehmer mit der Beförderung von Paketen beauftragt, gelten die Absätze 3a, 3b Satz 1, 3e und 3f entsprechend. [2]Absatz 3b Satz 2 gilt entsprechend mit der Maßgabe, dass die Präqualifikation die Voraussetzung erfüllt, dass der Nachunternehmer in einem amtlichen Verzeichnis eingetragen ist oder über eine Zertifizierung verfügt, die jeweils den Anforderungen des Artikels 64 der Richtlinie 2014/24/EU des Europäischen Parlaments und des Rates vom 26. Februar 2014 über die öffentliche Auftragsvergabe und zur Aufhebung der Richtlinie 2004/18/EG (ABl. L 94 vom 28.3.2014, S. 65), die zuletzt durch die Delegierte Verordnung (EU) 2017/2365 (ABl. L 337 vom 19.12.2017, S. 19) geändert worden ist, entsprechen. [3]Für einen Unternehmer, der im Auftrag eines anderen Unternehmers Pakete befördert, gilt Absatz 3c entsprechend. [4]Beförderung von Paketen im Sinne dieses Buches ist

(a) die Beförderung adressierter Pakete mit einem Einzelgewicht von bis zu 32 Kilogramm, soweit diese mit Kraftfahrzeugen mit einem zulässigen Gesamtgewicht von bis zu 3,5 Tonnen erfolgt,

(b) die stationäre Bearbeitung von adressierten Paketen bis zu 32 Kilogramm mit Ausnahme der Bearbeitung im Filialbereich.

(3h) Die Bundesregierung berichtet unter Beteiligung des Normenkontrollrates zum 31. Dezember 2023 über die Wirksamkeit und Reichweite der Haftung für Sozialversicherungsbeiträge für die Unternehmer im Speditions-, Transport- und damit verbundenen Logistikgewerbe, die im Bereich der Kurier-, Express- und Paketdienste tätig sind und einen anderen Unternehmer mit der Beförderung von Paketen beauftragen, insbesondere über die Haftungsfreistellung nach Absatz 3b und Absatz 3f Satz 1.

(4) Die Haftung umfasst die Beiträge und Säumniszuschläge, die infolge der Pflichtverletzung zu zahlen sind, sowie die Zinsen für gestundete Beiträge (Beitragsansprüche).

(5) Die Satzung der Einzugsstelle kann bestimmen, unter welchen Voraussetzungen vom Arbeitgeber Vorschüsse auf den Gesamtsozialversicherungsbeitrag verlangt werden können.

(3g) [1]For an entrepreneur in the forwarding, transport and related logistics business who operates in the courier, express and parcel services sector and who commissions another entrepreneur to transport parcels, paragraphs 3a, 3b sentence 1, 3e and 3f apply accordingly. [2]Subparagraph 3b sentence 2 shall apply accordingly to the proviso that the prequalification fulfils the condition that the subcontractor is entered in an official register or has a certification which meets the requirements of Article 64 of Directive 2014/24/EU of the European Parliament and of the Council of 26 February 2014 of the European Parliament and of the Council of the European Union on public procurement and to repea the directive 2004/18/EC (OJ L 94, 28.3.2014, p. 65), as last amended by Delegated Regulation (EU) 2017/2365 (OJ L 337, 19.12.2017, p. 19). [3]For an operator who transports parcels on behalf of another operator, paragraph 3c applies accordingly. [4]For the purposes of this book, the carriage of parcels is

(a) the carriage of addressed parcels with an individual weight of up to 32 kilograms, provided that such carriage is carried out by motor vehicles with a maximum authorised weight of up to 3.5 tonnes

(b) the stationary processing of addressed parcels weighing up to 32 kilograms, with the exception of processing in branch offices.

(3h) The Federal Government, with the participation of the Normenkontrollrat, shall report by 31 December 2023 on the effectiveness and scope of the liability for social security contributions for entrepreneurs in the forwarding, transport and related logistics industry who operate in the courier, express and parcel services sector and commission another entrepreneur to transport parcels, in particular on the exemption from liability under paragraph 3b and paragraph 3f first sentence.

(4) The liability includes the contributions and late payment surcharges payable as a result of the breach of duty as well as interest on deferred contributions (contribution claims).

(5) The statutes of the collection agency may determine the conditions under which advances on the total social security contribution may be demanded from the employer.

§ 28f
Aufzeichnungspflicht, Nachweise der Beitragsabrechnung und der Beitragszahlung

(1) ¹Der Arbeitgeber hat für jeden Beschäftigten, getrennt nach Kalenderjahren, Entgeltunterlagen im Geltungsbereich dieses Gesetzes in deutscher Sprache zu führen und bis zum Ablauf des auf die letzte Prüfung (§ 28p) folgenden Kalenderjahres geordnet aufzubewahren. ²Satz 1 gilt nicht hinsichtlich der Beschäftigten in privaten Haushalten. ³Die landwirtschaftliche Krankenkasse kann wegen der mitarbeitenden Familienangehörigen Ausnahmen zulassen. ⁴Für die Aufbewahrung der Beitragsabrechnungen und der Beitragsnachweise gilt Satz 1.

(1a) ¹Bei der Ausführung eines Dienst- oder Werkvertrages im Baugewerbe oder durch Unternehmer im Speditions-, Transport- und damit verbundenen Logistikgewerbe, die im Bereich der Kurier -, Express- und Paketdienste tätig sind und im Auftrag eines anderen Unternehmers Pakete befördern, hat der Unternehmer die Entgeltunterlagen und die Beitragsabrechnung so zu gestalten, dass eine Zuordnung der Arbeitnehmer, des Arbeitsentgelts und des darauf entfallenden Gesamtsozialversicherungsbeitrags zu dem jeweiligen Dienst- oder Werkvertrag möglich ist. ²Die Pflicht nach Satz 1 ruht für einen Unternehmer im Speditions-, Transport- und damit verbundenen Logistikgewerbe, der im Bereich der Kurier-, Express- und Paketdienste tätig ist, solange er eine Präqualifikation oder eine Unbedenklichkeitsbescheinigung im Sinne von § 28e Absatz 3f Satz 1 und 2 oder eine Unbedenklichkeitsbescheinigung nach § 150 Absatz 3 Satz 2 des Siebten Buches vorlegen kann.

(2) ¹Hat ein Arbeitgeber die Aufzeichnungspflicht nicht ordnungsgemäß erfüllt und können dadurch die Versicherungs- oder Beitragspflicht oder die Beitragshöhe nicht festgestellt werden, kann der prüfende Träger der Rentenversicherung den Beitrag in der Kranken-, Pflege- und Rentenversicherung und zur Arbeitsförderung von der Summe der vom Arbeitgeber gezahlten Arbeitsentgelte geltend machen. ²Satz 1 gilt nicht, soweit ohne unverhältnismäßig großen Verwaltungsaufwand festgestellt werden kann, dass Beiträge nicht zu zahlen waren oder Arbeitsentgelt einem bestimmten Beschäftigten zugeordnet werden kann. ³Soweit der prüfende Träger der Rentenversicherung die Höhe der Arbeitsentgelte nicht oder nicht ohne unverhältnismäßig großen Verwaltungsaufwand ermitteln kann, hat er diese zu schätzen. ⁴Dabei ist für das monatliche Arbeitsentgelt eines Beschäftigten das am Be-

Section 28f
Obligation to keep records, proof of the contribution statement and payment of contributions

(1) ¹The employer shall keep remuneration records in German for each employee, broken down by calendar year, within the scope of this Act and shall keep them in an orderly manner until the end of the calendar year following the last examination (section 28p). ²Sentence 1 does not apply to employees in private households. ³The agricultural health insurance fund may permit exceptions in respect of family members who work with them. 4Sentence 1 applies to the storage of contribution statements and contribution receipts.

(1a) ¹When executing a service or work contract in the construction industry or by entrepreneurs in the forwarding, transport and associated logistics industry who are active in the courier, express and parcel services sector and who transport parcels on behalf of another entrepreneur, the entrepreneur must structure the remuneration documents and the contribution statements in such a way that it is possible to allocate the employees, the remuneration and the total social security contribution attributable to it to the respective service or work contract. ²The obligation under sentence 1 shall be suspended for an entrepreneur in the forwarding, transport and associated logistics business who is active in the courier, express and parcel services sector for as long as he can present a prequalification or a clearance certificate within the meaning of Article 28e paragraph 3f sentences 1 and 2 or a clearance certificate within the meaning of Article 150 paragraph 3 sentence 2 of Book 7.

(2) ¹If an employer has not properly fulfilled its obligation to keep records and if, as a result, the obligation to insure or contribute or the amount of contributions cannot be determined, the examining pension insurance institution may claim the contribution to health, long-term care and pension insurance and to employment promotion from the total of the remuneration paid by the employer. 2Sentence 1 does not apply if it can be established without disproportionate administrative effort that contributions were not payable or that remuneration can be attributed to a particular employee. 3In so far as the pension insurance institution carrying out the investigation cannot determine the amount of remuneration or cannot determine it without disproportionate administrative expense, it must estimate it. 4 The monthly remuneration of an employee must be taken into account in this calculation, taking into account the remu-

schäftigungsort ortsübliche Arbeitsentgelt mit-
zuberücksichtigen. ⁵Der prüfende Träger der
Rentenversicherung hat einen auf Grund der
Sätze 1, 3 und 4 ergangenen Bescheid insoweit
zu widerrufen, als nachträglich Versicherungs-
oder Beitragspflicht oder Versicherungsfreiheit
festgestellt und die Höhe des Arbeitsentgelts
nachgewiesen werden. ⁶Die von dem Arbeitgeber auf Grund dieses Bescheides geleisteten
Zahlungen sind insoweit mit der Beitragsforderung zu verrechnen.

(3) ¹Der Arbeitgeber hat der Einzugsstelle einen
Beitragsnachweis zwei Arbeitstage vor Fälligkeit der Beiträge durch Datenübertragung zu
übermitteln; dies gilt nicht hinsichtlich der Beschäftigten in privaten Haushalten bei Verwendung von Haushaltsschecks. ²Übermittelt der
Arbeitgeber den Beitragsnachweis nicht zwei
Arbeitstage vor Fälligkeit der Beiträge, so kann
die Einzugsstelle das für die Beitragsberechnung maßgebende Arbeitsentgelt schätzen, bis
der Nachweis ordnungsgemäß übermittelt wird.
³Der Beitragsnachweis gilt für die Vollstreckung
als Leistungsbescheid der Einzugsstelle und im
Insolvenzverfahren als Dokument zur Glaub-
haftmachung der Forderungen der Einzugsstelle. ⁴Im Beitragsnachweis ist auch die Steuernummer des Arbeitgebers anzugeben, wenn der
Beitragsnachweis die Pauschsteuer für geringfügig Beschäftigte enthält.

(4) ¹Arbeitgeber, die den Gesamtsozialversicherungsbeitrag an mehrere Orts- oder Innungs-
krankenkassen zu zahlen haben, können bei

1. dem jeweils zuständigen Bundesverband
   oder

2. einer Orts- oder Innungskrankenkasse

(beauftragte Stelle) für die jeweilige Kassenart
beantragen, dass der beauftragten Stelle der jeweilige Beitragsnachweis eingereicht wird. ²Dies
gilt auch für Arbeitgeber, die den Gesamtsozialversicherungsbeitrag an mehrere Betriebskran-
kenkassen zu zahlen haben, gegenüber dem jeweiligen Bundesverband. ³Gibt die beauftragte
Stelle dem Antrag statt, hat sie die zuständigen
Einzugsstellen zu unterrichten. ⁴Im Falle des
Satzes 1 erhält die beauftragte Stelle auch den
Gesamtsozialversicherungsbeitrag, den sie arbeitstäglich durch Überweisung unmittelbar an
folgende Stellen weiterzuleiten hat:

1. die Beiträge zur Kranken- und Pflegeversicherung an die zuständigen Einzugsstellen,

2. die Beiträge zur Rentenversicherung gemäß
   § 28k,

neration customary in the place of employment.
5 The examining pension insurance institution
must revoke a decision taken on the basis of
sentences 1, 3 and 4 in so far as it subsequently
establishes that the person concerned is subject to compulsory insurance or contribution
or is exempt from compulsory insurance and
provides evidence of the amount of the salary.
6 The payments made by the employer on the
basis of this decision must be offset against the
contribution claim.

(3) ¹ The employer shall send the collection
agency a statement of contributions by data
transmission two working days before the
contributions are due; this does not apply to
employees in private households if household
cheques are used. ²If the employer does not
send the statement of contributions two working days before the contributions are due, the
collection agency may estimate the remuneration to be taken into account in calculating
contributions until the statement of contributions is duly sent. ³For enforcement purposes,
the contribution statement shall be deemed to
be a notice of performance issued by the collection agency and, in insolvency proceedings,
as a document to substantiate the claims of the
collection agency. ⁴The contribution statement
must also indicate the employer's tax number if
the contribution statement includes the flat-rate
tax for marginally employed persons.

(4) ¹Employers who are required to pay the total
social security contribution to several local or
guild health insurance funds may apply to

1. the respective competent federal association
   or

2. a local or guild health insurance fund

(commissioned body) for the respective type
of health insurance fund request that the respective contribution statement be submitted
to the commissioned body. 2This also applies
to employers who have to pay the total social
security contribution to several company health
insurance funds, vis-à-vis the respective federal
association. 3If the delegated body accepts the
application, it must inform the competent collection agencies. 4In the case of sentence 1, the
delegated body shall also receive the total social
security contribution, which it must forward
directly to the following bodies by means of a
transfer on each working day:

1. the health and long-term care insurance
   contributions to the competent collection
   agencies,

2. the contributions to the pension insurance
   pursuant to § 28k,

3. die Beiträge zur Arbeitsförderung an die Bundesagentur für Arbeit.

⁵Die beauftragte Stelle hat die für die zuständigen Einzugsstellen bestimmten Beitragsnachweise an diese weiterzuleiten. ⁶Die Träger der Pflegeversicherung, der Rentenversicherung und die Bundesagentur für Arbeit können den Beitragsnachweis sowie den Eingang, die Verwaltung und die Weiterleitung ihrer Beiträge bei der beauftragten Stelle prüfen. ⁷ § 28q Absatz 2 und 3 sowie § 28r Absatz 1 und 2 gelten entsprechend.

§ 28g
Beitragsabzug

¹Der Arbeitgeber und in den Fällen der nach § 7f Absatz 1 Satz 1 Nummer 2 auf die Deutsche Rentenversicherung Bund übertragenen Wertguthaben die Deutsche Rentenversicherung Bund hat gegen den Beschäftigten einen Anspruch auf den vom Beschäftigten zu tragenden Teil des Gesamtsozialversicherungsbeitrags. ²Dieser Anspruch kann nur durch Abzug vom Arbeitsentgelt geltend gemacht werden. ³Ein unterbliebener Abzug darf nur bei den drei nächsten Lohn- oder Gehaltszahlungen nachgeholt werden, danach nur dann, wenn der Abzug ohne Verschulden des Arbeitgebers unterblieben ist. ⁴Die Sätze 2 und 3 gelten nicht, wenn der Beschäftigte seinen Pflichten nach § 280 Absatz 1 vorsätzlich oder grob fahrlässig nicht nachkommt oder er den Gesamtsozialversicherungsbeitrag allein trägt oder solange der Beschäftigte nur Sachbezüge erhält.

§ 28h
Einzugsstellen

(1) ¹Der Gesamtsozialversicherungsbeitrag ist an die Krankenkassen (Einzugsstellen) zu zahlen. ²Die Einzugsstelle überwacht die Einreichung des Beitragsnachweises und die Zahlung des Gesamtsozialversicherungsbeitrags. ³Beitragsansprüche, die nicht rechtzeitig erfüllt worden sind, hat die Einzugsstelle geltend zu machen.

(2) ¹Die Einzugsstelle entscheidet über die Versicherungspflicht und Beitragshöhe in der Kranken-, Pflege- und Rentenversicherung sowie nach dem Recht der Arbeitsförderung; sie erlässt auch den Widerspruchsbescheid. ²Soweit die Einzugsstelle die Höhe des Arbeitsentgelts nicht oder nicht ohne unverhältnismäßig großen Verwaltungsaufwand ermitteln kann, hat sie dieses zu schätzen. ³Dabei ist für das monatliche Arbeitsentgelt des Beschäftigten das am

---

3. contributions to the Federal Employment Agency for the promotion of employment.

⁵The commissioned agency shall forward the contribution statements intended for them to the competent collection agencies. ⁶The institutions responsible for long-term care insurance, pension insurance and the Federal Employment Agency may check the statement of contributions and the receipt, administration and forwarding of their contributions to the commissioned office. ⁷Article 28q paragraphs 2 and 3 and Article 28r paragraphs 1 and apply accordingly.

Section 28g
Deduction of contributions

¹The employer and, in the case of the assets transferred to the German Pension Insurance Federation in accordance with Article 7f paragraph 1 sentence 1 number 2, the German Pension Insurance Federation has a claim against the employee for the part of the total social security contribution to be borne by the employee. ²This claim may only be asserted by deduction from the employee's remuneration. ³Any omitted deduction may only be made up for the next three wage or salary payments and thereafter only if the deduction was not made through no fault of the employer. ⁴The second and third sentences do not apply if the employee fails to comply with his obligations under Article 280 paragraph 1 intentionally or through gross negligence or if he bears the total social security contribution alone or as long as the employee receives only remuneration in kind.

Section 28h
Catchment offices

(1) ¹The total social security contribution is payable to the health insurance funds (collection agencies). ²The collection agency shall monitor the submission of the contribution statement and the payment of the total social security contribution. ³Contribution claims that have not been met in time must be asserted by the collection agency.

(2) ¹The collection agency shall decide on the obligation to be insured and the amount of contributions in health, long-term care and pension insurance and under the law on employment promotion; it shall also issue the notice of appeal. ²If the collection agency is unable to determine the amount of remuneration or cannot determine it without disproportionate administrative effort, it must estimate it. ³The employee's monthly remuneration shall be based

Beschäftigungsort ortsübliche Arbeitsentgelt mit zu berücksichtigen. ⁴Die nach § 28i Satz 5 zuständige Einzugsstelle prüft die Einhaltung der Arbeitsentgeltgrenze bei geringfügiger Beschäftigung nach den §§ 8 und 8a und entscheidet bei deren Überschreiten über die Versicherungspflicht in der Kranken-, Pflege- und Rentenversicherung sowie nach dem Recht der Arbeitsförderung; sie erlässt auch den Widerspruchsbescheid.

(3) ¹Bei Verwendung eines Haushaltsschecks vergibt die Einzugsstelle im Auftrag der Bundesagentur für Arbeit die Betriebsnummer des Arbeitgebers, berechnet den Gesamtsozialversicherungsbeitrag und die Umlagen nach dem Aufwendungsausgleichsgesetz und zieht diese vom Arbeitgeber im Wege des Lastschriftverfahrens ein. ²Die Einzugsstelle meldet bei Beginn und Ende der Beschäftigung und zum Jahresende der Datenstelle der Rentenversicherung die für die Rentenversicherung und die Bundesagentur für Arbeit erforderlichen Daten eines jeden Beschäftigten. ³Die Einzugsstelle teilt dem Beschäftigten den Inhalt der abgegebenen Meldung schriftlich oder durch gesicherte Datenübertragung mit.

(4) Bei Verwendung eines Haushaltsschecks bescheinigt die Einzugsstelle dem Arbeitgeber zum Jahresende

1. den Zeitraum, für den Beiträge zur Rentenversicherung gezahlt wurden, und
2. die Höhe des Arbeitsentgelts (§ 14 Absatz 3), des von ihm getragenen Gesamtsozialversicherungsbeitrags und der Umlagen.

§ 28i
Zuständige Einzugsstelle

¹Zuständige Einzugsstelle für den Gesamtsozialversicherungsbeitrag ist die Krankenkasse, von der die Krankenversicherung durchgeführt wird. ²Für Beschäftigte, die bei keiner Krankenkasse versichert sind, werden Beiträge zur Rentenversicherung und zur Arbeitsförderung an die Einzugsstelle gezahlt, die der Arbeitgeber in entsprechender Anwendung des § 175 Absatz 3 Satz 2 des Fünften Buches gewählt hat. ³Zuständige Einzugsstelle ist in den Fällen des § 28f Absatz 2 die nach § 175 Absatz 3 Satz 3 des Fünften Buches bestimmte Krankenkasse. ⁴Zuständige Einzugsstelle ist in den Fällen des § 2 Absatz 3 die Deutsche Rentenversicherung Knappschaft-Bahn-See. ⁵Bei geringfügigen Beschäftigungen ist zuständige Einzugsstelle die Deutsche Rentenversicherung Knappschaft-Bahn-See als Träger der Rentenversicherung.

on the remuneration customary in the place of employment. ⁴The collection agency responsible under section 28i sentence 5 shall check compliance with the pay ceiling in the case of marginal employment under sections 8 and 8a and, if it is exceeded, shall decide whether the employee is subject to compulsory health, long-term care and pension insurance and employment promotion legislation; it shall also issue an objection notice.

(3) ¹If a household cheque is used, the collection agency shall, on behalf of the Federal Employment Agency, issue the employer's company number, calculate the total social security contribution and the apportionments in accordance with the Expenditure Compensation Act and collect these from the employer by means of the direct debit procedure. ²At the beginning and end of employment and at the end of the year, the collection agency shall report to the data centre of the pension insurance scheme the data required for the pension insurance scheme and the Federal Employment Agency for each employee. ³The collection agency shall inform the employee of the content of the submitted notification in writing or by secure data transmission.

(4) If a household cheque is used, the collection agency shall certify to the employer at the end of the year

1. the period for which pension insurance contributions have been paid, and
2. the amount of the salary (section 14(3)), the total social security contribution paid by him and the apportionments

Section 28i
Competent collecting agency

¹ The competent collecting agency for the total social security contribution is the sickness insurance fund which administers the health insurance. ²For employees who are not insured with any health insurance fund, pension insurance and employment promotion contributions shall be paid to the collection office chosen by the employer by analogous application of the second sentence of Article 175(3) of Book 5. ³In the cases covered by § 28f paragraph 2, the competent collection agency is the sickness insurance fund chosen in accordance with § 175 paragraph 3 sentence 3 of Book 5. ⁴The competent collecting agency in the cases referred to in Article 2(3) is the German Pension Insurance Knappschaft-Bahn-See (pension for miners, railway workers and seafarers). ⁵In the case of minor employment, the competent collecting agency is the German Pension Insurance.

Knappschaft-Bahn-See (pension for miners, railway workers and seafarers) as the pension insurance institution

<table>
<tr><td>

§ 28k
Weiterleitung von Beiträgen

</td><td>

Section 28k
Forwarding of contributions

</td></tr>
</table>

(1) ¹Die Einzugsstelle leitet dem zuständigen Träger der Pflegeversicherung, der Rentenversicherung und der Bundesagentur für Arbeit die für diese gezahlten Beiträge einschließlich der Zinsen auf Beiträge und Säumniszuschläge arbeitstäglich weiter; dies gilt entsprechend für die Weiterleitung der Beiträge zur gesetzlichen Krankenversicherung an den Gesundheitsfonds. ²Die Deutsche Rentenversicherung Bund teilt den Einzugsstellen die zuständigen Träger der Rentenversicherung und deren Beitragsanteil spätestens bis zum 31. Oktober eines jeden Jahres für das folgende Kalenderjahr mit. ³Die Deutsche Rentenversicherung Bund legt den Verteilungsschlüssel für die Aufteilung der Beitragseinnahmen der allgemeinen Rentenversicherung auf die einzelnen Träger unter Berücksichtigung der folgenden Parameter fest:

(1) ¹The collection agency shall forward to the competent institution of the long-term care insurance scheme, the pension insurance scheme and the Federal Employment Agency the contributions paid for them, including interest on contributions and default surcharges, on each working day; this shall apply mutatis mutandis to the forwarding of contributions to the statutory health insurance scheme to the Health Fund. ²The German Pension Insurance Federation shall inform the collection agencies of the competent pension insurance institutions and their contribution rates by 31 October of each year at the latest for the following calendar year. ³The German Pension Insurance Federation shall determine the distribution key for the allocation of the contribution income of the general pension insurance scheme to the individual institutions, taking into account the following parameters:

1. Für die Aufteilung zwischen Deutsche Rentenversicherung Bund und Regionalträgern:

   (a) Für 2005 die prozentuale Aufteilung der gezahlten Pflichtbeiträge zur Rentenversicherung der Arbeiter und der Rentenversicherung der Angestellten im Jahr 2003,
   (b) Fortschreibung dieser Anteile in den folgenden Jahren unter Berücksichtigung der Veränderung des Anteils der bei den Regionalträgern Pflichtversicherten gegenüber dem jeweiligen vorvergangenen Kalenderjahr.
2. Für die Aufteilung der Beiträge unter den Regionalträgern: Das Verhältnis der Pflichtversicherten dieser Träger untereinander.

3. Für die Aufteilung zwischen Deutsche Rentenversicherung Bund und Deutsche Rentenversicherung Knappschaft-Bahn-See: Das Verhältnis der in der allgemeinen Rentenversicherung Pflichtversicherten dieser Träger untereinander.

(2) ¹Bei geringfügigen Beschäftigungen werden die Beiträge zur Krankenversicherung an den Gesundheitsfonds, bei Versicherten in der landwirtschaftlichen Krankenversicherung an die Sozialversicherung für Landwirtschaft, Forsten und Gartenbau weitergeleitet. ²Das Nähere zur Bestimmung des Anteils der Sozialversicherung

1. for the distribution between German Pension Insurance Federation and regional institutions:

   (a) For 2005, the percentage allocation of the compulsory contributions paid to the pension insurance scheme for manual workers and the pension insurance scheme for salaried employees in 2003,
   (b) updating these proportions in the following years, taking into account the change in the proportion of persons compulsorily insured with the regional bodies compared with the respective previous calendar year.
2. for the distribution of contributions among the regional bodies: the ratio of those compulsorily insured by these bodies among themselves.

3. For the distribution between the Federal German Pension Insurance Fund and the Knappschaft-Bahn-See Pension Insurance Fund: the ratio of those insured compulsorily in the general pension insurance scheme of these institutions among themselves.

(2) ¹For minor jobs, health insurance contributions are passed on to the Health Fund, for those insured in the agricultural health insurance scheme, to the Social Insurance Scheme for Agriculture, Forestry and Horticulture. ²The details for determining the share of social insurance for agriculture, forestry and horticulture,

für Landwirtschaft, Forsten und Gartenbau, insbesondere über eine pauschale Berechnung und Aufteilung, vereinbaren die Sozialversicherung für Landwirtschaft, Forsten und Gartenbau und die Spitzenverbände der beteiligten Träger der Sozialversicherung.

in particular by means of a flat-rate calculation and distribution, shall be agreed between the social insurance for agriculture, forestry and horticulture and the umbrella organisations of the participating social insurance institutions.

§ 28l
Vergütung

(1) ¹Die Einzugsstellen, die Träger der Rentenversicherung und die Bundesagentur für Arbeit erhalten für

1. die Geltendmachung der Beitragsansprüche,

2. den Einzug, die Verwaltung, die Weiterleitung, die Abrechnung und die Abstimmung der Beiträge,

3. die Prüfung bei den Arbeitgebern,

4. die Durchführung der Meldeverfahren,

5. die Ausstellung der Sozialversicherungsausweise und

6. die Durchführung des Haushaltsscheckverfahrens, soweit es über die Verfahren nach den Nummern 1 bis 5 hinausgeht und Aufgaben der Sozialversicherung betrifft,

eine pauschale Vergütung, mit der alle dadurch entstehenden Kosten abgegolten werden, dies gilt entsprechend für die Künstlersozialkasse. ²Die Höhe und die Verteilung der Vergütung werden durch Vereinbarung zwischen dem Spitzenverband Bund der Krankenkassen, der Deutschen Rentenversicherung Bund, der Bundesagentur für Arbeit und der Künstlersozialkasse geregelt; vor dem Abschluss und vor Änderungen der Vereinbarung ist die Sozialversicherung für Landwirtschaft, Forsten und Gartenbau anzuhören. ³In der Vereinbarung ist auch für den Fall, dass eine Einzugsstelle ihre Pflichten nicht ordnungsgemäß erfüllt und dadurch erhebliche Beitragsrückstände entstehen, festzulegen, dass sich die Vergütung für diesen Zeitraum angemessen mindert. ⁴Die Deutsche Rentenversicherung Knappschaft-Bahn-See wird ermächtigt, die ihr von den Krankenkassen nach Satz 1 zustehende Vergütung mit den nach § 28k Absatz 2 Satz 1 an den Gesundheitsfonds weiterzuleitenden Beiträgen zur Krankenversicherung für geringfügige Beschäftigungen aufzurechnen.

Section 28l
Compensation

(1) ¹The collection agencies, the pension insurance institutions and the Federal Employment Agency receive for

1. the assertion of contribution claims,

2. the collection, administration, forwarding, accounting and reconciliation of contributions,

3. the examination at the employers' premises,

4. the implementation of the notification procedures,

5. the issue of social security cards, and

6. the implementation of the budget cheque procedure in so far as it goes beyond the procedures laid down in points 1 to 5 and concerns social security tasks,

a lump-sum payment to cover all costs incurred; this applies accordingly to the artists' social security fund. ²The amount and distribution of the remuneration shall be regulated by agreement between the Federal Association of Health Insurance Funds, the German Pension Insurance Fund, the Federal Employment Agency and the social insurance fund for artists; the social insurance fund for agriculture, forestry and horticulture must be consulted before the agreement is concluded and before any changes are made. ³The agreement must also stipulate that if a collection agency fails to fulfil its obligations properly and this results in substantial arrears of contributions, the remuneration for this period must be reduced appropriately. ⁴The Deutsche Rentenversicherung Knappschaft-Bahn-See is authorised to offset the remuneration to which it is entitled from the health insurance funds in accordance with the first sentence above against the health insurance contributions to be passed on to the health fund for marginal employment in accordance with Article 28k(2), first sentence.

(2) Soweit die Einzugsstellen oder die beauftragten Stellen (§ 28f Absatz 4) bei der Verwaltung von Fremdbeiträgen Gewinne erzielen, wird deren Aufteilung durch Vereinbarungen zwischen den Krankenkassen oder ihren Verbänden und der Deutschen Rentenversicherung Bund sowie der Bundesagentur für Arbeit geregelt.

(2) Insofar as the collection agencies or the commissioned agencies (Section 28f (4)) make profits in the administration of third-party contributions, their allocation shall be regulated by agreements between the health insurance funds or their associations and the German Pension Insurance Association and the Federal Employment Agency.

§ 28m
Sonderregelungen für bestimmte Personengruppen

Section 28m
Special arrangements for certain categories of persons

(1) Der Beschäftigte hat den Gesamtsozialversicherungsbeitrag zu zahlen, wenn sein Arbeitgeber ein ausländischer Staat, eine über- oder zwischenstaatliche Organisation oder eine Person ist, die nicht der inländischen Gerichtsbarkeit untersteht und die Zahlungspflicht nach § 28e Absatz 1 Satz 1 nicht erfüllt.

(1) The employee shall pay the total security contribution if his employer is a foreign state, a supranational or intergovernmental organisation or a person not subject to domestic jurisdiction and does not fulfil the payment obligation under section 28e(1) first sentence.

(2) [1]Heimarbeiter und Hausgewerbetreibende können, falls der Arbeitgeber seiner Verpflichtung nach § 28e bis zum Fälligkeitstage nicht nachkommt, den Gesamtsozialversicherungsbeitrag selbst zahlen. [2]Soweit sie den Gesamtsozialversicherungsbeitrag selbst zahlen, entfallen die Pflichten des Arbeitgebers; § 28f Absatz 1 bleibt unberührt.

(2) [1]Home workers and domestic craftsmen may, if the employer fails to meet its obligation under section 28e by the due date, pay the total social security contribution themselves. [2]In so far as they pay the total social security contribution themselves, the employer's obligations shall cease; Section 28f subsection (1) shall remain unaffected.

(3) Zahlt der Beschäftigte oder der Hausgewerbetreibende den Gesamtsozialversicherungsbeitrag, hat er auch die Meldungen nach § 28a abzugeben; bei den Meldungen hat die Einzugsstelle mitzuwirken.

(3) If the employee or the domestic craftsman pays the total social insurance contribution, he shall also submit the notifications under section 28a; the collection agency shall cooperate in the notifications.

(4) Der Beschäftigte oder der Hausgewerbetreibende, der den Gesamtsozialversicherungsbeitrag gezahlt hat, hat gegen den Arbeitgeber einen Anspruch auf den vom Arbeitgeber zu tragenden Teil des Gesamtsozialversicherungsbeitrags.

(4) The employee or the domestic craftsman who has paid the total social security contribution shall be entitled to claim from the employer the part of the total social security contribution to be borne by the employer.

§ 28n
Verordnungsermächtigung

Section 28n
Authorisation by decree

Das Bundesministerium für Arbeit und Soziales wird ermächtigt, durch Rechtsverordnung mit Zustimmung des Bundesrates zu bestimmen,

The Federal Ministry of Labour and Social Affairs is empowered to determine by statutory order with the consent of the Bundesrat,

1. die Berechnung des Gesamtsozialversicherungsbeitrags und der Beitragsbemessungsgrenzen für kürzere Zeiträume als ein Kalenderjahr,

2. zu welchem Zeitpunkt die Beiträge als eingezahlt gelten, in welcher Reihenfolge eine Schuld getilgt wird und welche Zahlungsmittel verwendet werden dürfen,

1. the calculation of the total social security contribution and the contribution assessment thresholds for periods shorter than one calendar year

2. the date on which contributions are deemed to have been paid, the order in which a debt is repaid and the means of payment that may be used,

3. Näheres über die Weiterleitung und Abrechnung der Beiträge einschließlich Zinsen auf Beiträge und der Säumniszuschläge durch die Einzugsstellen an die Träger der Pflegeversicherung, der Rentenversicherung, den Gesundheitsfonds und die Bundesagentur für Arbeit, insbesondere über Zahlungsweise und das Verfahren nach § 28f Absatz 4, wobei von der arbeitstäglichen Weiterleitung bei Beträgen unter 2 500 Euro abgesehen werden kann,
4. Näheres über die Führung von Entgeltunterlagen und zur Beitragsabrechnung sowie zur Verwendung des Beitragsnachweises.

§ 28o
Auskunfts- und Vorlagepflicht des Beschäftigten

(1) Der Beschäftigte hat dem Arbeitgeber die zur Durchführung des Meldeverfahrens und der Beitragszahlung erforderlichen Angaben zu machen und, soweit erforderlich, Unterlagen vorzulegen; dies gilt bei mehreren Beschäftigungen sowie bei Bezug weiterer in der gesetzlichen Krankenversicherung beitragspflichtiger Einnahmen gegenüber allen beteiligten Arbeitgebern.

(2) ¹Der Beschäftigte hat auf Verlangen den zuständigen Versicherungsträgern unverzüglich Auskunft über die Art und Dauer seiner Beschäftigungen, die hierbei erzielten Arbeitsentgelte, seine Arbeitgeber und die für die Erhebung von Beiträgen notwendigen Tatsachen zu erteilen und alle für die Prüfung der Meldungen und der Beitragszahlung erforderlichen Unterlagen vorzulegen. ²Satz 1 gilt für den Hausgewerbetreibenden, soweit er den Gesamtsozialversicherungsbeitrag zahlt, entsprechend.

§ 28p
Prüfung bei den Arbeitgebern

(1) ¹Die Träger der Rentenversicherung prüfen bei den Arbeitgebern, ob diese ihre Meldepflichten und ihre sonstigen Pflichten nach diesem Gesetzbuch, die im Zusammenhang mit dem Gesamtsozialversicherungsbeitrag stehen, ordnungsgemäß erfüllen; sie prüfen insbesondere die Richtigkeit der Beitragszahlungen und der Meldungen (§ 28a) mindestens alle vier Jahre. ²Die Prüfung soll in kürzeren Zeitabständen erfolgen, wenn der Arbeitgeber dies verlangt. ³Die Einzugsstelle unterrichtet den für den Arbeitgeber zuständigen Träger der Rentenversicherung, wenn sie eine alsbaldige Prüfung bei dem Arbeitgeber für erforderlich hält. ⁴Die Prüfung umfasst auch die Entgeltunterlagen der Beschäftigten, für die Beiträge nicht gezahlt wurden. ⁵Die Träger der Renten-

3. details on the forwarding and settlement of contributions, including interest on contributions and late payment surcharges, by the collection agencies to the institutions of long-term care insurance, pension insurance, the Health Fund and the Federal Employment Agency, in particular on the method of payment and the procedure under Section 28f(4), whereby forwarding on a working day basis may be waived for amounts of less than EUR 2 500.
4. details on the keeping of payroll records and on the statement of contributions as well as on the use of the contribution statement.

Section 28o
Obligation of the employee to provide information and to present it

(1) The Employee shall provide the Employer with the information required to carry out the registration procedure and the payment of contributions and, where necessary, submit documents; this shall apply to all participating employers in the case of several jobs as well as in the case of receipt of further income subject to contributions in the statutory health insurance scheme.

(2) ¹The employee shall, on request, immediately provide the competent insurance institutions with information on the nature and duration of his employment, the remuneration received in this connection, his employers and the facts necessary for the collection of contributions, and shall submit all documents necessary for the verification of the notifications and the payment of contributions. ²Sentence 1 shall apply mutatis mutandis to the domestic craftsman insofar as he pays the total social security contribution.

Section 28p
Examination at the employers

(1) ¹The pension insurance institutions shall check with employers to ensure that they duly comply with their obligation to register and other obligations under this Act in connection with the total social security contribution; in particular, they shall check the accuracy of contribution payments and notifications (Article 28a) at least every four years. ²The checks shall be carried out at shorter intervals if the employer so requests. ³The collection agency shall inform the pension insurance institution responsible for the employer if it considers it necessary to carry out an examination with the employer as soon as possible. ⁴The examination shall also include the payroll records of employees for whom contributions have not been paid. ⁵As part of the examination, the pension insurance institutions

versicherung erlassen im Rahmen der Prüfung Verwaltungsakte zur Versicherungspflicht und Beitragshöhe in der Kranken -, Pflege- und Rentenversicherung sowie nach dem Recht der Arbeitsförderung einschließlich der Widerspruchsbescheide gegenüber den Arbeitgebern; insoweit gelten § 28h Absatz 2 sowie § 93 in Verbindung mit § 89 Absatz 5 des Zehnten Buches nicht. [6]Die landwirtschaftliche Krankenkasse nimmt abweichend von Satz 1 die Prüfung für die bei ihr versicherten mitarbeitenden Familienangehörigen vor.

(1a) [1]Die Prüfung nach Absatz 1 umfasst die ordnungsgemäße Erfüllung der Meldepflichten nach dem Künstlersozialversicherungsgesetz und die rechtzeitige und vollständige Entrichtung der Künstlersozialabgabe durch die Arbeitgeber.
[2]Die Prüfung erfolgt

1. mindestens alle vier Jahre bei den Arbeitgebern, die als abgabepflichtige Unternehmer nach § 24 des Künstlersozialversicherungsgesetzes bei der Künstlersozialkasse erfasst wurden,
2. mindestens alle vier Jahre bei den Arbeitgebern mit mehr als 19 Beschäftigten und
3. bei mindestens 40 Prozent der im jeweiligen Kalenderjahr zur Prüfung nach Absatz 1 anstehenden Arbeitgeber mit weniger als 20 Beschäftigten.

[3]Bei Arbeitgebern, die eine Betriebsstruktur mit Haupt- und Unterbetrieben mit jeweils eigener Betriebsnummer aufweisen, wird der Arbeitgeber insgesamt geprüft. [4]Das Prüfverfahren kann mit der Aufforderung zur Meldung eingeleitet werden. [5]Die Träger der Deutschen Rentenversicherung erlassen die erforderlichen Verwaltungsakte zur Künstlersozialabgabepflicht, zur Höhe der Künstlersozialabgabe und zur Höhe der Vorauszahlungen nach dem Künstlersozialversicherungsgesetz einschließlich der Widerspruchsbescheide. [6]Die Träger der Rentenversicherung unterrichten die Künstlersozialkasse über Sachverhalte, welche die Melde- und Abgabepflichten der Arbeitgeber nach dem Künstlersozialversicherungsgesetz betreffen. [7]Für die Prüfung der Arbeitgeber durch die Künstlersozialkasse gilt § 35 des Künstlersozialversicherungsgesetzes.

(1b) [1]Die Träger der Rentenversicherung legen im Benehmen mit der Künstlersozialkasse die Kriterien zur Auswahl der nach Absatz 1a Satz 2 Nummer 3 zu prüfenden Arbeitgeber fest. [2]Die Auswahl dient dem Ziel, alle abgabepflichtigen Arbeitgeber zu erfassen. [3]Arbeitgeber mit weniger als 20 Beschäftigten, die nicht nach Absatz 1a Satz 2 Nummer 3 zu prüfen sind,

shall issue administrative acts on the compulsory insurance and the amount of contributions in health, long-term care and pension insurance and under the law on the promotion of employment, including decisions of appeal against employers; in this respect, Article 28h(2) and Article 93 in conjunction with Article 89(5) of Book 10 shall not apply. [6]Notwithstanding the first sentence above, the agricultural health insurance fund shall carry out the examination for the family members who are insured with it.

(1a) [1]The examination under subsection 1 shall include the proper fulfilment of the registration obligations under the Social Insurance for Artists Act and the timely and complete payment of the social security contribution for artists by their employers.
[2]The audit shall be carried out

1. at least every four years in the case of employers who have been registered with the artists' social insurance fund as entrepreneurs liable to pay contributions under Section 24 of the Artists' Social Insurance Act
2. at least every four years for employers with more than 19 employees, and
3. at least 40 per cent of the employers with fewer than 20 employees who are due for examination pursuant to subsection 1 in the respective calendar year.

[3]In the case of employers who have a company structure with main and sub-companies, each with its own company number, the employer as a whole shall be audited. [4]The examination procedure may be initiated with a request to report. [5]The institutions of the German Pension Insurance Scheme shall issue the necessary administrative acts on the obligation to pay social security contributions for artists and on the amount of advance payments under the Artists' Social Security Act, including decisions on objections. [6]The pension insurance institutions shall inform the Artists' Social Security Fund of facts concerning employers' obligations to register and pay social security contributions in accordance with the Artists' Social Security Act. [7]Section 35 of the Artists' Social Insurance Act applies to the examination of employers by the Artists' Social Insurance Fund.

(1b) [1]The pension insurance institutions shall, in consultation with the social insurance fund for artists, lay down the criteria for selecting the employers to be audited under subsection 1a, second sentence, number 3. [2]The selection serves the purpose of covering all employers liable to pay contributions. [3]Employers with fewer than 20 employees who are not to be ex-

werden durch die Träger der Rentenversicherung im Rahmen der Prüfung nach Absatz 1 im Hinblick auf die Künstlersozialabgabe beraten. [4]Dazu erhalten sie mit der Prüfankündigung Hinweise zur Künstlersozialabgabe. [5]Im Rahmen der Prüfung nach Absatz 1 lässt sich der zuständige Träger der Rentenversicherung durch den Arbeitgeber schriftlich oder elektronisch bestätigen, dass der Arbeitgeber über die Künstlersozialabgabe unterrichtet wurde und abgabepflichtige Sachverhalte melden wird. [6]Bestätigt der Arbeitgeber dies nicht, wird die Prüfung nach Absatz 1a Satz 1 unverzüglich durchgeführt. [7]Erlangt ein Träger der Rentenversicherung im Rahmen einer Prüfung nach Absatz 1 bei Arbeitgebern mit weniger als 20 Beschäftigten, die nicht nach Absatz 1a Satz 2 Nummer 3 geprüft werden, Hinweise auf einen künstlersozialabgabepflichtigen Sachverhalt, muss er diesen nachgehen.

(1c) [1]Die Träger der Rentenversicherung teilen den Trägern der Unfallversicherung die Feststellungen aus der Prüfung bei den Arbeitgebern nach § 166 Absatz 2 des Siebten Buches mit. [2]Die Träger der Unfallversicherung erlassen die erforderlichen Bescheide.

(2) [1]Im Bereich der Regionalträger richtet sich die örtliche Zuständigkeit nach dem Sitz der Lohn- und Gehaltsabrechnungsstelle des Arbeitgebers. [2]Die Träger der Rentenversicherung stimmen sich darüber ab, welche Arbeitgeber sie prüfen; ein Arbeitgeber ist jeweils nur von einem Träger der Rentenversicherung zu prüfen.

(3) Die Träger der Rentenversicherung unterrichten die Einzugsstellen über Sachverhalte, soweit sie die Zahlungspflicht oder die Meldepflicht des Arbeitgebers betreffen.

(4) (weggefallen)

(5) [1]Die Arbeitgeber sind verpflichtet, angemessene Prüfhilfen zu leisten. [2]Abrechnungsverfahren, die mit Hilfe automatischer Einrichtungen durchgeführt werden, sind in die Prüfung einzubeziehen.

(6) [1]Zu prüfen sind auch steuerberatende Stellen, Rechenzentren und vergleichbare Einrichtungen, die im Auftrag des Arbeitgebers oder einer von ihm beauftragten Person Löhne und Gehälter abrechnen oder Meldungen erstatten. [2]Die örtliche Zuständigkeit richtet sich im Bereich der Regionalträger nach dem Sitz dieser Stellen. [3]Absatz 5 gilt entsprechend.

amined under paragraph 1a, second sentence, number 3, shall be advised by the pension insurance institutions in the context of the examination under paragraph 1 with regard to the social security contribution for artists. [4]For this purpose, they shall receive information on the social security contribution for artists with the audit notification. [5]Within the framework of the examination referred to in paragraph 1, the competent pension insurance institution shall obtain confirmation from the employer, in writing or electronically, that the employer has been informed of the social security contribution for artists and will report any facts that are subject to the contribution. [6]If the employer does not confirm this, the examination under subsection 1a sentence 1 shall be carried out without delay. [7]If, in the course of an audit pursuant to subsection 1, a pension insurance institution finds indications of facts liable to pay social security contributions for artists in the case of employers with fewer than 20 employees who are not audited pursuant to subsection 1a, second sentence, number 3, it must investigate these facts.

(1c) [1]The pension insurance institutions shall inform the accident insurance institutions of the findings of the examination at the employers' premises in accordance with Article 166(2) of Book Seven. [2]The accident insurance institutions shall issue the necessary notices.

(2) [1]In the area covered by the regional institutions, local jurisdiction is determined by the location of the employer's payroll office. [2]The pension insurance institutions shall agree on which employers they will audit; an employer shall be audited by only one pension insurance institution at a time.

(3) The pension insurance institutions shall inform the collection agencies of facts concerning the employer's obligation to pay or to report.

(4) (deleted)

(5) [1]Employers are obliged to provide appropriate auditing aids. [2]Accounting procedures which are carried out with the aid of automatic equipment must be included in the audit.

(6) [1]Audits must also include tax advisory offices, computer centres and similar institutions which settle wages and salaries or make reports on behalf of the employer or a person commissioned by the employer. [2]In the case of regional bodies, local competence is determined by the location of the headquarters of these bodies. 3Section 5 applies accordingly.

(6a) ¹Für die Prüfung nach Absatz 1 gilt § 147 Absatz 6 Satz 1 und 2 der Abgabenordnung entsprechend mit der Maßgabe, dass der Rentenversicherungsträger eine Übermittlung der Daten im Einvernehmen mit dem Arbeitgeber verlangen kann. ²Die Deutsche Rentenversicherung Bund bestimmt in Grundsätzen bundeseinheitlich das Nähere zum Verfahren der Datenübermittlung und der dafür erforderlichen Datensätze und Datenbausteine. ³Die Grundsätze bedürfen der Genehmigung des Bundesministeriums für Arbeit und Soziales, das vorher die Bundesvereinigung der Deutschen Arbeitgeberverbände anzuhören hat.

(7) ¹Die Träger der Rentenversicherung haben eine Übersicht über die Ergebnisse ihrer Prüfungen zu führen und bis zum 31. März eines jeden Jahres für das abgelaufene Kalenderjahr den Aufsichtsbehörden vorzulegen. ²Das Nähere über Inhalt und Form der Übersicht bestimmen einvernehmlich die Aufsichtsbehörden der Träger der Rentenversicherung mit Wirkung für diese.

(8) ¹Die Deutsche Rentenversicherung Bund führt ein Dateisystem, in dem der Name, die Anschrift, die Betriebsnummer, der für den Arbeitgeber zuständige Unfallversicherungsträger und weitere Identifikationsmerkmale eines jeden Arbeitgebers sowie die für die Planung der Prüfungen bei den Arbeitgebern und die für die Übersichten nach Absatz 7 erforderlichen Daten gespeichert sind; die Deutsche Rentenversicherung Bund darf die in diesem Dateisystem gespeicherten Daten nur für die Prüfung bei den Arbeitgebern und zur Ermittlung der nach dem Künstlersozialversicherungsgesetz abgabepflichtigen Unternehmer verarbeiten. ²In das Dateisystem ist eine Kennzeichnung aufzunehmen, wenn nach § 166 Absatz 2 Satz 2 des Siebten Buches die Prüfung der Arbeitgeber für die Unfallversicherung nicht von den Trägern der Rentenversicherung durchzuführen ist; die Träger der Unfallversicherung haben die erforderlichen Angaben zu übermitteln. ³Die Datenstelle der Rentenversicherung führt für die Prüfung bei den Arbeitgebern ein Dateisystem, in dem neben der Betriebsnummer eines jeden Arbeitgebers, die Betriebsnummer des für den Arbeitgeber zuständigen Unfallversicherungsträgers, die Unfallversicherungsmitgliedsnummer des Arbeitgebers, das in der Unfallversicherung beitragspflichtige Entgelt der bei ihm Beschäftigten in Euro, die anzuwendenden Gefahrtarifstellen der bei ihm Beschäftigten, die Versicherungsnummern der bei ihm Beschäftigten einschließlich des Beginns und des Endes von deren Beschäftigung, die Bezeichnung der für jeden Beschäftigten zuständigen Einzugsstelle

(6a) ¹For the examination under subsection 1, Section 147(6), first and second sentences of the Tax Code shall apply accordingly, subject to the proviso that the pension insurance institution may require the data to be transmitted in agreement with the employer. ²The German Pension Insurance Association shall lay down the details of the data transmission procedure and the data records and data modules required for this purpose in principles that are uniform throughout Germany. ³The principles require the approval of the Federal Ministry of Labour and Social Affairs, which must first consult the Confederation of German Employers' Associations.

(7) ¹The pension insurance institutions must keep an overview of the results of their audits and submit it to the supervisory authorities by 31 March of each year for the previous calendar year. ²The supervisory authorities of the pension insurance institutions shall determine the details of the content and form of the overview by mutual agreement with effect for the pension insurance institutions.

(8) ¹The German Pension Insurance Federation shall maintain a file system in which the name, address, company number, the accident insurance institution responsible for the employer and other identification features of each employer are stored, as well as the data required for the planning of examinations at the employers' premises and the data required for the overviews in accordance with paragraph 7; the German Pension Insurance Federation process the data stored in this file system only for the purposes of examinations at the employers' premises and for determining the employers liable to pay contributions under the Artists' Social Security Act. ²A mark must be included in the file system if, under Article 166 paragraph 2 sentence 2 of Book 7, the examination of employers for accident insurance does not have to be carried out by the pension insurance institutions; the accident insurance institutions must provide the necessary data. ³The data centre of the pension insurance scheme shall keep a file system for the examination at the employers' premises in which, in addition to the company number of each employer, the company number of the accident insurance institution responsible for the employer, the accident insurance member number of the employer, the remuneration in euros of the employees employed by the employer who are liable to pay contributions to the accident insurance scheme are stored, the applicable danger tariff offices of his employees, the insurance numbers of his employees, including the beginning and end of their employment, the name of the collection agency responsible

sowie eine Kennzeichnung des Vorliegens einer geringfügigen Beschäftigung gespeichert sind. ⁴Sie darf die Daten der Stammsatzdatei nach § 150 Absatz 1 und 2 des Sechsten Buches sowie die Daten des Dateisystems nach § 150 Absatz 3 des Sechsten Buches und der Stammdatendatei nach § 101 für die Prüfung bei den Arbeitgebern speichern, verändern, nutzen, übermitteln oder in der Verarbeitung einschränken; dies gilt für die Daten der Stammsatzdatei auch für Prüfungen nach § 212a des Sechsten Buches. ⁵Sie ist verpflichtet, auf Anforderung des prüfenden Trägers der Rentenversicherung

1. die in den Dateisystemen nach den Sätzen 1 und 3 gespeicherten Daten,
2. die in den Versicherungskonten der Träger der Rentenversicherung gespeicherten, auf den Prüfungszeitraum entfallenden Daten der bei dem zu prüfenden Arbeitgeber Beschäftigten,
3. die bei den für den Arbeitgeber zuständigen Einzugsstellen gespeicherten Daten aus den Beitragsnachweisen (§ 28f Absatz 3) für die Zeit nach dem Zeitpunkt, bis zu dem der Arbeitgeber zuletzt geprüft wurde,
4. die bei der Künstlersozialkasse über den Arbeitgeber gespeicherten Daten zur Melde- und Abgabepflicht für den Zeitraum seit der letzten Prüfung sowie
5. die bei den Trägern der Unfallversicherung gespeicherten Daten zur Melde- und Beitragspflicht sowie zur Gefahrtarifstelle für den Zeitraum seit der letzten Prüfung

zu verarbeiten, soweit dies für die Prüfung, ob die Arbeitgeber ihre Meldepflichten und ihre sonstigen Pflichten nach diesem Gesetzbuch, die im Zusammenhang mit dem Gesamtsozialversicherungsbeitrag stehen, sowie ihre Pflichten als zur Abgabe Verpflichtete nach dem Künstlersozialversicherungsgesetz und ihre Pflichten nach dem Siebten Buch zur Meldung und Beitragszahlung ordnungsgemäß erfüllen, erforderlich ist. ⁶Die dem prüfenden Träger der Rentenversicherung übermittelten Daten sind unverzüglich nach Abschluss der Prüfung bei der Datenstelle und beim prüfenden Träger der Rentenversicherung zu löschen. ⁷Die Träger der Rentenversicherung, die Einzugsstellen, die Künstlersozialkasse und die Bundesagentur für Arbeit sind verpflichtet, der Deutschen Rentenversicherung Bund und der Datenstelle die für die Prüfung bei den Arbeitgebern erforderlichen Daten zu übermitteln. ⁸Sind für die Prüfung bei den Arbeitgebern Daten zu übermitteln, so dürfen sie auch durch Abruf im automatisierten Verfahren übermittelt werden, ohne dass es einer Genehmigung nach § 79 Absatz 1 des Zehnten Buches bedarf.

for each employee and an indication of the existence of marginal employment. ⁴It may store, modify, use, transmit or restrict in processing the data in the master data file in accordance with Article 150 paragraphs 1 and 2 of the Sixth Book and the data in the file system in accordance with Article 150 paragraph 3 of the Sixth Book and the master data file in accordance with Article 101 for the purposes of audits at employers; this also applies to the data in the master data file for audits in accordance with Article 212a of the Sixth Book. ⁵At the request of the examining pension insurance institution, it is obliged

1. the data stored in the file systems according to sentences 1 and 3,
2. the data of the employees of the employer to be examined which are stored in the insurance accounts of the pension insurance institutions and which relate to the examination period,
3. the data stored at the collection points responsible for the employer from the contribution statements (section 28f (3)) for the period after the date by which the employer was last audited,
4. the data stored by the artists' social security fund on the employer for the period since the last check, and
5. the data stored by the institutions of accident insurance on the obligation to register and pay contributions and on the dangerous goods tariff office for the period since the last inspection

insofar as this is necessary for the examination whether the employers duly fulfil their reporting obligations and their other obligations under this Code which are related to the total social security contribution, as well as their obligations as persons obliged to make contributions under the Artists' Social Security Act and their obligations under Book Seven for reporting and payment of contributions. 6 The data transmitted to the examining pension insurance institution must be deleted immediately after completion of the examination by the data centre and the examining pension insurance institution. 7The pension insurance institutions, the collection agencies, the Artists' Social Security Fund and the Federal Employment Agency are obliged to provide the German Pension Insurance Federation and the data centre with the data required for the examination at the employers' offices. 8If data are to be transmitted to the employers for the purposes of the examination, they may also be transmitted by retrieval in an automated procedure without the need for approval under Article 79(1) of Book 10.

(9) Das Bundesministerium für Arbeit und Soziales bestimmt im Einvernehmen mit dem Bundesministerium für Gesundheit durch Rechtsverordnung mit Zustimmung des Bundesrates das Nähere über

1. den Umfang der Pflichten des Arbeitgebers und der in Absatz 6 genannten Stellen bei Abrechnungsverfahren, die mit Hilfe automatischer Einrichtungen durchgeführt werden,
2. die Durchführung der Prüfung sowie die Behebung von Mängeln, die bei der Prüfung festgestellt worden sind, und
3. den Inhalt des Dateisystems nach Absatz 8 Satz 1 hinsichtlich der für die Planung der Prüfungen bei Arbeitgebern und der für die Prüfung bei Einzugsstellen erforderlichen Daten, über den Aufbau und die Aktualisierung dieses Dateisystems sowie über den Umfang der Daten aus diesem Dateisystem, die von den Einzugsstellen und der Bundesagentur für Arbeit nach § 28q Absatz 5 abgerufen werden können.

(10) Arbeitgeber werden wegen der Beschäftigten in privaten Haushalten nicht geprüft.

(11) ¹Sind beim Übergang der Prüfung der Arbeitgeber von Krankenkassen auf die Träger der Rentenversicherung Angestellte übernommen worden, die am 1. Januar 1995 ganz oder überwiegend mit der Prüfung der Arbeitgeber beschäftigt waren, sind die bis zum Zeitpunkt der Übernahme gültigen Tarifverträge oder sonstigen kollektiven Vereinbarungen für die übernommenen Arbeitnehmer bis zum Inkrafttreten neuer Tarifverträge oder sonstiger kollektiver Vereinbarungen maßgebend. ²Soweit es sich bei einem gemäß Satz 1 übernommenen Beschäftigten um einen Dienstordnungs-Angestellten handelt, tragen der aufnehmende Träger der Rentenversicherung und die abgebende Krankenkasse bei Eintritt des Versorgungsfalles die Versorgungsbezüge anteilig, sofern der Angestellte im Zeitpunkt der Übernahme das 45. Lebensjahr bereits vollendet hatte. ³ § 107b Absatz 2 bis 5 des Beamtenversorgungsgesetzes gilt sinngemäß.

§ 28q
Prüfung bei den Einzugsstellen und den Trägern der Rentenversicherung

(1) ¹Die Träger der Rentenversicherung und die Bundesagentur für Arbeit prüfen bei den Einzugsstellen die Durchführung der Aufgaben, für die die Einzugsstellen eine Vergütung nach § 28l Absatz 1 erhalten, mindestens alle vier Jahre. ²Satz 1 gilt auch im Verhältnis der Deut-

(9) The Federal Ministry of Labour and Social Affairs, in agreement with the Federal Ministry of Health, shall determine by statutory instrument, with the consent of the Bundesrat, the details of

1. the extent of the obligations of the employer and of the bodies referred to in paragraph 6 in the case of accounting procedures carried out by means of automated devices
2. the performance of the audit and the rectification of deficiencies found during the audit, and
3. the content of the file system pursuant to subsection (8) first sentence above with regard to the data required for the planning of audits at employers and the data required for audits at collection agencies, on the structure and updating of this file system and on the scope of the data from this file system which can be retrieved by the collection agencies and the Federal Employment Agency pursuant to section 28q subsection (5)

(10) Employers shall not be audited because of employees in private households.

(11) ¹Where, at the time of the transfer of the audit of employers from health insurance funds to the pension insurance institutions, employees who were wholly or predominantly involved in the audit of employers on 1 January 1995 have been taken over, the collective agreements or other collective agreements in force up to the time of the transfer shall apply to the employees taken over until the entry into force of new collective agreements or other collective agreements. ²Insofar as an employee taken over in accordance with the first sentence above is an employee subject to the Staff Regulations, the receiving pension insurance institution and the health insurance fund which has ceased to operate shall bear a proportionate share of the pension payments when the case arises, provided that the employee had already reached the age of 45 when he was taken over. ³Section 107b(2) to (5) of the Civil Servants' Pensions Act applies mutatis mutandis.

Section 28q
Examination at the collecting agencies and pension insurance institutions

(1) ¹The pension insurance institutions and the Federal Employment Agency shall inspect the performance of the tasks for which the collection agencies receive remuneration under Section 28l(1) at least every four years. ²Sentence 1 also applies in the relationship between the

schen Rentenversicherung Bund zur Künstlersozialkasse. ³Die Deutsche Rentenversicherung Bund speichert in dem in § 28p Absatz 8 Satz 1 genannten Dateisystem Daten aus dem Bescheid des Trägers der Rentenversicherung nach § 28p Absatz 1 Satz 5, soweit dies für die Prüfung bei den Einzugsstellen nach Satz 1 erforderlich ist. ⁴Sie darf diese Daten nur für die Prüfung bei den Einzugsstellen speichern, verändern, nutzen, übermitteln oder in der Verarbeitung einschränken. ⁵Die Datenstelle der Rentenversicherung hat auf Anforderung des prüfenden Trägers der Rentenversicherung die in dem Dateisystem nach § 28p Absatz 8 Satz 3 gespeicherten Daten diesem zu übermitteln, soweit dies für die Prüfung nach Satz 1 erforderlich ist. ⁶Die Übermittlung darf auch durch Abruf im automatisierten Verfahren erfolgen, ohne dass es einer Genehmigung nach § 79 Absatz 1 des Zehnten Buches bedarf.

(1a) ¹Die Träger der Rentenversicherung und die Bundesagentur für Arbeit prüfen bei den Einzugsstellen für das Bundesamt für Soziale Sicherung als Verwalter des Gesundheitsfonds im Hinblick auf die Krankenversicherungsbeiträge im Sinne des § 28d Absatz 1 Satz 1 die Geltendmachung der Beitragsansprüche, den Einzug, die Verwaltung, die Weiterleitung und die Abrechnung der Beiträge entsprechend § 28l Absatz 1 Satz 1 Nummer 1 und 2. ²Absatz 1 Satz 3 und 4 gilt entsprechend. ³Die mit der Prüfung nach Satz 1 befassten Stellen übermitteln dem Bundesamt für Soziale Sicherung als Verwalter des Gesundheitsfonds die zur Geltendmachung der in § 28r Absatz 1 und 2 bezeichneten Rechte erforderlichen Prüfungsergebnisse. ⁴Die durch die Aufgabenübertragung und Wahrnehmung entstehenden Kosten sind den Trägern der Rentenversicherung und der Bundesagentur für Arbeit aus den Einnahmen des Gesundheitsfonds zu erstatten. ⁵Die Einzelheiten des Verfahrens und der Vergütung vereinbaren die Träger der Rentenversicherung und die Bundesagentur für Arbeit mit dem Bundesamt für Soziale Sicherung als Verwalter des Gesundheitsfonds.

(2) Die Einzugsstellen haben die für die Prüfung erforderlichen Unterlagen bis zur nächsten Einzugsstellenprüfung aufzubewahren und bei der Prüfung bereitzuhalten.

German Pension Insurance Federation and the Künstlersozialkasse. ³In the file system referred to in Article 28p paragraph 8 sentence 1, the Federal German Pension Insurance Fund shall store data from the notice of the pension insurance institution in accordance with Article 28p paragraph 1 sentence 5, insofar as this is necessary for the examination at the collection agencies in accordance with sentence 1. ⁴It may only store, modify, use, transmit or restrict the processing of this data for the purposes of examination at the collection agencies. ⁵At the request of the examining pension insurance institution, the data centre of the pension insurance scheme must transfer the data stored in the file system in accordance with § 28p paragraph 8 sentence 3 to the examining institution, insofar as this is necessary for the examination in accordance with sentence 1. ⁶The transmission may also be carried out by retrieval in an automated procedure, without the need for approval under Article 79 paragraph 1 of the Tenth Book.

(1a) ¹The pension insurance institutions and the Federal Employment Agency shall check with the collection agencies for the Federal Social Insurance Office as administrator of the health fund with regard to health insurance contributions within the meaning of Section 28d paragraph 1 sentence 1 the assertion of contribution claims, the collection, administration, forwarding and accounting of contributions in accordance with Section 28l paragraph 1 sentence 1 numbers 1 and 2. ²Paragraph 1 sentences 3 and 4 shall apply mutatis mutandis. ³The bodies responsible for the audit in accordance with sentence 1 shall forward to the Federal Social Security Office, as administrator of the Health Fund, the audit results required to assert the rights referred to in § 28r paragraphs 1 and 2. ⁴The costs incurred by the transfer of tasks and the performance of these tasks shall be reimbursed to the pension insurance institutions and the Federal Employment Agency from the revenues of the Health Fund. ⁵The details of the procedure and the remuneration shall be agreed between the pension insurance institutions and the Federal Employment Agency and the Federal Social Security Office as administrator of the Health Fund.

(2) The collection agencies shall keep the documents required for the audit until the next collection agency audit and shall have them available at the audit.

(3) [1]Die Einzugsstellen sind verpflichtet, bei der Darlegung der Kassen- und Rechnungsführung aufklärend mitzuwirken und bei Verfahren, die mit Hilfe automatischer Einrichtungen durchgeführt werden, angemessene Prüfhilfen zu leisten. [2]Der Spitzenverband Bund der Krankenkassen, die Deutsche Rentenversicherung Bund und die Bundesagentur für Arbeit treffen entsprechende Vereinbarungen. [3]Die Deutsche Rentenversicherung Knappschaft-Bahn-See und die landwirtschaftliche Krankenkasse können dabei ausgenommen werden.

(4) [1]Die Prüfung erstreckt sich auf alle Stellen, die Aufgaben der in Absatz 1 genannten Art für die Einzugsstelle wahrnehmen. [2]Die Absätze 2 und 3 gelten insoweit für diese Stellen entsprechend.

(5) [1]Die Einzugsstellen und die Bundesagentur für Arbeit prüfen gemeinsam bei den Trägern der Rentenversicherung deren Aufgaben nach § 28p mindestens alle vier Jahre. [2]Die Prüfung kann durch Abruf der Arbeitgeberdateisysteme (§ 28p Absatz 8) im automatisierten Verfahren durchgeführt werden. [3]Bei geringfügigen Beschäftigungen gelten die Sätze 1 und 2 nicht für die Deutsche Rentenversicherung Knappschaft-Bahn-See als Einzugsstelle.

§ 28r
Schadensersatzpflicht, Verzinsung

(1) [1]Verletzt ein Organ oder ein Bediensteter der Einzugsstelle schuldhaft eine diesem nach diesem Abschnitt auferlegte Pflicht, haftet die Einzugsstelle dem Träger der Pflegeversicherung, der Rentenversicherung und der Bundesagentur für Arbeit sowie dem Gesundheitsfonds für einen diesen zugefügten Schaden. [2]Die Schadensersatzpflicht wegen entgangener Zinsen beschränkt sich auf den sich aus Absatz 2 ergebenden Umfang.

(2) Werden Beiträge, Zinsen auf Beiträge oder Säumniszuschläge schuldhaft nicht rechtzeitig weitergeleitet, hat die Einzugsstelle Zinsen in Höhe von zwei vom Hundert über dem jeweiligen Basiszinssatz nach § 247 des Bürgerlichen Gesetzbuchs zu zahlen.

(3) [1]Verletzt ein Organ oder ein Bediensteter des Trägers der Rentenversicherung schuldhaft eine diesem nach § 28p auferlegte Pflicht, haftet der Träger der Rentenversicherung dem Gesundheitsfonds, der Krankenkasse, der Pflegekasse und der Bundesagentur für Arbeit für einen diesen zugefügten Schaden; dies gilt entsprechend gegenüber den Trägern der Unfallversicherung

(3) [1]The collection agencies are obliged to provide information in the presentation of the cash and accounting records and to provide appropriate auditing aids in procedures carried out with the aid of automatic equipment. [2]The National Association of Health Insurance Funds, the German Pension Insurance Fund Federation and the Federal Employment Agency shall conclude corresponding agreements. [3]The German Pension Insurance Knappschaft-Bahn-See (pension for miners, railway workers, seafarers) and the agricultural health insurance fund may be exempted from these agreements.

(4) [1]The audit shall extend to all bodies performing tasks of the type specified in paragraph 1 for the collection agency. [2]Paragraphs 2 and 3 shall apply mutatis mutandis to these bodies.

(5) [1]The collection agencies and the Federal Employment Agency shall jointly examine the duties of the pension insurance institutions under Section 28p at least every four years. [2]The examination may be carried out by retrieving the employer file systems (Article 28p paragraph 8) in an automated procedure. [3]In the case of minor employment, sentences 1 and 2 shall not apply to the German Pension Insurance Knappschaft-Bahn-See (pension for miners, railway workers, seafarers) as a collection agency.

Section 28r
Liability for damages, interest

(1) [1]If an organ or an employee of the collection agency culpably violates an obligation imposed on it under this section, the collection agency shall be liable to the institution of the long-term care insurance, the pension insurance and the Federal Employment Agency as well as the Health Fund for any damage caused to them. [2]The liability to pay compensation for loss of interest is limited to the extent resulting from paragraph 2.

(2) If contributions, interest on contributions or late payment surcharges are culpably not forwarded in time, the collection agency shall pay interest at a rate of two percent above the respective base rate pursuant to Section 247 of the German Civil Code.

(3) [1]If an institution or an employee of the pension insurance institution culpably violates an obligation imposed on it under Section 28p, the pension insurance institution shall be liable to the health fund, the health insurance fund, the nursing care insurance fund and the Federal Employment Agency for any damage caused to them; this shall apply mutatis mutandis to the

für die Prüfung nach § 166 Absatz 2 des Siebten Buches. [2]Für entgangene Beiträge sind Zinsen in Höhe von zwei vom Hundert über dem jeweiligen Basiszinssatz nach § 247 des Bürgerlichen Gesetzbuchs zu zahlen.

institutions of accident insurance for the purposes of the examination under Section 166(2) of Book 7. [2]For lost contributions, interest at two percent above the respective base rate in accordance with Article 247 of the German Civil Code shall be paid.

§ 106
Elektronischer Antrag auf Ausstellung einer Bescheinigung über die anzuwendenden Rechtsvorschriften bei Beschäftigung nach Artikel 12 Absatz 1 der Verordnung (EG) Nr. 883/2004 und bei Ausnahmevereinbarungen nach Artikel 16 der Verordnung (EG) Nr. 883/2004

Section 106
Electronic application for a certificate of the applicable legislation in the case of employment under Article 12(1) of Regulation (EC) No 883/2004 and in the case of derogations under Article 16 of Regulation (EC) No 883/2004

(1) [1]Gelten für vorübergehend in einem anderen Mitgliedstaat der Europäischen Union, in einem Vertragsstaat des Abkommens über den Europäischen Wirtschaftsraum oder in der Schweiz Beschäftigte die deutschen Rechtsvorschriften über soziale Sicherheit nach Artikel 12 Absatz 1 der Verordnung (EG) Nr. 883/2004 des Europäischen Parlaments und des Rates vom 29. April 2004 zur Koordinierung der Systeme der sozialen Sicherheit (ABl. L 166 vom 30.4.2004, S. 1, L 200 vom 7.6.2004, S. 1), die zuletzt durch die Verordnung (EU) Nr. 465/2012 (ABl. L 149 vom 8.6.2012, S. 4) geändert worden ist, so hat der Arbeitgeber einen Antrag auf Ausstellung einer entsprechenden Bescheinigung über die Fortgeltung der deutschen Rechtsvorschriften (A1-Bescheinigung) für diesen Beschäftigten an die zuständige Stelle durch Datenübertragung aus einem systemgeprüften Programm oder mittels einer maschinell erstellten Ausfüllhilfe zu übermitteln. [2]Die zuständige Stelle hat den Antrag elektronisch anzunehmen, zu speichern und zu nutzen. [3]Ist festgestellt, dass die deutschen Rechtsvorschriften über soziale Sicherheit gelten, erfolgt die Übermittlung der Daten der A1-Bescheinigung innerhalb von drei Arbeitstagen durch Datenübermittlung an den Arbeitgeber, der diese Bescheinigung unverzüglich auszudrucken und seinen Beschäftigten auszuhändigen hat.

(1) [1]Whereas German social security legislation pursuant to Article 12(1) of Regulation (EC) No 883/2004 of the European Parliament and of the Council of 29 April 2004 on the coordination of social security systems (OJ L 166, 30.4.2004, p. 1, L 200, 7.4.2004, p. 1) is applicable to workers temporarily employed in another Member State of the European Union, in a State party to the Agreement on the European Economic Area or in Switzerland 6.2004, p. 1), as last amended by Regulation (EU) No 465/2012 (OJ L 149, 8.6.2012, p. 4), the employer must submit an application for the issue of a corresponding certificate of the continued application of German legislation (A1 certificate) for that employee to the competent body by means of data transmission from a system-checked programme or by means of a computerised completion aid. [2]The competent authority must accept, store and use the application electronically. [3]If it is established that German social security legislation applies, the data of the A1 certificate shall be transmitted within three working days by data transmission to the employer, who shall print out the certificate without delay and hand it over to his employees.

(2) [1]In den Fällen, in denen die deutschen Rechtsvorschriften über soziale Sicherheit auf Grund einer Vereinbarung nach Artikel 16 der Verordnung (EG) Nr. 883/2004 gelten sollen, gilt für das Antragsverfahren Absatz 1 entsprechend. [2]Beschäftigte haben in diesem Fall zusätzlich eine schriftliche Erklärung an die zuständige Stelle zu senden, in der sie bestätigen, dass eine solche Vereinbarung in ihrem Interesse liegt.

(2) [1]In cases where German social security legislation is to apply on the basis of an agreement under Article 16 of Regulation (EC) No 883/2004, paragraph 1 shall apply accordingly to the application procedure. [2]In this case, employees must additionally send a written declaration to the competent authority confirming that such an agreement is in their interest.

(3) Das Nähere zum Verfahren und zu den Inhalten des Antrages und der zu übermittelnden Datensätze nach den Absätzen 1 und 2 regeln der Spitzenverband Bund der Krankenkassen, die Deutsche Rentenversicherung Bund, die Deutsche Gesetzliche Unfallversicherung e. V. und die Arbeitsgemeinschaft berufsständischer Versorgungseinrichtungen e. V. in Gemeinsamen Grundsätzen, die vom Bundesministerium für Arbeit und Soziales zu genehmigen sind; die Bundesvereinigung der Deutschen Arbeitgeberverbände ist vorher anzuhören.

(3) Further details of the procedure and the content of the application and the data records to be transferred in accordance with subsections 1 and 2 shall be regulated by the Federal Association of Health Insurance Funds, the German Pension Insurance Fund Federation, the German Statutory Accident Insurance Association and the Working Group of Professional Associations and Employers' Associations.

XV. Social Security Code VII –
Compulsory Accident Insurance (Excerpt)

Sozialgesetzbuch (SGB) Siebtes Buch (VII) –
Gesetzliche Unfallversicherung (Auszug)

Stand: 28.03.2021

§ 110
Haftung gegenüber den
Sozialversicherungsträgern

(1) ¹Haben Personen, deren Haftung nach den §§ 104 bis 107 beschränkt ist, den Versicherungsfall vorsätzlich oder grob fahrlässig herbeigeführt, haften sie den Sozialversicherungsträgern für die infolge des Versicherungsfalls entstandenen Aufwendungen, jedoch nur bis zur Höhe des zivilrechtlichen Schadenersatzanspruchs. ²Statt der Rente kann der Kapitalwert gefordert werden. ³Das Verschulden braucht sich nur auf das den Versicherungsfall verursachende Handeln oder Unterlassen zu beziehen.

(1a) ¹Unternehmer, die Schwarzarbeit nach § 1 des Schwarzarbeitsbekämpfungsgesetzes erbringen und dadurch bewirken, dass Beiträge nach dem Sechsten Kapitel nicht, nicht in der richtigen Höhe oder nicht rechtzeitig entrichtet werden, erstatten den Unfallversicherungsträgern die Aufwendungen, die diesen infolge von Versicherungsfällen bei Ausführung der Schwarzarbeit entstanden sind. ²Eine nicht ordnungsgemäße Beitragsentrichtung wird vermutet, wenn die Unternehmer die Personen, bei denen die Versicherungsfälle eingetreten sind, nicht nach § 28a des Vierten Buches bei der Einzugsstelle oder der Datenstelle der Rentenversicherung angemeldet hatten.

(2) Die Sozialversicherungsträger können nach billigem Ermessen, insbesondere unter Berücksichtigung der wirtschaftlichen Verhältnisse des Schuldners, auf den Ersatzanspruch ganz oder teilweise verzichten.

Section 110
Liability to social security institutions

(1) ¹If persons whose liability is limited under sections 104 to 107 have caused the insured event intentionally or through gross negligence, they shall be liable to the social insurance institutions for the expenses incurred as a result of the insured event, but only up to the amount of the civil claim for compensation. ²The capital value may be claimed instead of the pension. ³The fault need only relate to the action or omission causing the insured event.

(1a) ¹Untrepreneurs who perform undeclared work in accordance with Section 1 of the Act to Combat Undeclared Work and thereby have the effect that contributions under Chapter Six are not paid, are not paid in the correct amount or are not paid on time shall reimburse the accident insurance institutions for the expenses which they have incurred as a result of insured events when performing the undeclared work. ²Incorrect payment of contributions is presumed if the employers had not registered the persons with whom the insured events occurred with the collection agency or the data centre of the pension insurance fund in accordance with § 28a of the Fourth Book.

(2) The social insurance institutions may waive the claim for compensation in whole or in part at their reasonable discretion, in particular taking into account the economic circumstances of the debtor.

§ 150
Beitragspflichtige

(1) ¹Beitragspflichtig sind die Unternehmer, für deren Unternehmen Versicherte tätig sind oder zu denen Versicherte in einer besonderen, die Versicherung begründenden Beziehung stehen. ²Die nach § 2 versicherten Unternehmer sowie die nach § 3 Abs. 1 Nr. 1 und § 6 Abs. 1 Versicherten sind selbst beitragspflichtig. ³Für Versicherte nach § 6 Absatz 1 Satz 2 ist die jeweilige Organisation oder der jeweilige Verband beitragspflichtig. ⁴Entsprechendes gilt in den Fällen des § 6 Absatz 1 Satz 3.

(2) ¹Neben den Unternehmern sind beitragspflichtig

1. die Auftraggeber, soweit sie Zwischenmeistern und Hausgewerbetreibenden zur Zahlung von Entgelt verpflichtet sind,
2. die Reeder, soweit beim Betrieb von Seeschiffen andere Unternehmer sind oder auf Seeschiffen durch andere ein Unternehmen betrieben wird.

²Die in Satz 1 Nr. 1 und 2 Genannten sowie die in § 130 Abs. 2 Satz 1 und Abs. 3 genannten Bevollmächtigten haften mit den Unternehmern als Gesamtschuldner.

(3) ¹Für die Beitragshaftung bei der Arbeitnehmerüberlassung gilt § 28e Abs. 2 und 4 des Vierten Buches, für die Beitragshaftung bei der Ausführung eines Dienst- oder Werkvertrages im Baugewerbe gelten § 28e Absatz 3a bis 3f sowie § 116a des Vierten Buches und für die Beitragshaftung bei der Ausführung eines Dienst- oder Werkvertrages durch Unternehmer im Speditions-, Transport- und damit verbundenen Logistikgewerbe, die im Bereich der Kurier-, Express- und Paketdienste tätig sind und im Auftrag eines anderen Unternehmers adressierte Pakete befördern, gilt § 28e Absatz 3g des Vierten Buches entsprechend. ²Der Nachunternehmer oder der von diesem beauftragte Verleiher hat für den Nachweis nach § 28e Absatz 3f des Vierten Buches eine qualifizierte Unbedenklichkeitsbescheinigung des zuständigen Unfallversicherungsträgers vorzulegen; diese enthält insbesondere Angaben über die bei dem Unfallversicherungsträger eingetragenen Unternehmensteile und diesen zugehörigen Lohnsummen des Nachunternehmers oder des von diesem beauftragten Verleihers sowie die ordnungsgemäße Zahlung der Beiträge.

Section 150
Contributors

(1) ¹Contributors are the entrepreneurs for whose companies insured persons work or with whom insured persons have a special relationship that constitutes the basis of the insurance. ²The entrepreneurs insured under § 2 and the persons insured under § 3 paragraph 1 No. 1 and § 6 paragraph 1 are themselves liable to pay contributions. ³For insured persons under § 6 paragraph 1 sentence 2, the respective organisation or association is liable to pay contributions. ⁴The same shall apply accordingly in the cases of section 6 subsection (1) sentence 3.

(2) ¹In addition to the entrepreneurs, the following are liable to pay contributions

1. the clients, insofar as they are obliged to pay remuneration to intermediate masters and domestic craftsmen
2. the shipowners, insofar as other entrepreneurs are involved in the operation of seagoing vessels or if an enterprise is operated on seagoing vessels by others.

²The authorised representatives named in sentence 1 nos. 1 and 2 as well as those named in § 130 paragraph 2 sentence 1 and paragraph 3 shall be jointly and severally liable with the entrepreneurs

(3) ¹Section 28e, paragraph (e) applies to the liability for contributions in the case of temporary employment. 2 and 4 of the Fourth Book, Section 28e(3a) to (3f) and Section 116a of the Fourth Book shall apply to contribution liability in the execution of a service or work contract in the construction industry, and Section 28e(3g) of the Fourth Book shall apply mutatis mutandis to contribution liability in the execution of a service or work contract by entrepreneurs in the forwarding, transport and associated logistics industry who operate in the courier, express and parcel services sector and transport addressed parcels on behalf of another entrepreneur. ²The subcontractor or the lender commissioned by it must submit a qualified clearance certificate from the competent accident insurance institution as evidence under Article 28e paragraph 3f of the Fourth Book; this certificate must contain in particular information on the parts of the company registered with the accident insurance institution and the corresponding wage totals of the subcontractor or the lender commissioned by it, as well as the proper payment of contributions.

(4) Bei einem Wechsel der Person des Unternehmers sind der bisherige Unternehmer und sein Nachfolger bis zum Ablauf des Kalenderjahres, in dem der Wechsel angezeigt wurde, zur Zahlung der Beiträge und damit zusammenhängender Leistungen als Gesamtschuldner verpflichtet.

§ 151
Beitragserhebung bei überbetrieblichen arbeitsmedizinischen und sicherheitstechnischen Diensten

¹Die Mittel für die Einrichtungen nach § 24 werden von den Unternehmern aufgebracht, die diesen Einrichtungen angeschlossen sind. ²Die Satzung bestimmt das Nähere über den Maßstab, nach dem die Mittel aufzubringen sind, und über die Fälligkeit.

(4) In the event of a change in the person of the employer, the previous employer and his successor shall be jointly and severally liable for payment of the contributions and related benefits until the end of the calendar year in which the change was notified.

Section 151
Collection of contributions from inter-company occupational health and safety services

[1]The funds for the facilities under Article 24 shall be provided by the entrepreneurs who are affiliated to these facilities. [2]The statutes shall determine the details of the scale on which the funds are to be raised and the due date.

XVI. Commercial Code (Excerpt)

Handelsgesetzbuch – HGB (Auszug)

Stand: 12.12.2019

§ 128
Persönliche Haftung der Gesellschafter

[1]Die Gesellschafter haften für die Verbindlichkeiten der Gesellschaft den Gläubigern als Gesamtschuldner persönlich. [2]Eine entgegenstehende Vereinbarung ist Dritten gegenüber unwirksam.

Section 128
Personal Liability of the partners

[1]The partners shall be personally and jointly and severally liable to the creditors for the partnership's obligations. [2]Any agreement to the contrary shall be ineffective vis-à-vis third parties.

XVII. Stock Corporation Act (Excerpt)

Aktiengesetz – AktG (Auszug)

Stand: 12.12.2019

§ 18
Konzern und Konzernunternehmen

(1) ¹Sind ein herrschendes und ein oder mehrere abhängige Unternehmen unter der einheitlichen Leitung des herrschenden Unternehmens zusammengefaßt, so bilden sie einen Konzern; die einzelnen Unternehmen sind Konzernunternehmen. ²Unternehmen, zwischen denen ein Beherrschungsvertrag (§ 291) besteht oder von denen das eine in das andere eingegliedert ist (§ 319), sind als unter einheitlicher Leitung zusammengefaßt anzusehen. ³Von einem abhängigen Unternehmen wird vermutet, daß es mit dem herrschenden Unternehmen einen Konzern bildet.

(2) Sind rechtlich selbständige Unternehmen, ohne daß das eine Unternehmen von dem anderen abhängig ist, unter einheitlicher Leitung zusammengefaßt, so bilden sie auch einen Konzern; die einzelnen Unternehmen sind Konzernunternehmen.

§ 76
Leitung der Aktiengesellschaft

(1) Der Vorstand hat unter eigener Verantwortung die Gesellschaft zu leiten.

(2) ¹Der Vorstand kann aus einer oder mehreren Personen bestehen. ²Bei Gesellschaften mit einem Grundkapital von mehr als drei Millionen Euro hat er aus mindestens zwei Personen zu bestehen, es sei denn, die Satzung bestimmt, daß er aus einer Person besteht. ³Die Vorschriften über die Bestellung eines Arbeitsdirektors bleiben unberührt.

(3) ¹Mitglied des Vorstands kann nur eine natürliche, unbeschränkt geschäftsfähige Person sein. ²Mitglied des Vorstands kann nicht sein, wer

1. als Betreuter bei der Besorgung seiner Vermögensangelegenheiten ganz oder teilweise einem Einwilligungsvorbehalt (§ 1903 des Bürgerlichen Gesetzbuchs) unterliegt,

Section 18
Group of enterprises and group member companies

(1) ¹Where a controlling enterprise and one or several controlled enterprises are combined under the common management of the controlling enterprise, they form a group; the individual enterprises are group member companies. ²Where a control agreement is in place between enterprises (section 291), or where one enterprise has been integrated into another (section 319), the enterprises are to be regarded as enterprises combined under common management. ³The assumption is that a controlled enterprise forms a group with the controlling enterprise.

(2) Where legally independent enterprises are combined under common management without one enterprise being controlled by the other, they likewise form a group of enterprises; the individual enterprises are group member companies.

Section 76
Management of the stock corporation

(1) The management board is to manage the affairs of the company on its own responsibility.

(2) ¹The management board may consist of one or several persons. ²In the case of companies having a share capital of more than three million euros, the management board is to be comprised of at least two (2) persons unless the by-laws stipulate that it is to consist of one (1) person. ³The regulations governing the appointment of a member of the board responsible for human resources and social welfare matters (*Arbeitsdirektor*) shall remain unaffected.

(3) ¹Solely a natural person having legal capacity without any restrictions may be a member of the management board. ²No-one may be a member of the management board who

1. As a person under custodianship as concerns matters of his property, is subject wholly or in part to a reservation of consent (section 1903 of the Civil Code (BGB));

2. aufgrund eines gerichtlichen Urteils oder einer vollziehbaren Entscheidung einer Verwaltungsbehörde einen Beruf, einen Berufszweig, ein Gewerbe oder einen Gewerbezweig nicht ausüben darf, sofern der Unternehmensgegenstand ganz oder teilweise mit dem Gegenstand des Verbots übereinstimmt,

3. wegen einer oder mehrerer vorsätzlich begangener Straftaten

   (a) des Unterlassens der Stellung des Antrags auf Eröffnung des Insolvenzverfahrens (Insolvenzverschleppung),

   (b) nach den §§ 283 bis 283d des Strafgesetzbuchs (Insolvenzstraftaten),

   (c) der falschen Angaben nach § 399 dieses Gesetzes oder § 82 des Gesetzes betreffend die Gesellschaften mit beschränkter Haftung,

   (d) der unrichtigen Darstellung nach § 400 dieses Gesetzes, § 331 des Handelsgesetzbuchs, § 313 des Umwandlungsgesetzes oder § 17 des Publizitätsgesetzes,

   (e) nach den §§ 263 bis 264a oder den §§ 265b bis 266a des Strafgesetzbuchs zu einer Freiheitsstrafe von mindestens einem Jahr

verurteilt worden ist; dieser Ausschluss gilt für die Dauer von fünf Jahren seit der Rechtskraft des Urteils, wobei die Zeit nicht eingerechnet wird, in welcher der Täter auf behördliche Anordnung in einer Anstalt verwahrt worden ist

[3]Satz 2 Nr. 3 gilt entsprechend bei einer Verurteilung im Ausland wegen einer Tat, die mit den in Satz 2 Nr. 3 genannten Taten vergleichbar ist.

(4) [1]Der Vorstand von Gesellschaften, die börsennotiert sind oder der Mitbestimmung unterliegen, legt für den Frauenanteil in den beiden Führungsebenen unterhalb des Vorstands Zielgrößen fest. [2]Liegt der Frauenanteil bei Festlegung der Zielgrößen unter 30 Prozent, so dürfen die Zielgrößen den jeweils erreichten Anteil nicht mehr unterschreiten. [3]Gleichzeitig sind Fristen zur Erreichung der Zielgrößen festzulegen. [4]Die Fristen dürfen jeweils nicht länger als fünf Jahre sein.

2. Based on a court ruling or an enforceable decision by an administrative authority, is prohibited from exercising a profession, a professional activity, a trade, or commercial activities, inasmuch as the purpose of the stock corporation corresponds, as a whole or in part, to the subject matter addressed by the prohibition;

3. Has been convicted for one or several criminal offences committed intentionally and consisting of any of the following:

   (a) Failure to file the application for opening insolvency proceedings (delay in filing a petition for insolvency),

   (b) Criminal offences pursuant to sections 283 to 283d of the Criminal Code (StGB) (insolvency offences),

   (c) Provision of false information pursuant to section 399 of the present Act or section 82 of the Limited Liability Companies Act (GmbHG),

   (d) False representation of facts pursuant to section 400 of the present Act, section 331 of the Commercial Code (HGB), section 313 of the Transformation Act (UmwG), or section 17 of the Act on the Financial Accounting by Certain Enterprises and Corporate Groups (PublG), or who

   (e) Has been convicted pursuant to sections 263 to 264a or sections 265b to 266a of the Criminal Code (StGB) to imprisonment of at least one (1) year;

This disqualification shall apply for the duration of five (5) years from the date on which the corresponding judgment has become final and conclusive; in this context, that period shall not be included in the computation in which the perpetrator was detained in an institution upon the order of governmental authorities.

[3]The second sentence, no. 3 shall apply mutatis mutandis in the case of a conviction being handed down abroad for an offence that is comparable to the offences set out in no. 3 of the second sentence.

(4) [1]The management board of companies that are listed on the stock exchange or that are subject to co-determination rights shall stipulate target values for the percentage of women working in positions at the first and second management levels below the management board. [2]Where the percentage of women is lower than 30 percent at the time the target values are stipulated, the target values stipulated may not be lower than the percentage respectively attained at that time. [3]Concurrently, periods are to be set within which the target values are to be attained. [4]In each case, the periods may not be longer than five years.

§91
Organisation; Buchführung

(1) Der Vorstand hat dafür zu sorgen, daß die erforderlichen Handelsbücher geführt werden

(2) Der Vorstand hat geeignete Maßnahmen zu treffen, insbesondere ein Überwachungssystem einzurichten, damit den Fortbestand der Gesellschaft gefährdende Entwicklungen früh erkannt werden.

§93
Sorgfaltspflicht und Verantwortlichkeit der Vorstandsmitglieder

(1) [1]Die Vorstandsmitglieder haben bei ihrer Geschäftsführung die Sorgfalt eines ordentlichen und gewissenhaften Geschäftsleiters anzuwenden. [2]Eine Pflichtverletzung liegt nicht vor, wenn das Vorstandsmitglied bei einer unternehmerischen Entscheidung vernünftigerweise annehmen durfte, auf der Grundlage angemessener Information zum Wohle der Gesellschaft zu handeln. [3]Über vertrauliche Angaben und Geheimnisse der Gesellschaft, namentlich Betriebs- oder Geschäftsgeheimnisse, die den Vorstandsmitgliedern durch ihre Tätigkeit im Vorstand bekanntgeworden sind, haben sie Stillschweigen zu bewahren. [4]Die Pflicht des Satzes 3 gilt nicht gegenüber einer nach § 342b des Handelsgesetzbuchs anerkannten Prüfstelle im Rahmen einer von dieser durchgeführten Prüfung.

(2) [1]Vorstandsmitglieder, die ihre Pflichten verletzen, sind der Gesellschaft zum Ersatz des daraus entstehenden Schadens als Gesamtschuldner verpflichtet. [2]Ist streitig, ob sie die Sorgfalt eines ordentlichen und gewissenhaften Geschäftsleiters angewandt haben, so trifft sie die Beweislast. [3]Schließt die Gesellschaft eine Versicherung zur Absicherung eines Vorstandsmitglieds gegen Risiken aus dessen beruflicher Tätigkeit für die Gesellschaft ab, ist ein Selbstbehalt von mindestens 10 Prozent des Schadens bis mindestens zur Höhe des Eineinhalbfachen der festen jährlichen Vergütung des Vorstandsmitglieds vorzusehen.

Section 91
Organisation; accounting

(1) The management board is to ensure that the required journal, required general ledger, and other required records are kept.

(2) The management board is to take suitable measures, and in particular is to institute a monitoring system, in order to allow developments jeopardising the company's continued existence to be identified at an early point in time.

Section 93
Duty of the members of the management board to exercise skill and care, liability and responsibility

(1) [1]In managing the affairs of the company, the members of the management board are to exercise the due care of a prudent manager faithfully complying with his duties. [2]No dereliction of duties shall be given in those instances in which the member of the management board, in taking an entrepreneurial decision, was within his rights to reasonably assume that he was acting on the basis of adequate information and in the best interests of the company. [3]The members of the management board are to respect the secrecy of any confidential information and secrets of the company, particularly trade secrets or business secrets, of which they have become aware in the context of their activities in the management board. [4]The obligation set out in the third sentence shall not apply vis-à-vis an audit and enforcement panel recognised pursuant to section 342b of the Commercial Code (HGB) in the context of an audit performed by this panel.

(2) [1]Members of the management board acting in dereliction of their duties are liable as joint and several debtors to compensate the company for any damage resulting therefrom. [2]Where it is in dispute whether or not they exercised the due care of a prudent manager faithfully complying with his duties, the onus of proof shall be on them. [3]Where the company has taken out insurance to protect a member of the management board against risks arising from his professional activities for the company, the insurance policy is to provide for a deductible of at least ten (10) percent of the damage, up to a minimum of one hundred and fifty (150) percent of the annual fixed remuneration of the member of the management board.

(3) Die Vorstandsmitglieder sind namentlich zum Ersatz verpflichtet, wenn entgegen diesem Gesetz Einlagen an die Aktionäre zurückgewährt werden,

1. den Aktionären Zinsen oder Gewinnanteile gezahlt werden,
2. eigene Aktien der Gesellschaft oder einer anderen Gesellschaft gezeichnet, erworben, als Pfand genommen oder eingezogen werden,
3. Aktien vor der vollen Leistung des Ausgabebetrags ausgegeben werden,

4. Gesellschaftsvermögen verteilt wird,

5. Zahlungen entgegen § 92 Abs. 2 geleistet werden,
6. Vergütungen an Aufsichtsratsmitglieder gewährt werden,
7. Kredit gewährt wird,
8. bei der bedingten Kapitalerhöhung außerhalb des festgesetzten Zwecks oder vor der vollen Leistung des Gegenwerts Bezugsaktien ausgegeben werden.

(4) ¹Der Gesellschaft gegenüber tritt die Ersatzpflicht nicht ein, wenn die Handlung auf einem gesetzmäßigen Beschluß der Hauptversammlung beruht. ²Dadurch, daß der Aufsichtsrat die Handlung gebilligt hat, wird die Ersatzpflicht nicht ausgeschlossen. ³Die Gesellschaft kann erst drei Jahre nach der Entstehung des Anspruchs und nur dann auf Ersatzansprüche verzichten oder sich über sie vergleichen, wenn die Hauptversammlung zustimmt und nicht eine Minderheit, deren Anteile zusammen den zehnten Teil des Grundkapitals erreichen, zur Niederschrift Widerspruch erhebt. ⁴Die zeitliche Beschränkung gilt nicht, wenn der Ersatzpflichtige zahlungsunfähig ist und sich zur Abwendung des Insolvenzverfahrens mit seinen Gläubigern vergleicht oder wenn die Ersatzpflicht in einem Insolvenzplan geregelt wird.

(5) ¹Der Ersatzanspruch der Gesellschaft kann auch von den Gläubigern der Gesellschaft geltend gemacht werden, soweit sie von dieser keine Befriedigung erlangen können. ²Dies gilt jedoch in anderen Fällen als denen des Absatzes 3 nur dann, wenn die Vorstandsmitglieder die Sorgfalt eines ordentlichen und gewissenhaften Geschäftsleiters gröblich verletzt haben; Absatz 2 Satz 2 gilt sinngemäß. ³Den Gläubigern

(3) The members of the management board shall be under obligation to provide compensation particularly in those instances in which, in contravention of the present Act

1. Contributions are restituted to the stockholders,
2. Stockholders are paid interest or participate in the profits,

3. Treasury shares of stock in the company or in some other company have been subscribed to, purchased, accepted in pledge, or redeemed,
4. Shares of stock are issued prior to the issue price for them having been fully paid in,
5. The company's assets are distributed,

6. Payments are made in contravention of section 92 (2),
7. Loans are granted,
8. Shares of a new issue are issued in the context of the conditional capital increase and this is done outside of the purpose specified therefor or prior to the equivalent value having been fully paid.

(4) ¹The obligation to provide compensation shall not arise vis-à-vis the company where the action taken is based on a lawful resolution adopted by the general meeting. ²The fact that the supervisory board has endorsed the action does not preclude the obligation to provide compensation. ³The company may waive its claims to compensation, or conclude a compromise regarding these claims, only once three (3) years have lapsed since the arisal of the claim, and only in those cases in which the general meeting approves this being done and no minority, the aggregate of whose shares is at least equivalent to one tenth of the share capital, raises an objection and has it recorded in the minutes. ⁴The limitation in time shall not apply where the party obligated to provide compensation is unable to pay his debts as they become due and concludes a compromise with his creditors in order to avert insolvency proceedings or if the compensation obligation is provided for in an insolvency plan.

(5) ¹The company's claim to compensation may also be asserted by its creditors insofar as they cannot obtain satisfaction from the company. ²However, this shall apply in cases other than those governed by subsection (3) only in those instances in which members of the management board have grossly violated their duty to exercise the due care of a prudent manager faithfully complying with his duties; subsection (2),

gegenüber wird die Ersatzpflicht weder durch einen Verzicht oder Vergleich der Gesellschaft noch dadurch aufgehoben, daß die Handlung auf einem Beschluß der Hauptversammlung beruht. ⁴Ist über das Vermögen der Gesellschaft das Insolvenzverfahren eröffnet, so übt während dessen Dauer der Insolvenzverwalter oder der Sachwalter das Recht der Gläubiger gegen die Vorstandsmitglieder aus.

(6) Die Ansprüche aus diesen Vorschriften verjähren bei Gesellschaften, die zum Zeitpunkt der Pflichtverletzung börsennotiert sind, in zehn Jahren, bei anderen Gesellschaften in fünf Jahren.

§ 111
Aufgaben und Rechte des Aufsichtsrats

(1) Der Aufsichtsrat hat die Geschäftsführung zu überwachen.

(2) ¹Der Aufsichtsrat kann die Bücher und Schriften der Gesellschaft sowie die Vermögensgegenstände, namentlich die Gesellschaftskasse und die Bestände an Wertpapieren und Waren, einsehen und prüfen. ²Er kann damit auch einzelne Mitglieder oder für bestimmte Aufgaben besondere Sachverständige beauftragen. ³Er erteilt dem Abschlußprüfer den Prüfungsauftrag für den Jahres- und den Konzernabschluß gemäß § 290 des Handelsgesetzbuchs. ⁴Er kann darüber hinaus eine externe inhaltliche Überprüfung der nichtfinanziellen Erklärung oder des gesonderten nichtfinanziellen Berichts (§ 289b des Handelsgesetzbuchs), der nichtfinanziellen Konzernerklärung oder des gesonderten nichtfinanziellen Konzernberichts (§ 315b des Handelsgesetzbuchs) beauftragen.

(3) ¹Der Aufsichtsrat hat eine Hauptversammlung einzuberufen, wenn das Wohl der Gesellschaft es fordert. ²Für den Beschluß genügt die einfache Mehrheit.

(4) ¹Maßnahmen der Geschäftsführung können dem Aufsichtsrat nicht übertragen werden. ²Die Satzung oder der Aufsichtsrat hat jedoch zu bestimmen, daß bestimmte Arten von Geschäften nur mit seiner Zustimmung vorgenommen werden dürfen. ³Verweigert der Aufsichtsrat seine Zustimmung, so kann der Vorstand verlangen, daß die Hauptversammlung über die Zustimmung beschließt. ⁴Der Beschluß, durch

second sentence, shall apply *mutatis mutandis*. ³The obligation to provide compensation shall not be cancelled vis-à-vis the creditors by a waiver by the company or by its concluding a compromise, nor shall the fact that the action is based on a resolution adopted by the general meeting cancel this obligation. ⁴Where insolvency proceedings have been opened for the company's assets, the insolvency administrator or the insolvency monitor shall exercise the right of the company's creditors against the members of the management board for the duration of said proceedings.

(6) The claims governed by the present regulations shall become statute-barred, in the case of companies that were listed on a stock exchange at the time at which the dereliction of duties occurred, after ten (10) years; in the case of other companies after five (5) years.

Section 111
Taks and rights of the supervisory board

(1) The supervisory board is to supervise the management board.

(2) ¹The supervisory board may inspect and audit the books and records of the company as well as its assets, particularly the company's cash and the inventory of securities and goods. ²It may also instruct individual members to perform these tasks, or may commission special experts for certain tasks. ³The supervisory board shall instruct the auditor of the annual accounts to audit the annual accounts and consolidated financial statements pursuant to section 290 of the Commercial Code (HGB). ⁴Moreover, the supervisory board may instruct that an external audit be performed of the substance of the non-financial statement or of the separate non-financial report (section 289b of the Commercial Code (HGB)), or of the consolidated non-financial statement or the separate consolidated non-financial report (section 315b of the Commercial Code (HGB)).

(3) ¹The supervisory board is to convene a general meeting where this is required by the company's best interests. ²It shall suffice for the corresponding resolution to be adopted by a simple majority.

(4) ¹The measures to be taken by the management may not be transferred to the supervisory board. ²However, it is to be determined in the by-laws or by the supervisory board that certain types of business transactions may only be implemented with the supervisory board's consent. ³Where the supervisory board refuses to grant such consent, the management board may demand that the general meeting adopt a

den die Hauptversammlung zustimmt, bedarf einer Mehrheit, die mindestens drei Viertel der abgegebenen Stimmen umfaßt. ⁵Die Satzung kann weder eine andere Mehrheit noch weitere Erfordernisse bestimmen.

(5) ¹Der Aufsichtsrat von Gesellschaften, die börsennotiert sind oder der Mitbestimmung unterliegen, legt für den Frauenanteil im Aufsichtsrat und im Vorstand Zielgrößen fest. ²Liegt der Frauenanteil bei Festlegung der Zielgrößen unter 30 Prozent, so dürfen die Zielgrößen den jeweils erreichten Anteil nicht mehr unterschreiten. ³Gleichzeitig sind Fristen zur Erreichung der Zielgrößen festzulegen. ⁴Die Fristen dürfen jeweils nicht länger als fünf Jahre sein. ⁵Soweit für den Aufsichtsrat bereits eine Quote nach § 96 Absatz 2 gilt, sind die Festlegungen nur für den Vorstand vorzunehmen.

(6) Die Aufsichtsratsmitglieder können ihre Aufgaben nicht durch andere wahrnehmen lassen.

§ 116
Sorgfaltspflicht und Verantwortlichkeit des Aufsichtsratsmitglieder

¹Für die Sorgfaltspflicht und Verantwortlichkeit der Aufsichtsratsmitglieder gilt § 93 mit Ausnahme des Absatzes 2 Satz 3 über die Sorgfaltspflicht und Verantwortlichkeit der Vorstandsmitglieder sinngemäß. ²Die Aufsichtsratsmitglieder sind insbesondere zur Verschwiegenheit über erhaltene vertrauliche Berichte und vertrauliche Beratungen verpflichtet. ³Sie sind namentlich zum Ersatz verpflichtet, wenn sie eine unangemessene Vergütung festsetzen (§ 87 Absatz 1).

resolution concerning such consent. ⁴The resolution by which the general meeting grants its consent shall require a majority of at least three quarters of the votes cast. ⁵The by-laws may neither stipulate a greater majority ratio, nor may they impose further requirements.

(5) ¹The supervisory board of companies that are listed on the stock exchange or that are subject to co-determination rights shall stipulate target values for the percentage of women sitting on the supervisory board and the management board. ²Where the percentage of women is lower than 30 percent at the time the target values are stipulated, the target values stipulated may not be lower than the percentage respectively attained at that time. ³Concurrently, periods are to be set within which the target values are to be attained. ⁴In each case, the periods may not be longer than five years. ⁵Inasmuch as a quota pursuant to section 96 (2) already applies to the supervisory board, the stipulations shall be made solely for the management board.

(6) The members of the supervisory board may not have others perform the tasks incumbent on them.

Section 116
Duty of the members of the supervisory board to exercise skill and care, liability and responsibilities

¹Section 93 shall apply mutatis mutandis to the duty of the members of the supervisory board to exercise skill and care as well as to their liability and responsibilities, to the exception of subsection (2), third sentence concerning the duty of the members of the management board to exercise skill and care as well as their liability and responsibilities. ²In particular, the members of the supervisory board shall be under an obligation of secrecy regarding any confidential reports they may have received as well as their confidential deliberations. ³Particularly, they shall be under obligation to provide compensation should they have established remuneration that is inappropriate (section 87 subsection (1)).

XVIII. Limited Liability Companies Act (Excerpt)

Gesetz betreffend die Gesellschaften mit beschränkter Haftung – GmbHG (Auszug)

Stand: 17.07.2017

§43
Haftung der Geschäftsführer

(1) Die Geschäftsführer haben in den Angelegenheiten der Gesellschaft die Sorgfalt eines ordentlichen Geschäftsmannes anzuwenden.

(2) Geschäftsführer, welche ihre Obliegenheiten verletzen, haften der Gesellschaft solidarisch für den entstandenen Schaden.

(3) ¹Insbesondere sind sie zum Ersatze verpflichtet, wenn den Bestimmungen des § 30 zuwider Zahlungen aus dem zur Erhaltung des Stammkapitals erforderlichen Vermögen der Gesellschaft gemacht oder den Bestimmungen des § 33 zuwider eigene Geschäftsanteile der Gesellschaft erworben worden sind. ²Auf den Ersatzanspruch finden die Bestimmungen in § 9b Abs. 1 entsprechende Anwendung. ³Soweit der Ersatz zur Befriedigung der Gläubiger der Gesellschaft erforderlich ist, wird die Verpflichtung der Geschäftsführer dadurch nicht aufgehoben, daß dieselben in Befolgung eines Beschlusses der Gesellschafter gehandelt haben.

(4) Die Ansprüche auf Grund der vorstehenden Bestimmungen verjähren in fünf Jahren.

§52
Aufsichtsrat

(1) Ist nach dem Gesellschaftsvertrag ein Aufsichtsrat zu bestellen, so sind § 90 Abs. 3, 4, 5 Satz 1 und 2, § 95 Satz 1, § 100 Abs. 1 und 2 Nr. 2 und Abs. 5, § 101 Abs. 1 Satz 1, § 103 Abs. 1 Satz 1 und 2, §§ 105, 107 Absatz 3 Satz 2 und 3 und Absatz 4, §§ 110 bis 114, 116 des Aktiengesetzes in Verbindung mit § 93 Abs. 1 und 2 Satz 1 und 2 des Aktiengesetzes, § 124 Abs. 3 Satz 2, §§ 170, 171, 394 und 395 des Aktiengesetzes entsprechend anzuwenden, soweit nicht im Gesellschaftsvertrag ein anderes bestimmt ist.

Section 43
Directors' liability

(1) The directors shall conduct the company's affairs with the due care of a prudent businessman.

(2) Directors who breach the duties incumbent upon them shall be jointly and severally liable to the company for any damage arising.

(3) ¹In particular, they shall be obligated to compensate where payments have been made in contravention of section 30 from those company assets which are required to maintain the share capital or the company's own shares have been purchased in contravention of the provisions set out in section 33. ²The provisions set out in section 9b (1) shall apply mutatis mutandis to a claim for compensation. ³Where compensation must be paid to satisfy the company's creditors, the directors' obligation shall not be abrogated on account of the fact that they acted in compliance with a resolution passed by the shareholders.

(4) The claims based on the aforementioned provisions shall become statute-barred after five years.

Section 52
Supervisory board

(1) If the articles of association stipulate that a supervisory board is to be appointed, section 90 (3), (4), (5), first and second sentences, section 95, first sentence, section 100 (1) and (2), no. 2, and subsection (5), section 101 (1), first sentence, section 103 (1), first and second sentences, section 105, section 107 (3), second and third sentences, and subsection (4), sections 110 to 114 and section 116 of the Stock Corporation Act in conjunction with section 93 (1) and (2), first and second sentences, of the Stock Corporation Act, section 124 (3), second sentence, sections 170, 171, 394 and 395 of the Stock Corporation Act shall apply mutatis mutandis, unless otherwise provided in the articles of association.

(2) ¹Ist nach dem Drittelbeteiligungsgesetz ein Aufsichtsrat zu bestellen, so legt die Gesellschafterversammlung für den Frauenanteil im Aufsichtsrat und unter den Geschäftsführern Zielgrößen fest, es sei denn, sie hat dem Aufsichtsrat diese Aufgabe übertragen. ²Ist nach dem Mitbestimmungsgesetz, dem Montan Mitbestimmungsgesetz oder dem Mitbestimmungsergänzungsgesetz ein Aufsichtsrat zu bestellen, so legt der Aufsichtsrat für den Frauenanteil im Aufsichtsrat und unter den Geschäftsführern Zielgrößen fest. ³Liegt der Frauenanteil bei Festlegung der Zielgrößen unter 30 Prozent, so dürfen die Zielgrößen den jeweils erreichten Anteil nicht mehr unterschreiten. ⁴Gleichzeitig sind Fristen zur Erreichung der Zielgrößen festzulegen. ⁵Die Fristen dürfen jeweils nicht länger als fünf Jahre sein.

(3) ¹Werden die Mitglieder des Aufsichtsrats vor der Eintragung der Gesellschaft in das Handelsregister bestellt, gilt § 37 Abs. 4 Nr. 3 und 3a des Aktiengesetzes entsprechend. ²Die Geschäftsführer haben bei jeder Änderung in den Personen der Aufsichtsratsmitglieder unverzüglich eine Liste der Mitglieder des Aufsichtsrats, aus welcher Name, Vorname, ausgeübter Beruf und Wohnort der Mitglieder ersichtlich ist, zum Handelsregister einzureichen; das Gericht hat nach § 10 des Handelsgesetzbuchs einen Hinweis darauf bekannt zu machen, dass die Liste zum Handelsregister eingereicht worden ist.

(4) Schadensersatzansprüche gegen die Mitglieder des Aufsichtsrats wegen Verletzung ihrer Obliegenheiten verjähren in fünf Jahren.

(2) ¹Where a supervisory board is to be appointed in accordance with the One-Third Participation Act, the meeting of shareholders shall set targets regarding the proportion of women on the supervisory board and the proportion of women directors, unless it has delegated this task to the supervisory board. ²Where a supervisory board is to be appointed in accordance with the Co-determination Act, the Act on Co-determination in the Coal, Iron and Steel Industry or the Supplementary Co-determination Act, the supervisory board shall set targets regarding the proportion of women on the supervisory board and the proportion of women directors. ³If the proportion of women is below 30 per cent when the targets are set, then the targets may no longer fall below the previously achieved proportion of women. ⁴At the same time, deadlines are to be set by which these targets are to be achieved. ⁵The deadlines may not exceed five years in each case.

(3) ¹If the members of the supervisory board are appointed before the company is entered in the Commercial Register, section 37 (4), nos 3 and 3a, of the Stock Corporation Act shall apply mutatis mutandis. ²Whenever there is a change in the members of the supervisory board, the directors shall without undue delay submit to the Commercial Register a list of the members of the supervisory board indicating their family name, given name, profession and place of residence; in accordance with section 10 of the Commercial Code, the court shall give notice that the list has been submitted to the Commercial Register.

(4) Claims for compensation against the members of the supervisory board on account of a violation of their obligations shall become statute-barred after five years.

XIX. Competition Register Act (Excerpt)

Gesetz zur Einrichtung und zum Betrieb eines Registers zum Schutz des Wettbewerbs um öffentliche Aufträge und Konzessionen – (Wettbewerbsregistergesetz – WRegG) (Auszug)

Stand: 29.07.2017

§2
Eintragungsvoraussetzungen

(1) In das Wettbewerbsregister sind einzutragen:

1. rechtskräftige strafgerichtliche Verurteilungen und Strafbefehle, die wegen einer der folgenden Straftaten ergangen sind:
   (a) in § 123 Absatz 1 des Gesetzes gegen Wettbewerbsbeschränkungen aufgeführte Straftaten,
   (b) Betrug nach § 263 des Strafgesetzbuchs und Subventionsbetrug nach § 264 des Strafgesetzbuchs, soweit sich die Straftat gegen öffentliche Haushalte richtet,
   (c) Vorenthalten und Veruntreuen von Arbeitsentgelt nach § 266a des Strafgesetzbuchs,
   (d) Steuerhinterziehung nach § 370 der Abgabenordnung oder
   (e) wettbewerbsbeschränkende Absprachen bei Ausschreibungen nach § 298 des Strafgesetzbuchs;

2. rechtskräftige strafgerichtliche Verurteilungen und Strafbefehle sowie rechtskräftige Bußgeldentscheidungen, die wegen einer der folgenden Straftaten oder Ordnungswidrigkeiten ergangen sind, sofern auf Freiheitsstrafe von mehr als drei Monaten oder Geldstrafe von mehr als 90 Tagessätzen erkannt oder eine Geldbuße von wenigstens zweitausendfünfhundert Euro festgesetzt worden ist:
   (a) nach § 8 Absatz 1 Nummer 2, den §§ 10 bis 11 des Schwarzarbeitsbekämpfungsgesetzes vom 23. Juli 2004 (BGBl. I S. 1842), das zuletzt durch Artikel 1 des Gesetzes vom 6. März 2017 (BGBl. I S. 399) geändert worden ist,

Section 2
Registration requirements

(1) The following shall be entered in the competition register

1. final criminal convictions and orders issued for one of the following crimes:
   (a) offences listed in Section 123 (1) of the Act against Restraints of Competition,
   (b) Fraud pursuant to section 263 of the German Criminal Code and subsidy fraud pursuant to section 264 of the German Criminal Code, insofar as the offence is directed against public budgets,
   (c) Withholding and embezzlement of remuneration in accordance with section 266a of the German Criminal Code
   (d) tax evasion according to section 370 of the German Fiscal Code or
   (e) agreements restricting competition in the case of invitations to tender pursuant to section 298 of the German Penal Code;

2. final criminal convictions and penalty orders as well as final penalty decisions issued for one of the following offences or administrative offences, provided that a prison sentence of more than three months or a fine of more than 90 daily rates has been imposed or a fine of at least two thousand five hundred euros has been determined
   (a) in accordance with section 8 paragraph 1 number 2, sections 10 to 11 of the Act on the Prevention of Undeclared Work of 23 July 2004 (BGBl. I p. 1842), which was last amended by Article 1 of the Act of 6 March 2017 (BGBl. I p. 399),

(b) nach § 404 Absatz 1 und 2 Nummer 3 des Dritten Buches Sozialgesetzbuch – Arbeitsförderung – (Artikel 1 des Gesetzes vom 24. März 1997, BGBl. I S. 594, 595), das zuletzt durch Artikel 6 Absatz 8 des Gesetzes vom 23. Mai 2017 (BGBl. I S. 1228) geändert worden ist,

(c) nach den §§ 15, 15a, 16 Absatz 1 Nummer 1, 1c, 1d, 1f und 2 des Arbeitnehmerüberlassungsgesetzes in der Fassung der Bekanntmachung vom 3. Februar 1995 (BGBl. I S. 158), das zuletzt durch Artikel 1 des Gesetzes vom 21. Februar 2017 (BGBl. I S. 258) geändert worden ist,

(d) nach § 21 Absatz 1 und 2 des Mindestlohngesetzes vom 11. August 2014 (BGBl. I S. 1348), das zuletzt durch Artikel 6 Absatz 39 des Gesetzes vom 13. April 2017 (BGBl. I S. 872) geändert worden ist, oder

(e) nach § 23 Absatz 1 und 2 des Arbeitnehmer-Entsendegesetzes vom 20. April 2009 (BGBl. I S. 799), das zuletzt durch Artikel 6 Absatz 40 des Gesetzes vom 13. April 2017 (BGBl. I S. 872) geändert worden ist, oder

3. rechtskräftige Bußgeldentscheidungen, die nach § 30 des Gesetzes über Ordnungswidrigkeiten, auch in Verbindung mit § 130 des Gesetzes über Ordnungswidrigkeiten, wegen Straftaten nach Nummer 1 oder Straftaten oder Ordnungswidrigkeiten nach Nummer 2 ergangen sind.

(2) ¹In das Wettbewerbsregister werden ferner Bußgeldentscheidungen eingetragen, die wegen Ordnungswidrigkeiten nach § 81 Absatz 1 Nummer 1, Absatz 2 Nummer 1 in Verbindung mit § 1 des Gesetzes gegen Wettbewerbsbeschränkungen ergangen sind, wenn eine Geldbuße von wenigstens fünfzigtausend Euro festgesetzt worden ist. ²Nicht eingetragen werden Bußgeldentscheidungen, die nach § 81 Absatz 3 Buchstabe a bis c des Gesetzes gegen Wettbewerbsbeschränkungen ergangen sind.

(3) ¹Die Eintragung von strafgerichtlichen Entscheidungen und Bußgeldentscheidungen nach Absatz 1 Nummer 1 und 2 und von Entscheidungen gegen eine natürliche Person nach Absatz 2 erfolgt nur, wenn das Verhalten der natürlichen Person einem Unternehmen zuzurechnen ist. ²Das ist der Fall, wenn die natürliche Person als für die Leitung des Unternehmens Verantwortliche gehandelt hat, wozu auch die Überwachung der Geschäftsführung oder die sonstige Ausübung von Kontrollbefugnissen in leitender Stellung gehört.

(b) according to section 404 paragraph 1 and 2 number 3 of the Third Book of the Social Security Code – Promotion of Employment – (Article 1 of the Act of 24 March 1997, Federal Law Gazette I p. 594, 595), which was last amended by Article 6 paragraph 8 of the Act of 23 May 2017 (Federal Law Gazette I p. 1228)

(c) in accordance with sections 15, 15a, 16 (1) No. 1, 1c, 1d, 1f and 2 of the German Act on the Provision of Temporary Workers in the version of the announcement of 3 February 1995 (Federal Law Gazette I p. 158), last amended by Article 1 of the Act of 21 February 2017 (Federal Law Gazette I p. 258),

(d) in accordance with section 21 (1) and (2) of the Minimum Wage Act of 11 August 2014 (Federal Law Gazette I p. 1348), which was last amended by Article 6 (39) of the Act of 13 April 2017 (Federal Law Gazette I p. 872), or

(e) in accordance with section 23 paras. 1 and 2 of the Law on the Posting of Employees of 20 April 2009 (Federal Law Gazette I p. 799), which was last amended by Article 6 para. 40 of the Law of 13 April 2017 (Federal Law Gazette I p. 872), or

3. final decisions on fines imposed pursuant to section 30 of the Act on Administrative Offences, also in conjunction with section 130 of the Act on Administrative Offences, for offences under No. 1 or offences or administrative offences under No. 2

(2) ¹The Competition Register shall also record decisions imposing fines for administrative offences under Section 81 (1) No. 1, (2) No. 1 in conjunction with Section 1 of the Act against Restraints of Competition if a fine of at least fifty thousand euros has been imposed. ²Fines imposed pursuant to Article 81(3)(a) to (c) of the Act against Restraints of Competition shall not be registered.

(3) ¹The registration of criminal court decisions and decisions imposing fines pursuant to paragraph 1, points 1 and 2, and of decisions against a natural person pursuant to paragraph 2 shall be made only if the conduct of the natural person is attributable to an undertaking. ²This shall be the case where the natural person has acted as a person responsible for the management of the undertaking, including the supervision of management or other exercising of control in a managerial capacity.

(4) ¹Unternehmen im Sinne dieses Gesetzes ist jede natürliche oder juristische Person oder eine Gruppe solcher Personen, die auf dem Markt die Lieferung von Waren, die Ausführung von Bauleistungen oder die Erbringung von sonstigen Leistungen anbietet. ²Erlischt eine juristische Person oder eine Personenvereinigung mit Unternehmenseigenschaft nachträglich, steht dies der Eintragung nicht entgegen.

(4) ¹For the purposes of this Act, an enterprise shall mean any natural or legal person or group of such persons who offers to supply goods, execute works or provide other services on the market. ²If a legal person or an association of persons with corporate status subsequently ceases to exist, this shall not prevent its registration.

XX. Income Tax Act (Excerpt)

Einkommensteuergesetz – EStG (Auszug)

Stand: 21.12.2019

§ 1
Steuerpflicht

(1) [1]Natürliche Personen, die im Inland einen Wohnsitz oder ihren gewöhnlichen Aufenthalt haben, sind unbeschränkt einkommensteuerpflichtig. [2]Zum Inland im Sinne dieses Gesetzes gehört auch der der Bundesrepublik Deutschland zustehende Anteil

1. an der ausschließlichen Wirtschaftszone, soweit dort
   (a) die lebenden und nicht lebenden natürlichen Ressourcen der Gewässer über dem Meeresboden, des Meeresbodens und seines Untergrunds erforscht, ausgebeutet, erhalten oder bewirtschaftet werden,
   (b) andere Tätigkeiten zur wirtschaftlichen Erforschung oder Ausbeutung der ausschließlichen Wirtschaftszone ausgeübt werden, wie beispielsweise die Energieerzeugung aus Wasser, Strömung und Wind oder
   (c) künstliche Inseln errichtet oder genutzt werden und Anlagen und Bauwerke für die in den Buchstaben a und b genannten Zwecke errichtet oder genutzt werden, und
2. am Festlandsockel, soweit dort
   (a) dessen natürliche Ressourcen erforscht oder ausgebeutet werden; natürliche Ressourcen in diesem Sinne sind die mineralischen und sonstigen nicht lebenden Ressourcen des Meeresbodens und seines Untergrunds sowie die zu den sesshaften Arten gehörenden Lebewesen, die im nutzbaren Stadium entweder unbeweglich auf oder unter dem Meeresboden verbleiben oder sich nur in ständigem körperlichen Kontakt mit dem Meeresboden oder seinem Untergrund fortbewegen können; oder
   (b) künstliche Inseln errichtet oder genutzt werden und Anlagen und Bauwerke für die in Buchstabe a genannten Zwecke errichtet oder genutzt werden.

Section 1
Tax Liability

(1) Natural persons who have a place of residence or habitual abode in Germany are subject to unlimited income tax. Within the meaning of this Act, the share to which the Federal Republic of Germany is entitled shall also be deemed to be part of the domestic territory

1. in the exclusive economic zone, provided that
   (a) the living and non-living natural resources of the waters above the sea-bed, the seabed and its subsoil are explored, exploited, conserved or managed
   (b) other activities for economic exploration or exploitation of the Exclusive Economic Zone, such as power generation from water, current and wind; or
   (c) artificial islands are constructed or used and installations and structures are constructed or used for the purposes referred to in points (a) and (b); and
2. on the continental shelf, as far as there
   (a) the natural resources of which are being explored or exploited; for this purpose, natural resources means the mineral and other non-living resources of the sea-bed and its subsoil and those living creatures belonging to sedentary species which, at the exploitable stage, are either fixed on or under the sea-bed or can move only in permanent physical contact with the sea-bed or its subsoil; or
   (b) artificial islands are constructed or used and installations and structures are constructed or used for the purposes referred to in point (a).

(2) [1]Unbeschränkt einkommensteuerpflichtig sind auch deutsche Staatsangehörige, die

1. im Inland weder einen Wohnsitz noch ihren gewöhnlichen Aufenthalt haben und
2. zu einer inländischen juristischen Person des öffentlichen Rechts in einem Dienstverhältnis stehen und dafür Arbeitslohn aus einer inländischen öffentlichen Kasse beziehen,

sowie zu ihrem Haushalt gehörende Angehörige, die die deutsche Staatsangehörigkeit besitzen oder keine Einkünfte oder nur Einkünfte beziehen, die ausschließlich im Inland einkommensteuerpflichtig sind. [2]Dies gilt nur für natürliche Personen, die in dem Staat, in dem sie ihren Wohnsitz oder ihren gewöhnlichen Aufenthalt haben, lediglich in einem der beschränkten Einkommensteuerpflicht ähnlichen Umfang zu einer Steuer vom Einkommen herangezogen werden.

(3) [1]Auf Antrag werden auch natürliche Personen als unbeschränkt einkommensteuerpflichtig behandelt, die im Inland weder einen Wohnsitz noch ihren gewöhnlichen Aufenthalt haben, soweit sie inländische Einkünfte im Sinne des § 49 haben. [2]Dies gilt nur, wenn ihre Einkünfte im Kalenderjahr mindestens zu 90 Prozent der deutschen Einkommensteuer unterliegen oder die nicht der deutschen Einkommensteuer unterliegenden Einkünfte den Grundfreibetrag nach § 32a Absatz 1 Satz 2 Nummer 1 nicht übersteigen; dieser Betrag ist zu kürzen, soweit es nach den Verhältnissen im Wohnsitzstaat des Steuerpflichtigen notwendig und angemessen ist. [3]Inländische Einkünfte, die nach einem Abkommen zur Vermeidung der Doppelbesteuerung nur der Höhe nach beschränkt besteuert werden dürfen, gelten hierbei als nicht der deutschen Einkommensteuer unterliegend. [4]Unberücksichtigt bleiben bei der Ermittlung der Einkünfte nach Satz 2 nicht der deutschen Einkommensteuer unterliegende Einkünfte, die im Ausland nicht besteuert werden, soweit vergleichbare Einkünfte im Inland steuerfrei sind. [5]Weitere Voraussetzung ist, dass die Höhe der nicht der deutschen Einkommensteuer unterliegenden Einkünfte durch eine Bescheinigung der zuständigen ausländischen Steuerbehörde nachgewiesen wird. [6]Der Steuerabzug nach § 50a ist ungeachtet der Sätze 1 bis 4 vorzunehmen.

(4) Natürliche Personen, die im Inland weder einen Wohnsitz noch ihren gewöhnlichen Aufenthalt haben, sind vorbehaltlich der Absätze 2 und 3 und des § 1a beschränkt einkommensteuerpflichtig, wenn sie inländische Einkünfte im Sinne des § 49 haben.

(2) [1]Also subject to unlimited income tax are German nationals who

1. have neither a domicile nor their habitual residence in Germany, and
2. are in an employment relationship with a domestic legal person under public law and receive wages from a domestic public fund,

and members of their household who are German citizens or who receive no income or only income that is exclusively subject to income tax in Germany. [2]This only applies to natural persons who are only subject to income tax in the state in which they have their residence or habitual abode to an extent similar to the limited income tax liability.

(3) [1]Upon application, natural persons shall also be treated as having unlimited income tax liability if they have neither a residence nor their usual place of abode in Germany, provided they have domestic income within the meaning of section 49. [2]This shall only apply if at least 90 per cent of their income in a calendar year is subject to German income tax or if the income not subject to German income tax does not exceed the basic exemption under Section 32a (1) sentence 2 number 1; this amount shall be reduced to the extent that this is necessary and appropriate under the circumstances in the taxpayer's country of residence. [3]Domestic income which, under a convention for the avoidance of double taxation, may be taxed only to a limited extent is deemed not to be subject to German income tax. [4]Income which is not subject to German income tax and which is not taxed abroad is not taken into account when determining the income in accordance with sentence 2, provided that comparable income is tax-free in Germany. [5]A further prerequisite is that the amount of income not subject to German income tax is proven by a certificate issued by the competent foreign tax authority. [6]The tax deduction pursuant to § 50a must be made irrespective of sentences 1 to 4.

(4) Subject to paragraphs 2 and 3 and section 1a, natural persons who have neither a domicile nor their habitual residence in Germany shall be subject to limited income tax liability if they have domestic income within the meaning of section 49.

§ 2
Umfang der Besteuerung, Begriffsbestimmungen

(1) ¹Der Einkommensteuer unterliegen

1. Einkünfte aus Land- und Forstwirtschaft,
2. Einkünfte aus Gewerbebetrieb,
3. Einkünfte aus selbstandiger Arbeit,
4. Einkünfte aus nichtselbständiger Arbeit,
5. Einkünfte aus Kapitalvermögen,
6. Einkünfte aus Vermietung und Verpachtung,
7. sonstige Einkünfte im Sinne des § 22,

die der Steuerpflichtige während seiner unbeschränkten Einkommensteuerpflicht oder als inländische Einkünfte während seiner beschränkten Einkommensteuerpflicht erzielt. Zu welcher Einkunftsart die Einkünfte im einzelnen Fall gehören, bestimmt sich nach den §§ 13 bis 24.

(2) ¹Einkünfte sind

1. bei Land- und Forstwirtschaft, Gewerbebetrieb und selbständiger Arbeit der Gewinn (§§ 4 bis 7k und 13a),
2. bei den anderen Einkunftsarten der Überschuss der Einnahmen über die Werbungskosten (§§ 8 bis 9a).

Bei Einkünften aus Kapitalvermögen tritt § 20 Absatz 9 vorbehaltlich der Regelung in § 32d Absatz 2 an die Stelle der §§ 9 und 9a.

(3) Die Summe der Einkünfte, vermindert um den Altersentlastungsbetrag, den Entlastungsbetrag für Alleinerziehende und den Abzug nach § 13 Absatz 3, ist der Gesamtbetrag der Einkünfte.

(4) Der Gesamtbetrag der Einkünfte, vermindert um die Sonderausgaben und die außergewöhnlichen Belastungen, ist das Einkommen.

(5) ¹Das Einkommen, vermindert um die Freibeträge nach § 32 Absatz 6 und um die sonstigen vom Einkommen abzuziehenden Beträge, ist das zu versteuernde Einkommen; dieses bildet die Bemessungsgrundlage für die tarifliche Einkommensteuer. ²Knüpfen andere Gesetze an den Begriff des zu versteuernden Einkommens an, ist für deren Zweck das Einkommen in allen Fällen des § 32 um die Freibeträge nach § 32 Absatz 6 zu vermindern.

Section 2
Scope of Taxation; Definitions

(1) ¹The following shall be subject to income tax

1. income from agriculture and forestry,
2. income from commercial operations
3. income from self-employment,
4. income from employment,
5. income from capital assets,
6. income from renting and leasing,
7. other income within the meaning of sec. 22,

which the taxpayer generates during his unlimited income tax liability or as domestic income during his limited income tax liability. The type of income to which the income belongs in the individual case is determined in accordance with sec. 13 to 24.

(2) ¹Income is

1. in the case of agriculture and forestry, commercial operations and self-employment, the profit (sec.4 to 7k and 13a),
2. in the case of other types of income, the surplus of income over income-related expenses (sec. 8 to 9a).

In the case of income from capital assets, Article 20 paragraph 9 shall replace Articles 9 and 9a subject to the provisions of Article 32d paragraph 2.

(3) The sum of the income, reduced by the amount of the old-age pension, the amount of the pension for single parents and the deduction in accordance with section 13(3), is the total amount of income.

(4) The total amount of income, reduced by special expenses and extraordinary burdens, is the income.

(5) ¹The income, reduced by the allowances under Section 32(6) and by the other amounts to be deducted from the income, is the taxable income; this constitutes the basis of assessment for income tax under collective agreements. ²If other laws link the concept of taxable income to the concept of taxable income, the income in all cases under Article 32 must be reduced by the allowances under Article 32(6) for the purpose of such income.

(5a) [1]Knüpfen außersteuerliche Rechtsnormen an die in den vorstehenden Absätzen definierten Begriffe (Einkünfte, Summe der Einkünfte, Gesamtbetrag der Einkünfte, Einkommen, zu versteuerndes Einkommen) an, erhöhen sich für deren Zwecke diese Größen um die nach § 32d Absatz 1 und nach § 43 Absatz 5 zu besteuernden Beträge sowie um die nach § 3 Nummer 40 steuerfreien Beträge und mindern sich um die nach § 3c Absatz 2 nicht abziehbaren Beträge. [2]Knüpfen außersteuerliche Rechtsnormen an die in den Absätzen 1 bis 3 genannten Begriffe (Einkünfte, Summe der Einkünfte, Gesamtbetrag der Einkünfte) an, mindern sich für deren Zwecke diese Größen um die nach § 10 Absatz 1 Nummer 5 abziehbaren Kinderbetreuungskosten.

(5b) Soweit Rechtsnormen dieses Gesetzes an die in den vorstehenden Absätzen definierten Begriffe (Einkünfte, Summe der Einkünfte, Gesamtbetrag der Einkünfte, Einkommen, zu versteuerndes Einkommen) anknüpfen, sind Kapitalerträge nach § 32d Absatz 1 und § 43 Absatz 5 nicht einzubeziehen.

(6) [1]Die tarifliche Einkommensteuer, vermindert um [neue Fassung: den Unterschiedsbetrag nach § 32c Absatz 1 Satz 2,] die anzurechnenden ausländischen Steuern und die Steuerermäßigungen, vermehrt um die Steuer nach § 32d Absatz 3 und 4, die Steuer nach § 34c Absatz 5 und den Zuschlag nach § 3 Absatz 4 Satz 2 des Forstschäden-Ausgleichsgesetzes in der Fassung der Bekanntmachung vom 26. August 1985 (BGBl. I S. 1756), das zuletzt durch Artikel 18 des Gesetzes vom 19. Dezember 2008 (BGBl. I S. 2794) [neue Fassung: das zuletzt durch Artikel 412 der Verordnung vom 31. August 2015 (BGBl. I S. 1474)] geändert worden ist, in der jeweils geltenden Fassung, ist die festzusetzende Einkommensteuer. [2]Wurde der Gesamtbetrag der Einkünfte in den Fällen des § 10a Absatz 2 um Sonderausgaben nach § 10a Absatz 1 gemindert, ist für die Ermittlung der festzusetzenden Einkommensteuer der Anspruch auf Zulage nach Abschnitt XI der tariflichen Einkommensteuer hinzuzurechnen; bei der Ermittlung der dem Steuerpflichtigen zustehenden Zulage bleibt die Erhöhung der Grundzulage nach § 84 Satz 2 außer Betracht. [3]Wird das Einkommen in den Fällen des § 31 um die Freibeträge nach § 32 Absatz 6 gemindert, ist der Anspruch auf Kindergeld nach Abschnitt X der tariflichen Einkommensteuer hinzuzurechnen; nicht jedoch für Kalendermonate, in denen durch Bescheid der Familienkasse ein Anspruch auf Kindergeld festgesetzt, aber wegen § 70 Absatz 1 Satz 2 nicht ausgezahlt wurde.

(5a) [1]Where non-taxable legal norms link the terms defined in the preceding paragraphs (income, sum of income, total amount of income, income, taxable income), for their purposes these figures shall be increased by the amounts to be taxed in accordance with § 32d paragraph 1 and § 43 paragraph 5 and by the amounts exempt under § 3 number 40 and reduced by the amounts not deductible under § 3c paragraph 2. [2]Where non-tax legal provisions link the terms referred to in paragraphs 1 to 3 (income, sum of income, total amount of income), these amounts shall be reduced for their purposes by the childcare costs deductible under section 10(1)(5).

(5b) Insofar as legal provisions of this Act are linked to the terms defined in the above paragraphs (income, sum of income, total amount of income, income, taxable income), investment income pursuant to Section 32d(1) and Section 43(5) shall not be included.

(6) [1]The standard income tax, reduced by [new version: the difference pursuant to the second sentence of Paragraph 32c(1)], the foreign taxes to be credited and the tax reductions, increased by the tax pursuant to Paragraph 32d(3) and (4), the tax pursuant to Paragraph 34c(5) and the surcharge pursuant to the second sentence of Paragraph 3(4) of the Forstschäden-Ausgleichsgesetz (Law on Compensation for Damage to Forestry), as amended by the Notice of 26 September 2003, shall be reduced by [new version: the difference pursuant to the second sentence of Paragraph 32c(1)]. August 1985 (BGBl. I p. 1756), last amended by Article 18 of the Act of 19 December 2008 (BGBl. I p. 2794) [new version: last amended by Article 412 of the Ordinance of 31 August 2015 (BGBl. I p. 1474)], as amended, is the income tax to be assessed. [2]If, in the cases referred to in section 10a(2), the total amount of income has been reduced by special expenses under section 10a(1), the entitlement to a supplement under section XI shall be added to the standard income tax in order to determine the income tax to be fixed; when determining the supplement to which the taxpayer is entitled, the increase in the basic supplement under the second sentence of section 84 shall not be taken into account. [3]If, in the cases referred to in § 31, the income is reduced by the allowances under § 32(6), the entitlement to child benefit under Section X is to be added to the standard income tax; this does not apply, however, to calendar months in which an entitlement to child benefit was established by notice of the family fund but was not paid out because of § 70(1), second sentence.

(7) ¹Die Einkommensteuer ist eine Jahressteuer. ²Die Grundlagen für ihre Festsetzung sind jeweils für ein Kalenderjahr zu ermitteln. ³Besteht während eines Kalenderjahres sowohl unbeschränkte als auch beschränkte Einkommensteuerpflicht, so sind die während der beschränkten Einkommensteuerpflicht erzielten inländischen Einkünfte in eine Veranlagung zur unbeschränkten Einkommensteuerpflicht einzubeziehen.

(8) Die Regelungen dieses Gesetzes zu Ehegatten und Ehen sind auch auf Lebenspartner und Lebenspartnerschaften anzuwenden.

2. Einkünfte der Einnehmer einer staatlichen Lotterie, wenn sie nicht Einkünfte aus Gewerbebetrieb sind;

3. Einkünfte aus sonstiger selbständiger Arbeit, z. B. Vergütungen für die Vollstreckung von Testamenten, für Vermögensverwaltung und für die Tätigkeit als Aufsichtsratsmitglied;

4. Einkünfte, die ein Beteiligter an einer vermögensverwaltenden Gesellschaft oder Gemeinschaft, deren Zweck im Erwerb, Halten und in der Veräußerung von Anteilen an Kapitalgesellschaften besteht, als Vergütung für Leistungen zur Förderung des Gesellschafts- oder Gemeinschaftszwecks erzielt, wenn der Anspruch auf die Vergütung unter der Voraussetzung eingeräumt worden ist, dass die Gesellschafter oder Gemeinschafter ihr eingezahltes Kapital vollständig zurückerhalten haben; § 15 Absatz 3 ist nicht anzuwenden.

(2) Einkünfte nach Absatz 1 sind auch dann steuerpflichtig, wenn es sich nur um eine vorübergehende Tätigkeit handelt.

(3) ¹Zu den Einkünften aus selbständiger Arbeit gehört auch der Gewinn, der bei der Veräußerung des Vermögens oder eines selbständigen Teils des Vermögens oder eines Anteils am Vermögen erzielt wird, das der selbständigen Arbeit dient. ²§ 16 Absatz 1 Satz 1 Nummer 1 und 2 und Absatz 1 Satz 2 sowie Absatz 2 bis 4 gilt entsprechend.

(4) ¹§ 13 Absatz 5 gilt entsprechend, sofern das Grundstück im Veranlagungszeitraum 1986 zu einem der selbständigen Arbeit dienenden Betriebsvermögen gehört hat. ²§ 15 Absatz 1 Satz 1 Nummer 2, Absatz 1a, Absatz 2 Satz 2 und 3, §§ 15a und 15b sind entsprechend anzuwenden.

(7) ¹The income tax is an annual tax. The basis for its determination shall be determined for one calendar year at a time. ²If both unlimited and limited income tax liability exists during a calendar year, the domestic income earned during the limited income tax liability shall be included in an assessment for unlimited income tax liability.

(8) The provisions of this Act on spouses and marriages shall also apply to life partners and civil partnerships.

2. income of the receivers of a state lottery, if they are not income from business operations;

3. income from other independent work, e. g. remuneration for the execution of wills, for asset management and for activities as a member of the supervisory board;

4. income earned by a participant in an asset-managing company or community whose purpose is to acquire, hold and sell shares in corporations as remuneration for services rendered in furtherance of the company or community purpose, if the entitlement to the remuneration has been granted on condition that the shareholders or community members have received back their paid-up capital in full; section 15 (3) shall not apply.

(2) Income as referred to in paragraph 1 shall be taxable even if the activity in question is only temporary.

(3) ¹Income from self-employment shall also include the profit made on the disposal of the assets or an independent part of the assets or a share of the assets serving the purpose of self-employment. ²Article 16 paragraph 1 sentence 1 numbers 1 and 2 and paragraph 1 sentence 2 and paragraphs 2 to 4 apply accordingly.

(4) ¹Section 13 subsection (5) shall apply mutatis mutandis if the property was part of a business property serving the purpose of independent work during the 1986 assessment period. ²§ 15, subsection 1, sentence 1, number 2, subsection 1a, subsection 2, sentences 2 and 3, §§ 15a and 15b shall apply mutatis mutandis.

§ 37
Einkommensteuer-Vorauszahlung

(1) ¹Der Steuerpflichtige hat am 10. März, 10. Juni, 10. September und 10. Dezember Vorauszahlungen auf die Einkommensteuer zu entrichten, die er für den laufenden Veranlagungszeitraum voraussichtlich schulden wird. ²Die Einkommensteuer-Vorauszahlung entsteht jeweils mit Beginn des Kalendervierteljahres, in dem die Vorauszahlungen zu entrichten sind, oder, wenn die Steuerpflicht erst im Laufe des Kalendervierteljahres begründet wird, mit Begründung der Steuerpflicht.

(2) (weggefallen)

(3) ¹Das Finanzamt setzt die Vorauszahlungen durch Vorauszahlungsbescheid fest. ²Die Vorauszahlungen bemessen sich grundsätzlich nach der Einkommensteuer, die sich nach Anrechnung der Steuerabzugsbeträge (§ 36 Absatz 2 Nummer 2) bei der letzten Veranlagung ergeben hat. ³Das Finanzamt kann bis zum Ablauf des auf den Veranlagungszeitraum folgenden 15. Kalendermonats die Vorauszahlungen an die Einkommensteuer anpassen, die sich für den Veranlagungszeitraum voraussichtlich ergeben wird; dieser Zeitraum verlängert sich auf 23 Monate, wenn die Einkünfte aus Land- und Forstwirtschaft bei der erstmaligen Steuerfestsetzung die anderen Einkünfte voraussichtlich überwiegen werden. ⁴Bei der Anwendung der Sätze 2 und 3 bleiben Aufwendungen im Sinne des § 10 Absatz 1 Nummer 4, 5, 7 und 9 sowie Absatz 1a, der §§ 10b und 33 sowie die abziehbaren Beträge nach § 33a, wenn die Aufwendungen und abziehbaren Beträge insgesamt 600 Euro nicht übersteigen, außer Ansatz. ⁵Die Steuerermäßigung nach § 34a bleibt außer Ansatz. ⁶Bei der Anwendung der Sätze 2 und 3 bleibt der Sonderausgabenabzug nach § 10a Absatz 1 außer Ansatz. ⁷Außer Ansatz bleiben bis zur Anschaffung oder Fertigstellung der Objekte im Sinne des § 10e Absatz 1 und 2 und § 10h auch die Aufwendungen, die nach § 10e Absatz 6 und § 10h Satz 3 wie Sonderausgaben abgezogen werden; Entsprechendes gilt auch für Aufwendungen, die nach § 10i für nach dem Eigenheimzulagengesetz begünstigte Objekte wie Sonderausgaben abgezogen werden. ⁸Negative Einkünfte aus der Vermietung oder Verpachtung eines Gebäudes im Sinne des § 21 Absatz 1 Satz 1 Nummer 1 werden bei der Festsetzung der Vorauszahlungen nur für Kalenderjahre berücksichtigt, die nach der Anschaffung oder Fertigstellung dieses Gebäudes beginnen. ⁹Wird ein Gebäude vor dem Kalenderjahr seiner Fertigstellung angeschafft, tritt an die Stelle der Anschaffung die Fertigstellung. ¹⁰Satz 8 gilt nicht für negative Einkünfte aus der

Section 37
Income Tax Advance Payment

(1) ¹On 10 March, 10 June, 10 September and 10 December, the taxpayer shall make advance payments of income tax which he is likely to owe for the current assessment period. ²The advance payment of income tax shall arise at the beginning of the calendar quarter in which the advance payments are to be made or, if the tax liability is only established in the course of the calendar quarter, with the justification of the tax liability.

(2) (omitted)

(3) ¹The tax office shall determine the advance payments by means of an advance payment notice. ²The advance payments shall in principle be calculated on the basis of the income tax which has arisen after crediting the tax deductions (Section 36(2)(2)) in the last assessment. ³Until the end of the 15th calendar month following the assessment period, the tax office may adjust the advance payments to the income tax which is expected to be payable for the assessment period; this period is extended to 23 months if the income from agriculture and forestry is expected to outweigh other income when the tax is first assessed. ⁴When applying sentences 2 and 3, expenses within the meaning of section 10(1) nos. 4, 5, 7 and 9 as well as paragraph 1a, sections 10b and 33 and the deductible amounts under section 33a shall not be taken into account if the expenses and deductible amounts do not exceed EUR 600 in total. ⁵The tax reduction under section 34a shall not be applied. ⁶When applying sentences 2 and 3, the special expenses deduction under section 10a(1) shall not be taken into account. ⁷Until the acquisition or completion of the properties within the meaning of section 10e (1) and (2) and section 10h, expenses which are deducted as special expenses in accordance with section 10e (6) and section 10h sentence 3 shall also be disregarded; the same shall also apply mutatis mutandis to expenses which are deducted in accordance with section 10i for properties which are eligible under the Home Ownership Allowance Act, such as special expenses. ⁸Negative income from the letting or leasing of a building within the meaning of section 21 (1) sentence 1 number 1 shall only be taken into account in determining the advance payments for calendar years beginning after the acquisition or completion of that building. ⁹If a building is acquired prior to the calendar year of its completion, its completion shall take the place of acquisition. ¹⁰Sentence 8 shall not apply to negative income from the letting or leasing of a building for which special

Vermietung oder Verpachtung eines Gebäudes, für das Sonderabschreibungen nach § 7b dieses Gesetzes oder erhöhte Absetzungen nach den §§ 14a, 14c oder 14d des Berlinförderungsgesetzes in Anspruch genommen werden. [11]Satz 8 gilt für negative Einkünfte aus der Vermietung oder Verpachtung eines anderen Vermögensgegenstands im Sinne des § 21 Absatz 1 Satz 1 Nummer 1 bis 3 entsprechend mit der Maßgabe, dass an die Stelle der Anschaffung oder Fertigstellung die Aufnahme der Nutzung durch den Steuerpflichtigen tritt. [12]In den Fällen des § 31, in denen die gebotene steuerliche Freistellung eines Einkommensbetrags in Höhe des Existenzminimums eines Kindes durch das Kindergeld nicht in vollem Umfang bewirkt wird, bleiben bei der Anwendung der Sätze 2 und 3 Freibeträge nach § 32 Absatz 6 und zu verrechnendes Kindergeld außer Ansatz.

(4) [1]Bei einer nachträglichen Erhöhung der Vorauszahlungen ist die letzte Vorauszahlung für den Veranlagungszeitraum anzupassen. [2]Der Erhöhungsbetrag ist innerhalb eines Monats nach Bekanntgabe des Vorauszahlungsbescheids zu entrichten.

(5) [1]Vorauszahlungen sind nur festzusetzen, wenn sie mindestens 400 Euro im Kalenderjahr und mindestens 100 Euro für einen Vorauszahlungszeitpunkt betragen. [2]Festgesetzte Vorauszahlungen sind nur zu erhöhen, wenn sich der Erhöhungsbetrag im Fall des Absatzes 3 Satz 2 bis 5 für einen Vorauszahlungszeitpunkt auf mindestens 100 Euro, im Fall des Absatzes 4 auf mindestens 5 000 Euro beläuft.

(6) [1]Absatz 3 ist, soweit die erforderlichen Daten nach § 10 Absatz 2 Satz 3 noch nicht nach § 10 Absatz 2a übermittelt wurden, mit der Maßgabe anzuwenden, dass

1. als Beiträge im Sinne des § 10 Absatz 1 Nummer 3 Buchstabe a die für den letzten Veranlagungszeitraum geleisteten
   (a) Beiträge zugunsten einer privaten Krankenversicherung vermindert um 20 Prozent oder
   (b) Beiträge zur gesetzlichen Krankenversicherung vermindert um 4 Prozent,
2. als Beiträge im Sinne des § 10 Absatz 1 Nummer 3 Buchstabe b die bei der letzten Veranlagung berücksichtigten Beiträge zugunsten einer gesetzlichen Pflegeversicherung

anzusetzen sind; mindestens jedoch 1 500 Euro. [2]Bei zusammen veranlagten Ehegatten ist der in Satz 1 genannte Betrag von 1 500 Euro zu verdoppeln.

depreciation pursuant to Section 7b of this Act or increased deductions pursuant to Sections 14a, 14c or 14d of the Berlin Promotion Act are claimed. [11]Sentence 8 shall apply mutatis mutandis to negative income from the letting or leasing of another asset within the meaning of § 21 (1) sentence 1 numbers 1 to 3 with the proviso that the acquisition or completion is replaced by the commencement of use by the taxpayer. [12]In the cases of § 31, in which the required tax exemption of an amount of income in the amount of the minimum subsistence level of a child is not fully effected by the child benefit, allowances under § 32, paragraph 6 and child benefit to be offset shall not be taken into account when applying sentences 2 and 3.

(4) [1]If the advance payments are subsequently increased, the last advance payment for the assessment period shall be adjusted. [2]The increased amount shall be paid within one month of notification of the advance payment notice.

(5) [1]Advance payments shall only be fixed if they amount to at least EUR 400 per calendar year and at least EUR 100 for a date of advance payment. [2]Fixed advance payments shall only be increased if the amount of the increase in the case of paragraph 3, sentences 2 to 5 for an advance payment date amounts to at least EUR 100 and in the case of paragraph 4 to at least EUR 5 000.

(6) [1]Subsection (3) shall apply to the extent that the required data pursuant to section 10 subsection (2) sentence 3 have not yet been transmitted in accordance with section 10 subsection (2a), provided that

1. as contributions within the meaning of § 10 paragraph 1 number 3 letter a, the contributions paid for the last assessment period
   (a) contributions in favour of a private health insurance reduced by 20 per cent or
   (b) Contributions to statutory health insurance reduced by 4 percent,
2. as contributions within the meaning of § 10 paragraph 1 number 3 letter b, the contributions taken into account in the last assessment in favour of a statutory long-term care insurance scheme

with a minimum of EUR 1 500. [2]In the case of spouses assessed together, the amount of EUR 1 500 mentioned in the first sentence is to be doubled.

§ 38
Erhebung der Lohnsteuer

(1) ¹Bei Einkünften aus nichtselbständiger Arbeit wird die Einkommensteuer durch Abzug vom Arbeitslohn erhoben (Lohnsteuer), soweit der Arbeitslohn von einem Arbeitgeber gezahlt wird, der

1. im Inland einen Wohnsitz, seinen gewöhnlichen Aufenthalt, seine Geschäftsleitung, seinen Sitz, eine Betriebsstätte oder einen ständigen Vertreter im Sinne der §§ 8 bis 13 der Abgabenordnung hat (inländischer Arbeitgeber) oder
2. einem Dritten (Entleiher) Arbeitnehmer gewerbsmäßig zur Arbeitsleistung im Inland überlässt, ohne inländischer Arbeitgeber zu sein (ausländischer Verleiher).

²In den Fällen der internationalen Arbeitnehmerentsendung ist das nach Satz 1 Nummer 1 in Deutschland ansässige aufnehmende Unternehmen inländischer Arbeitgeber, wenn es den Arbeitslohn für die ihm geleistete Arbeit wirtschaftlich trägt oder nach dem Fremdvergleichsgrundsatz hätte tragen müssen; Voraussetzung hierfür ist nicht, dass das Unternehmen dem Arbeitnehmer den Arbeitslohn im eigenen Namen und für eigene Rechnung auszahlt. ³Der Lohnsteuer unterliegt auch der im Rahmen des Dienstverhältnisses von einem Dritten gewährte Arbeitslohn, wenn der Arbeitgeber weiß oder erkennen kann, dass derartige Vergütungen erbracht werden; dies ist insbesondere anzunehmen, wenn Arbeitgeber und Dritter verbundene Unternehmen im Sinne von § 15 des Aktiengesetzes sind.

(2) ¹Der Arbeitnehmer ist Schuldner der Lohnsteuer. ²Die Lohnsteuer entsteht in dem Zeitpunkt, in dem der Arbeitslohn dem Arbeitnehmer zufließt.

(3) ¹Der Arbeitgeber hat die Lohnsteuer für Rechnung des Arbeitnehmers bei jeder Lohnzahlung vom Arbeitslohn einzubehalten. ²Bei juristischen Personen des öffentlichen Rechts hat die öffentliche Kasse, die den Arbeitslohn zahlt, die Pflichten des Arbeitgebers. ³In den Fällen der nach § 7f Absatz 1 Satz 1 Nummer 2 des Vierten Buches Sozialgesetzbuch an die Deutsche Rentenversicherung Bund übertragenen Wertguthaben hat die Deutsche Rentenversicherung Bund bei Inanspruchnahme des Wertguthabens die Pflichten des Arbeitgebers.

Section 38
Collection of the Wage Tax

(1) ¹For income from employment, income tax shall be levied by deduction from the salary (wage tax), if the salary is paid by an employer who

1. has a residence, habitual abode, management, registered office, permanent establishment or permanent representative within the meaning of sec. 8 to 13 of the German Fiscal Code (domestic employer) or
2. hires out employees to a third party (hirer) for work in Germany without being a domestic employer (foreign hirer).

²In cases of international employee assignment, the receiving enterprise resident in Germany pursuant to sentence 1 number 1 shall be a domestic employer if it bears the wage for the work performed for it economically or should have borne it according to the arm's length principle; a precondition for this is not that the enterprise pays the wage to the employee in its own name and for its own account. ³Wage tax is also payable on wages granted by a third party in the context of the employment relationship if the employer knows or can see that such remuneration is paid; this is to be assumed in particular if the employer and the third party are affiliated companies within the meaning of Section 15 of the German Stock Corporation Act.

(2) ¹The employee is the debtor of the wage tax. ²The wage tax arises at the point in time when the wage accrues to the employee.

(3) ¹The employer shall withhold the wage tax from the employee's salary for the employee's account each time the salary is paid. ²In the case of legal entities under public law, the public fund which pays the wage shall have the obligations of the employer. ³In the cases of the value credit balances transferred to the German Pension Insurance Federation in accordance with sec. 7f paragraph 1 sentence 1 number 2 of Book 4 of the Social Security Code, the German Pension Insurance Federation has the obligations of the employer when the value credit balance is used.

(3a) ¹Soweit sich aus einem Dienstverhältnis oder einem früheren Dienstverhältnis tarifvertragliche Ansprüche des Arbeitnehmers auf Arbeitslohn unmittelbar gegen einen Dritten mit Wohnsitz, Geschäftsleitung oder Sitz im Inland richten und von diesem durch die Zahlung von Geld erfüllt werden, hat der Dritte die Pflichten des Arbeitgebers. ²In anderen Fällen kann das Finanzamt zulassen, dass ein Dritter mit Wohnsitz, Geschäftsleitung oder Sitz im Inland die Pflichten des Arbeitgebers im eigenen Namen erfüllt. 3Voraussetzung ist, dass der Dritte

1. sich hierzu gegenüber dem Arbeitgeber verpflichtet hat,
2. den Lohn auszahlt oder er nur Arbeitgeberpflichten für von ihm vermittelte Arbeitnehmer übernimmt und
3. die Steuererhebung nicht beeinträchtigt wird.

⁴Die Zustimmung erteilt das Betriebsstättenfinanzamt des Dritten auf dessen Antrag im Einvernehmen mit dem Betriebsstättenfinanzamt des Arbeitgebers; sie darf mit Nebenbestimmungen versehen werden, die die ordnungsgemäße Steuererhebung sicherstellen und die Überprüfung des Lohnsteuerabzugs nach § 42f erleichtern sollen. ⁵Die Zustimmung kann mit Wirkung für die Zukunft widerrufen werden. ⁶In den Fällen der Sätze 1 und 2 sind die das Lohnsteuerverfahren betreffenden Vorschriften mit der Maßgabe anzuwenden, dass an die Stelle des Arbeitgebers der Dritte tritt; der Arbeitgeber ist von seinen Pflichten befreit, soweit der Dritte diese Pflichten erfüllt hat. ⁷Erfüllt der Dritte die Pflichten des Arbeitgebers, kann er den Arbeitslohn, der einem Arbeitnehmer in demselben Lohnabrechnungszeitraum aus mehreren Dienstverhältnissen zufließt, für die Lohnsteuerermittlung und in der Lohnsteuerbescheinigung zusammenrechnen.

(3a) ¹Insofar as an employee's claims for remuneration under a contract of employment or a previous contract of employment are directed directly against a third party with residence, management or registered office in Germany and are fulfilled by the latter by payment of money, the third party shall have the obligations of the employer. ²In other cases the tax office may allow a third party with residence, management or registered office in Germany to fulfil the employer's obligations in his own name. ³The condition is that the third party

1. has undertaken to do so vis-à-vis the employer
2. pays the salary or only assumes employer's obligations for employees he has placed and
3. the collection of taxes is not affected.

⁴Such approval shall be granted by the third party's permanent establishment tax office upon the third party's request and in agreement with the employer's permanent establishment tax office; it may be provided with ancillary provisions to ensure the proper collection of tax and to facilitate the verification of the deduction of income tax pursuant to section 42f. ⁵Such consent may be revoked with effect for the future. ⁶In the cases of sentences 1 and 2, the provisions relating to the wage tax procedure shall be applied with the proviso that the third party takes the place of the employer; the employer shall be released from its obligations to the extent that the third party has fulfilled these obligations. ⁷If the third party fulfils the employer's obligations, the employer may add up the wages which an employee receives from several employment relationships in the same payroll period for the purposes of the wage tax calculation and in the wage tax certificate.

§41a
Anmeldung und Abführung der Lohnsteuer

(1) ¹Der Arbeitgeber hat spätestens am zehnten Tag nach Ablauf eines jeden Lohnsteuer-Anmeldungszeitraums

1. dem Finanzamt, in dessen Bezirk sich die Betriebsstätte (§ 41 Absatz 2) befindet (Betriebsstättenfinanzamt), eine Steuererklärung einzureichen, in der er die Summen der im Lohnsteuer-Anmeldungszeitraum einzubehaltenden und zu übernehmenden Lohnsteuer angibt (Lohnsteuer-Anmeldung),

Section 41a
Registration and Payment of Income Tax

(1) ¹No later than on the tenth day after the end of each income tax registration period, the employer shall

1. submit a tax return to the tax office in whose district the permanent establishment (section 41 paragraph 2) is located (permanent establishment tax office), in which he states the sums of the wage tax to be withheld and assumed in the wage tax registration period (wage tax registration)

2. die im Lohnsteuer-Anmeldungszeitraum insgesamt einbehaltene und übernommene Lohnsteuer an das Betriebsstättenfinanzamt abzuführen.

²Die Lohnsteuer-Anmeldung ist nach amtlich vorgeschriebenem Datensatz durch Datenfernübertragung zu übermitteln. ³Auf Antrag kann das Finanzamt zur Vermeidung unbilliger Härten auf eine elektronische Übermittlung verzichten; in diesem Fall ist die Lohnsteuer-Anmeldung nach amtlich vorgeschriebenem Vordruck abzugeben und vom Arbeitgeber oder von einer zu seiner Vertretung berechtigten Person zu unterschreiben. ⁴Der Arbeitgeber wird von der Verpflichtung zur Abgabe weiterer Lohnsteuer-Anmeldungen befreit, wenn er Arbeitnehmer, für die er Lohnsteuer einzubehalten oder zu übernehmen hat, nicht mehr beschäftigt und das dem Finanzamt mitteilt.

(2) ¹Lohnsteuer-Anmeldungszeitraum ist grundsätzlich der Kalendermonat. ²Lohnsteuer-Anmeldungszeitraum ist das Kalendervierteljahr, wenn die abzuführende Lohnsteuer für das vorangegangene Kalenderjahr mehr als 1 080 Euro, aber nicht mehr als 5 000 Euro betragen hat; Lohnsteuer-Anmeldungszeitraum ist das Kalenderjahr, wenn die abzuführende Lohnsteuer für das vorangegangene Kalenderjahr nicht mehr als 1 080 Euro betragen hat. ³Hat die Betriebsstätte nicht während des ganzen vorangegangenen Kalenderjahres bestanden, so ist die für das vorangegangene Kalenderjahr abzuführende Lohnsteuer für die Feststellung des Lohnsteuer-Anmeldungszeitraums auf einen Jahresbetrag umzurechnen. ⁴Wenn die Betriebsstätte im vorangegangenen Kalenderjahr noch nicht bestanden hat, ist die auf einen Jahresbetrag umgerechnete für den ersten vollen Kalendermonat nach der Eröffnung der Betriebsstätte abzuführende Lohnsteuer maßgebend.

(3) ¹Die oberste Finanzbehörde des Landes kann bestimmen, dass die Lohnsteuer nicht dem Betriebsstättenfinanzamt, sondern einer anderen öffentlichen Kasse anzumelden und an diese abzuführen ist; die Kasse erhält insoweit die Stellung einer Landesfinanzbehörde. ²Das Betriebsstättenfinanzamt oder die zuständige andere öffentliche Kasse können anordnen, dass die Lohnsteuer abweichend von dem nach Absatz 1 maßgebenden Zeitpunkt anzumelden und abzuführen ist, wenn die Abführung der Lohnsteuer nicht gesichert erscheint.

2. to pay over the total amount of wage tax withheld and paid during the wage tax registration period to the permanent establishment tax office.

²The wage tax registration is to be transmitted by remote data transmission according to the officially prescribed data set. ³Upon application, the tax office may waive electronic transmission in order to avoid undue hardship; in this case, the wage tax registration must be submitted according to the officially prescribed form and signed by the employer or a person authorised to represent him/her. ⁴The employer is released from the obligation to submit further wage tax registrations if he no longer employs employees for whom he has to withhold or take over wage tax and informs the tax office accordingly.

(2) ¹In principle, the wage tax registration period is the calendar month. ²The wage tax registration period is the calendar quarter if the wage tax to be paid for the previous calendar year was more than EUR 1,080 but not more than EUR 5,000; the wage tax registration period is the calendar year if the wage tax to be paid for the previous calendar year was not more than EUR 1,080. ³If the permanent establishment did not exist for the whole of the previous calendar year, the wage tax to be paid for the previous calendar year must be converted to an annual amount in order to determine the wage tax registration period. ⁴If the permanent establishment did not exist in the previous calendar year, the wage tax to be paid for the first full calendar month after opening the permanent establishment, converted to an annual amount, is decisive.

(3) ¹The supreme tax authority of the Land may determine that the wage tax is not to be declared to the permanent establishment tax office but to another public fund and transferred to it; the fund shall be given the status of a Land tax authority in this respect. ²The permanent establishment tax office or the competent other public fund may order that the wage tax be declared and paid at a different time from the one specified in paragraph 1 if the payment of the wage tax does not appear to be assured.

(4) ¹Arbeitgeber, die eigene oder gecharterte Handelsschiffe betreiben, dürfen die gesamte anzumeldende und abzuführende Lohnsteuer, die auf den Arbeitslohn entfällt, der an die Besatzungsmitglieder für die Beschäftigungszeiten auf diesen Schiffen gezahlt wird, abziehen und einbehalten. ²Die Handelsschiffe müssen in einem inländischen Seeschiffsregister eingetragen sein, die deutsche Flagge führen und zur Beförderung von Personen oder Gütern im Verkehr mit oder zwischen ausländischen Häfen, innerhalb eines ausländischen Hafens oder zwischen einem ausländischen Hafen und der Hohen See betrieben werden. ³Die Sätze 1 und 2 sind entsprechend anzuwenden, wenn Seeschiffe im Wirtschaftsjahr überwiegend außerhalb der deutschen Hoheitsgewässer zum Schleppen, Bergen oder zur Aufsuchung von Bodenschätzen oder zur Vermessung von Energielagerstätten unter dem Meeresboden eingesetzt werden. ⁴Ist für den Lohnsteuerabzug die Lohnsteuer nach der Steuerklasse V oder VI zu ermitteln, so bemisst sich der Betrag nach Satz 1 nach der Lohnsteuer der Steuerklasse I.

(4) ¹Employers who operate their own or chartered merchant ships may deduct and withhold the entire wage tax to be declared and paid which is attributable to the wages paid to the crew members for the periods of employment on these ships. ²The merchant ships must be entered in a domestic shipping register, fly the German flag and be operated for the transport of persons or goods in traffic with or between foreign ports, within a foreign port or between a foreign port and the high seas. ³Sentences 1 and 2 shall be applied mutatis mutandis if seagoing vessels are used in the business year predominantly outside German territorial waters for towing, salvage or exploration of mineral resources or for surveying energy deposits under the sea bed. ⁴If the wage tax is to be determined according to tax classes V or VI for the deduction of wage tax, the amount pursuant to sentence 1 shall be determined according to the wage tax of tax class I.

§ 42d
Haftung des Arbeitgebers und Haftung bei Arbeitnehmerüberlassung

(1) Der Arbeitgeber haftet

1. für die Lohnsteuer, die er einzubehalten und abzuführen hat,

2. für die Lohnsteuer, die er beim Lohnsteuer-Jahresausgleich zu Unrecht erstattet hat,
3. für die Einkommensteuer (Lohnsteuer), die auf Grund fehlerhafter Angaben im Lohnkonto oder in der Lohnsteuerbescheinigung verkürzt wird,
4. für die Lohnsteuer, die in den Fällen des § 38 Absatz 3a der Dritte zu übernehmen hat.

(2) Der Arbeitgeber haftet nicht, soweit Lohnsteuer nach § 39 Absatz 5 oder § 39a Absatz 5 nachzufordern ist und in den vom Arbeitgeber angezeigten Fällen des § 38 Absatz 4 Satz 2 und 3 und des § 41c Absatz 4.

(3) ¹Soweit die Haftung des Arbeitgebers reicht, sind der Arbeitgeber und der Arbeitnehmer Gesamtschuldner. ²Das Betriebsstättenfinanzamt kann die Steuerschuld oder Haftungsschuld nach pflichtgemäßem Ermessen gegenüber jedem Gesamtschuldner geltend machen. ³Der Arbeitgeber kann auch dann in Anspruch genommen werden, wenn der Arbeitnehmer zur Einkommensteuer veranlagt wird. ⁴Der Arbeitnehmer kann im Rahmen der Gesamtschuldnerschaft nur in Anspruch genommen werden,

Section 42d
Employer's Liability and Liability in Case of Temporary Employment

(1) The employer shall be liable

1. for the wage tax which he has to withhold and pay

2. for the wage tax which he has wrongly refunded in the annual wage tax adjustment
3. for income tax (payroll tax), which is reduced due to incorrect information in the payroll account or in the payroll tax certificate
4. for income tax, which in the cases of section 38(3a) must be borne by the third party.

(2) The employer shall not be liable to the extent that wage tax is to be claimed subsequently under section 39(5) or section 39a(5) and in the cases indicated by the employer under section 38(4), second and third sentences, and section 41c(4).

(3) ¹Insofar as the employer's liability extends, the employer and the employee shall be joint and several debtors. ²The permanent establishment tax office may assert the tax debt or liability debt against each joint and several debtor at its discretion. ³The employer can also be held liable if the employee is assessed for income tax. The employee can only be held liable in the context of joint and several liability,

1. wenn der Arbeitgeber die Lohnsteuer nicht vorschriftsmäßig vom Arbeitslohn einbehalten hat,

2. wenn der Arbeitnehmer weiß, dass der Arbeitgeber die einbehaltene Lohnsteuer nicht vorschriftsmäßig angemeldet hat.

(4) ¹Für die Inanspruchnahme des Arbeitgebers bedarf es keines Haftungsbescheids und keines Leistungsgebots, soweit der Arbeitgeber

1. die einzubehaltende Lohnsteuer angemeldet hat oder

2. nach Abschluss einer Lohnsteuer-Außenprüfung seine Zahlungsverpflichtung schriftlich anerkennt.

²Satz 1 gilt entsprechend für die Nachforderung zu übernehmender pauschaler Lohnsteuer.

(5) Von der Geltendmachung der Steuernachforderung oder Haftungsforderung ist abzusehen, wenn diese insgesamt 10 Euro nicht übersteigt.

(6) ¹Soweit einem Dritten (Entleiher) Arbeitnehmer im Sinne des § 1 Absatz 1 Satz 1 des Arbeitnehmerüberlassungsgesetzes in der Fassung der Bekanntmachung vom 3. Februar 1995 (BGBl. I S. 158), das zuletzt durch Artikel 26 des Gesetzes vom 20. Dezember 2011 (BGBl. I S. 2854) geändert worden ist, zur Arbeitsleistung überlassen werden, haftet er mit Ausnahme der Fälle, in denen eine Arbeitnehmerüberlassung nach § 1 Absatz 3 des Arbeitnehmerüberlassungsgesetzes vorliegt, neben dem Arbeitgeber. ²Der Entleiher haftet nicht, wenn der Überlassung eine Erlaubnis nach § 1 des Arbeitnehmerüberlassungsgesetzes in der jeweils geltenden Fassung zugrunde liegt und soweit er nachweist, dass er den nach § 51 Absatz 1 Nummer 2 Buchstabe d vorgesehenen Mitwirkungspflichten nachgekommen ist. ³Der Entleiher haftet ferner nicht, wenn er über das Vorliegen einer Arbeitnehmerüberlassung ohne Verschulden irrte. ⁴Die Haftung beschränkt sich auf die Lohnsteuer für die Zeit, für die ihm der Arbeitnehmer überlassen worden ist. ⁵Soweit die Haftung des Entleihers reicht, sind der Arbeitgeber, der Entleiher und der Arbeitnehmer Gesamtschuldner. ⁶Der Entleiher darf auf Zahlung nur in Anspruch genommen werden, soweit die Vollstreckung in das inländische bewegliche Vermögen des Arbeitgebers fehlgeschlagen ist oder keinen Erfolg verspricht; § 219 Satz 2 der Abgabenordnung ist entsprechend anzuwenden. ⁷Ist durch die Umstände der Arbeitnehmerüberlassung die Lohnsteuer schwer zu ermitteln, so ist die Haftungsschuld mit 15 Prozent des zwischen Verleiher und Entleiher vereinbarten Entgelts ohne Umsatzsteuer anzunehmen, solange der Entleiher nicht

1. if the employer has not deducted the wage tax from the salary in accordance with the regulations

2. if the employee knows that the employer has not duly declared the withheld income tax.

(4) ¹No notice of liability and no offer of benefits shall be required for recourse against the employer if the employer

1 has declared the wage tax to be withheld or

2. acknowledges his payment obligation in writing after completion of an external wage tax audit.

²Sentence 1 shall apply accordingly to the subsequent claim for flat-rate wage tax to be assumed.

(5) The assertion of the subsequent tax claim or liability claim shall be waived if it does not exceed a total of 10 euros.

(6) ¹Where employees within the meaning of section 1(1) first sentence of the Act on the Provision of Temporary Workers in the version promulgated on 3rd February 1995 (Federal Law Gazette I p. 158), as last amended by Article 26 of the Act of 20th December 2011 (Federal Law Gazette I p. 2854), are provided to a third party (hirer) for the purpose of performing work, the hirer shall be liable in addition to the employer, except in cases where the provision of temporary workers under section 1(3) of the Act on the Provision of Temporary Workers. ²The hirer shall not be liable if the temporary employment is based on a permit pursuant to section 1 of the temporary employment act in its currently applicable version and if he proves that he has complied with the obligations to cooperate provided for under section 51, first paragraph, point 2, letter d. ³Furthermore, the hirer shall not be liable if he erred in assuming the existence of a temporary employment agency without fault. ⁴The liability is limited to the wage tax for the period for which the employee was made available to him. ⁵If the liability of the hirer is sufficient, the employer, the hirer and the employee are jointly and severally liable. ⁶The hirer may only be held liable for payment if enforcement against the employer's domestic movable assets has failed or does not promise success; section 219 sentence 2 of the German Tax Code is to be applied accordingly. ⁷If it is difficult to determine the wage tax due to the circumstances of the temporary employment agency, the liability debt is to be assumed to be 15 percent of the remuneration agreed between the lender and the hirer, excluding value added tax, as long as the hirer does not provide cred-

glaubhaft macht, dass die Lohnsteuer, für die er haftet, niedriger ist. [8]Die Absätze 1 bis 5 sind entsprechend anzuwenden. [9]Die Zuständigkeit des Finanzamts richtet sich nach dem Ort der Betriebsstätte des Verleihers.

(7) Soweit der Entleiher Arbeitgeber ist, haftet der Verleiher wie ein Entleiher nach Absatz 6.

(8) [1]Das Finanzamt kann hinsichtlich der Lohnsteuer der Leiharbeitnehmer anordnen, dass der Entleiher einen bestimmten Teil des mit dem Verleiher vereinbarten Entgelts einzubehalten und abzuführen hat, wenn dies zur Sicherung des Steueranspruchs notwendig ist; Absatz 6 Satz 4 ist anzuwenden. [2]Der Verwaltungsakt kann auch mündlich erlassen werden. [3]Die Höhe des einzubehaltenden und abzuführenden Teils des Entgelts bedarf keiner Begründung, wenn der in Absatz 6 Satz 7 genannte Prozentsatz nicht überschritten wird.

(9) [1]Der Arbeitgeber haftet auch dann, wenn ein Dritter nach § 38 Absatz 3a dessen Pflichten trägt. [2]In diesen Fällen haftet der Dritte neben dem Arbeitgeber. [3]Soweit die Haftung des Dritten reicht, sind der Arbeitgeber, der Dritte und der Arbeitnehmer Gesamtschuldner. [4]Absatz 3 Satz 2 bis 4 ist anzuwenden; Absatz 4 gilt auch für die Inanspruchnahme des Dritten. [5]Im Fall des § 38 Absatz 3a Satz 2 beschränkt sich die Haftung des Dritten auf die Lohnsteuer, die für die Zeit zu erheben ist, für die er sich gegenüber dem Arbeitgeber zur Vornahme des Lohnsteuerabzugs verpflichtet hat; der maßgebende Zeitraum endet nicht, bevor der Dritte seinem Betriebsstättenfinanzamt die Beendigung seiner Verpflichtung gegenüber dem Arbeitgeber angezeigt hat. [6]In den Fällen des § 38 Absatz 3a Satz 7 ist als Haftungsschuld der Betrag zu ermitteln, um den die Lohnsteuer, die für den gesamten Arbeitslohn des Lohnzahlungszeitraums zu berechnen und einzubehalten ist, die insgesamt tatsächlich einbehaltene Lohnsteuer übersteigt. [7]Betrifft die Haftungsschuld mehrere Arbeitgeber, so ist sie bei fehlerhafter Lohnsteuerberechnung nach dem Verhältnis der Arbeitslöhne und für nachträglich zu erfassende Arbeitslohnbeträge nach dem Verhältnis dieser Beträge auf die Arbeitgeber aufzuteilen. [8]In den Fällen des § 38 Absatz 3a ist das Betriebsstättenfinanzamt des Dritten für die Geltendmachung der Steuer- oder Haftungsschuld zuständig.

ible evidence that the wage tax for which he is liable is lower. [8]Paragraphs 1 to 5 shall apply accordingly. [9]The jurisdiction of the tax office depends on the location of the permanent establishment of the lender.

(7) Insofar as the user is an employer, the lender shall be liable as a user in accordance with paragraph 6.

(8) [1]With regard to the wage tax of temporary workers, the tax office may order that the hirer must withhold and pay over a certain part of the remuneration agreed with the lender if this is necessary to secure the tax claim; paragraph 6 sentence 4 shall apply. [2]The administrative act may also be adopted orally. [3]The amount of the part of the remuneration to be withheld and paid need not be justified if the percentage specified in paragraph 6 sentence 7 is not exceeded.

(9) [1]The employer shall also be liable if a third party bears the obligations of the latter under section 38(3a). [2]In such cases the third party shall be liable in addition to the employer. [3]Insofar as the liability of the third party is sufficient, the employer, the third party and the employee shall be joint and several debtors. [4]Paragraph 3, sentences 2 to 4, shall apply; paragraph 4 shall also apply to claims against the third party. [5]In the case of section 38 subsection 3a, second sentence, the third party's liability shall be limited to the wage tax to be levied for the period for which he has undertaken to the employer to deduct wage tax; the relevant period shall not end before the third party has notified his permanent establishment tax office of the termination of his obligation to the employer. [6]In the cases referred to in the seventh sentence of Section 38(3a), the amount by which the amount of payroll tax to be calculated and withheld for the entire salary during the pay period exceeds the total amount of payroll tax actually withheld is to be determined as the liability debt. [7]If the liability debt concerns several employers, it must be divided among the employers in the event of incorrect wage tax calculation in proportion to the wages and, for wage amounts to be recorded subsequently, in proportion to these amounts. [8]In the cases referred to in Section 38(3a), the tax office of the third party's permanent establishment is responsible for asserting the tax or liability debt.

XXI. Fiscal Code (Excerpt)

Abgabenordnung – AO (Auszug)

Stand: 21.12.2019

§44
Gesamtschuldner

(1) [1]Personen, die nebeneinander dieselbe Leistung aus dem Steuerschuldverhältnis schulden oder für sie haften oder die zusammen zu einer Steuer zu veranlagen sind, sind Gesamtschuldner. [2]Soweit nichts anderes bestimmt ist, schuldet jeder Gesamtschuldner die gesamte Leistung.

(2) [1]Die Erfüllung durch einen Gesamtschuldner wirkt auch für die übrigen Schuldner. [2]Das Gleiche gilt für die Aufrechnung und für eine geleistete Sicherheit. [3]Andere Tatsachen wirken nur für und gegen den Gesamtschuldner, in dessen Person sie eintreten. 4Die Vorschriften der §§ 268 bis 280 über die Beschränkung der Vollstreckung in den Fällen der Zusammenveranlagung bleiben unberührt.

§153
Berichtigung von Erklärungen

(1) [1]Erkennt ein Steuerpflichtiger nachträglich vor Ablauf der Festsetzungsfrist,

1. dass eine von ihm oder für ihn abgegebene Erklärung unrichtig oder unvollständig ist und dass es dadurch zu einer Verkürzung von Steuern kommen kann oder bereits gekommen ist oder

2. dass eine durch Verwendung von Steuerzeichen oder Steuerstemplern zu entrichtende Steuer nicht in der richtigen Höhe entrichtet worden ist,

so ist er verpflichtet, dies unverzüglich anzuzeigen und die erforderliche Richtigstellung vorzunehmen. [2]Die Verpflichtung trifft auch den Gesamtrechtsnachfolger eines Steuerpflichtigen und die nach den §§ 34 und 35 für den Gesamtrechtsnachfolger oder den Steuerpflichtigen handelnden Personen.

(2) Die Anzeigepflicht besteht ferner, wenn die Voraussetzungen für eine Steuerbefreiung, Steuerermäßigung oder sonstige Steuervergünstigung nachträglich ganz oder teilweise wegfallen.

Section 44
Joint and several debtors

(1) [1]Persons who concurrently owe or are liable for the same obligation arising from the tax debtor-creditor relationship or who must be assessed jointly shall be joint and several debtors. [2]Unless otherwise stipulated, each joint and several debtor shall owe the entire obligation.

(2) [1]Fulfilment by a joint and several debtor shall also take effect for the other debtors. [2]The same shall apply to the set-off and any securities provided. [3]Other facts shall only take effect for and against the joint and several debtor personally affected by them. The provisions of sections 268 to 280 with regard to the limitation of enforcement in the case of joint assessment shall remain unaffected.

Section 153
Correction of returns

(1) [1]Where a taxpayer subsequently realises before the period for assessment has elapsed

1. that a return submitted by him or for him is incorrect or incomplete and that this can lead or has already led to an understatement of tax, or

2. that a tax amount payable by way of tax mark or tax stamp was not paid in the correct amount,

he shall be obliged to indicate such without undue delay, and to effect the necessary corrections. [2]This obligation shall also concern the taxpayer's universal successor and the persons acting for the universal successor or the taxpayer pursuant to sections 34 and 35.

(2) The notification obligation shall further apply where the conditions for tax exemption, tax reduction or other tax privileges subsequently cease to exist, whether in full or in part.

(3) Wer Waren, für die eine Steuervergünstigung unter einer Bedingung gewährt worden ist, in einer Weise verwenden will, die der Bedingung nicht entspricht, hat dies vorher der Finanzbehörde anzuzeigen.

(3) In the case of goods for which a tax privilege has been granted subject to specific conditions, any person who wishes to use such goods in a manner that does not comply with the specified conditions shall be obliged to notify the revenue authority accordingly in advance.

§ 233a
Verzinsung von Steuernachforderungen und Steuererstattungen

Section 233a
Interest accrual on tax deficiencies and tax refunds

(1) ¹Führt die Festsetzung der Einkommen-, Körperschaft-, Vermögen-, Umsatz- oder Gewerbesteuer zu einem Unterschiedsbetrag im Sinne des Absatzes 3, ist dieser zu verzinsen. ²Dies gilt nicht für die Festsetzung von Vorauszahlungen und Steuerabzugsbeträgen.

(1) ¹Where the assessment of income tax, corporation tax, capital tax, VAT or trade tax leads to a differential within the meaning of subsection (3) below, interest shall be charged on this differential. ²This shall not apply to the assessment of prepayments and withheld taxes.

(2) ¹Der Zinslauf beginnt 15 Monate nach Ablauf des Kalenderjahrs, in dem die Steuer entstanden ist. ²Er beginnt für die Einkommen- und Körperschaftsteuer 23 Monate nach diesem Zeitpunkt, wenn die Einkünfte aus Land- und Forstwirtschaft bei der erstmaligen Steuerfestsetzung die anderen Einkünfte überwiegen. ³Er endet mit Ablauf des Tages, an dem die Steuerfestsetzung wirksam wird.

(2) ¹The period of interest accrual shall begin 15 months after expiration of the calendar year in which the tax has arisen. ²With respect to income tax and corporation tax, it shall begin 23 months after this date where the income from agricultural and forestry undertakings is more than other income when the tax is first assessed. ³It shall end on expiration of the date when the tax assessment comes into effect.

(2a) Soweit die Steuerfestsetzung auf der Berücksichtigung eines rückwirkenden Ereignisses (§ A175 Abs. Absatz 1 Satz 1 Nr. 2 und Abs. 2) oder auf einem Verlustabzug nach § 10d Abs. 1 des Einkommensteuergesetzes beruht, beginnt der Zinslauf abweichend von Absatz 2 Satz 1 und 2 15 Monate nach Ablauf des Kalenderjahres, in dem das rückwirkende Ereignis eingetreten oder der Verlust entstanden ist.

(2a) Notwithstanding subsection (2), first and second sentences, above, where the tax assessment is based on an event with retroactive effect (section 175 (1), first sentence, number 2 and section 175 (2)) or a loss deduction pursuant to section 10d (1) of the Income Tax Act, the period of interest accrual shall begin 15 months after expiration of the calendar year in which the event with retroactive effect occurred or the loss was incurred.

(3) ¹Maßgebend für die Zinsberechnung ist die festgesetzte Steuer, vermindert um die anzurechnenden Steuerabzugsbeträge, um die anzurechnende Körperschaftsteuer und um die bis zum Beginn des Zinslaufs festgesetzten Vorauszahlungen (Unterschiedsbetrag). ²Bei der Vermögensteuer ist als Unterschiedsbetrag für die Zinsberechnung die festgesetzte Steuer, vermindert um die festgesetzten Vorauszahlungen oder die bisher festgesetzte Jahressteuer, maßgebend. ³Ein Unterschiedsbetrag zugunsten des Steuerpflichtigen ist nur bis zur Höhe des zu erstattenden Betrags zu verzinsen; die Verzinsung beginnt frühestens mit dem Tag der Zahlung.

(3) ¹The assessed tax minus the withheld taxes to be credited, the corporation tax to be credited and the prepayments assessed up to the beginning of the period of interest accrual (differential) shall form the basis for calculating the interest. ²With respect to capital tax, the assessed tax minus the assessed prepayments or the annual tax assessed to date shall form the basis of the differential for calculating the interest. ³Interest shall be charged on a differential in the taxpayer's favour only up to an amount equal to the amount to be refunded; interest shall begin to accrue at the earliest on the date of payment.

(4) Die Festsetzung der Zinsen soll mit der Steuerfestsetzung verbunden werden.

(4) The assessment of interest should be issued in conjunction with the tax assessment.

(5) ¹Wird die Steuerfestsetzung aufgehoben, geändert oder nach § 129 berichtigt, ist eine bisherige Zinsfestsetzung zu ändern; Gleiches gilt, wenn die Anrechnung von Steuerbeträgen zurückgenommen, widerrufen oder nach § 129 berichtigt wird. ²Maßgebend für die Zinsberechnung ist der Unterschiedsbetrag zwischen der festgesetzten Steuer und der vorher festgesetzten Steuer, jeweils vermindert um die anzurechnenden Steuerabzugsbeträge und um die anzurechnende Körperschaftsteuer. ³Dem sich hiernach ergebenden Zinsbetrag sind bisher festzusetzende Zinsen hinzuzurechnen; bei einem Unterschiedsbetrag zugunsten des Steuerpflichtigen entfallen darauf festgesetzte Zinsen. ⁴Im Übrigen gilt Absatz 3 Satz 3 entsprechend.

(6) Die Absätze 1 bis 5 gelten bei der Durchführung des Lohnsteuer-Jahresausgleichs entsprechend.

(7) ¹Bei Anwendung des Absatzes 2a gelten die Absätze 3 und 5 mit der Maßgabe, dass der Unterschiedsbetrag in Teil-Unterschiedsbeträge mit jeweils gleichem Zinslaufbeginn aufzuteilen ist; für jeden Teil-Unterschiedsbetrag sind Zinsen gesondert und in der zeitlichen Reihenfolge der Teil-Unterschiedsbeträge zu berechnen, beginnend mit den Zinsen auf den Teil-Unterschiedsbetrag mit dem ältesten Zinslaufbeginn. ²Ergibt sich ein Teil-Unterschiedsbetrag zugunsten des Steuerpflichtigen, entfallen auf diesen Betrag festgesetzte Zinsen frühestens ab Beginn des für diesen Teil-Unterschiedsbetrag maßgebenden Zinslaufs; Zinsen für den Zeitraum bis zum Beginn des Zinslaufs dieses Teil-Unterschiedsbetrags bleiben endgültig bestehen. ³Dies gilt auch, wenn zuvor innerhalb derselben Zinsberechnung Zinsen auf einen Teil-Unterschiedsbetrag zuungunsten des Steuerpflichtigen berechnet worden sind.

§ 235
Verzinsung von hinterzogenen Steuern

(1) ¹Hinterzogene Steuern sind zu verzinsen. ²Zinsschuldner ist derjenige, zu dessen Vorteil die Steuern hinterzogen worden sind. ³Wird die Steuerhinterziehung dadurch begangen, dass ein anderer als der Steuerschuldner seine Verpflichtung, einbehaltene Steuern an die Finanzbehörde abzuführen oder Steuern zu Lasten eines anderen zu entrichten, nicht erfüllt, so ist dieser Zinsschuldner.

(2) ¹Der Zinslauf beginnt mit dem Eintritt der Verkürzung oder der Erlangung des Steuervorteils, es sei denn, dass die hinterzogenen Beträge ohne die Steuerhinterziehung erst später fällig geworden wären. ²In diesem Fall ist der spätere Zeitpunkt maßgebend.

(5) ¹Where the tax assessment is cancelled, amended or corrected pursuant to section 129, any previous assessment of interest shall be amended; the same shall apply where the crediting of tax amounts is withdrawn, revoked or corrected pursuant to section 129. ²The differential between the assessed tax and the previously assessed tax, both reduced by the amounts of withheld tax and corporation tax to be credited, shall form the basis for calculating interest. ³The resulting interest amount shall be supplemented by the assessable interest up to this point; where the differential is in the taxpayer's favour, assessed interest shall be added to this amount. ⁴In other respects, subsection (3), third sentence, above shall apply accordingly.

(6) Subsections (1) to (5) above shall apply accordingly to the annual adjustment of wages tax.

(7) ¹In applying subsection (2a) above, subsections (3) and (5) above shall apply under the proviso that the differential is to be divided into sub-differentials, each sub-differential being comprised of sub-amounts with the same starting date for the accrual of interest; interest shall be calculated for each sub-differential separately and in the chronological order of the sub-differentials, beginning with the interest on the sub-differential with the earliest commencement date of interest accrual. ²Where a sub-differential in the taxpayer's favour results, assessed interest shall be charged on this amount at the earliest from the beginning of the decisive period of interest accrual for this sub-differential; interest for the period up to the beginning of this sub-differential's period of interest accrual shall remain permanently. ³This shall also apply where, previously within the same interest calculation, interest had been calculated on a sub-differential in the taxpayer's favour.

Section 235
Interest accrual on evaded taxes

(1) ¹Interest shall be charged on evaded taxes. ²The debtor of the interest shall be the person to whose advantage the taxes have been evaded. ³Where tax evasion is committed by a person other than the tax debtor failing to fulfil his obligation to remit withheld taxes to the revenue authority or to pay taxes imposed on another, this person shall be the debtor of the interest.

(2) ¹The period of interest accrual shall begin upon occurrence of the understating of the taxes or attainment of the tax advantage unless the evaded amounts would have fallen due at a later date had the taxes not been evaded. ²In this case, the later point in time shall be decisive.

(3) ¹Der Zinslauf endet mit der Zahlung der hinterzogenen Steuern. ²Für eine Zeit, für die ein Säumniszuschlag verwirkt, die Zahlung gestundet oder die Vollziehung ausgesetzt ist, werden Zinsen nach dieser Vorschrift nicht erhoben. ³Wird der Steuerbescheid nach Ende des Zinslaufs aufgehoben, geändert oder nach § 129 berichtigt, so bleiben die bis dahin entstandenen Zinsen unberührt.

(4) Zinsen nach § 233a, die für denselben Zeitraum festgesetzt wurden, sind anzurechnen.

§ 370
Steuerhinterziehung

(1) Mit Freiheitsstrafe bis zu fünf Jahren oder mit Geldstrafe wird bestraft, wer

1. den Finanzbehörden oder anderen Behörden über steuerlich erhebliche Tatsachen unrichtige oder unvollständige Angaben macht,
2. die Finanzbehörden pflichtwidrig über steuerlich erhebliche Tatsachen in Unkenntnis lässt oder
3- pflichtwidrig die Verwendung von Steuerzeichen oder Steuerstemplern unterlässt

und dadurch Steuern verkürzt oder für sich oder einen anderen nicht gerechtfertigte Steuervorteile erlangt.

(2) Der Versuch ist strafbar.

(3) ¹In besonders schweren Fällen ist die Strafe Freiheitsstrafe von sechs Monaten bis zu zehn Jahren. ²Ein besonders schwerer Fall liegt in der Regel vor, wenn der Täter

1. in großem Ausmaß Steuern verkürzt oder nicht gerechtfertigte Steuervorteile erlangt,

2. seine Befugnisse oder seine Stellung als Amtsträger oder Europäischer Amtsträger (§ 11 Absatz 1 Nummer 2a des Strafgesetzbuchs) missbraucht,
3. die Mithilfe eines Amtsträgers oder Europäischen Amtsträgers (§ 11 Absatz 1 Nummer 2a des Strafgesetzbuchs) ausnutzt, der seine Befugnisse oder seine Stellung missbraucht,
4. unter Verwendung nachgemachter oder verfälschter Belege fortgesetzt Steuern verkürzt oder nicht gerechtfertigte Steuervorteile erlangt,
5. als Mitglied einer Bande, die sich zur fortgesetzten Begehung von Taten nach Absatz 1 verbunden hat, Umsatz- oder Verbrauchssteuern verkürzt oder nicht gerechtfertigte Umsatz- oder Verbrauchssteuervorteile erlangt oder

(3) ¹The period of accrual of interest shall end upon payment of the evaded taxes. ²Interest pursuant to this provision shall not be levied in a period to which a late-payment penalty applies or for which the payment is deferred or implementation suspended. ³Where upon conclusion of the period of interest accrual the tax assessment notice is cancelled, amended or corrected pursuant to section 129, the interest accrued up to this time shall remain unaffected.

(4) Zinsen nach § 233a, die für denselben Zeitraum festgesetzt wurden, sind anzurechnen.

Section 370
Tax evasion

(1) A penalty of up to five years' imprisonment or a monetary fine shall be imposed on any person who

1. furnishes the revenue authorities or other authorities with incorrect or incomplete particulars concerning matters that are relevant for tax purposes,
2. fails to inform the revenue authorities of facts that are relevant for tax purposes when obliged to do so, or
3. fails to use revenue stamps or revenue stamping machines when obliged to do so

and as a result understates taxes or derives unwarranted tax advantages for himself or for another person.

(2) Attempted perpetration shall be punishable.

(3) ¹In particularly serious cases, a penalty of between six months and ten years' imprisonment shall be imposed. ²In general, a particularly serious case is one in which the perpetrator

1. deliberately understates taxes on a large scale or derives unwarranted tax advantages,

2. abuses his authority or position as a public official or European public official (section 11(1) number 2a of the Criminal Code),

3. solicits the assistance of a public official or European public official (section 11(1) number 2a of the Criminal Code) who abuses his authority or position,

4. repeatedly understates taxes or derives unwarranted tax advantages by using falsified or forged documents, or

5. as a member of a group formed for the purpose of repeatedly committing acts pursuant to subsection (1) above, understates value-added taxes or excise duties or derives unwarranted VAT or excise duty advantages.

6. eine Drittstaat-Gesellschaft im Sinne des § 138 Absatz 3, auf die er alleine oder zusammen mit nahestehenden Personen im Sinne des § 1 Absatz 2 des Außensteuergesetzes unmittelbar oder mittelbar einen beherrschenden oder bestimmenden Einfluss ausüben kann, zur Verschleierung steuerlich erheblicher Tatsachen nutzt und auf diese Weise fortgesetzt Steuern verkürzt oder nicht gerechtfertigte Steuervorteile erlangt.

(4) ¹Steuern sind namentlich dann verkürzt, wenn sie nicht, nicht in voller Höhe oder nicht rechtzeitig festgesetzt werden; dies gilt auch dann, wenn die Steuer vorläufig oder unter Vorbehalt der Nachprüfung festgesetzt wird oder eine Steueranmeldung einer Steuerfestsetzung unter Vorbehalt der Nachprüfung gleichsteht. ²Steuervorteile sind auch Steuervergütungen; nicht gerechtfertigte Steuervorteile sind erlangt, soweit sie zu Unrecht gewährt oder belassen werden. ³Die Voraussetzungen der Sätze 1 und 2 sind auch dann erfüllt, wenn die Steuer, auf die sich die Tat bezieht, aus anderen Gründen hätte ermäßigt oder der Steuervorteil aus anderen Grunden hatte beansprucht werden können.

(5) Die Tat kann auch hinsichtlich solcher Waren begangen werden, deren Einfuhr, Ausfuhr oder Durchfuhr verboten ist.

(6) ¹Die Absätze 1 bis 5 gelten auch dann, wenn sich die Tat auf Einfuhr- oder Ausfuhrabgaben bezieht, die von einem anderen Mitgliedstaat der Europäischen Union verwaltet werden oder die einem Mitgliedstaat der Europäischen Freihandelsassoziation oder einem mit dieser assoziierten Staat zustehen. ²Das Gleiche gilt, wenn sich die Tat auf Umsatzsteuern oder auf die in Artikel 1 Absatz 1 der Richtlinie 2008/118/EG des Rates vom 16. Dezember 2008 über das allgemeine Verbrauchsteuersystem und zur Aufhebung der Richtlinie 92/12/EWG (ABl. L 9 vom 14.1.2009, S. 12) genannten harmonisierten Verbrauchsteuern bezieht, die von einem anderen Mitgliedstaat der Europäischen Union verwaltet werden.

(7) Die Absätze 1 bis 6 gelten unabhängig von dem Recht des Tatortes auch für Taten, die außerhalb des Geltungsbereiches dieses Gesetzes begangen werden.

6. uses a third-country company (as defined in section 138(3)) over which he can directly or indirectly exercise controlling or decisive influence alone or jointly with related parties (as defined in section 1(2) of the External Tax Relations Act), where such use is for the purpose of concealing facts that are relevant for tax purposes and in this way understating his taxes or obtaining unwarranted tax benefits on an ongoing basis.

(4) ¹Taxes shall be deemed to have been understated in particular where they are not assessed at all, in full or in time; this shall also apply even where the tax has been assessed provisionally or assessed subject to review or where a self-assessed tax return is deemed to be equal to a tax assessment subject to review. ²Tax advantages shall also include tax rebates; unwarranted tax advantages shall be deemed derived to the extent that these are wrongly granted or retained. ³The conditions of the first and second sentences above shall also be fulfilled where the tax to which the act relates could have been reduced for other reasons or the tax advantage could have been claimed for other reasons.

(5) The act may also be committed in relation to goods whose importation, exportation or transit is banned.

(6) ¹Subsections (1) to (5) above shall apply even where the act relates to import or export duties which are administered by another Member State of the European Communities or to which a Member State of the European Free Trade Association or a country associated therewith is entitled. ²The same shall apply where the act relates to value-added taxes or harmonised excise duties on goods designated in Article 3 (1) of Council Directive 92/12/EEC of 25 February 1992 (OJ L 76, p. 1) which are administered by another Member State of the European Communities.

(7) Irrespective of the lex loci delicti, the provisions of subsections (1) to (6) above shall also apply to acts committed outside the territory of application of this Code.

§ 371
Selbstanzeige bei Steuerhinterziehung

(1) [1]Wer gegenüber der Finanzbehörde zu allen Steuerstraftaten einer Steuerart in vollem Umfang die unrichtigen Angaben berichtigt, die unvollständigen Angaben ergänzt oder die unterlassenen Angaben nachholt, wird wegen dieser Steuerstraftaten nicht nach § 370 bestraft. [2]Die Angaben müssen zu allen unverjährten Steuerstraftaten einer Steuerart, mindestens aber zu allen Steuerstraftaten einer Steuerart innerhalb der letzten zehn Kalenderjahre erfolgen.

(2) [1]Straffreiheit tritt nicht ein, wenn

1. bei einer der zur Selbstanzeige gebrachten unverjährten Steuerstraftaten vor der Berichtigung, Ergänzung oder Nachholung

    (a) dem an der Tat Beteiligten, seinem Vertreter, dem Begünstigten im Sinne des § 370 Absatz 1 oder dessen Vertreter eine Prüfungsanordnung nach § 196 bekannt gegeben worden ist, beschränkt auf den sachlichen und zeitlichen Umfang der angekündigten Außenprüfung, oder

    (b) dem an der Tat Beteiligten oder seinem Vertreter die Einleitung des Straf- oder Bußgeldverfahrens bekannt gegeben worden ist oder

    (c) ein Amtsträger der Finanzbehörde zur steuerlichen Prüfung erschienen ist, beschränkt auf den sachlichen und zeitlichen Umfang der Außenprüfung, oder

    (d) ein Amtsträger zur Ermittlung einer Steuerstraftat oder einer Steuerordnungswidrigkeit erschienen ist oder

    (e) ein Amtsträger der Finanzbehörde zu einer Umsatzsteuer-Nachschau nach § 27b des Umsatzsteuergesetzes, einer Lohnsteuer-Nachschau nach § 42g des Einkommensteuergesetzes oder einer Nachschau nach anderen steuerrechtlichen Vorschriften erschienen ist und sich ausgewiesen hat oder

2. eine der Steuerstraftaten im Zeitpunkt der Berichtigung, Ergänzung oder Nachholung ganz oder zum Teil bereits entdeckt war und der Täter dies wusste oder bei verständiger Würdigung der Sachlage damit rechnen musste.

Section 371
Voluntary disclosure of tax evasion

(1) [1]Whoever, in relation to all tax crimes for a type of tax, fully corrects the incorrect particulars submitted to the revenue authority, supplements the incomplete particulars submitted to the revenue authority or furnishes the revenue authority with the previously omitted particulars shall not be punished pursuant to section 370 on account of these tax crimes. [2]The information provided must cover all tax crimes for one type of tax that have not become time-barred, and at least all tax crimes for one type of tax within the last 10 calendar years.

(2) [1]Exemption from punishment shall not apply if,

1. prior to the correction, supplementation or subsequent furnishing of particulars in connection with voluntarily disclosed tax crimes that have not become time-barred,

    (a) the person involved in the act, his representative, the beneficiary as referred to in section 370(1), or the beneficiary's representative has been notified of an audit order in accordance with section 196, limited to the material and temporal scope of the ordered external audit, or

    (b) the person involved in the act or his representative has been notified of the initiation of criminal proceedings or administrative fine proceedings, or

    (c) a public official from the revenue authority has already appeared for the purpose of carrying out a tax audit, limited to the material and temporal scope of the external audit, or

    (d) a public official has already appeared for the purpose of investigating a tax crime or tax-related administrative offence, or

    (e) a public official from the revenue authority has already appeared and provided proof of identity for the purpose of conducting a VAT inspection in accordance with section 27b of the VAT Act, a wages tax inspection in accordance with section 42g of the Income Tax Act or an inspection in accordance with other tax law provisions, or

2. one of the tax crimes had already been fully or partially detected at the time of the correction, supplementation or subsequent furnishing of particulars and the perpetrator knew this or should have expected this upon due consideration of the facts of the case,

3. die nach § 370 Absatz 1 verkürzte Steuer oder der für sich oder einen anderen erlangte nicht gerechtfertigte Steuervorteil einen Betrag von 25 000 Euro je Tat übersteigt, oder
4. ein in § 370 Absatz 3 Satz 2 Nummer 2 bis 6 genannter besonders schwerer Fall vorliegt.

²Der Ausschluss der Straffreiheit nach Satz 1 Nummer 1 Buchstabe a und c hindert nicht die Abgabe einer Berichtigung nach Absatz 1 für die nicht unter Satz 1 Nummer 1 Buchstabe a und c fallenden Steuerstraftaten einer Steuerart.

(2a) ¹Soweit die Steuerhinterziehung durch Verletzung der Pflicht zur rechtzeitigen Abgabe einer vollständigen und richtigen Umsatzsteuervoranmeldung oder Lohnsteueranmeldung begangen worden ist, tritt Straffreiheit abweichend von den Absätzen 1 und 2 Satz 1 Nummer 3 bei Selbstanzeigen in dem Umfang ein, in dem der Täter gegenüber der zuständigen Finanzbehörde die unrichtigen Angaben berichtigt, die unvollständigen Angaben ergänzt oder die unterlassenen Angaben nachholt. ²Absatz 2 Satz 1 Nummer 2 gilt nicht, wenn die Entdeckung der Tat darauf beruht, dass eine Umsatzsteuervoranmeldung oder Lohnsteueranmeldung nachgeholt oder berichtigt wurde. ³Die Sätze 1 und 2 gelten nicht für Steueranmeldungen, die sich auf das Kalenderjahr beziehen. ⁴Für die Vollständigkeit der Selbstanzeige hinsichtlich einer auf das Kalenderjahr bezogenen Steueranmeldung ist die Berichtigung, Ergänzung oder Nachholung der Voranmeldungen, die dem Kalenderjahr nachfolgende Zeiträume betreffen, nicht erforderlich.

(3) ¹Sind Steuerverkürzungen bereits eingetreten oder Steuervorteile erlangt, so tritt für den an der Tat Beteiligten Straffreiheit nur ein, wenn er die aus der Tat zu seinen Gunsten hinterzogenen Steuern, die Hinterziehungszinsen nach § 235 und die Zinsen nach § 233a, soweit sie auf die Hinterziehungszinsen nach § 235 Absatz 4 angerechnet werden, innerhalb der ihm bestimmten angemessenen Frist entrichtet. ²In den Fällen des Absatzes 2a Satz 1 gilt Satz 1 mit der Maßgabe, dass die fristgerechte Entrichtung von Zinsen nach § 233a oder § 235 unerheblich ist.

---

3. the tax understated pursuant to section 370(1) or the unwarranted tax advantage derived by someone for himself or for another person exceeds the amount of 25,000 euros per act, or
4. a particularly serious case exists as specified in section 370(3), second sentence, numbers 2 to 6.

²In the event that exemption from punishment is ruled out in accordance with the first sentence, numbers 1a) and 1c) above, this shall not preclude the submission of a correction in accordance with subsection (1) above in connection with tax crimes for one type of tax that do not fall under the scope of the first sentence, numbers 1a) and 1c) above.

(2a) ¹Insofar as tax evasion has been committed by breaching the obligation to submit a complete and accurate provisional VAT return or wages tax return on time, exemption from punishment shall apply, notwithstanding subsection (1) and subsection (2), first sentence, number 3 above, if the perpetrator corrects the incorrect particulars submitted to the competent revenue authority, supplements the incomplete particulars submitted to the competent revenue authority, or furnishes the competent revenue authority with the previously omitted particulars. ²Subsection (2), first sentence, number 2 above shall not apply if the act was detected upon the discovery that a provisional VAT return or wages tax return was corrected or submitted late. ³The first and second sentences above shall not apply to tax returns relating to the calendar year. ⁴In order for a voluntary disclosure relating to a tax return for a particular calendar year to be deemed complete, it shall not be compulsory to correct, supplement or subsequently furnish particulars for provisional returns concerning time periods following that calendar year.

(3) ¹Where tax has already been understated or tax advantages have already been derived, exemption from punishment shall be granted to the person involved in the act only if he pays, within the reasonable period of time allowed to him, the taxes which were evaded to his benefit through the perpetration of the act, the interest payable on the evaded taxes in accordance with section 235, and the interest payable under section 233a insofar as such interest is charged on the interest payable on the evaded taxes in accordance with section 235(4). ²In cases covered by the first sentence of subsection (2a) above, the first sentence above shall apply with the proviso that the timely payment of interest in accordance with section 233a or section 235 is immaterial.

(4) [1]Wird die in § 153 vorgesehene Anzeige rechtzeitig und ordnungsmäßig erstattet, so wird ein Dritter, der die in § 153 bezeichneten Erklärungen abzugeben unterlassen oder unrichtig oder unvollständig abgegeben hat, strafrechtlich nicht verfolgt, es sei denn, dass ihm oder seinem Vertreter vorher die Einleitung eines Straf- oder Bußgeldverfahrens wegen der Tat bekannt gegeben worden ist. [2]Hat der Dritte zum eigenen Vorteil gehandelt, so gilt Absatz 3 entsprechend.

(4) [1]Where the notification provided for in section 153 is punctually and duly filed, a third party who failed to make the statements referred to in section 153 or who made such statements incorrectly or incompletely shall not be prosecuted unless he or his representative was previously notified of the initiation of criminal or administrative fine proceedings resulting from the act. [2]Subsection (3) above shall apply accordingly where the third party has acted for his own benefit.

§ 378
Leichtfertige Steuerverkürzung

Section 378
Reckless understatement of tax

(1) [1]Ordnungswidrig handelt, wer als Steuerpflichtiger oder bei Wahrnehmung der Angelegenheiten eines Steuerpflichtigen eine der in § 370 Abs. 1 bezeichneten Taten leichtfertig begeht. [2]§ 370 Abs. 4 bis 7 gilt entsprechend.

(1) [1]Whoever as a taxpayer or a person looking after the affairs of a taxpayer recklessly commits one of the acts described in section 370(1) shall be deemed to have committed an administrative offence. [2]Section 370(4) to (7) shall apply accordingly.

(2) Die Ordnungswidrigkeit kann mit einer Geldbuße bis zu fünfzigtausend Euro geahndet werden.

(2) The administrative offence may be punished with a monetary fine of up to 50,000 euros.

(3) [1]Eine Geldbuße wird nicht festgesetzt, soweit der Täter gegenüber der Finanzbehörde die unrichtigen Angaben berichtigt, die unvollständigen Angaben ergänzt oder die unterlassenen Angaben nachholt, bevor ihm oder seinem Vertreter die Einleitung eines Straf- oder Bußgeldverfahrens wegen der Tat bekannt gegeben worden ist. [2]Sind Steuerverkürzungen bereits eingetreten oder Steuervorteile erlangt, so wird eine Geldbuße nicht festgesetzt, wenn der Täter die aus der Tat zu seinen Gunsten verkürzten Steuern innerhalb der ihm bestimmten angemessenen Frist entrichtet. [3]§ 371 Absatz 4 gilt entsprechend.

(3) [1] A monetary fine shall not be set insofar as the perpetrator corrects the incorrect particulars submitted to the revenue authority, supplements the incomplete particulars submitted to the revenue authority, or furnishes the revenue authority with the previously omitted particulars before he or his representative has been notified of the initiation of criminal or administrative fine proceedings resulting from the act. [2]Where tax has already been understated or tax advantages have already been derived, a monetary fine shall not be set if the perpetrator pays, within the reasonable period of time allowed to him, the taxes that were understated to his benefit on the basis of this act. [3]Section 371(4) shall apply accordingly.

XXII. Value Added Tax Act (Excerpt)

Umsatzsteuergesetz – UstG (Auszug)

Stand: 21.12.2019

§ 2
Unternehmer, Unternehmen

(1) [1]Unternehmer ist, wer eine gewerbliche oder berufliche Tätigkeit selbständig ausübt. [2]Das Unternehmen umfasst die gesamte gewerbliche oder berufliche Tätigkeit des Unternehmers. [3]Gewerblich oder beruflich ist jede nachhaltige Tätigkeit zur Erzielung von Einnahmen, auch wenn die Absicht, Gewinn zu erzielen, fehlt oder eine Personenvereinigung nur gegenüber ihren Mitgliedern tätig wird.

(2) Die gewerbliche oder berufliche Tätigkeit wird nicht selbständig ausgeübt,

1. soweit natürliche Personen, einzeln oder zusammengeschlossen, einem Unternehmen so eingegliedert sind, dass sie den Weisungen des Unternehmers zu folgen verpflichtet sind,

2. wenn eine juristische Person nach dem Gesamtbild der tatsächlichen Verhältnisse finanziell, wirtschaftlich und organisatorisch in das Unternehmen des Organträgers eingegliedert ist (Organschaft). [2]Die Wirkungen der Organschaft sind auf Innenleistungen zwischen den im Inland gelegenen Unternehmensteilen beschränkt. [3]Diese Unternehmensteile sind als ein Unternehmen zu behandeln. [4]Hat der Organträger seine Geschäftsleitung im Ausland, gilt der wirtschaftlich bedeutendste Unternehmensteil im Inland als der Unternehmer.

(3) [aufgehoben]

§ 14
Ausstellen von Rechnungen

(1) [1]Rechnung ist jedes Dokument, mit dem über eine Lieferung oder sonstige Leistung abgerechnet wird, gleichgültig, wie dieses Dokument im Geschäftsverkehr bezeichnet wird. [2]Die Echtheit der Herkunft der Rechnung, die Unversehrtheit ihres Inhalts und ihre Lesbarkeit müssen gewährleistet werden. [3]Echtheit der Herkunft bedeutet die Sicherheit der Identität des Rechnungsausstellers. [4]Unversehrtheit des Inhalts bedeutet, dass die nach diesem Gesetz erforderlichen Angaben nicht geändert wurden.

Section 2
Entrepreneur, Company

(1) [1]Entrepreneur is anyone who independently pursues a commercial or professional activity. [2]The enterprise comprises the entire commercial or professional activity of the entrepreneur. [3]Commercial or professional activity is any sustainable activity aimed at generating income, even if the intention to make a profit is absent or if an association of persons only acts in relation to its members.

(2) Commercial or professional activity is not exercised independently,

1. insofar as natural persons, individually or in groups, are integrated into a company in such a way that they are obliged to follow the instructions of the entrepreneur,

2. if a legal entity is financially, economically and organisationally integrated into the company of the controlling company in accordance with the overall picture of the actual circumstances (fiscal unity). [2]The effects of the fiscal unity are limited to internal services between the parts of the company located in Germany. [3]These parts of the company must be treated as one company. [4]If the controlling company has its business operations abroad, the economically most important part of the company in Germany is deemed to be the company

(3) [repealed].

Section 14
Issuing of invoices

(1) [1]Invoice is any document with which a delivery or other service is settled, regardless of how this document is referred to in business dealings. [2]The authenticity of the origin of the invoice, the integrity of its content and its legibility must be guaranteed. [3]Authenticity of origin means the certainty of the identity of the issuer of the invoice. [4]The integrity of the content means that the information required by this Act has not been altered. [5]Each trader shall determine how the authenticity of the origin, the

⁵Jeder Unternehmer legt fest, in welcher Weise die Echtheit der Herkunft, die Unversehrtheit des Inhalts und die Lesbarkeit der Rechnung gewährleistet werden. ⁶Dies kann durch jegliche innerbetriebliche Kontrollverfahren erreicht werden, die einen verlässlichen Prüfpfad zwischen Rechnung und Leistung schaffen können. ⁷Rechnungen sind auf Papier oder vorbehaltlich der Zustimmung des Empfängers elektronisch zu übermitteln. ⁸Eine elektronische Rechnung ist eine Rechnung, die in einem elektronischen Format ausgestellt und empfangen wird.

(2) ¹Führt der Unternehmer eine Lieferung oder eine sonstige Leistung nach § 1 Abs. 1 Nr. 1 aus, gilt Folgendes:

1. führt der Unternehmer eine steuerpflichtige Werklieferung (§ 3 Abs. 4 Satz 1) oder sonstige Leistung im Zusammenhang mit einem Grundstück aus, ist er verpflichtet, innerhalb von sechs Monaten nach Ausführung der Leistung eine Rechnung auszustellen;

2. führt der Unternehmer eine andere als die in Nummer 1 genannte Leistung aus, ist er berechtigt, eine Rechnung auszustellen. ²Soweit er einen Umsatz an einen anderen Unternehmer für dessen Unternehmen oder an eine juristische Person, die nicht Unternehmer ist, ausführt, ist er verpflichtet, innerhalb von sechs Monaten nach Ausführung der Leistung eine Rechnung auszustellen. ³Eine Verpflichtung zur Ausstellung einer Rechnung besteht nicht, wenn der Umsatz nach § 4 Nummer 8 bis 29 steuerfrei ist. ⁴§ 14a bleibt unberührt.

²Unbeschadet der Verpflichtungen nach Satz 1 Nr. 1 und 2 Satz 2 kann eine Rechnung von einem in Satz 1 Nr. 2 bezeichneten Leistungsempfänger für eine Lieferung oder sonstige Leistung des Unternehmers ausgestellt werden, sofern dies vorher vereinbart wurde (Gutschrift). ³Die Gutschrift verliert die Wirkung einer Rechnung, sobald der Empfänger der Gutschrift dem ihm übermittelten Dokument widerspricht. ⁴Eine Rechnung kann im Namen und für Rechnung des Unternehmers oder eines in Satz 1 Nr. 2 bezeichneten Leistungsempfängers von einem Dritten ausgestellt werden.

(3) Unbeschadet anderer nach Absatz 1 zulässiger Verfahren gelten bei einer elektronischen Rechnung die Echtheit der Herkunft und die Unversehrtheit des Inhalts als gewährleistet durch

1. eine qualifizierte elektronische Signatur oder

integrity of the content and the legibility of the invoice are guaranteed. ⁶This can be achieved by any internal control procedures that can provide a reliable audit trail between the invoice and the service. ⁷Invoices shall be sent on paper or, subject to the agreement of the recipient, electronically. 8An electronic invoice is an invoice issued and received in an electronic format.

(2) ¹If the entrepreneur carries out a delivery or other service in accordance with Article 1 paragraph 1 No. 1, the following shall apply:

1. If the Company makes a taxable supply of work (Section 3(4), first sentence) or other service in connection with real property, it is obliged to issue an invoice within six months of making the service;

2. If the Contractor performs a service other than the service referred to in No. 1, he shall be entitled to issue an invoice. ²If he carries out a transaction to another entrepreneur for his company or to a legal entity which is not an entrepreneur, he is obliged to issue an invoice within six months of the performance of the service. 3 There is no obligation to issue an invoice if the turnover is tax-exempt under Article 4 Nos 8 to 29. 4 § 14a remains unaffected.

²Irrespective of the obligations under sentence 1 no. 1 and 2 sentence 2, an invoice may be issued by a service recipient designated in sentence 1 no. 2 for a delivery or other service provided by the company if this has been agreed in advance (credit note). ³The credit note loses the effect of an invoice as soon as the recipient of the credit note objects to the document sent to him. ⁴An invoice may be issued by a third party in the name of and on behalf of the Company or of a recipient of services referred to in sentence 1 no. 2.

(3) Without prejudice to other procedures permitted under paragraph 1, the authenticity of the origin and the integrity of the content of an electronic invoice shall be deemed guaranteed by

1. a qualified electronic signature, or

2. elektronischen Datenaustausch (EDI) nach Artikel 2 der Empfehlung 94/820/EG der Kommission vom 19. Oktober 1994 über die rechtlichen Aspekte des elektronischen Datenaustausches (ABl. L 338 vom 28.12.1994, S. 98), wenn in der Vereinbarung über diesen Datenaustausch der Einsatz von Verfahren vorgesehen ist, die die Echtheit der Herkunft und die Unversehrtheit der Daten gewährleisten.

(4) ¹Eine Rechnung muss folgende Angaben enthalten:

1. den vollständigen Namen und die vollständige Anschrift des leistenden Unternehmers und des Leistungsempfängers,
2. die dem leistenden Unternehmer vom Finanzamt erteilte Steuernummer oder die ihm vom Bundeszentralamt für Steuern erteilte Umsatzsteuer-Identifikationsnummer,
3. das Ausstellungsdatum,
4. eine fortlaufende Nummer mit einer oder mehreren Zahlenreihen, die zur Identifizierung der Rechnung vom Rechnungsaussteller einmalig vergeben wird (Rechnungsnummer),
5. die Menge und die Art (handelsübliche Bezeichnung) der gelieferten Gegenstände oder den Umfang und die Art der sonstigen Leistung,
6. den Zeitpunkt der Lieferung oder sonstigen Leistung; in den Fällen des Absatzes 5 Satz 1 den Zeitpunkt der Vereinnahmung des Entgelts oder eines Teils des Entgelts, sofern der Zeitpunkt der Vereinnahmung feststeht und nicht mit dem Ausstellungsdatum der Rechnung übereinstimmt,
7. das nach Steuersätzen und einzelnen Steuerbefreiungen aufgeschlüsselte Entgelt für die Lieferung oder sonstige Leistung (§ 10) sowie jede im Voraus vereinbarte Minderung des Entgelts, sofern sie nicht bereits im Entgelt berücksichtigt ist,
8. den anzuwendenden Steuersatz sowie den auf das Entgelt entfallenden Steuerbetrag oder im Fall einer Steuerbefreiung einen Hinweis darauf, dass für die Lieferung oder sonstige Leistung eine Steuerbefreiung gilt,
9. in den Fällen des § 14b Abs. 1 Satz 5 einen Hinweis auf die Aufbewahrungspflicht des Leistungsempfängers, und
10. in den Fällen der Ausstellung der Rechnung durch den Leistungsempfänger oder durch einen von ihm beauftragten Dritten gemäß Absatz 2 Satz 2 die Angabe „Gutschrift".

2. electronic data interchange (EDI), as defined in Article 2 of Commission Recommendation 94/820/EC of 19 October 1994 on the legal aspects of electronic data interchange (OJ L 338, 28.12.1994, p. 98), where the agreement relating to that interchange provides for the use of procedures guaranteeing the authenticity of the origin and integrity of the data.

(4) ¹An invoice must contain the following information:

1. the full name and address of the supplier and the recipient of the service
2. the tax number issued to the entrepreneur providing services by the tax office or the VAT registration number issued to him by the Federal Central Tax Office,
3. the date of issue,
4. a consecutive number with one or more series of numbers, which is assigned once by the issuer of the invoice to identify the invoice (invoice number),
5. the quantity and type (customary trade description) of the delivered goods or the scope and type of other services,
6. the time of delivery or other performance; in the cases of paragraph 5, first sentence, the time of receipt of the remuneration or part of the remuneration, if the time of receipt is fixed and does not coincide with the date of issue of the invoice,
7. the remuneration for the delivery or other service, broken down according to tax rates and individual tax exemptions (§ 10) as well as any reduction of the remuneration agreed in advance, unless it is already taken into account in the remuneration,
8. the applicable tax rate as well as the amount of tax payable on the remuneration or, in the case of tax exemption, an indication that the supply or other service is exempt from tax,
9. in the cases set out in § 14b (1) sentence 5, a reference to the obligation of the service recipient to keep records, and
10. in cases where the invoice is issued by the service recipient or by a third party commissioned by him in accordance with paragraph 2, sentence 2, the indication „credit".

²In den Fällen des § 10 Abs. 5 sind die Nummern 7 und 8 mit der Maßgabe anzuwenden, dass die Bemessungsgrundlage für die Leistung (§ 10 Abs. 4) und der darauf entfallende Steuerbetrag anzugeben sind. ³Unternehmer, die § 24 Abs. 1 bis 3 anwenden, sind jedoch auch in diesen Fällen nur zur Angabe des Entgelts und des darauf entfallenden Steuerbetrags berechtigt.

(5) ¹Vereinnahmt der Unternehmer das Entgelt oder einen Teil des Entgelts für eine noch nicht ausgeführte Lieferung oder sonstige Leistung, gelten die Absätze 1 bis 4 sinngemäß. ²Wird eine Endrechnung erteilt, sind in ihr die vor Ausführung der Lieferung oder sonstigen Leistung vereinnahmten Teilentgelte und die auf sie entfallenden Steuerbeträge abzusetzen, wenn über die Teilentgelte Rechnungen im Sinne der Absätze 1 bis 4 ausgestellt worden sind.

(6) Das Bundesministerium der Finanzen kann mit Zustimmung des Bundesrates zur Vereinfachung des Besteuerungsverfahrens durch Rechtsverordnung bestimmen, in welchen Fällen und unter welchen Voraussetzungen

1. Dokumente als Rechnungen anerkannt werden können,
2. die nach Absatz 4 erforderlichen Angaben in mehreren Dokumenten enthalten sein können,
3. Rechnungen bestimmte Angaben nach Absatz 4 nicht enthalten müssen,
4. eine Verpflichtung des Unternehmers zur Ausstellung von Rechnungen mit gesondertem Steuerausweis (Absatz 4) entfällt oder
5. Rechnungen berichtigt werden können.

(7) ¹Führt der Unternehmer einen Umsatz im Inland aus, für den der Leistungsempfänger die Steuer nach § 13b schuldet, und hat der Unternehmer im Inland weder seinen Sitz noch seine Geschäftsleitung, eine Betriebsstätte, von der aus der Umsatz ausgeführt wird oder die an der Erbringung dieses Umsatzes beteiligt ist, oder in Ermangelung eines Sitzes seinen Wohnsitz oder gewöhnlichen Aufenthalt im Inland, so gelten abweichend von den Absätzen 1 bis 6 für die Rechnungserteilung die Vorschriften des Mitgliedstaats, in dem der Unternehmer seinen Sitz, seine Geschäftsleitung, eine Betriebsstätte, von der aus der Umsatz ausgeführt wird, oder in Ermangelung eines Sitzes seinen Wohnsitz oder gewöhnlichen Aufenthalt hat. ²Satz 1 gilt nicht, wenn eine Gutschrift gemäß Absatz 2 Satz 2 vereinbart worden ist. ³Nimmt der Unternehmer in einem anderen Mitgliedstaat an einem der besonderen Besteuerungsverfahren entsprechend Titel XII Kapitel 6 der Richtlinie 2006/112/EG des Rates vom 28. November 2006 über das gemeinsame Mehrwertsteuersystem (ABl. L 347

²In the cases covered by Article 10 paragraph 5, numbers 7 and 8 shall be applied on condition that the basis of assessment for the benefit (Article 10 paragraph 4) and the amount of tax payable thereon are specified. ³Entrepreneurs who apply § 24 paragraphs 1 to 3 are, however, also in these cases only entitled to state the remuneration and the amount of tax payable on it.

(5) ¹If the entrepreneur collects the remuneration or part of the remuneration for a delivery or other service not yet performed, paragraphs 1 to 4 shall apply mutatis mutandis. ²If a final invoice is issued, the partial payments received before the delivery or other service is carried out and the tax income attributable to them shall be deducted if invoices within the meaning of paragraphs 1 to 4 have been issued for the partial payments.

(6) The Federal Ministry of Finance may, with the consent of the Bundesrat, decide by statutory order to simplify the taxation procedure, in which cases and under which conditions

1. documents can be recognised as invoices
2. the information required under paragraph 4 may be contained in several documents,
3. invoices do not have to contain certain information according to paragraph 4,
4. an obligation on the part of the company to issue invoices with a separate tax statement (paragraph 4) does not apply or
5. invoices can be corrected.

(7) ¹If the trader carries out a turnover in the country for which the recipient of the service is liable for tax under Article 13b and the trader has neither his registered office nor his management, a permanent establishment from which the turnover is exported or which is involved in the provision of this turnover, in the country, or, in the absence of a registered office, his domicile or habitual residence within the territory of the country, the rules applicable to invoicing shall, by way of derogation from paragraphs 1 to 6, be those of the Member State in which the trader has his registered office, central administration, a permanent establishment from which the transaction is carried out or, in the absence of a registered office, his domicile or habitual residence. ²Sentence 1 does not apply if a credit note has been agreed in accordance with paragraph 2 sentence 2. 3 If the trader participates in another Member State in one of the special tax procedures under Chapter 6 of Title XII of Council Directive 2006/112/EC of 28 November 2006 on the common system of value added

vom 11.12.2006, S. 1) in der jeweils gültigen Fassung teil, so gelten für die in den besonderen Besteuerungsverfahren zu erklärenden Umsätze abweichend von den Absätzen 1 bis 6 für die Rechnungserteilung die Vorschriften des Mitgliedstaates, in dem der Unternehmer seine Teilnahme anzeigt.

tax (OJ L 347, 11.12.2006, p. 1), as amended, the transactions to be declared in the special tax procedures shall be subject, by way of derogation from paragraphs 1 to 6, to the rules of the Member State in which the trader declares his participation.

§ 14c
Unrichtiger oder unberechtigter Steuerausweis

(1) ¹Hat der Unternehmer in einer Rechnung für eine Lieferung oder sonstige Leistung einen höheren Steuerbetrag, als er nach diesem Gesetz für den Umsatz schuldet, gesondert ausgewiesen (unrichtiger Steuerausweis), schuldet er auch den Mehrbetrag. ²Berichtigt er den Steuerbetrag gegenüber dem Leistungsempfänger, ist § 17 Abs. 1 entsprechend anzuwenden. ³In den Fällen des § 1 Abs. 1a und in den Fällen der Rückgängigmachung des Verzichts auf die Steuerbefreiung nach § 9 gilt Absatz 2 Satz 3 bis 5 entsprechend.

(2) ¹Wer in einer Rechnung einen Steuerbetrag gesondert ausweist, obwohl er zum gesonderten Ausweis der Steuer nicht berechtigt ist (unberechtigter Steuerausweis), schuldet den ausgewiesenen Betrag. ²Das Gleiche gilt, wenn jemand wie ein leistender Unternehmer abrechnet und einen Steuerbetrag gesondert ausweist, obwohl er nicht Unternehmer ist oder eine Lieferung oder sonstige Leistung nicht ausführt. ³Der nach den Sätzen 1 und 2 geschuldete Steuerbetrag kann berichtigt werden, soweit die Gefährdung des Steueraufkommens beseitigt worden ist. ⁴Die Gefährdung des Steueraufkommens ist beseitigt, wenn ein Vorsteuerabzug beim Empfänger der Rechnung nicht durchgeführt oder die geltend gemachte Vorsteuer an die Finanzbehörde zurückgezahlt worden ist. ⁵Die Berichtigung des geschuldeten Steuerbetrags ist beim Finanzamt gesondert schriftlich zu beantragen und nach dessen Zustimmung in entsprechender Anwendung des § 17 Abs. 1 für den Besteuerungszeitraum vorzunehmen, in dem die Voraussetzungen des Satzes 4 eingetreten sind.

Section 14c
Incorrect or unjustified tax statement

(1) ¹If the entrepreneur has separately shown a higher amount of tax in an invoice for a delivery or other service than that which he owes for turnover under this Act (incorrect tax statement), he shall also owe the additional amount. ²If he corrects the tax amount vis-à-vis the recipient of the service, Section 17 (1) shall apply accordingly. ³In the cases set out in § 1 paragraph 1a and in cases where the waiver of tax exemption under § 9 is reversed, paragraph 2 sentences 3 to 5 shall apply mutatis mutandis.

(2) ¹Anyone who shows an amount of tax separately in an invoice although he is not entitled to show the tax separately (unauthorised tax statement) shall owe the amount shown. ²The same applies if a person settles accounts like a performing trader and shows a tax amount separately, although he is not a contractor or does not carry out a delivery or other service. ³The amount of tax owed under sentences 1 and 2 may be corrected insofar as the threat to tax revenue has been removed. ⁴The threat to tax revenue is removed if the recipient of the invoice has not made a deduction or the input tax claimed has been refunded to the tax authorities. ⁵The correction of the tax amount owed must be applied for separately in writing to the tax office and, after its approval, must be carried out by analogous application of § 17 paragraph 1 for the taxable period in which the conditions of sentence 4 occurred.

§ 15
Vorsteuerabzug

(1) ¹Der Unternehmer kann die folgenden Vorsteuerbeträge abziehen:

1. die gesetzlich geschuldete Steuer für Lieferungen und sonstige Leistungen, die von einem anderen Unternehmer fur sein Unternehmen ausgeführt worden sind. ²Die Ausübung des Vorsteuerabzugs setzt voraus, dass der Unternehmer eine nach den §§ 14, 14a ausgestellte Rechnung besitzt. ³Soweit der gesondert ausgewiesene Steuerbetrag auf eine Zahlung vor Ausführung dieser Umsätze entfällt, ist er bereits abziehbar, wenn die Rechnung vorliegt und die Zahlung geleistet worden ist;
2. die entstandene Einfuhrumsatzsteuer für Gegenstände, die für sein Unternehmen nach § 1 Absatz 1 Nummer 4 eingeführt worden sind;
3. die Steuer für den innergemeinschaftlichen Erwerb von Gegenständen für sein Unternehmen, wenn der innergemeinschaftliche Erwerb nach § 3d Satz 1 im Inland bewirkt wird;
4. die Steuer für Leistungen im Sinne des § 13b Absatz 1 und 2, die für sein Unternehmen ausgeführt worden sind. ²Soweit die Steuer auf eine Zahlung vor Ausführung dieser Leistungen entfällt, ist sie abziehbar, wenn die Zahlung geleistet worden ist;
5. die nach § 13a Abs. 1 Nr. 6 geschuldete Steuer für Umsätze, die für sein Unternehmen ausgeführt worden sind.

²Nicht als für das Unternehmen ausgeführt gilt die Lieferung, die Einfuhr oder der innergemeinschaftliche Erwerb eines Gegenstands, den der Unternehmer zu weniger als 10 Prozent für sein Unternehmen nutzt.

(1a) ¹Nicht abziehbar sind Vorsteuerbeträge, die auf Aufwendungen, für die das Abzugsverbot des § 4 Abs. 5 Satz 1 Nr. 1 bis 4, 7 oder des § 12 Nr. 1 des Einkommensteuergesetzes gilt, entfallen. ²Dies gilt nicht für Bewirtungsaufwendungen, soweit § 4 Abs. 5 Satz 1 Nr. 2 des Einkommensteuergesetzes einen Abzug angemessener und nachgewiesener Aufwendungen ausschließt.

Section 15
Input tax deduction

(1) ¹The entrepreneur may deduct the following input tax amounts

1. the tax due under the law for supplies and other services carried out by another entrepreneur for his business. ²The exercise of the right to deduct input tax requires that the entrepreneur is in possession of an invoice issued in accordance with §§ 14, 14a. ³In so far as the tax amount shown separately is attributable to a payment made before these transactions were carried out, it is already deductible when the invoice is available and payment has been made;
2. the import turnover tax incurred for goods which have been imported for his company in accordance with § 1 Para. 1 No. 4;
3. the tax on the intra-Community acquisition of goods for his undertaking if the intra-Community acquisition is effected in Germany in accordance with the first sentence of § 3d;
4. the tax on services within the meaning of section 13b(1) and (2) which have been performed for his undertaking. ²Insofar as the tax is payable on a payment made before these services are performed, it is deductible when the payment has been made;
5. the tax due under section 13a(1)(6) for transactions carried out for his business.

²The supply, import or intra-Community acquisition of an object which the entrepreneur uses for his business for less than 10 per cent of its value is not deemed to have been carried out for the business.

(1a) ¹Intradable input tax income shall not be deductible if it relates to expenses to which the prohibition of deduction under section 4(5) sentence 1 nos. 1 to 4, 7 or section 12 no. 1 of the Income Tax Act applies. ²This does not apply to entertainment expenses insofar as § 4, paragraph 5, sentence 1, no. 2 of the German Income Tax Act excludes the deduction of reasonable and weighted expenses.

(1b) [1]Verwendet der Unternehmer ein Grundstück sowohl für Zwecke seines Unternehmens als auch für Zwecke, die außerhalb des Unternehmens liegen, oder für den privaten Bedarf seines Personals, ist die Steuer für die Lieferungen, die Einfuhr und den innergemeinschaftlichen Erwerb sowie für die sonstigen Leistungen im Zusammenhang mit diesem Grundstück vom Vorsteuerabzug ausgeschlossen, soweit sie nicht auf die Verwendung des Grundstücks für Zwecke des Unternehmens entfällt. [2]Bei Berechtigungen, für die die Vorschriften des bürgerlichen Rechts über Grundstücke gelten, und bei Gebäuden auf fremdem Grund und Boden ist Satz 1 entsprechend anzuwenden.

(2) [1]Vom Vorsteuerabzug ausgeschlossen ist die Steuer für die Lieferungen, die Einfuhr und den innergemeinschaftlichen Erwerb von Gegenständen sowie für die sonstigen Leistungen, die der Unternehmer zur Ausführung folgender Umsätze verwendet:

1. steuerfreie Umsätze;
2. Umsätze im Ausland, die steuerfrei wären, wenn sie im Inland ausgeführt würden.

3. [aufgehoben]

[2]Gegenstände oder sonstige Leistungen, die der Unternehmer zur Ausführung einer Einfuhr oder eines innergemeinschaftlichen Erwerbs verwendet, sind den Umsätzen zuzurechnen, für die der eingeführte oder innergemeinschaftlich erworbene Gegenstand verwendet wird.

(3) Der Ausschluss vom Vorsteuerabzug nach Absatz 2 tritt nicht ein, wenn die Umsätze

1. in den Fällen des Absatzes 2 Satz 1 Nr. 1

   (a) nach § 4 Nr. 1 bis 7, § 25 Abs. 2 oder nach den in § 26 Abs. 5 bezeichneten Vorschriften steuerfrei sind oder
   (b) nach § 4 Nummer 8 Buchstabe a bis g, Nummer 10 oder Nummer 11 steuerfrei sind und sich unmittelbar auf Gegenstände beziehen, die in das Drittlandsgebiet ausgeführt werden;

2. in den Fällen des Absatzes 2 Satz 1 Nr. 2

   (a) nach § 4 Nr. 1 bis 7, § 25 Abs. 2 oder nach den in § 26 Abs. 5 bezeichneten Vorschriften steuerfrei wären oder

(1b) [1]If the entrepreneur uses a property both for the purposes of his enterprise and for purposes outside the enterprise or for the private needs of his staff, the tax on supplies, imports and intra-Community acquisitions as well as on other services in connection with this property shall not be deductible unless it is attributable to the use of the property for the purposes of the enterprise. [2]In the case of rights to which the provisions of civil law on real property apply and in the case of buildings on third-party land, sentence 1 shall apply accordingly.

(2) [1]The tax shall not be deductible in respect of the supply, importation or intra-Community acquisition of goods or other services used by the customer to carry out the following transactions:

1. exempt transactions;
2. transactions carried out abroad which would be exempt if they were carried out within the country.

3. [repealed].

[2]Items or other services which the entrepreneur uses to carry out an import or an intra-Community acquisition must be included in the turnover for which the imported or intra-Community acquired item is used.

(3) The exclusion of deduction of input tax pursuant to paragraph 2 shall not apply where the transactions

1. in the cases set out in paragraph 2, first sentence, no. 1

   (a) are tax-exempt under section 4 nos. 1 to 7, section 25(2) or under the provisions designated in section 26(5), or
   (b) are exempt from tax under Article 4(8) (a) to (g), (10) or (11) and relate directly to goods exported to the third country;

2. in the cases referred to in paragraph 2, first sentence, No 2

   (a) would be tax-exempt under section 4 nos. 1 to 7, section 25(2) or under the provisions referred to in section 26(5), or

(b) nach § 4 Nummer 8 Buchstabe a bis g, Nummer 10 oder Nummer 11 steuerfrei wären und der Leistungsempfänger im Drittlandsgebiet ansässig ist oder diese Umsätze sich unmittelbar auf Gegenstände beziehen, die in das Drittlandsgebiet ausgeführt werden.

(4) ¹Verwendet der Unternehmer einen für sein Unternehmen gelieferten, eingeführten oder innergemeinschaftlich erworbenen Gegenstand oder eine von ihm in Anspruch genommene sonstige Leistung nur zum Teil zur Ausführung von Umsätzen, die den Vorsteuerabzug ausschließen, so ist der Teil der jeweiligen Vorsteuerbeträge nicht abziehbar, der den zum Ausschluss vom Vorsteuerabzug führenden Umsätzen wirtschaftlich zuzurechnen ist. ²Der Unternehmer kann die nicht abziehbaren Teilbeträge im Wege einer sachgerechten Schätzung ermitteln. ³Eine Ermittlung des nicht abziehbaren Teils der Vorsteuerbeträge nach dem Verhältnis der Umsätze, die den Vorsteuerabzug ausschließen, zu den Umsätzen, die zum Vorsteuerabzug berechtigen, ist nur zulässig, wenn keine andere wirtschaftliche Zurechnung möglich ist. ⁴In den Fällen des Absatzes 1b gelten die Sätze 1 bis 3 entsprechend.

(4a) Für Fahrzeuglieferer (§ 2a) gelten folgende Einschränkungen des Vorsteuerabzugs:

1. Abziehbar ist nur die auf die Lieferung, die Einfuhr oder den innergemeinschaftlichen Erwerb des neuen Fahrzeugs entfallende Steuer.

2. Die Steuer kann nur bis zu dem Betrag abgezogen werden, der für die Lieferung des neuen Fahrzeugs geschuldet würde, wenn die Lieferung nicht steuerfrei wäre.

3. Die Steuer kann erst in dem Zeitpunkt abgezogen werden, in dem der Fahrzeuglieferer die innergemeinschaftliche Lieferung des neuen Fahrzeugs ausführt.

(4b) Für Unternehmer, die nicht im Gemeinschaftsgebiet ansässig sind und die nur Steuer nach § 13b Absatz 5, nur Steuer nach § 13b Absatz 5 und § 13a Absatz 1 Nummer 1 in Verbindung mit § 14c Absatz 1 oder nur Steuer nach § 13b Absatz 5 und § 13a Absatz 1 Nummer 4 schulden, gelten die Einschränkungen des § 18 Absatz 9 Satz 5 und 6 entsprechend.

(5) Das Bundesministerium der Finanzen kann mit Zustimmung des Bundesrates durch Rechtsverordnung nähere Bestimmungen darüber treffen,

(b) would be exempt from tax under § 4(8) (a) to (g), (10) or (11) and the recipient is established in the third territory or these transactions relate directly to goods exported to the third territory.

(4) ¹If a trader uses only part of an item supplied, imported or acquired within the Community for his business or of another service used by him to carry out transactions which exclude the right to deduct input tax, that part of the respective input tax amounts which is economically attributable to the transactions which exclude the right to deduct input tax shall not be deductible. ²The trader may determine the non-deductible partial amounts by means of an appropriate estimate. ³The non-deductible part of the input tax amounts may only be determined in the ratio of the transactions which exclude input tax deduction to the transactions which give rise to the right to deduct input tax if no other economic allocation is possible. ⁴In the cases referred to in paragraph 1b, sentences 1 to 3 shall apply mutatis mutandis.

(4a) The following restrictions on the right to deduct input tax apply to vehicle suppliers (section 2a):

1. Only the tax due on the supply, import or intra-Community acquisition of the new vehicle is deductible.

2. the tax can only be deducted up to the amount which would be due for the supply of the new vehicle if the supply were not exempt.

3. The tax may be deducted only at the time when the supplier of the vehicle makes the intra-Community supply of the new vehicle.

(4b) For traders who are not established in the Community territory and who owe only tax under Section 13b(5), only tax under Section 13b(5) and Section 13a(1)(1) in conjunction with Section 14c(1) or only tax under Section 13b(5) and Section 13a(1)(4), the restrictions of Section 18(9), sentences 5 and 6 shall apply accordingly.

(5) The Federal Ministry of Finance may, with the consent of the Bundesrat, adopt more detailed provisions by statutory order,

1. in welchen Fällen und unter welchen Voraussetzungen zur Vereinfachung des Besteuerungsverfahrens für den Vorsteuerabzug auf eine Rechnung im Sinne des § 14 oder auf einzelne Angaben in der Rechnung verzichtet werden kann,
2. unter welchen Voraussetzungen, für welchen Besteuerungszeitraum und in welchem Umfang zur Vereinfachung oder zur Vermeidung von Härten in den Fällen, in denen ein anderer als der Leistungsempfänger ein Entgelt gewährt (§ 10 Abs. 1 Satz 3), der andere den Vorsteuerabzug in Anspruch nehmen kann, und
3. wann in Fällen von geringer steuerlicher Bedeutung zur Vereinfachung oder zur Vermeidung von Härten bei der Aufteilung der Vorsteuerbeträge (Absatz 4) Umsätze, die den Vorsteuerabzug ausschließen, unberücksichtigt bleiben können oder von der Zurechnung von Vorsteuerbeträgen zu diesen Umsätzen abgesehen werden kann.

1. in which cases and under which conditions, in order to simplify the taxation procedure for the deduction of input tax, an invoice within the meaning of § 14 or individual details on the invoice may be waived,
2. under what conditions, for what taxable period and to what extent, in order to simplify or avoid hardship in cases where a person other than the recipient of the service grants a remuneration (§ 10 (1) sentence 3), the other person can claim the input tax deduction, and
3. when, in cases of minor tax significance, in order to simplify or avoid hardship in the allocation of input tax amounts (paragraph 4), transactions which exclude the right to deduct input tax may be disregarded or input tax amounts may not be allocated to these transactions.

I. Industrial Code (Excerpt)

Gewerbeordnung – GewO (Auszug)

Stand: 22.11.2019

Titel VIII
Arbeitnehmer
I. Allgemeine arbeitsrechtliche Grundsätze

Title VIII
Employees
I. General principles of labour law

§ 106
Weisungsrecht des Arbeitgebers

[1]Der Arbeitgeber kann Inhalt, Ort und Zeit der Arbeitsleistung nach billigem Ermessen näher bestimmen, soweit diese Arbeitsbedingungen nicht durch den Arbeitsvertrag, Bestimmungen einer Betriebsvereinbarung, eines anwendbaren Tarifvertrages oder gesetzliche Vorschriften festgelegt sind. [2]Dies gilt auch hinsichtlich der Ordnung und des Verhaltens der Arbeitnehmer im Betrieb. [3]Bei der Ausübung des Ermessens hat der Arbeitgeber auch auf Behinderungen des Arbeitnehmers Rücksicht zu nehmen.

Section 106
Employer's Right to Issue Instructions

[1]The employer may, at its reasonable discretion, specify the content, place and time of the work performance in more detail, provided that these working conditions are not specified by the employment contract, provisions of a works agreement, an applicable collective bargaining agreement or statutory provisions. [2]This also applies to the order and conduct of employees in the company. When exercising its discretion, the employer must also take account of any disabilities of the employee.

Titel XI
Gewerbezentralregister

Title XI
Register of business centres

§ 149
Einrichtung eines Gewerbezentralregisters

(1) Das Bundesamt für Justiz (Registerbehörde) führt ein Gewerbezentralregister.

(2) [1]In das Register sind einzutragen

1. die vollziehbaren und die nicht mehr anfechtbaren Entscheidungen einer Verwaltungsbehörde, durch die wegen Unzuverlässigkeit oder Ungeeignetheit
   (a) ein Antrag auf Zulassung (Erlaubnis, Genehmigung, Konzession, Bewilligung) zu einem Gewerbe oder einer sonstigen wirtschaftlichen Unternehmung abgelehnt oder eine erteilte Zulassung zurückgenommen oder widerrufen,

Section 149
Establishment of a Central Business Register

(1) The Federal Office of Justice (registration authority) shall maintain a central register of businesses.

(2) [1]The following shall be entered in the register

1. the enforceable and no longer contestable decisions of an administrative authority which, on grounds of unreliability or unsuitability
   (a) an application for admission (licence, permit, concession, authorisation) to a trade or other economic activity is rejected or a granted authorisation is withdrawn or revoked

(b) die Ausübung eines Gewerbes, die Tätigkeit als Vertretungsberechtigter einer Gewerbetreibenden oder als mit der Leitung eines Gewerbebetriebes beauftragte Person oder der Betrieb oder die Leitung einer sonstigen wirtschaftlichen Unternehmung untersagt,

(c) ein Antrag auf Erteilung eines Befähigungsscheines nach § 20 des Sprengstoffgesetzes abgelehnt oder ein erteilter Befähigungsschein entzogen,

(d) im Rahmen eines Gewerbebetriebes oder einer sonstigen wirtschaftlichen Unternehmung die Befugnis zur Einstellung oder Ausbildung von Auszubildenden entzogen oder die Beschäftigung, Beaufsichtigung, Anweisung oder Ausbildung von Kindern und Jugendlichen verboten oder

(e) die Führung von Kraftverkehrsgeschäften untersagt wird

2. Verzichte auf eine Zulassung zu einem Gewerbe oder einer sonstigen wirtschaftlichen Unternehmung während eines Rücknahme- oder Widerrufsverfahrens wegen Unzuverlässigkeit oder Ungeeignetheit,

3. rechtskräftige Bußgeldentscheidungen, insbesondere auch solche wegen einer Steuerordnungswidrigkeit, die aufgrund von Taten ergangen sind, die

(a) bei oder in Zusammenhang mit der Ausübung eines Gewerbes oder dem Betrieb einer sonstigen wirtschaftlichen Unternehmung oder

(b) bei der Tätigkeit in einem Gewerbe oder einer sonstigen wirtschaftlichen Unternehmung von einem Vertreter oder Beauftragten im Sinne des § 9 des Gesetzes über Ordnungswidrigkeiten oder von einer Person, die in einer Rechtsvorschrift ausdrücklich als Verantwortlicher bezeichnet ist,

begangen worden sind, wenn die Geldbuße mehr als 200 Euro beträgt,

4. rechtskräftige strafgerichtliche Verurteilungen wegen einer Straftat nach den §§ 10 und 11 des Schwarzarbeitsbekämpfungsgesetzes, nach den §§ 15 und 15a des Arbeitnehmerüberlassungsgesetzes oder nach § 266a Abs. 1, § 266a Absatz 2 und § 266a Absatz 4 des Strafgesetzbuches, die bei oder im Zusammenhang mit der Ausübung eines Gewerbes oder dem Betrieb einer sonstigen wirtschaftlichen Unternehmung begangen worden ist, wenn auf Freiheitsstrafe von mehr als drei Monaten oder Geldstrafe von mehr als 90 Tagessätzen erkannt worden ist.

(b) prohibits the exercise of a trade or business, the activity of an authorised representative of a trader or of a person charged with the management of a trade or business, or the operation or management of any other economic activity

(c) an application for a certificate of competence under Section 20 of the Explosives Act is rejected or a certificate of competence issued is withdrawn,

(d) within the framework of a business enterprise or other economic undertaking, the authority to employ or train apprentices or the employment, supervision, instruction or training of children and young people is withdrawn or the employment, supervision, instruction or training of children and young people is prohibited or

(e) prohibiting the conduct of road transport operations

2. waiver of an admission to a trade or other economic activity during a withdrawal or revocation procedure due to unreliability or unsuitability

3. legally binding decisions imposing fines, in particular also those for an infringement of tax regulations, which have been issued on the basis of acts which

(a) in or in connection with the exercise of a trade or business or the operation of any other economic activity; or

b) in the case of activity in a trade or other commercial enterprise, by a representative or agent within the meaning of section 9 of the Law on Administrative Offences or by a person who is expressly designated as responsible in a legal provision,

where the fine is more than EUR 200

4. final criminal convictions for a criminal offence under Sections 10 and 11 of the Act to Combat Illegal Employment, under Sections 15 and 15a of the Law on Temporary Employment or under Section 266a (1), Section 266a (2) and Section 266a (4) of the German Criminal Code, committed in the course of or in connection with the exercise of a trade or business or the operation of another business enterprise, if a prison sentence of more than three months or a fine of more than 90 daily rates has been imposed.

[2]Von der Eintragung sind Entscheidungen und Verzichte ausgenommen, die nach § 28 des Straßenverkehrsgesetzes in das Fahreignungsregister einzutragen sind.

[2]Decisions and waivers which are to be entered in the register of fitness to drive in accordance with section 28 of the Road Traffic Act are excluded from registration.

II. Regulation (EC) No 883/2004 of the European Parliament and of the Council of 29 April 2004 on the coordination of social security systems

Verordnung (EG) Nr. 883/2004 des Europäischen Parlaments und des Rates vom 29. April 2004 zur Koordinierung der Systeme zur sozialen Sicherheit

Stand: 29.04.2004

The full text of the Regulation is available in several languages at:
https://eur-lex.europa.eu/legal-content/DE/LSU/?uri=CELEX:32004R0883

III. Regulation (EC) No 593/2008 of the European Parliament and of the Council of 17 June 2008 on the law applicable to contractual obligations (Rome I – Excerpt)

Verordnung (EG) Nr. 593/2008 des Europäischen Parlaments und des Rates vom 17. Juni 2008 über das auf vertragliche Schuldverhältnisse anzuwendende Recht (Rom I – Auszug)

Stand: 17.06.2008

The full text of the Regulation is available in several languages at:
https://eur-lex.europa.eu/legal-content/DE/TXT/?uri=CELEX:32008R0593

IV. Regulation (EC) No 987/2009 of the European Parliament and of
the Council of 16 September 2009
laying down the procedure for implementing Regulation (EC)
No 883/2004 on the coordination of social security systems

Verordnung (EG) Nr. 987/2009 des Europäischen Parlaments und des
Rates vom 16. September 2009 zur
Festlegung der Modalitäten für die Durchführung der Verordnung
(EG) Nr. 883/2004 über die Koordinierung der Systeme der sozialen
Sicherheit

Stand: 16.09.2009

The full text of the Regulation is available in
several languages at:
https://eur-lex.europa.eu/legal-content/DE/
ALL/?uri=CELEX:32009R0987

PART 3
ANNEXES

A. Helpful Weblinks

Link to the website of the Federal Employment Agency:
www.arbeitsagentur.de

Homepages Federal Employment Agencies Düsseldorf / Kiel / Nuremberg (Responsibilites see below):
https://www.arbeitsagentur.de/vor-ort/duesseldorf/unternehmen
https://www.arbeitsagentur.de/vor-ort/kiel/startseite
https://www.arbeitsagentur.de/vor-ort/nuernberg/startseite

Information Page of the Federal Employment Agency for information on „Temporary Agency Employment":
https://www.arbeitsagentur.de/unternehmen/personalfragen/arbeitnehmerueberlassung

Migration Check of the Federal Employment Agency (Examination whether and if so, what kind of Work Permit is required):
https://www.arbeitsagentur.de/fuer-menschen-aus-dem-ausland/voraussetzungen-arbeiten-in-deutschland
https://www.arbeitsagentur.de/fuer-menschen-aus-dem-ausland/migration-check-english

Link to the Application Form: Temporary Agency Employment Permit:
https://www.arbeitsagentur.de/datei/antragueberlassungaueg2a_ba013421.pdf

Link to the Minimum Wage Reporting Portal of the Customs Administration:
https://www.meldeportal-mindestlohn.de/Meldeportal/form/display.do?%24context=3784B-36F969E9C2EAC21

Link to the Download of the Information Sheet Concerning Temporary Employment in accordance with sec. 11 para. 2 AÜG:
https://www.arbeitsagentur.de/unternehmen/download-center-unternehmen

Link to the Addresses of Institutions responsible for Issuing the Portable Document A1:
https://europa.eu/youreurope/citizens/work/social-security-forms/contact_points_pd_a1.pdf

Information Page of the Customs on Employment/Work:
https://www.zoll.de/DE/Fachthemen/Arbeit/arbeit_node.html

Clearingstelle German Federal Pension Fund:
https://www.clearingstelle.de/drv.html

Overview of the local audit office of the German Federal Pension Fund:
https://www.deutsche-rentenversicherung.de/DRV/DE/Experten/Arbeitgeber-und-Steuerberater/Betriebspruefdienst/Pruefbueros/pruefbueros.html

Home Page of the German Federal Pension Fund on Status Declaratory Procedure:
https://www.deutsche-rentenversicherung.de/SharedDocs/Formulare/DE/Formularpakete/01_versicherte/01_vor_der_rente/_DRV_Paket_Versicherung_Statusfeststellung.html

Federal Gazette, e. g., for an Overview of General Binding Collective Bargaining Agreements:
https://www.bundesanzeiger.de/pub/de/start;wwwsid=B8BAD438BE3F29AB68E550BD-06582BEC.web07-pub?0

General and Further Information on the Current Minimum Wage:
https://www.bmas.de/DE/Themen/Arbeitsrecht/Mindestlohn/mindestlohn.html

Corpus juris: (most of them are only available in German)
https://www.gesetze-im-internet.de/

Noerr Dawn Raid:
https://www.dawnraid.de/

Noerr External Personell:
https://www.noerr.com/fpe

B. Helpful Addresses

Employment Agency	*Düsseldorf*	*Kiel*	*Nuremberg*
Address	Agentur für Arbeit Düsseldorf 40180 Düsseldorf	Agentur für Arbeit Kiel 24131 Kiel	Agentur für Arbeit Nürnberg 90300 Nürnberg
Competence - **Federal state**	Hesse North Rhine-Westphalia	Schleswig-Holstein Mecklenburg-Western Pomerania Hamburg Lower Saxony Bremen Berlin Brandenburg Saxony-Anhalt Thuringia Saxony	Bavaria Baden-Württemberg Rhineland-Palatinate Saarland
Competence - **Foreign countries**	Bulgaria Great Britain Ireland Painted Netherlands Poland Romania and **All other non EU/EEA countries**	Denmark Estonia Finland Iceland Latvia Lithuania Norway Sweden Slovak Republic Czechia Hungary	Belgium France Greece Italy Liechtenstein Luxembourg Austria Portugal Slovenia Spain Cyprus

C. Glossary of Key Words

I. English/German

A

accident insurance	Unfallversicherung
Act on Payment of Wages and Salaries on Holidays and in Case of Illness (Continuation of Remuneration Act)	Entgeltfortzahlungsgesetz (EFZG)
Act on Temporary Employment	Gesetz zur Arbeitnehmerüberlassung (AÜG)
Act on the Codetermination of Employees in the Mining, Iron and Steel Manufacturing Industry	Montan-Mitbestimmungsgesetz
administrative fine	Geldbuße
administrative offence	Ordnungswidrigkeit
after-effect	Nachwirkung
agent	Auftragnehmer
Aliens Department	Ausländerbehörde
allowance relationship	Zuwendungsverhältnis
ancillary service obligation	Nebenleistungspflicht
articles of incorporation	Gesellschaftsvertrag
assignment	Überlassung
assistant	Erfüllungsgehilfe
authority	Behörde

B

Basic Law	Grundgesetz (GG)
blocking agreement	Sperrabrede
blocking period	Sperrzeit
body of persons	Personenvereinigung
borrowing	Entleih

C

cash method	Zuflussprinzip
Certificate of good conduct	Führungszeugnis
chain hiring	Kettenüberlassung
civil partner	Lebenspartner (eingetragen)
Coal & Steel Co-Determination Act	Montan-Mitbestimmungsgesetz
Code of Civil Procedure	Zivilprozessordnung (ZPO)

Codetermination Act	Mitbestimmungsgesetz (MitbestG)
codetermination right	Mitbestimmungsrecht
collecting agency	Einzugsstelle
collective bargaining agreement	Tarifvertrag
Collective Bargaining Agreements Act	Tarifvertragsgesetz (TVG)
companion plant	Nebenbetrieb
company car	Dienstwagen
company pension scheme	betriebliche Altersvorsorge
joint works council	Gesamtbetriebsrat
Compliance Management System	Compliance Management System
compulsory insurance	Pflichtversicherung
consortium	Arbeitsgemeinschaft
consortium agreement	Arbeitsgemeinschaftsvertrag
construction business	Baugewerbe
consultation with the works council	Anhörung des Betriebsrates
continued remuneration	Entgeltfortzahlung
contractor	Werkunternehmer
contract to produce a work	Werkvertrag
control agreement	Beherrschungsvertrag
covenant of non-competition	Wettbewerbsverbot
cover relationship	Deckungsverhältnis
criminal offence	Straftat
cross-border-merger	grenzüberschreitende Verschmelzung
customer	Besteller

D

declaration of intent	Willenserklärung
default of acceptance	Annahmeverzug
devolution	Aufgabenverlagerung
directives, instructions	Weisungen
Managing director(s)	Geschäftsführer
directorate	Geschäftsleitung
Directive on Temporary Agency Employment EU 2008/104 EC	Leiharbeitsrichtlinie EU 2008/104 EC
disclosure statement	Offenlegungspflicht
dismissal	Kündigung
Dismissal Protection Act	Kündigungsschutzgesetz (KSchG)
termination agreement	Aufhebungsvertrag
D&O liablity procedure	Organhaftungsprozess

documentation requirement	Dokumentationspflicht
duty of disclosure	Aufklärungspflicht
Due diligence	Sorgfaltspflicht

E

employee	Angestellter/Arbeitnehmer
employer	Arbeitgeber
employers' association	Arbeitgeberverband
employer's right to issue instructions	Weisungsrecht
Employment Agency	Agentur für Arbeit
employment contract	Arbeitsvertrag
employment law	Arbeitsrecht (individuell)
Employment Services	Arbeitsvermittlung
entity	Rechtsträger
equal treatment	Gleichbehandlung
establishment	Betrieb
excerpt from the trade/commercial register	Handelsregisterauszug
execution	Zwangsvollstreckung
externally determined	fremdbestimmt

F

false self-employed	Scheinselbstständige
false self-employment	Scheinselbstständigkeit
fault	Verschulden
Federal Employment Agency	Bundesagentur für Arbeit
Federal Labour Court	Bundesarbeitsgericht (BAG)
Federal Vacation Act	Bundesurlaubsgesetz (BUrlG)
fine	Geldstrafe
fixed-term employment agreement	befristeter Arbeitsvertrag
freelancer	freier Mitarbeiter
function area	Funktionsbereich

G

general binding of collective bargaining agreements	Allgemeinverbindlichkeit von Tarifverträgen
General Equal Treatment Act	Allgemeines Gleichbehandlungsgesetz (AGG)
generally binding	allgemeinverbindlich
generally binding collective bargaining agreements	allgemeinverbindliche Tarifverträge
general protection against dismissal	allgemeiner Kündigungsschutz

German Civil Code	Bürgerliches Gesetzbuch (BGB)
German Commercial Code	Handelsgesetzbuch (HGB)
German Federal Pension Fund	Deutsche Rentenversicherung Bund
German Federation of Trade Unions	Deutscher Gewerkschaftsbund
gross total	Bruttosumme
group	Konzern
group works council	Konzernbetriebsrat

H

Health and Safety at Work Act	Arbeitsschutzgesetz (ArbSchG)
Health and Safety laws	Arbeitsschutzrecht
health insurance	Krankenversicherung
health insurance fund	Krankenkasse
hirer	Entleiher
hirer's undertaking	Entleihunternehmen
hiring	Einstellung
hiring Out	Verleih
holiday	Urlaub
holiday pay	Urlaubsentgelt
Home Employment Act	Heimarbeitsgesetz (HAG)

I

Income Tax Act	Einkommensteuergesetz (EStG)
information requirement	Informationspflicht
in-house collective bargaining agreement	Firmentarifvertrag
input tax	Vorsteuer
input tax reduction	Vorsteuerabzug
instruction-bound	weisungsgebunden
interest on arrears	Säumniszuschlag
interest on grandfathering	Bestandschutzinteresse
indeterminate obligation	Gattungsschuld

J

joint establishment	gemeinsamer Betrieb
jointly and severally liable debtors	Gesamtschuldner

L

labour court	Arbeitsgericht
Labour Court Act	Arbeitsgerichtsgesetz (ArbGG)
labour court proceedings	Arbeitsgerichtsverfahren

labour law	Arbeitsrecht (kollektiv)
Law on Documenting Essential Applicable Conditions for Employment Relationship	Nachweisgesetz (NachwG)
Law on the Participation of Employees in a European Company (SE participation Act)	SE-Beteiligungsgesetz (SEBG)
Law on the Participation of Employees in a European Cooperative (SCE participation Act)	SCE-Beteiligungsgesetz (SCEBG)
legal concept	Rechtsfigur
legal entity	juristische Personen
liability	Haftung
liability for wage tax	Lohnsteuerpflicht
liability regardless of negligence or fault	verschuldensunabhängige Haftung
licensing authority	Erlaubnisbehörde
limited liability company	Gesellschaft mit beschränkter Haftung (GmbH)
local tax office	Betriebsstättenfinanzamt

M

management	Geschäftsführung
management agreement	Führungsvereinbarung
management board	Vorstand
management board member	Vorstandsmitglied
management system	Leitungsapparat
manager	Geschäftsleiter
mandatary	Beauftragter
maximum assignment length	Überlassungshöchstdauer
merger	Verschmelzung
Minimum Wage Notification Portal	Meldeportal Mindestlohn
mixed operation	Mischbetrieb

N

natural person	natürliche Person
non-solicitation	Abwerbeverbot
notice period	Kündigungsfrist

O

objective reasons	sachlicher Grund/sachliche Gründe
obligation to cooperate	Mitwirkungspflicht
obligation to hold the records in readiness	Bereithaltungspflicht
obligation to monitor	Überwachungspflicht
obligation to obtain permission	Erlaubnispflicht
obligation to produce supporting documents	Nachweispflicht

obligee	Gläubiger
obligor	Schuldner
One-Third Participation Act	Drittelbeteiligungsgesetz (DrittelbG)
opening clause	Öffnungsklausel
operating agreement	Dienstvereinbarung
order imposing a collective bargaining agreement to be generally binding	Allgemeinverbindlichkeitserklärung
organisational unit	Organisatorische Einheit
overtime (work)	Überstunden

P

paragraph (para.)	Absatz
partial retirement	Altersteilzeit
partnership with legal capacity	rechtsfähige Personengesellschaft
part of an establishment	Betriebsteil
Part-Time and Fixed-Term Employment Act	Gesetz über Teilzeitarbeit und befristete Arbeitsverträge – Teilzeit- und Befristungsgesetz (TzBfG)
permit	Erlaubnis
personally dependent	persönlich abhängig
person entitled to services	Dienstberechtigter
person obliged to services	Dienstverpflichteter
placement	Vermittlung
placement fee	Vermittlungsgebühr
placement officer	Arbeitsvermittler
plant section	Betriebsteil
Posted Workers Law	Arbeitnehmerentsendegesetz (AEntG)
preliminary VAT-return	Umsatzsteuervoranmeldung
principal	Auftraggeber
principle of equality	Gleichstellungsgrundsatz
principle of equal treatment	Gleichbehandlungsgrundsatz
principle of origin	Entstehungsprinzip
principle of territoriality	Territorialprinzip
product area	Produktbereich
promise recipient	Versprechensempfänger
promisor	Versprechender
proxy holder	Prokurist
public holidays	Feiertage

R

readiness to help	Dienstbereitschaft
Regional Court [City]	Landgericht [Ort]
registered office	Sitz (einer Gesellschaft)
registration requirement	Meldepflicht
remuneration	Vergütung
residence permit	Aufenthaltserlaubnis
residence title	Aufenthaltstitel
Residence title for specific purposes	Aufenthaltsgestaltung
(statutory) rest periods	Ruhezeiten
retention requirement	Aufbewahrungspflicht
right of recourse	Regressanspruch

S

section (sec.)	Paragraph
self-denunciation	Selbstanzeige
sentence (sent.)	Satz
service agreement	Dienstvertrag
service provider	Dienstleister
service provision agreement	Dienstverschaffungsvertrag
sham service contract	Scheindienstvertrag
sham contract to produce a work	Scheinwerkvertrag
short-time work	Kurzarbeit
small business	Kleinbetrieb
small business owner	Kleinunternehmer
social security authorities	Sozialversicherungsträger
Social Security Code	Sozialgesetzbuch (SGB)
social security contributions	Sozialversicherungsbeiträge
Social Security Fund Cooperative Agreement	Sozialversicherungstarifvertrag
social security laws	Sozialversicherungsrecht
status quo declaration	Festhaltenserklärung
statutory pension insurance	Rentenversicherung
statutory social insurance	gesetzliche Sozialversicherung
statutory health insurance fund	gesetzliche Krankenkasse
stock corporation	Aktiengesellschaft (AG)
Stock Corporation Act	Aktiengesetz (AktG)
stock options	Aktienoptionen
supervisory authority	Aufsichtsbehörde
supervisory board	Aufsichtsrat
surety	Bürge

T

tax authorities	Finanzbehörden
Tax Code	Abgabenordnung (AO)
tax law	Steuerrecht
tax office	Finanzamt
temporary agency employment	Arbeitnehmerüberlassung
temporary agency employment permit	Arbeitnehmerüberlassungserlaubnis
temporary agency worker	Leiharbeitnehmer
temporary agency employment contract	Arbeitnehmerüberlassungsvertrag
(temporary) employment contract	Leiharbeitsvertrag
(temporary) employment relationship	Leiharbeitsverhältnis
temporary work agency	Verleiher
termination agreement	Aufhebungsvertrag
torts	Deliktsrecht
total social insurance contribution	Gesamtsozialversicherungsbeitrag
trade union	Gewerkschaft
Treaty on the Functioning of the European Union (TFEU)	Vertrag über die Arbeitsweise der Europäischen Union (AEUV)

U

underlying debt relationship	Valutaverhältnis
undertaking	Unternehmen
unemployment benefits	Arbeitslosengeld
unemployment insurance	Arbeitslosenversicherung
unexhausted remedies	Vorausklage

V

value added tax (VAT)	Umsatzsteuer
Value added tax Act	Umsatzsteuergesetz
VAT payable amount	Umsatzsteuerzahlart
VAT-return	Umsatzsteuererklärung

W

wage tax	Lohnsteuer
wage tax class	Lohnsteuerklasse
wage tax return	Lohnsteueranmeldung
wage tax withholding	Lohnsteuerabzug
warning	Verwarnung
warning notice	Abmahnung
working day	Arbeitstag

working hours	Arbeitszeit
Working Time Act	Arbeitszeitgesetz (ArbZG)
work permit	Arbeitsgenehmigung
works agreement	Betriebsvereinbarung
works council	Betriebsrat
works council member	Betriebsratsmitglied
Works Constitution Act	Betriebsverfassungsgesetz (BetrVG)
(statutory) written form	Schriftform

II. German/English

A

Abgabenordnung (AO)	Tax Code
Abmahnung	warning notice
Absatz	paragraph (para.)
Abwerbeverbot	non-solicitation
Agentur für Arbeit	Employment Agency
Aktiengesellschaft	stock corporation
Aktiengesetz (AktG)	Stock Corporation Act
Aktienoptionen	stock options
allgemeiner Kündigungsschutz	general protection against dismissal
Allgemeines Gleichbehandlungsgesetz (AGG)	General Equal Treatment Act
allgemeinverbindlich	generally binding
allgemeinverbindliche Tarifverträge	generally binding collective bargaining agreements
Allgemeinverbindlichkeit von Tarifverträgen	general binding of collective bargaining agreements
Allgemeinverbindlichkeitserklärung	order imposing a collective bargaining agreement to be generally binding
Altersteilzeit	partial retirement
Anhörung des Betriebsrates	consultation with the works council
Annahmeverzug	default of acceptance
Arbeitgeber	employer
Arbeitgeberverband	employers' association
Arbeitnehmer	employee
Arbeitnehmerüberlassung	temporary agency employment
Arbeitnehmerüberlassungsgesetz (AÜG)	Act on Temporary Employment
Arbeitnehmerentsendegesetz (AEntG)	Posted Workers Law
Arbeitsgenehmigung	work permit

Arbeitsgemeinschaft	consortium
Arbeitsgemeinschaftsvertrag	consortium agreement
Arbeitsgericht	labour court
Arbeitsgerichtsgesetz (ArbGG)	Labour Court Act
Arbeitsgerichtsverfahren	labour court proceedings
Arbeitslosengeld	unemployment benefits
Arbeitslosenversicherung	unemployment insurance
Arbeitsrecht (individuell)	employment law
Arbeitsrecht (kollektiv)	labour law
Arbeitsschutzgesetz (ArbSchG)	Health and Safety at Work Act
Arbeitsschutzrecht	Health and Safety laws
Arbeitstag	working day
Arbeitsvermittler	placement officer
Arbeitsvermittlung	employment services
Arbeitsvertrag	employment contract
Arbeitszeit	working hours
Arbeitszeitgesetz (ArbZG)	Working Time Act
Aufbewahrungspflicht	retention requirement
Aufenthaltserlaubnis	residence permit
Aufenthaltsgestaltung	residence title for specific purposes
Aufenthaltstitel	residence title
Aufhebungsvertrag	termination agreement
Aufgabenverlagerung	devolution
Aufklärungspflicht	duty of disclosure
Aufsichtsbehörde	supervisory authority
Aufsichtspflicht	obligatory supervison
Aufsichtsrat	supervisory board
Auftraggeber	principal
Auftragnehmer	agent
Ausländerbehörde	Aliens Department

B

Baugewerbe	construction business
Beauftragter	mandatary
befristeter Arbeitsvertrag	fixed-term employment agreement
Beherrschungsvertrag	control agreement
Behörde	authority
Betriebsteil	plant section
Bereithaltungspflicht	obligation to hold the records in readiness

Bestandschutzinteresse	interest on grandfathering
Besteller	customer
Betrieb	establishment
betriebliche Altersvorsorge	company pension scheme
Betriebsstättenfinanzamt	local tax office
Betriebsrat	works council
Betriebsratsmitglied	works council member
Betriebsteil	part of an establishment
Betriebsvereinbarung	works agreement
Betriebsverfassungsgesetz (BetrVG)	Works Constitution Act
Bruttosumme	gross total
Bundesagentur für Arbeit	Federal Employment Agency
Bundesarbeitsgericht	Federal Labour Court
Bundesurlaubsgesetz (BUrlG)	Federal Vacation Act
Bürge	surety
Bürgerliches Gesetzbuch (BGB)	German Civil Code

C

Compliance Management System	Compliance Management System

D

Deckungsverhältnis	cover relationship
Deliktsrecht	torts
Deutsche Rentenversicherung Bund	German Federal Pension Fund
Deutscher Gewerkschaftsbund	German Federation of Trade Unions
Dienstberechtigter	person entitled to services
Dienstbereitschaft	readiness to help
Dienstleister	service provider
Dienstverpflichteter	person obliged to services
Dienstverschaffungsvertrag	service provision agreement
Dienstvertrag	service contract
Dienstvereinbarung	operating agreement
Dienstwagen	company car
Dokumentationspflicht	documentation requirement
Drittelbeteiligungsgesetz (DrittelbG)	One-Third Participation Act

E

Einkommensteuergesetz (EStG)	Income Tax Act
Einstellung	hiring
Einzugsstelle	collecting agency

Entleih	Borrowing
Entleiher	hirer
Entleihunternehmen	hirer's undertaking
Entgeltfortzahlung	continued remuneration
Entgeltfortzahlungsgesetz (EFZG)	Act on Payment of Wages and Salaries on Holidays and in Case of Illness (Continuation of Remuneration Act)
Entstehungsprinzip	principle of origin
Erfüllungsgehilfe	assistant
Erlaubnis	permit
Erlaubnisbehörde	licensing authority
Erlaubnispflicht	obligation to obtain permission

F

Feiertage	public holidays
Festhaltenserklärung	status quo declaration
Finanzamt	tax office
Finanzbehörden	tax authorities
Firmentarifvertrag	in-house collective bargaining agreement
freier Mitarbeiter	freelancer
fremdbestimmt	externally determined
Funktionsbereich	function area
Führungsvereinbarung	management agreement
Führungszeugnis	certificate of good conduct

G

Gattungsschuld	indeterminate obligation
Geldbuße	administrative fine
Geldstrafe	fine
gemeinsamer Betrieb	joint establishment
Gesamtbetriebsrat	joint works council
Gesamtschuldner	jointly and severally liable debtors
Gesamtsozialversicherungsbeitrag	total social insurance contribution
Geschäftsführer	managing director(s)
Geschäftsführung	management
Geschäftsleiter	manager(s)
Geschäftsleitung	directorate
Gesellschaft mit beschränkter Haftung (GmbH)	limited liability company
Gesellschaftsvertrag	articles of incorporation

Gesetz über Teilzeitarbeit und befristete Arbeitsverträge (TzBfG)	Part-Time and Fixed-Term Employment Act
gesetzliche Krankenkasse	statutory health insurance fund
gesetzliche Sozialversicherung	statutory social insurance
Gewerkschaft	trade union
Gläubiger	obligee
Gleichbehandlung	equal treatment
Gleichbehandlungsgrundsatz	principle of equal treatment
Gleichstellungsgrundsatz	principle of equality
grenzüberschreitende Verschmelzung	cross-border-merger
Grundgesetz (GG)	Basic Law

H

Haftung	liability
Handelsgesetzbuch (HGB)	German Commercial Code
Handelsregisterauszug	Excerpt from the commercial/trade register
Hauptleistungspflichten	primary service obligations
Heimarbeitsgesetz (HAG)	Home Employment Act

I

Informationspflicht	information requirement

J

juristische Personen	legal entity

K

Kennzeichnungspflicht	obligation to label
Kettenüberlassung	chain hiring
Kleinbetrieb	small business
Kleinunternehmer	small business owner
Konkretisierungspflicht	obligation to concretise
Konzern	group
Konzernbetriebsrat	group works council
Krankenkasse	health insurance fund
Krankenversicherung	health insurance
Kündigung	dismissal
Kündigungsfrist	notice period
Kündigungsschutzgesetz (KSchG)	Dismissal Protection Act
Kurzarbeit	short-time work

L

Landgericht [Ort]	Regional Court [City]
Lebenspartner (eingetragen)	civil partner
Legalitätspflicht	obligation to legality
Leiharbeit	temporary employment
Leiharbeitnehmer	temporary agency worker
Leiharbeitsrichtlinie	Directive on Temporary Agency Employment EU 2008/104 EC
Leiharbeitsverhältnis	(temporary) employment relationship
Leiharbeitsvertrag	(temporary) employment contract
Leitungsapparat	management system
Lohnsteuer	wage tax
Lohnsteuerabzug	wage tax withholding
Lohnsteueranmeldung	wage-tax return
Lohnsteuerklasse	wage tax class
Lohnsteuerpflicht	liability for wage tax

M

Meldepflicht	registration requirement
Meldeportal	Minimum Wage Notification Portal
Mischbetrieb	mixed operation
Mitbestimmungsgesetz (MitbestG)	Co-Determination Act
Mitbestimmungsrecht	codetermination right
Mitwirkungspflicht	obligation to cooperate
Montan-Mitbestimmungsgesetz	Coal & Steel Co-Determination Act

N

Nachweisgesetz (NachwG)	Law on Documenting Essential Applicable Conditions for Employment Relationship
Nachweisspflichten	obligation to produce supporting documents
Nachwirkung	after-effect
natürliche Person	natural person
Nebenbetrieb	companion plant
Nebenleistungspflichten	ancillary service obligations

O

Organhaftungsprozess	D&O liability procedure
Ordnungswidrigkeit	administrative offence
Offenlgungspflicht	Disclousre Statement
Öffnungsklausel	opening clause
Organisatorische Einheit	organisational unit

P

Paragraph (§)	section (sec.)
Personenvereinigung	body of persons
persönlich abhängig	personally dependent
Pflichtversicherung	compulsory insurance
Produktbereich	product area
Prokurist	proxy holder

R

Rechtsfähige Personengesellschaft	partnership with legal capacity
Rechtsfigur	legal concept
Rechtsträger	entity
Regressanspruch	right of recourse
Rentenversicherung	statutory pension insurance
Ruhezeiten	(statutory) rest periods

S

sachlicher Grund/sachliche Gründe	objective reasons
Satz	sentence (sent.)
Säumiszuschlag	interest on arrears
SCE Beteiligungsgesetz (SCEBG)	Law on the Participation of Employees in a European Cooperative (SCE participation act)
Scheindienstvertrag	sham service contract
Scheinwerkvertrag	sham contract to produce a work
Scheinselbstständige	false self-employed
Scheinselbstständigkeit	false self-employment
Schriftform	(statutory) written form
Schuldner	obligor
SE Beteiligungsgesetz (SEBG)	Law on the Participation of Employees in a European Company (SE participation act)
Selbstständiger	self-employed person
Selbstanzeige	self-denunciation
Sitz (einer Gesellschaft)	registered office
Sorgfaltspflicht	Due Diligence
Sozialgesetzbuch (SGB)	Social Security Code
Sozialversicherungsbeiträge	social security contributions
Sozialversicherungsrecht	social security laws
Sozialversicherungstarifvertrag	social security fund cooperative agreement
Sozialversicherungsträger	social security authorities
Sperrabreden	blocking agreements

Sperrzeit	blocking period
Straftat	criminal offence
Steuerrecht	tax law

T

Tarifvertrag	collective bargaining agreement
Tarifvertragsgesetz	Collective Bargaining Agreement Act
Teilzeit- und Befristungsgesetz (TzBfG)	Part-Time and Fixed-Term Contracts Act
Territorialprinzip	principle of territoriality

U

Überlassung	assignment
Überlassungshöchstdauer	maximum assignment length
Überstunden	overtime (work)
Überwachungspflicht	obligation to monitor
Umsatzsteuer	value-added tax (VAT)
Umsatzsteuererklärung	VAT return
Umsatzsteuergesetz	Value-Added Tax Act
Umsatzsteuervoranmeldung	Preliminary VAT-return
Umsatzsteuerzahlpflicht	VAT payable amount
Unfallversicherung	accident insurance
Unternehmen	undertaking
Urlaub	holiday
Urlaubsentgelt	holiday pay

V

Valutaverhältnis	underlying debt relationship
Vergütung	remuneration
Verleih	hiring Out
Verleiher	temporary work agency
Vermittler	placement officer
Vermittlungsgebühr	placement fee
Verschmelzung	merger
Verschulden	fault
verschuldensunabhängige Haftung	liability regardless of negligence or fault
Versprechender	promisor
Versprechensempfänger	promise recipient
Vertrag über die Arbeitsweise der Europäischen Union (AEUV)	Treaty on the Functioning of the European Union (TFEU)
Verwarnung	warning

Vorausklage	unexhausted remedies
Vorstand	management board
Vorstandsmitglied	management board member
Vorsteuer	input tax
Vorsteuerabzug	input tax reduction

W

Weisungen	directives, instructions
weisungsgebunden	instruction-bound
Weisungsrecht	employer's right to issue instructions
Werktag	working day
Werkunternehmer	contractor
Werkvertrag	contract to produce a work
Wettbewerbsverbot	covenant of non-competition
Willenserklärung	declaration of intent

Z

Zivilprozessordnung (ZPO)	Code of Civil Procedure
Zuflussprinzip	cash method
Zuwendungsverhältnis	allowance relationship
Zwangsvollstreckung	execution